PHL

54060000036599

D0507763

THE
**PAUL HAMLYN
LIBRARY**

DONATED BY
THE PAUL HAMLYN
FOUNDATION
TO THE
BRITISH MUSEUM

opened December 2000

WITHDRAWN

VILLAGE RECORDS

VILLAGE RECORDS

JOHN WEST

With a Foreword by
W. G. Hoskins

PHILLIMORE

First published in 1962 by
MACMILLAN AND COMPANY LIMITED

2nd edition published in 1982
3rd edition published in 1997 by
PHILLIMORE & CO. LTD.,
Shopwyke Manor Barn, Chichester, West Sussex

© John West, 1962, 1982, 1997

ISBN 1 86077 040 1

Printed and bound in Great Britain by
BUTLER & TANNER LTD.
London and Frome

THIS BOOK IS DEDICATED TO
MY FATHER

Contents

✧

List of Illustrations

✧

Foreword

✧

More than fifty years ago the then Board of Education expressed the view that the best approach to the teaching of history in schools was through the history of the particular locality in which the pupils lived. Nothing has happened officially since that momentous statement, but teachers have not been idle. All over the county a growing number of them have tried to carry out this precept in their own ways. These teachers work in primary schools, secondary modern and grammar schools, and in adult education classes; for one of the great attractions of local history is that it appeals equally to the intelligent schoolchild and the elderly retired man or woman.

But to study or to teach local history is not as easy as it sounds. There is a great dearth of qualified teachers and of books which train children and adults in the technique of the subject. Professional historians have been of little help in this connection. They have tended to make the subject sound too difficult, even intimidating, and to warn off beginners. But what is needed is encouragement, not this freezing-out of people anxious to study and enjoy the history of their own beloved corner of England. It was in order to help and encourage beginners (and others) in the field of English local history that I wrote *Local History in England* recently. But that short book could not answer all the questions that a good pupil or student would ask, or deal with all the difficulties that might well arise in a particular locality. So here is Mr. John West to give more detailed advice about the materials available for the study of village history, and the best way to handle them. It is a book of practical advice, intended for the student working on his own, for the guidance of the organiser and members of a group who are studying their own village, or for teachers in primary and secondary schools who are anxious to make the teaching of English history come alive through the study of their own parish and neighbourhood. Among many other ideas, Mr. West provides a series of practical exercises in documentary study, backed up by carefully-chosen facsimile illustrations to familiarise the reader with the look of his raw materials. The first look at some documents can be discouraging, not to say baffling; but Mr. West takes the reader by the hand and shows him (or her) step by step how to make sense of something that looks unintelligible to all but an expert.

As far as possible Mr. West has followed the documentary history of a single Worcestershire village and its immediate neighbourhood. This gives continuity to his book and shows what can be done with a single small place. But he would be the first to emphasise that every village in England has its own minor (and sometimes major) variations from the common pattern, and that the student must be constantly on the watch for these variations. It is this variety of detail, within the common broad pattern of history, that makes the study of local history so entrancing and so full of unexpected pleasures. Every community is unique: but there are many documents common to all, common questions to be answered and methods of study common to all of them.

As a lecturer in history at a well-known training college, Mr. West could not be better placed for the spreading of his enthusiasm and ideas. Through the teachers (as I myself know well) one influences pupils of all ages from ten to eighty. The history class becomes a pleasure to teacher and taught, and no longer a dreary half-misunderstood chore. It used to infuriate me to see my eleven-year-old daughter grappling vaguely with 'subjects' like Castlereagh's foreign policy, but knowing nothing of the history of the Oxfordshire parish in which we then lived, of the fact, for example, that in the field next to our own garden there lay the visible remains of the 'lost' medieval village of Steeple Barton. No wonder so many grown-ups loathe the very word 'history'. Not every child will fall in love with history just because local history is taught by an enlightened teacher, but some will at least have the chance to do so; and many will leave school with a curiosity and an interest that will last as long as life itself.

There is perhaps one suggestion which I may add to the many admirable suggestions made by Mr. West in this book, though I think it is implicit in his remarks on local maps and elsewhere. It is that students of local history, whether children or adults, should use the records for an ulterior purpose. They should use them, or those that are appropriate, *to reconstruct the past landscape of their parish and village*. All the materials for such a reconstruction are contained in this book. There might be an Anglo-Saxon landscape, even a Roman landscape if the local materials are there. There should certainly be a Norman landscape based upon the interpretation of Domesday Book. We may regard Domesday Book, looked at aright, as the first great guide-book to rural England, and use it to restore to the map the vanished landscape of the 11th century. In no other country in the world is it possible to do things like this.

The medieval landscape might be reconstructed from extents and other records, then perhaps the Tudor and Stuart landscapes if there are sufficient estate and manorial papers available; and finally one could make a very detailed picture of the parish landscape as it was about a hundred years ago, a period for which the records are usually abundant. In this way the dry words of the records come alive, and we see how the landscape of today is really a palimpsest, written over again and again, with ancient features appearing here and there among the modern for those who have eyes to see. Every country walk will then have a new meaning, every corner of the parish will be peopled with ghosts of old men and old buildings.

Those who study Mr. West's book carefully, who use it as he intends it to be used, and who also use their own imagination on the realities behind the records, will find it of inestimable value, not only in Worcestershire but in almost any part of rural England.

W. G. HOSKINS

October 1961

William George Hoskins CBE (1908-1992), a West Countryman of yeoman stock, became England's most influential local history teacher. He began his studies of peasant farming and landscape in Leicester in 1948, as Head of the University's new School of Local History. A seminal pilot study of Wigston Magna set the scene for three invaluable guides: *The Making of the English Landscape*, *Local History in England* and *Fieldwork in Local History* which stressed the essential combination of landscape and documents. He was never too proud to be considered 'popular', as his lively TV series *Landscapes of England* proved. Hoskins was a master-teacher who could make the bare bones of the landscape come to life. Tolerant of inexperience, as this generous Foreword shows, he was eager for children's involvement in the study of local history.

Preface to the Third Edition

✧

The preface to our second edition observed that 'there have been many changes in the world of education and local studies since *Village Records* was first published in 1962'. Since 1982, the rising tide of change has become a flood, not only in the continually extending range of sources available, but also in the vastly increasing legion of searchers. This is no sudden change: the pursuit of local history has always attracted many different types of enthusiasts, other than the earlier class of 'training college students' for whom *Village Records* was originally written. What then, are the differences in 1997?

Recession, with unanticipated leisure hours due to unemployment or early retirement, now prompts another generation to search out the records of their past, whilst popular television stimuli such as *Time Team* combine to send searchers to the archives in droves. Most of these persistent workers seek information about their family history, their house and home locality. They are joined in the search rooms by the professionals, teachers and ambitious authors, aspiring exponents of their craft; these groups occasionally combine in busy local study groups. Thus, the whole field of local studies has become open to all, to an extent that could not have been visualised in 1962, when our first Preface merely remarked that 'books on local history have become increasingly popular of recent years'.

In 1982, considerable progress had already been made at all levels of local studies and there was optimism in the recommendations of Lord Blake's Committee to review Local History. The terms of reference of this independent body, set up by the then Standing Conference for Local History in 1977, were 'to make an assessment of the pattern of interest, activity, and of study, in local history in England and Wales; and to make recommendations for meeting any needs revealed by amateur and professional local historians for support and services.' The Committee recorded 701 written submissions by record offices, museums, local historical societies, schools and universities; fourteen meetings received official representatives and public conferences were held with local historians in Bolton and Swansea. Their Report, published in 1979, advocated the promotion of 'a strong independent national organisation for local history' and the establishment of a Diploma in Local History, analogous to the C.B.A.'s Diploma in Archaeological Practice. 180 detailed recommendations aimed to improve access to local advice, study materials, accommodation and equipment, and advocated the formation of local Institutes of Historical Research in areas where there were then no university or polytechnic.

For younger students, the Schools Council continued to promote *History Around Us*, for examination at both CSE and O-level. The prevalence of examination course work promoted countless local projects and there was, at last, an A-level in local history. Leicester had the only university local history department, as it has today, and 39 other universities and polytechnics offered local history as part of a wider study. Most history teachers in secondary schools were enthusiastic about the use of local documentary sources; teachers' centres flourished, their chief product the ubiquitous Archive Study Unit. The popularity of these documentary packs, reminiscent of Cape's ancient *Jackdaws*, was confirmed by the Historical Association's publication, in 1987, of *Archival Teaching Materials*, edited by G.R. Batho and J.S. Thompson at the University of Durham. This described and indexed 645 units available for study. The Introduction remarked that 'By the mid-1980s it has become unthinkable that the candidate's ability to assess evidence should not be examined at O-, OA- or A- levels'.

The situation today is far more fluid and our view of all-round progress is less optimistic, at least in the case of schoolchildren's opportunities. Teachers now describe their situation less confidently as 'a melting pot'. In some other areas, the climate of recession is also inclement and the forecast uncertain. Archive providers and users of all types are beset by market forces, rising costs, reduction of grants, staffing cuts, shortage of working time, closure of resources centres, curricular change of priorities in schools and colleges, and, looming over record offices, the shadow of yet another bout of local government reorganisation. North Yorkshire's archivist warns us, for example, that: 'The situation of record offices in Yorkshire is complicated, and the latest round of government reorganisation (in which Humberside was abolished) has only added to the confusion. I do not know whether you will have space to list all of the repositories, let alone attempt to define the boundaries of their holdings, but staff of most offices can usually direct enquirers to the appropriate place if they cannot provide information themselves.' Making as much virtue of this necessity as possible, '*Village Records*' gazetteers attempt to direct the searcher primarily to the archives of the ancient counties, leaving their whereabouts in 2001 to the good offices of the archivists, wherever they may find themselves by then. There are, nevertheless, some welcome signs of growth and opportunity. It may be true that the whole field of local studies in 1997 has become less institutional, less well endowed or officially maintained but it may also have become more independent. Our resources are certainly more subject to notorious 'market forces'; this is the age of the private customer rather than the well-maintained and carefully directed student.

By far the most promising educational development, for younger children at least, has been the firm inclusion in the National History Curriculum of a prescribed local history unit for Key Stage 2, from 7-11. This important groundwork has so far survived all the repeated shuffling and deletion of various prescriptive options. Opportunities for secondary school pupils are less well defined, as there is no prescribed unit of local study for KS3 (11-14) and no National History Curriculum for History from 14-16. History courses and examinations for these older pupils are still in the course of development. The losses, of CSE's less formal course work after 1988 and examination courses like the Northern Board's GCSE in local history in 1997, for example, are grievous but the AEB still offers the possibility of local source work at A-level. The key elements of the New Order of 1994 offer hopeful requirements of the study of source materials at all levels from KS1-3: 'pupils should have opportunities to extend their knowledge by learning about (*the prescribed*) programmes of study in depth and through a local study,' and ' ... using a range of sources of information, including documents and printed sources'. The Schools (Council) History project survives with an element of course work on 'History around us', otherwise 'sources' are not necessarily local records. This 'melting pot' is still far from the 'structured and recognised programme of local history teaching to replace the present unsystematic and sporadic bursts of activity ...' .

The most vigorous national development was certainly the establishment, in 1982, of the British Association for Local History, as an outcome of the Blake Committee's recommendation of 'a strong independent national organisation'. Now firmly established on a businesslike footing with 2,000 members, the Association organises regular conferences and courses for local historians and is a source of regular publication. In addition to two quarterly journals, an impressive list of study guides includes, for example, an introduction to tithes, a manual of self-help on Tudor and Stuart handwriting and a practical guide on *Writing Local History* by David Dymond.[1] Like *Village Records*, the BALH makes a wide appeal to 'people from all walks of life: local historians, teachers, archivists, librarians, broadcasters, museum staff and family historians ... working individually or in a group, on the history of your house, your family, your village or your town, searching in the archives at a local record office; attending evening classes on local history or the local environment; or visiting buildings and sites of historical interest'. Its publications emphasise 'applying principles and methods to local research and study, so that you can benefit from the work of others'.

Family historians too, since 1974, have had their own national association, the Federation of Family History Societies, which exists 'to bring together societies with a common interest in genealogy, heraldry and allied subjects'. Membership in 1994 was 100 organisations in the UK and 50 overseas and the Federation's considerable record of publication, of guides to local records of all sorts, family news and digests, is recognised in almost every documentary section of this book. From finding the whereabouts of record offices to searching out their archives, for detailed identification and instruction on county collections of documents such as hearth tax returns, tithe awards, local newspapers, probate documents, census returns and quarter and family sessions papers, local historians of all sorts are indebted to the Federation.

The Blake Report also made three recommendations regarding training and teaching, perceiving a need for work leading to the award of non-graduate Certificates or Diplomas, possibly through the medium of the Open University, for first degree courses in local history and an M.A. in local history. In fact, the availability of study courses of all sorts developed steadily after 1979; there are now several University Certificates and many part-time M.A. courses. As yet there is no B.A. in local history, though most University History departments, like York, introduce a strong element of local source material at examination and dissertation level. In 1992, Robert Howard, editor of *Local History Magazine*, published a national *Guide* to courses which gave details of over one hundred local history related courses at all levels.

Arranged by counties, this list revealed 'that there are two kinds of courses on offer: those which involve students in study and research in order to achieve a specific goal, and those which inform participants rather than involve them'. The latter included several short-term courses, for example: Reading University's *20-week Introduction to Local History*, 'a guide to sources in local and national record offices and the techniques of using them', Leigh-on-Sea's *Do it Yourself Local History*, 'designed to assist the local historian in getting the most out of records and sources in 10 weeks', a 20-week guide to *Sources for Local History, 1550-1750* at the Lancashire Record Office or two residential weekends at Ipswich on *Latin and Paleography for Local History*.

---

[1] D. Dymond, *Writing Local History: A Practical Guide*, BALH/Phillimore, 1988.

Qualifying courses were also listed. These included: a three-year course in Local History organised by Nottingham University, which is still available from October 1997, not only at Nottingham but also at local centres in Lincoln and Derby, Loughborough and Sleaford. The Advanced Certificate qualifies non-graduate entrants to undertake the University's M.A. in Local History. A two-year Certificate Course in Regional and Local History at Hull University which is also taught at Grimsby and Bishop Grosseteste College, Lincoln and constitutes the first stage in Hull's four-year part-time B.A. in Regional and Local History. Keele also creates an opportunity for non-graduate entry with a two-year, part-time Certificate in Local History which offers open access, with 'no entrance requirements beyond an enthusiasm for the subject and a willingness to learn'; a Certificate pass with distinction 'is an appropriate qualification for registration on the M.A. course in Local History'. The Certificate is shortly to become a Diploma: 'There is talk about a part-time B.A. in Local History but there are no immediate plans for this'. A similar Certificate is available at York, where non-graduate entry to the University's two-year Certificate course qualifies able students for transfer to M.A. studies at the end of the first or second year.

Certificate courses are usually autonomous, or offered, like Liverpool's two-year, part-time Diploma in Local History, jointly with the Centre for Continuing Education. Leeds University's Part-time Education Department offers four B.A. (Hons.) degree programmes in Local and Regional History, each in conjunction with another subject: Economic and Social History, History, Geography, Sociology or a Certificate course in Archaeology. Students achieve a Certificate in Higher Education after two years of study, a Diploma after four years and a full honours degree in five or six years. The University's policy of flexible commitment aims 'to make entry as simple and easy as possible for mature students'; there is a wide range of entry requirements including, for example, professional courses qualifications in nursing and accountancy. 'The first fifteen students of the above degree graduated last summer (1995) and several are now undertaking post-graduate study in Local and Regional History through the School of History.' Part-time M.A. courses in local history are also offered by several universities' History faculties, for example at Liverpool, Nottingham, Sheffield, Birmingham and Wolverhampton is offered, but graduate qualifications for admission to these degrees are usually high. Bristol's M.A. in Local History offer post-graduate courses, on a non-faculty basis by the university's departments of adult and continuing education.

In 1996 Robert Howard followed up this survey with a questionnaire to 189 'mature' students.[2] He points out that the over-50s now outnumber all other age-groups and make up 75 per cent of all local history students; 43 per cent of his sample were over sixty. These are students who are prepared to travel from 31-40+ miles (24 per cent) to attend courses and whose future intentions include a continuing attending local history courses (45 per cent), undertaking a local history MA course (16 per cent), writing a local history book or making a video (5 per cent) or taking up history related employment (5 per cent). An alternative viewpoint in this issue 'highlights the fact that there are alternative methods of study, which, if more widely available, may well rival university and college "award" courses in terms of popularity among local historians'. Kieran Costello, Museums Education Officer with Bristol Museums and Art Education Service, based on Bristol Record Office, advocates the provision of LEA Community Education courses to be organised by local record offices and museums.

---

[2] 'Local History Students—Universities target the "oldies" ', *Local History Magazine*, no.56, July/August 1996.

He points out that 'the vast majority of adult learners to date have not expressed any interest in achieving qualifications'.[3]

At the grass roots, in terms of the availability of primary and secondary sources, the picture is as positive as ever. For all types of searcher, whether they be those who once, long ago, were not offended by the description 'amateur historian', the student who is not too proud to be helped as a novice, or the professional researcher preparing an article for a learned journal, opportunities continue to increase in spite of financial cuts and shortage of staff. Documents are available by the thousand, if not as originals, then on microfilm, microfiche, database and photocopied 'parish packs'. As the secretary of the National Council on Archives was evidently proud to claim in 1991: 'Throughout the network there is increasing concern to provide the sort of service which the customer wants'.

Another newcomer since our second edition is *Local History*, a bi-monthly magazine at £13.50 per annum. This newsletter was established in 1984 as a private venture by Robert and Sue Howard, at 3 Devonshire Promenade, Nottingham. The editor 'has always held the view that local history activity should be organised from the bottom up, with local history societies banding together at local authority level wherever possible ... certainly at county level and, ideally, at regional level as well'. To that end, he has recently produced Countyfile 1995 at £1.50 to *Local History* subscribers. This fourth annual directory lists more than 60 societies, 'for the most part these are county based local history associations, but in some parts of the country there are local history umbrella groups covering towns and conurbations'.

Over many years *Village Records* has assumed a modest cult status amongst amateur historians, even to a curious assumption by very young teachers of the author's probable long-ago demise (much exaggerated!). The publishers are reassuring about their intention to remodel the text and illustrations in a modern format without doing violence to its venerable format. In return, the author has endeavoured to make the text as relevant to a later generation of record searchers. Some of us may regret the inevitability of change, more especially in the loss of so many of the friends and teachers who are still remembered in the book's acknowledgment lists, and even of a few of the creative institutions which our first and second editions so confidently recommended. We can, however, agree that the measure of advantage and uncertainty in the future of local history, whether in boom or recession, is still fairly well balanced. In a new, uncertain age this middle-aged book, originally devised as a set of ancient finger-posts for the uninitiated, can now be supplemented by a nationwide series of more detailed documentary maps. Most of the signs still point in the same direction; a few have been slightly re-orientated in this edition.

Village Records attempts to meet a diversity of searchers' needs by extensive, up-to-date additions to each documentary section's general reading list and county gazetteer. In many of these additional sources for local study, the watchword is now 'revision' and re-assessment of an earlier, traditional interpretation of familiar scenes. The results of some of these trends are examined in Chapter One and explained more fully in extensions to those documentary sections which are currently under review. Otherwise, our aims and objectives remain basically the same as those expressed in the first preface, only slightly abridged and edited.

Thus, we still maintain that: 'This book does not profess to be a complete outline of English local history, nor yet the entire history of one midland village, but provides a series of

---

[3] K. Costello, 'Networking education provision in local history', *Local History Magazine*, no.56, July/August 1996.

practical exercises in documentary study. The illustrations are the most important part of the book, intended as facsimiles for careful study, not merely as pictures. These studies are not intended for the expert, but rather for the amateur historian who has only begun to discover the fascination of documentary study and needs a handbook for guidance. County archivists have assured me of the necessity of such a book; if it can indeed equip a student with a better understanding of the nature and use of some archives, and thus prevent the occasional friction that arises between archivists and students who have been inadequately prepared, the book will fulfil a very real need.'

As far as possible, a realistic selection of documents has been made, but the author is well aware that many more might have been included. One or two more obscure records, such as *Inquisitiones post mortem*, have nevertheless been included in order to give some idea of how difficult, as well as how absorbing such documentary studies can be. Every document included does, in some special way, bring the history of a village to life. In making choices, the following principles have been observed. Firstly, each document should be one of the more important landmarks of English local history; secondly, no document set which has an exclusively regional significance has been included and, wherever available, each example is taken from the records of Chaddesley Corbett in Worcestershire; thirdly, precedence has been given to those records which can be found in printed translation. In many cases, documents such as inventories have been chosen which offer the possibility of work with different levels of ability, including children.

A consistent pattern has been followed for each of the four sets of records which comprise four chapters of English history. Each set is introduced by a brief outline of the major factors of social and administrative change which produced its records. Each documentary study is self-contained, introduced by a resumé of its administrative background and its application to the landscape, life and work of the village. A description of the archive's physical size, shape and calligraphy is also given with reference to a clear facsimile, parallel transcript and, if necessary, a translation. Next, reference is made to handlists or indexes of any national or regional collections with special reference to Worcestershire calendars and indexes. Each section concludes with a county gazetteer of printed texts and explanatory articles in print. All these reading lists have been brought up-to-date in 1995.

Thus the book is offered as a working tool which, it is hoped, will save the student a good deal of frustration in a task which is sometimes too lightly undertaken. This is a guide which seems to have inspired a particular affection amongst amateur enthusiasts. It has been a satisfying experience over the past 30 years to have encountered so many friends of *Village Records*, from Chaddesley Corbett to Melbourne. It is offered again, in this new edition, to those enthusiastic readers who have made its re-issue feasible.

Acknowledgements

✧

The author's grateful acknowledgments were due to the following colleagues and authorities as they were in 1962:

The Principal and Governors of Shenstone College, and the Officers of the Local Education Authority, for their kindly encouragement of the work done in this connection with students and local teachers.

Miss M. Spurway, B.A., Shenstone College, for her help and advice in correcting the MS.

Mr. A.H. Stow, B.Sc., Shenstone College, for photographing the effigies (Plate VIII).

Mr. F.W.B. Charles, B.Arch., F.R.B.A., for producing the drawings of 17th-century houses (Figs. 2-6).

Mr. E.H. Sargeant, F.L.A., County Archivist for Worcestershire, and his colleagues, Miss M.A. Henderson, A.L.A., and Mr. G.E.S. Parker, for permission to reproduce Plates VI, XII, XIII, XVI-XVIII and Fig. 8, and for their unfailing patience in instructing students in the proper study of their County's Records.

Mr. W.E. Tate, M.A., F.S.A., for his assistance and generous practical advice on the section on Parish Documents.

Dr. P.T. Underdown, for permission to reproduce Plate XIX, which is taken from the Worcester Teachers' Archives Teaching Unit.

His Excellency the Viscount Cobham, G.C.M.G., T.D., for permission to reproduce Plate III.

Miss June Thomas, Shenstone College, for her rubbing of the Chaddesley Brass (Fig. 1).

Birmingham Reference Library, for permission to reproduce Plates III, VIII and Fig. 10.

Rev. J.A. Thursfield, M.A., sometime Vicar of Chaddesley Corbett, and the Churchwardens of the parish, for their permission to take the brass-rubbing (Fig. 1), to photograph the effigies (Plate VIII), and to reproduce Plate XI.

The Trustees of the British Museum, for permission to reproduce Plate I.

The Controller of H.M. Stationery Office and the Keeper of the Public Records, for their permission to reproduce Plates VII, XV and XIX the photographs of which are Crown Copyright.

The many County Archivists of English and Welsh County Record Offices, who supplied the information given on printed source material for their counties, and gave invaluable advice on the approach to original records.

Charlie Amies and all our other friends at the *Talbot Inn*, for their ready expert knowledge of 'shopickes' and 'swingletrees'.

Professor Coghill and Penguin Books Ltd, for their permission to quote the lines from his translation of *The Canterbury Tales* (Penguin Classics, 1951).

Warwick Corporation, for their permission to reproduce the portion of their Estate Map (Plate IX).

The extract from the Ordnance Survey 1" Sheet No. 130 (Plate XIX), is reproduced with the sanction of the Controller of H.M. Stationery Office. Crown copyright reserved.

and, with as much gratitude, in 1997 to:

Judith Baldry of Manchester Central Library's Archives department for information about Lancashire parish registers.

Dr. Robert Bearman, Senior Archivist to the Shakespeare Birthplace Trust Records Office, for his help with the Throckmorton papers.

Stephen K. Blades, Assistant Secretary, for information about the List and Index Society.

P.H.W. Booth, MA, FRHistS, Director of Studies for the MA and Diploma in Local History at the University of Liverpool, for information about these courses.

Mrs. Valerie Chapman and the librarians and archivists at Wolverhampton Reference Library.

Dr. M.D. Costan, Staff Tutor in Historical Studies, Department of Continuing Education, the University of Bristol for information about the MA in Local History.

Mrs. F. de Courcy, General Secretary of the Lancashire Parish Register Society for information about the Society's most recent publications.

Miss J. Crowther, Local Studies Librarian at Hull Central Library, for information about the Library's collection of county maps.

Helen Dyson, Programme Co-ordinator in the Part Time Education Department of the University of Leeds, for information about Local and Regional History degrees and certificates.

Jonquil Elliott of the British Library for information about Christopher Saxton's maps.

Professor Barbara English of Hull University for information and advice on university Certificate courses.

Mrs. K. Haslem for help with Gloucestershire Record Office's deposits of tithe documents.

Stephen Hobbs, Diocesan Archivist at Wiltshire CRO for information on probate records.

Alan Hodges of Smestow School, for information about curricular requirements.

Robert Howard of the Local History Press, for information on regional societies and courses.

Dr. D.B.M. Huffer, for help with UCAS information.

C. Jeens, County Archivist of Warwickshire, for his help with the Throckmorton papers.

Dr. John Lally, for all his continuing help, both academic and curricular.

Philip Morgan of Keele University's Department of History for information about the University's courses in Local History.

Mrs. M. de Motte, Manchester Library Archives Dept. on Lancashire parish registers.

Dr. John Palmer, for information about the University of Hull's Domesday database.

Mike D. Raftery, Assistant Local Studies Librarian at Leicestershire Record Office, for information about the county's ancient maps.

James Rivington, Publications Officer of the British Academy, for up-to-date information about *Anglo-Saxon Charters*.

Dr. C.D. Rogers of the Manchester Metropolitan University, Hon. General Editor of the Lancashire Parish Register Society for generous help with cross-county parishes.

H. Martin Stuchfield, Hon Secretary to the Monumental Brass Society for information on up-to-date publications.

Francoise Vassie, Continuing Education Officer at the University of York for information about the University's Certificate in Local History.

A.M. Wherry, BA, DAA, County Archivist at Worcester Record Office for assistance with reproduction of Chaddesley Probate Accounts and to all the archivists at Worcester for their help with many other enquiries, especially Martin Taylor for help with tithe maps, M. Quarrell for assistance with Photographs, Margaret Tohill for information about Worcestershire commercial directories and Val Morris for help with identifying probate accounts.

Kate Woolley and her colleagues at Tettenhall Regis Library, also all the librarians at the Wolverhampton Central Library, but **not** including the computerised index.

The librarians at Birmingham Reference Library's Local History department.

To the many County Archivists who have advised on the updating of their guides and handlists.

My special thanks to Nicola Willmot of Phillimore, for her patient work on a complicated amalgam of texts, and to Margaret, my wife, for all her help throughout the third edition.

Finally, a special tribute to the late F.I.S. McKendrick, the editor who accepted the original draft of *Village Records* in 1961 and gave friendly guidance to the first edition. Freddie died in November 1995, and will be sadly missed.

Abbreviations

✧

Please note that *italic* type refers to the actual title of a publication. In the same way, abbreviations in *italic*, may also indicate the *Proceedings* or *Transactions* of a society or institution.

AASRP	Association of Archaeological Societies Reports and Papers
AC	*Archologia Cantiana*
ASLC	Antiquarian Society of Lancashire & Cheshire
App.	Appendix
Arch. J.	*Archaeological Journal*
Arch. Soc.	Archaeological Society
BALH	British Association for Local History
B.A.No.	Bulk Accession No.
BAS	Birmingham Archaeological Society
BBOASJ	*Berkshire, Buckinghamshire & Oxfordshire Archaeological Society Journal*
BGAS	Bristol & Gloucestershire Archaeological Society
BHRS	Bedfordshire Historical Records Society
Bourn. Nat. Hist. Soc.	Bournemouth Natural History Society
BPRS	Buckinghamshire Parish Records Society
Bradford Hist. & Antiq. Soc.	Bradford Historical & Antiquarian Society
Bristol Rec. Soc.	Bristol Record Society
BRS	Buckinghamshire Record Society
Caern. Antiq. Soc.	Caernarvonshire Antiquarian Society
CAS	Cambridge Antiquarian Society
CASFC	Carmarthen Antiquarian Society & Field Club
CHAS	Cambridgeshire & Huntingdonshire Archaeological Society
C.C.	County Council
CNWAAHSJ	*Chester & North Wales Architectural, Archaeological & Historical Society Journal*
CUP	Cambridge University Press
CWAAS	Cumberland & Westmorland Antiquarian & Archaeological Society
DANHSJ	*Derbyshire Archaeological & Natural History Society Journal*
DASLA	Devon Association of Science, Literature & Art
DAT	*Devonshire Association Transactions*
DCNQ	*Devon and Cornwall Notes & Queries*
DCRS	Devon & Cornwall Record Society
Dev. Soc.	Devonshire Society
DNHAFC	Dorset Natural History & Antiquarian Field Club
DNHAS	Dorset Natural History & Archaeological Society
DNPRS	Durham & Northumberland Parish Records Society

EANQ	*East Anglian Notes & Queries*
EAS	Essex Archaeological Society
EHAS	East Hertfordshire Archaeological Society
EHR	English Historical Review
EPNS	English Place-Name Society
E. Rid. Ant. Soc.	East Riding Antiquarian Society
FFHS	Federation of Family History Societies
Hants. Rec. Soc.	Hampshire Rcord Society
HFCAS	Hampshire Field Club & Archaeological Society
Hist. Rec. Soc.	Historical Records Society
H.M.S.O.	Her Majesty's Stationery Office
HSLC	Historical Society of Lancashire & Cheshire
I.p.m.	Inquisitiones post mortem
J.	*Journal*
J. Brit Arch. Assocn	*Journal of the British Archaeological Association*
JRIC	J.R. Inst. of Cornwall
Kent Rec. Soc.	Kent Record Society
LAHS	Leicestershire Archaeological & Historical Society
LAS	Lancashire Archaeological Society
LCAS	Lancashire & Cheshire Archaeological Society
LCRS	Lancashire & Cheshire Records Society
LeAS	Leicestershire Archaeological Society
Lincs. Rec. Soc.	Lincolnshire Record Society
LMAS	London & Middlesex Archaeological Society
Loc. Rec. Ser.	Local Records Series
LPRS	Lancashire Parish Registers Society
LRS	Lincolnshire Record Society Parish Registers Section
MBS	Monumental Brass Society
Merioneth Hist. & Rec. Soc.	Merioneth Historical & Record Society
Middx. & Herts. N. & Q.	*Middlesex & Hertfordshire Notes & Queries*
Misc.	*Miscellanea*
n.d.	no date
Norf. Antiq. Misc.	Norfolk Antiquarian Miscellany
Norf. Arch. Soc.	Norfolk Archaeological Society
Northants. Nat. Hist. Soc.	Northamptonshire Natural History Society
Northants. Rec. Soc. Pubs.	Northamptonshire Record Society Publications
N. Rid. Rec. Soc.	North Riding Record Society
n.s.	New Series
N. Staffs. FC	North Staffordshire Field Club
OAS	Oxford Archaeological Society
OHS	Oxfordshire Historical Society
ORS	Oxford Record Society
o.s.	Old Series
Parish Reg. Soc.	Parish Registers Society
PRO	Public Record Office
Pub.	Publications of …
RANHS	Rutland Archaeological & Natural History Society
Rec. Ser.	Records Series
Rec. Soc.	Records Society

Ref. Library	Reference Library
Ruislip Nat. Hist. Soc.	Ruislip Natural History Society
SAC	*Sussex Archaeological Society Collections*
SAHAAS	St Albans & Hertfordshire Architectural and Archaeological Society
SANHS	Somerset Archaeological & Natural History Society
SAS	Surrey Archaeological Society
SASNQ	*Sussex Archaeological Society Collections Notes & Queries*
SDNHAS	Somerset & Dorset Natural History & Archaeological Society
SDNQ	*Somerset & Dorset Notes & Queries*
ShANHS	Shropshire Archaeological & Natural History Society
ShAS	Shropshire Archaeological Society
SIANH	Suffolk Institute of Archaeology and Natural History
Sociol. Rev.	*Sociological Review*
Som. Rec. Soc.	Somerset Record Society
SRS	Sussex Record Society
Staffs. Rec. Soc.	Staffordshire Record Society
SuAS	Sussex Archaeological Society
SurRS	Surrey Record Society
S. Wales Rec. Soc.	South Wales Record Society
TSRS	Thoroton Society Record Series
VCH	*Victoria County History Series*
WANHM	*Wiltshire Archaeological & Natural History Magazine*
WANHS	Wiltshire Archaeological & Natural History Society
WAS	Worcestershire Archaeological Society
Wm. Salt Arch. Soc.	William Salt Archaeological Society
Worcs. Arch. Soc.	Worcestershire Archaeological Society
Worcs. Hist. Soc.	Worcestershire Historical Society
W.P.R.M.	Worcestershire Parish Registers (Marriages)
W. Wales Hist. Rec. Soc.	West Wales Historical Records Society
YAS	Yorkshire Archaeological Society
Yorks. Arch. & Top. Soc.	Yorkshire Archaeological & Topographical Society
YPRS	Yorkshire Parish Register Society

CHAPTER I

The Approach to Local Documents

✧

What are our aims, as local historians? What do we expect to learn from a closer acquaintance with original documents? It is very difficult to generalise about these objectives, as we have already remarked on the wide diversity of age and aspirations of those who search the records in local archive repositories. Disparity of interests creates tensions as well as differences of aims and needs. A minority of professional teachers, together with those amateurs who share their more exalted aims of research and possible publication, are often critical of the weight which the larger body of amateur 'fans' imposes on a library's staff and equipment and especially on their own table space. Local historians are wary of the invasion of genealogists and family historians, just as national historians once denigrated local history as gossip about the parish pump.

None of the multifarious efforts of diligent searchers should be patronised or dismissed as in some sense unprofessional or insufficiently academic. This author has always reacted strongly against those scholars and educationists who denigrate children's formative efforts with contemptuous inverted commas in reference to their 'research'. There is no simple hierarchy or rank in the discipline of local studies, but it is essential that each of us considers the objectives and limits of our ongoing search. We must also be aware that these may change with an increase of knowledge. Nowhere is this more evident than in the increasing length of the county gazetteers and general reading lists which are appended to every chapter of this up-to-date edition. Our first task in orientating our approach to local records must therefore be to make ourselves aware of the aims and objectives of the masters in each documentary field before we venture to attempt our own interpretation.

Changes in interpretation mark the passage of time for those of us who remember our first-hand experience of the post-war enthusiasm created by such masters as the late W.G. Hoskins, who wrote so kindly a foreword to our first edition, Bill Tate who first opened the *Parish Chest*, F.G. Emmison, who made Essex Record Office a model of archive custody and publication, or Professor Rodney Hilton, who brought medieval society to life for us. New names now mark the title-pages; Peter Sawyer, Zvi Razi, Della Hooke and Denis Stuart are among those authorities whose research is cited in this edition of *Village Records* as being most pertinent to our documentary studies. Bridging the time-scale with considerable relevance to our next chapter, is Dr. Margaret Gelling, whose article on 'The Present State of English Place-name Studies'[1] looks back to her original work, written in 1952. Acknowledging continuous

---

[1] M. Gelling, 'The Present State of English Place-Name Studies', *The Local Historian*, vol.21, no.4, November 1991.

development in her field during four decades, she remarks that: 'My paper requires a considerable amount of up-dating. It would, of course, be deplorable if that were not the case, since forty years' hard labour by my colleagues and myself would then have produced merely confirmation of what was already known.' This is an admirable lead for any local historian to follow.

Extreme revisionists may persuade us that Hoskins's vision of the English landscape is no longer completely acceptable as a whole view of local change; nor does Stenton's view of Domesday as 'an ordered description of a national economy' or Darby's geographical approach remain unchallenged.[2] For the searcher, these encounters with revision of familiar ideas can be a difficult lesson to learn unless we recognise some essential purpose in change, rather than seeing it for its own sake. These changes and our independent judgment of their worth are signs that History is still alive and well. Some long-established interpretations of familiar sources tend to change merely because of the availability of more and more evidence of the same type for comparison and contrast. This additional evidence may lead to a different understanding of the actual meanings of the words and phrases used throughout the text, as, for example, when *virgate* is suddenly seen to mean something different from the traditional 30-acre servile tenant's holding and becomes a mere tax code.

Nowhere is the trend to re-interpretation more vigorous and essential to remark than in Chapter Two's introduction to the Domesday Survey. Re-assessment, even statistical *regression*, are the watchwords of many a new authority bold enough to challenge the findings of Stenton, Maitland or the Anglo-Saxon Chronicle. Sometimes revision seems to involve merely semantic issues, a different reading of the same words or a logic-chopping, monocausal approach to what once seemed to be a straightforward study, in which most of the traps for the unwary were already well enough marked. Perhaps the more significant lesson for the searcher to learn from such studies is never to assume that the evidence always says only what it seems to say in so many words; no document is sacrosanct, very few exactly prove what their bare words indicate.

Other re-interpretations are suggested by a new awareness of formerly neglected types of record which can and should be studied in connection with the master document. Geld rolls, when correlated with Domesday, reveal a different meaning of *demesne* and *value*; forest court rolls identify a numerous population unrecorded in the manorial records; probate accounts fill in details of the livelihood of those who had no will or inventory to tell their tales because the deceased died intestate. These and other re-assessments of the same or different evidence are reviewed more fully in each documentary chapter.

Re-interpretation of any historical event or situation may also arise from changes in the outlook, attitude or emphasis—or, perhaps, prejudice—of the researcher. Nowadays, in studies as diverse as manorial records, probate proceedings or enclosure proceedings, younger students are likely to be more preoccupied with the sociology of the local scene than with its property, agriculture or landscape. Those records are more likely to be scrutinised for previously neglected evidence of social negotiation and tensions than measurement of boundaries and acreage. In this new context too, it is not only political correctness which ensures that more attention is likely to be paid to the influence and welfare of womenfolk in manor and parish, as several of our periodical references will show.[3]

---

[2] See, for example: A.R. Bridbury, 'Domesday Book, a re-interpretation', *English Historical Review*, 105, April 1990; J.D. Hamshere, J. McDonald and G.D. Snooks, 'Regressing Domesday Book', *Economic History Review*, 40, May 1987; D.M. Palliser, 'Domesday Book and "The Harrying of the North" ', *Northern History*, 29, 1993.

[3] See, for example: P. Carter, 'Poor relief strategies; women,children and enclosures', *The Local Historian*, vol.25, no.3, August 1995; J. Goldberg, 'Women in later medieval archives', *Journal of the Society of Archivists*, 15 (1), Spring 1994; H.M. Jewell, 'Women in the court rolls of the manor of Wakefield', *Northern History*, 26, 1990; C. Cross, 'Northern women in the early modern period; female testators of Hull and Leeds, 1520-1650', *Yorkshire Archaeological Journal*, 59, 1987.

How far should amateur historians expect to concern themselves with abstruse historical revisions, the processes of the diplomatic or the niceties of cliometrics and error theory? Is it not patronising to suggest to the ordinary reader that 'such things need not concern you at your own level'? In most cases we have included any relevant new works on the understanding that, abstruse or not, they may well concern us all. It is simplistic to divide record searchers into different, productive and non-productive species. As soon as any of us begins to make notes about the data which we have retrieved, we begin to be authors and should expect to observe and be judged by rigorous professional standards. We can never stop short at information retrieval and brief factual notes of data retrieved. Inevitably we will extend our notes to make comparisons and, probably, our own commentary and generalisations. Having discovered great-great-grandfather as a collier of 1840, shall we not wish to know more of general conditions in the 19th-century coal industry and make judgments on family conditions, standards and costs of living? It may then be but a short step towards membership of a local studies group and access to a home computer.

A growing body of research and publication demonstrates how the computer itself can create a new impetus to re-interpretation of records as familiar as parish registers:

> Twenty years ago these were used largely for either the study of local trends in the three vital series of baptisms, marriages and burials or for biographical/genealogical research. Whilst no archivist can claim that genealogical enquiries are not still the major demand placed upon registers, their use has been revolutionised in demographic research and in social and demographic history, more generally by the advent of the computer and of increasingly specialised software in this field ... Taxation and rating documents such as the late 17th-century hearth-tax returns and 18th- and 19th-century poor rate assessments can be pressed into new uses once they are in machine-readable form. They can be made to reveal much about the social structures of localities and regions on a comparative basis ...[4]

Dramatic developments in the possibilities of desktop publishing have immeasurably widened the possibility and scope of printed studies by local groups or even dedicated lone searchers of their local archives. This then is the meeting point of searcher, researcher and author, the point at which it is essential for any reader of this book to consult, not only the chosen documentary sources in his own locality, but also the general reading lists which bring that study up-to-date and possibly revise her most precious misunderstandings. To this end, each documentary section has a paragraph or two, additional to those written in 1962 or 1982, which indicate some of the main changes which have taken place in our reading and understanding of the documents in question.

The purpose of this collection of documentary studies is to familiarise students with a selection of characteristic sources for local study and to enable them to relate those documents to their own locality and to the wider field of contemporary knowledge and research in that field. It is by no means a complete series; many more documents might have been included and must certainly be investigated by the student who wishes to make a more complete village survey. It should however be borne in mind that few and fortunate are those villages which possess a complete series of 'typical' records for every stage of their history. There are, nevertheless, certain fairly recognisable landmarks in documentary history, some of which have been selected as *Village Records*.

---

[4] Pat Hudson, 'A New History from Below: Computers and the Maturing of Local and Regional History', *The Local Historian*, vol.25, no.4, November 1995.

To give unity to the study, examples have been taken from one particular village, Chaddesley Corbett in Worcestershire, wherever possible. If the necessary document has not been found for that village, a specimen has been sought in neighbouring villages. Further examples are taken from Worcestershire but all are of a type which is common to villages all over England. In each case, a hand-list is provided for students in other counties, indicating whether the particular document is available within their own county or for their own village. Here, most of the information given with the Worcestershire specimen will apply.

How then do we set about making our own collection of sources from which to compile a local history of people or places of special interest to us? Our study is divided into two main parts, essential groundwork and access to archives. The first aim must be to teach ourselves as much as we can about the **origin** of the document which we intend to study and the sort of information we can expect it to contain, and, equally important, what sort of information we should **not** expect to find there. All record sources or *archives* were compiled for some administrative purpose, with no intention to inform or instruct posterity. If then, we choose to use them for this different purpose, we must first find out something of the administrative framework into which they fit. Each chapter's documents are therefore accompanied by explanatory text, with notes on further reading.

Next, we need to know what the original document **looked like**. Each facsimile is intended to show the original's shape, size and superficial appearance. Information is then given as to where each local record may be found, even if the need to use such an original does not eventually arise. In its original form an archive may be illegible, unidentifiable, or both. It is as well that the student should know of these difficulties, their nature and extent; this is impossible if one has never seen a facsimile. Adequate preparation may, we hope, prevent over-zealous local historians appearing before overworked archivists with requests to examine documents which they should not expect to find in that repository and which they will be unable to decipher, if found. More constructively, it may help the student to know which types of record will be both available and intelligible. Many students are too easily discouraged by initial difficulties which can be overcome by preliminary study. Where then, is the best place to begin?

Original records will be found in two main forms, either in printed collections, or as separate originals. Printed versions can be seen in most large provincial reference libraries, with some inevitable regional bias. The printed records of the medieval manors of Wakefield, Bridlington, Aldborough, Bingley and Kirkheaton, for example, and many more which have been published at length by the Yorkshire Archaeological Society, will certainly be found in Birmingham University and the City Reference Libraries, as well as in Leeds, but less conspicuous transactions, such as Suffolk's *East Anglian Miscellany*, with its records of Sudbury or Hepworth, may be confined to Ipswich. For those whose main reference library is far from home, these volumes can usually be obtained, after some delay, by courtesy of a nearby lending library, on inter-library loan or as photocopied articles if these are reasonably brief.

In the search rooms, our investigations are widely extended by the availability, not only of printed guidebooks, but also of serried ranks of micro-readers and computerised indexes. Printed guides to county collections of specific sources, such as the invaluable series published the Federation of Family History Societies, proliferate in reference libraries and record offices. New editions of standard reference works, published by national Records Societies are matched by a continuing output of learned and informative articles in the transactions of county historical societies. These sources are examined more closely at the end of this chapter and are also listed in our general reading lists for each documentary section.

Students are well served by a variety of periodical journals, newsletters or magazines, all of which aim to cater for a wide range of interests and experience. The genealogical field is kept up-to-date by the quarterly publication of *Family History*, journal of the Institute of Heraldic & Genealogical Studies, edited by Cecil R. Humphery-Smith at Northgate, Canterbury and available on annual subscription of £13.50. The *Genealogists' Magazine*, is also published quarterly for a subscription of £12 a year, by the Society of Genealogists. It aims to inform 'anyone interested int he study of genealogy or family history as amateur or professional'. *The Local Historian* flourishes as the official journal of the British Association for Local History, regularly updating documentary sources cited in *Village Records* with readable, well informed articles. This successor to *The Amateur Historian* (1952-67), which is well worth a wealth of reference in our reading lists, is now supplemented by BALH's *Local History News*, also published quarterly, containing 'topical reports of local societies, record offices, libraries, museums and of issues concerning local historians'. Both journals are sent to members in return for a subscription of £19, and a concise Index to *The Local Historian* is available to subscribers at £2.00, with available back numbers. Many counties, like Lancashire, Leicestershire, Shropshire, Suffolk and North Devon and other independent localities like Altrincham and Cheltenham also publish their own Local History or Family History Journal.

For information about major record-publishing societies, consult the *Directory of British Associations* (13th edition, 1996-1997), edited by S.P.A. and A.J.W. Henderson and published by CPD Research Publications, which should be available in your reference library. The index lists 19 entries under *Records—Historical*, two as Parish Registers societies, 15 for *Historical Buildings* and 95 under *Archaeology*, plus another 15 more specialised *Archaeology: industrial* societies. Although the societies indexed are mainly the major county record publishing associations, there are many entries for more independent organisations such as the Newcastle on Tyne Society of Antiquaries and Wolverton and District Archaeological Society in Buckinghamshire. Less familiar titles, such as the Black Country Society or the Historical Landscape Group, are not included in these lists but may be separately entered, alphabetically, so that the index merits a careful search for your particular interest. Each society's entry gives basic details of secretary's name, address, telephone number, membership total and subscriptions. Activities such as meetings, conferences, excavations and study groups are also listed, with a statement of the group's objectives and main fields of research. Reference is made to published handbooks, newsletters, yearbooks, journals and occasional leaflets.

A similar source of information will be found in *Local History Magazine*'s 'CountyFile'. A full list of county- and area-based local history associations and related groups appeared in issue no.52 for November/December 1995 and was followed by the fifth annual directory in 1996. CountyFile lists more than 60 associations, mostly county-based history societies and a few 'local history umbrella groups covering towns and conurbations'. Information includes a statement of each society's aims, for example: 'To collect and make accessible materials for the history of the county' (Bedfordshire Historical Record Society), subscription rates, contact addresses, and a list of publications, periodical volumes or transactions. CountyFile is an ongoing appendix to a thoroughly practical magazine with an annual subscription of £14.70

for six issues, each of which includes the updated CountyFile contact list. A compendium version is available separately at £1.50. Each number of *Local History* also offers a comprehensive survey of current local societies' periodicals, each entry summarising its issue's contents of articles.

The latest news about local history societies' prospects from this vigorous source[1] informs us that 'groups undertaking local history projects related to the environment can obtain grants of £2,000 towards 50 per cent of their costs'. Projects which have already received rural funds include a Hampshire study of parish boundaries, a Derbyshire survey of field patterns, a trail leaflet for the area around Cadbury Hill and numerous parish map projects.

Most listed associations are at county and regional level; usually small local groups are not included. Most listed associations are at county or regional level; small local groups are not usually included in published handlists. To find a more homely group to join, for local research, we return again to our friendly reference library. In some fortunate cases a local or regional list is printed and offered for sale. Wolverhampton Libraries, for example, list 14 secretaries' addresses in the Black Country and Staffordshire under *Local History* and adds two more under *Genealogy*. Each entry also gives the group's aims, as in the case of the Walsall Family History Group which exists 'to help and entertain family history researchers', or the Albrighton and District Historical Society offering 'historical talks at winter meetings. Visits to places of interest in the summer'. The boom in local society membership which we noticed in 1982 has continued all over England, but the situation is so fluid that most central libraries keep unprinted lists of local or regional societies under the counter for individual reference and regular up-dating. Chelmsford Library, for example, can provide a searcher with information on 238 local history 'and amenities' societies; Leeds records 47 local and family history history groups in the metropolitan area, matched by about 50 in and around Stafford.

A few of these active groups, however small, make regular contributions to the field of local publication. Especially active, for example, is the Hull and Humberside Local History Unit with an impressive list of articles such as Robert Curry's *Family History, a Beginner's Guide* and Gordon Ostler's *Lost Villages of the Humber Estuary*, both published in 1990. Also active in various documentary fields are, or have been, the producers of Totnes Community Archives, the WEA Waltham Branch, Staine Hundred Local Historical Society, the Farnham & District Museum Society and the Altrincham Historical Society. Their publications and those of many more local study groups are listed in the county gazetteers which follow each documentary section of this book. For those who see themselves as founders of study groups rather than joiners, there is a useful BALH guide to *Running a History Society* by Mary Paget, published by Phillimore in 1988.

Manuscript and printed originals are more usually found in national repositories such as the British Library and the Bodleian in Oxford or, more accessibly in County Record Offices. Some originals, such as maps, census returns, newspapers and a few manuscript parish records may still survive in libraries, either as originals or collected on microfilm. The dwindling numbers of originals which remain *in situ*, in parish chests or private collections, are probably beyond the reach of the amateur searcher, offering no support or information services or adequate study space. Because the County Record Office is likely to be further from home, offers less legible originals and in some cases has a more forbidding aspect than the more familiar library, we are well advised to start nearer home, with printed sources. Most large

---

reference libraries now offer a separate Archives or Local History department; this may be housed in another building. Once essential background data, from the *Victoria County History*, the catalogue of the British Library on computer, the transactions of the county historical society and articles in *The Local Historian*, have been assimilated, the student may feel well enough equipped to visit the CRO and ask to see original records which he/she now knows to be there. Applications for access to original documents should always be as explicit as possible.

There are two main sources of practical guidance to the prospective CRO visitor; both of them are usually on hand in reference libraries. *Record Offices: How to Find Them*, by Jeremy Gibson and Pamela Peskett, is published by the Federation of Family History Societies (Benson Room, Birmingham & Midland Institute, Margaret Street, Birmingham B3 3BS) at £3.00 including p&p. The 7th edition was published in 1996. This essential guide gives not only addresses and telephone numbers, but also clear 2-10":1 mile town maps showing CRO location, bus stops, railway stations and car parks. Any published genealogical guide to the records is also noted, with occasional comment on their main classes. Any other more specialised issue of the copious FFHS series is always well worth consulting in preparation for documentary study in local archives.

A similar guide to *Record Repositories in Great Britain, A Geographical Directory* (Royal Commission on Historical Manuscripts, HMSO, 9th edition, 1991 @ £3.50) contains most of the FFHS's information, except the maps, but adds archivists' names and titles of published guides to the deposited records. Fax as well as telephone numbers, are given, also any requirement of a reader's ticket. The difference between this guide and the FFHS edition, which is primarily concerned with the local availability of genealogical records, is its wider national scope. Thus, it includes the same amount of information about national record offices, university and college libraries, charitably endowed organisations and institutes and specialised collections in addition to county repositories.

Since *Village Records* first offered advice to inexperienced searchers, the whole aspect of County Record Offices has changed, not only in the shape of modern, more commodious buildings and hi-tech facilities, but in their somewhat inconvenient popularity. Gone are the more free-and-easy days when, as one of a small group of initiates, the privileged searcher could monopolise whole boxes or piles of archives for the day and perhaps be offered a cup of coffee in the repair room. Today's search room is more likely to be overcrowded and understaffed and security is rigid. It may be necessary to book a seat and table-space in advance and certainly notice **must** be given of any need to use a micro-reader; some classes of document may also need advance warning and, if microfilmed, may not be available as originals (a real difficulty for short-sighted readers in sunlit rooms). A reader's ticket will usually be issued, requiring **printed** evidence of identity; a few offices charge a fee for admission. Most of these tickets are associated with the County Archive Research Network (CARN), which gives admission to record offices other than the county of issue. A visitor's book will ask the purpose of the visit; bags and outdoor clothing must be surrendered and work must be done in pencil without excessive handling of old parchment or paper.

Helpful staff will always offer advice on how to fill out application forms for documents and point out essential indexes and catalogues. In some cases only a limited number of original documents, as few as six, will be issued during any one day. In some counties different records are held in more than one building so that it is as well to know where your own chosen class of archives is stored. Time limits are set, so that no issues are made after a certain hour. It is essential that all these points are checked beforehand—most offices will send their leaflet of instructions in a self-addressed envelope to prevent us from being in the wrong place at the wrong time.

Most archivists welcome a **brief** telephone call of introduction, stating the date and time of a proposed visit, the purpose of the search and the sets of documents to be consulted; they will offer advice on the accessibility of those records, times of opening and available equipment. Do not, however, expect to have a lengthy telephone consultation or ask for *ab initio* information about the records you need. The archivist is entitled to expect that you already know what you want to see and what you expect to find. More guidance may be offered in the search room but you will soon observe how hard-pressed archivists are; we must never under-rate the high degree of their responsibility for precious documents and the sheer inconvenience of continuous storage and access. It is usual for searchers to work in pairs on their family history or village study; this is acceptable, but as the search room is supposed to be a relatively silent area, continual discussion is very irritating to other searchers. Lap-top computers are rarely permitted, except in special cases such as a research task, index or database, seen to be of value to the archives. This is well worth an enquiry but cannot be taken for granted. It goes without saying that mobile telephones carried in the arrested briefcase should be switched OFF before work begins.

Once the precious original is obtained at last, preparation should have already equipped you to recognise its shape, style and possible content; it should not, for instance, come as a complete surprise to find that your sample is written in Latin or in a spiky, unfamiliar hand. Try to discover the physical size and shape of the document before it is brought up to you, so that again you are not taken by surprise. Printed transcripts of similar documents should have warned you if the content, language or calligraphy is likely to confound you and have familiarised you with the form and phraseology of such records, their customary abbreviations and specialised vocabulary. If you realised, from print, that it would be useless to continue further with a study of similar originals before you have had more practice in reading facsimiles, you will have saved both yourself and the archivists a great deal of time and frustration.

In spite of more modern reprographic equipment, high standard copying of documents in libraries and record offices is less effective than it used to be in the archaic age of photographic copies in black-and-white negative or positive. Copying of originals is now more restricted, and may indeed be prohibited in some fragile or oversize cases. Otherwise, the ubiquitous office copier at standard rates is fairly reliable for permitted documents or printed pages, if sometimes grey-on-grey. The most convenient machine, prompt, selective and effective, when it works well, is the micro-reader-copier. For serious reproduction or publication of facsimiles only a professional photograph is suitable. The Historical Manuscripts Commission's *Directory* offers information on those repositories which offer photographic services as well as microfilm copies. Copyright regulations are far-reaching and explicitly printed on all official copies; it must be made very clear if your intention is to use a copy for desktop publishing, so that permission may—or may not—be gained.

For those who become interested, as so many do, in making a more permanent record of their notes and conclusions, first read *Writing Local History* by David Dymond (BALH,

1988). There are many models and modes of compilation as well as booklet format. The production of Archive Study Units on selected themes and topics, in vogue from 1962 to 1982, has to some extent fallen off in more recent years, largely due to the demise of so many teachers' resources centres. Exceptional survivors of this genre are the documentary wallets produced by the Borthwick Institute at Peasholme Green in York. These, proudly said to be 'selling well' (at £2.95 inc. p&p) include guides to early handwriting and other collections on special topics which are listed in the Yorkshire gazetteers. Otherwise, publication mainly continues more formally by University departments of Extended Education, as at Reading and Hull in 1990 and by Museums such as Derbyshire, Nottingham, Leicester and Doncaster. Some CROs still offer documentary packs and Essex still, as ever, leads in this field, publishing SEAX portfolios of documents and illustrations on: *Essex Towns, 1540-1640, Law and Order in Essex* and *Agriculture in Essex c.1840-1900.*

An interesting offshoot is the idea of 'parish packs', pioneered in 1987 by David Bromwich, local studies librarian for Somerset. These were prepared and deposited in sets of six A4 booklets for 500 parishes in the county as a useful starter set for beginners. They include a first edition 25" OS map, population tables from 1801-1981 and a whole series of photocopies, from Domesday, lay subsidy rolls, hearth tax etc. There is also a whole run of commercial directory entries from 1840 to 1935 and relevant extracts from Pevsner's *Buildings of England.* The intention is 'to devolve information to the level of the smallest branch libraries as close as possible to the places they describe and to the people who live there and want to study them'. Sets were also deposited with the Schools Library Service Resources Centre. The idea has been taken up in Devon and might well recommend itself to other county libraries.

Now we are moving along the information super-highway, into the Millennium of the Computer. This progress will involve not only rapid catalogue searching and home word-processing, nor even simple access to ever-larger data bases, but far more reliance on effective methods of computer assisted learning.[6] A brief list of a few of the many available books about the wider possibilities of computers in local history is given at the end of this chapter. These show that software packages for compilation of the researcher's own data-bases and other types of computer assisted learning are already in use. Some of these, like *Gaol*, a computerised analysis of 19th-century prison records in the Bedfordshire county record office may appear at first sight to be too eclectic and localised for the general searcher. They demonstrate a form of study, however, which our own studies of other records might well take in future, even though at present this type of programme is prone to alarmingly rapid obsolescence as state-of-the-art hardware continually outruns the capacity of ready-made discs. *Gaol*[7] itself is no longer compatible with the present generation of computers. Programming adequately large samples which are capable of reliable cross-reference and statistical analysis is labour intensive and becomes uneconomic when one realises, as with the excellent Quarry Bank census programme, that so much useful material, for one reason or another, has fallen into disuse, as have so many more of the packages recommended by the Historical Association as recently as 1986.[8]

The more flexible, up-to-date uses of the Internet[9] and CD-ROM have both a more immediate and longer-term significance than obsolescent software packs. They extend the range of search, whether in schools and library networks or on lone 'techies' home computers. Susan Howard offers a realistic explanation of the facilities which the Internet can offer to the

---

[6] See, for example: *Exploring History with Computers*, edited by J. Wilkes, Council for Educational Technology MEP Readers, 1985.

[7] F. Milligan, 'Gaol'—using modern technology to encourage historical enquiry in schools, *Bedfordshire Magazine*, Summer 1987, pp.17-20.

[8] A. Dickinson, F. Blow and M. Wild, *History and New Technology: suggestions and considerations*, The Historical Association, 1986.

[9] Susan Howard, 'The Internet', *Local History magazine*, no.54, March/April and no.56, July/August 1996.

local history searcher. She gives lucid information about types of modem, service providers and software, with clearly tabulated examples of available functions. The uses of 'domain name', URL (Universal Resources Location), web sites, e-mail addresses (local history.co.uk) and access to mailing lists (e.g. compiled by BALH and the Institute of Historical Research) are all carefully explained. This is a persuasive, practical guide to many more ideas and skills than this elderly Luddite, lacking the essential hardware, will ever be able to master. It is a commonplace division of the generations that for some of us these unsettling prospects, so much less reassuring than the painstaking manual search of card-indexes and photostats, are capable of arousing reactions of insecurity and computer-rage. Even so, recent experience of children using the British Library's CD-ROM *Medieval Realms* has given this author a glimpse of the possibilities of a really large Windows-compatible data base.[10] For this lo-tech reader enough excitement was already caused by the publication in 1992 of Phillimore's complete *Domesday Book: Indexes of Persons, Places* and *Subjects*. The extension of students' reference capacity by these extensive works is immense. It marks the author's conversion to some possibilities of computerised study that, since *Medieval Realms 1995*, his mind boggles at the infinite capacity for cross-reference and comparisons, county to county, which those indexes will no doubt offer on the home computer—someday? Meanwhile, we still need books, but books and computers are only there to guide us to the documents and help us to interpret them in the light of the most recent research.

GENERAL WORKS ON DOCUMENTARY STUDY

A present drawback to easy reference is the current state of publishing and its rapid changes. Many of the references available from 1962-1982 are no longer in print. Many of those publishers are no longer in business; unprofitable books regularly fall out of print and become difficult to trace. Film strips recommended for younger students can no longer compete with CD-ROMs; even the British Library and the Public Record Office sell of old stock. The searcher for any abstruse work which is difficult to find or even to identify with a complete reference is fortunate if the local reference library is, like Birmingham, Manchester and about 30 other libraries, universities and colleges with similar cataloguing systems, a member of BLCMP (The British Library Computer Mark Project). Also known to librarians as the Union Name Catalogue, this is a more searching programme than *British Books in Print* and will often trace works which are in fact out of print.

In revising the second edition's bibliographies, as far as possible, priority has been given to those books listed in Whittaker's *Books in Print*, July 1995 and more recent editions up-dated. A few monumental ancient volumes such as Birch's *Cartularium Saxonicum* or Kemble's *Codex Diplomaticus*, though not available to the student in a hurry, cannot be ignored and some out-of-print books have not been replaced by newer alternatives. On the assumption that most major works and a full range of periodical *Transactions* will be found in reliable reference libraries, only the most essential out-of-print works have been included in the general reading list. Other study guides are listed in their appropriate documentary sections where all relevant works, whether in or out of print, are included.

---

[10] J. West and J. Lally, *Medieval Realms 1995*, Historical Association and British Library, 1995.

BACKGROUND INFORMATION BOOKS

M. Aston, *Interpreting the Landscape*, Batsford, 1988

J. Bristow, *The Local Historian's Glossary and Vade Mecum*, University of Nottingham, 2nd edition, 1994

J. Campbell-Kease, *A Companion to Local History Research*, A & C Black, 1989

A.J. Camp, *Tracing Your Ancestors*, Gifford, 1970

R. Dunning, *Local History for Beginners*, Phillimore, 1980

D. Dymond, *Writing Local History, a Practical Guide*, BALH/Phillimore, 1988

S. Friar, *The Batsford Companion to Local History*, Batsford, 1991—Short encyclopedic articles with black-and-white line drawings and useful bibliographies for each subject and document.

G. Hamilton-Edwards, *In Search of Ancestry*, Phillimore, 1983

A. Henstock, *Tracing the History of your House*, Nottingham Local History Association, 1988

D. Hey (ed.), *The Oxford Companion to Local and Family History* (O.U.P., 1996) is an invaluable reference book in encyclopedic form, 'intended as a starting point for those professional scholars and amateur researchers who are working in those fields and serves as a valuable source of information for the general reader'. An impressive list of contributors includes eminent librarians, genealogists, archivists and dons, such as Anthony Camp, Dr. D. Huw Owen, Dr. Joan Thirsk and Dr. Margaret Gelling. 'The *Companion* provides information on archives: how to use them and where they can be found and defines terms commonly used in Local and Family History research'. 509 pages of alphabetical entries range from one-line definitions of, eg. *abstract* or *pinder* to 3-8 pages on *buildings, domestic, court, place-names, popular culture, Welsh local and family history* or *women local and family historians*. This is an essential day-to-day reference book.

W.G. Hoskins, *Local History in England*, Longman, 1984; and: *Making of the English Landscape*, Hodder, 1992

A.L. Humphreys, *A Handbook to County Bibliography*, 1974

D. Iredale, *Discovering Local History*, Shire, 1991

J. Richardson, *The Local Historian's Encyclopedia*, Phillimore, 1993

K. Tiller, *English Local History: An Introduction*, 1992

A.J. Willis & K. Proudfoot, *Genealogy for Beginners*, Phillimore, 1997

GUIDES TO ARCHIVE SOURCES AND ADMINISTRATION

Record Repositories in Great Britain, a Geographical Directory, Historical Manuscripts Commission, pbk., HMSO, 1993

F.G. Emmison, *Introduction to Archives*, Phillimore, 1977

F.G. Emmison & I. Gray, *County Records*, Historical Association 'Helps for History Students', 1994

J. Foster & J. Sheppard, *British Archives: A Guide to Archive Resources in the United Kingdom*, Macmillan, 1995. 1,109 entries, arranged by towns, of 'relatively accessible' archives, with a 46-page Index to Collections, a 7-page Index to Key Collections and a 15-page list of useful publications, uncluding periodical articles.

J. Gibson & P. Peskett, *Record Offices and How to Find Them*, Federation of Family History Societies, 7th edition, 1996

S. Guy, *English Local Studies Handbook; a guide to resources for each county, including libraries, record offices, societies, journals and museums*, University of Exeter Press, 1992

C.R. Humphery-Smith, *A Genealogist's Bibliography*, Phillimore, 1985

D. Iredale, *Enjoying Archives; what they are, where to find them and how to use them*, Phillimore, 1985

K.A. Johnson & M.R.Sainty (eds.), *Genealogical Research Directory 1995*, 'A key reference work for national and worldwide family history'

G. Martin & P.O. Spufford, *The Records of the Nation; Public Record Office 1848-1988*, Boydell Press, 1990

A. Morton and G. Donaldson, *British and National Archives and the Local Historian*, Historical Association H.88, 1980

E.L.C. Mullins, *Texts and Calendars; an analytical guide to serial publications*, Royal Historical Society, vol.1, 1958; vol.2, 1983

M. Nicksom, *The British Library, A Guide to the Catalogues and Indexes of the Department of Manuscripts*, 1978

W.B. Stephens, *Sources for English Local History*, Phillimore, 1994

Several Record Offices publish guides to their archives which contain notes on classification and types of documents, some with a few well-produced facsimiles. These may well be used as textbooks on documentary study sources. See, for example:

F. Hull, *Guide to the Kent County Archives Office*, Kent County Council, 1971

N.W. Kingsley, *Handlist of the Contents of the Gloucestershire County Record Office*, Glos. CRO., 1988

R. Whittaker, 'Worcester Records in the Hereford and Worcester Record Office', *Genealogists' Magazine*, vol.21, no.10, June 1985 and no.11, September 1985

BOOKS ON HANDWRITING AND STUDY SKILLS

J.H. Baxter & C. Johnson, *Medieval Latin Word List*, O.U.P., 1950

L.E. Boyle, *Medieval Latin Paleography, A Bibliographical Introduction*, University of Toronto Press, 1984

Chester Record Office Local History Packs: *Old Handwriting Starter Pack*; *Family History Organizer*; *Record Office Survival Kit*; *Archive Conservation Pack*; *Family History Starter Pack*, Chester City Record Office, 1995

E. Danbury, *Palaeography for Local and Family Historians*, Phillimore, 1997

F.G. Emmison, *How to Read Local Archives 1550-1700*, Historical Association Helps for Students of Local History, 1994; *Archives and Local History*, Phillimore, 1978

J. Fines, *Reading Historical Documents*, Blackwell, 1988—offers a guide to the study of historical records.

E.B. Fryde *et al*, *Handbook of British Chronology*, 3rd edition, Royal Historical Society, 1986

E.A. Gooder, *Latin for Local History, An Introduction*, Longman, 1961

D. Gosden, *Starting to Read Medieval Latin Manuscripts*, (an introduction for students of medieval history and genealogists who wish to venture into Latin texts), Llanerch, 1993

H.E.P. Grieve, *Examples of English Handwriting, 1150-1750*, Essex Record Office, 5th edition, 1981— Reproductions of documents with accompanying transcriptions and alphabets.

L.C. Hector, *The Handwriting of English Documents*, facsimile reprint, 1980

R.E. Latham, *A Dictionary of Medieval Latin from British Sources*, O.U.P., 1975

E. McLaughlin, *Reading Old Handwriting* (from Elizabeth I to Victoria), FFHS, 1987; *Latin for Family Historians*, FFHS, 1986

C. Trice Martin, *The Record Interpreter*, a facsimile of the 1910 edition, a collection of abbreviations with Latin-English glossary of words used in historical manuscripts, Phillimore, 1994

L. Munby, *Reading Tudor and Stuart Handwriting*, BALH/Phillimore, 1988

K.C. Newton, *Medieval Local Records, A Reading Aid*, Historical Association H83, 1971

A. Rycraft, *English Medieval Handwriting*, Borthwick Wallet no.3, Borthwick Institute, 1971; *Sixteenth and Seventeenth Century Handwriting, series 1*, Borthwick Wallet no.1, Borthwick Institute, 1969; *Sixteenth and Seventeenth Century Handwriting, series 2*, Borthwick Wallet no.2, Borthwick Institute, 1969

K.C. Sidwell, *Reading Medieval Latin*, C.U.P. pbk., 1995

D. Stuart, *Latin for Local and Family Historians*, Phillimore, 1995

E.E. Thoyts, *How to Read Old Documents*, a standard 90-year-old work on handwriting contractions in all periods, Phillimore, 1980

F. Tremblay, *Medieval Latin Lexicography*, Mellen U.S., 1989

LOCAL HISTORY AND ARCHIVES FOR SCHOOLS

Archives and Education: Conference Proceedings, 1984, Society of Archivists, 1985

BALH, *Teaching Local History Leaflets*, 1995—Teachers' Notes including background information, teaching strategies and a glossary, with four pages of primary and secondary sources, pictures and text and activities for pupils. A set of introductions by no means confined to the classroom, but also useful for amateur historians. Available at £3.50 per leaflet from: Ashwell Education Services, Merchant Taylors' Centre, Ashwell, Baldock, Herts. SG7 5LY. Titles in the series include: *The Victorians* by Emma Steed; *Medieval Life* by Stephanie Luxford; *Roman Life* by Emma Steed; *The Tudors* by Mary Tither; *World War II* by Emma Steed; *The New Poor Law* by Rosemary Little.

R. David and M. Huggins, 'Local History in the National Curriculum', *The Local Historian*, vol. 23, no.3., August 1991

R. Dunning, 'Archive Packs and Archive Teaching Units', *The Local Historian*, vol.12, no.8, 1977

J. Fines, *Domesday Book in the Classroom: A Guide for Teachers*, Phillimore, 1982

T. Lomas, 'The Teaching of Local History in Schools', *The Local Historian*, vol.18, no.4, November 1988

D. Smith and J. Turtle, 'Local History Research in Schools: The role of the Gloucestershire Record Office', *The Local Historian*, vol.19, no.1, February 1989

K.M. Thompson, *The Use of Archives in Education*, Society of Archivists, 1982

COMPUTERS AND HISTORY

'Computer Projects, an Information Exchange', *The Local Historian*, vol.16, no.7, August 1985

D. Hawgood, *Internet for Genealogy*, Parchment, Oxford, 1996

P. Hudson, 'A New History from Below: Computers and the Maturing of Local and Regional History', *The Local Historian*, vol.25, no.4, November 1995

S. Jackson, 'Using Micro-Databases in Local History: Bromborough Pool, 1861', *The Local Historian*, vol.16, no.5, February 1985

D. and J. Mills, 'Rural mobility in the Victorian censuses; experience with a micro-computer program', *The Local Historian*, vol.18, no.2, May 1988

S.J. Page, 'Research Methods and Techniques: Researching Local History: Methodological Issues and Computer-assisted Analysis', *The Local Historian*, vol.23, no.1, February 1993

K. Randell, *The Use of the Computer in the study and learning of History*, Historical Association, 1984

K. Schurer, 'Census Enumeration Returns and the Computer', *The Local Historian*, vol.16, no.6, May 1985

J. Spavold, 'Using a Relational Database: The Example of Church Gresley (Berks.) Inventories', *The Local Historian*, vol.26, no.2, May 1996; and: 'Children and Databases: An Analysis of Data Entry and Query Formulation', *Journal of Computer Assisted Learning*, no.5, 1989

J. Wilkes, *Exploring History with Computers*, Council for Educational Technology MEP Readers, 1985

CHAPTER II

Saxon and Early Norman Documents

✧

The centuries before the Norman Conquest were an age of migration and settlement, of the foundations of an English race and a Saxon language. During this period there emerged also the central institutions of monarchy and of the Christian Church in England. After the conversion, in England as on the continent, Church and State worked closely together to preserve peace and order. From A.D. 600 to 1035 there developed a body of accepted law and social custom, interpreted by the King's officers, household thegns and clerics of the royal chapel.

At a local level, most English villages originate from these centuries of settlement; pre-Saxon remains, whether prehistoric, Roman or Celtic, are usually fragmentary and isolated in lowland England. It is the forest clearings and homesteads of the immigrant Saxon warbands which are recorded in the village's earliest record—its place-name—and which are delimited and defined by charter and parish boundaries. The parish church too, though little if any of the original fabric may now survive, often stands upon its Saxon site.

In local government, the territorial divisions of shire and diocese, hundred and archdeaconry, vill and parish, developed together to replace the original tribal kingdoms which gave them identity. The fundamental bonds of society, kindred and tithing, folk-moot and personal status were recorded and interpreted, together with personal responsibilities of fyrd service, geld, law and order, in the unsystematic repetitions of ancient laws by the successors of Ethelbert of Kent, Offa of Mercia, and Ine of Wessex, down to the more complex codes of Alfred and Canute. Under the Saxon kings, personal status and responsibility, between king and gesith, thegn, earl and shire-reeve, were continually recorded and defined in accordance with custom. Responsibility for service to the community only gradually became associated with territorial grants, and was not fully developed until feudalism was introduced by the Norman kings.

This was an age of assimilation and growth; the tribal divisions of the heptarchy coalesced into the Saxon kingdom of Alfred's successors; Christianity was superimposed upon a pagan society; repeated Norse invasions contributed their own institutions, language and social customs. All this was comprised in a loose federation of earldoms under a Saxon royal house. It is a common mistake to seek, in this age, the origins of English 'nationalism' and 'democratic' institutions; in 1066 Mercia, Northumbria and Wessex still survived, committed only by personal loyalties to their Saxon kings.

The Norman Conquest introduced extensive administrative changes, but involved little disturbance of the existing social structure. The Norman kings were conservative in their adaptation of the offices and machinery of Saxon local government, adding, in feudalism, a territorial military government based upon a more rigidly conditional contract. This innovation in the relationship of crown, church and baronage may have replaced the more personal ties of Saxon government, but was, even so, able to co-exist with the older institutions of shire, hundred, tithing, vill and township. As for the peasantry, under new Norman-French manorial overlords, their daily routine went on undisturbed.

During both Saxon and Norman periods, the vernacular English tongue survived in literary and business forms, alongside the universal Latin of Church and Law, and the Norman-French of feudalism, just as the Saxon writ was preserved in the Anglo-Norman charter. Thus the monarchy retained much of its Anglo-Saxon basis of authority and law, conserving and interpreting the ancient customs of Canute and the Confessor. Nowhere is this period of transition and adaptation more clearly recorded than in the great Domesday Survey of William I.

SAXON CHARTERS AND PLACE-NAMES

THE DOCUMENT

The Anglo-Saxon charter, more accurately known as the diploma or 'book', was a document which recorded the conveyance of land, or rights over land. There are many examples for the period from *c.*690 to the Norman Conquest, and they are a most important source for the history of that period. The entire document, written in half-uncial or cursive script, was in Saxon (later in Latin with land boundaries described in Saxon) and developed an elaborate form. This comprised seven main parts:

  (i)   the preamble, or invocation;
  (ii) the proem, some pious observation on the transitory nature of earthly wealth, or on the virtues of charity, giving the title of the donor in majestic terms;
  (iii) the gift, of lands or rights;
  (iv) the sanction, a curse or anathema on any who break the terms of the charter;
  (v)   the perambulation of the bounds of the gift;
  (vi) the date;
  (vii) the attestation, with the names of the donors and witnesses (not autographs).

The purpose of the charter was confirmation of a grant by the king to a follower, a thegn, or a religious body, or, later, by a noble or ecclesiastic to his own dependents. The document appears to be a simple conveyance of property, but is more properly considered as an alienation of royal or seigneurial rights over such lands. The recipient was granted immunity from payments and dues formerly rendered to the king himself, 'tribute', food-rents, repair of royal houses, public duties and legal fines. Usually the most important royal rights, fyrd service and work on bridges and defences, were specifically retained in the king's hands. The chief purpose of such a grant was often the foundation of a religious house, with security of possession, and freedom from public burdens.

Charters are of particular value in local study, in that they show the progress and nature of land distribution and ordered settlement immediately after the Saxon invasions. They add to our knowledge of the position of the local kings (for example, the Hwiccas, and their relationship with their Mercian overlords), and show something of the prestige and property of the Church. The perambulations are especially interesting as defining the bounds of villages and hamlets by reference to natural and man-made features, many of which may still be in evidence. Their boundaries often ante-date the parochial division. Their evidence of place-names is particularly revealing in determining Celtic survivals, extent of Norse invasion and settlement, and occasionally evidence of prehistoric sites which have not survived.

The student must not expect to find original charters locally, as these are mostly collected in the great national repositories.[1] Our nearest acquaintanceship will more usually be with a photograph, obtained from these archives. The examples illustrated are fairly typical and, though more clearly legible than many later documents, their language is a problem for those who have not studied elementary Latin or Early English. It is soon apparent that the formula used, wordy and repetitive in the Latin portions, more concise for the Saxon boundaries, does in fact follow a pattern which is soon recognisable with practice. The Saxon vocabulary is limited and quite quickly learned, but makes use of a number of archaic letters (particularly the forms of *r, s, th t, w,* and *f*), which at first sight make quite ordinary words appear unfamiliar. The beginner is thus well-advised to confine himself for some time to modern printed editions wherever available. There are many fine collections of charters, with very adequate translation, explanatory text, and, often, topographical data and map references.

A charter is often the first written evidence of the existence of an English village, but place-names which it records refer to settlements which had already existed, sometimes for centuries, before any written record was made. Thus the place-names themselves are records, usually the most ancient evidence, of the existence of towns and vills, which can tell us much about the earliest settlers and the places which they chose for habitation. The single word, or two, of a village's name can afford a tremendous amount of information to the expert. It usually throws light upon the origin and progress of settlement during the otherwise 'dark' ages of Celtic subjection and Anglo-Saxon occupation. The immigration of new racial groups and their mode of settlement are thus recorded, and regional differences in place-names can reveal the survival of Celtic inhabitants, or the extent and even the direction of Germanic and Scandinavian invasions from the sixth to the tenth century.

So also are often disclosed the strategic or communication points which made settlement possible, in reference to the water supply, the portways, fording-places, bridges and markets. Other names emphasise the natural features which first impressed the primitive settlers, the oak and ash groves, the ancient burial mounds, the hawks' and eagles' eyries, the marsh and fen, the hard flinty rocks and ridges. Nor does the development of place-names end with the Saxon settlement. The extent of Viking penetration can to a large extent be measured and mapped by reference to the location of Scandinavian place-names; later still, the Norman baronial families, the Giffards, the Wyvilles and d'Abitots, added their family names to existing villages, and the feudal 'system' is still revealed in villages which were once the demesnes of earls and bishops, kings and abbots, or the fees of Corbetts and Mortimers. Even later history

---

[1] Staffordshire and Kent are exceptional. In the William Salt Library, Stafford, are eight original Staffordshire Charters. Kent Archives Office holds the original of King Wihtred's Charter of A.D. 699, and supplies facsimiles, with a translation and transcript.

is revealed in the family names of outlying farms and hamlets, once owned by Elizabethan gentry whose families had prospered since the Dissolution. In the field- and street-names of medieval towns can be traced the physical growth and shape of its walls and fields; even the Industrial Revolution has recorded the positions of mills and forges now extinct, just as the names of streets and parks today may commemorate local worthies and national events soon forgotten.

As Professor Hoskins pointed out, 'few subjects contain so many pitfalls as the study of place-names'.[2] To explain the derivation of a village's name calls for specialised linguistic and historical knowledge; conjecture upon the 'obvious' origins can frequently be totally misleading, as Hoskins shows. The student has, however, the resources of specialist research readily to hand in the large number of place-name dictionaries which are available from local libraries. *The Oxford Dictionary of English Place-Names* (E. Ekwall [ed.], Oxford, 3rd ed., 1947) is an invaluable guide for the whole country. Most counties are provided with their own dictionary, which will usually include not only village names, but also the origins of names of farms, hamlets, woods and brooks, with reference to the documents in which each new form of the name has been found.

There are, indeed, few fields of local study more productive of regular and ongoing publication than the investigation of place-names. Some of this output is seen by critics as misplaced, encouraging superfluous anecdote and tourist-guide guesswork. 'More nonsense', according to another leading authority, 'has been written on place-names than on any subject, except perhaps than that of surnames'.[3] John Field lists more than 100 place-name books and articles, not only major dictionaries, but also those periodical publications, which can be used locally to flesh out the broader regional outlines.[4] His bibliography also lists authorities on the place-names of Wales, Ireland, Scotland and the Isle of Man. Field points out the disadvantage of any alphabetical listing, which inevitably separates names which should be closely associated for interpretation at ground level and we are warned of the misleading conclusions which can be drawn from 'over-hasty use of place-name dictionaries'.

The main contribution in this field, for nearly seventy years, has been that of the English Place-Name Society and its eminent contributors to more than 50 place-name dictionaries. Thirty substantial county volumes draw, more recently, on documents and archaeological evidence from beyond the PRO and British Library, which were not included in earlier publications. More attention too, is lately paid to Celtic, Gaelic and Scandinavian elements in English place-names, particularly where these are seen to mingle, not only on the most westerly and northern frontiers; the fundamental importance of river-, field- and street-names is also recognised.

Appreciation of the vital significance of place-names as virtual documents of early Anglo-Saxon and Norse settlement and the probable survival and assimilation of Celtic inhabitants has long been recognised. As this brief introduction pointed out in 1962: 'A study of place-names is essential if we are to discover the origin of settlement'. This awareness now leads to more careful distinction between those non-Germanic derivations which either pre-date mid-fifth-century invasion or survive the first decades of eighth-century settlement. Margaret Gelling suggests that: 'English place-names which incorporate words borrowed from the Latin may indicate continuity of settlement from Romano-British times'. She points to a 1960s revision of the perceived importance of '-*ing*' names as the earliest evidence of Saxon tribal

[2] W.G. Hoskins, *Local History in England*, Longmans, 1959, p. 10.
[3] P.H. Reaney, *The Origins of English Place-names*, 1960.
[4] J. Field, 'What to read on place-names in Britain', *The Local Historian*, 17., no.7, August 1987, citing P.H. Reaney.

settlement and offers a new reading of the suffixes '*tun*' and '*ley*' as late eighth-century settlement terms. We have certainly needed to re-think our first edition's imaginative play on 'the clearings in the forest where Saxon warrior bands, led by shadowy giants named Ceadda, Wulfweard or Eadbald, first built their stockades and halls', at places like Chaddesley, Wolverley and Abberley. The personal names are real, the Saxon settlers were there, but the dating of the name is not as early as we may have thought. Indeed, even hasty reference to Ekwall would have reminded us that our earliest evidence of the first two names is found in ninth-century charters and Abberley not until *c.*1180! In the same way, most northern Danish names are now post-dated as probable evidence of secondary Norse, rather than of early Viking immigration.[5] In the Celtic context, another important contribution has been the publication of Rivet and Smith's *The Place-Names of Roman Britain* in 1979.

On a different time-scale, more recent attention is also paid to the relevance of place-names to early medieval history, as well as to those names which originated in post-medieval periods. No more helpful development could now take place than the projected replacement of Eilert Ekwall's standard *Dictionary of English Place-names*, first published 60 years ago, by a new version by Victor Watts. Publication date by C.U.P. is as yet conjectural, 'possibly by April 1997'.

It is essential that local students be encouraged to apply a microcosmic focus to any local survey by first mapping all available place-name derivations on large-scale maps which show the topographical features of the local landscape, including contours, notes on aspect and land-use. Secondly, we must be sure to seek out any local evidence to expand the outlines of a county dictionary, including not only local historical societies' transactions, but also any first-hand documentary sources, such as charters, Domesday and later medieval records which may be in print. The map should also include the names and origins of hills, brooks and fields, taken from early maps, tithe awards and enclosure records. Minor variations in spelling should be carefully recorded.

Pre-occupation with landscape features is nowadays an important feature of the interpretation of settlement. The main trend in revisionist studies has been the realisation that 'topographical' names of Celtic and early Saxon origin are more important than the 'habitative' names which once seemed to dominate our view of the earliest Anglo-Saxon landscape. Margaret Gelling offers us a revealing insight into the very *thinking* of the earliest Saxon immigrants as they surveyed the Celtic land which they would occupy. 'Many of these [topographical] terms have a quasi-habitative sense, describing the position of the settlement in relation to the landscape feature and conveying information about its likely size and economic prospects. The possibilities for growth and development for a settlement on a hill called *dun* or in the type of valley called *denu* are much greater than those for a settlement on a *hyll*, by a *hoh*, or in the sort of valley called *cumb* or *hop* ... The Anglo-Saxon topographical vocabulary is a subtle code which can be deciphered by relating names to their surroundings.'[6] This argument is graphically illustrated by a photograph of a hill which is an unfavourable '*hoh*' and shows us what a Saxon thought his heel looked like.

Because the danger exists that the less well-known village names, and particularly names of fields and lanes, may become lost for want of use or of written record, the amateur student can perform a useful service in the careful collection and recording of names which he may discover by word of mouth from older inhabitants, or from maps and records which are not

[5] M. Gelling, 'Recent Work on English Place Names', *The Local Historian*, 11, 1974, and 'The Present State of English place-name studies', *The Local Historian*, 22, no.3, August 1992.
[6] M. Gelling, 'Topographical Settlement Names', *The Local Historian*, 12, no.6, 1977; *Place Names in the Landscape*, Dent, 1992.

easily accessible. 'If, therefore, the local historian encounters place-names within his parish for which he can find no authoritative explanation in print, he should simply record the spellings (with references and dates) as he finds them and leave it to others to decide what they mean' (W.G. Hoskins, *op. cit.*, p.10). The English Place-Name Society exists to further the study of hitherto unknown place-names.

FURTHER READING

W. Addison, *Understanding English Place-names*, Batsford, 1978

K. Bailey, 'Anglo-Saxon Charters and the Local Historian', *The Local Historian*, 17, no.2, May 1986

N. Brooks, 'Anglo-Saxon Charters, the work of the last 30 years', *Anglo-Saxon England 3*, 1974

K. Cameron, *English Place Names*, Batsford, 1977; *The Significance of English Place Names*, British Academy Proceedings, no.62, 1976

K. Cameron and M. Gelling, *Place-name evidence for the Anglo-Saxon invasion and Scandinavian Settlement*, English Place-Name Society, 1976

G.J. Copley, *English Place-names and their origins*, 1968; *Archaeology and Place-Names in the Fifth and Sixth centuries*, British Archaeological Reports, British series 147, 1986

B. Cox, 'The Place-names of the Earliest English records', *English Place-Name Society Journal*, no.8, 1976

J. Earle, *Handbook of Charters and Saxonic Documents*, Oxford, 1888

E. Ekwall, *The Concise Oxford Dictionary of English Place Names*, O.U.P., 4th edition, 1980; and: *English River-Names*, 1928

J. Field, 'What to read on place-names in Britain', *The Local Historian*, 17, no.7, August 1987 (includes references to Scotland and N. Ireland); *Discovering Place Names*, Shire Publications, 1971; *Place Names of Great Britain and Ireland*, David and Charles, 1980

H.P.R. Finberg, *The Formation of England 550-1042*, Paladin, 1976

M. Gelling, *Early Charters of the Thames Valley*, Leicestershire University Press, 1980; *Place-Names in the Landscape*, London, 1984; *Signposts to the Past. Place-names and the History of England*, Phillimore, 1988; 'Recent Work on English Place Names', *The Local Historian*, 11, 1974; 'Topographical Settlement Names', *The Local Historian*, 12, no.6, 1977; 'The Present State of English place-name studies', *The Local Historian*, 22, no.3, August 1992; *Place Names in the Landscape*, Dent, 1992

N. Gould, *Looking at Place Names*, Havant, 1978

J. Brown Johnston, *Place Names of Scotland*, Wakefield S.R.P., re-issue of 1934 edition, 1970

P. McClure, 'Surnames from English Place Names as Evidence of Mobility in the Middle Ages', *The Local Historian*, 13, 1978; and: 'Patterns of Migration in the Late Middle Ages; the Evidence of Place Name Surnames', *Economic History Review*, no.32, 1979

A. Mawer and F.M. Stenton, *Introduction to the Survey of English Place Names and the Chief Elements used in English Place Names*, C.U.P. and EPNS, 1, 1924

A.D. Mills, *A Dictionary of English Place-Names*, O.U.P., 1991

W.F.H. Nicolaisen, M. Gelling and M. Richards, *The Names of Towns and Cities in Britain*, Batsford, 1970

A.L.F. Rivet and A.H. Smith, *The Place-Names of Roman Britain*, Batsford, 1979

P.H. Sawyer, *Anglo-Saxon Charters: an annotated list and bibliography*, Royal Historical Society Guides and Handbooks no.8, 1968

A.H. Smith, *English Place Name Elements*, C.U.P. and E.P.N.S., vols.25 and 26, 1971

C.J. Spittal and J. Field, *A Readers' Guide to the Place-Names of the United Kingdom: A Bibliography of Publications 1920-1989 on the Place Names of Great Britain, Northern Ireland, the Isle of Man and the Channel Islands*, Paul Watkins, Stamford, 1990

F.M. Stenton, *Anglo-Saxon England*, O.U.P., new paperback edn. 1989

VCH volumes usually include a chapter on 'Anglo-Saxon Remains', which will offer archaeological evidence to confirm what we seem to learn from Saxon charters and place-names. Further archaeological information must be sought in the Transactions of the local Archaeological Society.

HANDLISTS AND NATIONAL COLLECTIONS IN PRINT

For printed versions for various Counties see Robert Somerville, *Handlist of Record Publications* (British Records Association, Pamphlet no.3, Section 101) and E.L.C. Mullins, *Texts and Calendars* (Royal Historical Society, 1958). Both give references to texts printed by English Record Societies for all periods of history, and should therefore be consulted for texts of all types of documents given in this book, in addition to the county handlists published at the end of each section.

W. de G. Birch, *Cartularium Saxonicum*, London, 1885-99. (Referred to in place-name dictionaries and other reference books as B.C.S.) This is the standard printed collection, in Latin and Saxon, of the texts of English charters down to A.D. 957.

J.M. Kemble, *Codex Diplomaticus*, Eng. Hist. Soc. London, 6 vols., 1839-48. (K.C.D.) This also gives full texts of charters in Latin and Saxon. Both these books are chiefly useful for tracing originals in the British Museum, as Museum MSS reference numbers are given in footnotes to each charter, e.g. MS Cott. (*Cottonian Collection*), Tib. (*Tiberius—the divisions of this collection are given Roman Imperial names*), A xiii, f(*olio*) 182b. This is sufficient reference to enable the Museum to find and copy the original charter. It should be noted whether this is in fact original, or a later medieval copy from the cartulary, or charter collection, of the abbey involved. Birch and Kemble take one main text, and interpolate, in footnotes, any variations or glosses which appear in later versions; these are indicated by letters A, B, C, etc. in the note.

PRINTED EDITIONS FOR WORCESTERSHIRE

H.P.R. Finberg, *The Early Charters of the West Midlands*, Leics. Univ. Press, 1960.

G.B. Grundy, *Saxon Charters of Worcestershire*, Transactions of the Birmingham Archaeological Society, 1931. This gives a full translation, original text and references to boundary positions on the OS Map, and refers to B.C.S. for identification of each charter. As the list of other counties' charters shows, Grundy has done a great deal to record these documents in different parts of the country. It is sometimes suggested that some of his boundary identifications are ill-defined; but the beginner in this field will find his work invaluable, and a source of inspiration for much interesting field work.

D. Hooke, *Worcestershire Anglo-Saxon Charter Bounds*, Boydell Press, 1990 and *The Anglo-Saxon Landscape in the Kingdom of the Hwicce*, Manchester U. P., 1985.

A. Mawer and F.M. Stenton, *The Place-names of Worcestershire*, C.U.P., 1927.

The most momentous recent development for our study of local charters has been the publication of Della Hooke's complete collection of *Worcestershire Anglo-Saxon Charter Bounds* in 1990. This is a collection of 233 charters, listed by centuries from the seventh to the eleventh and located by OS references. Seventy-eight of these contain Saxon boundary clauses, each one individually surveyed and mapped with its bounds given in translation and all available sources both chief manuscripts and secondary printed sources cited, including concordance with Birch's, Sawyer's and Finberg's earlier identifications. Our own example from the hamlet of Cookley in Wolverley (Plate I and p.17) is analysed on pp.169-174, as the latest, in 1067, of four copies including a lost original granted by King Edgar (959-975), granting this land to his *comes*, Beorhtnoth (*Sawyer no.726*).

Worcestershire Villages[7] with Charters Cited by Grundy

Abberton (DH)
Abbots Morton (DH)
Acton Beauchamp (He.)
Bedwardine
Bengeworth (DH)
Bentley Pauncefoot
Beoley (DH)
Bransford
Bredicot (DH)
Broadwas (DH)
Broadway (DH)
Bushey
Chaceley (Gl.) (DH)
Church Honeybourne (DH)
Claines (DH)
Cleeve Prior (DH)
Cofton Hackett
Cotheridge (DH)
Crowle (DH)
Cutsdean (Gl.)
Daylesford (Gl.)
Doddenham
Elmley Castle (DH)
Evesham (DH)
Feckenham (DH)
Great Hampton
Great Malvern
Great Witley

Grimley (DH)
Hartlebury (DH)
Harvington (DH)
Hill Croome
Himbleton (DH)
Hindlip (DH)
Holt (DH)
Huddington (DH)
Iccomb (Gl.)
Inkberrow (DH)
Kemerton (DH)
Kempsey
Kings Norton (DH)
Knighton (DH)
Leigh (DH)
Lenchwick
Lindridge
Little Hampton
Longdon
Mamble
Martin Hussingtree (DH)
Martley
Naunton Beauchamp (DH)
Newland
North Piddle (DH)
Norton-juxta-Kempsey
Oddingley (DH)
Offenham

Ombersley (DH)
Overbury and Conderton (DH)
Pendock (DH)
Pensax (DH)
Peopleton
Pershore (DH)
Pirton
Powick
Redditch
Redmarley D'Abitot (Gl.)
Rock
Salwarpe (DH)
Sedgeberrow (DH)
Severn Stoke
Shipston-on-Stour (War.)
Stockton-on-Teme
Stoke Prior (DH)
Stoulton (DH)
Strensham
Teddington (Gl.)
Tidmonton (War.)
Tredington
Tutnal and Cosley
Upton-on-Severn (DH)
Washbourne (Gl.)
Whittington (DH)
Wichenford
Wolverley (DH)

Grundy's list is now superseded by Della Hooke's collection of Worcestershire charters and their bounds, of which 46 are marked here (DH). She adds the following 24 charters with boundary clauses:

Bentley, Bickmarsh and Ullington, Bredon's Norton, Child's Wickham, Clopton, Cofton, Cookley, Croome d'Abitot, Cudley, Dormston, Flyford Flavell, Hampton, Ismere, Kington, Langham, Little Witley, Old Swinford, Perry, Powick, Tardebigge, Upper Arley, Wican, Wick Episcopi, Yardley.

Another important Worcestershire and Midlands source-book by Della Hooke is *The Anglo-Saxon Landscape: The Kingdom of the Hwicce* (Manchester University Press, 1985). The origins of this Anglo-Saxon tribal kingdom can be traced in the early seventh century, long after the earlier westward invasions. Its territorial boundaries appear to be identical with those of the Romano-British kingdom of the Dobunni and also with the mid-seventh-century diocese of

---

[7] Including some villages since taken into other counties (Gloucestershire, Herefordshire and Warwickshire).

TRANSCRIPT
B.C.S. 1134 (Boundaries only are given)
Ærest of usmere on hearecan beorh of þam (1) beorge
10 ... on cuðredes (2) treow (3). of þam treowe on þa dic and
lang dic þonsture. þonne of sture ðæt eft on þa dic
andlang (4) dic þæt on horsa broc andlang broces on ce
nunga ford of þan forda utan wið þone wudu ðæt
to kynefares stane. of þan stane on hoccan stige. of
15 ... þære stige on mære wylle. of ðam wylle on ða dic and
lang dic on sture. of sture on mær dene andlang de
ne to wind ofre. of wind ofre on ðone stapul of þam
stapole on þone weg. andlang weges in ðæ slæd of
þam slaede on lyttan dune andlang weges þæt eft
20 ... on usmere.

NOTES

(1) Note the use of the rune 'thorn', the hard 'th' here and elsewhere in the text.

(2) Note the rune representing the sort 'th'.

(3) Here we see the Saxon 'w' or 'wen'

(4) The Saxon 'g' is used in vernacular writing. Compare the 'g' used in the Latin text in lines 1-8.

TRANSLATION
(Amended, with notes that follow, from G.B. Grundy's
Saxon Charters of Worcestershire, pp.274-6)
'First from Usa pond to Heareca's barrow; from the barrow
10 ... to Cuthred's tree; from the tree to the ditch; a-
long the ditch to the Stour; then from the Stour again to the ditch;
along the ditch to Horse Brook; along the brook to Cenunga's ford; from the ford outside the wood
to Kinver stone; from the stone to Hocca's path; from
15 ... the path to boundary stream; from the stream to the ditch; a-
long the ditch to the Stour; from the Stour to boundary valley; along the valley to wind slope; from wind slope to the post; from the
post to the way; along the way to the valley; from
the valley to the little hill; along the way again
20 ... to Usa pond.'

NOTES
'*Usmere*' is preserved in the local name 'Ismere House': the actual pond is now called Podmore Pond.
'*Hearecan Barrow*' is the small hill north-north-east of Axborough Farm.
'*Horse Brook*' is the stream joined by Chalk Brook at Coldridge Wood.
'*Cenunga Ford*' survives in the modern 'Kingsford'.
'*Cynefar's Stone*': this is the same name as 'Kinver'.
'*The Windbank*' is the high land in the south-east corner of the parish.
'*The Little Hill*' is the high land in the south-east corner of the parish.
'*The Way*' was a road which ran formerly down the east part of the south boundary of Wolverley. The modern road is just inside this, but part of the line of the line of the old road is clearly marked on the boundary to the east of Hurcott Farm by parallel lines of hedges which have obviously been at one time the boundaries of another 'way'.
'*The Slaed*' is the valley at the head of which Ismere House stands.

Plate I. The Wolverley Charter, AD 964
(British Library, Cotton MS. Tiberius. A xiii f. 185v.) Actual size: 23.5 x 13.4cm
This is an 11th-century copy of the Charter of 964. Note the attestation of King William I and Queen Matilda at the end of the preceding Charter (11; 1 and 3).

Ego Willelmus rex anglorum meam donatione ...
dño factam signaculo scissime crucis confirm...

Ego Mathilda regina c̄scribo. Ego Aldrec ...
Ego Odo.   ep̄s.   Ego Wlstanus.   ...
Ego Agelinnus.   abb̄   Ego Wlf... ...
Ego Willelmus.   dux.   Ego Roger ... ...
Ego Ricard.   scrob. Ego Urs ... ...
Ego Osebearn.   min. Ego Rodbeard ... ...
    ... þise ofusmeþe onheartan broth. orþan ...
        oneudþredes qurop. ofþan qu ... onhæ ...
    lang die þonstune. þonne of scuþe ... onhæ ...
    ⁊lang die þæt onhoþsa bþoc ano... ... ...
    nunga foþd ofþanfoþda utan ... þone þ... ...
    to kyneþaþes stane. ofþanstane onhoccan ... of
    þaþie sæge onmæþ þylle. ofþam þylle ouþa die ...
    lang die onstune. of scuþe onmaþ ... ...
    ne ropmdofþie. of piþo ofþie ondune ... ...
    stapole onþoþie þeg. and lang þeges mdæ ... ⁊
    þam slade onlyttan dune. and lang ... ...
    on us meþe..

P
X   OHANTE DÑO ... ...
        HYLE² rex mere ... ...
    eassatam cui uocabulum est ouuhamtyþe ...
    tiotis anime mee adecclesiam ... ...
    nebedian engernensis ep̄i eouor ... ...
    hereditaretur. Acta est aute hec mea ... ...
    dccc xui indictione uii die iii k̄ ... ...

Worcester, see of the 'Bishops of the Hwicce' with Worcester as its capital and cathedral city. Hwiccan rule extended over almost the whole of Worcestershire, south-west Warwickshire and all of Gloucestershire west of Severn, with some minor claims, later relinquished, in northern Somerset, Wiltshire and Herefordshire. Hooke demonstrates how this territorial influence is affirmed by eighth-century charter evidence.

Sawyer conveniently lists 12 authentic charters (nos. 51-63) by Hwiccan rulers, kings and *sub-reguli*, granted to their kinsmen, *ministri*, monks and abbesses between A.D. 676 and 777, sometimes with the consent of the superior kings of Mercia. Of particular relevance to our own studies are a grant by King Oshere of land at Ripple in 680, by Uhtred at Aston in Stoke Prior (767), at Fladbury by King Ealdred in 777, by Aethelward at Ombersley in 706 and by Uhtred again at Kemerton in 756. The last two charters have bounds which are surveyed by Hooke. Sawyer also lists several charters by self-styled 'Bishops of the Hwicce', for example: (no.1251) Ecgwine in 714, founding Evesham Abbey with grants at Fladbury, Evesham, Chedbury and Twyford and Wilfrith (no.1254) to his *comes*, Leppa, granting land at Bibury in Gloucestershire, a charter with bounds.

Hooke surveys the whole landscape of this Hwiccan territory with important identification and linkage of early territorial groupings (pp.75-113) of estates all over Worcestershire. A particularly important example is taken from Wolverley itself, citing an earlier charter than our illustration. This, a grant of 10 *cassatae* of land by King Aethelbald of Mercia to his *comes*, Cyneberht, gives the boundary of this grant at Ismere by the Stour. The Usmere 'pond' of our later charter is described more graphically as '*Husmerae, the province to which the ancients had assigned the name Husmerae*'. Hooke sees this as 'a folk-name relating to an extensive region' (*op cit.* p.80) and demonstrates from this and associated charter evidence and later manorial records how 'the full pattern of interlinked estates becomes evident'. She concludes that 'This may suggest that all this territory in northern Worcestershire should be ascribed to the *Husmerae*, but this is not an uncommon water name' (as in the Cookley charter's *usmere*). Thus we find, in 1995, that the charter evidence for Worcestershire is far more complex and far-reaching than our simple illustration suggested in 1962, because so much more fieldwork and documentary publication has become available to the local historian.

PRINTED COLLECTIONS OF CHARTERS AND COUNTY PLACE-NAME DICTIONARIES

For Charters, the most accessible finding list is P.H. Sawyer's *Anglo-Saxon Charters, an Annotated List and Bibliography*, published by the Royal Historical Society in 1968. This lists 1,875 documents in all, divided into sections on: royal charters granted from the seventh-century kings of Kent to Edward the Confessor and King Harold in 1066 *(1-1163)*, grants by the laity *(1164-1243)*, grants by bishops *(1244-1409)* and other ecclesiastics *(1410-1428)*, with other miscellaneous texts, bequests and wills. A typical entry identifies the grantor, beneficiary with date and place of the grant and the language of the charter. This is followed by details of the original manuscripts and printed versions, with comments on the authenticity or otherwise of each charter. Thus Plate I is identified as:

726 AD 964 King Edgar to Beorhtnoth, his *comes*; grant of land at Cookley in Wolverley, Worcs. *Latin with English bounds.*

Four manuscript versions are cited, including the lost original and reference to 'variant readings of the bounds from B.M.Cotton Tib A xiii, fo.185v., appended to a copy (s.xi/xii) of a charter of King William I, dated 1067' (see caption on page 17). Sawyer affirms this charter's authenticity.

Regional Editions

K. Cameron and M. Gelling, *Place-name evidence for the Anglo-Saxon Invasion and Scandinavian settlements*, E.P.N.S., 1976

H. Edwards, *The Charters of the early West Saxon Kingdom*, with maps and plans, Oxford U.P.,1988

H.P.R. Finberg, *The Early Charters of Wessex*, Leics. Univ. Press, 1964; *The Early Charters of the West Midlands: Gloucestershire, Herefordshire, Worcestershire and Shropshire*, Leics.U.P., 2nd edition, 1972

M. Gelling, *The Early Charters of the Thames Valley*, Leics.Univ. Press, 1979; *The West Midlands in the Early Middle Ages*, Leics.Univ. Press, 1992

C.R. Hart, *The Early Charters of Eastern England*, 1966; *The Early Charters of Northern England and the North Midlands*, 1975

The British Academy has undertaken the publication of an important *Corpus of Anglo-Saxon Charters*, in association with Oxford University Press. So far (1996) five volumes have been published, of charters for Rochester, Burton Abbey, Sherborne, St Augustine's, Canterbury and Shaftesbury. Full reference to each of these collections is made in the appropriate county entry of this gazetteer. A Supplementary Volume (1) of *Facsimiles of Anglo-Saxon Charters*, edited by S.E. Kelly, was published by O.U.P. in 1995.

Note: In this, and the later bibliographies of local publications, wherever the pre-1974 county only is titled, the old name of that county is given; also, where reference is made only, for example, to *Yorkshire*.

(listed in order of publication date)

Bedfordshire   W.W. Skeat, *The Place-names of Bedfordshire*, Cambridge, 1906; G.H. Fowler, *Some Saxon Charters of Bedfordshire*, BHRS, 1920; F.G. Gurney, *Yittingaford and the 10th Century bounds of Chalgrave and Innsdale*, BHRS, 1920; A. Mawer and F.M. Stenton, *The Place-Names of Bedfordshire and Huntingdonshire*, 3, EPNS, 1926; L.R. Conisbee, 'Animals in Bedfordshire Place Names', *Bedfordshire Magazine*, 16, 1978.

Berkshire   E. and J. Stevenson, *Chronicon Monasterii de Abingdon*, 2 vols., Rolls Series, 1857; J.E. Field, 'The Saxon charters of Brightwell, Sotwell and Mackney, Berkshire', *BBOASJ*, XI and XII, 1905 and 1906; J.E. Field, 'Earmundeslea at Appleton, Berkshire', *BBOASJ*, XIII, 1907; W.W. Skeat, *The Place-names of Berkshire*, Oxford, 1911; F.M. Stenton, *The Place-Names of Berkshire*, Reading, 1911; G.B. Grundy, 'Berkshire charters', *BBOASJ*, XXVII-XXXII (with index), 1922-8; M. Gelling, *The Place Names of Berkshire*, C.U.P. and EPNS, XLIX-LII, 1973-76.

Buckinghamshire   A. Mawer and F.M. Stenton, *The Place-Names of Buckinghamshire*, 2, Place-Name Soc., 1925; F.G. Parson, 'Some additional notes on the name of "Risborough" ', *Recs. of Bucks.*, XIII, 1934-40.

Cambridgeshire   W.W. Skeat, *The Place-names of Cambridgeshire*, Cambridge, 1904; P.H. Reaney, *The Place-Names of Cambridgeshire*, 19, EPNS, 1925; and: *The Place Names of Cambridgeshire and Ely*, C.U.P. and EPNS, XIX, 1943; T.A.M. Bishop, 'Notes on Cambridge Mss.', *Camb. Bibl. Soc.*, II, 1954-8.

Cheshire   W. de Gray Birch, 'On some manuscripts relating to St. Werburgh's Abbey, Chester, preserved in the British Museum', *Journal of the Chester Arch. and Hist. Soc.*, n.s., III, 1888-90; J. Tait, *The Chartulary or Register of the Abbey of St. Werburgh, Chester*, Chetham Soc., n.s., LXXIX, 1920; J.McNeal Dodgson, 'Place-names and Street-names of Chester', *Journal of Chester Arch. Soc.*, 55, 1968. For *Carrington* see *Greater Manchester*; G. Kristensson, 'The place-name "Carrington" ', *Notes and Queries*, no.22, 1975; J.McNeal Dodgson, *The Place-names of Cheshire*, EPNS, 48, 54, 1981.

Cornwall   E.H. Pedler, *The Anglo-Saxon Episcopate of Cornwall*, 1856; T.F.G. Dexter, *Cornish Names*, London, 1926; J. Alexander, 'Bishop Conan and St. Buryan', *DCNQ*, XV, 1928; H.P.R. Finberg, *The Early Charters of Devon and Cornwall*, 1953; R. Pool, *Place Names of West Penwith*, Federation of Old Cornwall Societies, 1973; E.G.R. Hooper, *'Merther' Place-names in Cornwall, Old Cornwall*, no.8, 1976; O.J. Padel, *Cornish Place-Name Elements*, EPNS, 56 and 57, 1985; and: *A Popular Dictionary of Cornish Place-names*, Alison Hodge, 1988.

Cumberland   W.J. Sedgefield, *The Place-Names of Cumberland and Westmorland*, M.U.P., 1915; A.M. Armstrong, A. Mawer, F.M. Stenton, and B. Dickins, *The Place Names of Cumberland*, C.U.P. and EPNS, XX-XXII, 1950-2.

Derbyshire   B. Walker, *The Place-names of Derbyshire*, Derby, 1914; W. Fraser, *Field-Names of South Derbyshire*, 1947; K.Cameron, *Place-names of Derbyshire*, Cambridge, 1959; A. Saltman, *The Cartulary of Dale Abbey*, Historical MSS. Commission, no. 11, and Derbs. Arch. Soc., Records Series, no. 2, 1967; and: *The Cartulary of the Wakebridge Chantries at Crich*, Derbs. Arch. Soc., Records Series, no. 6, 1971.

Devonshire   R.J. King, 'Copplestone Cross; and a charter of Edgar, A.D.974', *TDA.*, VIII, 1876; J.B. Davidson, 'Some Anglo-Saxon boundaries, now deposited at the Albert Museum, Exeter', *TDA*, VII, 1876; and: 'On some ancient documents relating to Crediton Minster', *TDA*, X, 1878; and: 'On the early history of Dawlish', *TDA*, XIII, 1881; and: 'On some Anglo-Saxon charters at Exeter', *Journ. Brit. Arch. Assoc.*, XXXIX, 1883; and: 'Seaton before the Conquest', *TDA*, XVII, 1885; O.J. Reichel, 'Church right and church charters in Devonshire', *Devon N. & Q.*, I, 1900; T.W. Rundell, 'The early charters of Crediton, *DCNQ*, VII, 1912-13; B. Blomé, *The Place-Names of North Devonshire*, Uppsala, 1929; F. Rose-Troup, 'The Edgar charter and the South Hams', *TDA*, LXI, 1929; and: 'The ancient monastery of St. Mary and St. Peter at Exeter 680-1050', *TDA*, LXIII, 1931; J.E.B. Gover, A. Mawer and F.M. Stenton, *The Place-Names of Devon*, 8, 9, EPNS, 1931, 1932; J.A. Alexander, 'The Saxon conquests and settlements', *TDA*, 64, 1932; W. Pope, 'Copplestone Charter', *DCNQ*, XVII, 1932-3; F. Rose-Troup, 'Anglo-Saxon charters of Devonshire', *DCNQ*, XVII, 1932-3; and: 'The Anglo-Saxon charter of Bramford, Devon', *TDA*, LXX, 1938; and: 'The Anglo-Saxon charter of Ottery St. Mary', *TDA*, LXXI, 1939; and: 'Crediton charters of the tenth century', *TDA*, LXXIV, 1942; O.J. Padel, 'Some Early Tavistock Charters', *EHR*, LXII, 1947; and: 'The Manor of Roborough', *DCNQ*, no.23, 1947-9; H.P.R. Finberg, 'The Making of a Boundary' in *Devonshire Studies*, 1952; and: *The Early Charters of Devon and Cornwall*, Univ. Leics., Dept. Local Hist., Occasional Paper no.2, 1953; and: 'Supplement to the early charters of Devon and Cornwall', in W.G. Hoskins' *Westward Expansion of Wessex*, Univ. Leics., Dept. Local Hist., Occasional Papers, 13, 1960; H.S.A. Fox, 'The Boundary of Uplyme', *TDA*, 102, 1970; J. Hall, 'Archaeology and the Place Names of Devon', *Devon Archaeological Society Proceedings*, no.34, 1976; *Anglo-Saxon boundaries related to Devon*, Devonshire Association Report and Transactions 122, 1990; D. Hooke, *Pre-Conquest Charter Bounds of Devon and Cornwall*, Boydell Press, 1994.

Dorset   W.B. Barrett, 'Wyke Regis, Dorset; Ethelred's charter, c.988', *SDNQ*, IX, 1905; A. Fagersten, *The Place-Names of Dorset*, Uppsala, 1933; G.B. Grundy, 'A Series of Papers dealing with Boundary Clauses of Saxon Charters relating to Dorset' (articles with some translations), *DNHAS*, LV-LXI, 1933-9; H.P.R. Finberg, 'Sherborne, Glastonbury and the expansion of Wessex', *R. Hist. Soc.* (5th series), III, 1953; C.R. Hart, 'Some Dorset charter boundaries', *DNHAS*, LXXXVI, 1964; G.C. Taylor, 'Lost Dorset place-names', *DNHAS*, LXXXVIII, 1966; B. Kerr, 'Dorset Fields and their names', *DNHAS*, 1967; A.D. Mills, *The Place-Names of Dorset*, EPNS (part 1) 52, 1977; (part 2) 53, 1980; (part 3) 59-60, 1989; (part 4) in preparation (1996); and: *The Major Place-Names of Dorset*, EPNS, 1986; M.A. O'Donovan, *Charters of Sherborne*, British Academy Anglo-Saxon Charters III, 1988; S.E. Kelly, *Charters of Shaftesbury Abbey*, British Academy Anglo-Saxon Charters V, 1996.

Durham   A. Mawer, *The Place-Names of Northumberland and Durham*, C.U.P., 1920.

Essex   P.H. Reaney, *The Place-Names of Essex*, 12, EPNS, 1935; C.R. Hart, *The Early Charters of Essex: The Norman Period*, Leics. Univ. Press, 1957; and: *The Early Charters of Essex: The Saxon Period,* Leics. Univ. Press, 1957; and: *The Early Charters of Essex*, 1971.

Flintshire   E. Davies, *Flintshire Place-Names*, 1959.

Glamorgan   H.C. Jones, *Place-Names in Glamorgan*, Risca, Starling Press, 1978.

Gloucestershire   T. Phillipps, 'Three unedited Saxon charters, from the cartulary of Cirencester Abbey', *Archaeologia*, XXVI, 1836; J.Y. Akerman, 'An account of Saxon remains at Kemble, with observations of a grant of land at Ewelme (Oxon.)', *Archaeologia*, XXXVII, 1857; C.R. Hart, *Historia et cartularium monasterii S. Petri Gloucestriae*, 3 vols., Rolls Series, 1863-7; Rev. J. Earle, 'Ancient charters relating to Woodchester', *Trans. BGAS*, V, 1880-1; T. Kerslake, 'A Gloucestershire parish a thousand years ago', *Antiquarian Magazine*, III, 1883; C.S. Taylor, 'Berkeley Minster', *BGAS*, XIX, 1894-5; and: 'Deerhurst, Pershore and Westminster', *BGAS*, XXV, 1902; and: 'Osric of Gloucester', *BGAS*, XXVI, 1903; W. St C. Baddeley, *Place-Names of Gloucestershire*, Gloucester, 1913; L.E.W.O. Fullbrook-Leggatt, 'Saxon Gloucestershire', *BGAS*, LVII, 1935; G.B. Grundy, 'Saxon Charters and Field Names of Gloucestershire', *BGAS*, LVII, 1935-6; H.P.R. Finberg, *Gloucestershire, an illustrated essay on the history of the landscape*, 1955; and: *Roman and Saxon Withington; a Study in Continuity*, Univ. Leics., Dept. Local Hist., Occasional Paper no.8, 1955; and: 'Some early Gloucestershire estates', *Glos. Studies*, 1957; E.S. Linley, 'The Anglo-Saxon charters of Stoke Bishop', *BGAS*, LXXVIII, 1959; H.P.R. Finberg, *The Early Charters of the West Midlands*, Leics. Univ. Press, 1960; A.H. Smith, *The Place Names of Gloucestershire*, C.U.P. and EPNS, XXXVIII-XLI, 1960-3; C.D. Ross, *The Cartulary of Cirencester Abbey, Gloucestershire*, 2 vols., 1964; M. Devine, *The Cartulary of Cirencester Abbey*, 3 vols., O.U.P., 1977.

Gwent   E.T. Davies, *The Place-names of Gwent*, 1982.

Hampshire   F.J. Baigent, *A Collection of Records and Documents relating to the Hundred and Manor of Crondal*, Hants. Rec. Soc., 1891; F.H. Baring, 'Letter ... concerning Wonston in the tenth century', *HFCAS*, VI, 1907-10; R.T. Andrews, 'The charters of Oxhey A.D. 790', *The Antiquary*, XLVIII, 1912; J.C. Hughes, 'An unrecognized charter of Alverstoke', *HFCAS*, VIII, 1917-19; V. H. Galbraith, 'Royal Charters to Winchester', *EHR*, XXXV, 1920; O.G.S. Crawford, *The Andover District*, 1922; A.W. Goodman, *The Manor of Goodbegot in the City of Winchester*, 1923; and: *Chartulary of Winchester Cathedral*, 1927; G.B. Grundy, 'The Saxon Land Charters of Hampshire, with notes on place and field-names', *Arch. Journal*, 2nd series, XXVIII, 1921, XXIV, 1927 and XXXIV, 1928; G.D. Dunlop, *Pages from the History of Highclere, Hampshire*, 1940; G. Civil, 'Saxon Gosport and a royal charter of Alverstoke', *HFCAS*, XVIII, Part 1, 1953; L.A. Burgess, *The Origins of Southampton*, Univ. Leics. Dept. Local History, Occasional Paper no.16, 1964; R. Coates, *The Place-names of Hampshire*, Batsford, 1989 and EPNS, 1993.

Herefordshire   C.S. Greaves and J. Lee-Warner, 'Charter of Cuthwulf, Bishop of Hereford, A.D. 840', *Arch. J.*, XXX, 1873; J.W. Leigh, 'Some archives and seals of Hereford cathedral', *TWNFC*, XVII, Part 2, 1901; W.W. Capes, *Charters and Records of Hereford Cathedral*, Cantilupe Soc., 1908; and: *The Register of Richard de Swinfield, Bishop of Hereford (1283-1317)*, Cantilupe Soc. 1909; A.T. Bannister, *The Place-Names of Herefordshire*, Cambridge, 1916; C.B. Judge, 'Anglo-Saxonica in Hereford Cathedral Library', *Harvard Studies and Notes in Philology and Literature*, XVI, 1934; H.P.R. Finberg, *The Early Charters of the West Midlands*, Leics. Univ. Press, 1960; J. and M. West, *A History of Herefordshire*, Chapter IV, 1985.

Hertfordshire   W.W. Skeat, *The Place-Names of Hertfordshire*, Hertford, 1904; J.E.B. Gover, A.Mawer and F.M.Stenton, *Place-Names of Hertfordshire*, Cambridge, 1938; A. Mawer and F.M. Stenton, *The Place-Names of Hertfordshire*, 15, Place-Name Soc., 1938; J. Field, *The Place Names of Dacorum District*, Dacorum College, 1977.

Huntingdonshire   W.W. Skeat, *The Place-names of Huntingdonshire*, Cambridge, 1904; A. Mawer and F.M. Stenton, *The Place-Names of Bedfordshire and Huntingdonshire*, 3, Place-Name Soc., 1926; C. Hart, *Early Charters of Eastern England*, Leicester, 1966.

Isle of Man   J.J. Kneen, *The Place-Names of the Isle of Man*, 1925-9; M. Gelling, 'Place-Names of the Isle of Man', *Journal of the Manx Museum*, no.7, 1970-1.

Isle of Wight   H. Kokeritz, *Place-names of the Isle of Wight*, Uppsala, 1940.

Kent   L.B. Larking, 'On the Sunnenden charters', *AC*, I, 1858; R.C. Jenkins, *The Chartulary of the Monastery of Lyminge*, 1867; J.K. Wallenberg, 'Studies in Old Kentish charters', *Studia Neophilologica*, I, 1928; G. Ward, 'Saxon Lydd', *AC*, XLIII, 1931; and: 'Sand Tunes Boc', *AC*, XLIII, 1931; and: 'The Saxon charters of Burmarsh', *AC*, XLV, 1933; and: 'The river Limen at Ruckinge', *AC*, XLV, 1933; J.K. Wallenberg, *Kentish Place Names*, Uppsala, 1931; and: *The Place-Names of Kent*, Uppsala, 1934; G. Ward, various works in *AC*: 'The Lathe of Aylesford in 975', XLVI, 1934; 'The topography of some Saxon charters relating to the Faversham district', XLVI, 1934; 'The Westenhanger charter of 1035', XLVII, 1935; 'The Wilmington Charter of A.D. 700', XLVIII, 1936; 'Saxon records of Tenterden', XLIX, 1937; 'King Oswin—a forgotten ruler of Kent', L, 1938; 'The life and records of Eadbert, son of King Wihtred', LI, 1939; 'The age of St Mildred's church, Canterbury', LIV, 1941; 'King Wihtred's charter of A.D. 699', LX, 1947; 'Dudda's land in Canterbury', LXIV, 1951; 'The Saxon history of the town and port of Romney', LXV, 1952; 'Forged Anglo-Saxon charters', LXXI, 1957; R.F. Jessup, 'Notes on a Saxon charter of Higham', *AC*, LV, 1942; P.H. Reaney, 'A survey of Kent place-names', *AC*, 73, 1959; and: 'Place-names and early settlement in Kent', *AC*, 76, 1961; A. Campbell (ed.), *Charters of Rochester*, British Academy Anglo-Saxon Charters I, 1973; K.J. Edwards, 'Recent developments in the study of place-names on the Anglo-Saxon settlement', *AC*, 88, 1973; J. Glover, *The Place Names of Kent*, Batsford, 1976; P. Kitson, 'Some unrecognised Old English and Anglo-Latin verse in a boundary summary from an Anglo-Saxon charter of Rochester', *Notes & Queries* 34, June 1987; S.E. Kelly, *Charters of St.Augustine's Abbey Canterbury and Minster-in-Thanet.*, British Academy Anglo-Saxon Charters IV, 1995.

Lancashire   H.C. Wyld and T.O. Hirst, *The Place-Names of Lancashire*, 1911; E. Ekwall, *The Place-Names of Lancashire*, M.U.P., 1928; A.N. Webb, *The Cartulary of Burscough Prior, 1189- 1510*, Chetham Society and M.U.P., 1970; D. Mills, *The Place Names of Lancashire*, Batsford, 1986.

Leicestershire   J. Bourne, *Place Names of Leicestershire and Rutland*, Leics. C.C. Libraries, 2nd edition 1981; C.R. Hart, *The Early Charters of Northern England and North Midlands*, Leics. University Press, 1975.

Lincolnshire   G.S. Streatfield, *Lincolnshire and the Danes*, 1884; F.M. Page, *The Estates of Crowland Abbey*, Cambridge, 1934; 'An early Boston charter', *Lincolnshire Hist. & Arch.*, 23, 1988; K. Cameron, J. Field and J. Insley, *The Place Names of Lincolnshire, Parts 1-3*, English Place-Name Society 58, 1985 and 64-5, 1991-2.

London & Middlesex   J.J. Park, *The topography and natural history of Hampstead*, 1818; J.M. Kemble, 'An Anglo-Saxon Document relating to Lands at Send (Surrey), and Sunbury in Middlesex, in the time of Edgar, and the Writ of Court on the Accession of Archbishop Aethelnoth to the See of Canterbury', *Arch. J.*, XIV, 1875; J.W. Hales, 'Notes on two Anglo-Saxon charters relating to Hampstead in the times of Kings Eadgar and Aethelred', *LMAS*, VI, 1890; A. Giraud Browning and R.E.G. Kirk, 'The Early History of Battersea', *Surrey Arch. Colls.*, X, 1891; J.E.B. Gover, *The Place-Names of Middlesex*, London, 1922; F.E. Harmer, 'Three Westminster writs of King Edward the Confessor', *Trans. EHR*, LI, 1936; M. Gibbs, *Early Charters of the Cathedral Church of St Paul, London*, Camden Third Series, LVIII, 1939; J.E.B. Gover, A. Mawer and F.M. Stenton, *The Place-Names of Middlesex*, 18, Place-Name Soc., 1942; 'The Sunbury Charter of King Edgar, c. A.D. 900', privately printed, 1951. (King Edgar's Charter, granting land at Sunbury to his kinsman, Aelfheh, c.A.D. 962, with reference in the legend to an earlier Charter in the possession of the Aethelstan family, possibly before A.D.900. With facsimile of the Charter), W.H. Tapp (Westminster Abbey Muniments); W.H. Tapp and F.W.M. Draper, 'The Saxon Charter of Sunbury-on-Thames', *LMAS*, n.s., 10, 1951; E. Ekwall, *Street-names of London*, 1954; M. Gelling, 'The boundaries of the Westminster charters', *LMAS*, n.s., XI, Part 3, 1954; V. Bott, *Brent Place Names*, Brent Library Service, 1977; J. Field, *Place Names of Greater London*, Batsford, 1980; A.C.B. Urwin, *Saxon Twickenham; The Evidence of the Charters of 709-948 A.D.*, Twickenham Local Hist. Soc., 1981.

Norfolk   J. Hunter, 'The history and topography of Ketteringham', *Norf. Arch.*, III, 1852; C.W. Goodwin, 'On two ancient charters in the possession of the Corporation of Kings Lynn', *Norf. Arch.*, IV, 1855; J. Rye, *A Popular Guide to Norfolk Place Names*, 1991; K. Sandred and B. Lindstrom, *Place-Names of Norfolk*, 1989.

Northamptonshire   F.M. Stenton, 'Facsimiles of early charters for Northamptonshire', *Northants. Rec. Soc.*, 4, 1930; J.E.B. Gover, A. Mawer and F.M. Stenton, *The Place-Names of Northamptonshire*, 10, Place-Name Soc., 1933; G.R. Elvey, *Luffield Priory Charters*, Northants. Records Soc., 22 and 26, 1957 and 1973; J.D. Martin, *Cartularies and Registers of Peterborough Abbey*, Northants. Records Soc., 28, 1975; C. Hart, 'A Charter of King Edgar for Brafield on the Green', *Northants. Past & Present*, 7, 1987-8.

Northumberland   A. Mawer, *The Place-Names of Northumberland and Durham*, C.U.P., 1920; G. Watson, *Goodwife Hot and others: Northumberland's Past as shown in its Place Names*, Oriel Press, Newcastle-upon-Tyne, 1970; Beckershall, *The Place Names of Northumberland*, Graham, 1975.

Nottinghamshire   H. Mutschmann, *The Place-Names of Nottinghamshire*, Cambridge, 1914; J.E.B. Gover, A. Mawer and F.M. Stenton, *The Place-Names of Nottinghamshire*, 17, Place-Name Soc., 1940; P. Lythe, *The Southwell Charter of 956 A.D; an Exploration of its Boundaries*, Southwell & District Local History Society, 1984.

Oxfordshire   H. Alexander, *Place-Names of Oxfordshire*, O.U.P., 1912; G.B. Grundy, *Saxon Oxfordshire*, ORS, XV, 1933; M. Gelling, *The Place-names of Oxfordshire*, Cambridge, 1953; J. Cooper, 'Four Oxfordshire Charter Boundaries', *Oxoniensia 50*, 1985; B. McIlroy, *Harwell, Village for a Thousand Years*, Harwell Parish Council, 1985.

Shropshire   W.H. Duigan, 'The will of Wulfgate of Donnington', *TSANHS*, 2nd series, III, 1891; W.H. Stevenson and W.H. Duignan, 'Anglo-Saxon Charters relating to Shropshire', *ShAS*, 4th series, Pt.I, LVI, 1911; E.W. Bowcock, *Place-Names of Shropshire*, Shrewsbury, 1923; A.L. Moir, *Bromfield Priory and Church in Shropshire*, 1947; H.M. Auden, 'Frodesley', *TSAS*, LII, 1947-8; H.P.R. Finberg, *The Early Charters of the West Midlands*, Leics. Univ. Press, 1960; G. Foxall, *Shropshire Field-Names*, 1980; D.C. Cox, 'The unpublished charters of King Stephen for Wenlock Priory', *ShAS*, 66, 1989; M. Gelling and H.D.G. Foxall, *Place-Names of Shropshire*, EPNS 62, 63, 1990.

Somerset   F.H. Dickinson, 'The Banwell Charters', *SANHS*, XXIII, 1877; and: 'West Monkton charter', *SANHS*, XXVIII, 1882; J.B. Davidson, 'On the charters of King Ine', *SANHS*, XXX, Part 2, 1884; H.C. Maxwell-Lyte and T.S. Holmes, *Burton and Montacute Cartularies*, Som. Rec. Soc., VIII, 1894; W. Hunt, *Two Chartularies of the Priory of St Peter at Bath*, Som. Rec. Soc., 1893; T. Hugo, 'Athelney Abbey', *SANHS*, XLIII, 1897; E.H. Bates, 'Two Cartularies of the Benedictine Abbeys of Muchelney and Athelney', *Som. Rec. Soc.*, XIV, 1899; C.S. Taylor, 'Bath, Mercian and West Saxon', *BGAS*, XXIII, 1900; W.H.P. Greswell, 'King Ine's grant of Brent to Glastonbury', *SDNQ*, VII, 1901; J.S. Hill, *Place-Names of Somerset*, 1913; J. Armitage Robinson, *The Saxon Bishops of Wells*, British Academy, Supp. Papers, IV, 1918; and: 'Westwood manor and Farleigh Hungerford', *SDNQ*, XVIII, 1925; Sir H.C. Maxwell-Lyte, *Historical Notes on some Somerset manors, formerly connected with the honour of Dunster*, Som. Rec. Soc. (extra series), 1931; G.B. Grundy, *The Saxon Charters and Field Names of Somerset*, SANHS, 1935; and in *SANHS*, LXXIII-LXXX, 1927-34; A.G.C. Turner, 'Notes on some Somerset place-names', *SANHS*, XCV, 1950; and: 'A selection of North Somerset place-names', *SANHS*, XCVI, 1951; R.W. Dunning, *The Hythe Cartulary*, Somerset Record Office, 1968; A. Sandison, *Rimpton in Somerset: 1000 Years of Village History, 1938-1939*, 1983; Dom. A. Watkin, *The Great Chartulary of Glastonbury*, Som. Rec. Soc., 59, 63, 64.

South Glamorgan   G.O. Pierce, *Place-Names of Dinas Powys Hundred*, 1968.

Staffordshire   W.H. Duignan and W.F. Carter, 'King Ethelred's charter confirming the foundation of Burton Abbey and the will of Wulfric Spott, the founder', *Midland Antiquary*, IV, 1886; W.H. Duignan and W.H. Stevenson, *Charter of Wulfrun to the Monastery at 'Hamtun' (Wolverhampton)*, 1888; J.T. Jeffcock, *A Record of the 900th Anniversary of the granting of the charter of the pious Lady Wulfrun in A.D. 994, to the Collegiate Church of Wolverhampton*, 1894; A. Anscombe and W.H. Stevenson, 'The charter relating to St Peter's, Wolverhampton', *N. & Q.*, 9th. series, III, 1899; W.H. Duignan, *Notes on Staffordshire Place-Names*, London, 1902; C.G.O. Bridgeman, *Staffordshire Pre-Conquest Charters* (translation and notes), Wm. Salt Arch. Soc., 1916 (There are also eight original Staffordshire charters in the William Salt Library, Stafford); and: 'Wulfric Spot's will', *Collections for a History of Staffordshire*, Wm. Salt Arch. Soc., 1916; I.H. Jeayes, (*Calendar of*) *Burton Abbey Muniments*, Staffs Rec. Soc., 1937; A. Saltman, *The Cartulary of Tutbury Priory*, Hist. MSS. Commission no.2 and Staffordshire Records Soc., 4th series, 4, 1962; P.H. Sawyer, *The Charters of Burton Abbey*, British Academy Anglo-Saxon Charters II, 1979; D. Hooke, *The Landscape of Anglo-Saxon Staffordshire; the charter evidence*, University of Keele, 1983; J.P. Oakden, *The Place-Names of Staffordshire*, EPNS, 55, 1984.

Suffolk   H.W.C. Davis, 'The liberties of Bury St Edmunds', *EHR*, XXIV, 1909; W.W. Skeat, *Place-Names of Suffolk*, Camb. Antiq. Soc., 1913; D.C. Douglas, 'Fragments of an Anglo-Saxon survey from Bury St Edmunds', *EHR*, XLIII, 1928; R. Mortimer, *Leiston Abbey Cartulary and Butley Priory Charters*, Suffolk Records Soc., 1979; C.Harper-Bill, *Bythburgh Prior Cartulary*, Suffolk Records Soc., 1980; *Deben Valley Place-name survey: Parish volumes*, Ipswich, 1984; C. Hart and A. Syme, 'The earliest Suffolk charter (King Edgar's grant of Chelsworth)', *Suffolk Inst. of Arch. & Hist.*, 36, 1987.

Surrey   G.R. Corner, 'On the Anglo-Saxon Charters of Frithwald, Aelfred and Edward the Confessor to Chertsey Abbey', *Surrey Arch. Colls.*, L, 1858; J.E.B. Gover, A. Mawer and F.M. Stenton, *The Place-Names of Surrey*, II, EPNS, 1934; E. Manning, *Saxon Farnham*, Phillimore, 1970; R. Dugmore, *Puttenham under the Hog's Back*, Phillimore, 1972.

Sussex   W.H. Blaauw, 'Buncton, the grant of part of a wood in Cealtborgstead by Ealdwulf, A.D. 791', *SAC*, VII, 1856; W. de Gray Birch, 'Notes on some Anglo-Saxon charters of the seventh and eighth centuries relating to Sussex', *J. Br. Arch. Assn.*, XLII, 1886; and: *The Anglo-Saxon Charter of Oslac, Duke of the South Saxons, A.D. 780*, 1892; E. Heron Allen, *Selsey Bill; Historic and Prehistoric*, 1911; W.D. Peckham, 'Ceadwalla's charter and the Hundred of Manwood', *Sussex N. & Q.*, I, 1927; and: 'The text of Ceadwalla's charter', *Sussex N. & Q.*, II, 1928; M.S. Holgate, 'The canon's manor of South Malling', *SAC*, LXX, 1929; A. Mawer and F.M. Stenton, *The Place-names of Sussex*, Cambridge, 1929-30; A. Mawer,

The Place Names of Sussex, Part 1: Rapes of Chichester; Part 2: Rapes of Lewes, Pevensey and Hastings, C.U.P. and EPNS, VI and VII, 1929-30; G. Ward, 'The Haeselersc charter of 1018', *SAC*, LXXVII, 1936; W.D. Peckham, *The Chartulary of the High Church of Chichester*, Sussex Record Soc., XLVI, 1942-3; G. Ward, 'King Nothelm's charter', *Sussex Co. Mag.*, XX, 1946; G. Maitland, 'Lindfield church from Saxon times', *Sussex N. & Q.*, XII, 1948-9; E.E. Barker, 'Sussex Anglo-Saxon charters', *SAC*, LXXXVIII, 1949; E.A. Fisher, *Saxon Charters of Sussex*, 1970; J. Glover, *Place Names of Sussex*, Batsford, 1975; P. Brandon, *The South Saxons*, Phillimore, 1978; M. Gardiner, 'Saxon settlement and land division in the Western Weald', *SAC*, 122, 1984.

Wales   D. Davies, *Welsh Place Names and their Meanings*, Brecon, 1977; Howard C. Jones, *Place Names in Glamorgan*, Risca, Starling Press, 1978.

Warwickshire   W. de Gray Birch, *The Anglo-Saxon charter of King Edward the Confessor to Coventry Minster*, 1889; W.H. Duignan, *Warwickshire Place-Names*, London, 1912; J.E.B. Gover, A. Mawer and F.M. Stenton, *Place-Names of Warwickshire*, 13, EPNS, 1936; M. Gelling, 'Some Notes on Warwickshire Place Names', *Birmingham and Warwickshire Archaeological Society*, no.86, 1974; H. Maynard, 'The use of the place-name elements "mor" and "mersc"', *Avon Valley, Birmingham and Warwickshire Archaeological Society and Transactions*, no.86, 1974.

Westmorland   W.J. Sedgefield, *The Place-names of Cumberland and Westmorland*, Manchester, 1915; A.H. Smith, *The Place Names of Westmorland*, C.U.P. and EPNS, XLII and XLIII, 1964 and 1966; R. Gambles, *Lake District Place-Names*, 1980.

Wiltshire   W. Hamper, 'Disquisition on a passage in king Athelstan's grant to the abbey of Wilton', *Archaeologia*, XXII, 1829; J.Y. Akerman, 'Some account of the possessions of the abbey of Malmesbury', *Archaeologia*, XXXVII, 1857; W.H. Jones, 'On an Anglo-Saxon charter relating to the parish of Stockton in Wiltshire', *Wilts. Arch. Mag.*, XII, 1870; and: 'On some ancient charters relating to North Newenton', *Wilts. Arch. Mag.*, XIX, 1881; A. Du Boulay Hill, 'The Saxon boundaries of Downton, Wiltshire', *Wilts. Arch. Mag.*, XXXVI, 1909-10; E. Ekblom, *The Place-names of Wiltshire*, Uppsala, 1917; G.B. Grundy, 'The Saxon land-charters of Wiltshire', *Arch. J.*, 2nd series, XXVI, 1919; and: 'The Saxon Land-Charters of Wiltshire', *Arch. J.*, LXXVI, 1919, LXXVII, 1920; O.G.S. Crawford, 'The Anglo-Saxon bounds of Bedwyn and Burbage', *Wilts. Arch. Mag.*, XLI, 1921; W. Goodchild, 'Tisbury in the Anglo-Saxon charters', *Wilts. Arch. Mag.*, XLIV, 1929; H.C. Brentnall, 'The Saxon bounds of Overton', *Report of Marlboro' College Nat. Hist. Soc.*, LXXXVII, 1939; J.E.B. Gover, A. Mawer and F.M. Stenton, *The Place-Names of Wiltshire*, 16, EPNS, 1939; J.H.P. Pafford, 'Bradford-on-Avon, the Saxon boundaries in Ethelred's charter of 1001 A.D.', *Wilts. Arch. Mag.*, LIV, 1951-2; T.R. Thomson, 'The Early Bounds of Pirton and a Pagan Sanctuary', *Wilts Arch. Mag.*, no.CCI, 55, 1954; and: 'The Bounds of Ellandune', *Wilts Arch. Mag.*, nos.CCIV, CCV, 56, 1956; and: 'The early bounds of Wanborough and Little Hinton,' *Wilts. Arch. Mag.*, LVII, 1958-60; T.R. Thomson and R.E. Sandell, 'Saxon land-charters of Wiltshire', *Wilts. Arch. Mag.*, LVIII, 1963; C.C. Taylor, 'The Saxon Boundaries of Frustfield, Wilts', *Arch and Natural Hist. Magazine*, 59, 1964; D.J. Donney, 'Two tenth-century charters concerning lands at Avon and Collingbourne, Wilts.', *Arch. and Natural Hist. Magazine*, 64, 1969; K.H. Rogers, 'Lacock Abbey Charters', *Wilts. Records Soc. Pubs.*, no.34, 1978.

Worcestershire   C.H. Turner, *Early Worcester Mss*, Oxford, 1916.; A. Mawer and F.M. Stenton, *The Place-names of Worcestershire*, Cambridge, 1927; G.B. Grundy, 'Saxon charters of Worcestershire', *Birm. Arch. Soc.*, LII, 1927 and LIII, 1928; I. Atkins, 'The church of Worcester from the eighth to the twelfth century', *Antiquaries Journal*, XVII, 1937; N.R. Ker, 'Heming's Cartulary; a description of the two Worcester Cartularies in Cotton Tiberius A.xiii', in *Studies in Medieval History presented to F.M. Powicke*, ed: R.W. Hunt, W.A. Pantin and R.W. Southern, Oxford, 1948; E. John, 'An alleged Worcestershire charter of the reign of Edgar', *Bulln. of John Rylands Lib.*, XLI, 1958; A.E.E. Jones, *Anglo-Saxon Worcester*, Worcester, 1958; D. Hooke, *The Anglo-Saxon Landscape in the Kingdom of the Hwicce*, M.U.P., 1985; P. Sims-Williams, 'St.Wilfred and two charters dated AD676 and 680 (Bath and Ripple, Worcs)', *Journal of Ecclesiastical History*, 39, April 1988; D. Hooke, 'Worcestershire Anglo-Saxon Charter Bounds', *Studies in Anglo-Saxon History II*, Boydell Press, 1990.

Yorkshire   G. Oliver, *The History and Antiquities of the Town and Minster of Beverley*, Beverley, 1829; G. Poulson, *Beverlac*, 1829 (containing one pre-Norman charter); F.W. Moorman, *Place-Names of the West Riding of Yorkshire*, 1910; W.H. Stevenson, 'Yorkshire surveys and other eleventh century documents in the York Gospels', *EHR*, XXVII, 1912; W. Farrer, *Early Yorkshire Charters*, I, Yorks. Arch. Soc., 1914 (containing six pre-Norman charters, with transcripts, translations and commentary); A. Goodall, *Place-Names of South-West Yorkshire*, Cambridge, 1914; A.H. Smith, *The Place-Names of the East Riding of Yorkshire and York*, EPNS, XIV, 1937; and: *The Place-Names of the West Riding of Yorkshire*, EPNS, XXX-XXXVIII, 1961-3; C. Trevis Clay, *Early Yorkshire Charters*, Yorkshire Archaeological Society, Record Series (extra series), 10, 1965; G. Fellows-Jensen, *Scandinavian Settlement Names in Yorkshire*, 1972; and: 'Place-names and settlement history; a review, with a select bibliography of works mostly published since 1960', *Northern History*, 13, 1977; and: 'Place-names and settlement in the North Riding of Yorkshire', *Northern History*, 14, 1978.

ORIGINAL DOCUMENTS TO BE FOUND AT:

British Library.
Bodleian Library.

THE DOMESDAY SURVEY

THE DOCUMENT

William I's survey of his English lands is described by the Anglo-Saxon chronicler of Peterborough, *sub anno* 1085 (MS. 'E').[8] 'Then he sent his men all over England into every shire to ascertain how many hundreds of 'hides' of land there were in each shire, and how much land and livestock the king himself owned in the country, and what annual dues were lawfully his from each shire. He also had it recorded how much lands his archbishops had, and his diocesan bishops, his abbots and his earls, and—though I may be going into too great detail—and what or how much money it was worth. So very thoroughly did he have the inquiry carried out that there was not a single 'hide', not one virgate of land, not even—it is shameful to record it, but it did not seem shameful to him to do—not even one ox, nor one cow, nor one pig which escaped notice in his survey. And all the surveys were subsequently brought to him.'

The purpose of the inquiry was thus partly a feudal reckoning, partly a census, but chiefly an assessment of value and land-use for geld or tax. The survey was taken by Royal Commissioners, by sworn inquest from a local jury, consisting of the Sheriff, the lord of each manor, the parish priest, and the reeve of each hamlet with six villeins from each village. A regular pattern of questions was usually followed:

(i) What is the name of the manor?

(ii) Who was the tenant in King Edward the Confessor's time? (T.R.E., i.e. *Tempore Regis Edwardi*.) This was not seen to be essential information, is often omitted and the uncertain Saxon names cause difficulties of identification and interpretation. Names may be of Saxon ***sub***-tenants, not the un-named pre-Norman overlord and *antecessor*.

(iii) Who is the present tenant? (T.R.W., i.e. *Tempore Regis Willelmi*.)

(iv) How many 'hides' does the manor contain? (This is an assessment of 'rateable value' for purpose of tax-collection. It may or may not be identical with the total area of the entire manor, or its demesne land. It is customary to calculate this area by equating one 'hide' with 120 acres, but there appear to be regional and other variations, so that this can give a misleading total.)

---

[8] *The Anglo-Saxon Chronicle*, translated by G.N. Garmonsway. J.M. Dent & Sons, Everyman's Library, 1990, p. 216.

(v) How many ploughs are accounted for in the lord's demesne, and how many in villeinage? How many more ploughs, if any, could be accounted for? This is probably a fiscal, not agricultural, reckoning.

(vi) How many inhabitants are there, divided by classes: villagers (*villani*), smallholders (*bordarii*), cottagers (*cotarii*), slaves (*servi*), parish priests, etc.? (The numbers given are, presumably, in family units, which can possibly be used to find an average aggregate population by claculating 4-5 members to a family.)

(vii) What are the areas of woodland, of meadow, of pasture? (These statistics are often difficult to use comparatively, as they may be regionally variable, and include many archaic units of measurement, e.g. the 'lewa' in the Chaddesley example, Plate II.[9])

(viii) How many mills and fishponds are there, and what is their annual value?

(ix) What was the total value of the manor, T.R.E., and what is its present value, T.R.W.?

The documents, which were probably not completed in final 'book' form until about 1100, were arranged by counties. The Book itself consists of closely-written folios, entered on both sides of the leaf in double columns. A county's entries usually begin with a description of certain ancient customs, particularly referring to methods of tax-assessment and collection, special forms of local administration of justice and inquest, and, occasionally, special military or other services peculiar to the shire or its chief townships. This is followed by a list of the feudal tenants-in-chief of the county (see Plate II), beginning with the king, followed by the great ecclesiastics, bishops and abbeys, both English and French, and continuing with the lay tenants in order of precedence. These are numbered, and the same order is followed throughout the survey of the county. Thus each tenant-in-chief's lands are dealt with separately and completely, in whatever part of the county they may lie, although usually arranged with some reference to hundreds in which the groups of manors will be found.

The calligraphy is small, but clear, in law-Latin, closely abbreviated. This makes the original document difficult to read or understand, until the reader is familiar with the formulae and common abbreviations, which are limited to about a hundred basic technical terms. An elementary knowledge of Latin is sufficient to enable a reader to follow the text; particularly necessary is an understanding of such points as the contraction 't' indicating the past tense, e.g. *Val. et Valt*. Once such points are made clear a simple glossary of abbreviations and their meanings is sufficient to help even a student without much knowledge of Latin to familiarise himself with selected samples of the original. Even this is hardly necessary, as good transcripts and translations are usually readily accessible. Quite young children can derive great satisfaction from finding themselves able to pick out individual names from a text, which they accept with interest as an illustration of what the 900-year-old original really looks like.

It is far less certain in 1997 than it seemed at the time of our first edition that the Survey offers us what Stenton described, in 1971 as: 'an ordered description of a national economy'.[10] A more critical account of the survey described it in 1990 as: 'incomplete, selective, often inaccurate, indecisive, inconsistent, even from time to time apparently capricious in its choice of information'.[11]

[9] For assistance with all such problems of land-use, refer to H.C. Darby, *The Domesday Geography of Eastern England*, C.U.P., 1952, and *The Domesday Geography of Midland England*, ed. H.C. Darby and I.B. Terrett, C.U.P., 1954. Also see Domesday Chapters in V.C.H. for any county.

[10] Sir Frank Stenton, *Anglo-Saxon England*, 3rd edition, Oxford, Clarendon Press, 1971(-1987), p.656.

[11] David Roffe, 'Domesday Book and northern society, a re-assessment', *English Historical Review*, no.105, April 1990, p.311.

Re-assessment was already well in hand in the year of the Survey's ninth centenary in 1986.[12] Since then, scholars have approached Domesday Book from several directions. The more esoteric re-appraisals investigate possible origins of Domesday forms in Carolingian and even Roman diplomatic. Nearer home, precedents have been sought in Anglo-Saxon tradition, in documents such as hidage lists and charter bounds. Other scholars find supplementary material in the evidence of earlier minster or collegiate churches, and extents of ancient demesne. These studies draw attention to the previously underestimated nature of pre-Conquest lordship and dependence and lead on to a new appraisal of the survival of Anglo-Saxon tenancies in Domesday manors. This approach challenges the earlier view of Domesday society as the outcome of a tenurial revolution which had entirely substituted Norman baronial overlordship for a lower class of free Saxon tenants. Even the essentially feudal barter of military service for land has been undermined by a new emphasis on the Norman kings' employment of wage-earning mercenaries. Like Domesday itself, even feudalism may not be what we once thought it was.[13]

As to the book itself, research has focused on comparison of the texts of different circuits and exposed significant variations between individual counties. There has been a more intensive study of the palaeography of the rolls, their orthography, re-binding and marginal notation. The effects of different sequences of drafting, re-writing and final compilation have been thoroughly scrutinised. Terms such as *ploughs*, *hides* or *waste* appear to have different shades of meaning from county to county; some scribes evidently modified their descriptions of manorial structures and tenants' holdings as they went along. Computer analysis of the texts will create new possibilities of extensive cross-reference and comparisons.

More meaningful to the amateur local historian is the central idea of a new textual interpretation which is generally agreed, *mutatis mutandis*. This asserts[14] that Domesday was **only** a tax assessment, based upon the ancient Anglo-Saxon unit of land which could support a *ceorl's* liability for fyrd and feorm, the *hide*, *sulung* or *carucate*. 'Hidage tells us about taxable capacity' (Bridbury, *op.cit.*, p.289). The ancient hidage was parcelled out to counties in supposedly arbitrary totals: 3,200 for Nottinghamshire, 1,200 each for Bedfordshire and Worcestershire, 500 for Staffordshire, etc. Domesday was intended to be an up-to-date, post-Conquest Exchequer record of this ancient fiscal system, related *entirely* to the major landowners' liability, county by county, for payments and exemptions which are later found in the counties' 12th-century geld rolls. Although the Conqueror certainly intended to check the liability for geld of his feudal tenants-in-chief and main tenants, their assessments are listed county by county, rather than as feudal baronial rolls, because these were the existing pre-Conquest administrative and fiscal units.

If we are persuaded to see Domesday as **only** a tax return, rather than as we wrote in 1962: 'partly a feudal reckoning, partly a census, but chiefly an assessment of value and land-use for geld and tax', then our perspective on each manor is modified. Domesday entries do not give complete pictures of the entire demesne, village population and livestock of each manor, but record only those assets which were assessed to pay tax. We can count only those villeins and bordars who contributed to their lord's tax assessment; it was no intention of the

[12] G.A. Loud, 'Domesday Book after nine hundred years', *Northern History*, no.23, 1987, pp.231-5, reviewing P. Sawyer (ed.), *Domesday Book: A Re-assessment*, Edward Arnold, 1985.

[13] C. Warren Hollister, 'The Norman Conquest and English Feudalism', *American History Review*, LXVI, no.3, April 1961.

[14] eg. A.R. Bridbury, 'Domesday Book, a re-interpretation', *English Historical Review*, no.105, April 1990, p.284: 'Domesday Book was an income-tax inquiry in the fullest sense possible at the time'.

Commissioners to measure their land-holdings, count their livestock and number the population. The record is not, as we may once have thought, a complete picture of each lord's demesne and every villein's tenement. *Value* means tax liability, not gross national product.

Similarly, totals of a manor's ploughs total only their annual taxable value, not the combined arable capacity of demesne and villeinage. In those many cases where the record notes a shortage or surplus of ploughs this is not an estimate of potential arable production but of over- or under-assessment of liability for tax. In this context, *acres* and *virgates* are not land measurements, but portions of hides returned as tax codes. If, as at Alton in Hampshire[15] on the lands of the Church of St Peter, Winchester: 'There were 10 hides of which the villagers who dwelt there paid 5 …,' those villagers do not 'hold' hides as arable acreage, but rather are assessed in terms of fiscal hidage. Their totals *sometimes* correspond *approximately*, with the overall hidage of the manor, in demesne and villeinage. Such calculations are commonplace in most counties. At Staines in Middlesex, Iver (Bucks.) and Long Eaton (Dbs.) for example,[16] servile and free tenants are said to hold hides or virgates, whole or in fractions. Any assessment based on matching totals is at the mercy of Domesday's erratic arithmetic: 'a cobbled-up job providing evidence of very different values for the survey of very different places'.[17]

The Anglo-Saxon chronicler, we are told[18] was 'misinformed' if he implied that every pig in England was numbered. Those lists of cattle which he deplored were not a complete manorial stock-taking; they counted only demesne livestock liable for tax. Domesday Book, in fact—or theory—was *not* a census, nor a set of estimates of the gross agrarian product, nor a feudal basis for knights' fees, but an income tax return. Were not those different aspects of Anglo-Norman society and manorial economy not inextricably inter-woven?

Much revisionist theory is not entirely new; it was debated as long ago as 1895 by Round and Maitland. 'What was the hide? However unwilling we may be to face this dreary old question we cannot escape it … Let it be granted that, long before the Norman Conquest, the hide has become a unit in an unwieldy system of taxation, which has been governed by false assumptions and vitiated by caprice, until the fiscal hide in a given case may widely diverge from its original or indeed from any fixed type.'[19] Stenton also realised that 'the number of hides assigned to a village for purposes of taxation can rarely have coincided with the number of arable tenements it contained'. On the unreliability of attempted calculations, he also remarks that hidage totals 'sometimes look like the results of a game with figures played by clerks with no interest in reality'.[20] Like most revisionist viewpoints, re-assessment of Domesday begs many questions and is relentlessly monocausal. If, as we are told, demesne was returned as exempt from taxation, and if it is not a total population which was numbered for tax, then we cannot possibly know how many more went scot free. It would be rash to assume that the Conqueror accepted a lenient tax-assessment of only a minority of his conquered people. The chronicler, perhaps, know him better than that.

We shall see, when we consider later manorial records that a specialised type of record may exclude population which did not come within the record's purview; court rolls are unreliable records of *total* medieval population and the same is certainly true of Domesday.

[15] *Domesday Book 4: Hampshire*, fo.43a, VI: Land of St Peter's Winchester, ed. Julian Munby, Phillimore 1982.
[16] *Domesday Book 11: Middlesex*, fo.128b, IV: The Abbot of St Peter's, 5: Staines: '… 3 villagers ½ hide each, 4 villagers with 1 hide, etc.', ed. Sara Wood, Phillimore, 1975; *13: Buckinghamshire*, fo.149b, XIX: Land of Robert d'Oilly, 1: Iver: '… 5 of these villagers have 6 hides ', ed. Elizabeth Teague and Veronica Sankaran, Phillimore, 1978; *27: Derbyshire*, fo.273b: II: Land of the Bishop of Chester, 22: Long Eaton: '… 22 freemen and 10 smallholders under them have 9 carucates of this land and 13 ploughs; the other 3 carucates of land are the villagers' …'.
[17] E. Miller, book review in *Northern History*, 1987, p.219.
[18] A.R. Bridbury, *op.cit.*, pp.298-300.
[19] F.W. Maitland, *Domesday Book and Beyond*, C.U.P., 1897, Fontana, 1960, p.419.
[20] Sir Frank Stenton, *op.cit.*, p.648.

'Successive critiques of the text have demonstrated that Domesday Book is incomplete, selective, often inaccurate, indecisive, inconsistent, even from time to time capricious, in its choice of information'.[21] Lacking the, as yet unfinished, Hull Database the reader longs for a complete, personal CD-ROM database of the Phillimore *Indexes*! Until we have such a resource we must accept that Domesday is not a reliable source of manorial extents.

Other re-assessments of Domesday are more regionally confined, but no less critical: It was always evident, for example, that the Domesday returns from Tosti Godwinsson's northern earldom were in many unfamiliar ways more unreliable than, or rather incomparable with the survey of midland and southern England. Indeed, it has been well said that: 'the picture of Northern society which Domesday provides is not always internally consistent'.[22] The surveyors of Circuit No.6, numbering the carucates of Yorkshire, Lincolnshire, Nottinghamshire, Derbyshire and Huntingdonshire, learned their definitions of the manor from unfamiliar tenures such as *socages*, *thanages* and *drengages*. Faced with the complex editing of a strange variety of sources, the Commissioners produced what has been referred to as a 'scissors-and-paste' compilation.[23] Much of the standard information on sub-tenants and other vital resources has been abbreviated by a novice scribe whose work 'indicates carelessness on a scale that borders on incompetence'.[24]

Given so many northern inconsistencies and anomalies, it is not surprising that some earlier interpretations of Domesday evidence, taken at face value, prove to be misleading. In no case is this more so than in the long-standing tradition of the 'harrying of the north' by the Conqueror's men-at-arms in revenge for the widespread rebellions of 1069-70. Re-assessments of this situation offer precaution against taking the apparent meaning of any traditional form of words or statement of facts for granted and making too ready assumptions of cause and effect. If there were any 'simple facts' they would be that, as many nearly contemporary chroniclers recount, four almost successful risings of the people of Northumberland, supported by rival Scottish and Danish contenders for the English throne, were punished by violent ethnic cleansing. The castles and borough of York were captured and hundreds of Frenchmen murdered. 'When the king learnt this, he marched northward with all the levies he could muster and plundered and utterly laid waste all that shire'.[25] In Yorkshire there was almost total destruction of 794 Yorkshire manors, with extensive wastage also in Nottinghamshire, Derbyshire, Staffordshire and Cheshire.

There are several sources of debatable evidence for the long-term effects of this punitive harrying; as to the actual cause there seems to be no dispute. Firstly, there are the lurid accounts of 12th-century chroniclers, alleging depopulation for 60 miles wide and 55 miles long. Secondly there is the Domesday record of 45 per cent of Yorkshire manors entered as 'waste' in 1087. Such records of apparent retribution, still effective 17 years after the event, seemed to be borne out by the closure of 10 northern mints and discoveries of hidden coin-hoards, closely dated to 1070. Yet there is, as yet, little if any archaeological evidence of burned destruction layers in towns or village excavations. More dubious too, is the traditional interpretation of more than 100 identified planned villages in Yorkshire as possible re-population of deserted Domesday manors as 12th-century Cistercian colonies. The question remains: how much long-term effect of harrying does Domesday confirm?

[21] D. Roffe, *op.cit.*, p.311.
[22] D. Roffe, *op.cit.*, p.334.
[23] D.M. Palliser, *op.cit.*, p.15.
[24] D. Roffe, *op.cit.*, p.313.
[25] Anglo-Saxon Chronicle, MS.D (Worcester Chronicle) sub anno 1068/9, ed. G.N. Garmonsway, *op.cit.*, p.204.

TRANSCRIPT

1 . . . . .   HIC ANNOTANT(UR) TENENTES TERRA(RUM) IN WIRCESTRESCIRE   1

.I. REX WILLELMUS.	.XV. Radulfus de Todeni.
.II. Eccl(esi)a de Virecestre.	.XVI. Radulfus de Mortemer.
.III. Ep(iscopu)s de Hereford.	.XVII. Robertus de Stadford.
.IIII. Eccl(esi)a S Dyonisii.	.XVIII. Rogerius de Laci.
.V. Eccl(esi)a de Coventreu.	.XIX. Osbernus filius Ricardi.
.VI. Eccl(esi)a de Cormelies.	.XX. Gislebert(us) filius Turoldi.
.VII. Eccl(esi)a de Glouuecestre.	.XXI. Drogo filius ponz.
.VIII. Eccl(esia de Westmonast(erio).	.XXII. Herald(us) filius Radulfi.
.IX. Eccl(esi)a de Persore.	.XXIII. Willelm(us) filius Ansculfi.
.X. Eccl(esi)a de Euesham.	.XXIIII. Willhelm(us) filius Corbucion.
.XI. Ep(iscopu)s Baiocensis.	.XXV. Willhelmus Goizenboded.
.XII. Eccl(esi)a S Guthlaci.	.XXVI. Vrso de Abetoth.
.XIII. Clerici de Wrehantone.	.XXVII. Hugo Lasne.
II	
.XII. Comes Rogerius.	.XXVIII. Eldue (1).

5 . . . . . (right: . . . . 5)
10 . . . . . (right: . . . . 10)
15 . . . . . (right: . . . . 15)

TRANSCRIPT

II
1 . . . . . XXVI. EDDEVE q(ue)da(m) femina ten(et) de rege. CEDESLAI.IN
           CRESSELAV H(UN)D(REDO)   1
           Ipsa tenuit T.R.E. Ibi. xxv. hide cu(m) .viii. Bereuuiches. Ex his
           .x. hide erant quiete a geldo. teste comitatu.
           In d(omi)nio sunt .iii. car(uce). (et) (2) xxxiii. vill(ani) (et) xx
           –bord(arii) (et) ii. p(res)b(yt)ri cu(m).
5 . . . . iiii. bord(ariis). Inter om(ne)s h(abe)nt. xxv. car(ucas). Ibi. viii. inter
           –seruos (et) ancillas.   5
           (et) .iii molini redd(unt) .xii. su(m)mas annone. In Wirecestre .ii. burg(en)
           –ses.
           redd(unt). xii. den(arois). (et) In Wich. v. saline redd(unt). xxi solid(os)
           —(et) iiii. den(arious).
           Ibi Silva de. ii leuuis. (et) alia silua de .1. leuua.
           T.R.E. (et) modo val(et). .xii. lib(ros).
10 . . . . . WILMAR(IUS) tenuit HILHAMATONE. Ibi .i. virg(ata) t(er)re. (et)est Wasta.
           T.R.E. val(eba)t .xii. denar(ios).   10
           In ESCH HUND(REDO) iaceNT (3) .x. hide in FRECHEHA(M), (et) iii. hide in
           –HOLEWEI.
           (et) scripte suNT in brevi de Hereford.
           In DODINTRET H(UN)D(REDO) iacent. xiii hide de MERTELAI (et) v. hide
15 . . . . . de SVCHELEI que hic placitaNT (et) geldaNT (et) ad Hereford redd(un)t
           firm(m) sua(m) (et) sunt scripte in breve regis.   15

(1) The actual entry for Eldeve (below) names her Eddeve.
(2) Note the special sign for 'et'.
(3) Note the conjoining of capitals N and T here an on lines 13 and 15. In the 11th and 13th centuries frequently occur medially in a word.
(4) Each of these lines, which was complete in the original, has been divided in printing

Plate II. Extracts from Worcestershire Domesday Survey, 1087.
   (i)   List of chief tenants of lands. (Fo.172).
   (ii) The Chaddesly entry. (Fo.178).
Composite page, enlarged. Actual size: 11.5 x 15cm. (Photograph taken from OS zincograph facsimile, 1862, at Worcestershire County Record Office.)

1

HIC ANNOTANT TENENTES TERRAM IN WIRECESTRESCIRE.

I.	Rex Willelmus.	XV.	Radulfus de Todeni.
II.	Ecclia de Wirecestre.	XVI.	Radulfus de Mortemer.
III.	Eps de Hereford.	XVII.	Robertus de Stadford.
IIII.	Ecclia S Dyonisii.	XVIII.	Rogerius de Laci.
V.	Ecclia de Covurtreu.	XIX.	Osbernus filius Ricardi.
VI.	Ecclia de Cormelies.	XX.	Gislebertus filius Turoldi.
VII.	Ecclia de Glouuecestre.	XXI.	Drogo filius Ponz.
VIII.	Ecclia de Westmonast.	XXII.	Heraldus filius Radulfi.
IX.	Ecclia de Persore.	XXIII.	Willelmus filius Ansculfi.
X.	Ecclia de Euesham.	XXIIII.	Willelmus filius Corbucion.
XI.	Eps Baiocensis.	XXV.	Willelmus Goizenboded.
XII.	Ecclia S Guthlaci.	XXVI.	Urso de Abetot.
XIII.	Clerici de Wolauarcone.	XXVII.	Hugo Lasne.
XIIII.	Comes Rogerius.	XXVIII.	Eadeue.

(i)

Esseue qdam femina ten de rege Cresselai. IN CRESSELAI HD.
Ipsa tenuit T.R.E. Ibi xxv hidæ cu vii Berewiches. Ex his
x hidæ erant quietæ a geldo, teste comitatu.
In dnio sunt iiii car. 7 xxxiii uilli 7 xx bord 7 ii pbri cu
iiii bord. Int oms hnt xxv car. Ibi viii int seruos 7 ancillas.
7 iiii molini redd xii summas annonæ. In Wirecestre ii burgses
redd xii den. 7 In Wich v salinæ redd xxi solid 7 iiii den.
Ibi silua de ii leuuis. 7 alia silua de i leuua.
T.R.E. 7 modo ual xii lib.

Wlmar tenuit Bihanmaroue. Ibi i uirg træ. 7 est wasta.
T.R.E. ualb xii denar.
In Essehame iacent x hidæ in Bechelha. 7 iii hidæ in Holewei.
7 scriptæ sunt in breui de Hereford.
In Dodintret hd iacent xiiii hidæ de Mertelai 7 v hidæ
de Sudelei. quæ hic placitant 7 geldant. 7 ad Hereford redd
firmā suā 7 sunt scriptæ in breui regis.

15
(ii)

TRANSLATION

1 . . . . .   HERE ARE ENTERED THE HOLDERS OF LAND IN WORCESTERSHIRE 1

.I. KING WILLIAM.	.XV. Ralf de Todeni.		
.II. The Church of Worcester.	.XVI. Ralf de Mortemer.		
.III. The Bishop of Hereford.	.XVII. Robert de Stadford.		
5 . . . . . .IIII. The Church of St Denis.	.XVIII. Roger de Laci.	 5
.V. The Church of Coventry.	.XIX. Osbern fitz Richard.		
.VI. The Church of Cormeilles.	.XX. Gilbert fitz Turold.		
.VII. The Church of Gloucester.	.XXI. Drogo fitz Ponz.		
.VIII. The Church of Westminster.	.XXII. Harold fitz Ralf.		
10 . . . . . .IX. The Church of Pershore.	.XXIII. William fitz Ansculf.	 10
.X. The Church of Evesham.	.XXIIII. William fitz Corbucion.		
.XI. The Bishop of Bayeux.	.XXV. William Goizenboded.		
.XII. The Church of St Guthlac.	.XXVI. Urse d'Abitot.		
.XIII. The Clerks of Wolverhampton.	.XXVII. Hugh Lasne.		
15 . . . . . .XII. Earl Roger.	.XXVIII. Eldeve.	 15

(i)

TRANSLATION

II

1 . . . . . XXVI. EDDEVE, a certain woman, holds CEDESLAI, IN CRESSELAU HUNDRED, of the King.   1
The same woman held it T.R.E. There are 25 hides, with 8 Berewicks. Of these,
10 hides were quit of geld, so the county testifies.
In demesne are 3 ploughs, and 33 villagers, and 20 smallholders, and 2 priests with
5 . . . .   4 smallholders. Among them all, they have 25 ploughs. There are 8 slaves and   5
maidservants, and 3 mills render 12 loads of grain. In Worcester 2 burgesses
render 12 pence, and in Wich 5 salt pans pay 21s. and 4d.
There are 2 leagues of woodland, and another wood of 1 league.
T.R.E. and now, it is worth £12.
10 . . . . .   WULMAR held HILHAMPTON. There is 1 virgate of land there, which is waste.   10
T.R.E. it was worth 12 pence.
IN ESCH HUNDRED lie 10 hides in FECKENHAM & 3 hides in HOLEWEI.
and they are entered in the 'writ' for Hereford.
IN DODDINGTREE HUNDRED lie 13 hides at MARTLEY & 5 hides
15 . . . .   in SECKLEY which plead here and pay geld here, but pay   15
their 'farm' at Hereford and are written in the King's entry.

(ii)

Of all the sources the most explicit certainly seemed to be Domesday's quasi-statistics. Typical entries for nearly 800 Yorkshire manors briefly state, for example, that: 'In Middleham, 5 carucates taxable, 3 ploughs possible, Gillepatric had a manor there. Now Ribald has it. **Waste**; In Leyburn, 7½ carucates taxable, 5 ploughs possible. Asketil and Authulfr had 2 manors there. Now Wiuhomarch has them. **Waste**; In Garriston, 3 carucates taxable, 2 ploughs possible. Thorketil had a manor there. Now Geoffrey has it. **Waste**.'[26] These are only three of 169 Yorkshire manors of Count Alan the Red of Penthièvre; 72 more of his fief in the North Riding were also described as 'waste'.

The obvious conclusion must surely be that Domesday recorded long-lasting effects of Norman devastation? To question, as some historians do, whether a relatively small but ferocious and well-armed feudal task force could have wreaked so much damage in so short a time probably underestimates the rapacity of an 11th-century army unimaginably more ferocious than the boyish enthusiasm of the SAS. The rest of the argument rests on play on Domesday words, even to query whether 'waste' means exactly what it appears to say. Confusion is worse confounded when the appeal to ambiguity by one revisionist appears to collide with a different ambiguous interpretation by another. When one authority claims that 'waste' manors still 'had some resources, population or value recorded', we remember that 'resources' in ploughs or livestock may be dismissed as tax-codes, not hard assets. Even so, we must remember that 'a less coherent body of date probably emerged from the north than from other regions'.[27]

In every region, therefore, we must be prepared to examine the evidence closely enough to form our own opinions on the various myths which such an icon as Domesday Book may have created and be careful not to substitute new myths for old. Whatever the current or future re-interpretations may be, there can be no doubt that Domesday and its satellites are an incomparable national record. 'There is every reason why the explorers of ancient English history should be hopeful. We are beginning to learn that there are intricate problems to be solved, and yet they are not insoluble. A century hence the student's materials will not be in the shape in which he finds them now ... There are discoveries to be made, but also there are habits to be formed.'[28]

FURTHER READING

D. Bates, *A Bibliography of Domesday Book*, Boydell, 1986

A.R. Bridbury, 'Domesday Book, a re-interpretation', *English Historical Review*, 105, April 1990

C.C. Clifford and G.R. Versey, *Domesday Gazetteer*, C.U.P., 1975

H.C. Darby, *Domesday England*, 1977

Domesday Studies: Papers read at the Novocentenary Conference of the Royal Historical Society and Institute of British Geographers, Boydell Press, for the RHS, 1987

H. Ellis, *A General Introduction to Domesday Book*, facsimile reprint of the first edition of 1883, London, 1971

J. Fines, *Domesday Book in the Classroom: A Guide for Teachers*, Phillimore, 1982

R. Welldon Finn, *Domesday Book, A Guide*, Phillimore, 1973

V.H. Galbraith, *Domesday Book and its Place in Administrative History*, O.U.P., 1974

E.M. Hallam, *Domesday Book through Nine Centuries*, Thames & Hudson, 1987

J.D. Hamshere and M.J. Blakemore, 'Computerising Domesday Book', Area, 8, 1976

J.D. Hamshere, J. McDonald and G.D. Snooks, 'Regressing Domesday Book', *Economic History Review*, 40, May 1987 (includes: Tax Assessments in Domesday England and the suitability of Domesday for climatic analysis)

S.P.J. Harvey, 'Domesday Book and Anglo-Norman Governance', *Royal Historical Society Transactions*, no.25, 1970

---

[26] *Domesday Book 30: Yorkshire*, fo.309a-313b, VI: Land of Count Alan, ed. Margaret L. Faull and Marie Stinson, Phillimore, 1986.
[27] D.M. Palliser, *op.cit.*, p.15, citing Roffe, p.313.
[28] F.W. Maitland, *op.cit.*, 1897-1960, p.596.

P. Hindle, *Maps for Local History*, Batsford, 1988

J.C. Holt, *Domesday Studies*, Royal Historical Society, 1987

F. Macdonald, *Domesday Book, A Teachers' Guide*, Macdonald Education, 1986

J. McDonald and G.D. Snooks, *Domesday Economy, a New Approach to Anglo-Norman History*, Clarendon Press, Oxford, 1986

S.J. Madge, *Domesday of Crown Lands*, 1968

F.W. Maitland, *Domesday Book and Beyond*, C.U.P., 1897, Fontana, 1960

P. Morgan, 'What to read on Domesday Book', *The Local Historian*, 17, no.1, February 1986; and: *Domesday Book and the Local Historian*, Historical Association H95, 1994

C.H. Nelson, *The Normans in South Wales, 1070-1171*, 1966

D.M. Palliser, 'Domesday Book and "The Harrying of the North" ', *Northern History*, 29, 1993 (suggests that 'while it would be wrong to conclude that William I's punitive actions in 1069-70 were not catastrophic, yet the Yorkshire Domesday itself, with its "scissors-and-paste" approach, cannot be used straightforwardly as a simple index of land still lying waste seventeen years after a recorded devastation and as a result of that devastation, despite the impressive testimony to that effect by a daunting line of scholars.')

D. Roffe, 'Domesday Book and Northern Society, a re-assessment', *English Historical Review*, 105, April 1990

I.J. Sanders, *English Baronies: A Study of their Origin and Descent, 1066-1327*, 1960

P. Sawyer (ed.), *Domesday Book; A Reassessment*, Edward Arnold, 1985, a set of nine essays, as follows: 'Domesday Studies since 1886', by P. Sawyer; 'The Precursors of Domesday: Roman and Carolingian Land Registers', by J. Percival; 'The Paleography of the Domesday Manuscripts', by A.R. Rumble; 'The Domesday Satellites', by H.B. Clarke; '1066-1086: A Tenurial Revolution?', by P. Sawyer; 'Taxation and the Ploughland in Domesday Book', by S.P.J.Harvey; 'Secular Minster Churches in Domesday Book', by J. Blair; 'Domesday Book and the Boroughs', by G.H. Martin; 'Domesday Book and the Computer', by J. Palmer. This book points to recent years' 'particular attention to the methods of the enquiry, leading to a better understanding of its purpose and a greater awareness of both the possibilities and limitations of Domesday Book as a source'.

P. Sawyer, *Domesday Heritage; Towns and Villages of Norman England through 900 years*, 1986

F.M. Stenton, *Anglo-Saxon England*, Oxford, 1971, paperback edition, 1989

R. Welldon Finn, 'Domesday Book and Anglo-Norman Governance', *Royal Historical Transactions*, no.25, 1970

PRINTED EDITIONS FOR WORCESTERSHIRE

Domesday Book, 16, Worcestershire, ed. F. and C. Thorn, Phillimore, 1982.

The *VCH of Worcestershire*, 1 (1901) has the full county text on pp. 235-280 with an introduction and map by J.H. Round.

J.D. Hamshere, 'A computer-assisted study of Domesday Worcestershire' in T.R. Slater and P.J. Jarvis (eds.), *Field and Forest: an Historical Geography of Warwickshire and Worcestershire*, Norwich, 1982.

There were several other regional drafts and surveys being made within the generation when the two volumes of Great and Little Domesday were being compiled. There are, for example, three later fragmentary surveys of Worcestershire, one of Oswaldslow Hundred *c.*1108-18, another fragment in an Evesham cartulary of *c.*1130 and another item for Droitwich *c.*1135. These afford some comparison with Domesday, showing further transfer of lands within the county immediately after the reign of William I.

PRINTED VERSIONS OF COUNTY DOMESDAY SURVEYS

In addition to those counties (shown below) which have so far published VCH volumes containing translations of their surveys, with excellent introductory chapters and commentary, many counties have other printed versions of their Domesday Survey, or articles analysing its contents. In 1861-2, the OS published a photo-zincograph of many counties' surveys from the original. Most counties have these facsimiles readily accessible, either at the County Record Office, or at the County Library. This is more convenient for taking photostat copies than attempting to obtain copies from the Public Record Office's originals. For information on these facsimiles, and other official record publications, such as calendars, guides and indexes of the major national documents held at the Public Record Office, and available from most large reference libraries, see Government Publications, Sectional List no.24, 'Record Publications' (H.M.S.O., 1958).

The essential Indexes to all county Domesday surveys are: *Domesday Book. Index Part One: Places, Part Two: Persons* (edited by J.McN. Dodgson and J.J.N. Palmer), and *Part Three: Subjects* (edited by J.D. Foy), Phillimore, 1992.

Each volume gives facsimile and facing transcription. 'Its aim has been to produce what the 11th-century compiler would have written if his language had been modern English, with two devices—standardised punctuation and paragraphs—already invented. The entries normally answer the Survey's questions and these are usually given as separate paragraphs, viz: 1, the place, its holder, its hides, ploughs and lordship, 2, population; 3, resources; 4, value; 5, additional notes. 'Maps are given for each county, with a key to all named places, and National Grid references with Hundred boundaries shown. Each volume has an introduction, indices of persons and of places, notes and glossary of technical terms'. This is, altogether, an invaluable source.

The invaluable *Domesday Geography* series by H.C. Darby *et al.* includes the following volumes which analyse the survey of each county, with distribution maps and statistical tables about settlement patterns and natural resources. In the county gazetteer below, each relevant volume is referred to for each of the 34 counties surveyed as, for example: (**DG: Midland**) etc. as follows:

H.C. Darby, *The Domesday Geography of Eastern England*, 1952 **DG: East**
H.C. Darby and I.B. Terrett, *The Domesday Geography of Midland England*, 1952 **DG: Midland**
H.C. Darby and I.S. Maxwell, *The Domesday Geography of Northern England*, 1952 **DG: North**
H.C. Darby and E.M.J. Campbell, *The Domesday Geography of South-East England*, 1952
   DG: South-East
H.C. Darby and R. Welldon Finn, *The Domesday Geography of South-West England*, 1952
   DG: South-West
See also: H.C. Darby and G.R. Vesey, *Domesday Gazetteer*, 1975.

Bedfordshire *VCH*, 1 (1904); W. Airy, *A Digest of the Domesday of Bedfordshire*, Bedford, 1881; G.H. Fowler, *Domesday Notes*, BHRS, 1, 1913, 1920; G.H. Fowler, *Bedfordshire in 1086; An Analysis and Synthesis of Domesday Book*, BHRS, 1922; W. Austin, *Domesday Water Mills of Bedfordshire*, BHRS, 1916; DG: South-East.
Berkshire *VCH*, 1 (1906); OS Facsimile; DG: South-East; *Domesday Book, 20,* trs. J. Morris, Phillimore, 1977; *Berkshire: Domesday Book, 5,* trs. J. Morris, Phillimore, 1979.
Buckinghamshire *VCH*, 1 (1905); OS Facsimile; DG: South-East; *Domesday Book, 13,* trs. J. Morris, Phillimore, 1978.
Cambridgeshire *VCH*, 1 (1938); OS Facsimile; *Domesday Book, 18,* ed. A. Rumble, Phillimore, 1981; *Domesday Book,* 18, ed. A. Rumble, trs. J. Fellows and S. Keynes, Phillimore, 1981; C.H. Evelyn White (ed.), Domesday Book: or great survey of England of William the Conqueror, A.D. 1086', *East Anglian* (3rd series), XI-XII, 1905-8; R.W. Finn, 'Some reflections on the Cambridgeshire Domesday', *Cambs. Antiq. Soc.*, LIII, 1960; DG: Eastern.
Cheshire OS Facsimile; J. Tait, *The Domesday Survey of Cheshire* (transcript, with translation), Chetham Soc., n.s., 1916; P. Dodd, 'Domesday Cheshire, some agricultural connotations', *LCAS Journal*, 68,

1985; DG: Northern; *Domesday Book, 26*, trs. P. Morgan. Phillimore, 1978; R.V.H. Burne, 'Domesday Book and Cheshire', *Journal of Chester and N. Wales Architectural and Hist. Soc.*, 49, 1962; B.M.C.Husain, 'Cheshire under the Norman Earls, 1066-1237', *History of Cheshire*, I (ed. J.J. Bagley), Cheshire Community Council, 1973.

Cornwall   *VCH*, 8 (1924); OS Facsimile; *Translation of Domesday Book*, P.R.O., 1875; I.S. Maxwell, *The Domesday settlements of Cornwall*, Historical Association, Cornwall, 1986; DG: South-West; *Domesday Book, 10*, trs. C.and F. Thorn, Phillimore, 1978.

Cumberland   *VCH*, I (1905); OS Facsimile; *Domesday Book, 26*, trs. P. Morgan, Phillimore, 1978.

Derbyshire   D. Roffe, *The Derbyshire Domesday*, Derbyshire Museum Service, 1986; DG: Northern; *Domesday Book, 27*, trs. S. Wood, Phillimore, 1978; K.C.Watson, *The Normans in the Peak District*, Peakland Archaeological Soc. Bulletin, no.25, 1970.

Devonshire   OS Facsimile; *The Devonshire Domesday and Geld Inquest* (extensions, parallel versions and translations, with index), Devon Assoc., 1884-92. (Contains the Devonshire portions of both the Exchequer and Exon Domesday.); *Domesday Book, 9* (in two parts), ed. C and F. Thorn, Phillimore, 1985; U. Earle, *Domesday Totnes, a survey of Totnes and its surrounding parishes as recorded in Domesday Book*, Totnes Community Archives, 1986; DG: South-West; H.P.R. Finberg, 'The Making of a Boundary', in *Devonshire Studies*, ed. W.G. Hoskins and H.P.R. Finberg, 1952; The Earl of Halsbury, 'The devolution of Ruald's fief', *DCNQ*, 27-8, 1956-61; W.G. Hoskins, 'A Domesday identification; Leigh Burton and Silverton', *DCNQ*, 24, 1950-1;

There are also numerous articles on the Devonshire Survey in *TDA*: H.P.R. Finberg, 'Ayshford and Boehill', 103, 1971; R.W. Finn, 'The Making of the Devonshire Domesdays', 89, 1957; H.S.A. Fox, 'The Boundary of Uplyme', 102, 1970; H. French and C.D. Lineham, 'Abandoned medieval sites in Widecombe in the Moor', 95, 1963; H.J. Hanham, 'A tangle untangled: the lordship of the manor and borough of Ashburton', 94, 1962; O.J. O'Reichel, 'Barnstaple and three sub-manors etc.', 49, 1917; and: 'The early descent of Devonshire estates belonging to the honour of Mortain and Okehampton', 38, 1906; and: 'Fees of the Bishop of Exeter', in *Testa de Nevil*, 34, 1902; and: 'Some doubtful and disputed Domesday identifications', 36, 1904; and: 'The Devonshire Domesday and the Geld Roll', 27, 1895; and: 'Berry Pomeroy and Stockleigh Pomeroy', 28, 1896; and: 'The Devonshire Domesday: The Hundreds of Devon', 26-8, 30, 33, 1894-1901; After O'Reichel's death, supplementary volumes of *The Hundreds of Devon* were published in the *TDA* from 1928-38, and an Index to the complete series was published in *TDA*, 74, 1942. O'Reichel also wrote: 'The Domesday churches of Devon', 30, 1898; and: 'Some suggestions to aid in identifying the place-names in Devonshire Domesday', 26, 1894; and: 'Walter of Douai's Domesday fief', *DCNQ*, 3, 1904-6; F.W. Morgan, 'The Domesday Geography of Devon', 72, 1940; Sir Frederick Pollock, 'The Devonshire Domesday', 25, 1893; H.H. Walker, 'Some medieval Devonshire boundaries in Torquay', 97, 1965.

Dorset   *VCH*, 2 (1908); OS Facsimile; J. Hutchins, *History of Dorset* (contains translation of Dorset Domesday), 3rd ed., London, 1861-70; W. Bawden, *Domesday Book for the County of Dorset* (translation and article), 1815; R.W. Eyton, 'A Key to Domesday, exemplified by an Analysis and Digest of the Dorset Survey', London, 1878 (now out of date on some important points); C.W.H. Dicker, 'The Normans in Dorset', *DNHAS*, XXI, 1910; M.F. Moore, 'The Feudal Aspects of the Domesday Surveys of Somerset and Dorset, in connection with the Barony of Moiun', *Bul. Inst. Hist. Res.*, IX, 1931-2; *Domesday Book, 7*, ed. C. and F. Thorn, trs. M. Newman, Phillimore, 1983; DG: South-West; C.D. Drew, 'The Manors of the Iwerne Valley', *DNHAS*, 69, 1947; R.W. Finn, 'The making of the Dorset Domesday', *DNHAS*, 81, 1959; W.O. Hassall, 'The Dorset properties of the nunnery of St Mary, Clerkenwell', *DNHAS*, 68, 1946; *The VCH of Dorset*, III, O.U.P., 1963, contains the Domesday Survey of the county.

Durham   *Domesday Book, The Boldon Book*, 35 (Northumberland and Durham), ed. D. Austin, Phillimore, 1982; DG: Eastern; J. Gyford, *Domesday Witham*, 1985; J. McDonald and G.D. Snooks, 'Were the tax assessments of Domesday England artificial?; The case of Essex', *Econ. H.R.*, 2nd series, 38, 1985; and: 'The determinants of manorial income in Domesday England; evidence from Essex', *Journal Econ. Hist.*, 45, 1985.

Essex: *VCH* (1903); OS Facsimile; *Domesday Book, 32*, ed. A. Rumble, trs. J. Plaister and V. Sankaran, Phillimore, 1983; John Drury, *Domesday Havering. The London borough of Havering in the 11th century as described in the Domesday Book of 1086*, Upminster, Farthings, 1989; W.R. Powell, 'Essex Domesday topography since 1903, place-name identification and problems', *Essex Arch. & Hist.*, 16, 1984-5; and:

Essex in Domesday Book, Essex Record Office, 1990; L.G.Walker, *Background to Domesday in Hertfordshire and Essex*, 1988; *Domesday Map of Essex*, Essex County Record Office.

Flintshire   J. Tait, 'Flintshire in Domesday Book', *Flints. Hist. Soc. Pubns.*, XI, 1925.

Gloucestershire: OS Facsimile; C.S. Taylor, *An Analysis of the Domesday Survey of Gloucestershire*, BGAS, 1887-9; A.S. Ellis, *Some account of the Landowners of Gloucestershire named in the Domesday Book*, BGAS, IV, 1880; C.S. Taylor, *The Norman Settlement in Gloucestershire*, Cirencester, 1779 (contains a facsimile); W. Bawden, *Translation of the Record called Domesday*, Doncaster, 1812 (also including Middlesex, Herts, Bucks, and Oxon); *Domesday Book, 15*, ed. J.S. Moore, Phillimore, 1982; J.S. Moore, 'The Gloucestershire section of the Domesday Book, geographical problems of the text', *BGAS*, 105, 1987; DG: Midland; D. Price, *The Normans in Gloucestershire and Bristol*, 1983; W.E. Wightman, 'The Palatine Earldom of William FitzOsbern in Gloucestershire and Worcestershire (1066-1071)', *EHR*, LXXVII, 1962; C.S. Taylor, 'Analysis of the Domesday Survey of Gloucestershire', *BGAS*, 1869.

Hampshire   *VCH*, 1 (1900); OS Facsimile; *Domesday Book, 4*, ed. J. Munby, Phillimore, 1982; DG: South-East; G. Stagg, *The New Forest in Domesday Book*, Hants. Field Club, New Forest Section, Report no.13, 1974; F. Barlow, *Winton Domesday: Winchester in the Early Middle Ages*, Oxford, Clarendon Press, 1976; J.E.H. Spaul, *Descriptio Andovere: A Survey of the Hundred of Andover in 1086, according to the Domesday Inquest*, Andover Local Archives Committee, 1974.

Herefordshire   *VCH*, 1 (1908); OS Facsimile; V.H. Galbraith and J. Tait, *Herefordshire Domesday*, Pipe Roll Soc., 1950; A.T. Bannister, *The Herefordshire Domesday*, Hereford, 1904; *Domesday Book, 17*, ed. C. and F. Thorn, Phillimore, 1983; DG: Midland; A.T. Bannister, 'The Herefordshire Domesday', *TWNFC*, 19 (iii), 1904; and: 'Richard's Castle and the Normans in Herefordshire', *TWNFC*, 25, 1925; J.G. Edwards, 'The Normans and the Welsh March', *British Academy*, XLII, 1956; V.H. Galbraith and J. Tait, *Herefordshire Domesday*, Pipe Roll Soc., LXIII, n.s., XXV, 1950; T.A. Gwynne, 'Domesday Society in Herefordshire', *TWNFC*, 41 (I), 1973; J.W. Tonkin, 'Herefordshire castles', *TWNFC*, 44 (I), 1982; D. Walker, 'Hereford and the Laws of Breteuil', *TWNFC*, 40, 1970; J. and M. West, *A History of Herefordshire*, Chapter VI, 1985; W.E. Wightman, *The Lacy Family in England and Normandy, 1066-1194*, 1966.

Hertfordshire: *VCH*, 1 (1902); OS Facsimile; Hon. F.K. Baring, *Domesday Tables for the County of Hertford*, Herts Local History Council, Hitchin Museum, 1962. (Photographic reprint of a valuable tabulation with an introduction.); L.G.Walker, *Background to Domesday in Hertfordshire and Essex*, 1988; DG: South-East; *Domesday Book, 12*, trs. M. Newman and S. Wood, Phillimore, 1976.

Humberside   B. English, *The Lords of Holderness, 1086-1270, A study in feudal society*, University of Hull and O.U.P., 1979.

Huntingdonshire: *VCH*, 1 (1926); OS Facsimile; DG: Eastern; *Domesday Book, 19*, trs. M. Newman and S. Wood, Phillimore, 1975; C. Hart, 'The Hidation of Huntingdonshire', *Cambridgeshire Antiquarian Soc.*, 61, 1968.

Kent   *VCH*, 3 (1932); OS Facsimile; *Domesday Book, 1*, ed. P. Morgan, Phillimore, 1983; DG: South-East; L.B. Larking, *The Domesday Book of Kent, with translation and appendix*, 1869; T. Tatton-Brown, 'The Topography and Buildings of Horton Manor, near Canterbury' (includes also: Thanington, Milton, Godmersham, Chartham and Chilsham), *AC*, 98, 1982.

Lancashire   *VCH*, 2 (1908); OS Facsimile; W. Farrer, *Notes on the Domesday Survey between Ribble and Mersey*, ASLC, XVI, 1899; W. Farrer, *Domesday Survey of North Lancashire*, ASLC, XVIII, 1900; DG: Northern; *Domesday Book, 26*, trs. P. Morgan, Phillimore, 1978.

Leicestershire   *VCH*, 1 (1906); OS Facsimile; D. Holly, 'The Domesday Geography of Leicestershire', *LeAS*, XX, 1939; W.K. Boyd, 'Survey of Leicestershire' (with facsimile), *Leics. Arch. & Archaeol. Soc.*, VIII, 1896; C.P. Adams, *The Norman Conquest of Leicestershire and Rutland*, Leics. Museums, 1986; DG: Midland; *Domesday Book, 22*, trs. P. Morgan, Phillimore, 1979.

Lincolnshire   OS Facsimile; C.W. Foster and T. Longley, *The Lincolnshire Domesday and Lindsey Survey*, Linc. Rec. Soc., XIX, 1924; *Domesday Book, 31* (in two parts), ed. P. Morgan and C. Thorn, Phillimore, 1986; DG: Eastern; G. Beresford, 'Goltho Manor, Lincolnshire', *Anglo-Norman Studies IV*, 1981; G.G. Bryant, *Domesday Book; How to Read it and What its Text Means. The Example of Waltham in Lincolnshire*, WEA, Waltham, 1985; G. Fellows-Jemsen, *Scandinavian Personal Names in Lincolnshire and Yorkshire*, 1968; and: 'On the Identification of Domesday Tenants in Lincolnshire', *Nomina*, 1986; C. Mahaney and D. Roffe, 'Stamford, the Development of an Anglo-Scandinavian Borough', *Anglo-Norman Studies V*, 1982.

London & Middlesex   OS Facsimile; F.H. Baring (arranged with notes by), *Domesday Tables for the Counties of Surrey, Berkshire and Middlesex,* St Catherine's Press, 1909; W. Bawden, *Translation of the Record called Domesday, so far as it relates to the Counties of Middlesex, Hertford, Buckingham, Oxford and Gloucester,* Longman Hurst, 1812; Sir Henry Ellis, *A General Introduction to Domesday Book; Accompanied by the Indexes of the Tenants-in-Chief and under-tenants at the time of the Survey, etc.* (with abstracts of population, 1087), 2 vols., Commissioners on the Public Records of the U.K., 1833; General Plantagenet Harrison, *Domesday Book, or the Great Survey of England ... Translation of the Part relating to Middlesex,* Head & Meek, 1876; *Domesday Book, or the Great Survey of England by William the Conqueror, A.D. 1086. A literal extension of the Latin text, and an English translation in relation to the County of Middlesex,* Vacher, 1862; W.D. Bushell, *Harrow in Domesday,* Macmillan, Cambridge, 1894; E. Griffith, 'Middlesex in the Time of the Domesday Survey', *LMAS,* I, 1860; M. Sharpe, *Antiquities of Middlesex; Accuracy of Domesday Land Measures in Middlesex, and their Roman origin,* Brentford, 1914; M. Sharpe, 'Middlesex in Domesday Book', *LMAS,* n.s., 7, 1937; West Drayton Local History Society, *Before and after Domesday. A chronology of Harmondsworth,* 1986; DG: South-East; *Domesday Book, 11,* trs. S. Wood, Phillimore, 1975; *VCH,* I (1969), contains the Domesday Survey of the county.

Monmouthshire   Monmouth had no separate Survey in 1086, but its present lands were surveyed under the counties of Gloucestershire and Herefordshire. The extracts from these Surveys have been translated in: J. Bradney, *History of Monmouthshire from the Coming of the Normans,* III, Pt.2, London, 1923; IV, Pt.I, London, 1929.

Montgomery   See *Domesday Book, 17* (Herefordshire), Phillimore; DG: Midland; J.C. Davies, *Lordships and manors in the county of Montgomery,* The Montgomery Collection, no.49, 1962.

Norfolk   *VCH,* 2 (1906); *Domesday Book, 33* (in two parts), ed. P. Brown, Phillimore, 1984; DG: Eastern; R.W. Finn, *Domesday Studies: The Eastern Counties,* 1967.

Northamptonshire   *VCH,* I (1902); OS Facsimile; C.P. Bayley, 'The Domesday Geography of Northamptonshire', *Northants Nat. Hist. Soc.,* XXIX, 1938 (article with maps); DG: Midland; F.H. Baring, 'The Hidation of Northamptonshire in 1086 and the pre-Domesday Hidation of Northamptonshire', *EHR,* 17, 1902; *Domesday Book, 21,* trs. P. Morgan, Phillimore, 1979.

Nottinghamshire   *VCH,* I (1906); OS Facsimile; M.W. Bishop, *Norman Nottinghamshire 1000-1150 AD,* Notts. County Council, 1986; G. Black and D. Roffe, *The Nottinghamshire Domesday, a reader's guide,* Nottingham Museums, 1986; DG: Northern; *Domesday Book, 28,* trs. C.Parker, S. Wood, Phillimore, 1977.

Oxfordshire   *VCH,* I (1939); OS Facsimile; DG: South-East; *Domesday Book, 13,* trs. C. Caldwell, Phillimore, 1978.

Radnorshire   L.C. Venables, 'Domesday Book in Radnorshire and the Border', *Rad. Soc.,* 2, 1932.

Rutland   *VCH,* I (1908); OS Facsimile; W. Bawden, *Translation of the Record called Domesday,* Doncaster, 1809 (also for Derby, Lincs, Yorks, Lancs, Westmorland and Cumberland); C.G. Smith, *Translation of that part of Domesday Book which relates to Lincolnshire and Rutlandshire,* London, 1870; C.P. Adams, *The Norman Conquest of Leicestershire and Rutland,* Leics. Museums, 1986; Prince Y. Galitzine, *Domesday Book in Rutland, the Dramatis Personae,* Rutland Record Society, 1986; DG: Midland; *Domesday Book, 29,* trs. C.Parker, Phillimore, 1980.

Shropshire   *VCH,* I (1908); OS Facsimile; D. Sylvester, 'Rural Settlement in Domesday Shropshire', *Social Rev.,* XXV, 1933; *Domesday Book, 25,* ed. F. and C. Thorn, Phillimore, 1986; DG: Midland; J.F.A. Mason, 'Roger of Montgomery and his sons', *Trans. R. Hist. Soc.* (5th series), 13, 1963;

   Various works in *Trans. Shrops. Arch. and Nat. Hist. Soc.:* W.J. Slack, 'The Shropshire Ploughman of Domesday Book', 1939; H.M. Auden, 'Frodesley', 52, 1947-8; R.W. Eyton, 'Notes on Domesday', 1, 1878; R. Lloyd Kenyon, 'The Domesday manors of Ruyton, Wikey and Felton', 2nd series, 12, 1900; J.F.A. Mason, 'Edric of Bayston', 55, 1954-6; and: 'The Officers and Clerks of the Norman Earls of Shropshire', 56, 1957-60; and: 'The Norman Earls of Shrewsbury', 57, 1961-4; R.C. Purton, 'Some accounts of the manor of Faintree', 2nd series, 5, 1893; and: 'Some accounts of the manor of Chetton', (2nd series), 6, 1894; and: 'Some accounts of the manors of Eudon Burnell and Eudon George', (2nd series), 6, 1894; and: 'Some accounts of Holdgate and the Cressets', (4th series), 6, 1916-17; and: 'Some accounts of the manor of Oldby, near Bridgnorth', 46, 1931; and: 'Some accounts of the manor of Okes in the parish of Pontesbury', 54, 1951-3.

Somerset   *VCH*, 1 (1906); OS Facsimile; R.W. Dunning, *Somerset in Domesday*, Somerset County Library, 1986; S.C. Morland, *Glastonbury, Domesday and related studies*, Glastonbury Antiquarian Society, 1991; DG: South-West; S. Everett, 'The Domesday geography of three Exmoor parishes', *SANHS*, 112, 1968; *Domesday Book, 8*, trs. C.Thorn, Phillimore, 1980.

Staffordshire   *VCH*, 4 (1958); OS Facsimile; R.W. Eyton, *Domesday Studies; an Analysis of the Staffordshire Survey*, London, 1881; H.M. Fraser, *The Staffordshire Domesday*, Stone, 1936; J.C. Wedgwood, *Early Staffordshire History, from the Map and from Domesday Book*, Wm. Salt Arch. Soc., 1916; C.G.O. Bridgeman, *Some Unidentified Domesday Vills, Wm. Salt Arch. Soc. n.s.,* 1923; C.F. Slade, *The Staffordshire Domesday: From VCH Staffordshire Vol.4*, Staffordshire County Library, 1985; DG: Midland; R.W. Eyton, *Domesday Studies; An analysis and digest of the Staffordshire survey*, 1881; *Domesday Book, 24*, trs. A. Hawkins and A. Rumble, Phillimore, 1976; 'Domesday Book for Staffordshire', Staffordshire County Council, *Local History Source Book*, no.10, 1971.

Suffolk   *VCH*, 1 (1902); OS Facsimile; *Domesday Book, 34* (in two parts), ed. A. Rumble, Phillimore, 1986; DG: Eastern; D.C. Douglas, *Feudal Documents from the Abbey of Bury St Edmunds*, 1932, (refers to Suffolk, Norfolk and Essex).

Surrey   *VCH*, 1 (1902); OS Facsimile; DG: South-East; *Domesday Book, 2*, trs. S. Wood, Phillimore, 1975.

Sussex   *VCH*, 1 (1905); OS Facsimile; DG: South-East; W.D. Parish, *Domesday Book in Relation to the County of Sussex*, 1886; *Domesday Book, 2*, trs. J. Mothersill, Phillimore, 1977.

Wales   National Library of Wales, *Exhibition Catalogue, Llyfr Domesday ac arolygon eraill yng Nyghymru/ Domesday and other surveys in Wales*, parallel English and Welsh texts, Aberystwyth, 1986; *Domesday Book, 26*, trs. P. Morgan, Phillimore, 1978.

Warwickshire   *VCH*, 1 (1904); OS Facsimile; W. Reader and E.P. Shirley, *Domesday Book for the County of Warwickshire*, Coventry, 1835; Warwick, 1879; C. Twamley, 'Notes on the Domesday of Warwickshire', *Arch. J.*, XXI, 1864; B. Walker, 'Some Notes on Domesday Book', *Trans. Birm. Arch. Soc.*, XXVI, 1900; B. Walker, 'The Hundreds of Warwickshire at the time of the Domesday Survey', *Antiquary*, XXXIX, 1903; R.H. Kinvig, 'The Birminghamshire District in Domesday Times', *Birmingham and its Regional Setting*, British Assocn., 1950; DG: Eastern; *Domesday Book, 23*, trs. J. Plaister, Phillimore, 1977.

Wiltshire   *VCH*, 2 (1955); OS Facsimile; DG: South-West; R.W. Finn, 'The making of the Wiltshire Domesday', *Wilts. Arch. & Nat. Hist. Mag.*, LII, 1949-50; M.W. Hughes, 'The Domesday Boroughs of Wiltshire', *WANHM*, LIV, 1951-2; W.H.R. Jones, *Domesday for Wiltshire*, 1865, contains extended texts of Exchequer and Exon. Domesdays; F.W. Morgan, 'The Domesday Geography of Wiltshire', *WANHM*, XLVIII, 1938; *Domesday Book, 6*, trs. C. and F. Thorn, Phillimore, 1979.

Worcestershire   *VCH*, 1 (1901); OS Facsimile; J.W. Willis-Bund, 'Worcestershire Domesday', *Assoc. of Arch. Socs. Reports & Papers*, XXII, 1894; DG: Midland.

Yorkshire   *VCH*, 2 (1910); OS Facsimile; R.H. Scaife, 'Domesday of Yorkshire', *Yorks Arch. J.*, XIII, XIV (reprinted 1896, transcript, translation and article, with index); A.B. Wilson-Barkworth, *Domesday Book for the East Riding of Yorkshire*, 1925; *Domesday Book, 30* (in two parts), ed. M.L. Faull and M. Stinson, Phillimore, 1986; N. Metcalf, *The Domesday Survey of the Doncaster Region*, Doncaster Museum & Arts Service, 1986; DG: Northern; M.W. Beresford, 'The lost villages of Yorkshire', *Yorks. Arch. Journal*, XXXVIII, 1955; A.S. Ellis, 'Some account of the landholders of Yorkshire named in Domesday', *Yorks. Arch. & Top. Journal*, IV, 1877 and V, 1879; W.H. Stevenson, 'Yorkshire surveys and other documents of the eleventh century in York gospels', *EHR*, XXVII, 1912; R. W. Finn, *The Making and Limitations of the Yorkshire Domesday*, St. Anthony's Press, York: *Borthwick Papers*, no. 4, 1972.

ORIGINAL DOCUMENTS TO BE FOUND AT:

The Public Record Office, Chancery Lane, London.

CHAPTER III

The Middle Ages

✧

The term 'Middle Ages' or 'medieval period' is often loosely used as a vague, even a misleading, description of the 11 centuries between the decay of the Roman Empire and the Renaissance. It is in fact misleading to assume that such a vast distance in time can be conveniently considered in one span. Several institutions which originate during this time, and which appear to be 'typically' medieval, still survive today; others which were equally characteristic were undergoing drastic change from the earliest times; many disappeared, or were completely transformed during the earlier centuries. It is more advisable to consider separately the period of Saxon migration, of Christian conversion, and repeated Norse incursions before the Norman Conquest, and to apply the term 'mediaeval' more particularly to the period from 1066 to the discovery of the New World and the Renaissance of learning. Even within this span of 400 years a further division should be made at the beginning of the 13th century, for the later Middle Ages were years of rapid transition and deep social upheaval. Nevertheless there are features of the Middle Ages which exhibit common characteristics, and which give the whole period a certain loose unity.

The traditional stereotype of medieval life tended to emphasise the period's extreme localism, a condition kept in place by numerous small-scale institutions such as manors, gilds, monasteries and corporate boroughs. At first sight these autonomous communities seem to shape the whole condition of medieval life and work; self-sufficient, with restrictive aims, they excluded 'foreigners' who came from neighbouring towns as well as people from other countries. The ground level of peasant economy certainly matches Hobbe's idea of a state of nature: 'solitary, poor, nasty, brutish and short', with very little evidence of Merrie England. The environment of the illiterate and superstitious village majority was confined to the length of a furrow, the conservative customs of the manor and the morality of the parish church with its mural threats of Hell. Nationally and overseas, geographical communication was primitive and the monetary economy was conditioned by a resulting restriction of trade. Thus, circulation of coinage was generally sluggish, accelerating only during exceptional periods of inflation during the 13th and late 15th centuries.

These observations tend to conceal a paradox. European society at large was in contrast with the more mundane local scene. Even if we choose to disregard the long duration of a period which makes generalisations unreliable, and ignore their revision by recent research, we cannot fail to notice that Christendom was an international union. Before the emergence of divisive nations Europe had one language of Latin scholarship and administration, one religion and a uniform hierarchy of social order. The upper levels of society were united by orders of chivalry and feudal bonds which extended the boundaries of fiefs and kingdoms beyond the frontiers of England, France or Germany. Monastic orders regulated life, work, worship, learning and architecture from Provence to Rievaulx, so that a boy might be sent from a Shropshire village to Evroult for his education and a monastic chronicler's career. Ruling class and bourgeoisie understood each other's conventions of royal court, barony, university, gild and cloister.

Nor was travelling completely confined: pilgrimages, crusades, fairs and markets, merchant venturers, university education, royal retinues, official embassies, episcopal and baronial peregrination, all these kept people, ideas and coinage actively mobile.[1] Even at a more local level, as Jusserand observed more than a hundred years ago,[2] wayfaring life was well organised, so that quite humble manorial officials, bailiffs and carters, ladies and their escorts, travelled regularly from village to village across the county boundaries. To return to the outworn stereotype, what does remain of 'localism', fortunately for the student, is a wealth of available documents reassuringly similar in style, format and content, which illustrate medieval society at its various levels, far and near.

Perhaps the most typically mcdicval of all institutions was that of military feudalism, evolved unsystematically as a remedy for the inadequacy of central government all over Western Europe. Feudalism imposed upon medieval society in England a code of personal relationships and a contract of territorial government with its own body of custom and legal forms which, however, never supplanted the older Saxon institutions of shire and hundred. During the Middle Ages the power of the monarchy was both personal and feudal in character; only slowly did the Angevins create a centralised machinery of bureaucratic government, working to achieve this through the departments of the royal household and its courts. Deeply conservative in the preservation and use of feudal custom and more ancient laws, medieval kings maintained order at home and conquests abroad, each according to his personal ability. Medieval society was divided into three main 'estates', baronage, ecclesiastics and peasantry, each with a specialised function, each, until the 14th century, divided by barriers of caste, of language and of law. Only slowly, from the amalgam of Latin, Norman-French and Anglo-Saxon, does an English tradition emerge, and only gradually does the bourgeois tradesman appear, to form a disintegrating middle class.

Throughout this period, responsibility for the administration of local affairs rested with the local aristocracy, rather than in any national policy. The authority of the Sheriff as a royal official was, at first, auxiliary to the franchises and liberties of the feudal classes. Only slowly does central government adopt a recognised function as law-maker and regulator of trade, justice, industry, wages and commerce. As the period continues, disintegrating forces emerge and develop. Peace and order fostered trade and wealth; the flow of currency, and particularly the revenues of the wool trade, provided resources and stimulus to central government. Commutation of services and payments in kind had, from an early date, tended to blur the divisions of medieval society; dynastic strife and an over-mighty baronage eventually brought the monarchy, and its people, to a crisis from which emerged Tudor government. Simultaneously, as new religious ideas foreshadowed the end of a truly Catholic age, as new discoveries and wider intercourse extended men's mental horizons, so feudalism and localism proved inadequate

[1] M.W. Labarge, *Medieval Travellers: The Rich and Restless*, Hamish Hamilton, 1982.
[2] Jean Jusserand, *English Wayfaring Life in the Middle Ages*, ed. L.T. Smith, London, 1950.

to control the shifting social pattern, and the Middle Ages drew to a close. This was a raw, brutal period, primitive and superstitious, yet threaded with a vein of simplicity and faith. Underlying all was the passive, inarticulate mass of the peasantry, bound to the land, their horizon at the end of a furlong.

The narrative history of wars and dynasties is contained in the great series of monastic chronicles which culminate in the 13th-century annals of the monks of St Albans. The documents chosen here do not pretend to show a cross-section of medieval life, but have been chosen to illustrate some aspects of daily life and duty on a Midland manor; the medieval abbot and chapter as estate managers; the tenuous connection of the vill with central government through the payment of royal taxes, and an example of the small manorial estate of the minor feudal gentry with whom the future lay.

MANORIAL COURT ROLLS

THE DOCUMENT

The manor court was the central institution of medieval village life. Each lord of the manor held a court there by right, and 'suit of court', the duty of attendance there, was one of the chief obligations of his tenants. The function of the court was chiefly administrative, supervising the organisation of the agrarian and social life of the manor, and continually interpreting its customs. The offences with which the court dealt in its judicial capacity were chiefly those concerned with tenure, services and dues within the manor. Other misdemeanours came within the authority of the shire and hundred courts, or royal and ecclesiastical courts; feudal affairs were managed by the king and barons in their baronial courts. In studying specific manors it may well be found that several jurisdictions are in fact combined in the same court-day. These may be Great Courts with Court Baron, or Courts Leet, to which had been added certain franchises to hear cases more usually tried in the shire or royal courts. The most common of these additions to the manorial court is that of the lord's right to take the local 'view of frankpledge', an ancient Saxon presentment by 'tithings' for the maintenance of peace and order. This can be very confusing for the beginner who has not fully understood the difference of function of one such court and another. In this study, 'manor court' has been used in its most restricted sense, that is, to describe the regular, three-weekly, 'customary' court which concerned itself only with the administration of the demesne and villeinage.

In the manor, the responsibilities of the lord's officials, steward, bailiffs and reeves, are recorded; so also are indicated the status of the villein, his services, rents and other obligations; payments of relief, heriot and merchet, all are recorded in the manorial court rolls. The lord's rights over the villagers and their tenements, as well as over his own demesne, are also apparent. We thus gain a very full picture of the life and work of the medieval manor, a picture which can be supplemented by further reference to manorial custumals, rent-rolls and accounts compiled by the lord's officials. Also invaluable for revealing the exact phraseology and detailed procedure of the court are the 'formularies' or treatises written by clerks and lawyers to instruct stewards in the proper legal forms and formalities.[3] These records are particularly numerous during the 13th and 14th centuries. Unfortunately, most of the surviving rolls, and

---

[3] See *The Court Baron; being precedents for use in seigneurial and other local courts, together with select pleas from the Bishop of Ely's Court of Littleport*, ed. F.W. Maitland and W. Paley Baildon, Selden Soc., 1891.

particularly those which have been published, record the administration of the greater estates of the lay and ecclesiastical nobility. Many previously accepted generalisations regarding the 'typical' manor are now being revised, as knowledge is gained of regional differences, of transitional periods, and particularly of the customs of the smaller estates.

The incomparable value of thousands of manorial court rolls from all over medieval England cannot be over-estimated as sources of information on the life, work and behaviour of manorial people, both servile villeins and free tenants. In 1980, Zvi Razi used the Halesowen court rolls and a computer to measure population trends from 1270 to 1348.[4] His interpretation of court-roll entries for demographic analysis registered, identified and located 3,435 villagers and reconstituted 677 families who were resident in Halesowen between 1270 and 1400. Using this data Razi was able to estimate the size of peasant families, the incidence of marriages and illegitimacy and the year-by-year rate of mortality in the manor. The death toll of the great plague of 1348-9 amounted to 40 per cent in Halesowen, with the hamlets of Illey and Hunnington suffering a 57 per cent loss.

More recent research casts doubt upon uncritical uses of court rolls for reconstructing medieval social structure.[5] (Razi himself was well aware of the inevitable limitations of his own large statistical sample.) It is pointed out that, as most of us already knew, that manorial population may account for no more than 60 per cent of the male population of a village and only 40 per cent of females. This is easily proved by the correlation of other medieval, non-manorial records, such as poll tax lists or lay subsidy rolls with the manorial records. In lectures to the English Genealogical Congress of 1984, entitled *Town, Manor and an Alternative Society* and again in 1986 on *People of the Medieval Forest*[6] it was possible to demonstrate, by supplementing court roll evidence with tax rolls and forest court proceedings, that 'there were more medieval people than a limited number of manorial documents reveals ... (that) ... this sporadically recorded population was more restlessly mobile, both socially and geographically than the rigid facade presented by manorial records suggests ... (and that) ... the royal forests provide a wealth of alternative records of named people, more numerous and socially mobile than the conservative society which manorial court rolls portray'.

List after list of surnames, taken from court rolls, lay subsidy rolls and forest eyres add more and more medieval inhabitants to the manorial tenants. It is a commonplace fact that manorial rentals exclude subtenants. As long ago as 1966, Professor Hilton reminded us that 'the number of tenants in any survey is not the same as the number of families in the manor; for the court records indicate that there was a considerable amount of sub-letting by the main tenants to families who might make no payment to the lord and so do not appear in his letters'.[7] Evasion of merchet payments, too, tends to conceal the incidence of marriage amongst manorial womenfolk. As to genealogical reconstruction, Razi pointed out the unreliable evidence of medieval surnames which remain unstable throughout the manorial records.

Even so, no amount of re-assessment can significantly reduce the importance of so great a national archive as the manorial documents of medieval England. Here indeed is a field in which computers can make a heyday of demographic reconstruction, as long as we are aware that, as was evident in our 1962 edition: 'Many previously accepted generalisations regarding the "typical" manor are now being revised ...'.

[4] Z. Razi, Life, *Marriage and Death in a Medieval Parish*, C.U.P., 1980.
[5] L.R. Poos and R.M. Smith, 'Legal windows on medieval population; Recent research on demography and the manor courts in medieval England', *Law Review*, no.2, 1984.
[6] J. West, *Town, Manor and the Alternative Society*, English Genealogical Congress: Select Papers given at the Congresses of 1978 and 1984 (1986).
[7] R.H. Hilton, *A Medieval Society*, 1966, p.76.

TRANSCRIPT

(See: *Court Rolls of the Manor of Hales*, vol.III, p.164)

1. . . . . (1) 'Cur(ia) de Romesl' die sab(batin)o p(ro)x(ime) (2) post festu(m) s(an)c(t)i Dionisij. Anno r(egni) r(egis) E(dwardi). Octavo. (3)
2. . . . . (1) Th(oma)s Sq(u)ier pro duab(us) defalt(is) in m(isericordi)a. p. (egius) Henr(icus) defulfen.
3. mi(sericordi) a. vjd. Jon(anne)s dehondeford' p(ro) hutesio levato in iuste (et) ideo in mi(sericordi)a. p(egius) Alanus de Tadenhurst,'
4. mi(sericordi) a. vjd. Will(elmu)s molendinar(ius) in mi(sericordi) a quia verberavit ancilla(m) Ric(ardi) de Edwyneshule. pl(egius) Ric(ardus) bound.
5. mi(sericordi) a. xij. (d') Hausia delaleye pr(ro) filia sua (q'fe struck through) videlicet de lerwite in mi(sericordi)a. pl(eigius) Th(oma)s filius ei(us).
6. mi(sericordi) a. vjd. Felicia Miteyns in (m) (4) i(sericordi)a q(u)ia deforciavit Ada(m) snow defeno suo (et) p(er)cussit filiu(m) suu(m). (et) ideo in mi(sericordi)a. pl(e)g(ius) Henr(icus) de folfen.
7. mi(sericordi) a. vjd. Ada(m) Snow q(u)ia cep(it) vacca(m) felic(ie) Miten. in iuste (et) detinuit ip(s)am (contr)a vadiu(m). (et) ideo in mi(sericordi)a. pl(e)g(ius) Joh(anne)s de monte.
8. M(emoran)d(um) q(uod) datus e(st) dies Ade snow de namio vi capto de custodia Tandi cl(er)ici die sab(bat)i p(ro)x(im)o.
9. M(emoran)d(um) de Will(elm)o de perie p(ro) t(r)ansg(r)essio(n)e f(a)c(t)a p(er) fr(atr)em suu(m) sup(er) blad(um) d(omi)ni.
10. dist(r)ict(i)o Nich(ola)s de Monte fec(it) defalta(m) (et) negat secta(m). (et) ideo distringat (ur) p(ro) defalta.
11. I(n)q(u)isit(i)o It(em) inq(u)isit(i)o inter familia(m) Henr(ici) defulfen (et) vxore(m) Will(elm)i Orme po(n)it(ur) in respectu usq(elm)i sab(bat) p(ro)x(imo) (5) videlicet de hutesio levato.
12. Th(oma)s demonte calu(m)pniat(ur) q(uia) destruit herbagiu(m) vicinor(um) cu(m) av(er)iis extraneor(um).

TRANSLATION

1. Court of Romsley held on the Saturday next after the feast of St Dionysius in the eighth year of the reign of King Edward.
2. Thomas Squier for two offences, amerced. Pledge Henry de fulfen.
3. Amercement 6d. John de Honeford for wrongfully raising the hue-and-cry. Pledge Alan de Tadenhurst.
4. Amercement 6d. William Miller amerced because he beat the maid-servant of Richard de Edwyneshulle. Pledge Richard Bound.
5. Amercement 12d. Hausia de la Leye fined for her daughter's *lerwite*. Pledge Thomas her son.
6. Amercement 6d. Felicia Miteyns is amerced because she forcibly deprived Adam Snow of his hay and beat his son. Pledge Henry de Folfen.
7. Amercement 6d. Adam Snow because he took a cow belonging to Felicia Miteyns and detained the same against his word. Pledge John de Monte.
8. Memorandum that a day has been appointed for Adam Snow, regarding his distress, taken by force from the custody of Tandy the cleric. Next Saturday.
9. Memorandum regarding William de Pirie, for trespass by his brother upon the lord's corn.
10. Distraint Nicholas de Monte defaulted and denied suit of court. The accused is distrained for default.
11. Inquest Item, the inquest between the family of Henry de Fulfen and William Orme's wife is placed in respite until next Saturday, that is regarding the raising of the hue and cry.
12. Thomas de Monte is accused of destroying his neighbours' pasture with the cattle of strangers.

(1) Note paragraph mark on this line and the next.
(2) A superior 'a' is used here as a sign of contraction.
(3) i.e., 8 Edw. I or 1280; the date of the feast-day was 12 October.
(4) *m* probably omitted in error because of proximity to 'in' preceding.

Plate III. Romsley Manor Court Roll 1280
(Birmingham Ref. Library MS. 346211. f. i, dorso)
Enlarged x 0.5: Actual size: 21.5 x 7.5cm

A great deal of research remains to be done into the work, services and wages of the lesser tenants and peasantry. There has, as yet, been little reference to changing agricultural techniques, and the reaction to changing conditions of supply and demand, or to the scale of profit and investment. The problems of wage-labour, encroachment on the waste and marginal land, commutation of services, and, in fact, the whole problem of the growth of a money economy,[8] all these need further examinations. Evidence of these changes can only be found by extensive regional studies, particularly of smaller estates, and by reference to other sources, such as manorial extents and compotus rolls.

The rolls themselves are usually found to be entered on membranes of vellum, measuring from 7 in. to 12 in. in width, and about 20 in. to 24 in. in length, stitched together in a bulky roll many feet long. The entry for a single court may vary in length from 2-3 in. to 2 ft. or more, the end of one court and the beginning of the next being quite clearly spaced and entitled. Most rolls are much yellowed, faded and damaged, though a fair proportion of them are still legible. The calligraphy is very difficult indeed, a cursive court hand, impossible for any but the advanced student to decipher, and then only after intensive work on printed originals. The language is Latin, with a complicated system of abbreviation, which is, however, fairly standardised, so that a really determined student who knows Latin can, with much practice, become familiar with the more common forms. This task is further hindered by the handwriting, which is often minute, and always spiky and sharply contracted in form. For any but research students the only feasible way of studying local Court Rolls is from the printed editions, which may be in Latin, or in translation.

In 1962, as the list of Worcestershire manors on page 58 shows, the author was unaware of the existence of any surviving Chaddesley court rolls and therefore used as manorial examples the best available nearby examples in print, those of Halesowen. After publication of the second edition of 1982 his attention was drawn to a small group of Chaddesley originals which are kept at the Shakespeare Birthplace Trust's Records Office in Stratford-upon-Avon. These had been amongst the large collection of Throckmorton family papers, once kept at Coughton Court in Warwickshire, but which had been transferred to Stratford at an early date. There, they are listed under accession numbers DR5 (2) Nos: 1920-3407 and date from c.1338 to c.1800, including a dozen court rolls, Nos: 2737-2748 from 4 November 1375 to 10 April 1402.

Each roll records the business of the manorial small court, combined with a view of frankpledge for the 11 village members: Chaddesley Corbett, Lower Chaddesley, Upper Chaddesley, Cakebole, Winterfold, Brockencote, Harvington, Bellington, Yieldingtree, Hill and Drayton. The manor court was intended to deal with cases of custom, services, rents, fines and transfers of land, often described as *messuages* and *virgates*. Normal manorial business includes records of amercements for failing to build houses or keep them in repair, penalties for un-scoured ditches, heriots surrendered as death duties and entry fines paid and fealty done for the taking over of tenements, usually a standard '*one messuage and half-virgate*' at 12d. entry fine and 4-5s. per annum in rent; the charge for one acre or a cottage was 2-3d. Suit of court and other 'fines, customs and services' are mentioned in agreements but not specified in any of these rolls. The '*visum*' was primarily concerned with the presentations of each hamlet's tithing-men on matters of law and order; in fact there is often an overlap of these different functions and similar cases appear in both parts of the roll.

---

[8] See M. Postan, 'The Rise of a Money Economy', in *Economic History Review*, Old Series, 14, 1944.

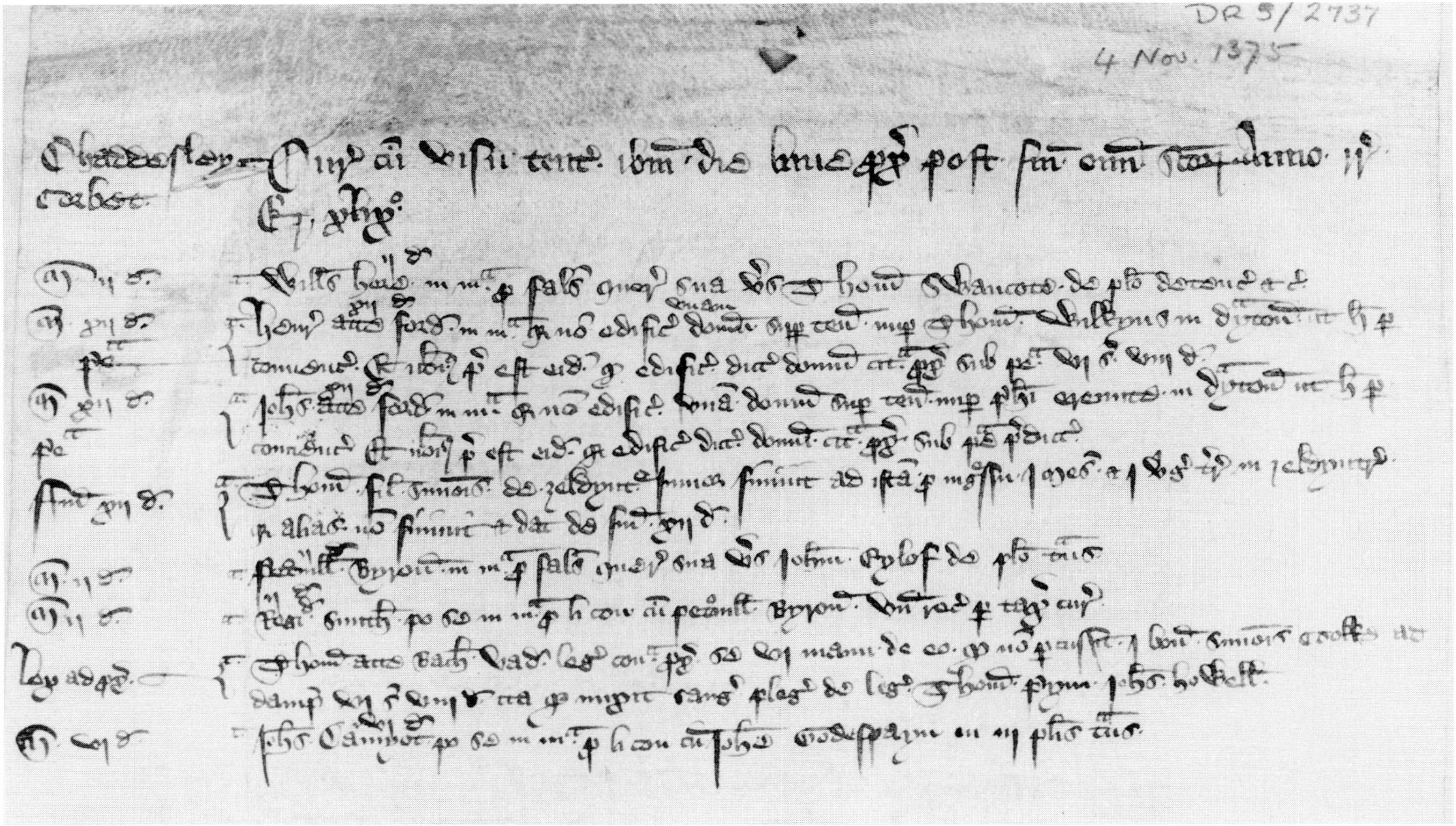

Plate IV

Court with View held at Chaddesley Corbett on 4 November 1375.

Printed by permission of the Stratford Birthplace Trust.

Ref: DRs/2737. Actual size: 22 x 13cm

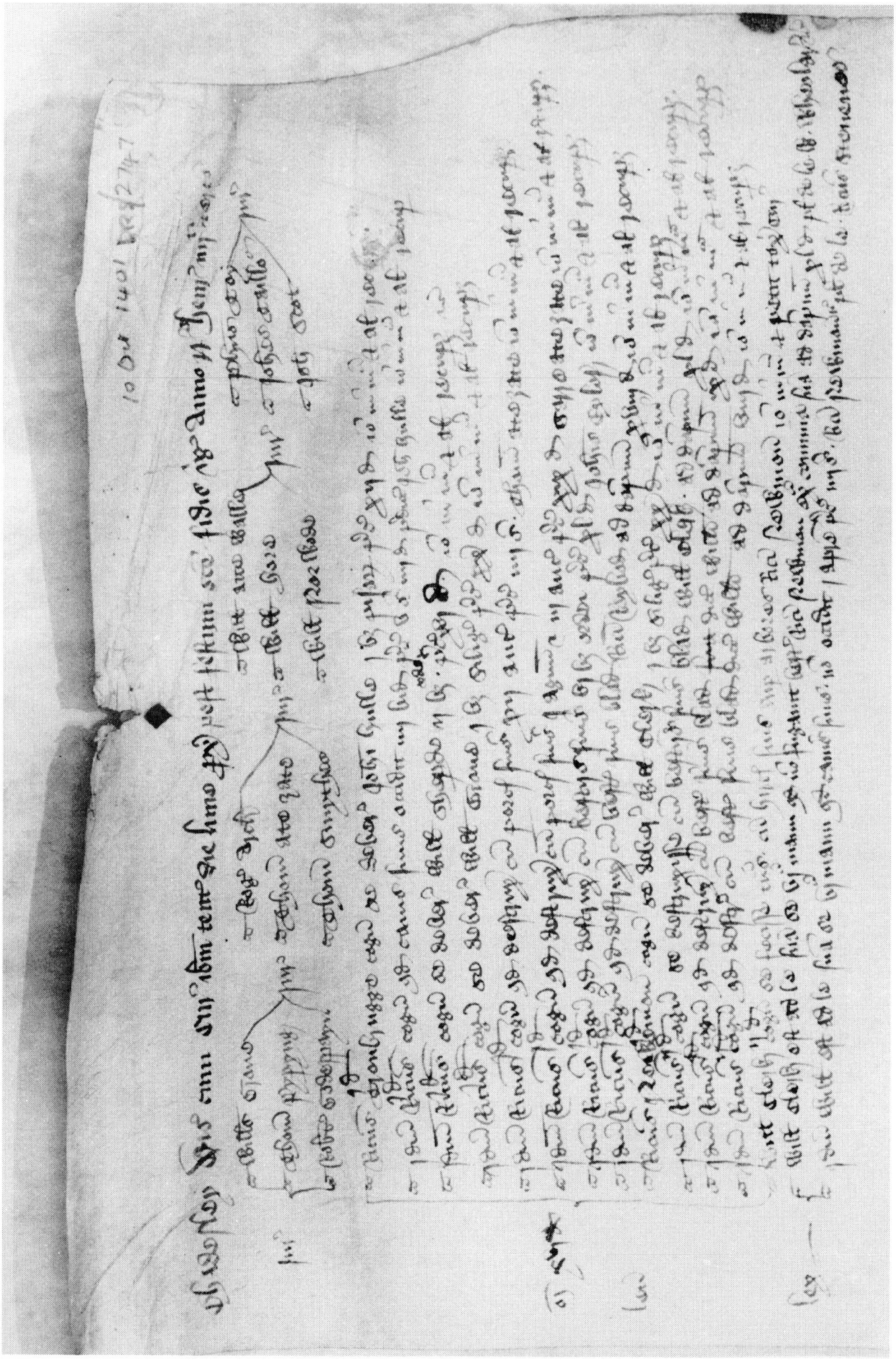

Plate V
View with Court held at Chaddesley Corbett on 10 October 1401.
Printed by permission of the Shakespeare Birthplace Trust.
Ref: DR5/2747. Actual size: 25 x 16.5cm

The two extracts illustrated are, firstly (Plate IV): 'Chaddesley Corbet, a Court with View held on the Monday next after the feast of All Saints (1st November) in the 49th year of the reign of King Edward III. (i.e. 4th.November 1375)'. This is the manorial section, in which we find amercements ranging from 2d. each for William Hore's false plea against Thomas Swancote and of Parnell Byron for falsely accusing John Eylof of trespass, to 12d. each from Henry atte Ford for failing to build a house on the tenement which had formerly belonged to Thomas Wilkyns and from John atte Ford for a similar offence on newly tenanted land in Drayton. Both are ordered to build before the next court under penalty of 6s. 8d. The amercement of 2d. for 'trespass' is also fixed at a standard rate; John Damyot pays 6d. for an agreement on three similar offences against John Godespayn. Thomas son of Simon pays a fine of 12d. for entry into one messuage and a virgate in Yieldingtree and Thomas atte Bache pledges himself six-handed to prove that he had not beaten Simon Cook's ox to the damage of 6s. 8d.; lacking family pledges he offers as 'pledges at law' Thomas Pym and John Howell. Overleaf from the illustrated extract, Peter Muleward comes to this court to take charge of the water-mill at Drayton for a rent of 26s. 8d. per annum and an undertaking to keep the mill and all its gear in good repair and Agnes Tomkyns 'the lord's native' pays her own marriage fee of 5s. in order to take a husband, Richard Perlar, who lived outside the manor.

The second extract (Plate V) reverses the court's title to that of 'View with Court' instead of the more usual 'Court with View' and illustrates the tithing-men's presentations. Held on 'Monday after the feast of St.Fides (6th October) in the second year of the reign of Henry IV (i.e. 10th October, 1401)', the roll begins with the names of 12 jurors and is unusual only in its list of eight offences by the same Richard Troubrugge. Richard was amerced 1d. each on two different kinds of charge: three debts of peas, winter wheat and barley and five claims of damages to his neighbours' stock. His dog had killed four of John Hull's sheep (worth 5s. 4d.); his pigs had killed 12 of Thomas atte Gate's geese (worth 4s.), one lamb and 3 geese (19d.) belonging to Sarah atte Gate, and his 'beasts' had destroyed six bushels of John Eylof's barley (40d.) and 18d. worth of Richard Reybod's wheat. The fact that this list continues with three cases of similar damage by Richard Newmon's animals might suggest that these crops lay open and unprotected by fences. William Clerk is to find six pledges at law to prove that he had not driven Newmon's animals from the common, that his dogs had not killed Richard's boar nor had his goats destroyed Newmon's trees. These disorders seem to indicate a restless, irresponsible social relationship of men and beasts. The restlessness took a violent turn when the tithing-men charge Richard Newmon with housebreaking—his victim, William Clerk!

Normally, the *decennarii* present '*omnia bene*', or the ale-tasters present as many as twenty villagers who have brewed ale and broken the assize; they are fined 2d. per brew for one to four offences, or perhaps pay these fines as routine licence payments. We learn that a tithing-man's responsibility began at the age of 12, when an adolescent Roger Godespayn of Drayton was amerced for default of attendance at court. Frankpledge also deals with routine inspection of the highways and ditches, either by default of an individual's section, or of a whole '*villata*'; at Brockencote in 1397 the tithing-men present that John Strong and Nicholas Boun have *forestalled* or obstructed the right-of-way of their neighbours, and that Richard Ermyte's hedges at Doubeslane grow over the road and obstruct other peoples' cartage; at Bellington, the enclosure of a common meadow by Thomas Goderych is also reported. The tithing too, can also concern themselves, in the very same court of 1375 in which the manorial responsibility of the Ford brothers was enforced, with four other tenants in Cakebole whose houses are ruinous, or record the absence of fugitive villeins like William Knyt, Richard Hobkyns, of Brockencote. Also on the view's roll, a jury of 12 swears to the liability of about twenty-five (some illegible) for payment of pannage of one penny per pig for very small numbers from one to five, which we might have assumed to be manorial business of the same type as 'Grastack' accounted for as manorial income on another court roll.

This handful of Chaddesley court rolls makes a virtue of 1962's necessity in choosing the printed Halesowen records as an introduction to manorial court rolls. Although they are by no means as comprehensive, they would repay a more careful reading of their difficult hands, if only for their indications of Chaddesley's manorial extent and topography. Fortunately we can now be more optimistic of the less professional student's chances of success with first-hand experience of medieval originals. Certainly the most important accession to the resources of any student of medieval paleography since the publication of Hector's *Handwriting of English Documents* is Denis Stuart's do-it-yourself manual of *Manorial Records*, published by Phillimore in 1992. This masterly set of 35 exercises uses facsimile documents to demonstrate how court rolls, rentals, extents, accounts and custumals should be read, transcribed and translated, with step-by-step notes in friendly style to explain each document's conventions and extend its contractions. As the publisher remarks: 'Surprisingly, this new book is the first full-length modern manual to offer a structured and comprehensive guide to their use'. Any student who completes this very practical course will be well equipped to read both the Chaddesley extracts in figs.1 and 2, their originals at Stratford, or the Halesowen court roll on page 51 and to check the accuracy of our own transcript. Would that this sort of master-class had been available in 1962!

FURTHER READING

W.O. Ault, *Open-Field Farming in Medieval England*, 1972
A.R. Baker and R.A. Butler, *Studies of Field Systems in the British Isles*, 1973
H.S. Bennett, *Life on the English Manor: a Study of Peasant Conditions*, Sutton, 1987
M. Beresford, *The Lost Villages of England*, 1983 (The seminal study of medieval depopulation and social mobility)
British Library, *Medieval Realms*, CD-ROM, 1995 has several transcripts from manorial records with explanatory texts. Manors are listed in their county gazetteers
R.R. Davies, 'Baronial Accounts, Incomes and Arrears in the Later Middle Ages', *Economic History Review*, no.21, 1968
C. Dyer, 'What to read on country and town in the Middle Ages', *The Local Historian*, 16. no.5, February 1985
M. Ellis, *Using Manorial Records*, PRO Publications with Royal Commission on Historical Manuscripts, 1994
J. Goldberg, 'Women in later medieval archives', *Journal of the Society of Archivists*, 15 (1), Spring 1994
P.D.A. Harvey, *Manorial Records*, British Records Association, 1984
and: *Manorial Records*, Historical Association's Short Guides to Records, no.47, 1993
R.H. Hilton, 'The Content and Sources of English Agrarian History before 1500', *Agricultural History Review*, 3, Part 1, 1955
G.A.J. Hodgett, *Agrarian England in the Later Middle Ages*, Historical Association, 1966
N.J. Hone, *The Manor and Manorial Records*, facsimile reprint of 1906 edition, 1971
E. Miller and J. Hatcher, *Medieval England: Rural Society and Economic Change 1068-1348*, Longman, 1978
P. Palgrave-Moore, *How to Locate and Use Manorial Records*, 1985
S.A.C. Penn, 'Female wage-earners in late 14th century England', *Agricultural History Review*, 35, 1987
C. Platt, *Medieval Britain from the Air*, 1984

D. Postles, 'Some recent research in medieval manorial court rolls', *Society of Archivists Journal*, 9, April 1988
J.A. Raftis, *Peasant Economic Development within the English Manorial System*, McGill, 1996
F. Sebohm, *The English Village Community*, a facsimile reprint of the first edition of 1833, 1971
D. Stuart, *Manorial Records*, Phillimore, 1992

The student who wishes to see the fields and houses of the medieval manor, its topography, open fields and crofts and tofts must use M.W. Beresford and J.K. St Joseph's, *Mediaeval England, an Aerial Survey*, C.U.P., 1958. This exciting, profusely illustrated book shows, in dozens of sample studies, the great value of combined application of documents, air-photography and field work to the study of town and village sites. It is also extremely readable, making otherwise complex terms and technicalities arrestingly clear.

HANDLISTS

Printed editions: A list of Court Rolls, Rentals, Survey and Account Rolls, printed by various County Historical and Record Societies, is given by Robert Somerville in *Handlist of Record Publications* (British Records Association, 1951, Sect. 98-104).

Deposited originals: A register of original Court Rolls held in repositories all over England is kept at the National Register of Archives, Quality Court, Chancery Lane, London, W.C.2. The information in this register is supplied and kept up-to-date by regional Record Offices, who themselves keep a copy of their own returns. Copies are kept at Worcestershire Record Office and Birmingham Reference Library, and can be consulted on request.

PRINTED EDITIONS FOR WORCESTERSHIRE

R.A. Wilson, *Court Rolls of the Manor of Hales, 1280-1303*, 3 vols., Worcs Hist. Soc., 1933. Including the manor court rolls of Romsley, this is the basic source of printed court rolls studied in this documentary section. The British Library's CD-ROM, *Medieval Realms*, 1995 includes extracts from the court rolls of Halesowen.
Z. Razi, *Life, Marriage and Death in a Medieval Parish*, C.U.P., 1983. This work is especially significant here, in that it is based entirely on the economy, society and demography of Halesowen from 1270 to 1400.
R.H. Hilton, *A Medieval Society. The West Midlands at the end of the Thirteenth Century*, Weidenfield and Nicolson, 1966 is the definitive basis of any study of the estates and records of Worcestershire and the other West Midland counties.
See also:
F.B.Andrews, 'Compotus Rolls of the Monastery of Pershore', *Birminghmam Arch.Soc.*, 57, 1935
A.F.C. Baber, *The Court Rolls of the Manors of Bromsgrove and Kings Norton*, Worcs. Hist. Soc., n.s., 46, 1963
C.J. Bond, 'The estates of Evesham Abbey; a preliminary survey of their medieval topography' and 'The medieval topography of the Evesham Abbey estates', *Vale of Evesham Hist.Research Papers*, 4, 1973 and 5, 1975
C. Dyer, *Lords and Peasants in a Changing Society* (about the Bishop of Worcester's estates), 1980
R.K. Field, 'Worcestershire peasant buildings, household goods and farming equipment in the later Middle Ages', *Medieval Archaeology*, IX, 1965

WORCESTERSHIRE ORIGINAL DOCUMENTS

These are to be found at the County Record Office, Worcester, and in Birmingham Reference Library. Both repositories keep P.R.O. registers of all manorial documents, including many records of manors in counties other than Worcestershire. Worcester has Rolls from 1273-1901; Birmingham from 1269-1831. (Additions to both registers are continually being made as more records are catalogued.) The following lists are a small selection of their Worcestershire Manor Court Rolls of the medieval period:

County Record Office

Bidford	from 1408	Eldersfield	from 1460
Birlingham	1448	Elmley Castle	1347
Bromsgrove	1335	Feckenham	1329
Cotheridge	1463	Hanbury	1378
Droitwich	1425	Hanley Castle	1376
Earls Croome	1400	Kempsey	1395
Eckington	1323	Powick	1314
Eckington	1429	Tardebigge	1273

Birmingham Reference Library

Areley	from 1429	Hales Borough	from 1272
Bentley Pauncefoot	1462	Hales Manor	1269
Bromsgrove	1255	Hampton Lovett	1409
Chadwick	1329	Huddington	1329
Clethale	1325	Rock	1302
Cotheridge	1306	Romsley	1293
Crowle	1361	Stildon	1302
Droitwich	1302	Stourbridge	1486
Elmley Lovett	1400	Swinford	1486
Frankley	1476	Warley	1302
Hagley	1413	Westwood	1302

FURTHER EXTRACTS FROM THE ROMSLEY COURT ROLLS

The following extracts have been selected, in addition to the transcript of the facsimile on Plate III, in order to give the student as full a picture as possible of the sort of business which came before a Manor Court. A full series of Court Rolls contains hundreds of cases which are often tediously repetitive, sometimes extremely technical. It is necessary for the student to understand that only a careful search will reveal those entries which add clear and interesting details to our picture of everyday manorial life. Each of the following extracts has been included for some such detail contained in it, of the status and services of freemen and villeins, their rights and disabilities, and the nature of their tenure, their everyday life and work, and the ways in which the lord's court could supervise their family lives. All these extracts are translated from the Latin transcript of the Court Rolls given in R. A. Wilson, op. cit. The MSS. numbers, printed in bold type, are those by which the originals can be found in Birmingham Reference Library.

29th November, 1280:
   Richard de Pirie is amerced for trespassing during the autumn, on the lord's cornfield.

(Ms. 346211/i dorso)

17th June, 1281:
   Henry de Fulfen acquires a piece of land in Bureaucharne, for marling [*ad marliandum*], and another piece at Smalecroft for 16 years. He pays the Lord 12d. for licence. Richard de Edwineshulle transfers to Henry de Fulfen *unam seylionem per xi croppos*. [This entry reveals the use of a 3-field rotation of crops

in Romsley, with the third year in fallow, if the period of 11 crops is equated with the 16 years of the first lease.]

Robert Wodecock pays 6d. for licence to transfer his land to the same Henry Fulfen. [Henry de Fulfen is an interesting character to follow through the Romsley Rolls, because of his continual efforts to consolidate and improve his land.]

The jury say that Thomas Faber enclosed a purpresture in the lord's waste-land, encroaching beyond the limits of his own fence [*extra haiam suam*]. [Note reference to appear to jury, and the reference to the fence around this tenant's land.]

Walter the Archer is distrained for having opened up the fence of his pasture without the lord's consent. He is ordered not to remove his part-share of a pig held by Thomas de la Leye, nor his two sheep at the house of Henry i' the Meadow, so that they may be available for distraint. John Baldrich amerced 6d. because he kept a field [*campum*] enclosed after the fence should have been removed.

[Here we see how the communal custom of the manor prevented individuals from making seasonal decisions for themselves about the cultivation of the land.] **(Ms. 346211/ii)**

27th October, 1281:

It is decided by the whole court that Richard de Volatu should be distrained for his non-payment of his share of a 'green wax' [i.e. Exchequer] levy. [A fairly unusual example of the royal administration impinging upon life within the manor.] **(Ms. 346211/ii dorso)**

23rd March, 1294:

William de Yieldingtree pays the lord 3s. as fine and relief for John his son to receive the inheritance of his mother, Matilda's land.

Henry Wodecote pays 6d. for licence to enter the dower of his step-mother, Agnes.

[References to payments of 'reliefs' and 'entry-fines' are, of course, quite common in all court rolls.] **(Ms. 346790)**

23rd June, 1294:

An enquiry by jurors, who state, regarding certain malefactors in the lord's woodland, that Matilda de Kelmestowe (fined 3d.), and Margery daughter of John de Kelmestowe, are in the habit of carting off the lord's wood, and of burning down hedges belonging to the lord and to their neighbours.

[There are very frequent references to the villagers' depredations in the woodland, an indication of the great value placed on wood, for fuel, houses and tools, a commodity which must literally be gained 'by hook or by crook'.]

Clement, son of Alexander of Kelmestowe, is convicted of taking away a cartload of brushwood, which had been left ready for carting to Wich. He pledges his fine, but does not find other pledges, because he is a villein [*nativus*].

[This is a typical illustration of the various disabilities of a villein's legal status in court. His oath and pledges have not the same value as those of a freeman.] **(Ms. 346790)**

30 October, 1296:

The jury state that, during last Summer, there was a certain vagrant going about the village of Romsley, and that one day, he came to Alicia de Edwineshulle's house, and carried off her wet linen, which he took to Offmore Wood. There he was caught by Walter de Bromwich, William atte Lithe's waggoner, and Henry ad Aulam, who took the clothes back from him, and also his own white tunic and three-bladed flail, and the money from his purse, they do not recollect how much. Nor do they know where the man went off to.

Richard de Edwineshulle . . . and II others . . . are amerced for failing to perform their service of gathering nuts.

The lord's Rent Roll is referred to, as evidence whether Henry Tandy ought to pay the lord 1d. more than 2s. Henry is amerced because it is proved that he tried to avoid paying his full rent.

(Ms. 346790/dorso)

24 July, 1301:

William de Yieldingtree is called to account for a certain piece of land, 6 perches in length, which lies next the land of the said William, and the lord asserts is part of his demesne. After much delay, William appears at a later court, and insists that the land in question was part of his father's freehold tenement, and that he cannot be forced to defend it, except by authority of a royal writ.

[This assertion of a legal principle, on the difference between a freehold and land held in villeinage, is typical of the way in which the free tenants frequently stand up to the Abbot in defence of their legal rights.]

Thomas Squire is accused of having cut turf from the lord's wasteland, and turfed his own with it, without the lord's permission. He appears before the court and insists that he had permission from Brother William the cellarer, whom he calls in witness of this.

[We find frequent references to the supervision of the manor by the Lord's manorial officials, particularly the cellarer, acting as his steward.]

At this court 22 tenants appear to do fealty and acknowledge the services which they owe for their tenements. Seven others were distrained for failing to appear and do likewise. The services mentioned are ploughing [*arrura*], harrowing [*hersura*], harvesting [*messura*], mowing [*falcatio*], and gathering nuts. e.g. 'Thomas atte Leye, a villein [*nativus*], acknowledges 3s. a year, to be paid at the four terms of the year, 3 days ploughing a year, 3 days harrowing after the ploughing is finished, and 3 days harvesting in the Autumn, finding his own meals and mowing the same amount as his neighbours.'

[In nearly all the later entries, Thomas is used as the typical villein for the purposes of service.]

'Henry Tandy does fealty to the Lord, and acknowledges his services, i.e. 2s. 5d. a year rent, to be paid in four parts, and 2 days' harvesting in the Autumn with meals provided at the Lord's table.'

'Richard Aleyn does fealty, and acknowledges 5d. a year in lieu of all services, and two suits of court.'

'William de Yieldingtree acknowledges 5d. a year in lieu of all services, and two suits of court.'

'William de Yieldingtree acknowledges a rent of 4d. a year paid in lieu of all services, and one pound of cummin for right of common pasture for his pigs and cattle at Offmoor.'

'William de Yieldingtree, accused of failing to do fealty properly, in that he omitted mention of suit of court, produces his charter [*cartam suam*], as evidence that he never owed suit of court.'

(Ms. 346791/i)

8th August, 1301:

'Christina o' the Grene, by special favour, has special licence to marry, for which the lord, waiving the customary "merchet", is prepared to accept only 12d.'

[The usual merchet was 12s. for marrying within the manor, and 2s. outside it.]

'William Pictor, who has previously done fealty, and acknowledged his services, now produces a charter, by which his ancestors held their ancient tenement, in return for giving the lord a pair of gloves [*pro uno pare cirocetarum*] at Christmas, in lieu of all services. He acknowledges 16d. for his other tenement.'

'The jury say on oath, that the wife of Richard, son of Malle, gathered more peas and vetches from the field in the Autumn that she was entitled to do, but only a small quantity. John Fox is similarly distrained for taking one sheaf.'

(Ms. 346791/i)

8th February, 1302:

'Action by the Lord against William de Yieldingtree, for having pulled down and removed the buildings of his wife's villein tenement [*de tenemento nativo*].'

[These occasional references to the hasty pulling down of villagers' houses and other buildings give us some idea of their flimsy construction, and explain why none of the small domestic buildings of this period have survived.]

'John de la Grene is amerced for 6d. for having redeemed a sentence of corporal punishment with cattle belonging to the lord.'

[This is the only reference in these Rolls to corporal punishment. The Abbot's court had no power to inflict the punishment itself.]

'Adam de la Grene is amerced for not having cleaned out his ditch.'

'Kemme Tandy is amerced 3 chickens for stealing the radishes which Brother Richard had bought from William de Westley.'

'The jury say that William le Peynter has ploughed on the Lord's waste-land.'

(Ms. 346791/i dorso)

Some Printed Manorial Court Rolls, Accounts, Custumals, etc.

The British Library's CD-ROM, *Medieval Realms* (1994) contains several manorial court roll extracts from printed sources in this Gazetteer, eg: Alrewas (Staffs.), Halesowen (Worcs.), Minchinhampton (Glos.), Wakefield (Yorks.), etc. Each set of entries has informative introductory notes and source references.

(listed chronologically by date of publication)

Bedfordshire   BHRS: J. Steele Elliott, *Stagsden and its Manors*, 1924; W. Farrer, *The Honour of Old Warndon*, 1927; W. Austin, *A Commutation of Villein Services*, 1931; B. Cook, *Newnham Prior, Rental of the Priory of Biddenham, 1505-6*, 1947; M.K. Dale, *Court Roll of Chalgrave Manor, 1278-1313*, 1947; J. Godber, *Two Cranfield Manors*, 1947; F.B. Stitt, *A Kempston Estate in 1341*, 1952; D.N. Hall, 'Modern surveys of medieval field systems', *Beds. Archaeological Journal*, no.7, 1972; M.J. Harrison, W.R. Mead and D.J. Pannett, 'A (four-county) Medieval ridge-and-furrow map', *Geographical Journal*, no.131, 1965 (includes also: *Buckinghamshire*, *Oxfordshire* and *Warwickshire*); The British Library CD-ROM *Medieval Realms*, 1995 has extracts from the court rolls of Chalgrave.

Berkshire   S.R. Scargill-Bird, *Custumals of Battle Abbey* (including manors in Berks), Camden Soc., n.s., 41, 1887; R.E.G. Kirk, *Accounts of the Obedientiaries of the Abbey of Abingdon*, Camden Soc., n.s., 51, 1892; N. Horne, 'Berkshire Court Rolls' (temp. Henry VI-VII), *Berks. Archit. & Arch. Soc. Quart. J.*, III, 1894; F.T. Wethered, *St Mary's Hurley in the Middle Ages*, London, 1898; S. Barfield, *Thatcham, Berkshire and its Manors*, Oxford, 1901; A.L. Humphreys, *Bucklebury; a Berkshire Parish*, Reading, 1932.

Buckinghamshire   W. Cunningham, 'Extracts from the Court Rolls of the manor of Winslow' (temp. Edw. III and Hen. VI), *Growth of English Industry*, 1, Cambridge, 1915; W. Bradbrook, 'Manor Court Rolls of Fenny Stratford and Eaton', *Records of Bucks*, XI, 1922; A.C.Chibnall, *Fiefs and fields of a Buckinghamshire village (Sherington)*, C.U.P., 1965; J.C.K. Cornwall, *Medieval peasant farmers*, Records of Bucks., no.20, 1975; R.A. Croft and D.C. Mynard, *A Guide to the Medieval Landscape of Milton Keynes*, Milton Keynes Archaeological Unit, 1984.

Caernarvonshire   H. Ellis, *The Record of Caernarvon-Extents of Manors in Caernarvon and Anglesey, 1353*, Record Commission, 1838; G.P. Jones and H. Owen, *Caernarvon Court Rolls, 1361-1402*, Caern. Hist. Soc., 1951.

Cambridgeshire   ... 'Compotus of the Manor of Newton', 1395, *East Anglian*, IV, 1869; F.W. Maitland and W.P. Baildon, *The Court Baron ... together with Select Pleas from the Bishop of Ely's Court of Littleport*, Selden Soc., 1891; F.W. Maitland, 'The history of a Cambridgeshire manor (Wilburton)', *EHR*, IX, 1894; W.M. Palmer, 'Village gilds of Cambridgeshire', *CHAS*, I, 1904; W.M. Palmer and H.W. Saunders, *Documents relating to Cambridgeshire Villages*, Cambridge, 1926; F.M. Page, 'The customary poor-law of three Cambridgeshire manors', *Camb. Hist. J.*, III, 1930; C.N.L. Brooke and M.M. Postan, *Carte Nativorum: a Peterborough Abbey Cartulary of the fourteenth century*, Northants. Records Soc., 2, 1945-6, reprinted 1960; H.C. Darby, *The Draining of the Fens*, C.U.P., 1956; M. Spufford, *A Cambridgeshire Community: Chippenham from settlement to enclosure*, Leics. Univ. Occasional Papers, no.20, 1965; H.C. Darby, *Medieval Cambridgeshire*, Oleander Press, 1977.

Carmarthenshire   F. Green, *Manorial Customs in Co. Carmarthen, 1554*, W. Wales Hist. Rec. Soc., VIII, 1919-21.

Cheshire   W. Beamont, *An Account of the Rolls of the Honour of Halton*, Warrington, 1879; R. Stewart-Brown, *The Wapentake of Wirral; a history of the hundred and hundred court*, Liverpool, 1907; and: 'The royal manor and park of Shotwick', *HSLC*, LXIV, 1912; D. Sylvester, 'The manor and the Cheshire landscape', *Lancs. and Cheshire Antiquarian Soc.*, no.70, 1960; *List of Documents relating to the manors of Chester Deanery*, University of Durham, 1967; R. Richards, *The manor of Gawsworth*, Morten, 1975; J.P. Greene, P.R. Hough *et al.*, 'Excavations in the medieval village of Norton', *Journal of Chester Arch. Soc.*, 60, 1977; M.J. Bennett, *Sources and problems in the study of social mobility: Cheshire in the Middle Ages*, HSLC, no.128, 1978; J. Phillip Dodd, 'The manor fields of Frodsham', *HSLC*, 128, 1978-9; P.H.W. Booth, 'Farming for profit in the fourteenth century: the Cheshire estates of the Earldom of Chester', *Journal of Chester Arch. Soc.*, 62, 1979; J. Phillip Dodd, 'The population of Frodsham manor, 1349-50', *HSLC*, 131, 1981.

Cornwall   L.M. Midgley, *Ministers' Accounts of the Earldom of Cornwall, 1296-7*, 2 vols., R. Hist. Soc. (Camden Series), LXVI (1942) and LXVIII (1945); J. Hatcher, *Rural Economy and Society in the Duchy of Cornwall, 1300-1500*, London, 1967.

Cumberland and Westmorland   R.F. Ferguson and W. Nanson, *Some Municipal Records of the city of Carlisle, including Court Leet extracts, 1597-1689*, CWAAS, extra series, VI, 1882.

Denbighshire   R.A. Roberts, *The Court Rolls of the lordship of Ruthin or Dyffryn Clwydd, of the reign of Edward I, preserved in the P.R.O. London*, Hon. Soc. of Cymmrodorion, Record Series, 1893; P. Vinogradoff and F. Morgan, *Survey of the Honor of Denbigh, 1334*, British Academy, 1914.

Derbyshire   C. Kerry, 'Court Rolls of Baslow', *DANHSJ*, XXII, 1900, and XXIII, 1901; C. Torr, *Wreyland Documents* (includes two 15th-century court rolls), Cambridge, 1910; R.H. Oakley, 'Atlow Court Rolls, 19 Edw. III-IV, Ric. II', *DANHSJ*, LXIII, 1953; F.N. Fisher, 'Egginton Court Rolls, 1306/7-1311/12', *DANHSJ*, LXXV, 1956; R.H. Oakley, 'Temple Normanton Court Rolls, 1447-1518', *DANHSJ*, LXXVIII, 1959; M. Gavaghan, *History of Pleasley Manor*, Gavaghan, 1964; P. Naylor, *Manors and Families of Derbyshire; 1 (A-L); 2 (M-Z)*, 1984.

Devonshire   Cruwys Morchard manor court roll (transcript of roll of 1511), *DCNQ.*, XX, 1939; C.D. Lineham, 'A forgotten manor in Widecombe-in-the-Moor (Dewdon)', *DAT*, 90, 1962; K. Uwaga, 'The economic development of some Devon manors in the thirteenth century', *DAT*, no.94, 1967; E.A. Wrigley, 'Mortality in pre-industrial England: the example of Colyton, Devon, over three centuries', *Daedelus*, XCVII, 1968; N. W. Alcock, 'An east Devon manor in the late Middle Ages, 1374-1430 (Manor Farm, Bishops Clyst)', *DAT*, no.102, 1970; and: 'An east Devon in the later Middle Ages; Leasing the demesne, 1423-1525 and 1526-1650', *Devonshire Association Trans.*, no.105, 1973; H.S.A. Fox, 'The chronology of enclosure and economic development in medieval Devon', *Economic History Review*, no.28, 1975; H.T. Miles, 'Excavations within a medieval village (Pilton)', *Devonshire Archaeological Soc.*, no.33, 1975; W.A. Roberts, *The Lords of Stokenham, South Devon, and their Feudal Manor*, 1980; W.A. Roberts, *Manorial Stokenham in the Fourteenth Century*, 1982; G. Beresford *et al.*, *Three deserted medieval settlements on Dartmoor (Houndtor, Hutholes and Dinna Clerks)*.

Dorset   J.S. Drew, 'Early account rolls of Portland, Wyke and Elwell', *DNHAS*, LXVI, 1944 and LXVII, 1945; C.D. Drew, 'The manors of the Iwerne Valley, Dorset', *DNHAS*, LXIX, 1947; E. Jervoise, 'The manor of Barton, Shaftesbury', *DNHAS*, LXXVI, 1954; J. Brocklebank, *Deserted medieval sites in Dorset*, *DNHAS*, no.94, 1972; A. Barnett, *The deserted medieval village of Winterborne Farringdon, Dorset Year Book*, 1975-5.

Durham   W. Greenwell, *Bishop Hatfield's Survey* (Reeves' Roll for Auckland, 1337-8 and Bailiffs' Roll for various episcopal manors, 1349-50), Surtees Soc., 1857; W.H. Longstaffe and J. Booth, *Halmota Prioratis Dunelmensis, containing extracts from the Halmote Court, or Manor Rolls of the Prior and Convent of Durham, 1296-1384*, Surtees Soc., 1889; B.K. Roberts, 'Village plans in County Durham: A preliminary statement', *Med. Arch.*, XVI, 1972.

Essex   A.J. Horwood, 'Custumal of the manor of Wykes, Hundred of Tendring', *E. Arch. Soc.*, n.s., I, 1878; J.A. Sparvel-Bayly, 'Records relating to Hadleigh Castle' (includes ministers' accounts, 1227-1544), *E. Arch. Soc.*, n.s., I, 1878; S.R. Scargill-Bird, *Custumals of Battle Abbey, 1283-1312* (including Custumals for manors in Essex), Camden Soc., n.s., 1887; 'Manor of Barrington's fee' (Latin text of a rental), *East Anglian*, n. s., V, 1894; A. Clark, 'Tithings Lists from Essex', 1329-43, *EHR*, XIX, 1904; E.B. Demarest, 'Consuetudo regis in Essex, Norfolk and Sussex', *EHR*, XLII, 1927; J.L. Fisher, 'Customs and services on an Essex manor (Netteswell) in the 13th century', *E. Arch. Soc.*, XIX, 1927; J.F. Nichols, 'The manor of Borley and its early descent', *E. Arch. Soc.*, XIX, 1927; and: 'An early 14th century petition from the tenants of Bocking to their manorial lord', *Econ. Hist. Rev.*, II, 1930; W.G. Benham, 'Notes from the Colchester court rolls of 1527-8. Some curious words', *Ess. Rev.*, LI, 1938; J.L. Fisher, 'The Harlow

Cartulary' (includes 15th-century manorial rentals and extents), *E. Arch. Soc.*, n.s., XXII, 1940; I.H. Jeayes, *Court Rolls of the Borough of Colchester*, Borough of Colchester, I, 1921, II, 1938, III, 1941; W.G. Benham, 'Manorial rolls of Fingringhoe, West Mersea and Pete Hall, 1547-58', *Ess. Rev. 1*, L, 1941 and LI, 1942; F.G. Emmison, 'Supplementary list of manorial documents in Essex Record Office', *Genealogists' Magazine*, IX, no.15, 1947; K.C. Newton, *Thaxted in the Fourteenth Century*, Essex CRO Pubns., XXXIII, 1960; J. Quaife, 'Reeve's Accounts of the Manor of Burnham', *E. Arch. Soc.*, 3rd series., II, 1967; K.C. Newton, *The Manor of Writtle: the development of a royal manor in Essex, 1086-1500*, Phillimore, 1970.

Gloucestershire   E.A. Fuller, 'Tenures of land by the customary tenants in Cirencester', *BGAS*, II, 1878; H.T. Ellacombe, *History of the Parish of Bitton*, 2 parts, Exeter, 1881-3; J. Maclean (ed.), *John Smyth's Berkeley Manuscripts* (3 vols.), BGAS, 1883-5; *Court Rolls of the Manor of English Bicknor, 1638*, BGAS, XI, 1886-7; *Ministers' Accounts of the Manor of Kingswood (nr. Wotton), 1240-1311*, BGAS, XXII, 1899; *Court Rolls of the Manor of Stonehouse, Kings Stanley, Woodchester and Achards, 1461-1533*, BGAS, LXVII, 1925; W. St Clair Baddeley, *A Cotteswold manor; being the manor of Painswick* (2nd ed.), London, 1929; *Minchinhampton Custumal, 1300*, BGAS, LIV, 1932; G. Beachcroft and A. Sabin, *Two Compotus Rolls of St Augustine's Abbey, Bristol, 1491-2, and 1511-12*, Bristol Rec. Soc., 1938; *Chamberlain's Accounts for Tewkesbury Abbey, 1352*, BGAS, LX, 1938; *Wick Rissington Manorial Accounts, 1337*, BGAS, LX, 1938; E.S. Scroggs, 'Calendar of Shrewsbury (Talbot) Manuscripts', *BGAS*, LX for 1938 (1939); R.H. Hilton, 'Winchcombe Abbey and the manor of Sherborne', *Univ. Birm. Hist. J.*, II, 1949-50; M. Paget, 'Cheltenham and Ashley; A study of manorial custom before 1625', *Local Historian*, 15, no.3, August 1982; The British Library CD-ROM, *Medieval Realms*, 1995 has extracts from the court rolls of Minchinhampton.

Hampshire   T. Hervey, *A History of the united parishes of Colmer and Priors Dean*, 1880; S.R. Scargill-Bird, *Custumals of Battle Abbey* (including manors in Hampshire), Camden Soc., n.s., 1887; J. Stevens, *A Parochial History of St Mary's Bourne, with an account of the manor of Hurstbourne Priors*, 1888; F.W. Maitland, *Select Pleas in Manorial and other Seigneurial Courts* (including transcripts from the Abbess of Romsey's Hundred of Whorwelsdown and manor of Ashton), Selden Soc., 1889; F.J. Baigent, *Collections of Charters and Documents relating to the Hundred and Manor of Crondall*, Part 1, Hants Rec. Soc., 1891; G.W. Kitchin, *The Manor of Manydown, Hampshire*, Hants Rec. Soc., 1895; F.J.C. Earnshaw, *Leet Jurisdiction in England ... illustrated by records of the Court Leet Rolls, 1550-1624*, Southampton Rec. Soc., 1905-8; A.W. Goodman, *The Manor of Goodbegot in the City of Winchester*, Winchester, 1923; N.B.S. and E.C. Gras, *The Economic and Social History of the English Village (Crawley, Hants., A.D. 909-1928)*, Cambridge, 1930; W.H. Beveridge, 'Wages in the Winchester manors', *Econ. Hist. Rev.*, VII, 1936; M.M. Postan and J.Z. Titow, 'Heriots and prices on Winchester manors', in Postan's *Essays on Medieval Agriculture and General Problems of the Medieval Economy*, Cambridge, 1973; D.L. Farmer, 'Grain fields on the Winchester manors in the later Middle Ages', *Economic History Review*, no.30, 1977.

Herefordshire   A.T. Bannister, 'Manorial customs on the Hereford bishopric estates', *EHR*, XLIII, 1928; H.M. Colvin, 'Holme Lacy; an episcopal manor and its tenants in the twelfth and thirteenth centuries, *Medieval Studies presented to Rose Graham* (eds. V. Ruffer and A.J. Taylor), Oxford, 1950; E.J. Cole, 'The Bailiff's Accounts for the Manor of Kingsland, 1389-90', *TWNFC*, XXXV, 1956; R.E. Hickling, 'Deserted medieval villages in Herefordshire', *Woolhope Naturalists' Field Club*, no.39, 1969.

Hertfordshire   F.W. Maitland, *Select Pleas in Manorial and other Seigneurial Courts, temp. Henry III and Edward I* (transcripts from the Rolls of the Manors of the Abbey of Bec, and the Abbot of Ramsey's manors in Huntingdonshire), I, Selden Soc., London, 1889; W. Cunningham, 'Compotus roll of the manor of Anstie, 2-3, Hen. IV', *Growth of English Industry*, I, 1915; R.L. Hine, *The History of Hitchin* (2 vols.), 1927-9; L.L. Rickman, 'Brief studies in the manorial and economic history of Much Hadham', *E. Herts. Arch. Soc.*, VII, 1934; K.R. Davis, *Deserted medieval villages of Hertfordshire*, Phillimore, 1973; P. Barton, *Manorial Economy and Society in Shenley; a Hertfordshire Manor in the 13th and 14th Centuries*, Herts. Pubns., 1987.

Huntingdonshire   C.G. Boxall, *Early Records of the Duke of Manchester's English Manorial Estates*, 1892; S.C. Ratcliff (ed.) and D. M. Gregory (trs.), *Elton Manorial Records, 1279-1351*, Roxburgh Club, 1946.

Kent   Sir Henry Ellis, 'Extent of the Royal Manor of Otford, 1573', *AC*, V, 1862-3; L.B. Larking, 'Rent roll of Roger de Scaccario, Lord of the manor of Addington, 1257-71', *Domesday Book of Kent*, 1869; S.R. Scargill-Bird, *Custumals of Battle Abbey* (including manors in Kent), Camden Soc., n.s., 1887; A.A. Arnold, 'A fourteenth century court roll of the manor of Ambree, Rochester, 1316-63', *AC*, XXIX, 1915; G.J. Turner and H.E. Salter, *The Register of St Augustine's Abbey, Canterbury*, 2 parts, British Academy,

1915, 1924; I.J. Churchill, *East Kent Records; a Calendar of some unpublished Deeds and Court Rolls*, Kent Arch. Soc., 1922; H.W. Knocker, 'The manor of Sundrish', *AC*, XLIV, 1932; Sir E. Harrison, 'The Court Rolls and other Records of the Manor of Ightham as a contribution to local History', *AC*, vols.XLVIII, XLIX, 1936-7; K.M.E. Murray, *Romney Custumal of the 14th Century*, Kent Rec. Soc., XVI, 1945; M.F. Bond, 'A Farnborough Court Roll of 1408', *AC*, LVII, 1946; and: 'Farnborough Manor in the 17th and 18th Centuries', *AC*, LIX, 1946; F.R.H. du Boulay, *Documents illustrative of medieval Kentish Society*, Kent Records Series, no.18, 1964; N.R. Goose, 'Wage labour on a Kentish manor (Meopham, 1307-75)', *AC*, 92, 1976; W.R. Mead and R.J.P. Kain, 'Ridge and furrow in Kent', *AC*, 92, 1976; C.L. Sinclair Williams, 'A rental of the manor of East Malling', in: *A Kentish Miscellany* (ed. F. Hull), *Kent. Arch. Soc. (Kent Recs.)*, 24, 1979.

Lancashire W. Beamont, *Warrington as described in a contemporary rent roll*, Chetham Soc., XVII, 1849; J. Harland, *A Volume of Court Leet Rolls in the Manor of Manchester in the 16th Century*, Chetham Soc., OS, 1864; J. Harland, *Three Lancashire Documents of the 14th and 15th Centuries including the Custom Roll and Rental of the Manor of Ashton-under-Lyne, 1422*, Chetham Soc., OS, 1868; P.A. Lyons, *Two Compoti of the Lancashire and Cheshire Manors of Henry de Lacy, Earl of Lincoln, 1294-1305*, Chetham Soc., OS, 1884; W. Beaumont, *Homage Roll of the Manor of Warrington, 1491-1517*, LCRS Misc., I, 1885; W. Farrer, *Court Rolls of Clitheroe*, 1897; W. Farrer, *Some Court Rolls of the Lordships, Wapentakes and Demesne Manor of Thomas, Earl of Lancaster, 1323-4*, LCRS, XLI, 1901; H.T. Crofton, *The History of the Ancient Chapel of Stretford*, Chetham Soc., XLV, 1901; J.T. Mandley, *The Portmote Records of Salford*, Chetham Soc., 46 & 48, 1902; W. Farrer, *Lancashire Inquests, Extents and Feudal Aids*, Pt. I (1205-1307), 1903; Pt. II (1310-33), 1907; Pt. III (1315-55), 1915, LCRS; H.T. Crofton, *The History of Newton Chapelry*, Chetham Soc., LIII, 1904; A. Hewitson, *Preston Court Leet Records, 1653-1813*, Preston, 1905; J. Brownbill, *The Ledger Book of Vale Royal Abbey*, LCRS, 1914; R. Cunliffe Shaw, *The Clifton Papers* (Manors of Lytham, Westby, Marton and Clifton), Preston, 1935; F.A. Bailey, *A Selection from the Prescot Court Leet and other records, 1447-1600*, LCRS, 1937; W.H. Chippindall, *A 16th-Century Survey, and year's accounts of the Estates of Hornby Castle, Lancs*, Chetham Soc., n.s., CII, 1939; R.S. France, 'Two custumals of the manor of Cockerham, 1326 and 1483', *Lancs. & Ches. Ant. Soc.*, LXIV, 1954.

Leicestershire G.T. Clark, 'Customary of the Manor and Soke of Rothley in the County of Leicester', *Archaeologia*, XLVII, 1883; H. Hartopp, 'Some unpublished documents relating to Nosely in Leicestershire', *Assoc. Arch. Socs. Reports & Papers*, XXV, 1900; G.H. Farnham, *Quorndon Records*, 1912; and: *Leicestershire medieval village notes* (6 vols.), 1929-33; R.H. Hilton, 'A thirteenth century poem on some disputed villein services (at Stoughton)' *EHR*, LVI, 1941; and: *The economic development of some Leicestershire estates in the 14th and 15th centuries*, 1947; and: 'Kibworth Harcourt, a Merton College manor in the thirteenth and fourteenth centuries', *LeAS*, 24, 1948; W.G. Hoskins, 'Studies in Leicestershire agrarian history', *LeAS*, 1949; and: *Essays in Leicestershire History*, 1950; R.H. Hilton, 'Medieval agrarian history', *VCH: Leicestershire*, II, 1955; W.G. Hoskins, 'Seven deserted village sites in Leicestershire', *LAHS*, 32, 1956; and: *The Midland Peasant. The economic and social history of a Leicestershire village* (Wigston Magna), 1957; and: 'The population of an English village 1086-1801; A study of Wigston Magna', *LeAS*, XXXIII, 1957; Deserted Medieval Village Research Group, 'A provisional list of deserted medieval villages in Leicestershire', *Leics. Arch. Soc.*, XXXIX, 1963-4; D.J. Rudkin, 'An excavation of an early medieval site at Buckminster', *LAHS*, no.47, 1971-2; P. Liddle, 'A late medieval enclosure in Donington Park', *LAHS*, no.53, 1977-8.

Lincolnshire A. Gibbons and W.E. Foster, 'Lists of Lincolnshire Court Rolls', *Lincs. N. & Q.*, I, 1889; W.O. Massingberd, *History of the parish of Ormsby-cum-Ketsby* (includes court rolls from 1410); and: 'Some ancient records relating to the Manor of Langton and its lords, 1202-1617', *AASRP*, XXII, 1894; A.R. Maddison, 'Manor of Ingoldmells-cum-Addlethorpe Court Rolls' (extracts, 1292-1503), *AASRP*, XXI, 1892; and: 'Rental of the Manor of Stallingborough, 1352', *AASRP*, XXIII, 1896; R.E.G. Cole, 'The royal burh of Torksey' (including a custumal of *c.*1238), *AASRP*, XXVIII, 1906; N. Neilson, *A Terrier of Fleet, Lincs*, British Academy, 1920; R.C. Dudding, *History of the manor and parish of Salesby with Thoresthorpe in the county of Lincoln*, 1922; C.W. Foster, *A History of the Village of Aisthorpe and Thorpe in the Fallows*, 1927; F. Hill, 'Manor of Hungate', *AASRP*, XXXVIII, 1927; R.C. Dudding, *History of the parish and manors of Alford with Rigsby and Ailby, with some account of Well, in the county of Lincolnshire*, 1930; F.W. East, 'The Heighington Terrier', *AASRP*, n.s. IV, 1952 and V, 1953; H.E. Hallam, 'Settlement and Society' (in south Lincs.), *Cambridge Studies in Econ. Hist.*, 1965; W.H. Hosford, 'The manor of Sleaford in the thirteenth century', *Notts. Med. Studies*, XII, 1968; G. Platts, 'Land and People in Medieval Lincolnshire', *History of Lincolnshire IV*, Society for Lincs. History and Archaeology, 1985.

London and Middlesex *Istleworth Syons Peace; concerning certain articles of agreement between ... the Earl of Northumberland, Lord of the Manor of Istleworth-Syon in the County of Middlesex, etc. and ... copyhold tenants of the said Manor,* Godbid (printer), 1657; F.E. Baines, *Records of the Manor, Parish and Borough of Hampstead in the County of London, to December, 1889,* Whittaker, 1890; F. Hitchin-Kemp, 'Clitterhouse Manor, Cricklewood, Hendon', *LMAS,* n.s., 5, 1929; W. McB. Marcham, *The Court Rolls of the Bishops of London's Manor of Hornsey, 1603-1701,* Grafton, 1929; and: 'The Court Rolls of Hornsey', *LMAS,* n.s., 6, Pt. 2, 1930; P. Davenport, *Old Stanmore,* Stanmore, 1933; N.G. Brett-James, 'Some Extents and Surveys of Hendon', in 4 parts, *LMAS,* n.s., 6, 1932; 7, 1933; 7, 1935; 7, 1937 (Parts 1-3 reprinted as *Some Extents and Surveys of Hendon,* Heffer, Cambridge, 1936; N.G. Brett-James, 'Ancient Customs of the Manor of Hendon, 1685', *LMAS,* n.s., 7, 1937; S.J. Madge, *The Early Records of Harringay, alias Hornsey,* Hornsey Public Libraries, 1938; and: *The Mediaeval Records of Harringay, alias Hornsey, from 1216-1307,* Hornsey Public Libraries, 1939; B. Garside, *The Ancient Manor Courts of Hampton-on-the-Thames during the 17th Century,* published by the author, 1948 and 1949; W. le Hardy, 'Harefield Deeds; the Tarleton Family Documents', *LMAS,* n.s., 10, 1951; W. le Hardy and E.D. Mercer, 'Manorial Records in the Middlesex County Record Office', 'Middlesex Manorial Records', *LMAS,* n.s., 10, 1951 and 11, 1954 (This list is in the course of being brought up to date in subsequent *Transactions);* W. McB. Marcham, *Some Court Rolls of the Manors of Tottenham, Middlesex, 1318-1503, and the Court Rolls of Cantelowes Manor, St Pancras, 1308-17,* Borough of Tottenham Libraries and Museum, 1956; L.E. Morris, 'A Custumal of Ruislip and Customs of the Manor of Ruislip', *LMAS,* 19, Pt. 1, 1956; 'Detailed List of Manor Rolls and other Manorial Documents, 1308-1732', Borough of Tottenham (Typescript), 1956; W. Hale, *The Domesday of St Pauls of the Year 1222; or Registrum de Visitatione Maneriorum per Robertum Decanum, and other original documents relating to the Manors and Churches belonging to the Dean and Chapter of St Paul's London in the 12th and 13th Centuries,* Camden Soc., 1858; W. McB. Marcham and C.H. Rock, *Some Court Rolls of the manors of Tottenham, Middlesex, 1318-1503 and Cantelowes, St. Pancras, 1308-17,* Tottenham Libraries and Museum, 1956; and: *Court Rolls of the Manor of Tottenham, 1510-1531,* Tottenham Public Libraries, 1960; F.H. Fenton, *Some recent work on the Tottenham Manor Rolls,* Edmonton Historical Society, 1961; R. Oram and F.H. Fenton, *Court Rolls of the manors of Bruces, Dawbenys and Pembrokes, 1377-1399,* Tottenham Public Libraries, 1961; W. McB. Marcham and F.H. Fenton, *Court Rolls of the Manor of Tottenham, 1558-1582,* Tottenham Public Libraries, 1963; D. Avery, *Manorial systems in the Edmonton Hundred in the late medieval and Tudor periods,* Edmonton Hundred Historical Society, 1964; H.M. Chew and W. Kellaway, *London Assize of Nuisance, 1301-1431,* London Record Society, 1973; M. Wilks and J. Bray, *Courts of the Manors of Bardon and Beddington, 1498-1552,* Sutton Library & Arts Services, 1983.

Monmouthshire A.J. Roderick, *Translation and Transcript of a minister's account, 1250-7, for the lordships of Abergavenny, Grosmont and Whitecastle,* Pub. of S. Wales Rec. Soc., no.2, 1950; no.3, 1954.

Norfolk H.W. Chandler, *Five Court Rolls of Great Cressingham, 1328-1584,* 1885; W. Hudson, *Leet Jurisdiction in Norwich during the 13th and 14th Centuries,* Selden Soc., 1892; F.G. Davenport, *The economic development of a Norfolk manor, 1086-1565 (Forncett),* London, 1906; W. Hudson, 'Traces of primitive agricultural organization as suggested by the survey of the manor of Martham, Norfolk, 1102-1292', *R. Hist. Soc.,* 4th series, I, 1918; L.J. Redstone, 'Three Carrow Account Rolls', *Norf. Arch.,* xxix, 1947; E.B. Burstall, 'The Pastons and their manor of Binham', *Norf. Arch.,* xxx, 1952; F.G. Davenport, *The Economic Development of a Norfolk Manor, 1086-1565,* Cass, 1967; B. Hanawatt, *Crime in East Anglia in the fourteenth century; Norfolk gaol delivery rolls, 1307-16,* Norfolk Record Soc., 1976; B. Campbell, 'The regional uniqueness of English field systems? Some evidence from eastern Norfolk', *Ag. Hist. Rev.,* XXIX, 1981; and: 'The extent and layout of common-fields in eastern Norfolk', *Norf. Arch.,* XXXVIII, 1981; and: 'Agricultural progress in medieval England; some evidence from eastern Norfolk', *Econ. Hist. Rev.,* XXXVI, 1983; The British Library CD-ROM, *Medieval Realms,* 1995 includes extracts from the manorial records of Dereham.

Northamptonshire L.B. Larking, 'Exemplification of the Records and Charters relating to the Manor of Moreton Pinkney, ... temp. Edw. II and Edw. III', *Collect. Top. & Gen.,* IV, 1837; I.H. Jeayes, 'On the Compotus Rolls of the Manor of Oundle', *Brit. Arch. Soc. J.,* xxxiv, 1878; C. Wise, *The Compotus of the Manor of Kettering, 1292,* Kettering, 1899; R.M. Serjeantson, *The Court Rolls of Higham Ferrers* (reprint from *AASRP,* XXXIII, 1915; XXXIV, 1917; D. Willis, *Estate Book of Henry de Bray of Harleston, Northants., 1289-1340,* R. Hist. Soc. Camden 3rd series, XXVII, 1916; W.T. Lancaster, 'A fifteenth century rental of Rothwell', Thoresby Soc., XXIV, *Miscellenea,* VII, 1919; F.M. Page, *Wellingborough Manorial Accounts, 1258-1323,* Northants Rec. Soc. Pub., VIII, 1936; W.T. Mellows and D.H. Gifford, *Peterborough Court Rolls, 1564-*

99, Northants Rec. Soc. Pub., XVIII, 1956; C.N.L. Brooke and M.M. Postan, *Carte Nativorum, a Peterborough Abbey cartulary of the 14th century*, Pubns. Northants. Rec. Soc., 20, 1960; T.H. Aston, *Wellingborough manorial accounts, 1258-1323*, Pubns. Northants. Records Soc., 8, 1965 (first edition originally published in 1936); J.K. Allison, M.W. Beresford and J.G. Hurst, *The Deserted Villages of Northamptonshire*, 1966; J. Greatrex, *Account Rolls of the obedientiaries of Peterborough*, Pubns. Northants. Rec. Soc., 33, 1984; C. Wise, 'Glimpses of Kettering in the 16th and 17th Centuries', *Northants Notes and Queries*, n.s., IV, V, VI.

Northumberland W.P. Hedley, 'Manor of Simonburn and Warks Park', *Arch. Aeliana*, 4th series, XXX, 1952; E. Miller, 'The tenants of Birting', *Procs. Soc. Ant. N.-on-T.*, 5th series, 1952; M.E. James, *Estate Accounts of the Earls of Northumberland, 1562-1637*, Surtees Soc., CLXIII for 1948, 1955; M.W. Beresford, 'Fallowfield, an early cartographic representation of a deserted village', *Medieval Archaeology*, no. 10, 1966; M.J. Alexander and B.K. Roberts, *The deserted village of Low Buston, Archaeologia Aeliana* (5th series), 6, 1978; A.F. and P.M.J. Pallister, 'A survey of the deserted medieval village of Newsham', *Architectural and Archaeological Soc. of Durham and Northumberland*, no.4, 1978.

Nottinghamshire L.V.D. Owen, 'Rental of Robert de Caunton', 'Extent of Langar and Barnston, *c*.1340', and 'An Annual Account Roll of the Manors of Scarrington, Car-Colston, Screveton and Orston, 1413-14' in *Miscellany of Notts Records*, Thoroton Soc., 1945; K.S.S. Train, *Second Miscellany of Nottinghamshire Records*, TSRS, XIV, 1951; M.W. Barley, *Documents relating to the manor and soke of Newark-on-Trent*, TSRS, XVI, 1956; A. Cameron, 'The deserted medieval village of Sutton Passeys', *Thoroton Soc.*, no.80, 1976; G. Coppack, 'The deserted medieval village of Keighton', *Thoroton Soc.*, no.75, 1971.

Oxfordshire J. Jordan, *A parochial history of Enstone* (includes court-roll extracts), 1857; E. Marshall, *The Early History of Woodstock manor and its environs*, 1873-4; S.R. Scargill-Bird, *Custumals of Battle Abbey, 1283-1312* (includes custumals of Oxford manors), Camden Soc., n.s., 1887; M.T. Pearman, *History of the manor of Bensington*, 1896;

Various papers published by ORS: W.A. Pantin, *Canterbury College, Oxford*, II, 1917 (accounts of payments from wardens of manors, 14th to 16th century); H. Barnett, *Glympton; the History of an Oxfordshire Manor* (includes Court Rolls, 1351-72), 1923; A.H. Cooke, *The Early History of Mapledurham* (extracts from Court Rolls, 1416-93, etc.), 1925; T.F. Hobson, *Adderbury Rectoria; Account Rolls, Deeds, and Court Rolls*, 1926; R.W. Jeffery, *The Manors and Advowsons of Great Rollright*, 1927; M.D. Lobel, *The History of Dean and Chalford* (extracts from Court Rolls, 1547), 1935; H.E. Salter, *Mediaeval Oxford* (includes a view of Frankpledge), 1936; W.O. Hassall, *Wheatley Records, 956-1956*, Rec. Sers., XXXVII, 1956; B.H. Harvey, *Custumal (1391) and Bye-laws (1386-1526) of the Manor of Islip*, Rec. Sers., XL, 1959;

H.M. Colvin, *A History of Deddington*, 1963; T.H. Lloyd, 'Some documentary sidelights on the deserted village of Brookend', *Oxoniensia*, XXIX, 1964; P.D. Adshead, *A medieval Oxfordshire village (Cuxham), 1240-1400*, O.U.P., 1965; P.D.A. Harvey, *Manorial records of Cuxham, 1200-1359*, Historical Manuscripts Commission and Oxfordshire Records Soc. Publications, no.50, H.M.S.O., London, 1976; The British Library CD-ROM, *Medieval Realms*, 1995 has extracts from the manorial records of Cuxham.

Shropshire T. Wright, 'Rental of the manor of Wroxeter, 1350', *ShAS*, XI, 1888; R.L. Kenyon, 'Manor of Ruyton', *ShAS*, 3rd series, I, 1901, II, 1902, and IV, 1904; L.H. Hayward, 'Ancient land-tenures, principally of Shropshire and the West Midlands', *ShAS*, XLIX, 1938; R.C. Purton, 'Documents relating to the manor of Church Stretton', *ShAS*, LIV, 1951-2; W.J. Slack, *The Lordship of Oswestry, 1393-1607*, Pubns. ShAS, 1952.

Somersetshire E. Smirke, 'The Custumal of Bleadon and agricultural tenures of the thirteenth century', *Memoirs of Wiltshire and Salisbury*, 1851; T.S. Holmes, *The History of the Parish and Manor of Wookey* (includes manorial accounts, 1329 and 1462), 1886; C.J. Elton, E. Hobhouse and T.S. Holmes, *Rentalia & Custumaria Michaelis de Ambresbury 1235-52*, Som. Rec. Soc., 1891; C.E.H. Chadwyck Healey, *History of part of West Somerset* (includes account rolls for Brendon and Porlock, 1419-19), 1901; F. Hancock, *History of the parish, manor and port of Minehead* (includes extracts from court rolls), 1903; A.L. Humphreys, 'Manorial Court Rolls, 1277-1908', *Materials for the History of the Town and Parish of Wellington*, Pt. 2, 1910; J.F. Chanter, 'Court rolls of the manor of Curry Rivel in the years of the Black Death, 1348-9' (translation), *SANHS*, LVI, 1911; H.C. Maxwell-Lyte, *Documents and Extracts illustrating the History of the Honour of Dunster*, Som. Rec. Soc., XXXIII, 1918; and: *Two Registers formerly belonging to the family of Beauchamp of Hatch* (14th century), Som. Rec. Soc., 1920; T.B. Dilkes, *Bridgwater Borough Archives* (includes court rolls of Bridgwater and Haygrove, 1200-1377), Som. Rec. Soc., 1933; T.J. Hunt, *The medieval customs of the manors of Taunton and Bradford-on-Tone*, Somerset County Record Office and Som. Rec. Soc., 1972.

Staffordshire   E. Salt, *The History of Standon parish, manor and church* (includes court rolls, 1338-1773), 1888; E.R.O. and C.G.O. Bridgeman, *History of the manor of Weston-under-Lizard*, Wm. Salt Arch. Soc. Collections, n.s., II, 1899; W.N. Landor, *Alweras Court Rolls, 1259-61*, Staffs Rec. Soc. Wm. Salt Arch. Soc., 1907; and: *Alweras Court Rolls, 1268-9; 1272-3*, Staffs Rec. Soc. Wm. Salt Arch. Soc., 1910; C.G.O. Bridgeman, *Notes on the manors of Aston and Walton, near Stone, in the thirteenth and fourteenth centuries*, Wm. Salt Arch. Soc. Collections, 3rd series, 1913; *Court Rolls of the Manor of Tunstall, 1326-1719*, N. Staffs Field Club, LIX-LXVI, 1924-5; 1931-2; J.R. Birrell, 'The forest economy of the Honour of Tutbury in the fourteenth and fifteenth centuries', *Univ. Birm. Hist. J.*, VIII, 1962; R.H. Hilton, 'Lord and peasant in Staffordshire in the Middle Ages', *North Staffs. Journal of Field Studies*, no.10, 1970; A.C.Pinnock, 'Staffordshire medieval population and prosperity: a study of available sources', *North Staffs. Journal of Field Studies*, no.14, 1974.

Suffolk   Lord John Hervey, 'Extent of Hadleigh Manor, 1302', *Suff. Inst. of Archaeol.*, 11, 1901-3; 3, 1863; L.T. Smith, *Commonplace Book of the Fifteenth Century* (refers to manorial customs of Stuston etc.), 1886; 'Custom Roll of the Manor of Earl Soham' (original in Ipswich and East Suffolk C.R.O.), *EANQ*, n.s., 2, 1887-8; J. Hervey, *Ickworth Survey Book, 1665*, Ipswich, 1893; 'Extent of the Manor of Hepworth', *EANQ*, n.s., 6, 1895-6; H. Prigg, *Icklingham Papers* (including Accounts of Richard le Veysyn, Bailiff of Icklingham Manor, 1342-3), Woodbridge, 1901; R.G.C. Livett, 'Some Fourteenth century documents relating to Herringswell' (includes court rolls, 1318-99), *East Anglian*, 3rd series, X, 1903-4 and XI, 1905-6; W.A. Copinger, *The Manors of Suffolk; Notes on their history and devolution* (7 vols.), 1905-11; H.W. Saunders, 'Bailiff's Roll of the Manor of Lawshall, 1393-4', *Suff. Inst. of Archaeol.*, 14, 1910-12; 'Court Roll for the Manor of Sudbury, 1488', *East Anglian Miscellany*, no.6370, 1922; E. Callard, *The Manor of Freckenham*, 1924; 'Rental, Thorndon Rectory Manor, 1650', *East Anglian Miscellany*, nos.7639, 7642, 1928; 'Bentley Manorial Rent Roll, 1638', *East Anglian Miscellany*, nos.9386, 9395, 9399, 1935; R. Lennard, 'An unidentified twelfth century custumal of Lawshall', *EHR*, LI, 1936; J.T. Munday, *Lakenheath manor of Clare fee, 1086-1331*, Munday, 1970; and: *Brandon manor rolls after the 1380s*, Munday, 1972; D.P. Dymond, 'The parish of Walsham-le-Willows: two Elizabethan surveys and their medieval background', *Suffolk Institute of Archaeology Procs.*, 33, 1974.

Surrey   *Extracts from the Court Rolls of Wimbledon*, Wimbledon Common Committee, 1866; S.R. Scargill-Bird, *Custumals of Battle Abbey, 1283-1312* (includes manors in Surrey), Camden Soc., n.s., 1887; F.B. Bickley, 'Extracts from the Court Rolls of the Manor of Dulwich, 1333-1693', in W. Young's *History of Dulwich College*, 1889; G.L. Gomme, *Court Rolls of Tooting Bec Manor, 1 (1394-1422)*, L.C.C., 1909; C. Deedes, *Register of the Manor of Ewell, 1408-23*, 1913; D.L. Powell, *Court Rolls of the Manor of Carshalton, 1359-1506*, SurRS, 1916; and: *List of Court Rolls, with some notes of other Manorial Records*, SurRS Pub., no.28, 1927; H.M. Briggs, *Surrey Manorial Accounts* (Maldon Farley and Thorneycroft), Surrey Rec. Soc., 1935; E. Thoms and H. Jenkinson, *Chertsey Abbey Court Rolls Abstract, 1327-48*, Surrey Rec. Soc., no.XXXVIII (21), 1937 and no.XLVIII (22, pt.2), 1954; D. Harper, *The cost of living in 1300 (Farnham)*, Farnham W.E.A., 1966; H.C.M. Lambert, *History of Banstead* (2 vols.) (contains manorial records).

Sussex   S.R. Scargill-Bird, *Custumals of Battle Abbey, 1283-1312* (includes manors in Sussex), Camden Soc., n.s., 1887; W. Hudson, 'The manor of Eastbourne, its early history', *SAC*, XLIII, 1900; and: 'On a series of rolls of the Manor of Wiston' (13th-16th centuries), *SAC*, LIII, 1910;

   Various papers published by SRS: C. Thomas-Stanford, *An Abstract of the Court Rolls of the Manor of Preston (Episcopi)*, 1921; W.D. Peckham, *Thirteen Custumals in the Sussex Manors of the Bishop of Chichester* (14th century), 1925; W.H. Godfrey, *The Book of John Rowe, Steward of the Manors of Lord Bergavenny, 1597-1622* (Comprising rentals, etc. of 27 manors in Sussex), 1928; E.J. Courthope and B.E.R. Formoy, *Lathe Court Rolls and Views of Frankpledge in the Rape of Hastings, 1387-1474*, 1934; A.J. Taylor, *Records of the Barony and Honour of the Rape of Lewes*, XLIV, 1940; S.P. Vivian, *The Manor of Etchingham cum Salehurst*, 1953; L.F. Salzman, *Ministers' Accounts of the Manor of Petworth, 1347-1353*, LV, 1955; J. Cornwall, 'Lay Subsidy Rolls for the County of Sussex 1524-5', 56, 1956; B.C. Redwood and A.E. Wilson, *Custumals of the Sussex Manors of the Archbishop of Canterbury*, LVII, 1958; A.E. Wilson, *Custumals of the manor of Laughton, Willingdon and Goring*, no.40, 1962; M. Clough, *The book of Bartholomew Bolney*, no.63, 1964;

   E.W. Holden, *Excavations at the deserted medieval village of Hangleton*, SAC, no.101, 1963; J.A. Brent, 'Alciston manor in the later Middle Ages', *SAC*, 116, 1968; G.R. Burleigh, 'An introduction to deserted medieval villages in East Sussex', *SAC*, 111, 1973; and: 'Further notes on deserted and shrunken medieval villages in Sussex', *SAC*, 114, 1976; F.G. Aldsworth, *Three medieval sites in West Dean parish*

(Chilgrove chapel, Monkton deserted medieval settlement and Binderton church), SAC, no.117, 1979; S. Farrant, *Sussex in the Medieval Period; A Bibliography*, Centre for Continuing Education, University of Sussex, Occ. Papers, no.10, 1980; C.F. Tebbutt, 'A deserted medieval farm settlement at Faulkners Farm, Hartfield', *SAC*, 119, 1981; M. Gardiner, 'Planned medieval land division in Withyham, East Sussex', *SAC*, 123, 1985.

Warwickshire W. Cooper, *Records of Beaudesert, Henley-in-Arden*, 1931; R.H. Hilton, *The Social Structure of rural Warwickshire in the Middle Ages*, Dugdale Soc. Occ. Papers, no.9, 1950; and: *Ministers' accounts of the Warwickshire estates of the Duke of Clarence, 1479-80*, Dugdale Soc. Pubs., no.21, 1952; C.D. Ross, *The Estates and Finances of Richard Beauchamp, Earl of Warwick*, Dugdale Soc. Occ. Papers, no.12, 1956; J.R. Birrell, 'The forest economy of Tutley in the fourteenth century and fifteenth century', *University of Birmingham Historical Journal*, no.8, 1962; C. Dyer, 'Population and agriculture on a Warwickshire manor in the later Middle Ages', *University of Birmingham Historical Journal*, no.11, 1968; D. Styles, *Ministers' accounts of the Collegiate church of St Mary's Warwick, 1432-85*, Dugdale Soc. Pubs., 26, 1969; C.J. Boyd, 'Deserted medieval villages in Warwickshire: a review of the field evidence', *Birmingham and Warwicks. Archaeological Soc. Trans.*, no.86, 1974.

Wiltshire G.P. Scrope, *History of the Manor and Barony of Castle Combe*, 1852; J.E.T. Rogers, 'Farmers' and Collectors' Accounts' (Alton Barnes, 1455-1531), *History of Agriculture*, III, 1884; S.R. Scargill-Bird, *Custumals of Battle Abbey, 1283-1312* (includes manors in Wilts), Camden Soc., n.s., 1887; C.R. Straton, *Survey of the Lands of William, First Earl of Pembroke*, Roxburgh Club, 1909; R.C. Payne, 'Agricultural conditions on the Wiltshire estates of the Duchy of Lancaster', *Brit. Inst. Hist. Res.*, XVIII, 1940; R.B. Pugh, 'The early history of the manors in Amesbury', *WANHM*, LII, no.187, 1947; T.R. Thompson, 'The custumal of Abingdon Court, Cricklade', *WANHM*, LII, no.189, 1948; S. Reynolds, 'Pleas in the Liberty of the Abbot of Battle at Bromham, 1289', Wilts. Arch. Soc. (Records Branch), XII, *Collectanea*, 1956; R.L. Rickard, *Progress Notes of Warden Woodward for the Wiltshire manors of New College, Oxford, 1659-75*, Wilts Arch. Soc., 1957; M.W. Farr, *Accounts and Surveys of the Wiltshire Lands of Adam de Stratton*, Wilts. Arch. Soc. (Records Branch), XIV, 1959; B. Farr, *The rolls of Highworth Hundred, 1275-1286*, WANHS, 1966; C.C. Taylor, 'Whiteparish: the study of a forest-edge parish', *WANHM*, 62, 1967; and: 'Three deserted medieval settlements in Whiteparish', *WANHM*, 64, 1969; R.B. Pugh, *Court rolls of the Wiltshire manors of Adam de Stratton*, Wilts. Records Soc. Pubs., 24, 1970.

Worcestershire F.B. Andrews, 'Compotus Rolls of the Monastery of Pershore', *Birm. Arch. Soc.*, 57, 1935; A.F.C. Baber, *The Court Rolls of the Manors of Bromsgrove and King's Norton*, Worcs. Hist. Soc., 46, n.s., 3, 1963; G.C. Dyer, 'The deserted medieval village of Woolasill', *Worcs. Arch. Soc.*, n.s., 1, 1965-6; C.J. Bond, 'The estates of Evesham Abbey; a preliminary survey of their medieval topography', and: 'The medieval topography of the Evesham Abbey estates', *Vale of Evesham Hist. Soc. Research Papers*, 4 and 5, 1973-5; The British Library CD-ROM, *Medieval Realms*, 1995 includes extracts from the court rolls of Stoke Prior.

Yorkshire H. Best, 'The manner and forme of a distringas or levy', *Rural Economy in Yorkshire, 1641*, Surtees Soc. XXXIII, 1857 (a 17th-century description of 'the forme and manner of collecting a subsidy ... and ... of ratinge, assessing and levying of polle money'.); P.A. Lyons, 'Compoti of the Yorkshire estates of Henry de Lacy', *Yorks. Arch. & Top. J.*, VIII, 1884; G.D. Lumb, 'Abstract of the Leeds Manor Rolls, 1650-1662', *Thoresby Soc. Misc.*, III, 1899; W. Paley Baildon, *Court Rolls of the Manor of Wakefield*, I (1274-97), 1901; II (1297-1309), 1906, Yorks Arch. Soc.; F. Collins, *Wills and Administration from Knaresborough Court Rolls*, I, Surtees Soc., 1902; W.T. Lancaster, 'Fourteenth century court rolls of the manor of Thorner, (38/9) Edw. III', *Pubns. Thoresby Soc., XV, Miscellanea*, V, 1906-9; W.T. Lancaster, 'Fourteenth-Century Court Rolls of the Manor of Thorner, 1365-6', *Thoresby Soc. Misc.*, V, 1909; J.C. Hodgson, *Percy Bailiffs' Rolls of the 15th Century*, Surtees Soc., 1921; J.S. Purvis, *Bridlington Court Rolls and Papers*, 1926; C.V. Collier, *Burton Agnes, 1632-1710*, YAS, LXXIV; *Miscellanea*, II, 1929; T. Lawson-Tancred and J.W. Walker, *Extracts from the Court Rolls of the Manor of Aldborough, 1338-9*, YAS, 1929; J. McNulty, *Chartulary of the Cistercian Abbey of St Mary of Sallay (Sawley)* (2 vols.), Yorks. Arch. Soc. Rec. Sers., LXXXVII, 1933, and XC, 1934 (vol.2 has the return for a 14th-century clerical taxation of Yorkshire.); A.G. Ruston and D. Witney, *Hooton Pagnell, the agricultural evolution of a Yorkshire village*, 1934; G.E. Kirk, 'A sixteenth century rental of the manor of Temple Newsam and its appurtenances', *Thoresby Soc. Misc.*, XXXIII, 1935; T.A.M. Bishop, *Monk Friston Extent, 1220*, YAS, XCIV, 1937; E.W. Crossley, *Court Rolls relating to the Manors of Cottingley, Bingley, Pudsey and Crossley Hall, 1615-17; Kirkheaton, 1333-1481, 1616-17*, YAS Misc., IV, 1937;

H.S. Darbyshire and G.D. Lumb, *The History of Methley* (extracts from the Court Rolls, 1331-1590), Thoresby Soc., 1937; M.W. Barley, 'Early Yorkshire manorial bye-laws', *YAS Journal*, XXXV, 1940; C. Whone, *Court Rolls of the Manor of Haworth, 1581-1870*, Bradford Hist. & Antiq. Soc. Loc. Rec. Ser., 1946; J. Le Patourel, 'Documents relating to the manor and borough of Leeds, 1066-1400', *Thoresby Soc.*, 45, 1957; R.A. Donkin, 'Settlement and depopulation of Cistercian estates during the twelfth and thirteenth centuries, especially in Yorkshire', *Brit. Inst. Hist. Res.*, XXXIII, 1960; and: 'The Cistercian order and the settlement of northern England', *Geog. Rev.*, LIX, 1969; H. Richardson, *Court Rolls of the manor of Acomb* (2 vols.), YAS Records Series, no.131, 1969; I. Kershaw, *Bolton Priory rentals and ministers' accounts, 1473-1539*, YAS Records Series, no.132, 1970; J.A. Sheppard, 'Metrological analysis of regular village plans in Yorkshire', *Ag. Hist. Rev.*, XXII, 1974; G.S. Haslop, 'A Selby kitchener's roll of the fifteenth century', *YAS Journal*, 48, 1976; A. Raistrick, *Monks and shepherds in the northern Dales, 1150-1780*, Yorkshire Dales National Park Committee, 1976; M.W. Beresford, 'Documentary evidence for the history of Wharram Percy', in: J.G. Hurst (ed.), *Wharram: A Study of Settlement in the Yorkshire Wolds*, 1979; D. Postles, 'Rural economy on the grits and sandstones of the South Yorkshire Pennines, 1086-1348', *Northern History*, no.15, 1979; M. Faull (ed.), *Medieval Manorial Records*, YAS (Medieval Section), 1983; C.M. Fraser and K. Emsley, *The Court Rolls of the Manor of Wakefield*, from October 1664-September 1665, YAS, 1986; H.M. Jewell, 'Women in the court rolls of the manor of Wakefield', *Northern History*, 26, 1990; A. Weikel, *The Court Rolls of the Manor of Wakefield from 1537 to 1539*, YAS, 1993; The British Library's CD-ROM, *Medieval Realms*, 1995 includes extracts from the court rolls of Wakefield.

LAY SUBSIDY ROLLS

THE DOCUMENT

These are the records of royal taxation upon moveable property from the 13th century to the 17th century. For the medieval period, the Subsidy Rolls record the assessments of the free householders of each village for a particular subsidy or tax. These were, during the 13th and 14th centuries, those taxes raised by Edward I and Edward II for their various campaigns in France, Scotland and Wales. The chief value of the Subsidy Rolls to the local historian lies in the evidence they provide, which can be combined with the information from other lists and returns, as the basis of a study of changes in medieval population and wealth. Incidental information includes the relative sizes of the county's towns; the mobility of medieval population; a comparison of social structure, village by village; comparison of villages held by lay or ecclesiastical lords; the development of place-names and surnames, and the latters' reflection of the development of crafts and trades. Worcestershire is unusual in that it possesses Rolls for both 1275 and 1327; this affords a useful comparison of the admitted resources of the county at those two dates, with some indications of social and economic change during the intervening years. These were times of civil war, misgovernment, and the recurrent disasters of plague and famine.

The Rolls consist, as the facsimile shows (Plate VI), of lists of names of inhabitants arranged village by village. Each name has a tax assessment in small Roman numerals, and a total for the whole village; there is no additional text or commentary. The lists of names are arranged in double columns, on long, narrow membranes of deeply-yellowed vellum, about 7in. in width, stitched together end-to-end, to form a giant roll of cartwheel proportions, unmanageable and swift to unroll and tangle if not firmly and carefully handled. The entries themselves, though written in the same spiky law-hand as the manor court rolls, are so simple in content, and so full of familiar names, that they present little difficulty to the reader. The

Christian names all follow the preposition 'de', and are therefore in the ablative case, e.g. Willo., Robto., Rogo., Gilbo. with strokes above the abbreviations to indicate omissions of letters. The surnames are rendered in Latin, or bastard French (Rogero le Tailleur, Roberto Molendinario, for Taylor, Miller, etc.). The names are of three main types; those denoting a person's abode (Petronilla de Clent, Willelmo de la More, etc.); those deriving from his status or occupation (Waltero Preposito, Hugone le Karetter, Johanne le Bonde); or patronymics (Johanne filio Osberti, etc.). Given a local printed edition of a county's Subsidy Rolls, there is no real need for a student to refer to the original; on the other hand, in the absence of such a transcript, a facsimile of the originals for a few villages, easily obtainable from the P.R.O., need present no real difficulty to the determined amateur.

Subsidy Rolls as a source for population studies

'The study of population changes is of fundamental importance in any local history' (W.G. Hoskins, *Local History in England*, p.139). It must be admitted here that the Lay Subsidy Rolls alone would be inadequate, and extremely unreliable, as the sole basis of such a study. It appears to have been an easy matter to escape assessment, for widespread evasion is evident, and the Rolls themselves are usually found, on further investigation, to list only a fraction of any village's total population. In view of these deficiencies, the document must be used with caution, and considered only in conjunction with other, more reliable documents which cannot be fully illustrated here. The information gained from medieval Subsidy Rolls must be added to, and compared with, the evidence of a village's population found elsewhere. The Hundred Rolls, where these survive, the records of other taxations, such as the poll-tax assessments of 1377-81, local tallage lists, and manorial extents, all contain details of medieval village population. For a really detailed study of population changes based upon documentary evidence, the student should use Dr Hoskins's study of Wigston Magna ('The Population of an English Village, 1086-1801', reprinted from *Transactions of the Leicestershire Archaeological and Historical Society*, XXXIII, 1957). The methods of study applied to this Leicestershire village should be used as a model for general application elsewhere, and the commentary upon the relative values of the documentary evidence carefully studied.

Later Subsidy Rolls and population returns

It must not be supposed that Subsidy Rolls come to an end at the close of the Middle Ages. After 1334, down to the reign of Charles II, however, the local assessments supply only total quotas for each village, and do not continue to provide us with lists of names of their inhabitants. Drastic changes in the prosperity of individual villages, even in some cases the total disappearance of a village, are occasionally recorded in the Rolls, so that relief and adjustment might be made in cases of exceptional need. Evidence on local population is sadly lacking for the 15th century. 'The local and central records for this century are generally less informative, or more sparse, than those for the centuries which precede it and come after' (*Local History in England*, p.142). During the 16th century, in Henry VIII's reign, a new type of subsidy was introduced by Parliament to supplement the older 'tenth' and 'fifteenth'. The new subsidy was a tax of 4s. in the pound on the annual value of land, and 2s. 8d. on the value of goods. Like the medieval subsidy, this assessment soon became fixed as a 'mere fiscal expression' for a fixed sum of £100,000, later £80,000, for the country as a whole. Thus the Tudor subsidy, in its turn, became fossilised and unrealistic, but its assessments, providing us as they do with records of the most comprehensive tax of this period, must be taken into consideration in any detailed study of 16th-century population changes. The great Lay Subsidy of 1524-5 is particularly important, and it has been said that 'the assessment rolls, where they survive, provide a directory of the upper, middle and lower classes, and are near enough to the earliest parish registers, to serve as some basis for genealogical tree-planting' (M.W. Beresford, 'The Lay Subsidies', Pt. 2, *Amateur Historian*, 4, no.3, 1959). It must, however, still be remembered that neither Subsidy Rolls nor any other single document can be relied on, in isolation, to provide us with valid statistics and accurate information. In addition to the later Subsidy Rolls, as with their medieval counterparts, attention must be given to the wide variety of other local and national records of population, whose evidence must be correlated and compared. These are seen to be of two main kinds, the records of subsidies and other forms of taxation, and registers and returns compiled to supply information on religious conformity. Some of those records given by Dr Hoskins[9] are listed here, but it is impossible to illustrate them all, or even to do them sufficient justice, in this collection of documents. They include:

1. Parish Registers and Churchwardens' Accounts (see Chapter IV, pp. 73-83).
2. Sixteenth-century Muster Rolls for the militia, available at the P.R.O.
3. Records of bishops' visitations, in the diocesan records.
4. Diocesan returns for the ecclesiastical census of 1563, at the British Library.
5. Registers of communicants, recusants and other nonconformists taken in 1603, also at the British Library.
6. Chantry certificates of communications for 1545.
7. Hearth Tax Returns for 1662-1689 (see Chapter IV, pp. 131-35).
8. The Protestation Returns of 1642, which listed all males in each parish who had taken the Oath of Protestation. These are to be found in the House of Lords' Library (see 5th Report, Historical Manuscripts Commission, 1876).

FURTHER READING

M.W. Beresford, 'The Lay Subsidies' (An article in two parts: Part 1.1290-1334; Part 2. after 1334. (*Amateur Historian*, 3, no.8, 1958 and 4, no.3, 1959, reprinted, Canterbury, 1963) and: 'Poll Taxes of 1377, 1379 and 1381', *Amateur Historian*, 3, no.7., 1958

R.E. Glasscock, *The Lay Subsidy of 1334*, Records of Social and Economic History, new series, no.2, O.U.P., 1975

H.L. Gray, 'Tables of enrolled customs and subsidy accounts, 1399-1482', in E. Power and M.Postan's *Studies in English Trade in the Fifteenth Century*, 1966

G.L. Harris, *King Parliament and Public Finance in Medieval England, to 1369*, Oxford, 1975

W.G. Hoskins, 'The Population of an English Village, 1086-1801', *LAHS*, XXXIII, 1957

Inventory or Calendar of Accounts, Assessments etc. (4.Henry III - 38 Hen.VIII), Deputy Keepers' Reports II, Appx.II and III, London, 1841-2

Nonarum Inquisitiones in Curia Scaccarii, temp.regis Edw.III, Records Commission, London, 1807. Records of a subsidy of one-ninth on corn and wool in every parish and on 'moveables' in every borough.

S.A. Peyton, 'The Village Polulation in Tudor Lay Subsidy Rolls', *English Historical Review*, 30, 1915

R. Somerville, *Handlist of Record Publications, Section 24*, British Records Association, 1951

J. Topham, 'A Subsidy Roll of 51 Edw.III', *Archaeologia*, VII, 1785

J.F. Willard, 'Parliamentary Taxes on Personal Property, 1290-1334', *Medieval Academy of America*, no.9, 1934

---

[9] W.G. Hoskins, *Local History in England,* Ch.10, 'Health, Disease and Population', pp.142-9.

1.

LADELEYE.

De Willelmo Turgys	xl.d'.
5. De Roberto Molendinario	.v.s'.
De Johanne Aldred	di'.m'.
De Hugone de Lodeley	di'.m'.
De Agnete vidua	xij.d'.
De Ricardo del Broc	iiij.s'.
10. De Thoma de Twygelbatche	di'.m'.
De Margeria vidua	xviij.d'.
De Ricardo de Hayle	iiijs'vj.d'.
De Thoma de Monte	di'm.
De Willelmo de Monte	iiij's'.
15. De Henrico le Barun	xijd.
Summa:	Lj.s'.

CHADDESLEYE.

De Willelmo Corbet	xlvjs'.viij.d'.
20. De Brun Arnald	sl.d'.
De Felicia	xvj.d'.
De Dobbe de Cakebale	v.s'.
De Stephano de Bosco	x.s'.
De Adam le Heremite	iiij.s.
25. De Ricardo Dunrych'.	v.s'.
De Petronilla de Clent	iiij.s'.
De Willelmo de Tenacre	iij.s'.
De Mathillda de la Ferne	iiij.s'.
De Johanne de Tenacre	xl.d'.
30. De Thoma de Tenacre	iiij.s'.
De Nicholao de la Brugge	iij.s'.
De Roberto de la More	iij.s'.
De Hawisia de Pleybmere	iiij.s'.
De Agnete Dunrych'	iij.s'.
35. De Margeria le Bes	iiij s'vj.d'.
De Ricardo Pym	xviij.d'.
De Simone Ore	iij.s'.vjd'.
De Rogero le Taillur'	vj.s'.
Summa:	vj. li'iij.s'. ij.d'.

40.

DRAYTON'.

MUTTON'   ... 1

De Nicholao de Mutton' iiij.li'xiiij.s'iiij.d'.		
De Willelmo Cole	xiiijd'.	
De Adam Leueson'	ij.s'.	... 5
De Adam Watemon	ii.s'.iiij.d'.	
De Waltero Godspede	xiiij.d'.	
De Roberto Stertinthehegge	xvj.d'.	
De Roberto Russel	svj.d'.	
De Willelmo filio Yuonis	xviiij.d'.	... 10
De Iuono filio Walteri	xvjd'.	
De Louecok	xxij.d'.	
De Ricardo Nistegalle	xvj.d'.	
De Thoma Carectario	xiiijd'.	
Summa:	Cix.s'x.d'.	... 15

WASSEBURN'.

De Rogers de Wasseburn'	xv.s'.	
De Ricardo le Bonde	iijs'.	... 20
De Ricardo de Alston'	iij.s'.	
De Ricardo Lucas	iij.s'.	
De Mauricio de Rotur'	iiij.s.	
De Henrico le Rous	ij.s'.	
De Roberto Rys	xij.d'.	... 25
De Milicia vidua	vij.s.	
De Toldo's	ij.s'.	
Summa:	xxxv.s'.	
		... 30

CROPPTHORN''

De Priore Wygornie	iiij.m'.	
De Rogero filio Henrici	vj.s'.	
De Waltero Burimon	viij.s'.	... 35
De Roberto Tony	iiij.s'.	
De Roberto Lyffe	xviij.d'.	
De Henrico Purs	v.s'.	
De Henrico Carectario	v.s'.	
De Osberto Preposito	iiij.s'.	... 40
De Johanne filio Osberti	iiij.s'.	

Plate VI. Lay Subsidy Roll for Chaddesley, etc. c.1280.
(Worcs. Record Office, 'Lechmere Roll'. Ref. 705:134.BA.1531/48.)
Actual size (as shown): 16 x 23cm (LADELEY-DRAYTON)

Radeleie

- Walto Turgys — xl d.
- Rob ... — c.s.
- ... Alured — ... m.
- Hugo de Radeleie — ... m.
- ... Gidia — xij d.
- Rico del Broc — iiij s.
- Thom de ... — ... m.
- Margña Gidia — xvij d.
- Rico del Hayle — iij s. vj d.
- Thom de ... — ... m.
- Walto de ... — iij s.
- Henr ... — xij d.

Chaddesleie

- Walto Coll — xlvij s. iiij d.
- Brun Arnald — xl d.
- ... — xvij d.
- Rob de ... — c.s.
- ... de ... — x.s.
- ... le ... —
- Rico ... — c.s.
- ... de Clent — iij s.
- Walto de Tenac — iij s.
- ... de la ferne — iij s.
- ... de Tenac — xl d.
- Thom de Tenac — iij s.
- ... de la Brugge — iij s.
- Rob de la ... — iij s.
- ... de ... — iij s.
- ... — iij s.
- Margña le Bes — iij s. vj d.
- Rico Pym — xvij d.
- Simone Ore — iij s. vj d.

- Rogo le Taillur — vj s.
- Sm ... iij s. ij d.

Drayton

Honiton

- ... de ... — iiij li. xij s. iij d.
- Walto Cole — xij d.
- ... Loueston — ij s.
- ... ... — ij s. iij d.
- Walto Godefrde — xij d.
- Rob ... — xvj d.
- Rob Russel — xvj d.
- Walto fil ... — xviij d.
- Simone fil Walter — xvj d.
- ... — xij d.
- Rico ... — xvj d.
- ... — xij d.
- **Sm. cxx s. x d.**

Wasseburn

- Rogo de Wasseburn — x s.
- Rico le Bonde — iij s.
- Rico de Alston — iij s.
- Rico Lucas — iij s.
- ... le ... — iij s.
- Henr le ... — iij s.
- Rob ... — iij s.
- William Gidia — iij s.
- ... — iij s.
- **Sm. xxxv s.**

Croppethom

- Priore ... — ...
- Rogo fil Henr — vj s.
- Walto Burnen — vj s.
- Rob Tony — iij s.
- Rob Lyffe — xij d.

- Henr Purs — vj s.
- Henr ... — vj s.
- Osb ... — iij s.
- ... fil Osb — iij s.

… 1
… 5
… 10
… 15
… 20
… 25
… 30
… 35
… 40

PRINTED EDITIONS FOR WORCESTERSHIRE

J. W. Willis-Bund and John Amphlett (eds.), *Lay Subsidy Roll for the County of Worcestershire, c.1280*, Worcs Hist. Soc., 1, 1893

F.J. Eld (ed.), *Lay Subsidy Roll, A.D. 1332-3, and nonarum inquisitiones, 1340, for the County of Worcestershire*, Worcs Hist. Soc., 10, 1899

J. Amphlett (ed.), *Lay Subsidy Rolls, A.D. 1346 and 1358, for the County of Worcestershire*, Worcs Hist. Soc., 12, 1900

J. Amphlett (ed.), *Lay Subsidy Roll, A.D. 1603, for the County of Worcestershire*, Worcs Hist. Soc., 13, 1901

J. Amphlett (ed.), *Lay Subsidy Rolls, 6 and 7 Henry VI, A.D. 1427-9, for the County of Worcestershire*, Worcs Hist. Soc., 14, 1902

GLOSSARY OF SURNAMES DERIVED FROM OCCUPATIONS

(Taken from the Worcestershire Lay Subsidy Rolls; for derivations of other surnames, see P.H. Reaney, *Dictionary of British Surnames,* Routledge and Kegan Paul, 3rd ed. 1991, and *The Origins of English Surnames*, pbk 1980, reprint under consideration 1996.)

Atte Mull	*miller*	Doule	*tanner*
Atte Novane	*baker*	Doware	*tanner*
Bachessor	*baker*	Dyer	*dyer*
Bagster	*baker*	Fernier	*baker*
Barat	*cap-maker*	Feure	*hunting-dog keeper*
Barker	*tanner*	Feute	*hunting-dog keeper*
Baxter	*baker*	Feutre	*hunting-dog keeper*
Bit	*fireman*	Feutrer	*hunting-dog keeper*
Blakestare	*cloth-bleacher*	Fewster	*pack-saddle maker*
Bollinger	*baker*	Filure	*yarn-spinner*
Bolutil	*miller*	Fithelare	*fiddler*
Brael	*girdle-maker*	Foet	*hunting-dog keeper*
Bralard	*girdle-maker*	Fot, Fotur	*hunting-dog keeper*
Braly	*girdle-maker*	Fullo	*cloth-fuller*
Breet	*cap-maker*	Furber	*arms-polisher*
Bultare	*fireman*	Furner	*baker*
Burden	*pilgrim*	Fustarius	*pack-saddle maker*
But	*fireman*	Heuster	*dyer*
Capyare	*cap-maker*	Hod	*pedlar*
Carboner	*charcoal-burner*	Holdare	*tenant*
Carectarius	*carter*	Holde	*tenant*
Ceinture	*girdle-maker*	Horel	*cap-maker*
Ceynter	*girdle-maker*	Hounte	*huntsman*
Colemon	*charcoal-burner*	Hunte	*huntsman*
Coliare	*charcoal-burner*	Kappe	*cap-maker*
Colier	*charcoal-burner*	Kembestere	*wool-comber, or carder*
Comber	*wool-comber, or carder*	Kempe	*wool-comber, orcarder*
Copper	*cooper*	Kytte	*pail-maker*
Couper	*cooper*	Legister	*lawyer*
Couverer	*cooper*	Linter	*cloth nap-cutter*
Cuper	*cooper*	Louf	*baker*
Cuver	*cooper*	Millward	*miller*
Cyreman	*cloth nap-cutter*	Mire	*mayor*
Deye	*dairyman*	Molendinarius	*miller*
Deyare	*dairyman*	Monner	*miller*
Dissare	*story-teller*	Mooldare	*baker*
Dodemon	*pedlar*	Muleward	*miller*

Mulnare	*miller*	Tannarius	*tanner*
Odde	*pedlar*	Telere	*flax-separator*
Ovane	*baker*	Teleware	*flax-separator*
Padgett	*pedlar*	Tenator	*tenant*
Pain	*baker*	Tenor	*tenant*
Palmer	*pilgrim*	Tente	*tenant*
Pannier	*baker*	Tenur	*tenant*
Patchett	*pedlar*	Teware	*flax-separator*
Paumer	*pilgrim*	Textor, Textrix	*weaver*
Peler	*tanner*	Tinctor	*dyer*
Peleter	*leather-dresser*	Tow	*flax-separator*
Pelliparius	*tanner*	Towelere	*flax-separator*
Pistor	*baker*	Towker	*fuller*
Playdour	*lawyer*	Tredel	*dyer*
Pollinger	*baker*	Troyare	*spinner*
Prepositus	*reeve*	Venur	*huntsman*
Roer	*fuller*	Vinur	*vintner*
Rommer	*pilgrim*	Vyn	*vintner*
Rowe	*fuller*	Vyttelare	*fiddler*
Rubbare	*fuller*	Wake	*night-watchman*
Segare	*story-teller*	Walker	*fuller*
Sengle	*girdle-maker*	Wastel	*baker*
Seynter	*girdle-maker*	Wayte	*night-watchman*
Shireman	*cloth nap-cutter*	Webbe	*dyer*
Sigare	*story-teller*	Wyn	*vintner*
Sinarius	*pail-maker*	Wynter	*vintner*
Stretch	*cloth nap-cutter*	Wyte	*night-watchman*
Taillur	*tailor*	Wyter	*cloth-bleacher*

PRINTED EDITIONS FOR OTHER COUNTIES

(See Robert Somerville, *Handlists of Record Publications*, Sect.24, British Records Association, 1951.)

The List and Index Society (Secretary c/o The Public Record Office) supplies, to members only, bound copies of unpublished PRO search room lists and indexes: Lists of Lay Subsidy Rolls include: No.44: Bedford-Essex (1969); No.54: Gloucester-Lincoln (1970); No.63: London-Somerset (1971); No.75: Staffordshire-Yorkshire (1972); No.87: Wales, Cinq Ports and Royal Household (1973).

(listed in chronological date of publication within the county)

Bedfordshire J.E. Brown, 'Clerical subsidies in the Archdeaconry of Bedford, 1390-2 and 1400-1', *Pubns. BHRS*, I, 1913; H. Jackson, *An Early Bedfordshire Taxation, 1237*, BHRS, 1915; H. Jenkinson, 'Some Bedfordshire assessments for the taxation of a ninth, 1297', *BHRS*, VIII, 1923; S.H.A. Hervey, *Two Bedfordshire Subsidy Lists, 1309 and 1332*, Suffolk Green Books, XVIII, 1925; A.T. Gaydon, *The taxation of 1297* (a translation of the local rolls of assessment for Barford, Biggleswade and Flitt Hundreds, and for Bedford, Dunstable, Leighton Buzzard and Luton), *Pubns. BHRS*, XXXIX, 1959.

Buckinghamshire A.C. Chibnall and A.V. Woodman, *Subsidy Roll for the County of Buckinghamshire, 1524*, BRS, VIII, 1950; A.C. Chibnall, *Early Taxation Returns* (1332), BRS, 14, 1966; F. Gurney, 'A Fourteenth-Century Subsidy List for Stone', *Records of Bucks*, X.

Caernarvonshire E.G. Jones, 'Caernarvonshire Subsidy Roll, 1597-8', *Bulln. of Board of Celtic Studies*, VIII, 1937; L. Owen, 'Lay Subsidy Rolls of the Tudor and Stuart Periods' (typescript available at the County Record Office).

Cambridgeshire W.M. Palmer, *List of Cambridgeshire Subsidy Rolls, 1250-1695*, East Anglian, VII-X and XII-XIII, 1898-1910; J.J. Muskett, *Lay Subsidies, Cambridgeshire, 1 Edw. III, 1326*, East Anglian, 3rd series, X-

XII, 1904-8.

Carmarthenshire   A.W. Matthews, 'Caermartren (Carmarthen): Subsidy rolls, 1628', *CASFC*, V, 1909.

Cornwall   J. Maclean, 'Poll-tax account for Cornwall, 51, Edw. III, 1377', *R. Inst. Corn. J.*, IV, 1872; *Subsidy Rolls, Muster, Hearth Tax Rolls and Probate Calendars for St. Constantine, Cornwall*, DCRS, 1910.

Cumberland and Westmorland   J.P. Steel, *Cumberland Lay Subsidy ... 6 Edw. III*, LCRS, XXXI, 1912; J.L. Kirby, 'Two tax accounts of the diocese of Carlisle, 1379-80', *CWAAS*, LII, 1952; J.L. and A.D. Kirby, 'The poll-tax of 1377 for Carlisle', *CWAAS*, n.s., LVIII, 1959; C.M. Fraser, 'The Cumberland and Westmorland Lay Subsidy for 1332', *CWAAS.*, no.66, 1966.

Derbyshire   J.P. Yeatman, *The Feudal History of the County of Derby* (5 vols., includes the subsidy roll of 1 Edw. III), 1886-1907; W.A. Carrington, 'Subsidy for the hundred of Scarsdale, 1599', *DANHSJ*, XXIV, 1902; J.C. Cox, 'Derbyshire in 1327-8', *DANHSJ*, XXX, 1908; S.O. Addy, 'Taxation by the oxgang in the subsidy roll for Scarsdale and High Peak, 1603', *DANHSJ*, XLIV, 1922.

Devonshire   T.W. Whale, 'The tax roll for Devon, 31 Edw. I', *Devon Assn. for Adv. Science, Litt. & Art*, XXXI, 1899; O.J. Reichel, *An Exeter manuscript* (translation, includes tenths and fifteenths, 1384), 1907; W.G. Hoskins, 'Cadbury and Thorverton subsidies (1591)', *DCNQ*, XX, 1938; A.M. Erskine, *The Devonshire Lay Subsidy of 1332*, DCRS, 38, n.s., XIV, 1969; T.L. Stoate, *Devon Lay Subsidy Rolls 1543-5*, 1986; and: *Devon Taxes 1581-1660*, 1988.

Dorset   E.A. Fry, 'Dorset Lay Subsidy Rolls, Edward I to Charles II', *SDNQs*, III, 1893 (translation); A.R. Rumble, *The Dorset Lay Subsidy Roll of 1327*, Pubns. Dorset Rec. Soc., 6, 1980; E.A. Fry, *Dorset Lay Subsidy Roll, 1327*; F.J. Pope, *Dorset Lay Subsidy Roll, 1332-3*; E.A. Fry, *Dorset Lay Subsidy Roll, 1640-1* (transcripts in Dorset County Museum Library).

Essex   G. Rickword, 'Taxations of Colchester, 1296 and 1301', *EAS*, IX, 1906; R.C. Fowler, 'An early Essex subsidy', *EAS*, XIX, 1927.

Flintshire   Flintshire Subsidy Roll, 1592', *Arch. Camb.*, 6th series, II, 1902.

Gloucestershire   R. Bigland, *Historical, monumental and genealogical collections relative to the County of Gloucestershire* (2 vols. gives subsidy lists for each parish), 1786-92; T. Phillips, *The 1327 Taxation*, 1856 (privately printed; copy available at Gloucester City library.); J. Maclean, 'The Aid levied in Gloucestershire, 20 Edw. III, to knight the Black Prince', *BGAS*, X, 1886; E.A. Fuller, 'The tallage of 6 Edw. II (1312) and the Bristol rebellion', *BGAS*, XIX, 1895; P. Franklin, *The Taxpayers of Medieval Gloucestershire*, an analysis of the Lay Subsidy Roll of 1327 with a new edition of the text, Alan Sutton, 1993; Middle Hill Press, *Gloucestershire Subsidy Roll, 1 Edw. III (1327)*, n.d.

Hampshire   J.G. Nichols, 'Taxation of the tenth and fifteenth in Hampshire', *Collecteana Topographica et Genealogica*, I, 1834; C.R. Davey, *The Hampshire Lay Subsidy Rolls, 1586*, Hants. C.C. 1981, and Hants. Record Series, 4, 1981; D.F. Vick, *Central Hampshire Lay Subsidy assessments 1558-1603*, 1987; and: *East Hampshire Lay Subsidy assessments 1558-1603*, 1988.

Humberside   S.R. Rigby, *The Grimsby Lay Subsidy Roll of 1297*, Lincolnshire Historical and Archaeological Soc., no.14, 1979.

Kent   R.P. Coates, 'Valuation of the town of Dartford, 29 Edw. I', *AC*, IX, 1874; J. Greenstreet, 'Assessments in Kent for an Aid to knight the Black Prince, 20 Edw. III', *AC*, X, 1876; and: 'The Kent Contribution to a loan to the King, A.D. 1542', *AC*, XI, 1877 (transcript); and: 'Subsidy Roll for the Hundred of Faversham, 14 Henry VIII', *AC*, XII, 1878 (transcript); H.H. Drake, 'The Hundred of Blackheath' (gives extracts from Subsidy roll of 1 Edw. III), 1886; from: E. Hasted, *The History and Topographical Survey of Kent* (2nd ed. 12 vols.), 1801; H.A. Hanley and C.W. Chalklin, *The Kent Lay Subsidy of 1334-5 (with an index and map of medieval Kent)*, Kent Archaeological Soc. (*Documents illustrative of Medieval Kentish Society*), 18, 1964; F.A. Cazel and A.P. Cazel, *Lay Subsidy Rolls for Kent, 1225 and 1232*, Pubns. Pipe Roll Soc., n.s., 45, 1976-7.

Lancashire   J.A.C. Vincent, *Lancashire Lay Subsidies*, LCRS, XXVII, 1893; J.P. Rylands, 'Exchequer Lay Subsidy Roll of the County of Lancaster, 1332', *LCRS Miscellanies*, II, 1896; J. Tait, *Taxation in Salford Hundred, 1524-1802*, Chetham Soc., 1924.

Leicestershire   W.G.D. Fletcher, 'The earliest Leicestershire Lay Subsidy Roll, 1327', *AASRP*, XIX, 1888, and XX, 1889; A.B. Clarke, 'Melton Mowbray Lay Subsidy, 1543', *LeAS*, XVIII, 1935; W.G. Hoskins, 'Wigston Magna lay subsidies', *LeAS*, XX, 1939; J.W.O. Wilshere, 'Appendix of Tax Returns, 1327-1666', *Parish Register Transcripts of Kirby Muxloe*, Kirby Muxloe, 1966.

London and Middlesex   J.C.L. Stahlschmidt, 'Lay Subsidy, London 1411-12', *Arch. J.*, XLIV, 1887; M.

Curtis, 'London Lay Subsidy for 1332', in *Finance and Trade under Edward III* (ed. G. Unwin), Pubns. Univ. Manchester, Hist. Series 32, 1918; E. Ekwall, *Two early London Subsidy Rolls* (1292 and 1319), 1951.

Merioneth B. Owen, 'A Merioneth Subsidy Roll, 1599', *J. Mer. Hist. Soc.*, II, 1953-6.

Montgomery W.A. Griffith, 'Lay Subsidy Roll for the Hundreds of Deythur [*sic*] etc.', *Powys Land Club (Montgomeryshire Collections)*, 38, 1918.

Norfolk G.H. Dashwood, 'Subsidy roll in the possession of Lynn Regis' (3 Edw. I), *Norf. Arch.*, I, 1847; W. Rye, *Some Rough Materials for a History for the Hundred of North Erpingham* (3 parts; part II includes subsidy rolls of 1, 6 and 18 Edw. III and 8 Edw. IV), Norwich, 1883-9; E.D. Stone, 'The Lay Subsidy of 1581' (Hundreds of Depwadem, South Greenhoe, Henstead, Mitford and Shropham), *Norf. Rec. Soc.*, XVII, 1944.

Northamptonshire J. Wake and J.E. Morris, *Musters Subsidies, etc. 1586-1623*, Northants Rec. Soc. Pub., III, 1926; The County Record Office holds 'a few subsidy rolls for various places' in manuscript form, also copies of subsidy rolls held at the Public Record Office for the period 1523-46. They are fairly complete for the county and the references are Microfilms 154-156.

Northumberland F. Bradshaw, 'Lay subsidy roll of 1296', *Arch. Aeliana*, 3rd series, XIII, 1916; C.M. Fraser, *The Northumberland Lay Subsidy Roll of 1296*, Soc. Ant. N.-on-T. Rec. Sers., I, 1968.

Nottinghamshire Original Subsidy Rolls occur among MSS. in the Savile and Neville Collections at C.R.O.

Oxfordshire J.E.T. Rogers, *Oxford City Documents, 1268-1665* (gives a calendar of subsidies 1312-1469), OHS, 1891; H.E. Salter, *Surveys and Tokens, 1543-1667*, OHS, 1923; M.D. Lobel, *The History of Dean and Chalford* (has subsidy returns for 1316 and 1327), ORS, XVII, 1935; M.M.B. Weinstock, *Hearth Tax Returns for Oxfordshire, 1665*, ORS, 1940.

Shropshire W.D.G. Fletcher, 'Poll-tax for the town and liberties of Shrewsbury, 1380', *SANHS*, 2nd series, II, 1890, and V, 1893; and: *The Shropshire Lay Subsidy Roll of 1327*, Oswestry, 1907; J.L. Hobbs, 'A Shrewsbury Subsidy Roll, 1445-6', *ShAS*, LIII, 1949-50; D. and R. Cromarty, *The wealth of Shrewsbury in the early 14th century*, ShANHS, 1993.

Somersetshire F.H. Dickinson, *Lay Subsidy Roll for 1327*, Som. Rec. Soc., 1889; E. Green, 'A Bath Poll-tax, 2 Ric. II'; and: 'Bath Lay subsidies, Hen. IV-Hen. VIII', *Bath Nat. Hist. & Ant. Field Club*, VI, 1889; F. Hancock, *Minehead in the County of Somerset* (has subsidy rolls 1-6 Edw. III), Taunton, 1903; E. Dwelly, *Directory of Somerset*, in *Dwelly's National Records*, Fleet, Hampshire, 1929; 1931; 1932 (extracts, transcripts, from various Rolls); Original Rolls for certain hundreds can be seen at the C.R.O.

Staffordshire Ed. Hon. G. Wrottesley, *Exchequer Subsidy Rolls, 1327*, Wm. Salt Arch. Soc., 1880; Ed. Hon. G. Wrottesley, *Subsidy Rolls, 1332-3*, Wm. Salt Arch. Soc., 1889; W.K. Boyd, 'Poll-tax of A.D. 1379-81 for the Hundreds of Offlow and Cuttlestone', *Wm. Salt Arch. Soc. Colls.*, xvii, 1896; S.A.H. Burne, *Subsidy Roll, 1640*, Staffs Rec. Soc., 1942.

Suffolk E. Powell, 'Transcripts of all poll-tax lists of 1381 which remain in the Record Office for the Hundreds of Thingo and Lackford', *R. Hist. Soc.*, n.s., VIII, 1894; and: *The Rising in East Anglia in 1381* (Appendix gives Suffolk poll-tax lists), Cambridge, 1896; H.A. Hervey Sydenham, 'Suffolk in 1327' (Subsidy), no.IX, II, *Suffolk Green Books*, Booth, Woodbridge, 1906; and: 'Suffolk in 1568' (Subsidy), no.XII, *Suffolk Green Books*, Booth, Woodbridge, 1909 (with a map); and: 'Suffolk in 1524' (Subsidy), no.X, *Suffolk Green Books*, Booth, Woodbridge, 1910 (with a map); C.H.E. White, *Great Domesday Book of Ipswich, Liber Sextus* (contains subsidy of 32 Hen. VI and a subsidy from Ipswich 1282).

Surrey J.F. Willard and H.C. Johnson, *Surrey Taxation Returns, 1332-1623*, SurRS, 1923; C. Webb, *A Calendar of Lay Subsidies pertaining to Western Surrey 1585-1603*, West Surrey Family History Society, 1985.

Sussex W.H. Blaauw, 'Subsidy Roll of the rape of Lewes, 1296', *SAC*, II, 1849; and: 'Subsidy collected from the clergy of Sussex in 1380', *SAC*, V, 1852; W.H. Hudson, 'The Manor of Eastbourne' (transcribes a Subsidy roll of *c.*1300 on pp.193-6), *SAC*, XLIII, 1900; and: 'Assessment of the Hundreds of Sussex to the king's tax, 1334', *SAC*, I, 1907; T.H. Noyes, 'Roll of a subsidy levied 13 Hen. IV (1412/13)', *SAC*, I, 1907; W. Hudson, *The Three Earliest Subsidies in 1296, 1327 and 1332*, SRS, 1910; J. Cornwall, *Lay Subsidy Rolls for Sussex, 1524-5*, Pubns. SRS, LVI, 1956; L.F. Salzman, 'Early taxation in Sussex', *SAC*, XCVIII, 1960, and XCIX, 1961.

Warwickshire W.F. Carter, 'Index Locorum to the Subsidy Roll of Warwickshire, 1327, showing the Hundred and Leet or Liberty in which each place is situate', *Midland Rec. Soc.*, vols. 3-4, 1899-1902; W. Fowler Carter and F.C. Wellstood, *Lay Subsidy Rolls for Warwicks, 1332*, Dugdale Soc., 1926.

Wiltshire E.M. Thompson, 'Records of Wiltshire Parishes' (has translations of some subsidy rolls), *Wilts. N. & Q.*, I-VI, 1895-1909; G.D. Ramsey, *Two Sixteenth-Century Taxation Lists, 1547 and 1576*, WANHS, 10, 1954; reprinted Devizes, 1969; J.L. Kirby, 'Clerical poll-taxes in the dioceses of Salisbury, 1377-81', WANHS (Records Branch), *Collecteana*, XLI, 1956; B. Farr, *The Rolls of Highworth Hundred, 1275-1287*, WANHS (Records Branch), 21-22, 1965-6.

Yorkshire A good deal of E. Riding material on Lay Subsidies will be found in *YAS*, Record Series. A descriptive catalogue of the whole series was published in CVIII, 1946; R.H. Scaife, *Survey of the County of York (Kirkby's Inquest), 1290*, Surtees Soc., 1867; J. Stansfield, 'Two Subsidy Rolls of Skyrack, 10 Edw. III', *Thoresby Soc. Miscellanea*, I, 1891; W. Brown, *Yorkshire Lay Subsidies, 1297*, YAS, 1894; and: *Yorkshire Lay Subsidies, 1301*, YAS, 1897; J.C. Cox, 'A poll-tax return of the East Riding, with some account of the peasant revolt of 1381', *E. R. Ant. Soc.*, XV, 1909; E. Lloyd, 'Poll-tax returns for the East Riding, 1381', *YAS J.*, XX, 1909; J.W.R. Parker, 'Lay Subsidy Rolls, 1 Edw. III, N. Riding and York', *YAS, Rec. Sers.*, LXXIV, *Miscellanea*, II, 1929; J.N. Bartlett, 'Poll-tax returns for the East Riding, 1379', *E. R. Ant. Soc.*, XXX, 1953.

ORIGINAL DOCUMENTS TO BE FOUND AT:

The Public Record Office, Chancery Lane, London.

Worcestershire Record Office hold an original Roll for the County, the so-called 'Lechmere Roll' of *c.*1280, from which the facsimile has been taken. This was found in private hands, and deposited at the Record Office.

INQUISITIONES POST MORTEM AND MANORIAL EXTENTS

THE DOCUMENTS

Inquisitiones Post Mortem. These records extend over 400 years, from the 13th century to the 17th century. At the death of any landowner whose position might be of concern to the royal government, a writ was sent to the Sheriff or Escheator of the county. This demanded the following information:

(i)   What land did the deceased hold at the time of his death?
(ii)   Of whom was it held?
(iii)   What was its annual value?
(iv)   What services were due from it?
(v)   Who was the heir?
(vi)   What was his age?

The answers given decided whether the land in question owed any obligation to the Crown; if there was an heir, and he held of the Crown, he must pay 'relief' for his land; if the heir was under age, he became the ward of the Crown, and his estates were administered for him. Such records are primary sources for local history. They have been extensively used in tracing genealogy and manorial tenure, particularly by the compilers of the Victoria County Histories, but they also contain essential evidence of rents, sergeanties and services, and manorial customs, particularly on the smaller manors. When accompanied by Extents (q.v.), they can be usefully compared with the Domesday Survey to demonstrate changes in population, settlement and agrarian structure during the 250 years which followed the Conquest. During the period covered by these records, the consolidation of Crown lands, and the fragmentation of the great estates, are clearly shown; particularly, in Worcestershire, the changing fortunes of the great noble families of Beauchamp, Clare, Mortimer and de Somery. Incidental information is also revealed, as to the extent of the royal forests, the importance of the salt industry, the occupations and employment of villagers and townsmen, the development of village place-names and personal surnames, and lay ownership of Church patronage. Most important of all is the information gained from these Inquisitions, and particularly from the extents, about the rise and prospering of the minor gentry, such as the Corbett family, and the structure of their estates.

Manorial Extents.[10] The Inquisition Post Mortem often includes a full description, or 'extent', of the manors of the deceased. The document illustrated (Plate VII) is an extent of the manor of Chaddesley Corbett, made at the death of Roger Corbett, in 1290. (Note the opening words, 'Extenta manerii . . .', from which this type of document takes its name.) This is the usual form of a medieval survey of manorial property and rights. Its purpose was to record the extent of a lord's lands, perquisites and income, and the obligations and services of his tenants. The information was collected by means of the verbal testimony of local witnesses, and is not a 'survey', in the modern sense of the measuring and mapping of land. (See later, more visual, manorial surveys, pp.102-3.) The information returned, as shown in the illustrated extent of Chaddesley Corbett, includes the acreage of the demesne, often with details of its cropping, rotation, and amount of seed required, and its yield in different kinds of crops. To this is added the acreages and values of the meadow-land, pasture, gardens, mills, woodland and dovecotes of the demesne. The customs of the manor are given, including the rate of pannage for swine, and details of commons, the value of aids, common fines, tolls and the value of the perquisites of the lord's court. This is usually followed by full details of the tenants of the manor, and their landholdings, classified in groups, from knights' fees and free tenants, to 'consuetudinarii', 'Monday-men', 'cotlanders', 'enchlonders' and many more whose names vary in different regions. The amount and nature of each man's rents and services are given, and there is usually a fair amount of detail regarding the conditions, frequency and duration of such labour, with special definitions of the conditions of 'bedrips' and 'boon-works'. The value of all the works and customs is recorded, totalled and summarised, with additional information on the advowson of the Church.

Thus, whilst the bare, rather formal, legal evidence of the Inquisition Post Mortem is invaluable to the genealogist, the extents are far more interesting to the local historian. Manor court rolls (p.48) offer us details of the working lives and activities of the living people of the manor, the extents provide us with the essential topographical and statistical detail as the backcloth of the scene. For purposes of first-hand study, these are the most difficult documents of the whole series given here. As the chosen example shows, the Inquisitions include all the typical difficulties of the other medieval records—the minute script, the extreme contraction of words, and the language of medieval Latin; also involved are legal and technical complications which can only be understood by a student with an adequate knowledge of feudalism. Unfortunately, most of the printed collections of Inquisitiones Post Mortem appear in calendar form, that is, they usually give only a précis of each document's contents, and the significant facts, names and dates. On the other hand, local publications usually quote extents in fairly full detail; the P.R.O. Calendar is very easy to consult, with each county clearly indicated in the

---

[10] *Extenta Manerii* (1275), Statutes of the Realm, 1.242.

TRANSCRIPT

1 … Extenta Manerii de chadesley facta per preceptum domini Regis die Mercurii in festo Translacionis sancti Wolstani Anno regni regis Edwardi xviijᵒ

2 … Coram Reginaldo le Portr vicecomite Wygorniensis per Mandatum Malcolmy de Harleg' Escaetoris domini Regis citra Trentam ad hoc

3 … assignato per sacramentum Stephani de Bosco Rogeri le Tayllur Henrici de Wunterfold' Thome de Stone Thome de Hetheye Johannis de Swa—

4 … necote Henrici le Tayllur Roberti de la Bache Simonis Ore Roberti de la More Johannis de Twenewode et Thome de Wodeham

5 … Jurati qui dicunt super sacramentum suum quod Rogerus Corbet nichil tenuit de Rege in Comitatu Wygorniensis. Dicunt etiam quod idem Rogerus Corbet

6 … tenuit Manerium de Chadelsey de Comite Glouceastrie et Ada mater dicti Rogeri dotata est de tercia parte eiusdem Manerii, ita quod

7 … idem Rogerus non obiit seysitus nisi de duabus partibus eiusdem Manerii que quidem due partes extendentur ut patet inferius. videlicet

8 … quod est ibi quoddam capitale Mesuagium cum gardenis et curtilagiis quod valet per annum x.s.salua sustenacione domorum. Dicunt etiam quod sunt

9 … ibi quatuor vinaria videlicet duo parua et duo maiora que valent per annum. xxvjs'. Dicunt etiam quod sunt ibit duo molendina aquatica

10 … cum suis stangnis que valent per annum.xxvj s'. viijd'. si sustineantur Dicunt etiam quod sunt ibi tres carucate terre in dominico, quarum.

11 … quelibet carucata terre continet C acras et valet quelibet acra per annum iiij.d'. Summa cuiuslibet caracute xls' et sic tota terra in dominico.

(1) These names appear in the Chaddesley Lay Subsidy Roll of ten years before (p.45).
(2) Two of the three mills of Domesday (p.23, line 6).
(3) See Domesday extract, p.23; 'In demesne there are three ploughs …'.
(4) I am idebted to Professor Rodney Hilton for enlightening me about the medieval 'long Hundred' which was, in fact, 120.

TRANSLATION

(See J.W. Willis-Bund, *Inquisitiones Post Mortem for Worcestershire*, Worcs. Hist. Soc., 1894 and 1909, no.xx, p.30.)

1 … The extent of the Manor of Chaddesley, made by the King's command on Wednesday the feast of St Wulfstan, in the 18th year of the reign of King Edward

2 … before Reginald Porter Sheriff of Worcester; by the command of Malcolm de Harlega, King's Escheator this side Trent

3 … by the oath of Stephen de Bosco (1), Roger le Tayllur (1), Henry de Wynterfold' Thomas de Stone, Thomas de Hetheye, John de Swa—

4 … necote, Henry le Tayllur, Robert de la Bache, Simon Ore (1), Robert de la More (1), John de Twenwode and Thomas de Wodeham

5 … The jury who say upon their oath that Roger Corbet held nothing of the King in the County of Worcester. They say also that the same Roger Corbet

6 … held the Manor of Chadesley of the Earl of Gloucester, and that Ada, the said Roger's mother holds, as dower, one third part of the same Manor, so that

7 … the said Roger died seised of only two parts of the whole Manor, which said two parts are described below, as follows

8 … There is there a capital messuage, with gardens and curtilages, worth yearly 10s, excluding maintenance of the houses. They say also that there are

9 … there four vineyards, that is two small and two larger, which are worth 26s. 8d. a year. They say also that there are two water-mills (2)

10 … with their pools which are worth 26s. 8d. a year if they are kept in repair. They say that there are three carucates of land (3) in demsne of which

11 … each carucate contains a hundred acres (4), each acre worth 4d. a year. Sum of each carucate 40s. Thus the total land in demesne

Plate VII. Extent of the Manor of Chaddesley which accompanies the Inquisition Post Mortem on Roger Corbett, 1290. (Public Record Office, MS. C. 133/56/25. mem. vi.) *Crown Copyright*. Actual size: 23 × 18cm

12 … is worth £6 per annum. They say that there are five acres of meadow in demesne fit for mowing, of which each acre is worth 2s. per annum. Sum. 10s.

13 … There is also a several pasture worth 21s. 4d. per annum, also a common pasture which

14 … is worth 2s. a year. They say also that there are two woods (5) which are within the bounds of the forest, from which nothing can be taken except by view of the forester

15 … except so much pannage as is worth half a mark a year. there are also free tenants there who, in all issues concerning their lands

16 … pay fixed rents of £4 14s. 9d. a year, also one free tenant who pays one pund of pepper a year.

17 … worth 10d. and a pound of cummin worth 1d. and four white cocks worth ½d. each. Sum of all the rent of the free tenants £4 15s. 10d.

18 … They say that there are 34 virgates (6) of land in villenage, each of which pays a fixed rent of 5s. a year. Sum—£8 10s.

19 … They say that the tallage of the villeins is worth 60s. a year and each virgate of the villeins' land owes three ploughing services a year, which is worth

20 … 2½d. per service. Sum of the ploughing service of each virgate 7½d. Sum of all the ploughing service 21s. 3d. They say that each of the villeins' virgates must

21 … reap each year from the Gules of August (7) until the lord shall have finished reaping, that is four days a week, and that is worth, the whole August's work from each virgate

22 … 2s. They say that each virgate of land owes carrying service twice a year to the bridge at Tewkesbury, and must fetch the lord's food within the County

23 … when it shall be necessary at the will of the lord. The carrying service is worth 7d. a year from each virgate. Sum—17s. They say that each virgate

24 … of land ought to give the lord two hens at Christmas, worth 2d. Sum—5s. 8d. In return for these hens, they will have from the demsne heather, bracken

25 … and dead wood within reason as uits them. They say that each virgate will give yearly a fixed payment which is called 'Grastak' 1d. Sum, 2s. 10d. Sum of the whole villenage, £17 4s. 9d.

(5) Domesday has '2 leagues of woodland and another wood of one league' (p.23).

12 … valet per annum vj.li'. Dicunt etiam quod sunt ibi quinque acrae prati falcabilis in dominico quorum quelibet acra valet per annum ij.s'. Summa: xs'.

13 … Dicunt etiam quod est ibi quedam pastura seperabilis que valet per annum. xxjs' iiij.d. Dicunt etiam quod est ibidem quedam pastura communis que

14 … valet per annum ijs'. Dicunt etiam quod sunt ibi duo Bosci infra metas foreste de quibus nichil possunt (sic) precipere nisi per visum forestarij

15 … nisi tantum pannagium quod valet per annum dimidiam marcam. Dicunt etiam quod sunt ibi liberi tenentes qui in omnibus exitibus terras eorum contingentibus

16 … de certo Reddunt per annum iiij.li.xiiij.s' ix.d' et preterea est ibi quidem liber tenens qui Reddit per annum unam libram piperis

17 … precii x.d'. et I libram cimini precii j.d' eet quatuos Wytecoci precii cuiuslibet obolum. Summa tocius Redditus liberorum tenencium iiij li.xv.s'. x.h'

18 … Dicunt etiam quod sunt ibi in villengaio xxxiiij. virgate terre quearum qualibet (sic) virgata terre Reddit per annum v.s' de certo Summa—viiij.li.xs'

19 … Dicunt etiam quod tallagium eorundem villanorum valet per annum lxs' et qualibet virgata terre eorundem villanorum debet tres arruras per annum et vale

20 … quelibet arrura ij.d' oboum. Summa arrure cuiuslibet virgate per annum. vij.d' ob Summa tocius arrure xxjs'. iij.d' Dicunt etiam quod qualibet (sic) virgate terre earundem (sic) villanorum.

21 … debet metere per annum a Gula Agusti (sic) vsque dominus permessuerit videlicet qualibet septimana per quatuor dies et valet operacio per totum Agustum cuiuslibet virgate terre ij.s'. Dicunt etiam quod quelibet virgate terre debet bis per annum facere aueragium ad pontem de Twyysbur' et querere excam domini infra Comitatum

22 … quando necesse fuerit ad voluntatem domini et valet aueracio cuiuslibet virgate terre per annum vj.d' Summa—xvij.s'. Dicunt etiam quod qualibet (sic) virgata

23 … terre debet dare domino duas gallinas ad Natalem Domini, precii ij.d'. Summa v.s'.vij.d' Et pro illis gallinas habebunt de dominico domini bruer(iam) feuger(iam)

24 … et mortuam boscam racionabilem prout eis sompetit. Dicunt etiam quod qualibet (sic) virgata terre dabit per annum pro quodam certo qui vocatur

25 … Grastak jd. Summa ij.s' x.d' Summa tocius villenagii— xvij.li.iiij.s'. ix.d'

27 ... They also say that of the 34 virgates, at the lord's will 8 virgates must work each week annually, except

28 ... three, that is (the weeks) of Christmas, Easter and Pentecost, for two days and they ought to be allowed at the end of the year one half their fixed rent, i.e., 2s. 6d.

29 ... as long as they perform these works.

30 ... They say that there are also 12 cottars whereof four shall render each year in lieu of all services 11s. 6d. and 8 others pay 8s. a year, that is

31 ... 12d. each, and must perform other lesser services, of mending the lady's linen, value of each such service 6d. Sum: 4s.

32 ... Thus, the sume of the total of cottars is 23s. 6d. (8)

27 ... Preterea intelligendum est quod de illis xxxiij. virgatis terre ad voluntatem domini debent octo virgate terre operari quelibet septimane per annum exceptis

28 ... tribus videlicet Natalis Domini, Pasche et Pentecostis per duos dies et debent eos allocari in fine anni.ii.s. vjd' videlicet medietatem certi redditus illorum

29 ... si faciunt illas operaciones.

30 ... Dicunt etiam sunt ibi xii Cotarii quorum quatuor reddent per annum pro omnibus ceruisiis xjs vjd' Et octo alii redunt per annum siij.s' videlicet

31 ... quibus corum xijd. et debent facere per annum alia minuta ceruisie ad linum domine Reparandum videlicet quelibet operacio vj.d' Summa iiijs'

32 ... et sic-Summa totalis cotarium xxiij.s' vj.d'

(8) The total value of the extent of the Manor, excluding the church, appears to be £32 6s. 9d. With the church, the total value of the Manor is £48 13s. 5d., more than four times the Domesday value of £12 (p.23, line 9).

margin in each case, and reference is made to extents, wherever given, though not in detail. Only the most advanced student can be expected to go beyond the printed calendars for information from his country's Inquisitions; fortunately, this is rarely necessary.

WORCESTERSHIRE EXTENTS

The following list gives a summary of those Worcestershire Inquisitions (I.p.m.) which include manorial extents, arranged chronologically. Down to 1327, the information is taken from J.W. Willis-Bund (*op. cit.*), to which work the initial page numbers refer. Worcestershire Inquisitions for the reign of Edward III have not been separately calendared; the extents for that reign are found in the 'Calendar of I.p.m. preserved at the P.R.O.', vols.VII-XIV, to which the later volume and page numbers refer.

I.9.	Norton near Evesham
	(I.p.m. Hugh Gutmund, 1266, 50 Hen. III, no.5)
I.2.	Wick
	(I.p.m. William Fitz Hamon, 1246, 29 Hen. III, no.55)
I.15-16.	Tatlinton, Edmundscote, Derlingscote and Hopwood
	(I.p.m. Robert Walraund, 1273, 1 Edw. I, no.6)
I.16-17.	Dudley, Weoley and Cradley
	(I.p.m. Roger de Someri, 1273, 1 Edw. I, no.15)
I.19.	Shelsley Beauchamp
	(I.p.m. Thomas Fitz Oto, 1274, 2 Edw. I, no.15)
I.19-20.	Martley
	(I.p.m. John Despenser, 1275, 3 Edw. I, no.2)
I.21-2.	Wychbold, Cotheridge and Home
	(I.p.m. Hugh)
I.26-7.	Shelsley Beauchamp
	(I.p.m. Sir William de Monte Casino, 1286, 16 Edw. I, no.27)
I.30-2.	Chaddelsey Corbett
	(I.p.m. Roger Corbett, 1290, 18 Edw. I, no.8)
I.33-4.	Chaddesley Corbett, 1291, 19 Edw. I, no.8)
	(I.p.m. Ada Corbett, 1291, 18 Edw. I, no.8)
I.34-7.	Weoley Park, Dudley and Cradley
	(I.p.m. Roger de Someri, 1291, 19 Edw. I, no.14)
I.41-2.	Middleton
	(I.p.m Philip Marmion, 1292, 20 Edw. I, no.36)
I.43-5	Dudley, Kidderminster, Hanley William, Kill, Kyre, Hanley Child, and 'Bastwood'
	(I.p.m. Robert Burnel, Bishop of Bath, 1293, 21 Edw. I, no.50)
I.49-52.	Dudley, Kidderminster, Hanley William, Hanley Child, and Eastham
	(I.p.m. Philip Burnel, 1294, 22 Edw. I, no.45*a*)
I.54.	Rushock
	(I.p.m. Henry l'Estormi, 1296, 23 Edw. I, no.51)
I.55-6.	Hanley Castle
	(I.p.m. Gilbert, Earl of Gloucester, 1296, 24 Edw. I, no.107*b*, *c.*
I.56-7.	Bushley
	(I.p.m. Gilbert, Earl of Gloucester, 1296, 24 Edw. I, no.107*b*, *c.*
I.58-9.	Frankley
	(I.p.m. Emma de Wethamstede, 1298, 26 Edw. I, no.1)
I.59-62.	Salewarpe, Naunton Beauchamp, Cumberton
	(I.p.m. William Beauchamp, Earl of Warwick, 1298, 26 Edw. I, no.41)
I.63-5.	Stoulton, and Wadborough
	(I.p.m. William Beauchamp, Earl of Warwick, 1298, 26 Edw. I, no.41)

II.1-2.   Inkberrow
            (I.p.m. Earl of Pembroke, 1296, 24 Edw. I, no.56)
II.2-3.   Kidderminster
            (I.p.m. Maud de Beauchamp, 1301, 29 Edw. I, no.33)
II.5-6.   Inkberrow
            (I.p.m. Maud de Mortimer, 1301, 29 Edw. I, no.53)
II.9-11.   Wychbold, and Cotheridge
            (I.p.m. Hugh de Mortimer, 1304, 32 Edw. I, no.48)
II.11-14.   Bewdley and Inkberrow
            (I.p.m. Edmund de Mortimer, 1304, 32 Edw. I, no.63a)
II.14.   Daylsford
            (I.p.m. Miles de Hastings, 1305, 33 Edw. I, no.64)
II.15-20.   Kidderminster
            (I.p.m. John Biset, 1307, 35 Edw. I, no.43)
II.20-6.   Bushley and Hanley Castle
            (I.p.m. Joan, wife of Gilbert de Clare, 1307, 35 Edw. I, no.47)
II.28.   Inkberrow
            (I.p.m. Joan, Countess of Pembroke, 1307, I Edw. II, no.58)
II.31-2.   Cotheridge and Wychbold
            (I.p.m. Maud, wife of Hugh de Mortimer, 1308, 1 Edw. II, no.59b)
II.35-8.   Tatlington and Edmundscote
            (I.p.m. John Walrand, 1309, 2 Edw. II, no.80)
II.38-9.   Abberley
            (I.p.m. Robert de Tony, 1309, 3 Edw. II, no.33)
II.40-1.   Tatlington
            (I.p.m. Walter de Gloucester, 1311, 5 Edw. II, no.66)
II.42-4.   Severn Stoke, and Tenbury
            (I.p.m. Robert de Clifford, 1314, 8 Edw. II, no.62)
II.46-8.   Hanley and Bushley
            (I.p.m. Gilbert de Clare, 1315, 8 Edw. II, no.68)
II.53.   Suckley
            (I.p.m. Edmund Burnel, 1315, 9 Edw. II, no.67)
II.56-103. Acton Beauchamp, Pirton, Salwarpe, Sheriffs Lench, Abberley, Elmley Castle,
            Comberton, Naunton Beauchamp, Wadborough, Stoulton, Little Inkberrow, and
            Temple Lawerne
            (I.p.m. Guy de Beauchamp, Earl of Warwick, 1316, 9 Edw. II, no.71)
II.112-14. Dudley, Weoley and Cradley
            (I.p.m. John de Somery, 1322, 16 Edw. II, no.72)
II.119-21. Naunton Beauchamp, Wadborough
            (I.p.m. Alice, wife of Guy de Beauchamp, 1324, 18 Edw. II, no.82)
II.121-2.   Inkberrow
            (I.p.m. John de Hastings, 1325, 18 Edw. II, no.83)
II.122.   Habberley
            (I.p.m. Hugh Mostel, 1319, 12 Edw. II, no.79)
II.123.   North Piddle
            (I.p.m. Stephen de Segrave, 1326, 19 Edw. II, no.91)
VII.13.   Elmerigg (Elmbridge)
            (I.p.m. Roger de Elmerigg, 1327, I Edw. III, no.34)
VII.97.   La Berwe (Berrow)
            (I.p.m. John de la Berwe, 1329, Edw. III, no.106)
VII.320.   Clifton, Shelsley, Churchill
            (I.p.m. John de Wysham, 1333, 6. Edw. III, no.454)
VII.412.   Kidderminster
            (I.p.m. John Biset, 1334, 8 Edw. III, no.605)
VII.501.   Bewdley
            (I.p.m. Edmund and Margaret de Mortuo Mari, 1336, 10 Edw. III, no.711)
VII.65.   Abberley

	(I.p.m. William la Zousche, 1337, 11 Edw. III, no.112)
VIII.79.	Hanley Castle and Bushley
	(I.p.m. Eleanor, late wife of Hugh le Despenser, 1337, 11 Edw. III, no.132)
VIII.113.	Northfield at Weoley
	(I.p.m. Roger de Swynnerton, 1338, 12 Edw. III, no.180)
VIII.200.	Cotheridge, Wychbold and Home
	(I.p.m. Joan, late wife of Richard Talbot, of Richard's Castle, 1341, 14 Edw. III, no.276)
VIII.294.	Crownest (Crowneast Court, St John in Bedwardine)
	(I.p.m. Baldwin de Frevill, 1343, 17 Edw. III, no.445)
VIII.495.	Kidderminster, Upton Snodsbury and Wick
	(I.p.m. John de Hadlowe, 1346, 20 Edw. III, no.667)
IX.249.	Queenhill
	(I.p.m. Joan, late wife of John de Wryecote, 1349, 23 Edw. III, no.251)
IX.330.	Hanley Castle and Martley
	(I.p.m. Hugh le Despenser, 1349, 23 Edw. III, no.428)
X.141.	Cure Wyard (Kyre Magna)
	(I.p.m. Robert Wyard, 1354, 28 Edw. III, no.161)
X.281.	Witley, Sutton Sturmy (in Tenbury), Nether Sapy, Goldecote (Goldicote House, Alderminster)
	(I.p.m. Hugh de Cokeseye, 1356, 30 Edw. III, no.329)
X.403.	Dudley
	(I.p.m. John de Sutton, 1359, 33 Edw. III, no.516)
X.415.	Hanley Castle and Martley
	(I.p.m. Elizabeth, late wife of Hugh Despenser, 1359, 33 Edw. III, no.523)
XI.17.	King's Norton
	(I.p.m. Thomas Belne, 1361, 35 Edw. III, no.25)
XI.174.	Forvelde (Fairfield, Belbroughton)
	(I.p.m. John Somenour, 1361, 35 Edw. III, no.193)
XI.180.	Cotheridge, Wychbold, Home
	(I.p.m. Juliana, late wife of John Talbot, of Richard's Castle, 1361, 35 Edw. III, no.205)
XI.372.	Suckley
	(I.p.m. Alina, late wife of Edward Burnel, 1363, 37 Edw. III, no.489)
XII.145.	Fairfield
	(I.p.m. John de Sudleye, 1367, 41 Edw. III, no.166)
XII.302.	Mitton
	(I.p.m. Agnes, late wife of Thomas Bradestone, 1369, 43 Edw. III, 325)
XIII.118.	North Piddle
	(I.p.m. Walter de Mauny, Knight, 1372, 46 Edw. III, no.148)
XIV.9.	Mitton and Kelmesham
	(I.p.m. Thomas, son of Robert de Bradestone, 1374, 48 Edw. III, no.10)
XIV.37.	Grafton and Upton Warren
	(I.p.m. John de Hastang, 1374, 48 Edw. III, no.36)
XIV.218.	Upton on Severn, Bushley and Hanley
	(I.p.m. Edward le Despenser, knight, 1375, 49 Edw. III, no.209)
XIV.229.	Wychbold, Cotheridge and Home
	(I.p.m. John Talbot, of Richard's Castle, knight, 1375, 49 Edw. III, no. 213)
XIV.260.	Kidderminster
	(I.p.m. Denise, late wife of Hugh Cokeseye, 1376, 50 Edw. III, no.251)

There are important collections of extents other than those which are to be found in connection with I.p.m. at the Public Record Office. The Midland student, for example, should be familiar with the extents of the Bishop of Worcester's manors, in Gloucestershire, Worcestershire and Warwickshire, for the 12th and 13th centuries, particularly the years 1282 and 1299. These are printed in *The Red Book of Worcester*, published by the Worcestershire Historical Society, in four parts, 1934-50, editor Marjory Hollings. The information given, often in three consecutive surveys, beginning with Domesday, makes a series of valuable comparative studies. The manors for which extents appear are:

Alvechurch (Worcs), Bibury (Glos), Bishop's Cleeve (Glos), Blockley (Glos), Bradley (Worcs), Bredon (Worcs), Fladbury (Worcs), Hampton Lucy (War), Hanbury (Worcs), Hartlebury (Worcs), Hatton (War), Henbury (Glos), Hopwood (Worcs), Kempsey (Worcs), Lapworth (War), Northwick (Worcs), Old Stratford (War), Paxford (Glos), Ripple (Worcs), Throckmorton (Worcs), Tredington (Worcs), Wast Hills (Worcs), Whiteladies Aston (Worcs), Whitstones (Worcs), Wick Episcopi (Worcs), Withington (Glos).

For collections of printed extents in other counties, see the gazetteer of manor court rolls and other manorial records (pp.37-42).

FURTHER READING

M.C.B. Dawes, *Calendarium Inquisitionum post Mortem ... preserved in the PRO: 15: 1-7, Ric.II*, HMSO,1970; *16: 7-15, Ric II*, HMSO, 1974

E. Kerridge, 'The Manorial Survey as an Historical Source', *Amateur Historian*, 7, no.1, 1966

R.E. Latham, 'Hints on Interpreting the Public Records: III: Inquisitiones post Mortem', *Amateur Historian*, 1., no.3., 1953

M. McGuiness, 'Documents in the Public Record Office, 2: Inquisitiones post Mortem', *Amateur Historian*, 6, no.4, 1965.

HANDLIST

A list of Inquisitions printed by various County Historical and Records Societies is also given by Robert Somerville in *Handlist of Record Publications* (British Records Association, 1951, Sect. 5).

PRINTED EDITIONS FOR WORCESTERSHIRE

J.W. Willis Bund, *The Inquisitiones Post Mortem for Worcestershire*, Pt.1 (1242-1299); Pt.2 (1300-1326), Worcs. Hist. Soc., 1894, 1909, with a valuable introduction;

H.S.Grazebrook, *The Barons of Dudley*, William Salt Arch. Soc.,*Collections*, IX, part II, 1889; (has translations of manorial extents, temp.Edw.I);

M. Hollings, *The Red Book of Worcester*, Worcs. Hist. Soc.,1934, 1950.

SOME OTHER PRINTED EDITIONS OF INQUISITIONS AND EXTENTS

For a national Survey, consult *Calendar of I.P.M. preserved at the P.R.O.*, 14 vols. P.R.O. Texts and Calendars published in 1904-54. (See Government Publications, 'Record Publications', Sectional List no.24, H.M.S.O., 1958, for reference to these and other record publications in print.) (listed chronologically by publication date)

Bedfordshire   G.H. Fowler, *Calendar of I.p.m. 1250-71*, BHRS, 1920; and: *Calendar of I.p.m. 1272-86*, BHRS, 1937; S. Houfe, 'Hawnes in Lady Sophia Carteret's day', *Bedfordshire Magazine*, no.17, 1979; A. Jones, 'Caddington, Kensworth and Dunstable in 1297', *Econ. Hist. Rev.*, no.32, 1979.

Berkshire   S.R. Scargill-Bird, *Custumals of Battle Abbey* (includes manorial extents in Berkshire), Camden

Soc., 41, 1887; F.T. Wethered, *Lands and Tythes of Hurley Priory*, Reading, 1909; M. Biddle, 'The Abbot ·
of Abingdon and the tenants of Winkfield', *Medium Aevum*, XXVIII, 1959.

Brecon   J.W. Willis-Bund, *The Black Book of St David's* (including Latin transcript and translation of an
extent of lands in this county), Hon. Soc. Cymmrodorion Rec. Sers., V, 1902.

Buckinghamshire   G. Herbert Fowler, 'Extents of the royal manors of Aylesbury and Brill, *c*.1155', *Recs.
Bucks.*, XI, no.7, 1926.

Caernarvonshire   H. Ellis, *The Record of Caernarvon* (extents of Caernarvon and Anglesey in 1335 and
1353; extent of lands of see of Bangor 1399, of Prestoll Abbey in 1375 and of Merioneth in 1420),
Record Comm., 1838.

Cambridgeshire   T. Stapleton, *Chronicon Petroburgense* (Appendix of surveys of the Abbey's manors,
1125-8), Camden Soc., 47, 1849; E. Miller, *The Abbey and Bishopric of Ely: the Social History of an Ecclesiastical
Estate from the Tenth to the Fourteenth Century*, C.U.P., 1969; S. Evans, *The Medieval Estate of the Cathedral
Priory of Ely*, Dean and Chapter of Ely, 1973; E. King, *Peterborough Abbey, 1086-1319: A Study in the Land
Market*, C.U.P., 1973; C.P. Hall and J.R. Ravensdale, *Terrarium Cantabrigiae: The West Fields of Cambridge*,
Cambridge Antiquarian Records Society Publications, 13, 1976; J.W. Clark, *Liber Memorandum Ecclesie
de Bernewelle, 1296* (Barnwell: contains an extent of the lands of the priory).

Cardiganshire   J.W. Willis-Bund, *The Black Book of St David's* (including Latin transcript and translation
of an extent of lands in this county), Hon. Soc. Cymmrodorion Rec. Sers., V, 1902.

Carmarthenshire   J.W. Willis-Bund, *The Black Book of St David's* (including Latin transcript and translation
of an extent of lands in this county), Hon. Soc. Cymmrodorion Rec. Sers., V, 1902.

Cheshire   PRO: *Index to inquisitions etc. (Edw. III-Charles I) Counties of Chester and Flint*, Deputy Keeper's
Reports (Welsh Records), XXV, 1864; R. Stewart-Brown, *Cheshire I.p.m. 1603-60*, LCRS, 84,1934, 86, 1935,
91, 1938; J.H.E. Bennett and J.C. Dewhurst, 'Cheshire Quarter Sessions 1559-1760', *LCRS*, 94, 1940;
'Survey and rental of the Manor of Dunham Massey, AD 1348-49', *Altrincham Historical Society Journal*,
no.4, December 1992.

Cornwall & Devonshire   E. Alexander Fry, *Calendar of I.p.m. for Cornwall and Devon, 1216-1649*, DCRS,
1906; M. Tangye, 'Deodand in the Manor of Telridy', *Old Cornwall*, no.8, 1979; T.L. Stoate, *Cornwall
Manorial rentals and surveys*, 1988.

Denbighshire   P. Vinogradoff and F. Morgan, *Survey of the Honour of Denbigh*, 1, 1914; T.P. Ellis, *The First
Extent of the lordship of Bromfield and Yale, A.D. 1315*, Hon. Soc. Cymmrodorion Rec. Sers., XI, 1924.

Dorset   'Abstract of Inquisitions post mortem, temp. Hen. III, for Somerset and Dorset', *Collecteana Top.
& Gen.*, II, 1835; E.A. Fry, 'On the Inquisitions Post Mortem for Dorset, 1216-1484', *DNHAS*, XVII,
1896; and: 'On the Inquisitions Post Mortem for Dorset, 1485-1648', *DNHAS*, XX, 1899; and: 'I.p.m.
for Dorset', *Somerset & Dorset Notes & Queries,* VIII et seq. from 1903; C.S. Frey, 'Dorset Inquisitions
post mortem', *SDNQ*, XXII, 1937.

Durham   W. Greenwell, *Boldon Buke* (Survey, 1183, of the manorial services due to the Bishop of Durham,
as typified in the manor of Boldon) Surtees Soc., 1852, also edited by G.T. Lapsley in: *VCH: Durham*,
1, 1905; W. Greenwell, *Bishop Hatfield's Survey, 1377-82*, Surtees Soc., XXXII, 1857; and: *Feodarium Prioratus
Dunelmensis* (a survey of the estates of the priory of Durham, compiled in the fifteenth century),
Surtees Soc., LVIII, 1872; PRO: *Abstracts or transcripts of inquisitiones post mortem, 1318-1448*, Deputy Keeper's
Reports (Durham Records), XLIV, 1883 and XLV, 1884-5; D. Austin, *Boldon Book, Northumberland and
Durham*, in *Domesday Book,* Supp. Vol. 35, Phillimore, 1982.

Essex   S.R. Scargill-Bird, *Custumals of Battle Abbey* (includes manorial extents in Essex), Camden Soc.,
1887; W. Cunningham, 'Extenta Manerii de Borle (Borley), 1 Edw. II', in *Growth of English Industry*, 1,
1915; J.F. Nichols, 'The extent of Lawling, 1310', *EAS*, XX, 1930-3; and: 'Milton Hall manor: extent of
1309 and an inventory of 1278', *Southend-on-Sea & District Ant. & Hist. Soc.*, II, 1934; J.L. Fisher, 'The
Harlow Cartulary' (rentals and extents), *EAS*, n.s., XXII, 1940; and: 'The Ledger Book of St John's
Abbey, Colchester' (calendar includes manorial extents), *EAS*, n.s., XXIV, 1951.

Flintshire   PRO: *Index to inquisitions etc. (Edw. III-Charles I) Counties of Chester and Flint*, Deputy Keeper's
Reports (Welsh Records), XXV, 1864; A. Jones, 'A fifteenth century document of Rhuddlan' (an extent
or list of burgesses and tenements), *Flints. Hist. Soc. Pubns.*, V, *Journal*, 1914-5.

Glamorgan   G.F. Clark, *Cartae et Alia Munimenta quae ad Dominium de Glamorgancia Pertinent* (6 vols.),
Cardiff, 1910.

Gloucestershire   W.H. Hart, *Historia et Cartularium Monasterii S. Petri Gloucestriae*, (3 vols.) Rolls Series,

1863-7 (III has manorial extents, 1265-7); H.T. Ellacombe, *History of the Parish of Bitton* (has I.p.m.), 1881-3; W.P.W. Phillimore and G.S. Fry, *I.p.m. 1236-1413; 1625-42*, Index Soc., 1891-1914.

Hampshire   F.G. Baigent, 'Inquests post mortem, charters etc., 1267-1707', *Collections ... Relating to the Hundred and Manor of Crondal, Pt. 1*, Hants. Rec. Soc., 3, 1891; R.H. D'Elboux, *Surveys of the manors of Robertsbridge, Sussex and Michelmarsh, Hampshire* (and of the demesne lands of Halden in Rolvenden, Kent, 1567-70), *SRS*, XLVII, 1944; L.A. Burgess, P.D.A. Harvey and A.D. Saunders, *The Southampton Terrier of 1454*, Historical Manuscripts Commission, Southampton Records Series, no.15, H.M.S.O., 1976; S.R. Scargill-Bird, *Custumals of Battle Abbey* (includes manorial extents in Hampshire).

Hertfordshire   R. Clutterbuck, *The History and Antiquities of the County of Hertford* (3 vols.), 1815-27, III's Appendix has surveys of the manors of Hatfield, Totteridge, Stevenage, Little Hadham and Kelshall, 1277; A.E. Levett, 'Studies in the manorial history of St Alban's Abbey' (with an Appendix of extent of Codicote, 1332), in: *Studies in Manorial History*, 1938.

Huntingdonshire   W.H. Hart and P.A. Lyons, *Cartularium Monasterii de Rameseia* (3 vols.), Rolls Series, 1884-93; C.G. Boxall, *Early Records of the Duke of Manchester's English Manorial Estates*, 1892 (includes St Ives, Houghton, Stukeley, etc. from 1086-1628),.

Kent   J. Greenstreet, 'Inquisitions post mortem, 1235-71', *AC*, II, 1859; III, 1860; IV, 1861; V, 1862-3; VI, 1864-5; and: 'Holders of knights' fees in Kent at the knighting of the king's eldest son, 38 Hen. III', *AC*, XII, 1878; H.E. Muhlfeld, *A Survey of the Manor of Wye*, Columbia Univ. Studies, N.Y., 1933; R.H. D'Elboux, *Surveys of the manors of Robertsbridge, Sussex and Michelmarsh, Hampshire* (and of the demesne lands of Halden in Rolvenden, Kent, 1567-70), *SRS*, XLVII, 1944; F.R.H. du Boulay, 'The Assembly of an Estate: Knole in Sevenoaks, 1275-1525', *AC*, no.89, 1974; N.R. Goose, 'Wage Labour in a Kentish Manor: Meopham, 1307-75', *AC*, no.92, 1976; S.R. Scargill-Bird, *Custumals of Battle Abbey* (includes manorial extents in Kent).

Lancashire   *Ducatus Lancastriae Calendarium Inquisitionum Post Mortem, Edw. I - Charles I*, Rec. Comm., 1823; J. Harland, *Mamecestre; Being chapters from the early history of the barony, the lordship or manor etc.* (3 vols., including extents of the manor in 1282, 1320 and 1322, Chetham Soc., LIII, LVI, LVIII, 1861-2; J. Harland, *Three Lancashire Documents of the fourteenth century* (De Lacy I.p.m. of 1311), Chetham Soc., 74, 1868; W. Langton, *Abstracts of Lancashire I.p.m.*, Chetham Soc., XCX, XCIX, 1875, 1876 (translations); PRO: *Calendar of Inquisitions post Mortem (Lancashire) Ric. II - Eliz.*, Deputy Keeper's Reports, XXXIX, 1878; W.D. Selby, *Lancashire and Cheshire Records preserved in the Public Record Office* (2 vols., including I.p.m.), LCRS, VII-VIII, 1882-3; E. Stokes, 'Calendar of the Duchy of Lancaster inquisitions post mortem, Edw. I - Hen. VIII', *Gen. Mag.*, II, 1899; III, 1900; IV, 1901; VI, 1903; W. Farrer, *Lancashire Inquests, Extents and Feudal Aids (1205-1355)*, LCRS (Pt. I: 1205-1307; Pt. II: 1310-33; Pt. III: 1333-55), 1903-15.

Leicestershire   W.G.D. Fletcher, 'Notes on Leicestershire Inquisitions Post Mortem', *Leics. Arch. & Archaeol. Soc.*, 6, 1884; W.G.D. Fletcher, A.H. Thompson and G.F. Farnham, 'Some unpublished documents relating to Leicestershire' (including I.p.m.), *AASRP*, XXIII, 1895.

Lincolnshire   T. Allen, *The History of the County of Lincoln* (with an extent of Boston in 1279), 1, 1833-4; W.O. Massingberd, 'Survey of the manor of Stow, 1283', *AASRP*, XXIX, 1898; and: 'Early Lincolnshire Inquisitions post Mortem (1241-82)', *AASRP*, XXV, 1900; N. Neilson, 'A Terrier of Fleet, Lincs. (1316)' and A.Ballard, 'An 11th century inquistion of St Augustine's Canterbury', *Brit. Academy* (Records of Social & Economic History), IV, 1920.

London and Middlesex   S.J. Madge and E.A. Fry, *Abstracts of Inquisitiones post Mortem for the City of London returned into the Court of Chancery*, I, 1485-1560; II, 1561-77; III, 1577-1603; W.H. Hale, *The Domesday of St Paul's of the year 1222* (contains a survey of 1222, rental of 1240, etc.), Camden Soc., o.s., 1858; W.P.W. Phillimore, *Inquisitiones Post Mortem for Middlesex and London, 1485-1645*, Clark, 1890; British Record Soc., Index Library, XXVI and XXXVI, 1896-1908; N.G. Brett-James, 'Some extents and surveys of Hendon' (with Latin transcript of a 1321 survey and the English version of the same, made in 1606), *LMAS*, n.s., VI, 1936; and: 'Extents and surveys of Hendon', *LMAS*, n.s., VII, 1937; G.D. Denoon and T. Roberts, 'The extent of Edgware, 1277', *LMAS*, n.s., VII, 1937.

Montgomery   T.P. Ellis, 'The Powys inquisitions, 1293-1311', *Powys-Land Club Collections*, XLI, 1930; W.A. Griffith, 'Lay Subsidy Rolls for the Hundreds of Deythur and Pool, 39 Elizabeth and 3 James I, and extracts from Harleian Mss. re. inquisition post mortem', *Powys-Land Club Collections*, XXXVIII, 19—.

Norfolk   G.A. Carthew, *The Hundred of Launditch and deanery of Brisley* (I.p.m. for Gressenhall), 1, Norwich, 1877-9; W.D. Selby, *Norfolk Records* (Index of Norfolk I.p.m.), II, 1886-92; W. Hudson, 'Three manorial extents of the thirteenth century' (translations of the extents of Bradcar in Shropham, Banham in Norfolk and Wykes in Bardwell, Suffolk, temp. Edw. I), *Norf. Arch.*, XIV, 1899; and: 'Traces of primitive agricultural organization as suggested by a survey of the manor of Martham, Norfolk, 1101-1292', *R. Hist. Soc.*, I, 1918.

Northamptonshire   T. Stapleton, *Chronicon Petroburgense* (Appendix of manorial surveys, 1125-8), Camden Soc., 47, 1849; J. Lister, 'Chapter House Records' (translations of several Northamptonshire extents of 1341), *Thoresby Soc.*, XXXIII, *Miscellanea*, X, 1935.

Northumberland   W. Greenwell, *Boldon Buke* (Survey, 1183 of the manorial services due to the Bishop of Durham, as typified in the manor of Boldon), Surtees Soc., 1852; Also edited by G.T. Lapsley in: *VCH: Durham*, I, 1905; M.T. Martin, 'Index to later Northumbrian inquisitions post mortem' (15 Hen. VIII - 21 Charles I) *Soc. Ant. N.-on-T.*, 3rd series, II, 1904; D Austin, 'Boldon Book, Northumberland and Durham', in *Domesday Book*, supplementary 35, Phillimore, 1982.

Nottinghamshire   W.P.W. Phillimore, *Abstracts of I.p.m. relating to Notts, 1485-1507*, 5 parts, Thoroton Soc., III, 1898-1905; W.P.W. Phillimore and J. Standish, *Abstract of Nottinghamshire I.p.m., 1242-1321 and 1485-1546* (2 vols.), Nottingham, 1898-1914;

  Various papers published as part of TSRS: Rev. J. Standish, *Abstracts of Inquisitiones Post Mortem relating to Notts 1279-1321*, VII, 1914; T.M. Blagg, *Abstracts of Inquisitiones Post Mortem relating to Notts, 1321-50*, in 3 parts, VI, 1937-9; and: 'An Extent of Langar and Barnstone, *c.*1340', *Miscellany of Nottinghamshire Records*, XI, 1945; V.W. Walker, 'An extent of Upton, 1431', *Second Miscellany of Nottinghamshire Records*, XI, 1951; K.S.S. Train, *Abstracts of I.p.m. relating to Notts, 1350-88; 1388-1403*, 2 parts, XII, 1948, 1952; M.W. Barley, *Documents relating to the Manor and Soke of Newark-on-Trent* (including surveys of 1225-31 and 1348-9), XVI, 1956; M.A. Renshaw, *I.p.m. relating to Notts, 1437-85*, XVII, 1956 (transcripts, with index);

  There are original documents at Nottinghamshire Archives, in the Savile, Craven-Smith-Milnes and Portland Collections.

Oxfordshire   A. Ballard, 'Three surveys of Bladon' (Domesday, 1229 and 1606), *Ox. Arch. Soc. Reports*, LVI, 1910; H. Salter, 'Oxfordshire Surveys of 1387', *Ox. Arch. Soc. Reports*, LVI, 1910; D.C. Douglas, 'Some early surveys of the abbey of Abingdon', *EHR*, XLIV, 1929; S.R. Scargill-Bird, *Custumals of Battle Abbey* (includes manorial extents in Oxfordshire).

Pembrokeshire   J.W. Willis-Bund, *The Black Book of St David's* (including Latin transcript and translation of an extent of lands in this county), Hon. Soc. Cymmrodorion Rec. Sers., V, 1902.

Shropshire   W.K. Boyd, 'Shropshire Inquisitions post mortem', 1254-1383, *ShANHS*, 2nd series, XI, 1899; and: 'Extent of the manor of Welch Hampton', *ShANHS*, 2nd series, XI, 1899; and: 'Extent of the manor of Cheswardine and a moiety of the manor of Childs Ercall', *ShANHS*, 3rd series, VIII, 1908; W.G.D. Fletcher, *Shropshire I.p.m.: Henry III-Charles I, 1245-1645*, ShAS, 10, 1926; W.J. Slack, 'The Condover Extents, 1283-1580', *ShAS*, L, 1939-40; and: *The Lordship of Oswestry, 1393-1607*, ShAS, 1952.

Somersetshire   'Abstract of Inquisitions post mortem, temp. Hen. III, for Somerset and Dorset', *Collecteana Top. & Gen.*, II, 1835; J.E. Jackson, *Liber Henrici de Solacio, Abbatis Glastonienis (Rental of 1189)*, Roxburghe Club, 1882; E.A. Fry, 'On the I.p.m. for Somerset from temp. Henry III to Richard II (1216-1485)', *SANHS*, XLIV, Pt.2, 1898 (index of names); and: 'On the I.p.m. for Somerset from Henry VII to Charles I (1485-1649)', *SANHS*, XLVII, Pt.2, 1901.

Staffordshire   Col. Wedgwood, *I.p.m. of the Audleys, 1273-1308*, Wm. Salt Arch. Soc., 1908; and: *Inquisitiones Post Mortem, 1223-1327*, Wm. Salt Arch. Soc., 1911 (translations); C.G.O. Bridgeman, 'The Burton Abbey twelfth century surveys', *Wm. Salt Arch. Soc. Collections*, 3rd series, XLI, 1916 (1918); The P.R.O. Calendars of I.p.m. from 1216-1374, and 1485-1509 are also available for reference at the Wm. Salt Library.

Suffolk   H. Pigot, 'Extenta manerii de Hadleghe, 1305', *Suff. Inst. Arch.*, III, 1863; W. Parker, *The History of Long Melford* (has manorial extents), 1873; W. Hudson, 'Three manorial extents of the thirteenth century' (translations of the extents of Bradcar and Banham in Norfolk and Wykes in Suffolk, temp. Edw. I), *Norf. Arch.*, XIV, 1899; J. Hervey, 'Extent of the manor of Hadleghe' (translation), *Suff. Inst. Arch.*, XI, 1903; E. Powell, *Suffolk Hundred of Blackbourne in the year 1283* (with extents of Coney Weston, Colford, Elmswell and Rickinghall in 1302), Cambridge, 1910.

Surrey   S.R. Scargill-Bird, *Custumals of Battle Abbey* (including manorial extents in Surrey), Camden Soc., 1887; H.C.M. Lambert, 'History of Banstead' (2 vols., including manorial extents) 1912-13.

Sussex   J.R. Daniel-Tyssen, 'Survey of the church of the College of Malling' (40 Edw. III and 21 Ric. II), *SAC*, XXI, 1869; S.R. Scargill-Bird, *Custumals of Battle Abbey* (including manorial extents in Sussex),

Camden Soc., 1887; L.F. Salzman, *Calendar of I.p.m. relating to Sussex, 1603-28*, SRS, 3, 1904; W. Hudson, 'On a series of rolls of the manor of Wiston' (13th-16th centuries, extents and rentals of Wiston, Chiltington, Heene etc.), *SAC*, LIII, 1910, and LIV, 1911; M.S. Holgate, *Sussex Inquisitions*, SRS, 33, 1927; R.H. D'Elboux, *Surveys of the manors of Robertsbridge, Sussex and Michelmarsh, Hampshire* (and of the demesne lands of Halden in Rolvenden, Kent, 1567-70), SRS, XLVII, 1944; M. Clough, *Two Estate Surveys of the FitzAlan Earls of Arundel*, SRS, LXVII, 1969.

Warwickshire *Extenta Manerii et Burgi de Veteri Stratford, 1252*, Middle Hill Press, 1840; J.W. Ryland, *Records of Wroxall Abbey and Manor* (includes court rolls, extents etc.), 1903; R.H. Hilton, *The Stoneleigh Leger Book* (with an estate survey of *c*.1393), Dugdale Soc. Pubns., XXIV, 1960; C.J. Bond, 'Deserted Medieval Villages in Warwickshire: A Review of the Field Evidence', *Birmingham and Warwickshire Archaeological Trans.*, no.86, 1974; P.R. Cross, *The Langley family and its cartulary*, Dugdale Soc. Occasional Papers, no.22, 1974.

Westmorland W. Farrer and J.F. Curwen, *Returns relating to the Barony of Kendale*, 2 vols., CWAAS Rec. Ser., 1923-4.

Wiltshire T. Phillipps, 'Survey of the manor and forest of Clarendon', *Archaeologia*, XXV, 1834; G.P. Scrope, *History of the Manor and Barony of Castle Combe, in the county of Wiltshire* (including an extent of 1454), 1852; S.R. Scargill-Bird, *Custumals of Battle Abbey* (including manorial extents in Wiltshire), Camden Soc., 1887; E.M. Thompson, 'Records of Wiltshire parishes' (including translations of extracts from I.p.m.), *Wilts. N. & Q.*, I-VI, 1895-1909; G.S. and E.A. Fry, *Calendar of I.p.m. Charles I*, British Rec. Soc., 1901 (abstracts); E.A. Fry, *Calendars of I.p.m. Edward II*, British Rec. Soc., 1908 (abstracts); E. Stokes, *Calendar of I.p.m. Edward III*, British Rec. Soc., 1914 (abstracts); W.R. Powell, 'Two royal surveys of Wiltshire during the Interdict' (surveys of manors of bishop, canons and monks), *Interdict Documents*, Pipe Roll Soc., LXII, n.s., XXXIV, 1958; N.W. Farr, *Accounts and Surveys of the Wiltshire Lands of Adam de Stratton*, WANHS Publications, no.13, 1959; A.E. Nash, 'The Mortality Pattern of Wiltshire lords of the manor', *Southern History*, no.2, 1980.

Yorkshire *Catalogue of I.p.m. for the County of Yorks, temp. James I and Charles I*, YAS, 1885; J.W. Morkill, 'The manor and park of Roundhay' (with abstracts of manorial extents), *Thoresby Soc. Pubns.*, II, *Miscellanea*, I, 1891; W. Brown, *Yorkshire Inquisitions of the reigns of Henry III and Edward I*, Yorks Arch. and Topographical Assoc. Rec. Ser., vols.12, 23, 31, 37, 1892-1906; W.H. Stevenson, 'Yorkshire surveys and other 11th century documents in the York Gospels', *EHR*, XXVII, 1912; E. Curtis, 'Sheffield in the fourteenth century: Two inquisitions post mortem' (Thomas Furnival, 1332, and William de Furnival, 1383), *Hunter Arch. Soc.*, I, 1914; J. Lister and H.P. Kendall, *Extent or Survey of the graveships of Rastrick, Hipperholme and Sowerby, 1309*, Halifax Ant. Soc., Rec. Sers., II, 1914; W. Paley Baildon and J.W. Clay, *I. p.m. relating to Yorks of the reigns of Henry IV and Henry V*, YAS, 1918; J. Lister, 'Chapter House records' (includes 14th-century extents of Leeds, Rothwell, Allerton, Bywater, Kippax and Ledston), *Pubns. Thoresby Soc.*, XXXIII, 1930; T.A.M. Bishop, 'The extent of Barton in Richmondshire, 1309', *YAS Journal*, XXXII, 1934; J. Lister, 'Chapter House Records' (translations of several Yorkshire extents of 1341), *Thoresby Soc.*, XXXIII, *Miscellanea*, X, 1935; T.A.M. Bishop, 'Extents of the Prebends of York, *c*.1295', *YAS, Rec. Sers.*, XCIV, *Miscellanea*, IV, 1936; and: 'Extent of Monk Friston 1320', *YAS, Rec. Sers.*, XCIV, *Miscellanea*, IV, 1937; H. King and A. Harris, *A Survey of the Manor of Settrington, 1599-1600*, YAS, Record Series, no.126, 1962; M.W. Barley, 'Castle Howard and the Village of Hinderskelfe', *North Yorkshire Antiquarian Journal*, no.58, Part 2, 1978.

ORIGINAL DOCUMENTS TO BE FOUND AT:

Public Record Office, Chancery Lane, London.

Reference to a printed Calendar, such as Willis-Bund's edition for Worcestershire, giving volume, page, village, date and tenant is sufficient to enable the original to be found.

MONUMENTAL BRASSES

THE DOCUMENT

The accompanying illustration of the monumental brass of Thomas Forest, from the church of Chaddesley Corbett, has been included to remind ourselves that 'documents', in their widest sense, comprise source material other than the written records. A document of the past can be any relic which illustrates some aspect of the life and history of its period. Thus, the houses in which people lived, the utensils which they used, the contents of museums, the fabric of the village church, all may be considered to be documentary material. Whilst all archives are documents, not all documents need be archives.

Monumental brasses are to be found in some 3,000 English parish churches and cathedrals; they range in date from the 13th to the 18th centuries, although only during the Middle Ages do we find examples of the true craftsmanship and clean-cut meticulous detail that is so essential. Although there are in fact many graceful brasses surviving from the Elizabethan, Jacobean and Restoration periods, later workmanship is usually shallow, and the plate thin; often these later brasses are in the form of palimpsests upon the reverse side of an older incision. The history of these figures is largely one of destruction and neglect, particularly during the Reformation and Commonwealth. They suffered also from the less intentional neglect of the 18th century, and the over-zealous restorations of the 19th century. Even so, England has the largest and finest surviving collection of church brasses in all Europe, larger than all other European countries together.

Their immense interest to the student of costume is obvious. Their value to the local historian, in supplying information on genealogy, heraldry, customs and social class-structure, is no less important. Before parish registers became available, brasses and effigies within the village church recorded the biographical detail and dates of its most notable personages. The story of armour and warfare can be read from the figures of knights, and many a village crusader portrayed by the lattener can be traced in the inquisitions, subsidy rolls and manorial records of the same village. The history of the wool-trade too, and its impact upon society and

---

Plate VIII. Effigies in St Cassian's Church, Chaddesley Corbett
(i)   Effigy of Roger Corbett, c.1290.
(ii)   Effigy of William Corbett, c.1306.

This figure of a 13th-century knight, in chain mail, is reputed by tradition to be Roger Corbett, the son of Ada Corbett, whose Inquisition Post Mortem is given in this Chapter. The family who added their name to that of the Saxon 'Chaddesley' were Lords of the Manor from c.1198 to c.1360. Roger's son William, also mentioned in the I.p.m., may well be the Rector of the parish, whose effigy, in mass vestments, is also found in the Church. William Corbett was involved in the rebellion against the Despensers in 1322, and soon after this the family lost precedence in the manor, although they continued to live there until the 19th century. Mrs. Grace Meredith, daughter of Edward Corbett, was mentioned here in the first edition, living at Lodge Farm. She died in 1964, and has a fitting memorial in the St Nicholas chapel of St Cassian's church. Thus ended the last living survival, in 800 years, of the Corbett family name in Chaddesley village.

(i)

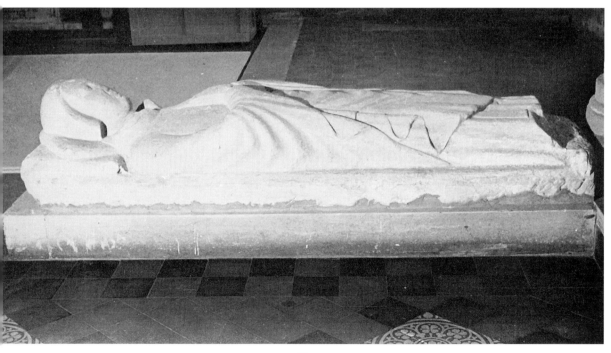

(ii)

government, is reflected in widespread woolmen's brasses. These are visual relics of burgess, merchant, priest and knight of the shire which help to illustrate and explain the origins of medieval Parliament.

These documents of the social life of the past are invaluable in bringing local history alive for children. They lend themselves easily to much practical, colourful interpretation, and brass-rubbing for its own sake creates tremendous interest in students of all ages. There is a number of scholarly and attractive books on the subject, and the locations of the brasses themselves have been carefully recorded; much practical advice and instruction is readily available in the transactions, portfolios and other publications of the MBS, and of the Oxford University Archaeological Society (see below). Although the possibilities are so obviously attractive, a word of warning must be added here. These brasses are precious, even *careful* unskilled rubbing can cause damage, and the position of the brass within the church can sometimes cause the brass-rubber to give unintentional offence. The amateur should on no account be encouraged to take his own rubbings before he has received adequate instruction and worked under supervision. The permission of the incumbent must, of course, be gained before any rubbing is taken; the best precaution of all is to undertake such work only with the agreement and advice of the MBS, or an experienced local expert. Courses on brass-rubbing have been arranged by the Educational Development Association and in some cathedrals and churches.

Our advice on this lovely activity was already tentative enough, but since this chapter was first written, the vastly increased attention to conservation has prohibited almost all amateur brassrubbing. Some churches and cathedrals, however, offer facilities for rubbing replicas at a commercial rate.

FURTHER READING

S. Beedell, *Brasses and Brass Rubbing*, Herman Publications, 1973

J. Bertram (ed.), *Monumental Brasses as Art and History*, Sutton, 1996

A.C. Bouquet, *Church Brasses*, Batsford, 1956

H.K. Cameron, *A Handlist of Monumental Brasses on the Continent of Europe*, MBS, 1970

M. Clayton, *Catalogue of the Rubbings of Brasses and Incised Slabs*, V & A Museum/HMSO, 1945

J. Coales, *The Earliest English Brasses (1270-1350)*, MBS, 1987

M. Cook, *Discovering Brasses and Brass Rubbings*, Shire Publications, 1976

D. Harley, *A Brief Introduction to Monumental Brasses*, Resources for Education 1992; *Monumental Brasses, a Topic Worth Studying*, Resources for Education, 1993

W. Lack, *Index to the Transactions, Bulletins and Portfolios of the MBS, 1887-1986*, MBS pbk, 1987

H.W. Macklin, *Monumental Brasses*, 1913

Sir J.G. Mann, *Monumental Brasses*, Penguin, 1957

The MBS, (c/o The Society of Antiquaries, Burlington House, Piccadilly, London W1V 0HS, Hon.Sec: W. Mendelsson) produces a list of useful publications, for example: N. Briggs, *Chapter and Verse, Documentary Sources for the Study of Monumental Brasses*, MBS, no.10, 1968; L. James, *Brasses and Medieval Piety*, MBS, 1967

M. Norris, *Monumental Brasses, the Craft*, Faber, 1978

M. Norris and M. Kellett, *Your Book of Brasses*, Faber, 1975

Oxford University Archaeological Society, from the Ashmolean Museum, Oxford, *Notes on Brass-Rubbing*, 1945. This booklet gave practical advice on methods of taking brass-rubbings, with a useful glossary of types of armour and garments depicted.

Portfolios of Plates of the MBS 1894-1984, Boydell Press, 1988

H.H. Trivick, *The Craft and Design of Monumental Brasses*, 1969

Monumental Brass of Thomas Forest,
Chaddesley Corbett, 1511
(Fig. I, p. 96)

The information given here is taken from F.J. Thacker's 'The Monumental Brasses of Worcestershire', an article in five parts, arranged in parishes, alphabetically, in *Transactions of the Worcestershire Archaeological Society*, new series, III (1925), IV (1927), XI (1934), XVI (1939), with Index. The biographical details of Thomas Forest can be found in J.R. Burton's *Kidderminster* (London, 1890).

'The brass shows Thomas Forest, *parcarius* of Dunclent Park (1511), in civil dress, and Margaret his wife, with 5 sons and 6 daughters. There is a marginal inscription, two shields with devices, and symbols of the four Evangelists at the four corners. The inscription and the two lower symbols are mutilated, the figures are much defaced. The brass is now a mural in its original slab, near the priest's door.

'*The male figure*. His hair is worn long and clubbed; he wears a long furred gown, thrown back to show the fur facings, the sleeves worn wide at the wrist, with fur cuffs. A tight-fitting under-garment is visible at the neck. From his girdle at his right side depends a *gypcière*, a hanging purse or game-pouch. (Chaucer's Franklin wore "a gipser all of silk, hong at his girdle".) The shoes are blunt and wide-toed.

'*The female figure*. His wife wears a long, close-fitting gown with a full skirt, loosely encircled by a long plain girdle terminating in an ornamental pendant. On her head she wears a *pedementa*, kennel, or diamond-shaped headdress, supported by wires and confining the hair in a close round cap at the back of the head, with long frontals or lappets hanging down each side of the face.

'*The badges on the shields*. These are not heraldic charges; one has a pair of arrows in saltire, the other a hunting-horn stringed.

'*The marginal inscription*. This is incomplete, but Habington, in his *Survey of Worcestershire*, I, p. 145, supplies the missing words. It reads: (ORATE PRO ANIMABUS) THOMAS FFOREST PARCARIJ DE DUNCLENT PARKE ET MARGARETE UXORIS EIUS AC AMNIUM PUERORUM SUORUM QUORUM (ANIMABUS PROPOTIETUR DEUS. AMEN). Each word is separated by horns, arrows, leaves, acorns and roses.

'*The symbols at the corners*. These are of the Evangelists: St Matthew portrayed as an angel in alb, girdle and amice; St Mark, a winged lion; St Luke, a winged ox; St John, an eagle (Ezekiel i. 10; Revelation iv. 7).

'*The Forester*. Dunclent Park, now in Stone parish, once formed part of the Forest of Feckenham, the Keeper of which, in 1389, was Geoffrey Chaucer. The brass of Thomas Forest shows the office to have been one of dignity and importance even as late as the sixteenth century. Chaddesley Corbett had been added to this royal forest by Henry II, and Peter Corbett was appointed chief Forester of the royal Midland forests during the reign of Edward I. A perambulation of 29 Edward I (1300-1) shows Chaddesley as contained within the Forest of Feckenham. This perambulation is printed in an article by J. Humphreys to be found in *Transactions and Proceedings of Birmingham Archaeological Society*, XLV, 1919. Feckenham Forest was finally disafforested in 1629.'

Manorial records of Kidderminster show that Thomas Forest was addressed as 'Forest Bayley of the Manor of Kidderminster' by the lord of that manor and Chaddesley in 1485, who

Fig. 1. Monumental brass of Thomas and Margaret Forest, 1511.

deals with a complaint of the Prior of Maiden Bradley of the high-handed conduct of his officers who 'have of late letted and denied the said Prioure and his Officers to Take and Felle their woods growing in his part of the seid Lordship' (full text of these letters in Burton, *op. cit.*, p. 38). Thomas Forest's will is available at the Worcestershire County Record Office (008.7: 35/1511) and is printed by Burton (pp. 67-8). He bequeaths gifts of money and 20 sheep to churches in Stone and Kidderminster, and his house and land to 'the Wardens of Our Ladys Chapel of Stone for everlasting times'.

For comparison with this brass, see Chaucer's description of the Yeoman:

> This Yeoman wore a coat and hood of green,
> And peacock-feathered arrows, bright and keen
> And neatly sheathed, hung at his belt the while
> - For he could dress his gear in yeoman style,
> His arrows never drooped their feathers low-
> And in his hand he bore a mighty bow.
> His head was like a nut, his face was brown.
> He knew the whole of woodcraft up and down.
> A saucy brace was on his arm to ward
> It from the bow-string, and a shield and sword
> Hung at one side, and at the other slipped
> A jaunty dirk, spear-sharp and well-equipped.
> A medal of St Christopher he wore
> Of shining silver on his breast, and bore
> A hunting-horn, well slung and burnished clean
> That dangled from a baldrick of bright green.
> *He was a proper forester I guess.*[11]

WORCESTERSHIRE BRASSES

The following is Thacker's list of Worcestershire brasses, much condensed. Those shown in italics are inscriptions only, the remainder are full figures in the style of dress indicated:

Alvechurch: 1524 (armour); *2680; 1684.*
Beoley: 1631; seventeenth century.
Birlingham: *c.*1617 (civil).
Birtsmorton: *c.*1500 (indents only).
Blockley: 1488 (cleric in academics); *1484;*
   1510 (cleric in vestments).
Bredon: 1650
Broadway: 1572 (armour); *1641.*
Bromsgrove: 1612; 1632.
Bushley: 1500 (civil); *1651.*
Chaddesley: 1511 (civil).
Daylesford: 1632 (civil). (now Glos.)
Dodderhill: 1630
Fladbury: 1445 (armour); 1458 (cleric
   in cope); *1460;* 1488 (armour); 1504
   (cleric in vestments); *1647*
Halesowen: 1669; 1676; 1784.
Huddington: 1641; 1642; 1653; 1658.
Kidderminster: 1415 (armour).

Longdon: 1523 (armour).
Mamble: *c.*1510 (armour).
Pershore Abbey: 1670.
Queenhill: 1624.
Redmarley: 1609. (now Glos.)
Ripple: 1596; 1652; 1668.
Spetchley: 1629, shield; 1658
Stockton: 1508 (civil).
Stoke Prior: 1606 (civil); 1609 (civil).
Stone: 1656; 1663.
Strensham: *c.*1390 (armour); 1405 (armour);
   1502 (armour); 1556 (armour).
Suckley: 1665.
Tredington: 1427 (cleric in cope); 1482
   (cleric in almuce); 1561 (woman).
Worcester Cathedral: 1481.
Worcester, St Helen's: 1622 (civil).[12]
Yardley: 1598 (civil and armour); *1625.*
   (now Birmingham)

---

[11] *The Canterbury Tales*, translated by Nevill Coghill, p. 20, Penguin Classics, 1951.

LOCAL PUBLICATIONS ON MONUMENTAL BRASSES

(listed under each county in order of publication date)

Bedfordshire   H.K. St. J. Sanderson, 'The brasses of Bedfordshire', *MBS*, 2, 1892-6; 3, 1897-9; G. Isherwood, *Monumental Brasses in the Bedfordshire Churches*, London, 1906; G.A.E. Ruck, 'Additions to the List from Bedfordshire, Northants, Oxfordshire, Rutland and Shropshire', *MBS*, 19, 1952; F.W. Kuhlicke, *The Gascoigne Brasses at Cardington*, MBS, no.11, 1971; E.N. Staines, 'Three Bedfordshire Brasses', *Bedfordshire Magazine*, no.15, 1977; A. Dowden, *The Wives of Sir William Gascoigne of Cardington*, MBS, no.12, 1978; W. Lack, H.M. Stuchfield and P. Whittemore, *The Monumental Brasses of Bedfordshire*, MBS, 1992.

Berkshire   H.T. Morley, *Monumental Brasses of Berkshire, 14th to 17th centuries*, Electric Press, Reading, 1924; H. Hinton and J. Hunt, *A Regency Collection of Brass-rubbings*, MBS, no.12, 1975; W. Lack, H.M. Stuchfield and P. Whittemore, *The Monumental Brasses of Berkshire*, MBS, 1993.

Buckinghamshire   H.K. St. J. Sanderson, 'Notes on brasses in some Buckinghamshire churches', *MBS*, vols.1, 1981; 3, 1897-99; 4, 1900; W. Lack, H.M. Stuchfield and P. Whittemore, *The Monumental Brasses of Buckinghamshire*, MBS, 1994.

Cambridgeshire   J.M. Neale (preface), *Illustrations of monumental brasses*, Cambridge, 1846; C.J.P. Cave, O.J. Charlton and R.A. Macalister, 'The brasses of Cambridgeshire', *MBS*, vols.2, 1892-6; 3, 1897-9; 4, 1899-1900; G. Montague Benton, *The Monumental Brasses of Cambridgeshire*, 2nd ed.,1902; J.W.E. Coneybeare, *Rides around Cambridge*, 1920; *Monumental Brasses in Cambridgeshire and the Isle of Ely*, Cambridge City Libraries, 1968; J. Bertram, *An Unrecorded Royal Brass at Peterborough*, MBS, no.10, 1968; F.A. Greenhill, *A Palimpsest at Christ's College, Cambridge*, MBS, no.11, 1969; J.R. Greenwood, *Haines's Cambridge School of Brasses*, MBS, no.11, 1969; H.K. Cameron, *Cambridge and the Study of Monumental Brasses*, MBS, no.12, 1977; P.J. Heseltine, *A Lost Brass from Isleham*, MBS, no.12, 1977; P.J. Heseltine, *The Figure Brasses of Cambridgeshire*, MBS, 1981; W. Lack, H.M. Stuchfield and P. Whittemore, *The Monumental Brasses of Cambridgeshire*, MBS, 1995.

Cheshire   J.L. Thornely, *The Monumental Brasses of Lancashire and Cheshire*, EP Publishing, 1975; W. Lack, H.M. Stuchfield and P. Whittemore, *The Monumental Brasses of Cheshire*, MBS, 1996.

Cornwall   E. Hadlow Wise Dunkin, *The Monumental Brasses of Cornwall*, Spottiswoode, London, 1882.

Cumbria   J.C. Page-Phillips, *Palimpsests at Greystoke, Cumberland*, MBS, no.11, 1969.

Derbyshire   H.E. Field, 'The monumental brasses of Derbyshire', *MBS*, vols.3, 1897-9; 5, 1904-9; H.F. Owen Evans, *The Brass to Rowland Eyre, Esquire and his wife, Gertrude, 1624, at Great Longstone, Derbyshire*, MBS, no.10, 1967; R. Lester, *Brasses and Brass Rubbings in the Peak District*, Mid-summer Publications, 1971.

Devonshire   W.R. Crabbe, *An Account of the Monumental Brasses remaining in the county of Devon*, reprints of four papers from *Exeter Diocesan Architectural Society*, 1859; J.C. Page-Phillips, *A Palimpsest at Tor Mohun*, MBS, no.10, 1968; P. Corbould, 'The Monumental Brasses of Devon', *Devonshire Association Report and Transactions*, no.100, 1969; A. Guy, *An Index of brass rubbings in the West Country Studies Library, Exeter*, Devon Library Services, 1991.

Dorset   W. de C. Prideaux, 'Ancient memorial brasses of Dorset', *DNHAS*, 23, 25, 27-9, 32, 34-7 and 40, 1902-19; and: 'Monumental brasses of Dorsetshire', *Brit. Assoc. J.*, 13, 1907.

Essex   M. Christy and W.W. Porteous, 'Some interesting Essex brasses', *EAS*, n.s., 7-10, 1900-9; R.H. D'Elboux, *The Monumental Brasses of Essex*, MBS, 1948; N. Briggs, *A Bibliography of Essex Brasses*, MBS, no.11, 1971; L. Norris and M. Norris, *A Palimpsest at Lambourne*, MBS, no.12, 1977; S. Frith, 'The brass rubbings in the Society's collections', *Ess. Hist. Soc.*, 2, 3rd series, 1979.

Gloucestershire   C.T. Davis, *Monumental Brasses of Gloucestershire*, Saifer, 1970 (facsimile of 1899 original); H.F. Owen, *Tormarton, Gloucestershire: Matrix for the Brass to Sir John de la Riviere, c.1350*, MBS, no.11, 1972.

Hampshire   C.J.P. Cave, 'List of Hampshire brasses', *MBS*, vols.5, 1904-9; 6, 1906-12; N. Surry, *A Lost Brass, formerly at Hordle, Hampshire*, MBS, no.10, 1968.

Herefordshire   C. Tudor Davis, *The Monumental Brasses of Herefordshire and Worcestershire*, 1885; A.J. Winnington Ingram, *Monumental Brasses in Hereford Cathedral*, Woolhope Club, 1956.

Hertfordshire   R. Holmes and A.E.L. Fox, *Andrew Willett, Puritan Divine and his Brass at Barley*, MBS, no.10, 1967; J.H. Busby, 'Indents of lost Brasses at Kimpton Church', *Hertfordshire Archaeology*, no.1, 1968; R.J. Busby, 'The Monumental Brasses of Hertfordshire', *Hertfordshire Past and Present*, no.10, 1970; and: 'Sidelights on Brasses in Hertfordshire Churches: Furneux Pelham; and Great Gaddesden',

---

[12] This church is now a department of the County Record Office.

Hertfordshire Archaeology, nos.1 and 2, 1970; H.K. Cameron and R.J. Busby, *A Palimpsest Brass at Clothall*, MBS, no.12, 1975; M. Rensten, *Hertfordshire Brasses: A Guide to the figurine brasses in Hertfordshire churches*, Herts. Pubns., 1982.

Huntingdonshire   H.W. Macklin, 'The Brasses of Huntingdonshire', *MBS*, 3, 1897-9; H.W. Macklin, 'The Brasses of Huntingdonshire', *MBS*, 1900; P. Heseltine, *The Brasses of Huntingdonshire*, Cambs. Libraries and MBS, 1987.

Isle of Wight   E.N. Staines, *Guide to the Monumental Brasses and Incised Slabs on the Isle of Wight*, 1972.

Kent   R. Hare Griffin, *List of Monumental Brasses remaining in the County of Kent in 1922*, Ashford and London, 1923; R. Griffin, 'Monumental brasses in Kent', *MBS*, 7, 1934-42; also in *AC 31, 1915*; 'References to brasses in "Archaeologia Cantiana" ', *MBS*, 7, 1934-42; R.H. D'Elboux, 'Kent brasses, some identifications', *MBS*, 9, 1954; I. Stewart, 'Knights in Armour and Their Ladies, the Monumental Brasses at Cobham Church, Kent', *Country Life*, no.146, December, 1969; I. Bethune, 'The Brasses and Incised Slabs at Milton Regis Parish Church', *AC*, 87, 1972.

Lancashire   L.M. Angus-Butterworth, 'Early Lancashire Brasses', *Ancient Monuments Society Trans.*, no.22, 1977-8.

Leicestershire   A.B. McDonald, 'Monumental brasses, with special reference to Leicestershire and Rutland', *RANHS*, 15th Annual Report, 1916.

Lincolnshire   J. Maugham and J. Fowler, *The Medieval Monumental Brasses of the Diocese of Lincoln*, Louth, 1855; N. Surry, *Folk Tradition and Brasses: Two examples from Lincolnshire*, MBS, no.10, 1968.

London and Middlesex   A full series of 'The Brasses of Middlesex' is published, parish by parish, in *Transactions of the London and Middlesex Archaeological Society (new series)* from 10, 1951, to 34, 1983 (and continuing), alphabetically by parishes from Acton to South Mimms, as listed below. The author in each case is H.K. Cameron. Volume numbers and the dates of the series of *Transactions* are also given here: Acton, Ashford, Bedfont, 10, 1951; Bow, Brentford, Bromley by Bow, Chelsea, Chiswick, Clerkenwell St James, 11, 1954; Cowley, Cranford, West Drayton, 18, 1955; Ealing, Edgware, Edmonton, Enfield, 19, 1958; Finchley, Fulham, Greenford, Hackney, Hadley, 20, 1959; Hampton, Harefield, 21, 1967; Harlington, 22, 1968-70; Harrow, 24, 1973; Hayes, 25, 1975; Hendon, Heston, 26, 1975; Hillingdon, Bedfont, 27, 1976; Hornsey, including Highgate, 28, 1977; Ickenham, 30, 1979; Isleworth, 31, 1980; Islington and Kilburn, 32, 1981; Kingsbury and Littleton, 33, 1982; South Mimms, 34, 1983; H.K. Cameron, 'The Brasses of Middlesex', *Middlesex Arch. Soc. Trans.*, no.22, 1969, and no.24, 1973; M.E. Speight, *The Charlton Brasses at Edmonton*, MBS, no.11, 1972; H.K. Cameron, 'The Brasses of Middlesex, Hayes', *LMAS*, no.25, 1974.

Norfolk   E.M. Beloe and W. Griggs, *A series of photo-lithographs of Monumental Brasses in Norfolk*, Kings Lynn, 1890; J.L. Andre, 'Female headresses exemplified by Norfolk brasses', *Norf. Arch.*, 14, 1898; M. Stephenson, 'Palimpsest brasses in Norfolk', *Norf. Arch.*, 15, 1902; J.R. Greenwood, *The Brasses of All Saints, Norwich*, MBS, no.12, 1977; J.R. Greenwood and M. Norris, *Brasses of Norfolk Churches*, Norfolk Churches Trust, 1977; J.M. Blatchley, *The Brasses of Sharrington*, MBS, no.12, 1978.

Northamptonshire   'Contributions to a complete exploration of Northamptonshire', extracted from Kelly's *Directory of Bedfordshire, Huntingdonshire and Northamptonshire*, 1894; A. Butler, 'Anne Boroeghe of Clerkenwell and Dingley', *Northamptonshire Past and Present*, no.5, 1977; N. Saul, *Two Fifteenth Century Brasses at Dodford*, MBS, no.12, 1977; F.A. Greenhill, *Some Additions to the Northamptonshire List*, MBS, no.12, 1978.

Nottinghamshire   J. Bramley, 'Nottinghamshire monumental brasses', *Thoroton Soc.*, 17, 1958.

Oxfordshire   H.F. Owen Evans, *A Palimpsest at Thame*, MBS, no.10, 1968; H. Hinton and J. Hunt, *A Regency Collection of Brass Rubbings*, MBS, no.12, 1975.

Rutland   A.B. McDonald, 'Monumental brasses, with special reference to Leicestershire and Rutland', RANHS, *15th Annual Report*, 1916.

Somersetshire   H. St. G. Gray, 'Index to monumental brasses mentioned or described in the "Proceedings of the Society", 1-52, 1849-1906', *SANHS*, 52, 1906 (also separately published, 1906, and continued in vols.77 and 78, 1932-3); G.H. Mitchell, 'Monumental brasses of the fifteenth century in Somerset', Wells Nat. Hist. & Arch. Soc., *Annual Report for 1920*; A.B. Connor, *Monumental Brasses in Somerset*, Kingsmead, Bath, 1970.

Staffordshire   W.C. Peck, 'A list of Staffordshire brasses to the end of the eighteenth century', *MBS*, 3, 1897-9; C. Masefield, 'Monumental brasses of Staffordshire', *N. Staffs. F.C.*, vols.47 and 48, 1912-14.

Suffolk   E. Farrer, *A List of Monumental Brasses remaining in the county of Suffolk*, Norwich, 1903; J.T. Munday, *A Lost Figure from Mildenhall; the Brass of Edward Warner*, MBS, no.11, 1969; J.A. Christian, *Identifying the Brasses at Assington*, MBS, no.11, 1975; L. and M. Norris, *A Palimpsest at Pettaugh*, MBS, no.12, 1977; T.M. Felgate, 'Knights on Suffolk Brasses', 1976; and: 'Ladies on Suffolk Brasses', *East Anglian Magazine*, 1989.

Surrey   M. Stephenson, 'List of monumental brasses in Surrey', *MBS*, 6, 1914; and: 'A list of monumental brasses in Surrey', *Surrey Arch. Colls.*, 25, 1910, continued in vols.26-33 and 40, 1911-1918 and 1925; B.S.H. Egan, *Brasses at Thames Ditton*, MBS, no.10, 1967; J.M. Blatchly, 'Further Notes on the Monumental Brasses of Surrey and the Collection of Rubbings at Castle Arch', *Surrey Arch. Colls.*, no.68, 1971; A. Stephenson, *Monumental Brasses in Surrey*, Saifer, 1971.

Sussex   H. Stuart Witley, 'A list of papers relating to monumental brasses in the "Collections of the Sussex Arch. Soc."', *MBS*, 3, 1897-9; R.K. Owen, *A Brief Description of 25 Sussex Monumental Brasses*, reprint from Hastings Museum Catalogue Exhibition, 1909; E.N. Staines, *A Lost Brass at Amberley*, MBS, no.10, 1967.

Warwickshire   E.W. Badger, *The Monumental Brasses of Warwickshire*, Birmingham, 1895; *Brass Rubbings from Shakespeare's Countryside*, a selection of the more interesting rubbings from monumental brasses from churches in the environs of Stratford-upon-Avon, Stratford-upon-Avon, 1970; 'M.B.S.: Monumental Brasses in Warwickshire', *Monumental Brass Soc.*, 1977.

Wiltshire   E. Kite, *The Monumental Brasses of Wiltshire*, facsimile of 1860 edition, Kingsmead Bookshop, Bath, 1960; M. Norris, *The Bennet Brasses at Norton Bavant and Westbury*, MBS, no.11, 1971; L.L. Hodge, *Guide to Wiltshire Brasses*, Compton Press, 1977.

Worcestershire   C. Tudor Davis, *The Monumental Brasses of Herefordshire and Worcestershire*, 1885; F.J. Thacker, 'Monumental brasses of Worcestershire', *Worcs. Arch. Soc.*, n.s., vols.3 and 4, 1970-2; S.J.G. Seamer, *Positions of Brasses in Worcestershire Churches*, MBS, no.12, 1977.

Yorkshire   Various published by *Yorks. Arch. J.*: M. Stephenson, 'Monumental brasses in the North Riding', 17, 1903; and: 'Monumental brasses in Yorkshire', 20, 1908; 'Articles on monumental brasses in Yorkshire published in the Journal', 20, 1908; M. Stephenson, 'Some additional brasses in the East Riding', 24, 1917; H. Lawrence, 'Monumental brasses in the East Riding of Yorkshire', 17, 1924; J.D. Watson, *The Morewood Brass at Bradfield*, MBS, no.12, 1978.

CHAPTER IV

The Sixteenth and Seventeenth Centuries

✧

The consolidation and renewal of royal authority by the Tudor dynasty introduced a new phase of national and regional development. The medieval wars with France had stimulated an independent spirit of English nationalism, which was constantly fostered by increasing trade and a prosperous commercial class. Among this changing society the Tudors found a reliable source of loyal support in middle-class dependence upon the Crown's good government and paternal care. The outworn local machinery of gild and manor, franchise and feudal contract, between central government and a regional baronial administration, had already broken down in faction and dynastic strife. People everywhere stood intimidated and bewildered by the perversion of law, justice and administrative offices at the hands of powerful private interests.

From this low ebb of national fortune, monarchy renewed its powers under the Tudors by dependence upon parish officials and the gentry of the shires. Voluntary, unpaid local magistrates were supervised and led by the conciliar courts and departments of central government. Within this remodelled framework peace and order were renewed, the Anglican Church was established, and a protective, paternal policy of national welfare and self-sufficiency was introduced and regulated by statute law. The application of these administrative and religious reforms, and attempted reforms, is recorded in the injunctions, orders, presentments, sessions and reports which kept the royal councils continually in touch with the social, political and religious life and problems of every region of the realm. It is the evidence of this reorganised administration which is chiefly reflected in the local documents of the period. The religious and civil contention of Stuart times, the struggles and conflict of crown, parliament and common lawyers for political sovereignty, are recorded only sporadically in most localities. More immediate and far-reaching is the abundant evidence of social change, and the premature stirrings of technical advance which culminates in economic revolution. All this can be clearly read from local records.

The 17th century, particularly, offered new opportunities for personal, as well as for more formal, written records. Wider-spread prosperity, secular education and the increase of a leisured middle class, raised a new literate gentry, who transmit the details of their everyday life and personal affairs in written forms. The studies of local antiquaries and map-makers, the diaries, private correspondence and estate papers of small gentlefolk, can all be added to the mass of administrative record to re-create a detailed and colourful picture of daily life in the English town and countryside.

COUNTY MAPS AND OTHER SURVEYS

THE DOCUMENTS

County Maps. Before the first Ordnance Survey maps of 1801, a wide variety of unofficial publications had for a long time been available, though not to the same scale and high degree of accuracy. Although such maps as that of Worcestershire in the Bodleian Library had been made as early as the 13th and 14th centuries, surviving examples are rare. County maps and atlases become increasingly common from *c*.1560, and continue to multiply throughout the 17th and 18th centuries. The earlier maps of Saxton, Norden and Speed do not show much detail. Relief is indicated, forests, parks, bridges, towns and villages are shown by semi-pictorial symbols, but roads are scantily marked, if at all. Incidental information is sometimes given, for example on local family heraldry or trades. Ogilby's *Travellers' Guides* (late 17th century), and similar guides, give more detail of landscape features and industrial sites. These maps are useful for land-use data, location and distribution of settlement, and information about the development of communications by roads and water-ways. They are also very useful in tracing place-name history and revealing the sites of abandoned villages, even lost prehistoric monuments. Several county maps include, in their margins, plans of the principal towns, which can be used to supplement information found in guide books, directories and coach time-tables. There may also be marginal information on the history of the county, particularly on battles fought locally. For more detailed local topographical studies, the larger scale of estate maps (q.v.), enclosure maps (pp.191-9), tithe maps (pp.199-217) and plans for development of public utilities, such as turnpike roads (pp.221-7), railways, canals and water-supply, deposited with the Clerks of the Peace (p.224), are more informative.

Estate Maps and Manorial Surveys. The revival of interest and progress in the techniques of surveying in the 16th century, created a new and growing demand for the employment of surveyors by landowners all over England. The profession of surveyor, at first a scholarly pastime (see the surveyor's book, chain and equipment among the chattels of Richard Evans of Bredon in 1594, p.168), soon became highly specialised and required formal training. Thus the latest equipment and the new technical proficiency of professional map-makers created new pictorial methods of recording the extent of estates, by means of maps, which soon superseded the previous written descriptions of landed property, common before this date. From the 16th to the 19th centuries, family papers usually include a series of maps of the families' estates which provide us with a complete and detailed picture of their development and planning. Estate maps are of particular importance in tracing the changes in fortunes and territorial influence of the landed gentry at several peak periods of changes and reallocation of land-tenure, with the redistribution of Church lands after the Reformation and Dissolution, with the fluctuation of fortunes and estates during the Civil War, and after the Restoration, and during the parliamentary enclosure movement of the 18th century.

The scale of estate maps is usually about 3 to 6 chains to the inch, and their generally high standard of decoration, the painstaking water-colour and pictorial representation of woodland, gates, fences, bridges and houses, adds a quaint and meticulous character which is very attractive.

The map of the part of the manor of Chaddesley Corbett which belonged to the Corporation of Warwick in 1697 is a pleasing example of this type of survey (Plate IX). This map is particularly important for the details of the village which it provides, with measurements of the buildings in bays, and particulars of roof structure, whether tile or thatch. A later (1745) map, drawn to a scale of 5 chains : 1 inch, once at Coughton Court, is now among the Throckmorton papers at Warwickshire CRO (*CR 1998/M13*). It shows the family's demesne, and the houses belonging to the lord of the manor, coloured in red; the land of each tenant is separately coloured, and the houses belonging to the Corporation of Warwick are coloured yellow. The possessions of other landowners in the parish have the owners' names written across the fields, and the entire map is of particular importance in showing as it does the lay-out of the fields and the village, and the position of the commons, half a century before the enclosure award of 1799.[1] Other estate maps record the holdings of individual tenant farmers separately, with field names and acreages entered; often a table of reference, or 'terrier', in one corner of the map tabulates the numbered fields, and lists their names, acreages and land-use. Occasionally an owner or tenant has used the map to sketch in his ideas and plans for the farm's future development, or its next year's crops, in hand-written comments across the fields. The large scale of these estate maps often reveals details of footpaths, waggon-ways and lanes, the exact position of toll-bars and surviving strips of copyhold land, which are not recorded elsewhere. Often a small section of the estate, or its boundary, will be the subject of a separate map. Also at Warwick (*CR 1998/M4*) we find another Throckmorton map of the northern boundary of Chaddesley Corbett in 1737. This is 'an exact Map of the Old and New Watercourses, beginning at Barnett Hill Brook, down to Dearne Ford, and from thence to the place where the two old Corn Mills[2] stood, one belonging to Major Brand in the Parish of Kidderminster, the other to Lady Yate in the Parish of Chaddesley, also the Boundary between Lord Foley's land, and Barnett Hill Warren belonging to Sir Robert Throckmorton'. The map also shows the position of two 'Blade Mills', one of which still stands today, and a line of boundary stones, 'which, 'twas agreed should be the bounds of the Manors of Kidderminster and Chaddesley, the Course of the Old Brook not being to be found'. These stones also survive, mostly in the bed of the stream where they have been thrown by farmers.

Estate maps are to be found amongst the estate papers of the families who were the village's principal land-owners. These may be stored amongst the family muniments, or deposited with the family solicitor, though many such collections, or photocopies of their maps, have been deposited in county archives. In view of the essential nature of maps to any continuous study of a county's landscape, this section, nominally of 16th- and 17th-century documents, is extended by examples of all types of surveys down to the early 19th century.

FURTHER READING

J.J. Bagley, 'County Maps and Town Plans', *Historical Interpretation 2: Sources of English History 1540 to the present day*, 1971

L. Bagrow, *History of Cartography*, 1964

A.R.H. Baker, 'Local History and Early Estate Maps', *Amateur Historian*, 5, no.3, 1962

G. Beech, 'Maps for Genealogy and Local History', *Genealogists' Magazine*, no.22, June 1987

G. de Boer and A.P. Carr, 'Early Maps as Historical Evidence for Coastal Change', *Geographical Journal*, no.135, 1969

T. Chubb, *The Printed Maps in the Atlases of Great Britian and Ireland, A Bibliography 1579-1870*, London, 1927

R. Douch, 'Geography and the Local Historian', *Amateur Historian*, 3, no.7, 1958

F.G. Emmison, 'Short Guides to Records, no.4: Estate Maps and Surveys', *History*, no.48, 1963

---

[1] See Plate XV.

[2] See the two mills mentioned in the Extent of 1290, (p.56), and the three mills recorded in the Domesday Survey of the manor (p.23).

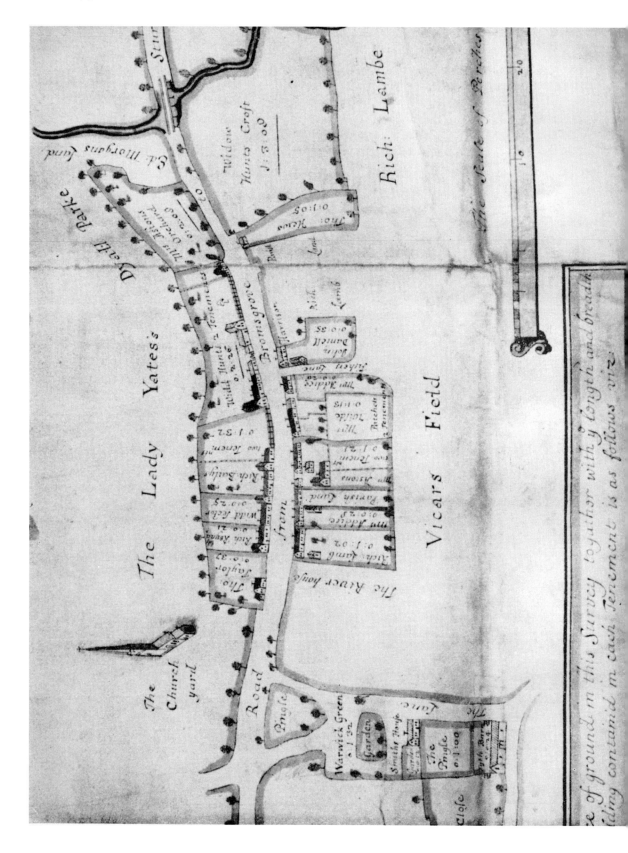

H.G. Fordham, *Some Notable Surveyors and Mapmakers of the Sixteenth to Eighteenth centuries and their work,* Cambridge, 1929

J.B. Harley, *Maps for the Local Historian: A Guide to British Sources,* 1977. This book was reprinted from a series of articles in *Amateur Historian* and *The Local Historian,* viz: 1. Maps and Plans of Towns, *AH,* 7, no.6, 1967; 2. Estate Maps, *AH,* 7, no.7, 1967; 3. Enclosure and Tithe Maps, *AH,* 7, no.8, 1967; 4. Maps of Communications, *LH,* 2, 1968; 5. Marine Charts, *LH,* 8, no.3, 1968; 6. County Maps, *LH,* 8, no.5, 1968; *The Evaluation of Early Maps; Towards a Methodology,* Amsterdam, 1968

J.B. Harley and C.W. Phillips, 'A Guide to Ordnance Survey Maps as Historical Sources', 1. 'One Inch to the Mile Maps of England and Wales', *Amateur Historian,* 5, no.5, 1962; 2. 'The Period Maps of the Ordnance Survey', 5., no.6, 1963; 3. 'The Maps of England and Wales on the 6 inch and 25 inch scales', 5, no.7, 1963; 'The Town Plans and Small scale Maps of England and Wales', 5, no.8, 1963

P.D.A. Harvey, *Maps in Tudor England,* British Library, 1993

P. Hindle, *Maps for Local History,* Batsford, 1988

'Historicus', 'Topography and Maps,' *Amateur Historian,* 3, no.3, 1957

J.E. Holehouse, 'The Golden Age of the County Map', *History Today,* no.24, 1974

A.M. Lambert, 'Early Maps and Local Studies', *Geography,* no.193, 41, Part 3, July 1956

L.B. Mayne, 'Maps from Saxton to Royal Ordnance', *Amateur Historian,* 1, no.12, 1954

R. Morden, *The County Maps from William Camden's 'Brittania' of 1695,* facsimile edition, David & Charles, 1972

R.A. Skelton, *County Atlases of the British Isles 1579-1850,* 1970

R.A. Skelton and P.D.A. Harvey, 'Local Maps and Plans before 1500', *Journal of the Society of Archivists,* no.3, 1969

R.A. Skelton and P.D.A. Harvey, *Local Maps and Plans from Medieval England,* Clarendon Press, Oxford, 1986

D. Smith, *Maps for the Local Historian and Collector,* Batsford,1988

R.V. Tooley, *A Dictionary of Mapmakers,* Map Collectors' Series, nos.16, 28, 40, 50 and 67, 1965-1970

H. Wallis and A. MacConnell, *Historians' Guide to Early British Maps. Guide to the Location of pre-1900 Maps of the British Isles preserved in the UK and Ireland,* C.U.P., 1994

I. Watt, *A Directory of United Kingdom Map Collections,* Map Collectors' Group Publications No.3. British Cartographic Society, 2nd edition, 1985

WORCESTERSHIRE ORIGINAL DOCUMENTS

At the County Record Office

See Ref: BA. 866. F. 899. 38/22, J. Severn Walker, *A Collection of Worcestershire Maps.* This is a bound volume, containing a mounted collection of county maps, including:

Saxton (1577)	Speed (1610)	Morden (1695)
Moll (1724)	Badeslade (1741)	Kitchin (1750)
Bickan 1753)	Bowen (1760)	Seale (1750)
Bowen (1767)	Cary (1787)	Young and Roper (1808)
Dix (1820)	Pigot (1837)	Moule (1837)
	O.S. from 1820	

Hereford and Worcestershire Record Offices now sell three facsimile maps for £2.00. These are: J. Roper: *City of Worcester 1808* (20 x 25.5cm); T. Moule's *Worcestershire 1837* (20 x 28cm); Christopher Saxton's *Herefordshire 1577* (38 x 30.5cm).

Plate IX. Part of a Map of the tenements in Chaddesley, belonging to the Corporation of Warwick in 1697.
Warwickshire County Record Office, ref: CR1618/WA/12/57.
Actual size: 82 x 72cm (whole map); Scale: 8 perches : 1 inch.
27.5 x 18cm (extract); scale: 10 perches : 1 inch (a perch was 5½ yards)

(i)

(ii)

Birmingham Reference Library

Here are also a large selection of county maps, turnpike plans, estate maps, tithe plans for various parishes, enclosure maps, canal, rail and other public utilities, catalogued under 'Worcesterhire'. County maps include:

Saxton (1577)	Speed (1610)	Janssonius (1646)
Kitchin (1777)	Harrison (1789)	Lodge (1790)
Pigot (1800)	Cary (1801)	Roper (1807)
Creighton and Starling (1831)		Bickley (1890)

See also: *Christopher Greenwood, County Map-maker and his Worcestershire map of 1822*, ed.J.B. Harley, Worcestershire Historical Society, 1962.

Reproductions of the more famous county maps have been published in book, or sheet form. See:

John Arlott, *John Speed's England; a Coloured Facsimile,* London, 1953.

E.G.R. Taylor, *John Speed's Atlas,* Penguin, 1951.

The British Library sells coloured facsimiles of Christopher Saxton's maps of English and Welsh counties, at £3.95 a sheet (about 50 x 63 cm); these are also available from the Stationery Office. Counties available include: Bedfordshire, Cambridgeshire, Huntingdonshire and Rutland; Cheshire; Caernarvonshire; Cardigan and Carmarthenshire; Cornwall; Cumberland; Denbighshire; Dorset; Durham; Essex; Glamorgan; Gloucestershire; Hampshire; Herefordshire; Kent; Surrey, Middlesex and Sussex; Leicestershire; Lincolnshire and Nottinghamshire; Monmouth; Montgomeryshire; Norfolk; Northamptonshire; Northumberland; Oxfordshire, Buckinghamshire and Berkshire; Pembrokeshire; Radnorshire and Brecknockshire; Shropshire; Somersetshire; Staffordshire; Suffolk; Warwickshire; Wiltshire; Worcestershire; Yorkshire (63 x 84cm).

GAZETTEER OF PRINTED EDITIONS AND OTHER REFERENCES

First consult: H. Wallis, *Historians' Guide to Early (pre-1900) British Maps*, Royal Historical Society Guides and Handbooks, no.18, 1994

See also: *The British Museum Catalogue of Printed Maps, Charts, Plans etc.*, 15 vols., 1967, with a British Library Supplement 1965-74, published in 1977 and intended to continue, possibly at 10-year intervals.

(listed chronologically in order of publication date)

Bedfordshire   G.H. Fowler, *Four pre-enclosure village maps* (strip-map of Oakley Reanes, 1795, with introduction to the study of field maps; pre-enclosure map of Renhold, 1781; strip-map of Apsley Guise, *c.*1745, with analysis of enclosure award, 1761; strip-map of Eversholt, 1764, with notes on strip-map of Houghton Regis, 1762), BHRS, *Quarto Memoirs*, 2, 1928-36; Catalogue of Maps in the Bedfordshire County Muniments, Bedford, 1930.

Berkshire   No published list; draft catalogue of the County Record Office's collection is available.

Plate X

(i)   Detail from Christopher Saxton's Map of Worcestershire, 1577

Original scale: ½ inch: 1 mile. Scale of extract shewn: 1 inch: 1 mile approx.

(ii)   Detail from Greenwood's Map of Worcestershire, 1822

Original scale: 1 inch: 1 mile. Scale of extract shewn: 1 inch: 1 mile approx.

Buckinghamshire   H.C. Schultz, 'An Elizabethan map of Wotton Underwood', *Hunt. Lib. Qua.*, III, 1939; U. Price, 'The Maps of Buckinghamshire, 1574-1800', *Records of Bucks*, XV, 1947-51; G. Wyatt, *Maps of Buckinghamshire*, Barracuda, 1978.

Cambridgeshire   'Cambridgeshire Maps, 1579-1800', *Camb. Antiq. Soc.*, 1905, 1907, 1908; *Cambridgeshire Maps, a Descriptive* Catalogue, 1579-1900, Cambridge, 1908; A.S. Bendall, *Maps, Land and Society: A History with carto-bibliography of Cambridgeshire estate maps, c.1600-1836*, C.U.P., 1992.

Carmarthenshire   G.R. Brigstocke, 'Index to the seats of Carmarthenshire, with names of owners as engraved upon the map drawn by Thomas Kitchin, *c*.1730-40', *CASFC*, VIII, 1912-13.

Cheshire   W. Harrison, 'Early Maps of Cheshire', *LCAS*, XXVI, 1909; H. Whitaker, *Descriptive List of the Printed Maps of Cheshire, 1577-1900*, Chetham Soc., 1943; E. Heawood (Introduction and notes), *English County Maps (16th-17th centuries) in the collection of the (Royal Geographical) Society*—21 Sheets folio, 2 vols.— *No.2: Chester by Saxton; No: 20: Cheshire, by Speed*, Royal Geographical Society, 1932; P.H. Burdett, *Survey of the County Palatinate of Chester. Facsimile of the 1777 Edition* HSLC, 1974.

Cornwall   J. Norden, *Speculi Britanniae pars; A topographical and historical description of Cornwall*, London, 1728; T. Tonkin, *Richard Carew's Survey of Cornwall, London 1602*, London, 1811; A.P. Jenkin, 'Scraps from old maps of Cornwall', *Old Cornwall*, I, 1925, Fed. Old Cornwall Socs.; R.C.E. Quixley, *Antique Maps of Cornwall and the Isles of Scilly*, Penzance, 1966; W.L.D. Ravenhill, 'The Newly Discovered Maps of Cornwall by John Norden', *Geographical Journal*, no.136, 1970; 'John Norden's Maps of Cornwall: A Problem in the Historical Cartography of South-west England', *Cartographer's Journal*, no.7, 1970; and: 'The Missing Maps from John Norden's Survey of Cornwall', *Exeter Essays in Geography*, Exeter, 1971; J.B. Harley and W.L.D. Ravenhill, 'Proposals for County Maps of Cornwall in 1699 and Devon in 1700', *Devon and Cornwall Notes and Queries*, no.32, Exeter, 1971; J. Norden, *Norden's Manuscript Maps of Cornwall and its Nine Hundreds*, facsimile edition, with introduction by W.L.D. Ravenhill, University of Exeter, 1972; J. Gascoyne, *A Map of the County of Cornwall, 1699*, facsimile reprint with Introduction by W.I.D. Ravenhill and O.J. Padel, DCRS, n.s., 34, 1991.

Cumberland   J.F. Curwen, 'A Descriptive Catalogue of the Printed Maps of Cumberland and Westmorland', *CWAAS*, n.s., XVIII, 1918.

Derbyshire   E.M. Yates, 'Map of Ashbourne in the sixteenth century', *DANHSJ*, no.80, 1960; and: 'Map of Over Haddon and Meadow Place, near Bakewell, c.1528', *Agricultural History Review*, 12, 1964; H. Nichols, *Local Maps of Derbyshire to 1770*, Derbs. Library Services, 1980.

Devonshire   K.M. Constable, 'The early Printed Plans of Exeter, 1587-1724', *Dev. Soc.*, 1932; D. Drake, 'Old maps of Devon', *DCNQ*, XX, 1938.

Dorset   H. Sumner, 'Old Maps of Hampshire, Dorset and Wilts', *Bourn. Nat. Hist. Soc.*, XI, 1918-19; P.D.A. Harvey, 'An Elizabethan Map of manors in North Dorset', *British Museum Quarterly*, no.29, 1965.

Durham   E. Heawood (Introduction and notes), *English County Maps (16th-17th centuries) in the collection of the (Royal Geographical) Society*—21 sheets folio, 2 vols.—*No.3, Durham by Saxton*, Royal Geographical Society, 1932; T. Corfe, *An Historical Atlas of County Durham*, Durham County Loc. Hist. Soc. 1992.

Essex   Essex County Record Office has a particularly fine selection of its county's maps, many of them published; J. Avery, 'Christopher Saxton, Draughtsman of the Earliest Known Map of Essex', *Essex Naturalist*, 11, 1901; W. Cole, 'John Norden's Map of Essex', *Essex Naturalist*, 1, 1887; T.W. Huck, 'Some Early Essex Maps and their Makers', *Essex Review*, XVIII, 1909; J.J. Green, 'Chapman and André's Map of Essex, 1777', *Essex Review*, XIX, 1910; E. Heawood (Introduction and notes), *English County Maps (16th-17th centuries) in the collection of the (Royal Geographical) Society*—21 sheets folio, 2 vols.—*No.17, Essex, Anon*, Royal Geographical Society, 1932; See also Essex Record Office Publications: no.3, *Maps in the Essex Record Office, 1566-1860*, 1947; no.16, *Maps in the Essex Record Office: Supplement*, 1952; no.25, *County Maps of Essex, 1576-1852*, 1952; no.11, *Atlas of Essex, 1777, by Chapman and André*, 1960; no.5, *Map of Essex, 1696, by John Oliver*, 1969; no.24, *Map of Essex, 1678, by Ogilby and Morgan*, 1957; no.29, *Map of Essex, 1594, by Norden*, 1959; no.4, *The Art of the Map-Maker in Essex*, 1947. no.35. *Joannes Blaeu, Map of Essex 1645*, 1961: no.36. *Mediaeval Essex*, 1962; H. Ellis, *John Norden, Speculi Britanniae pars; An historical and chorographical description of Essex*, Camden Soc., IX, 1840; F.G. Emmison, 'Survey of the manor of Woodham Ferrers, 1582', *Ess. Arch. Soc.*, n.s., XXIV, 1951; A.S. Mason, 'Chapman's Map of Essex', *Essex Journal*, 25, no.2, Summer 1990.

Gloucestershire   T. Chubb, *A Descriptive Catalogue of the Printed Maps of Gloucestershire*, BGAS, XXXV, 1912 (with additions in *BGAS*, XXXIX, LI, LII); *A Gloucestershire and Bristol Local Atlas: A selection of old maps and plans from the sixteenth to the nineteenth centuries*, BGAS, 1961.

Hampshire   G.W. Minns, 'Remarks on an old map of a portion of the ancient parish of Titchfield', *HFCAS*, V, 1900; E. Heawood (Introduction and notes), *English County Maps (16th-17th centuries) in the collection of the (Royal Geographical) Society*—21 sheets folio, 2 vols.—*No.4, Hampshire by Saxton; No.9, Hampshire by Norden*, Royal Geographical Society, 1932; C. Close, 'Ancient maps of Great Britain, with special reference to Hampshire', *HFCAS*, X, 1933; H. Sumner, 'Norden's survey of medieval coppices in the New Forest, 1609', *HFCAS*, X, 1933; E.G. Box, 'Hampshire in early maps and early road books', *HFCAS*, XIII, 1935; and: 'Norden's Plan of Hampshire, 1595', *HFCAS*, 1936.

Herefordshire   A facsimile copy of Moule's Map of Herefordshire (1577) is available from Hereford and Worcestershire Record Offices.

Hertfordshire   J. Norden, *Speculi Britanniae Pars; The description of Hertfordshire*, London, 1598; H.G. Fordham, 'Hertfordshire Maps 1529-1900', published in parts in *E. Herts Nat. Hist. Soc.*, 1901, 1903, 1905, 1907 (re-issued in one volume, 1907; most of the maps described are available at C.R.O.); E. Heawood (Introduction and notes), *English County Maps (16th-17th centuries) in the collection of the (Royal Geographical) Society*—21 sheets folio, 2 vols.—*No.5, Hertfordshire by Saxton; no.12, Hertfordshire, Anon*, Royal Geographical Society, 1932; D. Hodson, *The Printed Maps of Hertfordshire, 1577- 1900*, Map Collectors' Series, nos.53 and 59, 1969; and: no.65, 1970; P.A. Walne, *Catalogue of Manuscript Maps in Hertfordshire Record Office*, Herts. County Council, 1969; J. Wilkinson, 'John Norden's survey of Barley, Herts., 1593-1603', *Cambs. Ant. Recs. Soc.*, 2, 1974.

Huntingdonshire   P.G.M. Dickinson, *Maps in the County Record Office, Huntingdon*, 1968.

Isle of Man   J.C. Faulds (ed.), *Maps of the Isle of Man, 1280-1760*, 1975.

Kent   H. Nannen, 'Symonson's Map of Kent, 1596', *AC*, 30, 1914; E.G. Box, Lambarde's "Carde of this Shyre" third issue, with roads added', *AC*, XXXVIII, 1926; XXXIX, 1927 (article with illustrations); and: 'Notes on some West Kent roads in early maps and road books', *AC*, XLIII, 1931; E. Heawood (Introduction and notes), *English County Maps (16th-17th centuries) in the collection of the (Royal Geographical) Society*—21 sheets folio, 2 vols.—*No.10, Eastern part of Kent by Symonson; no.18, Kent and Sussex by Camden*, Royal Geographical Society, 1932; E.G. Box, 'Two sixteenth century maps of Kent, with further notes on early road books', *AC*, XLV, 1933; G.M. Livett, 'Early Kent Maps' (sixteenth century), *AC*, XLIX, 1937; and: 'Supplementary Notes on Early Kent Maps', *AC*, 1, 1938; A.R.H. Baker, 'Some Early Kentish estate maps and a note on their portrayal of field boundaries', *AC*, no.77, 1962; M. Baptist, 'Eighteenth century maps and estate plans of Bromley, Beckenham and Penge', *AC*, LXXXI, 1967; P. Symonson, *A new description of Kent in 1596* (facsimile), Southampton, 1968; I.M. Evans, 'A newly-discovered manuscript estate plan by Christopher Saxton, relating to Faversham in Kent', *Geographical Journal*, no.38, 1973; F. Hull, *Catalogue of Estate Maps, 1590-1840, in Kent County Archives Office*, 1973; Limited selection of maps available in C.R.O., particularly Andrews, Dury and Herbert's large-scale 1769 and 1779 editions. Photographs of sections of this can be obtained.

Lancashire   J. Gillow (annotated), 'Lord Burghley's map of Lancashire, 1590', *Catholic Rec. Soc.*, 4, *Miscellanea*, IV, 1907; W. Harrison, 'Early Maps of Lancashire and their Makers', *Lancs & Ches. Antiq. Soc.*, XXV, 1908; E. Heawood (Introduction and notes), *English County Maps (16th-17th centuries) in the collection of the (Royal Geographical) Society*—21 sheets folio, 2 vols.—*No.6, Lancashire by Saxton*, Royal Geographical Society, 1932; H. Whittaker, 'Maps of Lancashire', *Chetham Soc.*, CI, 1938 (Calendar); J.B. Harley, 'William Yates and Peter Burdett, their role in the mapping of Lancashire and Cheshire in the late eighteenth century', *HSLC*, 115, 1963; and: 'A proposed survey of Lancashire by Francis and Netlam Giles', *HSLC*, 116, 1964; W. Yates, *A Map of the County of Lancashire in 1786*, HSLC, 1968; *Maps of Manchester, 1650-1848*, Manchester Public Libraries, 1970; J.B. Harley (ed.), *William Yates's Map of the County of Lancaster, 1786*.

Leicestershire   The CRO's schedules of deposits and an old card index in the search room refer to three earlier sets of maps: the Bayman (19 maps 1610-1846), Halliday (10 maps) and Gimson (4 maps) Collections. The office also holds many other maps as part of other deposits which are similarly indexed. Since amalgamation with Leicester Reference Library in 1992 the CRO (at Long Street, Wigston Magna, LE18 2AH) also holds the library's earlier *Leicestershire Colleciton*. These comprise a substantial accession, beginning with Saxton's county map of 1576, and are variously indexed for the benefit of users at the office. A full catalogue is in preparation but there are no plans to publish any lists; B.L. Gimson and P. Russell, *Leicestershire Maps—A Brief Survey*, Leicester, 1947 (notes on early maps with some illustrations); R.K. Baum, *Antique Maps of Leicestershire*, Loughborough, 1972 (101 original issues from 1576 to 1850, of Leicestershire; Leicestershire and Rutland; Leicestershire and

Warwickshire; Derby, Nottingham and Leicester Shires; Northampton, Warwick, Leicester and Rutland. Cartographers include *inter alia*: Saxton (1576), Speed (1605, 1610), Bowen (1720-67), Prior (1777, 1787), Archer (1842-5) and an OS sheet of 1835).

Lincolnshire   G.R. Walshaw, 'An ancient Lincolnshire map (by William Hausarde, 1595)', *Linc. Mag.*, II, 1935; S. Bennett and N. Bennett, *An Historical Atlas of Lincolnshire*, University of Hull Press, 1993.

London & Middlesex   J. Norden, *Speculum Britanniae (Middlesex)*, London, 1593; P. Pratt, *Historic Chelsea in Maps*, 1980; J.J. Park, *Topography and Natural History of Hampstead*, 1814; Rocque, *An Exact Survey of the Cities of London, Westminster and the Country near ten miles around, 1754*, 1959; P.D. Whitting, *Some notes on a map of the parish of Hammersmith in 1853*, 1957;

From the *London Argus*: 'Sketch Map of the Parish of Fulham', XXIX, 2, 1897; Kensington, V, 1, 1897; Islington, XXV, 1, 1897; Clerkenwell, XLVIII, 2, 1898; Wandsworth, L, 2, 1898; Stoke Newington, LIII, 3, 1898; Streatham, LIX, 3, 1898;

I. Darlington and J. Howgego, *The Printed Maps of London, c.1553-1850*, 1960; A Series of Maps of West Middlesex ... No.2: Heston, Isleworth and Twickenham 1635, and No.3: Heston, Isleworth and Twickenham, 1800-1816, Geog. Assoc., W. Mx. Branch, 1961; J. C. Crace, *A Catalogue of Maps, plans and views of London ... collected by F. Crace*; M. Kelly, *Elizabethan London*, Town and Country Planning, no.33, 1965; M. Holmes, 'An unrecorded sixteenth century map of London', *Archaeologia*, no.100, 1966; E. Jones, 'London Life in Maps', *Geographical Magazine*, no.41, 1968; R. Hyde, 'Mapping London's Landlords; the ground plan of London, 1892-1915', *Guildhall Studies in London History*, no.1, 1973; W. Ravenhill, 'Joel Gascoyne's Stepney', *Guildhall Studies in London History*, no.2, 1977.

Monmouthshire   D.P.M. Michael, *The Mapping of Monmouthshire*, Regional Publications, 1985.

Montgomeryshire   E.G. Bowen, 'Map of the Trehelig common fields (end of the eighteenth century)', *Powys-Land Club, Collns.*, XLI, 1929.

Norfolk   W. Rye and H. Brittain, 'Rough Catalogue of Maps Relating to Norwich and Norfolk', *Norf. Antiq. Misc.*, Series II, Pt.1, 1906; T. Chubb and G.H. Stephen, *Descriptive List of the Printed Maps of Norfolk, 1574-1916*, Norwich, 1928; and: *The Printed Maps of Norfolk, 1574-1917*, 1928; B. Chambers, 'M.J. Armstrong in Norfolk, the progress of an eighteenth century county surveyor', *Geographical Journal*, no.130, 1964; J.C. Barringer, *An Introduction of Faden's Map of Norfolk (with facsimile Map)*, Norf. Rec. Soc., 42, 1973.

Northamptonshire   J. Norden, *Speculi Britanniae pars altera, or a delineation of Northamptonshire in the year 1610*, London, 1720; E. Heawood (Introduction and notes), *English County Maps (16th-17th centuries) in the collection of the (Royal Geographical) Society*—21 sheets folio, 2 vols., *No.13, Northamptonshire, Anon*, Royal Geographical Society, 1932; H. Whittaker, 'The Printed Maps of Northamptonshire, 1576-1900', *Northants Rec. Soc. Pubns.*, XIV, 1949. An index of printed and MS maps is also maintained at the C.R.O.; V.A.Hatley (Intro.), *Bryant's Map of the County of Northampton,1824-26*, Northants. Libraries, 1988.

Northumberland   H. Whitaker, *A Descriptive List of the Maps of Northumberland, 1576-1900*, 1949; *A Catalogue of an Exhibition of Old Maps of North- east England, 1600-1865*, Newcastle University Library Publications (extra series, no.8), 1967.

Nottinghamshire   F.A. Wordsworth, *Nottinghamshire Maps of the 16th, 17th, and 18th Centuries*, 1930. Nottinghamshire Archives holds a series of County Maps from 1607-1903, as well as numerous others in separate collections; S. Revill, 'A sixteenth century map of the river Trent, near Shelford', *Thoroton Soc.*, no.75, 1971; H. Nicholas, *Local Maps of Nottinghamshire to 1800, an Inventory*, Nottinghamshire County Council Leisure Services, 1987.

Oxfordshire   A. Holler, *Old Plans of Oxford*, OHS, XXXVIII, 1898; H. Hurst, *Oxford Topography*, OHS, XXXIX, 1899; H. Salter, *Survey of Oxford, 1772*, OHS, 1912; W. Ravenhill, 'An early eighteenth century cartographic record of an Oxfordshire manor', *Oxoniensia*, no.39, 1974.

Rutland   E. Heawood (Introduction and notes), *English County Maps (16th-17th centuries) in the collection of the (Royal Geographical) Society*—21 sheets folio, 2 vols., *No.14, Leicestershire and Rutland, Anon*, Royal Geographical Society, 1932.

Shropshire   A full list of Shropshire Maps, *The Printed Maps of Shropshire*, published by the Shropshire County Council, 1960; B. Trinder, *Robert Baugh's Map of Shropshire, 1808*, ShAS, 1984.

Somersetshire   C.W. Shickle, 'Notes on an old map of the parish of Walcot (1740)', *Bath Nat. Hist. & Antiq. Field Club*, IX, 1901; T. Chubb, *A Descriptive List of the Printed Maps of Somersetshire, 1575-1914*, SANHS, 1914 (Calendar, with illustrations); J.B. Harley and R.W. Dunning, *Somerset Maps (Day & Masters, 1782, Greenwood, 1822)*, Som. Rec. Soc., 76, 1981.

Staffordshire   C.E. Redmill, 'Bibliography of Staffordshire, with a list of maps', Geog. Assoc., *Geography*, XIV, 1901; E. Heawood (Introduction and notes), *English County Maps (16th-17th centuries) in the collection of the (Royal Geographical) Society*—21 sheets folio, 2 vols., *No.16, Staffordshire, Anon,* Royal Geographical Society, 1932; A.D.M. Phillips (ed.), *William Yates's Map of the County of Stafford, 1775,* Staffs. Record Society, 1985; S.A.H. Burne, *Early Staffordshire Maps,* N. Staffs. Field Club, vols. 54, 60. There are copies of most of the printed County Maps, from 1577 to the 19th century, in the William Salt Library.

Suffolk   *Suffolk Scene in Books and Maps,* East Suffolk County Library Exhibition, 1951; *Seven Centuries of Surveying in Suffolk,* Wolsey Art Gallery, Ipswich, 1954; D.P. Dymond, 'The county of Suffolk surveyed, by Joseph Hodskinson (1783)', *Suff. Rec. Soc.,* 15, 1972; J. Blatchey, *The Topography of Suffolk, 1561-1935* (brief biographies), Suffolk County Council, 1988; D. Dymond and E. Martin (eds.), *An Historic Atlas of Suffolk,* Suffolk County Council, 2nd edition, 1989; A MS. Catalogue of the large number of estate maps, deposited maps and plans for public undertakings, highway diversion maps, etc. is available at the C.R.O.

Surrey   R.L. Atkinson, 'Manuscript maps of Surrey; with a list of known examples in the Public Record Office', *Surrey Arch. Soc. Colls.,* XXXIII, 1920; H. Lambert, 'Banstead Maps', *Surrey Arch. Soc. Collns.,* XXXIV, 1921; W. Hooper, 'Rocque's Map of Surrey (and its date of publication)', *Surrey Arch. Soc. Colls.,* XL, 1922; H.A. Sharp, *Historical Catalogue of Surrey Maps,* Readers' Index, Croydon, 1928; E. Heawood (Introduction and notes), *English County Maps (16th-17th centuries) in the collection of the (Royal Geographical) Society*—21 sheets folio, 2 vols., *No.7, Surrey by Norden; No.11, Surrey, Anon,* Royal Geographical Society, 1932; 'Plan of the manor of Walworth, and the parish of Newington, Surrey, in the year 1681 (from an original in the possession of the Dean & Chapter, Canterbury)', *Pubns. London Top. Soc.,* no.65, 1932; *The Story of Surrey in Maps* (Catalogue of an exhibition, 1956 available at the C.R.O. who state that 'At present our printed maps are within our library system [the card index was transferred to a data-base]; however the data is about to be [by 1998] transferred to our county-wide computer system, so that map holdings of both the old offices at Kingston, Guildford and the Surrey Local Studies Library will be available, in due course over the Internet'); J.B. Harley, 'English County Map-making in the early years of the Ordnance Survey: the map of Surrey by Joseph Lindley and William Crossley', *Geographical Journal,* no.132, 1966.

Sussex   M.A. Lower, *A Survey of the Coast of Sussex in 1587,* Lewes, 1870; P.M. Johnston, 'Notes on an early map of Atherington manor (1606)', *SAC,* XLIV, 1901; E. Gerard, 'Some Notes on Some Early Printed Maps of Sussex and their Makers', *Library,* 3rd series, 6, 1916; E. Heron-Allen, 'Map of Selsey, 1672', *SAC N. & Q.* 4, LXVII, 1926; 'Early Sussex Maps', *Sussex County Magazine,* 1928; E. Heawood (Introduction and notes), *English County Maps (16th-17th centuries) in the collection of the (Royal Geographical) Society*—21 sheets folio, 2 vols., *No.8, Sussex, by Norden; No.18, Kent and Sussex, by Camden; No.19, Sussex, by Speed,* Royal Geographical Society, 1932; *Catalogue of Maps and Plans for an Exhibition of Local Maps,* Hastings Museum, 1936; F.W. Steer, *Catalogue of Sussex Estate Maps,* SRS, 61, 1968; J.H. Farrant, 'John Norden's Description of Sussex, 1595', *SAC,* no.116, 1978; D. Kingsley, 'Printed Maps of Sussex 1575-1900', *SRS,* 74, 1982.

Warwickshire   E. Heawood (Introduction and notes), *English County Maps (16th-17th centuries) in the collection of the (Royal Geographical) Society*—21 sheets folio, 2 vols., *No.15, Warwickshire. Anon,* Royal Geographical Society, 1932; P.A. Harvey and H. Thorpe, *The Printed Maps of Warwickshire, 1576-1900,* Warwickshire County Council, 1959.

Wiltshire   T. Chubb, 'A Descriptive Catalogue of the Printed Maps of Wiltshire, from 1576 to the Publication of the 25 in. Ordnance Survey of 1885', *Wilts Arch. Soc. Magazine,* XXXVII, 1912 (Catalogue); H. Sumner, 'Old maps of Dorset, Hampshire and Wiltshire', *Bourn. Nat. Hist. Soc.,* XII, 1932; J. Andrews, *Andrews and Drury's map of Wiltshire in 1773* (a reduced facsimile), WANHS (Records Branch), 8, 1952 (reprinted in 1968).

Worcestershire   J.B. Harley, 'Christopher Greenwood, county map-maker and his Worcestershire map', *Worcs. Hist. Soc.,* 45, 1962; J. Humphreys, 'Sheldon tapestry maps of Worcestershire', *Birm. Arch. Soc.,* 43, 1962; B.S. Smith, 'The Dougharty Family of Worcestershire, Estate Surveyors and Map-Makers, 1700-1760', *Worcestershire Historical Society Miscellany II,* n.s., no.5, 1967.

Yorkshire   T. Sheppard, 'East Yorkshire History in Plan and Chart', *E. Riding Antiq. Soc.,* XIX, 1912; W.B. Crump, 'The genesis of Warburton's Map of Yorkshire, 1720', *Pubns. Thoresby Soc.,* XXVIII, *Miscellanea,* 1928; H. Whittaker, *Descriptive List of Maps of Yorkshire and its Ridings, 1577-1900,* YAS Rec. Ser., LXXXVI, 1933; R.M. Butler, 'A late seventeenth century plan of York', *Antiquaries' Journal,* no.52, 1972; B. Dyson,

Yorkshire Maps and Plans in the Archives of the University of Hull, University of Hull, 1990; Hull Central Library has a card index to a massive collection of about 800 early maps of Yorkshire and East Yorkshire, arranged by date and including most of the eminent mapmakers' work. There is a separate collection of Hull maps, many village maps and a further collection catalogued by topic such as docks, railways, maritime charts, etc.; North Yorkshire C.R.O. publishes *Guide No.6: North Yorkshire Gazetteer of Townships and Parishes*. This lists the collection of maps and plans for North Yorkshire and the North Riding held there and is included in a useful list of the Record Office's other publications of texts and facsimiles. There is also a *Guide No.1: Calendars, Transcripts and Microfilms in the Record Office*.

PARISH RECORDS

THE DOCUMENTS

These are some of the most pertinent, because they are the most locally accessible of all village documents. A complete local study will always entail our leaving the village at an early stage, to seek out further evidence elsewhere. The topography and archaeology of a place can be studied, and the documentary evidence continually confirmed, on the ground, but the written source material is usually elsewhere. The secondary sources, which explain what we see or cannot see in the village, will be housed in reference libraries in neighbouring towns; the treasures and relics will be found in the nearby museum; most original documents must be sought at the County Records Office, or even in the great national repositories. Until very recently only the parish retained its records, relatively intact and on the spot. Unfortunately for the local student, a Parochial Registers and Records Measure passed in 1978 required parishes to make secure and costly provision for the documents, or make compulsory transfer of them to the County Record Office. Most parishes could only afford the second option. This regulation was intensified in 1993.

The English parish, as an ecclesiastical unit, dates back to the period of Saxon settlement and conversion; its boundaries often coincide with those of an earlier pagan land-grant. There were some 8,000 ancient parishes which came under the care of the medieval parish priest, but few villages are fortunate enough to retain any of their early records. Occasional medieval parochial assessment lists survive to illustrate the process of Subsidy Rolls in the making, with a few rare deeds and writs. It was not until Tudor times, however, that the declining authority of the manor and the township encouraged the new monarchy to resuscitate the parish, and develop it as an administrative unit. Independent of the control of the aristocracy, the parish was a conveniently autonomous, self-governing community, yet amenable to the authority of the established Church, subject to the patronage of the new Tudor gentry, and open to the supervision of the bishop's visitation and the J.P.s in Quarter Sessions. From 1538 the evidence of parochial growth multiplies, recording the widening spheres of competence and responsibility. As in the field of central conciliar government, the Tudors revived several already ancient parochial and manorial offices, and delegated to them, as to the J.P.s who supervised them, a new authority to administer their domestic affairs and effect the numerous statutes which maintained social order and regulated economic welfare. The records, reports and accounts of these, the Tudor descendants of the medieval churchwardens and overseers, the manorial constables and waywardens, are the documents which make up the contents of the parish chest. Though rarely complete, these may include, as well as the inevitable registers of the baptisms, marriages and burials of the village population, possibly from 1538, the churchwardens' accounts of the maintenance of the church fabric and the religious behaviour of priest and congregation, usually post-dating the registers; vestry minutes dating from the 16th century; the poor relief accounts from the 17th century; and the enclosure and tithe awards of the 18th century. Other miscellaneous papers may include the records of the parish school, almshouses and charities, terriers of the vicarage and glebe, burial certificates, briefs for the relief of distress in other parishes all over England, quarter sessions orders, apprenticeship indentures, royal writs requiring payment of subsidies, parish surveys, and militia books and muster rolls.

This dusty pile, the registers, vestry minutes and poor rate ledgers usually well-bound volumes, the remainder in assorted bundles and envelopes, may be found in several places. They will usually be kept in the vestry, often in the original parish chest, if not in the vestry safe. Others may be held at the vicarage in a safe or cupboard, or, in the case of minutes and ledgers, in the custody of the churchwardens, the parish council or its clerk. Most parishes have now deposited their earlier records at the County or Diocesan Record Office, which in any case will hold the bishop's transcripts of the registers, and other records which came directly under diocesan or county administration.

Thus are recorded, from Tudor times down to the decline of parochial authority during the 19th century, all the many aspects of the social, religious, economic and administrative life of the parish. Not all parishes possess a full surviving set of all such records; the most ancient church may house a disappointingly late and tedious series. On the other hand, an apparently 'new' church may often conceal an unexpected treasure from its earlier history. In searching parish records, one may seldom find the real object of the search, but may well disclose something much more interesting, because it is totally unexpected.

SOME DATES CONNECTED WITH THE HISTORY OF PARISH RECORDS

1538 Cromwell's Mandate; some parish registers begin.

1555 Statute for maintenance of the highways. Parish surveyors' accounts begin. Statute Labour levied.

1558 Accession of Elizabeth I. More parish registers begin.

1559 Act of Uniformity. Punishment of recusants and non-conformists.

1566 Statute enjoining churchwardens to enforce wearing of woollen caps on Sundays.

1598 Elizabeth I approves Canterbury Constitution. Many more parish registers begin.

1601 Great Poor Law Statute. Parish responsibility for paupers reorganised.

1650s The Cromwellian Interregnum. Gaps in parish registers. New secular official, the Parish Register, elected by ratepayers to perform marriages.

1662 Poor Law Settlement Act. Provision of settlement certificate.

1723 Poor Law Act; parishes to provide workhouses, some Parish Unions formed.

1753 Lord Hardwicke's Marriage Act. New Registers, bound volumes of printed forms, begin.

1795 Speenhamland 'System' of subsidising paupers' wages from the parish rates begins.

TRANSCRIPT

(i) 1 ...   Chadsley Corbett   ... 1
The Injungshions of owre Sovereind Lord
King Henrye the eyght weare readd fyrst
in Chadsley church the xxiij th. day of november
5 ...   in the xxx th. year of hys Raigne and in the year   ... 5
of our Lord 1538 the Dominicall ... [illegible]
          Christeninges the same year.
An. Do.   Anne the dawghter of William Sych December iiij th.
1538.   Silvester gleyshor January the xiii th.

(ii) 1 ...   Ri: Griffin Clarke preached at our Church the 25th.   ... 1
day of December 1662 upon Luk. 2.14 Glory be to god
in the highest on earth peace, good will towards men he being ordained (and liecensed) Minister by the Reverend Father in God Robert
5 ...   Lord Bp. of Lichfield and Coventry.   ... 5

(iii) 1 ...   William Broughton vicar.   ... 1
William Nock.
Thomas Barnett Church wardens.
Mermond. That November 24th. 1685 a certificate was
5 ...   granted to Gervais Burford to be touchd for the
Kings evill.

(iv) 1 ...   March 2nd. 1701. there was a certificate   ... 1
Exhibited to me of an unlawfull mar-
riage without Banns Licence or Stamp:
of Richard Bach and Eliz: Woodward
5 ...   of this parish but they have satisfyd the court   ... 5

Plate XI. Extracts from Chaddesley Corbett Parish Register, showing:
     (i)   Reference to Henry VIII's Injunctions of 1538.
     (ii)   A 'Strange Preacher', 1662.
     (iii)   Certificate to be touched for the 'King's Evil', 1685.
     (iv)   Unlawful Marriages, 1701.
(St Cassian's Church, Chaddesley Corbett.)
Size of register: 18 x 36cm; length of extracts: 2.5 x 6cm.

Chaddesley C...

The Injunctions of ... soueraine Lord
King Henry the eyght inward head first
in Chaddsley church the ... day of Nouember
in the ... yeare of hys Raigne In the yeare
of our Lord 1538 the Dominicall letter here

Cristninges the same yeare

An: do
1538   Anne the dawghter of william Gytt december iiij
        Siluster glosson Jannary the viijth

Ri: Griffin Clarke preached at our Church ye 29th
day of Nouember 1662 vpon Luk. 2.14. Glory be to god
in ye hyghest on earth peace, good will towards men &c
ing ordained a Minister by ye Reuerend father in god, Robert
Lord Bp of Lichfield & Couentry.

William Broughton vic:
  William nott   Church wardens
  Thomas Barnett

Memor: that Nouemb. 24th 1685 A Certificate was
granted to Geruas Buxford to be touchd for the
kings euill.

March 2nd 1701 there was a Certificate
Exhibited to me of an unlawfull mar=
riage without Banns Licence or Stamp
of Richard Barbe & Eliz: Woodward
of this parish, but they haue satisfyd ye court

1812   Rose's Act for more systematic registration in three separate registers. Registers to be kept in iron chests, many found today, stamped with date 1813.

1833   Lighting and Watching Act. New powers to wardens, constables and appointed inspectors.

1834   New Poor Law ends system of 'doles' from parish rates. Parish Unions established under Parish Guardians.

1835   Highways Act ends 'statute labour'.

1836   Statutory provision of civil registration of births and deaths.

1836   Great Tithe Act for general commutation of tithe payments, substituting a rent-charge. Many parishes still hold the tithe awards and plans from shortly after this date (see p.193).

1888 & 1894   Local Government Acts. County and District Councils formed. These acts remove the last surviving traces of parochial autonomy.

FURTHER READING

J. Bagley, 'Parish Registers, their Uses and Limitations', *Genealogists' Magazine*, 22, December 1987

M. Bennet, *Constables' Accounts*, Historical Association's Short Guides to Records, no.26, 1993

J.E. Bettey, *Church and Parish, A Guide for Local Historians*, 1987

L. Collins, *Marriage Licences, Abstracts and Indexes in the Library of the Society of Genealogists*, Society of Genealogists, 1981

D. Dymond, *Churchwardens' Accounts*, Historical Association's Short Guides to Records, no.25, 1995

L. Gibbens, *Church Records*, Federation of Family History Societies, 1994

J.S.W. Gibson, *Bishops' Transcripts and Marriage Licences, Bonds and Allegations. A Guide to their Location and Indexes*, FFHS, 2nd edn., 1982

J. Gibson and M. Walcot, *Where to find the International Genealogical Index*, FFHS, 1984

R. Hall, 'Parish Registers as a Source of Information', *The Local Historian*, 11, no.2, 1974

P.V. Harris, 'A Glossary of Terms from Parochial Records', *Amateur Historian*, 1, no.4, 1953

J. Kent, *The English Village Constable 1580-1642*, Clarendon Press, 1986

C.P. Ketchley, 'Practical Work on the Parish Chest', *Amateur Historian*, 2, no.3, 1954-5

E. McLaughlin, *Parish Registers: A McLaughlin Guide*, Federation of Family History Societies 2nd edn., 1988

C.J.Pickford, *Parish Registers*, Historical Association's Short Guides to Records, no.30, 1994

D. Robinson, *Bishops' Registers*, Historical Association's Short Guides to Records, no.32, 1994

D.J. Steel, *National Index of Parish Registers, 1: Sources of Births, Marriages and Deaths before 1837*, Society of Genealogists, 1960

J.A. Tallis, *Original Parish Registers in Record offices and Libraries*, Local Population Studies: Cambridge Group for the History of Populations and Social Structure, Matlock, 1976

W.E. Tate, *The Parish Chest*, Phillimore, 1983

K.M. Thompson, *Settlement Papers*, Historical Association's Short Guides to Records, no.28, and: *Apprenticeship and Bastardy Records*, Historical Association's Short Guides to Records, no.29, 1994

P.M. Tillot, 'Transcribing Parish Registers', *Amateur Historian*, 7, no.5, 1967

G.H. Tupling, 'Searching the Parish Records', a series of six articles in *The Amateur Historian*, viz: 1. The Parish registers, 1, no.7, 1953; 2. Vestry Minutes and Churchwardens' Accounts, 1, no.8, 1953; 3. Overseers' Accounts, 1, no.9, 1954; 4. Highway Surveyors' Accounts, 1, no.10, 1954; 5. Constables' Accounts, 1, no.11, 1954; 6. Terriers and Tithe and Enclosure Awards, 1, no.12, 1954

J. Whitehead and W.E. Tate, 'The Parish Constable', *Amateur Historian*, 1, no.2, 1952

E.A. Wrigley, 'Births and Baptisms; the Use of Anglican Baptism Registers as a Source of Information about Births in England before Civil Registration', *Population Studies*, no.31, 1977); and: 'Parish Registers and Population History', *Amateur Historian*, 6, no.6, 1965)

HANDLISTS

Published by the Society of Genealogists:

Catalogue of Parish Registers in possession of the Society of Genealogists, compiled by K. Blomfield, 2nd ed. 1937.

National Index of Parish Register Copies, compiled by K. Blomfield and H.K. Percy Smith, 1939.

PRINTED EDITIONS FOR WORCESTERSHIRE

(listed chronologically by publication date within parish)

W.P.W. Phillimore and W.F. Carter (eds.), *Worcestershire Parish Registers*, I, 'Marriages', London, 1901. (Contains transcripts of the Registers of twelve parishes in, or once in, the Diocese of Worcester. These are included in the following list of Worcestershire parishes, and marked WPR.M.) Transcripts of Registers and other Parish Records have been printed for the following parishes:

Alderminster (now War.)   1641-1812, WPR.M.

Alstone (now Glos.)   1550-1805, WPR.M.

Bengeworth   J.P. Shawcross, *The Parish Registers of Bengeworth*, Worcs Arch. Soc., O.S., XXXVI, 1921.

Beoley   E.A.B. Barnard, *Beoley Parish Accounts, 1656-1700*, Worcs Arch. Soc., n.s., XXV, 1948.

Bradley   1630-1812, Evesham, 1908.

Bromsgrove   E.A. Barnard, *The Earlier Parish Register of the parish of Bromsgrove*, Worcs. Arch. Soc., n.s., I, 1923.

Bushley   J. Rusling, *The Registers of Bushley, 1538-1812*, Worcs Parish Register Soc., 1913.

Churchill-in-Oswaldslow   R.A. Wilson, *The Registers of Churchill-in-Oswaldslow, 1564-1839*, Worcs. Parish Register Soc., 1914.

Church Lench   1702-1812, WPR.M.

Cropthorne   F.A. Crisp, *The Parish Registers of Cropthorne, Worcestershire, 1557-1717*, privately printed, 1896.

Dudley   E. Blockside, *Dudley Parish Registers, 1540-1650*, Dudley, 1894; A.A. Rollason, *Old Non-Parochial Registers of Dudley, comprising those of the Society of Friends, Old Meeting House, Independents, Wesleyan Methodists, Baptists and Methodist New Connection, 1662-1837*, Dudley, 1899.

Eastham   E.E. Lea, *The Registers of Eastham, with Hanley Child, Orleton and Hanley William, 1572-1812*, WPR.M.

Halesowen   E. Hobday, *The Registers of Halesowen, 1559-1643*, Parish Register Soc., 1910; F. Somers and E.H. Sargent, *Halesowen Churchwardens' Accounts, 1487-1582*, Worcs Hist. Soc., 1952.

Inkberrow   *Parochial Records of Local Government of Inkberrow in 1657*, Worcs Arch. Soc., O.S., XXX, 1909.

Kempsey   1609-1812, WPR.M.

Kington   1588-1836, WPR.M.

Knightwick and Doddenham   J. Bowstead Wilson, *The Parish Registers of Knightwick and Doddenham, 1538-1812*, London, 1891.

Oldswinford   H.E. Palfrey, *The Contents of Oldswinford Parish Chest*, Worcs Arch. Soc., n.s., XXI, 1944.

Over Areley   H.R. Mayo, *The Registers of Over Areley, 1564-1812*, Worcs Parish Register Soc., 1916.

Powick   *A List of the Parish Papers at Powick*, Worcs Arch. Soc., n.s., XXI, 1944.

Redditch   1508-1812, WPR.M.

Rous Lench   1539-1811, WPR.M.

Shipston-on-Stour   1571-1812, WPR.M.

South Littleton   E.A.B. Barnard, *The Churchwardens' Accounts of South Littleton, 1548-1571, and 1582-1693*, Worcs Arch. Soc., n.s., III, 1926.

Tidmington (now Warwicks.)   1693-1812, WPR.M.

Upton Snodsbury   E.H. Sargent, *Parish Registers of Upton Snodsbury, 1577-1837*, Worcs. Parish Registers, 2nd Series, I (typescript, 1950, available at C.R.O.).

Worcester   E.O. Browne, *The Register of Worcester Cathedral, 1693-1811*, Worcs. Parish Register Soc., 1913; J. Bowstead Wilson, *The Registers of St Alban's, Worcester, 1630-1812*, Parish Register Soc., 1896; J. Bowstead Wilson, *The Parish Book of St Helen's Church in Worcester; Parish Registers 1538-1812*, 2 vols., London, 1900;

A.S. Porter, *Churchwardens' Accounts of the Church of St Helen's, Worcester, 1519 and 1520*, Worcs. Hist. Soc., 1896; Jno. A. Copson, 'The Parish Records of St Martin's, Worcester', 1949 (typescript, C.R.O.); W.R. Buchanan-Dunlop, *The Parish Registers of St Michael's in Bedwardine, Worcester, 1546-1812*, Worcs. Parish Registers, 2nd series, 2, 1954 (typescript, C.R.O.); J. Amphlett, *Churchwardens' Account of St Michael's in Bedwardine, Worcester, 1539-1603*, Worcs. Hist. Soc., 1896; F.A. Crisp, *The Catholic Register of the City of Worcester, 1685-1837, 1887* (privately printed).

SOME PRINTED PARISH DOCUMENTS, CALENDARS AND OTHER SOURCES

C.R. Humphery-Smith, *The Phillimore Atlas and Index of Parish Registers*, 1995. There are several hundreds of parish registers and other parochial documents which have been published in transcript or Calendar form. Many of these can be found by reference to Burke's *Key to Parish Registers* and Mullins's *Texts and Calendars*. Some of this vast collection for various counties are listed below:

Bedfordshire   From BHRS: *Elizabethan Churchwardens' Accounts*; *Recusancy and Non-Conformity in Bedfordshire*; *The Paper Register of St Mary's Church, Bedford, 1539-58*; *Harlington Churchwardens' Accounts, 1677-1748*.

Berkshire   See County Record Office 'Guide';
  In *BBOSAJ*: 'Index to Berkshire marriage registers', VI; 'Index to Hurst parish register, 1585-1607 and 1613-1812 (men only)', XXVI; 'Church briefs (from Little Wittenham parish registers)', XVIII; 'Index to Ruscombe marriage register, 1559-1812 (men only)', X; 'List of briefs in the parish register (and churchwardens' accounts) of Ruscombe (1661-80)', XIX; 'Parish registers of St Lawrence, Reading (marriages, men only) 1605-99', XXV; Published by Par. Reg. Soc.: *Registers of Blewbury, Berks. 1588-1813*, 70; *Registers of Denchworth, Berks., 1540-1812*, 73.

Buckinghamshire   Bucks. CRO, *Notes for the Guidance of Genealogists*, Bucks. C.C., 1987;
  In *BBOASJ*: 'Rural parochial records', IX; 'Index to Bradfield parish register, 1559-1813', VIII;
  Published by Par. Reg. Soc.: *Register of St Mary's chapel in Fenny Stratford, co. Buckingham, 1730-1812*, 62; *Registers of Great Woolstone, Bucks. (baptisms, 1538-1811; marriages, 1538-1750 and 1789; burials, 1538-1810)*, 81; *Registers of Little Woolstone, Bucks. (baptisms and burials, 1596-1813; marriages, 1596-1810)*, 80;
  See *Publications of the Bucks. Par. Reg. Soc.* vols.1 (1902) to 20 (1916), as follows: 'Register of Addington (Baptisms & burials, 1558-1837; marriages, 1558-1908)', 20; 'Registers of Aston Abbots, 1559-1837 and Edgcott, 1538-1837', 15; 'A Transcript of the first volume of the Register of Chesham, with introductory notes, appendices and index', 4; 'Register of Drayton Parslow, 1559-1837', 17; 'The Early Register of Great Marlow, 1592-1611', 3; 'Register of Mentmore, 1685-1829', 11; 'Register of Olney, 1665-1812', 6, 7, 10, 12 and 13; 'Register of Raventone, 1568-1812', 14; 'Register of Stoke Poges, 1563-1653', 9 and 16; 'Register of Thoreton, 1562-1812', 2; 'Register of Walton (near Bletchley), 1598-1812', 1; 'Register of Wing, 1546-1812', 18 and 19; 'Register of Woughton-on-the-Green, 1558-1718', 5 & 8;
  In *Records of Bucks*: 'Aston Abbots Parish Registers', X; 'Bletchley parish register', VIII; 'Clifton Reynes Parish Account Book', XI; 'Hillesden Account Book, 1661-7', XI; 'The parish church of High Wycombe' (includes extracts from churchwardens' and overseers' accounts), VII and VIII; 'Newton Longville Parish Books (extracts, 1560-1840)', XI; 'Churchwardens' Accounts of Quainton', XII, 1927; 'Wavendon parish register', IX;
  E. M. Elvey, *The Courts of the Archdeaconry of Buckingham, 1483-1523*, BRS, no.19, 1975; *The Beaconsfield Parish Register, 1600-1837*, Beaconsfield and District Historical Society, 1973; L.H. Chambers, 'Extracts relating to Hertfordshire from the parish registers of Chesham, Bucks. (1541-1635)', *EHAS*, VII, 1923; 'Clifton Reynes parish account book 1665-1723', *Archit. & Arch. Soc. Bucks.*, XI, 1926.

Caernarvonshire   A. Hadley, *Conway Parish Registers, 1541-1793*, Strand, 1900.

Cambridgeshire   M. Farrer, *Genealogical Sources in Cambridgeshire*, County Council, 1979;
  From CHAS: 'Parish registers of Rampton, Cambs., 1599-1812', I; 'Notes from the registers and churchwardens' accounts of St. Mary, Over, Cambs.', II; 'Churchwardens' bills for the Deanery of Barton, Cambs., 1554', V;
  Churchwardens' Accounts of St Mary the Great, Cambridge 1504-1635, Cambs. Ant. Soc., 35; G. Reynolds, *Infant Mortality and Sex-ratios at Baptism, as shown by a reconstruction of Willingham*, Local Population Studies, no.22, 1979.

Carmarthenshire   'Carmarthenshire presentments 1671-79', *Cambrian Arch. Assoc. Arch. Cambrensis*, 6th series, XIX;

From *CASFC*: 'Llanarthney churchwardens' book 1801-29', IX; 'Llanfynydd churchwardens' accounts 1684', X; 'Churchwardens' presentments in Carmarthenshire', X-XV; 'Kidwelly churchwardens' presentments 1787', XIII; 'Llanfynydd churchwardens' presentments 1789'; 'Llanfihangel Uch Gwili chapel; churchwardens' presentments 1792', XIV.

Cheshire   *Cheshire Parish Registers* (vols.1-5), ed. W.P.W. Phillimore, T.M. Blagg and L. Choice, were published in the *Phillimore Parish Register Series*, from 1909 to 1914;

In *CNWAAHSJ*: 'Parish registers of Burton', XV; 'Trade and customs of Chester in the 17th and 18th centuries, as shown in some old parish registers', XVII; 'Churchwardens' accounts of the parish of St Bridget, Chester 1811-47', XI; 'Churchwardens' accounts of St Martin's Chester 1683-1816', XII;

In *LCAS*: 'Hatherlow chapel baptismal register, 1732-81', XLIV; 'Notes on Wilmslow parish registers (1558-1652)', XXXIII;

Published by LPRS: *The Register of Bruera Church, 1662-1812*, 1910; *Registers of Chester Cathedral, 1687-1812*, LIV; *The Register of Winwick Parish Church, Baptisms, 1563-1620: Marriages and Burials, 1600-1620*; *The Registers of St. Oswald's Parish Church, Winwick, Part 2: 1621-1660*, nos.10 and 113;

'Registers of St Mary's Birkenhead, 1721-1812', *HSLC*, LVIII; A. Anderson, *The Registers of the Parish of Bromborough in the County of Chester, 1600-1726*, Bromborough Parochial Church Council, 1962; F. Sanders, *The Parish Registers of Eastham, Cheshire, 1598-1700*, London, 1891; S. Thornley, *Frodsham Parish Church Registers, 1558-1812*, 3 vols., Worcester, 1906-13; *Registers of Prestbury, 1560-1635*, LCRS, 1881.

Cornwall   *Cornwall Parish Registers* (vols.1-24), ed. W.P.W. Phillimore, H. Glenross, W.J. Stephens and A.T. Sallaford, were published in the *Phillimore Parish Register Series* from 1900 to 1915; H. Peskett, *Guide to Parochial and Non-parochial Registers of Devon and Cornwall*, Devon and Cornwall Record Society (extra series), II, 1979; L.W.L. Lawson-Edwards, *Index to Cornish Nonconformist Registers deposited at the Public Record Office*, London, 1976;

From DCRS: *Register of baptisms, marriages and burials of Falmouth, Cornwall, 1663-1812*; *Register of marriages, baptisms and burials of the parish of St Mary, Truro, Cornwall, 1597-1837*;

In *JRIC*: T. Peter, 'Churchwardens' accounts of the parish of Camborne', *J. R. Inst. Cornwall J.*, XVII; 'Index to Cornish transcripts (of parish registers etc.) at Exeter and Bodmin', XIX.

Cumberland   The CWAAS, founded in 1866, published a Parish Registers Series of 51 volumes from 1912 to 1987. The following are of particular note: 'Parish Registers of Bridekirk, 1584-1812', XIV; 'Parish Registers of Crosthwaite, Part I: 1562-1600; Part II: 1600-1670; Part III: 1670-1812 (christenings and marriages)'; Part IV: 1670-1812 (burials)', XVI-XIX; 'Parish Registers of Crosthwaite and Lyth, 1569-1812', XXIII; 'Parish Register of Dacre, 1559-1716', I; 'Parish Registers of Holm Cultram, Part I: 1580-1597', XXXIV; 'Parish Registers of Lamplugh, 1581-1812', XXIV; 'Parish Registers of Newton Reigny 1571-1812', XXII; 'Parish Registers of Penrith, Part I: 1556-1604; Part II: 1605-1660; Part III: 1661-1713; Part IV: 1714-1769; Part V: 1770-1812', XXVI-XXX; 'Parish Registers of St Bees 1538-1837', XLI; 'Parish Registers of St Giles, Great Orton, 1568-1812', IV; 'Parish Registers of St James's, Whitehaven, Part I: Baptisms 1753-1837', XL; 'Parish Registers of Skelton, 1580-1812', VI; 'Parish Registers of Whicham, 1569-1812', XIII; 'Parish Registers of Wigton, Part I: 1604-1727; Part II: Baptisms 1728-97; marriages 1728-81; burials 1728-79; Indexes Parts I and II', XXXV and XXXVII;

The Registers of the Parish Church of Dalton-in-Furness, Part I: 1556-1620, Pubns. LPRS, no.100.

Derbyshire   In *DANHSJ*: 'Churchwardens' accounts of Chapel-en-le-Frith, 1729-1805', XXXIII; 'Registers and churchwardens' accounts of the parish of Duffield', XXXIX; 'Registers of Glossop parish church, 1620-1812', XXXVIII; 'Registers of the parish of Kedleston 1600-1812', xl; 'Notes on an old churchwardens' account book of St Werburgh in Derby', XXXIX; 'The earliest registers of the parish of Weston-upon-Trent 1565-1605', XLI;

Registers of Mickleover 1607-1812 and of Littleover 1680-1812, Pubns. Par. Reg. Soc., 65.

Devonshire   E. Windeatt, 'The Puritans in Devon' (with particular reference to the Joint-testimonie of the Ministers of Devon, 1648), *Cong. Hist. Soc.*, I, 1901;

By *D. Assoc. for Adv. Sc. Litt. & Art*: 'Early register of the parish of Fen Ottery, 1596-1680', XXXIII; 'Notes on Membury' (the parish, church, registers and churchwarden's book), LVIII;

By DCRS: *Guide to Parochial and Non-parochial Registers of Devon and Cornwall*, Devon and Cornwall Record Society (extra series), II; 'Churchwardens' accounts of Ashburton 1479-1580', 39; *Registers of*

Branscombe, 1539-1812; *Registers of Colyton, 1538-1837*; *Registers of Halberton, 1605-1837*; *Registers of Hartland, 1558-1837*; *Registers of Hemyock, 1635-1837*; *Registers of Lapford, 1567-1850*; *Registers of Lustleigh, 1608-1837*; *Registers of Ottery St Mary, 1601-1837*; *Registers of Parkham (1537-1812)*; *Register of births, marriages and burials of Parracombe, Devon, 1597-1836*; *Registers of Plymtree, 1538-1837*; *Registers of St Andrew's, Plymouth, 1581-1633*; *Registers of Topsham, 1600-1837*; *Registers of Widdicombe-in-the-Moor, 1573-1837*;

  J.J. Beckerlegge, 'Plympton records' (Overseers' accounts, 1780-1824; workhouse accounts, 1775-93), *Plymouth Inst. & C. & Corn. Nat. Hist. Soc.*, XVII, 1937; E. Lega-Weekes, 'Churchwardens' accounts of South Tawton', *Devon Assoc.*, XXXVIII-XLI, 1906.

Dorset W.P.W. Phillimore and I.E. Neville, *Dorset Parish Registers*, Phillimore & Co., 7 vols., 1906-14; 'Dorset Incumbents, 1542-1731' (in six parts), *SDNHAS*, LXX-LXXII, LXXVIII-LXXV; *Statistics of Dorset parishes, c.1600*, Dorset Natural History and Archaeological Soc., no.89;

  In *Dorset Records*: 'Registers of Caundle Bishop, 1570-1814', III; 'Registers of Holnest, 1589-1812', II; 'Registers of Long Burton, 1580-1812', I; 'Registers of Stourpaine, 1631-1799', VII; 'Registers of Thornford, 1677-1812', IX;

  By Par. Reg. Soc.: *Registers of Almer, 1538-1812*; *Registers of Beer Hackett, 1549-1812*; *Registers of Lydlinch, 1559-1812*; *Registers of Swanage, 1563-1812*; *Registers of Tarrant Hinton, 1545-1812*;

  By C.H. Mayo: *Parish Registers of Buckland Newton*, Dorchester, 1889; *Parish Registers of North Wootton, 1539-1786*, 1877.

Durham The DNPRS, founded in 1897, published 36 volumes of parish registers for both counties from 1898 to 1926: 'Registers of Bishop Middleham, 1559-1812', no.13; 'Registers of Castle Eden: baptisms 1661-1812; marriages 1698-1794', no.29; 'Registers of Coniscliffe; baptisms and marriages 1590-1812; burials 1591-1812', no.18; 'Registers of Dalton-le-Dale, 1653-1812', no.23; 'List of parochial and non-parochial registers relating to Durham and Northumberland', no.26; 'Registers of Ebchester 1619-1812', no.4; 'Registers of Middleton St George; baptisms 1652-1812; marriages and burials 1616-1812', no.12; 'Registers of Ryton; marriages 1581-1812', no.6; 'Registers of St Margaret's Durham; marriages 1558-1812', no.9; 'Registers of St Mary in the South Bailey, Durham; baptisms 1560-1812; marriages and burials 1559-1812', no.17; 'Registers of St Mary-le-Bow, Durham; baptisms and burials 1571-1812; marriages 1573-1812', no.27; 'Registers of St Nicholas's Church, Durham; 1: Marriages 1540-1812', no.32; 'Registers of Seaham; baptisms 1646-1812; marriages 1652-1812; burials 1653-1812', no.22; 'Registers of Sherburn Hospital; baptisms 1692-1812; marriages 1695-1763; burials 1678-1812', no.30; 'The Registers of Stanhope: Marriages 1613-1812', no.3; 'The Registers of Whickham: Marriages 1579-1812', no.1; 'Registers of Whitburn; baptisms 1611-1812; marriages and burials 1579-1812', no.10; 'Registers of Whorlton; baptisms 1626-1812; marriages 1713-1812; burials, 1669-1812', no.19; 'Registers of Winston; baptisms 1572-1812; marriages 1574-1812; banns 1754-1812; burials 1573-1812', no.35;

  By Pubns. Durham Hist Soc.: *Parish Registers of All Saints', Lanchester; 1: 1560-1603*; 'Parish Registers of Muggleswick 1784-1812'; *Parish Registers of St Cuthbert's Church, Satley, 1560-1812*;

  M.S. McCollum, *Durham Diocesan Records*, University of Durham, 1976.

Essex E.J. Erith, *Essex Parish Records, 1240-1894*, no.7, Essex Record Office Publication, 1950; A.D. Jones, *Parish Registers of Hatfield*, Hatfield Vicarage, 1974; G.E. Roebuck, *Walthamstow Marriages, 24 Feb. 1650 - 1 July 1837, abstracted from the parish registers*, Walth. Ant. Soc., Monograph no.25, 1931.

Gloucestershire Parish records for Gloucester diocese which are deposited at Gloucestershire Record Office are listed in the *Handlist of Contents of the Gloucestershire Record Office*, GCC, 1995. The Record Office can advise on the whereabouts of non-deposited records. A detailed guide to parish registers, indexes and transcripts is published as *A Handlist of Genealogical Records*, GCC, 1992. For records of parishes in Bristol diocese, contact Bristol Record Office;

  Gloucestershire Parish Registers (vols.1-11), ed. W.P.W. Phillimore, were published in the *Phillimore Parish Register Series*, from 1896 to 1905; D.J. Steel, *National Index of Parish Registers*, 5, Society of Genealogists, 1966 includes this county.

  By BGAS: *Tewkesbury Churchwardens' Accounts 1563-1624*; *Marriage Allegations in the Diocese of Gloucester, 2: 1681-1700*, 9; *The Registers of the Church of St. Mary's Dymock, 1538-1790*, no.4;

  The General Accounts of the Churchwardens of Chipping Campden 1626-1907, Campden Record Series, 1; *Register of Hanham and Oldland, Glos., 1584-1681*, Pubns. Par. Reg. Soc., 63; *A register book for (the parish of) St Mary de Lode (Gloucester), 1656-9*, Gloucester Cathedral Society Pubns., 1928; *Tidenham Parish Registers to 1754*, Chepstow Society, Pamphlet Series, no.10.

Hampshire A.J. Willis, *Hampshire Marriage Licences, 1607-1640* and *1669-1680*; *Papish Recusants, 1680*, Eastleigh, 1978; *Parish Registers of Bishopstoke, 1657-1812*, Eastleigh, 1977; 'Milford churchwardens' accounts', *Milford-on-Sea Record Soc. Mag.*, v.

Herefordshire A guide to Herefordshire parish registers, published by Friends of Hereford Record Office is available from Hereford and Worcester Record Offices; J. Harnden, *Parish Registers of Herefordshire*, Friends of Hereford Record Office, 1987; D.J. Steel, *National Index of Parish Registers, 1, 5*, includes both Herefordshire and Worcestershire;

Pubns. Par. Reg. Soc: M. Hopton, *Registers of Canon Frome, Herefordshire, 1680-1812*, 45; *Registers of Munsley, Herefordshire, 1662-1812*, 46;

'Bishop's transcripts at Hereford (1600-60)', *ShANHS*, VII; A.M. Godgson, *Registers of Little Malvern Priory, St. Giles, 1691-1837*, Birmingham and Midland Society for Genealogy and Heraldry, 1975; J. and M. West, 'Courtship map' of Woolhope in *A History of Herefordshire*, Phillimore, 1985;

Hertfordshire W.P.W. Phillimore, *Hertfordshire Parish Registers: Marriages, 1*; *Phillimore's Parish Register Series, no.XCI*, London, 1907, *no.CXXVII*, London, 1909; T.M. Blagg and J.H. Gurney, *Hertfordshire Parish Registers: Marriages, 3*; *Phillimore's Parish Register Series, no.CXL*, London, 1914;

By W. Brigg: *Hertfordshire Genealogist and Antiquary*, 3 vols., 1895, 1897 and 1898; *Parish Registers of Aldenham*, 2 vols., 1902 and 1910; *Parish Registers of St Alban's Abbey, 1538-1689*, supplement to *Hertfordshire Genealogist and Antiquary*, 1897;

EHAS: 'Barway churchwardens' accounts 1544-1714', v; 'Marriage Registers of Great and Little Wymondley, Ickleford, Willian, Norton, Holwell, Hexton and Digswill', 7; 'Extracts Relating to Hertfordshire from the Parish Registers of Chesham, Bucks', 7; 'An early Thundridge book of accounts (constable, churchwardens and overseers 1619-76)', VII; 'Churchwardens' books of Welwyn 1657-1732', V;

Herts. Record Society: *Early Churchwardens' Accounts of Bishop Stortford 1431-1558*; *Tudor Churchwardens' Accounts, 1*;

SAHAAS: H. Rudd, 'Churchwardens' accounts, with special reference to those at Bushey'; 'Sandridge parish accounts 1686-1780', I;

H.C. Gibbs, *Parish Registers of Hunsdon, 1546-1837*, London, 1915; W. Minet, *Register of the Parish of Little Hadham, 1559-1812*, Colchester, 1907; D.J. Browning and F.R. Pope, *The Registers of Rainford Chapel; Marriages 1813-37*, 1981; M. Aston, 'Iconoclasm at Rickmansworth, 1522; troubles of churchwardens', *Journal of Ecclesiastical History*, 40, October 1989.

Huntingdonshire 'Notes from the churchwardens' books of Great Gransden, Hunts.', *CHAS*, II.

Kent AC: 'Notes on the Records of Smarden Church', 9; 'Hythe Churchwardens' Accounts in the time of Henry IV', 10; 'Briefs in the Parish of Cranbrook', 14; 'Churchwardens' Accounts of Rainham, Kent, A.D.1517-19 and 1565-9', 15; 'Churchwardens' Accounts of St Dunstans Canterbury, 1484-1514', 16; 'Churchwardens' Accounts of St Dunstan's, Canterbury, 1508-80', 17; 'Church-wardens' Accounts, Edenbridge', 21; 'Extracts from the Parish Registers of Edenbridge', 21; 'Staplehurst register (1538-96)', XXVIII; 'Notes from the parish registers of Maidstone', XXIX; 'Extracts from some lost Kent registers', XXXI; 'Notes on 19th century alterations to High Halden church, with extracts from the parish books and registers', XXVI; 'Eltham churchwardens' accounts', 47-8; 'Chiddingstone early poor law accounts', 73; 'An early poor law account', 64;

Pubns. Par. Reg. Soc.: *Registers of Boughton-under-Blean, Kent; baptisms, 1558-1624; burials 1558-1625*, 49; *Registers of Lullingstone, Kent (1578-1812)*, 78; *Registers of Horton Kirbie, Kent, baptisms and marriages, 1684-1812; burials, 1678-1810*, 79;

A.J. Willis, *Canterbury Marriage Licences, 1751-1837* (3 vols.) Phillimore, and *Canterbury Licences General, 1568-1646*, Phillimore, 1971; C.E. Woodruff, *Parish Registers and Records in the Diocese of Canterbury*, Canterbury, 1922; W.E. Buckland, *Parish Registers and Records in the Diocese of Rochester*, Kent Arch. Soc. Rec. Set., 1912; C. Cotton, 'Churchwardens' accounts of St Andrew Canterbury, 1485-1625', *Kent Arch. Soc.*, XXXII, 1917; H.R. Plomer and F.R. Mercer, 'Churchwardens' Accounts of St Nicholas Strood and of Bethersden, 1515-73, *Kent Records*, 5, 1928.

Lancashire There are four useful sources of information about Lancashire parish registers. These are: The County Record Office at Preston, The Lancashire Parish Register Society (Hon. General Editor: Dr. Colin Rogers, Manchester Metropolitan University), the Manchester and Lancashire Family History Society (HQ and Library at Clayton House, 59 Piccadilly, Manchester M1 2AQ) and the Archives

Department of Manchester Central Library which holds many original registers, microfilm copies and transcripts. The Parish Register Society, since its foundation in 1897, has published one or two volumes a year, down to the registers of Todmarton as Vol.140 in 1996, and, since 1984, additional copies on microfiche. Published registers down to 1987 are listed below. The Society also issues, from time to time, *The Lancashire Parish Register Society Handbook*, the most recent number in 1995. This lists parishes alphabetically with their volume numbers and dates; it also includes details of Lancashire registers published by other organisations, lists some unpublished transcripts and a review of Bishops' transcripts. It also offers notes for the guidance of editors, transcribers and typists. The Manchester and Lancashire Family History Society publishes an occasional *Guide to the Registers in the Local Studies Unit of the Central Library*, affectionately known as 'the pink book'. The current edition is for 1992 but this is about to be brought up-to-date in 1996-7. *The Guide* lists all original registers and copies held by the Archives Department (tel. 0161 234 1900), a very helpful contact for the searcher.

Available at CRO and County Library, or on inter-library loan: *A Handlist of Genealogical Sources*, Lancashire County Record Office, 1986;

LCRS: *The Records of the Parish of Preston*, 104; *Prescot Churchwardens' Accounts, 1523-1607*, 104;

LPRS: *Registers of Aldingham in Furness, 1542-1695; Registers of Altham, 1596-1695; Parish registers of Ashton-under-Lyne: baptisms and marriages 1594-1720; burials 1596-1720,* LXV; *Parish Register of Aughton, 1541-1764,* 81; *Parish registers of Bentham, 1666-1812,* LXIX; *Parish Register of Billinge 1699-1812 (baptisms from 1696),* 123; *Registers of Bispham, baptisms, 1599-1754,* XXXIII; *Registers of Blackburn, 1600-60,* XLI; *2: 1653-80,* 93; *Registers of Blackley, near Manchester, 1655-1753; Registers of Blackrod, 1606-1701,* XXXVI; *Parish Registers of Blawith, 1728-1837, and Lowick 1718-1837,* 94; *Registers of Bolton: baptisms 1573-4, 1590-1660; marriages 1573, 1587-1660; burials 1573-4, 1587-1660,* L; *Registers of Bolton-le-Sands, 1655-1736; Registers of Brindle, 1558-1714,* XI; *Registers of Broughton, near Preston: baptisms 1653-1804; burials 1653-1803; marriages 1653-1759,* XLVIII; *Parish Register of Broughton-in-Furness, 1634-1812,* 90; *Parish Register of Burtonwood, 1668-1837,* 84; *Registers of Bury, I, Part I, 1590-1616; Part II, 1617-46* and *Registers of Bury, II, 1647-98,* I, X and XXIV; *Registers of Cartmel, 1559-1661,* XXVIII; *2: 1660-1723,* 96; *Registers of Caton, 1585-1718; Parish Register of Childwall, I: 1557-1680,* 106, *2: 1681-1753,* 122; *Registers of Chipping, 1559-1694,* XIV; *Registers of Chorley, 1548-1653,* XXXVIII; *Parish Register of Chorlton-cum-Hardy: baptisms 1639, 1737-1837; marriages 1737-51; burials 1753-1837; Parish Register of Church Kirk, 1600-1747,* 102; *Registers of Claughton, 1701-1813; Registers of Cockerham, 1595-1657,* XXI; *Registers of Colne, 1599-1653,* XVII; *Registers of Coniston, 1599-1700,* XXX; *Registers of Croston, I: christenings 1543-1685; marriages 1538-1727; burials 1538-1685; II: marriages and burials, 1690-1727,* VI and XX; *Registers of the Parish Church of Dalton-in-Furness, Part I, 1565-1621,* 100; *2: 1621-1691,* 104; *Registers of Deane, I: baptisms and marriages, 1604, 1613-1750; 2: burials 1604, 1613-1750,* LIII; *3: 1751-1812,* 79; *Registers of St Lawrence, Denton, 1695-1757,* XLVII; *Registers of the Church of St James, Didsbury, Part I: 1561-1653; Part II: 1654-1757,* VIII and IX; *Parish Register of Downham, 1606-1837,* 118; *Registers of Eccles, 1564-1632,* XXV; *Registers of Eccleston, 1603-94,* XV; *Parish Register of Farnworth (Widnes), 1538-1612,* 80; *2: 1612-98,* 97; *Parish Register of Formby, 1620-1780,* 112; *Parish registers of Garstang, 1567-1658; 1660-1734,* LXIII and LXVIII; *Parish Registers of Goosnargh: baptisms and burials 1639-1753; marriages 1639-1812,* LXIV; *Registers of Gorton, 1599-1741; Parish Register of Great Harwood, 1547-1812,* 75; *Registers of Gressingham: baptisms 1676-1812; Parish Register of Hale Chapel, 1572-1740,* 92; *Parish Register of Halsall 1606-1754,* 105; *Registers of Halton, 1592-1723,* XLIV; *Parish Register of Hambleton, 1695-1812; Parish Register of Heaton Norris: baptisms 1769-1845; burials 1767-1850,* 121; *Registers of Heysham: births and baptisms, deaths and burials 1658-1813; marriages 1659-1811; Parish Register of Hollinfare: baptisms 1654-1837; marriages 1705-44; burials 1709-1837,* 120; *Parish Register of Holme-in-Clivinger, 1742-1841,* 124; *Registers of Hornby, 1742-89; Parish Register of Huyton, 1578-1727,* 85; *Parish registers of Ingleton and Chapel-le-Dale* (originally in Lonsdale Deanery [La, We] and the Richmond [Y] archdeaconry; see also YPRS, p.129), *1607-1812,* LXXI; *Registers of Kirkby-in-Furness: baptisms, 1701-1812; burials 1681-1812; marriages 1728-1754,* XLIII; *Parish Register of Kirkham, I: 1539-1600,* 83; *2: 1601-1653,* 99; *Registers of Lancaster, I: 1599-1660; II: 1691-1748,* XXXII and LVII; *II: 1749-1786,* LXXXVIII; *Parish Register of Leigh, 1625-1700,* 87; *Earliest registers of Liverpool (St Nicholas's church), 1660-1704; Some of the earlier episcopal transcripts; Report on the ecclesiastical records in the diocese of Liverpool,* XXXV; *Parish Register of Liverpool, 2: 1705-1725,* 101; *Registers of Lytham: baptisms and burials, 1679-1761; marriages, 1679-1754; Registers of the Cathedral Church of Manchester, I: 1573-1616; II: baptisms and marriages 1616-55; burials 1616-53,* XXI, LV and LVI; *IV: 1653-1665,* 89; *Parish Register of St Mary's, Manchester, 1756-1888; marriages to 1837,* 77; *The Parish Register of Melling in Halsall: baptisms and burials 1607-1812; marriages 1603-1837,* 108; *Registers of Melling: baptisms 1625-1721; burials 1629-1721; marriages 1636-1752,* XL; *Registers of Middleton, I: 1541-1664; II: 1653-1729,* XII and XVIII; *1729-52; Registers of Newchurch in the township of Culceth, 1599-*

1812, XXII; *Registers of Newchurch-in-Rossendale, 1653-1723*, XLV; *Parish registers of North Meols, 1594-1731*, LXVI; *2: 1732-1812*, 72; *Registers of Ormskirk, 1557-1626*, XIII; *2: 1626-1678*, 98; *Registers of Over Kellet, 1648-1812*, XLII; *Registers of Padiham, 1573-1653*, XVI; *Registers of St Michael's, Pennington in Furness, 1612-1702*; *Registers of Penwortham, 1608-1753*, LII; *Registers of Pilling: baptisms 1630-1721; burials 1685-1719; marriages, 1630-1719*, XXXIX, 1910; *Registers of Poulton-le-Fylde, 1591-1677*, XIX; *Parish Register of Prescot, 1: 1573-1631*, 76; *2: 1632-1666*, 114; *The Registers of St Helen's Chapel in the Parish of Prescot, Part 2: 1788-1812*, III, 1972; *Registers of Preston, 1611-35*; *Registers of Prestwich, 1603-88*, XXXIV; *Registers of Prestwich, baptisms and burials, 1689-1711; marriages to 1712*, XLIX; *Registers of Radcliffe, Part I: Baptisms and burials 1557-1783; marriages 1560-1761; Part II: burials 1558-1783*, LX and LXI; *The Parish Register of Rainford: baptisms and burials 1702-1812; marriages 1704-1812*, 119; *Registers of Ribchester, 1598-1694*, XXVI; *Registers of Rochdale, 1642-1700*, LVIII; *Marriage registers of Rochdale, 1701-1801*, LXII; *Parish Register of Rufford, 1632-1812*, 115; *Parish Register of St Helens, 1: 1713-1787*, 106; *2: 1788-1812; marriages to 1837*, 111; *Registers of St Michael's on Wyre, 1659-1707*; *Parish Register of Sefton, 1597-1783*, 86; *Registers of Stalmine, 1583-1724*, LI; *Registers of Standish, 1560-1653*, XLVI; *Registers of Tatham, 1558-1812*, LIX; *2: 1813-37, and of Tatham Fells, 1745-1837*, 78; *Parish registers of Thornton-in-Lonsdale, 1576-1812*, LXVII; *Registers of Torver, near Coniston, 1599-1792*; *Parish Register of Todmorden, 1666-1780*, 117; *Parish Register of Tottington, 1799-1837*, 116; *Registers of Tunstall: baptisms, 1626-1812; burials 1627-1812; weddings 1625-1812*; *Parish Register of Turton, 1720-1812*, 82; *Registers of St Thomas the Martyr, Upholland, 1600-1735*, XXIII; *Registers of Urswick in Furness, 1608-95*, XXIX; *Registers of Walton-le-Dale, 1609-1812*, XXXVII; *2: 1663-1743*, 91; *Registers of Formby Chapel in the Parish of Walton on the Hill, 1620-1780*, 112, 1973; *Parish Register of West Derby Chapel in the Parish of Walton on the Hill, Baptisms, 1688-1837; Marriages, 1698-1847*, 110, 1971; *Parish registers of Warrington, 1591-1653*, LXX; *2: 1653-80*, 95; *3: 1681-1706*, 125; *Parish Register of Warton, 1568-1812*, 73; *Parish Register of Whalley, 2: 1605-53*, 74; *Parish Register of Winwick, 1: 1563-1620*, 109; *2: 1621-1660*, 113; *Registers of Woodplumpton, 1604-59*, XXVII; *2: 1659-1784*, 103; The following registers are published on microfiche: *Parish Register of Altcar, 1663-1809*, M9; *Parish Register of Ashton-in-Makerfield: baptisms 1698-1755; marriages 1700-53*, M3; *Parish Register of Cartmel, 3: 1724-71*, M4; *Register of Church Kirk, 1600-1747*, 102; *Parish Register of Formby, 2: 1781-1837*, M5; *Parish Register of Great Sankey, 1728-1837*, M1; *Parish Register of Maghull: christenings 1663-1812; marriages 1660-1754; burials 1660-1844*, M2; *Parish Register of Newchurch (Culceth): baptisms and burials 1813-41; and of Croft with Southworth: baptisms and burials 1833-41*, M8; *Register of Rufford Parish Church, 1632- 1812*, no.115; *Parish Register of Winwick, 3: 1661-1716*, M6; *4: 1716-56*, M7; *Registers of Woodplumpton: 1659-1784*, no.104; The LPRS's brochure lists those libraries which, as corporate members of the society, could be expected to provide these copies for reference;

E. Broxap, 'Extracts from Manchester churchwardens' accounts 1664-1710', Chetham Soc., *Miscellany*, n.s., IV, 1921; K. Leonard, *A Register of Births and Baptisms, Deaths and Burials, 1813-1837, in the Parish of Hawkshead*, London, 1971; *Parish and Nonconformist Registers in Manchester*, Manchester and Lancashire Family History Society, 1987; R. Peron, *Oldham Documents, A Collection*. Central Library, Oldham, 1975; G. Whittaker, D. Crowther and W.M. Spencer, 'Parochial Chapelry of Colne, Marriages from 1654-1754', *Colne Register Trans.*, Burnley, 1975; W.L. French, *Registers of Kirkby St. Chad's Chapel in the Parish of Walton on the Hill: Baptisms, 1610-1839*, Knowsley Borough Libraries, 1977.

Leicestershire *Survey of the Parish Registers in the County of Leicestershire: Deaneries of Gartree, I: II: III* (1953-7);

From *LeAS*: 'Leicestershire yeomen farmers and their pedigrees', 23, I, 1947; 'Ashby-de-la-Zouche ... Extracts from the parish registers', XV, 1927-8;

Reports & Papers, Ass. Arch. Socs.: 'Parish registers of Houghton-on-the-Hill, 1582-1639', XXV, 1900; 'Extracts from and notes on the parish registers of Misterton', XXVI, 1901; 'Parish registers of Ratby, 1695-1710', XXV, 1900;

Deaneries of East Goscote (in preparation, not yet available). Surveys made for the National Register of Archives. Copies are available for reference only at N.R.A., London, and at Leicester County Record Office; H. Hartopp, *Register of St Mary, Leicester, 1600-1738*, Pubns. Par. Reg. Soc., 64, 1909; J.E. Stocks and W.B. Bragg, *Market Harborough Parish Records to 1530*, London, 1890; J.R. Abney, *The Vestry Book and Accounts of the Churchwardens of St Mary's Leicester, 1652-1729*, Leicester, 1912; D.J. Browning, R.E. Cotton and L. Davenport, *The Registers of All Saints Parish Church, Oakham, in the County of Rutland, Marriages, 1754-1837*, Leicester University Genealogical Society, 1979; J. E. O. Wilshere, *the Parish Register Transcripts of Kirby Muxloe to 1702*, Kirby Muxloe, 1966, and *Parish Register Transcripts of Kirby Muxloe, 2: 1703-1837*, Leicester Research Services, 1970.

Lincolnshire By LRS: *Parish Registers of Alford and Rigsby, collated with Bishops' transcripts, 1538-1680*, V, 1917; *Parish Registers of Boston, 1: 1557-99; 2: 1599-1638*, I and III, 1914-15; *Parish Registers of Bourne, 1562-1650*, VII,

1921; *Parish Registers of Grantham, 1562-1632*, IV, 1916; *Parish Registers of the City of Lincoln: marriages 1538-1754*, IX, 1925; *Parish Registers of St Margaret in the Close, Lincoln, 1538-1837*, II, 1915; *Parish Registers of St Peter at Gowts, Lincoln: baptisms, 1540-1837; burials 1538-1837; marriages, 1826-1837*, VIII, 1923;

Mrs. Tempest and W.F. Curtoys, *Registers of Coleby, Lincs., 1561-1812*, Pubns Par. Reg. Soc., 48, 1903.

Monmouthshire Many of Monmouthshire's ancient documents are now held in the National Library of Wales at Aberystwyth. Gwent County Record Office at Cwmbran offers a useful printed list of those parish registers deposited in the National Library which are now available on microfilm at the Record Office. 181 parishes are listed, with particulars of baptisms, marriages and burials and their dates and it is hoped that more registers will be deposited in the near future. Readers wishing to consult records on microfilm *must* book in advance.

London and Middlesex W.P.W. Phillimore (*et al.*), *Middlesex Parish Registers: Marriages*, 1-9, London, 1909; C.W.F. Goss, 'Parish Registers for London and Middlesex', *LMAS*, n.s., 8, 1940; N.H. Graham, *The Genealogist's Consolidated Guide to the Parish Registers of the Inner London area, 1538-1837*, Orpington, 1976; and: *The Genealogist's Consolidated Guide to the Parish Registers of the Outer London Area, 1538-1837*, Orpington, 1979; *Registers of the Church of England Parishes within the City of London*, Guildhall Library, London, 1972; M. Robbins (intro.), *Middlesex Parish Churches* (tabulated information, gives dates of each church's registers), compiled from a survey made by LMAS, 1955;

Harl. Soc. publications: *Registers of St Vedast, Foster Lane, London, 1558-1837, and of St Michael le Quern, London, 1685-1837*, 2 vols., 29 and 30, 1902-3; *Registers of St Helen's Bishopsgate, London, 1575-1837*, 31, 1904; *Registers of St Mildred, Bread Street, 1658-1853, and of St Margaret Moses, Friday Street, 1558-1850, London*, 42, 1912; *Registers of All Hallows, Bread Street, 1538-1892, and of St John the Evangelist, Friday Street, 1653-1822, London*, 43, 1913; *Registers of St Mary le Bowe, Cheapside, All Hallows, Honey Lane and of St Pancras, Soper Lane, London, 1538-1852*, 44 and 45, 1914-15; *Registers of St Olave, Hart Street, London, 1563-1700*, 46, 1916; *Registers of St Stephen's Walbrook, and of St Benet Sherehog, London, 1557-1860*, 49 and 50, 1919-20; *Registers of St Mary, Mounthaw, London, 1568-1849*, 58, 1928; *Registers of St Mary Somerset, London, 1557-1853*, 2 vols., 59 and 60, 1929-30; *Registers of St Mary the Virgin, Aldermanbury, London, 1538-1722*, 61 and 62, 1931-2; *Registers of St Martin Outwich, London, 1670-1873*, 32, 1905; *Registers of marriages of St Mary le Bone, Middlesex, 1668-1812, and of Oxford Chapel, Vere Street, St Mary le Bone, 1736-54*, 9 vols., 47, 48 and 51-57, 1917-27; *Register of St Matthew, Friday Street, London, 1538-1812, and the united parishes of St Matthew and St Peter Cheap; marriages 1754-1812*, 63, 1923; *Registers of St Paul's Church, Covent Garden, London, 1653-1853*, 5 vols., 33-37, 1906-9; *Registers of St Benet and St Peter, Paul's Wharf, London, 1607-1837*, 4 vols., 1909-12;

LMAS: *Churchwardens' accounts of the parish of Allhallows, London Wall 1455-1536*, 1908; 'Parish of St Clement Danes; churchwardens' accounts and poor rate', V, 1923-8;

Greater London Record Office publications:*A Survey of the Parish Registers of the Diocese of Southwark*, 1978; *Survey of the Parish Registers of the Diocese of London*, 1972;

J.E.G. de Montmorency, *The Greenwich parish register, 1615-36/7*, Greenwich and Lewisham Ant. Soc., II, 1920; F. Wood, *St. Lukes, Charlton, Parish Registers, 1562-1653 and 1787-1812*, and *Deaths 1813-1850*, London, 1977 and 1979; W. Ward, *Registers of St. Margaret's Church, Westminster*, Harl. Soc. and O.U.P., 1968; G.C. Cunningham, 'St Martin-in-the-Fields churchwardens' accounts', Bacon Soc., *Baconiana*, 3rd series, XIII, 1915; J. Coburn, *Survey of the Parish Registers of the Diocese of Southwark, Inner London Area: Burials 1664-1666: Marriages 1675-1682*, Greater London Council, 1970; *Deposited Parish Records of Tottenham and Hornsey*, Haringey Borough Libraries, 1972; *accounts 1710-94)*, Walthamstow Antiq. Soc. Monographs 13, 14 and 16, 1925-7.

The Record Offices of London and Middlesex were combined in 1965; records of Middlesex were removed to the Greater London Record Office from 1979-82. R. Harris, *A Guide to the Parish Registers deposited in the Greater London Record Office*, 1992 includes those records previously held by Middlesex and others deposited elsewhere in London, for example at the Guildhall Library. This *Guide* is to be republished in May 1997 under the new title and auspices of what will then be the London Metropolitan Archives. Published volumes include:

Finchley—A.B. Collins, *Vestry Minutes, 1768-1840*, Finchley Public Libraries Committee, Pt.1, 1957; Pt. 2, 1958; W.B. Passmore, *Bygone Finchley* (extracts from Vestry Minutes), Warden, 1905; and: 'The Parish Registers of Finchley', *Middx. & Herts Notes & Queries*, 4, 1898; Hampton—B. Garside, *Parish Affairs in 'Hampton Town' during the seventeenth century, being mainly a description and interpretation of the Churchwardens' Accounts for the second half of the Century*, Dimbleby, printer, 1954; and: *Their Exits and their Entrances, an account of the Parish Registers of baptism, marriages and burials of Hampton-on-Thames for the 16th and 17th Century,* Scrimshire, printer, 1947; Harrow—*St Mary's Church; List of the Registers, Records, etc.,* Hazell, Watson and Viney, 1904; W.D. Cooper, 'The Parish Registers of Harrow-on-the-Hill, with special reference to the families of Bellamy and Page', *LMAS,* 1, 1899; Hornsey—F.W.M. Draper, 'Two Studies in the Hornsey Church Books', 1. Manor, Parish and Vestry; 2.The Poor, *LMAS,* n.s., 10, 1951; *An account of the Charities for Apprentices belonging to the Parish of Hornsey, Middlesex, with some suggestions for their better management and applications,* T. Blower, printer, 1856; T. Chapman, *An Account of the several Charities and Estates belonging to the Parish of St Mary Hornsey, Middlesex, extracted from the Parish Records,* Norris & Son, printers, 1853; Isleworth—*Parochial Charities; Report on the state of the Parish Charities by Moses Adams, 1839;* (Another edition of the same, revised to 1853 and having additional notes to c.1884.); Pinner—E. Hogg, 'Church Records', *Middx. & Herts Notes & Queries,* 1, 1895; St Marylebone—F.H.W. Sheppard, *Local Government in St Marylebone, 1688-1835,* Athlone Press, 1958; Staines—F.A. Crisp, *List of Parish Registers and other Genealogical works* (includes Registers of Staines, 1644-94), privately printed, 1899; Tottenham—*Account of various donations and benefactions, etc., for the benefit of the poor of the parish, and for the rent of houses and for loss of common rights,* Hunnings, printer, 1855; Twickenham—A. Burrell, *Church of St Mary the Virgin, Parish Register,* 1, 'Christenings, Weddings and Burials, 1538-1570'; Uxbridge—J.H. Thomas, 'MS. Parish Registers in the Uxbridge Deanery', *Antiquary,* 18, 1888; Willesden—F.A. Wood, *Registers of the Parish Church of St Mary, Willesden, from 1568-1865,* 4 vols., 1888.

Norfolk There are 12 volumes of Norfolk Parish Registers of Marriages published between 1899-1936. These are edited by W.P.W. Phillimore, Thomas Blagg and others, and published by Phillimore & Co., London.

Northamptonshire P.I. King, *Summary Guide to the Northants Record Office,* 1954;

Northants. Rec. Soc. Pub.: *Kettering Vestry Minutes, 1797-1853,* VI, 1933; *Peterborough Churchwardens' Accounts, 1467-1573,* IX, 1939;

R.L. Greenall, *The Parish Registers of Long Buckby, 1558-1689,* University of Leicester, 1971.

Northumberland The Durham and Northumberland Parish Register Society, founded in 1897, published 36 volumes of parish registers for both counties from 1898 to 1926.

Nottinghamshire W.P.W. Phillimore and T.M. Blagg, *Nottinghamshire Parish* Registers, 22 vols. (marriages only), London, 1898-1938; *Nottinghamshire Parish Registers on Microfilm 1538-1900,* Notts. County Council, 1984;

By G.W. Marshall: *Registers of Carburton, 1528-1815,* Worksop, 1888; *Registers of Edwinstow, 1634-1758,* Worksop, 1891; *Registers of Ollerton, 1592-1812,* Exeter, 1896; *Registers of Perlethorpe, 1528-1815,* Worksop, 1887; *Registers of Walesby, 1580-1792,* Par. Reg. Soc., 1898; *Registers of Wellow, 1713-1812,* Exeter, 1896; *Registers of Worksop, 1558-1771,* Guildford, 1894;

Par. Reg. Soc.: *Registers of Headon, 1566-1812,* 1898; *Registers of Farndon, 1695-1812,* 1902;

'The role of the parish constable in Gedling parish', *Nottingham Historian,* no.46, Spring-Summer 1991; W.P.W. Phillimore and Ward, *Nottingham Parish Registers, St Mary's and St Nicholas's* (marriages only), London, 1900-2; J.T. Godfrey, *Notes on St Mary's Parish Registers, 1566-1812,* Nottingham, 1901; T.M. Blagg, *Registers of Shelton, 1595-1812,* Worksop, 1899.

Oxfordshire D.J. Steel, *National Index of Parish Registers, 5,* Society of Genealogists, 1966, includes this county;

Banbury Historical Society: *Baptism and Burial Registers of Banbury, Part 3: 1723-1812,* 16, 1978; *Marriage Register of Banbury, Part 3: 1790-1837,* 1963; *Marriage Registers of Banbury, Part 2: 1724-1790,* 1962; *Marriage Registers of Banbury, Part 1: 1558-1724,* 1961; *Baptism and Burial Registers of Banbury, 1558-1653,* 1965.

Powys M. Yates, 'The Parish of Heyop, Church School and Parish Records', *Radnorshire Hist. Soc. Trans.,* no.46, 1976.

Shropshire *Shropshire Parish Documents,* Shrewsbury, c.1903; D.J. Steel, *National Index of Parish Registers, 5,* Society of Genealogists, 1966, includes this county.

Somersetshire J.E. King, *Inventory of Parochial Documents in the Diocese of Bath and Wells, and the County of Somerset,* Somerset C.C. Records Committee, 1938 (available from C.R.O.); *Handlist of the Board of Guardians in the County of Somerset preserved at the Somerset Record Office,* Somerset C.C. Records Committee, 1949 (O.P.; one loan copy available to individual students for limited period); Typescript lists of sixty parishes' records deposited are available at the C.R.O.; Bishop Hobhouse, *Churchwardens' Accounts for*

Croscombe, Pilton, Yatton, Tintinhull, Morebath and St Michael's Bath, from 1349-1560, Somerset Rec. Soc., 4, 1890.

Staffordshire   Staffs. Rec. Soc.: *Churchwardens' Accounts for Walsall, 1462-1531*, Wm. Salt Arch. Soc., 1928; *Bilston, an account of briefs collected 1685*, 1938; *Audley Terrier, 1708*, 1944;

Published by the Parish Register Society: *Parish Registers of St. Michael and All Angels, Adbaston, 1600-1812*, 1964-5; *Index to Barlaston Registers, 1573-1812*, 1977; *The Parish Registers of Bilston, 1684-1746*, 1937; *The Parish Registers of Bushbury*, 1560-1812, 1956-57; *Parish Registers of Chebsey, 1660-1812*, 1964-5; *Roman Catholic Registers of Chillington, Wolverhampton, Walsall, Cresswell and Wednesfield, 1751-1837*, 1958-9; *Parish Registers of Codsall, 1587-1840, 1862-3*; *Parish Registers of Ellenhall, 1539-1812*, 1944-5; *Parish Registers of Himley, 1665-1812*, 1968-9; *Parish Registers of Keele, 1540-1812*, 1944-5; *Parish Registers of Kingsley, 1561-1795*, 1967-8; *Parish Registers of Madeley, 1567-1812*, 1960-61; *The Parish Registers of Mucklestone, 1555-1761*, 1929; *Parish Registers of Newcastle under Lyme (2 vols.), 1563-1770*, 1931; *Parish Registers of Norton in the Moors, 1574-1751 and 1754-1837*, 1924; *Parish Registers of Pattingham, 1559-1812*, 1934; *Parish Registers of Penkridge, 1575-1735*, 1945-6; *The Parish Registers of Penn, 1570-1754*, 1921; *Parish Registers of Ranton, 1655-1812*, 1953-4; *Parish Registers of Rowley Regis (3 vols.), 1539-1812*, 1912; *Parish Registers of Rugeley, 1569-1722*, 1928; *Parish Registers of Seighford, 1561-1812*, 1977-8; *Parish Registers of St. Mary's Stafford, 1559-1671 and St. Chad's, Stafford, 1636-1811*, 1935-6; *Parish Registers of Tipton, 1513-1736*, 1923; *Parish Registers of Stoke on Trent (2 vols.) 1734-1797 and 1754-1812*, 1925-27; *The Parish Registers of Wednesfield, 1751-1837 and Tettenhall, 1602-1839* (2 vols.), 1930, 1967 and 1980; *Parish Registers of Walsall, 1646-1745*, 1974-5; *Parish Registers of Weeford, 1562-1812*, 1955; *The Parish Registers of West Bromwich, 1608-1659*, 1909; *The Parish Registers of Wolverhampton, 1539-1776* (3 vols.), 1932 and 1951-2; *Wolverhampton Parish Registers, 1735-1776*, 1973;

Parish Registers of St. Michael and All Angels, Adbaston, 1600-1727, Birmingham and Midland Society for Genealogy and Heraldry, 1970; and: *The Registers of Lichfield Cathedral, 1660-1754*, 1973-4;

H. M. Auden, *Parish Registers of Weston-under-Lizard*, Staffordshire Parish Society, 1933.

Suffolk   Phillimore, Blagg and Taylor (eds.), *Suffolk Parish Registers: Marriages*, 3 vols., Phillimore & Co., 1910, 1912, 1916;

By W. Brigg (privately printed): *Chevington, 1559-1812*, 1915; *Culford, 1560-1778*, 1909; *Ingham, 1538-1811*, 1909; *Timworth, 1565-1716*, 1909;

By F.A. Crisp (privately printed), *Brundish, 1562-1780*, 1885; *Carlton, 1538-1886*, 1886; *Chillesford, 1740-1876*, 1886; *Culpho, 1721-99*, 1886); *Ellough, 1540-1812*, 1886; *Frostenden, 1538-1791*, 1887; *Tannington, 1539-1660*, 1884; *Thorndon, 1538-1711*;

By S.H.A. Hervey: *St James, Bury St Edmunds, 1558-1800*, Suffolk Green Books, XVII, Booth, Woodbridge, 1916; *Denham, 1539-1850*, Bury St Edmunds, 1904; *Horringer, 1558-1850*, Booth, Woodbridge, 1900; *Ickworth, 1566-1890*, Wells, 1894; *Little Saxham, 1559-1850*, Booth, Woodbridge, 1901; *Rushbrook, 1567-1850*, Booth, Woodbridge, 1903; *Great and Little Welnetham, 1557-1850*, Suffolk Green Books, no.XV, Bury St Edmunds, 1910; *West Stow, 1558-1850 and Wordwell, 1580-1850*, Booth, Woodbridge, 1903;

By T.S. Hill: *Bramfield, 1536-96*, London, 1894; *Thorington, 1561-1881*, London, 1884;

A.T. Winn, *Records of the Borough of Aldeburgh: the Church*, Hertford, Austin & Sons, 1926; F.W. Warren, *Bardwell, 1538-1650*, London, 1892; P. Northeast, *Boxford Churchwardens' Accounts 1530-1561*, Suff. Rec. Soc., 23, 1982; J.J. Raven, *Cratfield Parish Papers; Transcripts of Accounts of the Parish, 1490-1642*, London, 1895; 'Extracts from the Parish papers of Flowton, relative to assessments made on that Parish during the Civil War, 1643', extracted from the *Antiquarian and Architectural Year Book*, Woodbridge, 1893; W.B. Bannerman, *Registers of Hollesley; Baptisms and marriages 1623-1812; Burials 1637-1812*, Pubns. Par. Reg. Soc., 82, 1920; E. Cookson, *St Nicholas, Ipswich, 1539-1710*, 1897 (private); C. Morley, *Monks' Soham, 1712-1919*, 1920 (private); J.R. Ollorenshaw, *Notes on the Church and Parish of Rattlesden, with copy of Parish Registers, 1558-1758*, 1900; 'Shotley Registers and Tombstones, 1571-1850', *Suffolk Green Books*, no.XVI (1); no.XVI (2); R.W.M. Lewis, *Walberswick Churchwardens' Accounts, 1450-99*, 1947 (privately printed); V.B. Redstone, *Bygone Woodbridge*, containing: Extracts from Parish Registers, 1545-1666; Churchwardens' Account Book, 1592-1689.

Surrey   Pubns. Surrey Par. Reg. Soc.: *Parish Registers of Abinger 1559-1806, Wotton 1596-1812, Oakwood chapel 1696-1814*, 9, 1927; *Registers of Addington 1559-1812, Chelsham 1669-1812 and Warlingham 1653-1812*, 5, 1907; *Registers of Beddington 1538-1673, Morden 1634-1812*, 10, 1912; *Registers of Beddington 1538-1673*, NO.76, 1917; *Registers of Chipstead 1656-1812, Titsey 1579-1812*, 7, 1909; *Registers of Coulsdon 1653-1812, Haslemere, Pt. I: 1573-1812*, 8, 1910; *Registers of Coulsdon 1653-1812*, no.75, 1916; *Registers of Gatton 1599-181, Sanderstead 1564-1812*,

6, 1908; *Registers of Godalming 1582-1688*, 2, 1904; *Registers of Farleigh 1679-1812*, *Registers of Tatsfield 1679-1812*, *Registers of Wanborough 1561-1675*, *Registers of Woldingham 1765-1812*, 4, 1906; *Registers of Haslemere, Baptisms 1594-1812, Marriages and burials 1573-1812*, no.57, 1906; *Registers of Merstham 1538-1812*, extra 1, 1914; *Registers of Merstham 1538-1812*, 1902; *Registers of Morden 1634-1812*, 1901; *Registers of Putney, I: 1620-1734, II: 1735-1812, III: 1774-1870*, 14 and 15, 1917-18; *Registers of Richmond* (2 vols.), 1 and 3, 1903-5; *Registers of Stoke D'Abernon 1619-1812, Haslemere, Pt. II: 1573-1812*, 9, 1911; *Registers of Stoke D'Abernon 1619-1812*, no.77, 1917; *Registers of Sutton 1636-1837*, extra 2, 1915; *Registers of Sutton 1636-1837*, no.74, 1915; *Parish Register of Wimbledon 1538-1812*, 8, 1924;

    Surrey Arch. Soc.: 'Bletchingley churchwardens' accounts 1546-52, XXIX, 1916; 'Wandsworth churchwardens' accounts 1558-73 and 1547-1630, XVII, 1902; and: 1631-9, XXIV, 1909; 'Weybridge parish registers', 17, 1902.

Sussex Sussex Family History Group, *Handlist of Parish Register Copies*, Brighton, 1977;

    SASNQ: 'Sussex marriage entries in London registers', I, II and IV, 1926-33; 'Early churchwardens' accounts of Arlington, 1455-79 , LIV, 1911; 'Extracts from the churchwardens' accounts of St Peter's the Less, Chichester', I-II, 1926-7; 'A churchwardens' presentment (East and West Lavant 1680)', I, 1926; 'Churchwardens' accounts of St Andrew's and St Michael's, Lewes 1522-1601 , XLV, 1902; 'Churchwardens' accounts of West Tarring 1514-79 , III, 1930-1.

Wales R.W. McDonald, 'The Parish Registers of Wales', *National Library of Wales Journal*, no.19, 1976; The National Library of Wales in Aberystwyth holds the largest existing collection of Welsh parish registers, from counties and parishes all over Wales. In addition, C.J. Williams and J. Watts-Williams, *Parish Registers of Wales*, Aberystwyth, 1986 (pending revision) gives dates and whereabouts of other registers held locally.

Warwickshire W.P.W. Phillimore, J. Harvey Bloom and J.L. Whitfield (eds.), *Warwickshire Parish Registers*, Phillimore Parish Register Series, from 1 in 1904; D.J. Steel, *National Index of Parish Registers*, 5, Society of Genealogists, 1966, includes this county; P.A. Bill, *The Warwickshire Parish Clergy in the Later Middle Ages*, Dugdale Soc. Occasional papers, no.17, 1967;

    Birm. Arch. Soc.: 'Warwick registers; notes on English history as told by account books and parish registers at Warwick, XLIII, 1918, and LXV, 1922; 'Churchwardens' accounts of the parish of Northfield 1606-1730', XXXIX, 1909; 'The parish registers of Morton Bagot', 63, 1939-40;

    Pubns. Dugdale Soc.: *Coventry Constables' presentments, 1629-1742*, XXXIV, 1986; *Registers of Edgbaston parish church 1636-1812* (2 vols.), VIII, 1928-36;

    Pubns. Par. Reg. Soc.: *Register of Solihull I: 1538-1668*, 53, 1904; *Registers of Stratford-on-Avon. Burials 1588-1622/3* (2 vols.), 55, 1897-1905; *Register of Wedington 1663-1812*, 51, 1904;

    E.R. Billington, *the Birmingham 'Smith' Index (Surnames from Parish Registers)*, Birmingham, 1977; and *Parish Registers and Churches in the Birmingham Area*, Birmingham Index, 1979; D. Wright, *Genealogy Index for Birmingham*, Birmingham and Midland Society for Genealogy and Heraldry, 1975; V.J. King and D. Wright, *Parish Registers in the Birmingham Reference Library*, Birmingham Public Libraries, 1975; S.A. Swain, *Parish Registers of St. Giles, Sheldon, 1558-1683*, Birmingham and Midland Society for Genealogy and Heraldry and Stourbridge Historical and Archaeological Society, 1977; T. Kemp, 'Extracts from the registers of Tanworth church 1558-1755 , *Warwks. Nat. & Archs. Field Club*, 1902.

Westmorland The CWAAS, founded in 1866, published a Parish Registers Series of 51 volumes for both counties from 1912 to 1987: 'A Sketch of the Church of Askham and some account of the early parish registers', n.s., IV, 1904; *Parish Registers of Barton, Baptisms and marriages 1666-1812; Burials 1666-1830*, V, 1917; *Parish Registers of Bolton, Westmorland 1647-1812*, XXXII, 1944; *Parish Registers of Brough under Stainmore, Part I: 1556-1706, Part II: 1707-1812*, IX and X, 1923 and 1924; *Parish Registers of Brougham 1645-1812*, XXXI, 1943; *Parish Registers of Cliburn 1565-1812*, XX, 1932; *Parish Registers of Crosby Garrett 1559-1812*, XXXIII, 1945; *Parish Registers of Crosby Ravensworth 1570-1812*, XXV, 1937; 'Ings Registers described', n.s., XIII, 1913; *Parish Registers of Kendal, Part I: Christenings 1558-1587, Part II: 1591-1595, Part III: Baptisms 1596-9, 1607-31, Marriages and burials 1591-9, Part IV: Marriages and burials 1606-31*, VII, VIII, XXXVI and XXXIX, 1912, 1922, 1952, 1960; 'Kirkby Lonsdale parish registers 1538-1812 , n.s., V, 1905; *Parish Registers of Lowther 1540-1812*, XXI, 1933; *Parish Registers of Middleton in Lonsdale 1570-1612*, XII, 1925; *Parish Registers of Milburn 1597-1744*, II, 1914; *Parish Registers of Morland, Part I: 1538-1812*, XXXVIII, 1960; *Parish Registers of Newbiggin 1571-1812*, XV, 1927; 'Shap Registers (Extracts)', n.s, XI, 1911; *Parish Registers of Warcop 1597-1744*, III, 1914.

Wiltshire Phillimore and Sadler, *Wiltshire Parish Registers, Marriages*, 1905-14; *Wilts Arch. Magazine*, Wilts

Arch. Soc. (extracts and lists *passim*); T.H. Baker, 'Churchwardens accounts of Mere 1556-1616 , *WANHS*, XXXV, 1907-8; W. Symons, 'Winterslow church reckonings 1542-1661 , *WANHM*, 36 (no.CXI), 1909.

Worcestershire The Worcestershire County Record Office publishes a guide: *Genealogical Resources in Worcestershire. No.1: Parish Registers and Transcripts*; W.P.W. Phillimore and W.F. Carter (eds.), *Worcestershire Parish Registers*, Phillimore Parish Register Series, from 1 in 1901;

Birmingham and Midland Society for Genealogy and Heraldry: J. and J.E. Beach, *The Parish Registers of St. Peter's Parish Church, Cradley, 1785-1839*; *Parish Registers of Christ Church, Oldbury, 1714-1812*, 1978; *Cradley Baptist Church Registers and Historical Records, 1783-1837*, 1980; L.G. Day, *Registers of the Parish of Northfield in Worcestershire, 1560-1765*, 1978; C.J. Voyce and A.Page, *Parish Registers of Oldswinford, 1719-1735*, 1977;

Pubns. Worcs. Par. Reg. Soc.: *Registers of Churchill in Oswaldslow, in the Deanery of Worcester East, 1564-1794; marriages to 1839*, 1914; *Registers of Eastham, (with Hanley Child and Orleton), with Hanley William, in the Deanery of Burford, 1572-1812*, 1915; *Registers of Over Arley, 1564-1812*, 1916; *Register of Worcester Cathedral, 1693-1811*, 1913;

R. Peacock, *Hagley from the 16th to the 19th centuries. Aspects of Hagley's history from the parish chest*, Hagley Parish Records Research Group, 1985; J.S. Roper, *The Parish Register of St. Edmund's Dudley, 1540-1611*, Dudley Public Libraries, 1961; E.A. Barnard, 'Churchwardens' accounts of the parish of South Littleton 1548-71 , *Worcs. Arch. Soc.*, III, 1926.

Yorkshire North Yorkshire County Record Office publishes *Guide No.2: Parish registers, census returns, land tax assessments, tithe apportionments and enclosure awards in the record office*, also *Guide No.5: North Yorkshire parish registers, including dates and whereabouts of parish registers, transcripts and microfilms*; M.W. Barley, *Parochial Documents of the Archdeaconry of the E. Riding*, YAS Rec. Ser., XCIX, 1939; W.P. Baker, *Parish Registers and Illiteracy in East Yorkshire*, East Yorks Local Hist. Soc., 1962;

Assoc. Archit. Soc. Reports & Papers: 'Holy Trinity church, Goodramgate, York; extracts from churchwardens' accounts 1557-1819 , XXX, 1908-9; 'Old parish account books of St John the Evangelist, York (1580-1800)', XXIX, 1907-8; 'Churchwarden's accounts of St Martin-cum-Gregory, York 1560-1670 and churchwardens' book 1670-1754 , XXXI, 1909-10;

Bradford Antiquary: 'Burial register of Bradford parish church', I-II, 1900-1; 'Transcript of the marriage registers of Bradford, Yorks, 1596-1708 , n.s., III-IV, 1902-3;

Halifax Ant. Soc. Papers: 'Elland churchwardens' accounts', 1927-28; 'Extracts from some Elland records 1729-1804', 1907; 'Notes and comments on the Halifax churchwardens' accounts I: 1620-1714; II: 1714-1800; III: 1714-1832, 1925;

Thoresby Soc.: 'Adel register, 1600 and 1606-1812; transcripts at York', 22, *Misc.*, 1912-15 and 5, 1893 (1895); *Register of the parish church of Leeds, 1695-1722; with Armley chapel 1665-1711; with Hunslet chapel, 1686-1724*, XIII, 1903-9; *Registers of the parish church of Leeds, 1722-57*, XX, 1911-14; *Registers of the parish church of Leeds; Baptisms and burials, 1757-76; marriages 1754-69*, XXV, 1923; 'St John's church, Leeds; the trustees' account book 1660-1766', XXIV, *Misc.*, 1919; 'Burials at St Paul's church, Leeds, 1796-1865 , XV, *Misc.*, 1909; 'Churchwardens' accounts, Methley', XI, *Misc.*, 1904; *Registers of the parish church of Methley, 1560-1812*, XII, 1903; 'Whitkirk register, 1600-1; transcripts at York', XXII, *Misc.*, 1912-15;

The Yorkshire Parish Register Society, from its foundation in 1899 until 1961 published 124 volumes of Yorkshire parish registers. With 125 in 1961 the Society became a section of the Yorkshire Archaeological Society which continues publication of the series (1987); *Registers of Addingham 1612-1812*, 66, 1920; *Parish Register of Aldborough (W.R.) I: 1538-1611*, 110, 1940; *Registers of Allerton Mauleverer; Marriages 1557-1812; baptisms 1562-1812; burials 1564-1812* and *Registers of Askham Richard in the Ainsty of York, 1579-1812*, 31, 1908; *Parish Register of Atwick (E.R.) 1538-1708*, 111, 1941; *Register of Aughton, 1610-1812*, 86, 1928; *Registers of the chapel of Austerfield in the parish of Blyth, 1559-1812*; *Register of Bentham 1666-1812*, 91, 1932; *Registers of Bingley, 1577-1686*, 9, 1901; *Registers of Blacktoft. East Yorks, 1700-1812* and *Registers of Scorborough 1653-1800*, 8, 1901; *Register of Bolton-by-Bolland, I: 1558-1724; II: 1725-1812*, 19 and 22, 1904-5; *Registers of Brantingham, East Yorks, 1653-1812*, 12, 1902; *Parish Register of Brodsworth 1538-1813*, 104, 1937; *Parish Register of Bubwith, I: Baptisms and burials 1600-1767; Marriages 1600-1753*, 99, 1935; *Registers of Burton Fleming, alias North Burton, 1538-1812*, 2, 1899; *Parish Register of Cantley 1539-1812*, 112, 1941; *Parish Register of Carlton-jexta-Snaith 1598-1812*, 96, 1934; *Registers of Cherry Burton, 1561-1740*, 15, 1903; *Register of Clapham I: 1595-1683*, 67, 1921; *Registers of Cowthorpe, marriages 1568-1812; christenings and burials 1568-1797*, 39, 1910; *Parish Registers of Coxworld Pt. I:*

1583-1666, 120, 1955; *Registers of Crofton 1615-1812*, 62, 1918; *Registers of Danby-in-Cleveland, 1585-1812*, 43, 1912; *Registers of Darrington, 1567-1812*, 49, 1913; *Registers of All Saints, Easingwold, 1599-1812*, 56, 1916; *Registers of the chapelry of East Rounton in the parish of Rudby-in-Cleveland 1595-1837* and *Register of All Saints, Weston, near Otley 1639-1812*, 54, 1916; *Registers of Emley 1600-1812*, 65, 1920; *Register of Eston, 1590-1812*, 76, 1924; *Registers of Farnham, Yorks, 1569-1812*, 56, 1905; *Register of Frickley with Clayton 1577-1812*, 95, 1933; *Registers of Garforth, 1631-1812*, 46, 1913; *Registers of Gargrave 1558-1812*, 28, 1907; *Parish Register of Gilling 1573-1812*, 113, 1942; *Parish Register of Gisburne Pt. 1: 1558-1745*, 114, 1943; and: *Pt. 2: 1745-1812*, 118, 1952; *Register of Great Ayton, 1600-1812*, 90, 1931; *Registers of Grinton in Swaledale; Baptisms and burials 1640-1807; marriages 1640-1802*, 23, 1905; *Register of Hackness, 1557-1783*, 25, 1906; *Registers of Halifax 1538-93. I: Baptisms; II: Marriages and burials*, 37 and 45, 1910-14; *Registers of Hampsthwaite; Marriages 1603-1807; Baptisms and burials 1603-1794*, 13, 1902; *Registers of Harewood; I: Baptisms 1614-1812; Marriages: 1621-1812*, 50, 1914; *Registers of Hartshead*, 17, 1903; *Registers of Hemsworth, 1654-1812*, 79, 1926; *Registers of Heptonstall, I: 1593-1660*, 78, 1925; *Parish Register of St Wilfrid's, Hickleton 1626-1812*, 109, 1940; *Registers of Hooton Pagnell 1538-1812*, 87, 1929; *Registers of the chapel of Horbury in the parish of Wakefield, 1598-1812*, 3, 1900; *Registers of Huggate Yorks., 1539-1812*, 35, 1901; *Register of Ilkley 1597-1812*, 83, 1927; *Registers of the churches of Ingleton and Chapel-le-Dale 1607-1812*, 94, 1933 (originally in Lonsdale Deanery [La, We] and the Richmond [Y] archdeaconry; see also LPRS, p.122); *Registers of St Andrew's Keighley I: 1562-1694; II 1649-1688; III: 1687-1736*, 77, 82 and 98, 1925-35; *Registers of St Andrew's, Kildwick-in-Craven; I: 1575-1622; II: 1623-78; III: 1678-1743; IV: Baptisms 1744-89; marriages 1744-54; burials 1744-71*, 47, 55, 69, 92, 1913-32; *Register of Kirby Hill, 1576-1812*, 75, 1924; *Parish Register of Kirkby Malham, 1: 1597-1690*, 106, 1938; *Registers of Kilburn 1600-1812*, 61, 1918; *Registers of Kirkleatham 1559-1812*, 59, 1917; *Registers of Kirklington 1568-1812*, 35, 1909; *Registers of Kippax, 1539-1812*, 10, 1901; *Registers of Ledsham, 1539-1812*, 26, 1906; *Registers of Linton-in-Craven, I: 1562-1779; II: 1779-1812*, 5 and 18, 1900-3; *Register of Maltby, 1597-1812*, 81, 1926; *Registers of Marske in Cleveland; Baptisms and marriages, 1570-1812; burials 1569-1812*, 16, 1903; *Register of Mirfield I: 1559-1700; II: Baptisms and burials 1700-76, marriages to 1754*, 64 and 72, 1919-23; *Parish Register of Myton upon Swale 1654-1812*, 121, 1956; *Registers of Otley, I: 1562-1672; II: Baptisms 1672-1753, marriages 1672-1750, burials 1672-1752*, 33 and 44, 1909-12; *Registers of Patrington, 1570-1731*, 6, 1900; *Parish Register of All Saints' Church, Pavement, 1: 1554-1690*, 100, 1935; and: *2: 1690-1738*, 102, 1936; *Registers of Pickhill-cum-Roxby; Marriages 1567-1812; Baptisms 1571-1812; Burials 1576-1812*, 21, 24, 32 and 48, 1904-13; *Parish Register of Pontefract 1585-1641*, 122, 1958; *Parish Registers of Raskelf 1747-1812*, 119, 1953; *Parish Register of Riccall 1669-1813*, 124, 1960; *Register of the civil marriages 1653-1660 belonging to Richmondshire and an Index to parish register transcripts belonging to the Archdeaconry of Richmond 1613-1848*, 101, 1936; *Parish Registers of Rillington 1638-1812*, 117, 1948; *Registers of Ripon, I: 1574-1628*, 80, 1926; *Registers of Rothwell, I: 1538-1689; II: Baptisms and burials 1690-1763, marriages 1690-1812; III: 1763-1812*, 27, 34 and 51, 1906-14; *Register of Saxton-in-Elmet 1538-1812*, 93, 1932; *Parish Register of Sculcoates, Pt. 1 1538-1772*, 123, 1959; *Register of Settrington 1559-1812*, 38, 1910; *Registers of Sheffield, I: Baptisms and marriages, 1560-1635; II: burials 1560-1634, baptisms and marriages 1635-53; III: burials 1635-53, baptisms and marriages 1653-86; IV: burials 1653-86, baptisms and marriages 1687-1703*, 58, 60, 68 and 74, 1917-24; *Registers of Snaith, I: Baptisms 1558-1657, marriages 1537-1657: II: Burials 1537-1656*, 57 and 63, 1917-19; *Registers of Stokesley, 1571-1750*, 7, 1901; *Parish Register of Swillington 1539-1812*, 115, 1944; *Registers of Tervington, Baptisms 1600-1812; marriages and burials 1599-1812*, 29, 1907; *Registers of Thirsk in the North Riding, 1556-1721*, 42, 1911; *Registers of Thornhill, I: Baptisms 1580-1742; marriages 1580-1745, burials 1580-1678; II: Baptisms 1743-1812, marriages 1746-53, burials, 1678-1812, Flocton baptisms, marriages and burials 1713-1812; III: marriages 1754-1812, banns 1788-1812, Flockton baptisms and burials 1717-1812*, 30, 40 and 53, 1907; *Register of Thornton-in-Lonsdale 1576-1812*, 89, 1931; *Registers of Waddington 1599-1812*, 88, 1930; *Registers of Wath-upon-Dearne; Baptisms and burials 1598-1778; Marriages 1598-1779*, 14, 1902; *Parish Register of Wensley, 1: 1538-1799*, 108, 1939; *Register of Whitby I: 1600-76*, 84, 1928; *Registers of Winestead in Holderness, 1578-1812*, 4, 1900; *Register of Wintringham 1558-1812*, 71, 1922; *Parish Register of Wragby, 1: 1538-1704; Church wardens' Accounts 1604-1626; Overseers of highways accounts 1626-1631; Wills 1555; Briefs 1661-1682*, 105, 1938; and: *2: 1704-1812*, 107, 1939; *Registers of Holy Trinity church, Goodramgate, York, 1573-1812*, 41, 1911; *Register of Holy Trinity, King's Court (or Christ Church) York, 1631-1812*, 85, 1928; *Registers of St Crux, York I: 1539-1716*, 70, 1922; *Parish Register of St Laurence, York 1607-1812*, 97, 1935; *Registers of St Martin Coney Street, York, 1557-1812*, 36, 1909; *Registers of St Mary, Bishophill Junior, York 1602-1812*, 52, 1915; *Registers of St Michael le Belfrey, York, I: 1565-1653; II: Marriages 1653-1772, baptisms and burials, 1653-1778*, I and II, 1899-1901; *Registers of St Olave, York I: 1538-1644*, 73, 1923;

YAS Par. Reg. Section: *Parish Register of Acomb, Vols. 1-10; 1663-1837 (Bishops' Transcripts 1634-1760)*, 129, 1966; *Parish Register of Almondbury, 1592-1652*, 135, 1976; and: *2: 1653-1682 (with map)*, 148, 1983; *Parish

Register of Askham Bryan, vols.1-6, 1697-1837 AND *Registers of Askham Richard 1813-1837*, 131, 1967; *Parish Register of Birstall. 1: 1558-1635, (with map)*, 146, 1981; *Parish Register of Bishopthorpe 1631-1837*, 150, 1985 (1986); *Parish Register of Bowes 1670-1837 and Bishops' Transcripts 1615-1700*, 128, 1965; *Parish Registers of Braithwell, 1: 1559-1774; vols.2-6: 1754-1837*, 1969; *Parish Register of Brandsburton 1558-1837*, 142, 1977; *Parish Register of Burghwallis, Baptisms 1596-1814; Marriages 1596-1814; Burials 1596-1669*, 148, 1983; *Parish Registers of Collingham 1579-1837* (with map and notes on early rectors), 141, 1976 (1978); *Parish Register of Drypool Vols. 1-6: Baptisms and burials 1572-1812; Marriages 1572-1807*, 125, 1961; *Parish Registers of Easingwold, Raskelf and Myton upon Swale 1813-37 with parish register transcripts for Raskelf 1600-1746/7 and Myton upon Swale 1598-1639/40* (with map), 145, 1980; *Parish Register of Giggleswick. 1: 1558-1669*, 147, 1982; and: *2: 1669-1769*, 151, 1986; *Parish Register of Heslington 1639-1837* (with plan), 144, 1979; *Parish Registers of Lythe, vols.1-3, 1634-1786; vols.4-11, 1754-1837*, 123 and 138, 1973; *Parish Register of Oswaldkirk, Vols. 1-10: 1536-1837*, 358, 1970; *Parish Register of Sheffield. 6: 1720-1736* (with map), 143, 1978; *Parish Register of Walton in Ainstey 1619-1837*, 126, 1963; *Parish Registers of Wensley, 2: 1701-1837* (part 1 of these registers was published by the Society in 1939), 1967; *Parish Register of St Crux, York. 2: Baptisms 1716-1837; Marriages and burials 1678-1837*, 149, 1984; *Parish Registers of St. Mary Castlegate, York, 1: 1604-1705*, 134, 1970; and: *2-4: 1705-1837*, 136, 1971;

G.E. Weddall, 'Churchwardens accounts and other documents relating to Howden', *YAS*, XIX, 19..; S.L. Ollard, 'A recently discovered register of Huggate church (17th century)', *Yorks. Arch. Journal*, XXVI, 1922; J.R. Wigfull, 'Early books of the parish register of Sheffield, 1560-1703 , *Hunter Arch. Soc.*, II, 1924; A.V. Hudson and J. W. Walker, 'Index to the parish register transcripts preserved in the diocesan registry, York', YAS Rec. Sers., 74, *Misc.*, II, 1929; J.S. Purvis, *Tudor Parish Documents of the Diocese of York*, Cambridge 1948.

ORIGINAL DOCUMENTS TO BE FOUND AT:

Parish chests (rarely).
Diocesan or County Record Offices (usually).

QUARTER SESSIONS PAPERS

THE DOCUMENTS

The court of Quarter Sessions was one of the chief instruments of Tudor local government. Its work was revised and defined in 1590, and the court continued to carry out these terms of reference until the Local Government Act of 1888. Sessions were held four times a year by unpaid Justices of the Peace whose task was both judicial and administrative. The powers delegated to them by the Tudor monarchy was very extensive, including jurisdiction over nearly every crime except treason. The J.P.s maintained law and order in their locality, and provided the vital contact between crown and localities, supervising the administration of the extensive national legislation by statute, and the work of the parish officers, constables, coroners, highway surveyors and overseers of the poor. By the 17th century the J.P.s were virtually rulers of the county.

Their sessions were of three kinds: discretionary, petty and Quarter Sessions. At Quarter Sessions oaths of loyalty to the government (allegiance and supremacy) were taken. Records of these sessions contain mainly recognisances for the appearance of malefactors, or for their future good behaviour, indictments (in Latin) and presentments. These last are statements in English, by local constables, or by the Grand Jury at sessions, of nuisance and negligence, and of other offences, chiefly larceny and assault, or of breaches of the many statutes. Miscellaneous papers, such as writs, letters, articles and petitions, deal with every aspect of village life. Frequently, parish constables were required to return information demanded by the justices, e.g. the number of alehouses in the village, rates charged by inns, growing of tobacco, extent of gambling, etc.

These Quarter Sessions papers are particularly valuable for the evidence they contain of Catholic recusancy and Puritan non-conformity, of vagrancy, enclosures, state of the highways, and local military musters. Trade or occupation of those named is usually given, so that the records are also invaluable in showing the incidence of crafts and industry in a county. These documents are essential to any study of everyday life in the 17th century, as nothing appears to have been considered too trivial to be brought before the court.

For assistance in deciphering these documents, see Lionel Munby, *Reading Tudor and Stuart Handwriting* (BALH, 1988) and Eve McLaughlin, *Reading Old Handwriting* (from Elizabeth I to Victoria) (FFHS, 1987).

FURTHER READING

F.G. Emmison and I. Gray, *County Records: Quarter Sessions, Petty Sessions, Clerk of the Peace and Lieutenancy*, Revised edition, 1987
J. Gibson, *Quarter Sessions Records for Family Historians*, FFHS, 3rd edition, 1995
J. Gleason, *The Justices of the Peace in England, 1558-1640*, Clarendon Press, Oxford, 1969
J.R. Lander, *English Justices of the Peace 1461-1509*, 1989
B. Osborne, *Justice of the Peace 1361-1848*, 1960

HANDLISTS

For availability of originals at County Record Offices, see Emmison and Gray, *County Records*, App. II. See also, Redstone and Steer, *Local Records*, Bibl. to Chs. XIV and XV, and also E.L.C. Mullins, *Texts and Calendars; An Analytical Guide to Serial Publications*, no.7, Royal Historical Society Guides and Handbooks Series, London, 1958, for editions printed by various County, Historical and Records Associations. Another list of printed sources appears in Robert Somerville's *Handlist of Record Publications*, no.7, Royal Historical and Society Guides and Handbooks Series, London, 1958, for editions printed by various County, Historical and Records Associations. Another version of this *Handlist* was published (Sect.72) by the British Records Association, 1951. Both are now out of print but accessible through the *Union Name Catalogue*.

PRINTED VERSION FOR WORCESTERSHIRE

J.W. Willis-Bund, *Worcestershire County Records: Calendar of Quarter Sessions Papers*, I (1591-1643), Worcs Hist. Soc., 1900. Reference to this volume enables the C.R.O. to trace originals.[3]

See also, J.W. Willis-Bund, *Social Life in Worcestershire in the first quarter of the Seventeenth Century, Illustrated by the Quarter Sessions Records*, Worcs Arch. Soc., O.S., XXIII, 1896, and *Religious Life in Worcestershire in the first quarter of the Seventeenth Century, Illustrated by the Quarter Sessions Records*, Worcs Arch. Soc., O.S., XXIV, 1898.

FURTHER EXAMPLES FROM QUARTER SESSIONS PAPERS, 1603-42

The following is a summary of some of the incidents and reports on the welfare and order of a typical Worcestershire village (Chaddesley Corbett), during the first half of the 17th century.

---

[3] The document illustrated (Plate XII) was found by reference to J.W. Willis-Bund, *Calendar of Quarter Sessions Papers*, I (1591-1643), p.644, no.206 (1637), Worcs Hist. Soc., 1900. This adds the reference number LXII/108, which is seen to have been added to the document. These references having been cited, the County Archivist had no difficulty in tracing the original.

TRANSCRIPT

1 ...   Wigorn Sh. The presentment of the Cunstables of
            Chadgsley Corbett.

    Imprimis, for Recusants we doe present

        Rychard Leayght
5 ...   Mary Bach Widdow
        Mary Hunt Widdow
        Parnell the wife of Gregory Muncke
        Elizabeth the wife of William Leight.
        Elizabeth Jourden

10 ...   Item, Our poore are well and sufficiently pvided for.

    Item, our Highwayes and bridges are in good repayre.

    Item, Rouges and vagabonds have beene punnished
        according to the Law.

    Item, Riots or Routs or unlawfull Assemblyes
15 ...   we know none.

    Item, Cardes or dicing or other unlawfull gamening
        we know none.

    Item, Our Alehouses are licensed to our knowledg

    for other matters worthy to present wee
20 ...   know none at this time.

    John Huntt
    Nycholas Kindon   Cunstables.

Plate XII
Constables' Presentment, Chaddesley Corbett, 1637
(Worcester Record Office Ref: 110.62/108.BA. 1.)
Actual size: 20.5 x 29cm

Megerssx   The presentment of the constables of
the dyther xorbete

Complaines for Recusants we doe presente

10: 62/108   Rychard Leavyst

Mary Bate widdow

Mary Hunt widdow

Marvell the wife of gregory munk

Elizabeth the wife of william Leayst

Elizabeth Jourden

Our poore are well and sufficiently provided for

our Hygheweyes and Brydges are in good repayer

Roges and vagabonds have beene punished
according to the Law

Riots or Routs or unlawfull dyssembbles
we know none

Cardes or dicing or other unlawfull gameninig
we know none

Our Alehouses are all licensed to our knowledge

for other matters worthy to present wee
know none at this time

John Hunt } constables
Nicholas Rendon

This is given to show a cross-section of village life at that time, as it is shown for one village by the Quarter Sessions papers. The many repetitive entries of indictments for assault and trespass, and the many recognisances to keep the peace, as well as numerous presentments of ale-sellers, both licensed and illegal, have been reduced to a single example or two. All the information is taken from the Calendar mentioned above, and reference numbers are given for each case.

1603. William Waldron and Benedicta his wife, and John Waldron and Margaret his wife, all of Belbroughton, are indicted for riotously and unlawfully assembling and felling trees on the close of Thomas Bourne of Chaddesley. (p.58, no.28; Ref. XII/60)

1603. Indictment of Joan, wife of George Carpenter and their daughter, for stealing four ash trees from the close of Francis Smith of Chaddesley. (p.57, no.27; XII/59)

1603/4. Indictment of John Doolittle, John Partridge and John Taylor, all of Stone, for assaulting Edward Broad of Chadsley and Stone, Gentleman. (p.39, no.39; XII/14)

1606. Presentment that there are in Chaddesley 20 dwelling houses, of which 8 are ale-houses. [What the Calendar does not say is that one of the ale-houses was a place of ill-repute, where there was frequent drunkenness, cutting of purses, prostitution, and even murder and 'keeping of men in "huddimucke" while their wives are looking for them'. This additional information is found by reference to the original document. Comparison with the village's present excellent licensed houses would be invidious!] (p.83, no.40; IV/37)

1609. Indictment of Thomas Badger, Husbandman, Elizabeth Badger, William Badger, Mary Badger, Spinster, Silvanus Brooke, Husbandman, Richard Cooper, Husbandman, and Richard Cowper, Husbandman, all of Chaddesley Corbett, for rescuing William Badger who had been arrested for debt at the suit of Thomas Nash, Gentleman, from the custody of Edward Gorney, William Dalbye and Richard Smyth, Sheriff's Bayliffs. (p.131, no.121; X/37)

1612. John Watts, Weaver, Ann his wife, George Watts, Weaver, and Lucy Watts, Spinster for entering the close of John Newnham at Chaddesley, and stealing apples. (p.171, no.78; XIX/26)

1615. Articles concerning the misdemeanour of Margaret Bache, wife of John Bache, Nailer, a common scold. She is a source of strife amongst her neighbours, and has been presented as a scold at the Leate holden for the Manor of Chaddesley. She was also presented at a visitation at Bromsgrove for 'misbehaving her tongue against her mother-in-law', in October 1603, and excommunicated. (p.211, no.126; XXII/77)

1619. Indictment of Katherine Underhill, Widow, for keeping 'a common tippling-house' at Chaddesley, before being licensed by any of the J.P.s of the County. A true Bill. (p.295, no.209; XXXII/25)

1619. Grand Jury Presentment that Thomas Onion of Chaddesley, Carpenter, and Ann his wife, being licensed to keep a common victualling house, keep great disorder there on the Sabbath day, with unlawful games, dice, cards, table-playing, etc. They also keep drunkards in their house, as many as 24 together, and Thomas is often very drunk himself. A true Bill. To be suppressed (p.299, no.244; XXX/97)

1619. Petition of John Wall, a poor prisoner in the County Gaol, to the J.P.s, showing that he granted a loan to John Newnham on a parcel of tenement with garden ground, at Chaddesley, for a period of 11 years. On the expiry of this period, he attempted to re-enter his property, but the said Newnham, under pretence of a title granted to him by the Bailiff and Burgesses of Warwick, brought several bills of forcible entry against the petitioner about 7 or 8 years past. Wall was fined and continued in the County Gaol, his estate being 'overthrown' by costs. The petitioner is still held in durance by the

Sheriff, who will neither accept bail or surety, as the petitioner has matters at hearing in the Court of Requests against the said Bailiff and Burgess of Warwick. He has no money left to make any further satisfaction, and prays that he may be released *Forma pauperis*, and for an allowance in the meantime, otherwise he will perish, 'living double-fettered with irons'. (p.306, no.310; XXX/80)

1627. Indictment of Griffin Meredith of Chaddesley, Labourer, for breaking and entering the dwelling-house of Francis Cooke at Chaddesley, and for stealing therefrom four plates, two candlesticks, two pairs of shoes, and two pairs of hose, of the value of 10 shillings. Not a true Bill. (p.246, no.195; LI/36)

1628. Articles of the behaviour of John Barber of Bellington in the parish of Chaddesley Corbett:

Imprimis, a slaunderer.
Item, a peace-breaker.
Item, a tale-bearer.
Item, an encloser and keeper-in of commons.
Item, a turner of the ancient stream out of her course.
Item, a layer of stumbling-blocks in the several highways, being a great denier of the passage of men or cattle.
Item, an eater, with his cattle, of other men's corn and grass by day and night.
Item, keeping a dog which hurts and bites men's cattle.
A contentious man with his neighbours, and given to law.
(p.452, no.166; LIII/78)

1633. Writ to the Sheriff, to summon the inhabitants of 27 parishes, including Chaddesley, to appear at the next Sessions to answer for various matters to be objected against them. (p.518, no.213; LVIII/50)

1634. Presented by William Stalle and Josiah Hunt, Constables of Chaddesley, that the bakers do not sell bread above 12 or 13 a dozen, watch and ward has been kept, there are none who sell ale without licence, or keep unlawful games; the highways and bridges are very well kept and maintained. Both the Constables brought to the stocks, and also the tithing-man sent, all rogues and vagrants, and have executed the law on them during the time of their office. (p.568, no.305; XXIV/96)

1637. Warrant under the hand and seal of John Wylde to the Constables of Chaddesley Corbett. Whereas William Griffin was about Easter last year apprenticed to John Norris, Yeoman, for eight years, and was well apparelled at the cost of the said Parish, yet the said Norris suffers him to wander up and down, and refuses to keep him in his service. Also, Edward Bennett, Scythesmith, has refused Aaron Reddishe, appointed to be bound to him at the monthly meeting on April 13th last, and was willing to take one William Hitchcox, which he also now refuses to do. The Constables are commanded to arrest the said John Norris, Edward Bennett, and William Griffin, and produce them at the next Quarter Sessions. (p.638, no.175; LXXXIV/78)

1640. Indictments of Josias Hunt of Harvington, Chaddesley, for building a cottage for the habitation of Roger Maholland at Harvington without laying four acres thereto. (p.682, no.144; LXXVII/121)

1640. Indictment of John Morris of Winterfould, Chaddesley, Yeoman, for assaulting Thomas Taylor, Constable of Chaddesley. A true Bill. (p.683, no.156; LXX/30)

1642. Grand Jury Presentment at Quarter Sessions: 'Concerning recusants, and imprimis, those who have absented themselves from their Parish Church or Chapel for the space of one month last past, we do present ... 32 parishes, including ... Chaddesley Corbett: Mary Bache, Widow, Richard Layte, Elizabeth the wife of William Layte, Anthony Monke, and Margaret his wife, and Elizabeth Jourdan.' (p.699, no.42; LXXIX/6)

PRINTED EDITIONS AND CALENDARS OF QUARTER SESSIONS PAPERS

Bedfordshire *Bedfordshire County Records Comprised in the Quarter Session Rolls* from 1714-1832, I (1651-1660), II, compiled by Hardy & Page, *c.*1910 (n.d.); J. Godber, *Guide to the Bedfordshire Record Office*, Beds. C.C., 1957; E.G. Kimball, *Sessions of the Peace for Bedfordshire, 1355-59 and 1363-64*, BHRS Publications, no.48, and Historical Manuscripts Commission, 1969.

Berkshire No Quarter Sessions records as yet published. All originals earlier than 1703 destroyed in fire *c.*1800. *Calendar of Sessions Rolls, 1736-50* available at Record Office; F. Hull, *Guide to Berkshire Record Office*, Berks. C.C. 1952.

Buckinghamshire W. le Hardy and G. Ll. Reckitt, *Buckinghamshire Sessions Records*, vols.I-III (1678-1712); W. le Hardy, vols.IV-VI (1712-24), published for Clerk of the Peace, Bucks, 1933-58 (in Calendar form); Quarter Sessions original records are available from 1678 to the present, at the C.R.O.; J.C.K. Cornwall, 'The County Treasurers, 1678-1889', *Records of Bucks*, XVI, Pt. 3, 1957-8.

Caernarvonshire W. Ogwen Williams, *Calendar of the Caenarvonshire Quarter Sessions Records*, I (1541-58), Caern. Hist. Soc., 1956 (calendar, with facsimiles and some transcripts, valuable introduction); and: *Tudor Gwynedd* (commentary on these Quarter Sessions Records), also 'The County Records', *Caern. His. Soc.*, X, 1949 (a review of the work of the court from the 16th to the 18th centuries); Originals dating from 1541 are available at the C.R.O.

Cheshire J.H.E. Bennet and J.C. Dewhurst, *Quarter Sessions Records of the County Palatine of Chester, 1559-1760*, Chester, 1940 (an index, with extracts).

Denbighshire (Clwyd) A.G. Veysey, *Handlist of the Denbighshire Quarter Sessions Records*, Clwyd Record Office, 1991.

Derbyshire J.C. Cox, *Three Centuries of Derbyshire Annals*, 2 vols., London, 1890; J.C. Cox, *Calendars of the Records of the County of Derby, 1558-1896*, 1899.

Devonshire A.H.A. Hamilton, *Quarter Sessions from Queen Elizabeth to Queen Anne; Illustrations of Local Government and History, drawn from original Records, chiefly of the County of Devon*, Sampson Low, 1878.

Dorset A.C. Cox, *Index to the Dorset County Records*, 1938 (obtainable from the Dorset County Museum).

Essex *Guide to the Essex Record Office*, Essex Record Office Publication no.1, 1946, 1948; D.H. Allen, *The Essex Quarter Sessions Order Book, 1652-61*, Essex CRO, Pubn. no.65, 1974; F.G. Emmison, *Guide to the Essex Quarter Sessions*, Essex Archaeological Soc. Occasional pubs., no.2 (revised edition of 1946 publication), Essex C.C. 1969.

Gloucestershire E. Kimball, 'Rolls of the Gloucestershire Sessions of the Peace, 1361-98', *BGAS*, LXII, 1942 (transcripts); I.E. Gray and A.T. Gaydon, *Gloucestershire Quarter Sessions Archives, 1660-1889, and other Official Records*, Glos. C.C., 1958 (descriptive catalogue); E. Moir, 'Local government in Gloucestershire, 1775-1800; a study of the Justices of the Peace', *BGAS Rec. Sers.*, 8, 1969; County Record Office, *A Short Handlist of the Gloucestershire Records*, Gloucester, 1968; E. Ralph, *Guide to Bristol Archives Office*, Bristol Corporation, 1971.

Gwynedd Caernarvon County Records Committee, *Caernarvon Records, the Caernarvon Record Office*, Caernarvon, 1968.

Hertfordshire *Hertford County Records: Sessions Rolls, 1581-1897*, vols.I, II, III; *Sessions Records of the Liberty of St. Albans Division, 1770-1840*, IV; *Sessions Books, 1619-1845*, vols.V-X (Calendars, published 1905-57); see also W. le Hardy, *Guide to the Hertfordshire Record Office*, Part I, Herts C.C., 1961.

Huntingdonshire There is nothing so far published from these records, but the C.R.O. has compiled lists and Calendars from the date when they begin, in 1734, to the end of 1860.

Kent The Archives Office has a full series of originals dating from 1595, and a typescript Calendar of the early Rolls is in progress there. For clear reference to these originals, see also Felix Hull's excellent *Guide to the Kent County Archives Office*, Kent C.C., 1971; R.D. Clarke, 'West Kent Quarter sessions orders in the reign of Charles I', *AC*, 80, 1965.

Lancashire J. Tait, *Lancashire Quarter Sessions Records*, Chetham Soc., LXXVII, 1919; E. Axon, *Manchester Quarter Sessions*, LCRS, XLII, 1902 (translations and transcripts); E. Axon, *Memoranda of Oswald and Nicholas Mosley of Ancoats, from the Manchester Sessions manuscripts*, Chetham Soc., n.s., XLVII, 1902; B.W. Quintrell, *Proceedings of the Lancashire Justices of the Peace at the Sheriff's Table during Assizes week, 1578-1694*, LCRS, 121, 1981; D. Wilkinson, 'The Commission of the Peace in Lancashire, 1603-42', *HSLC*, 132, 1982-3; R.S. France, *Guide to the Lancashire Record Office* (second edition), County Record Office,

Preston, 1962; J. Bierley Watson, 'The Lancashire Gentry and the Public Service, 1529-1558', *LCAS*, 73-4, 1963-4.

Leicestershire   Guide and Calendars in preparation.

Lincolnshire   S.A. Peyton, *Minutes of the Quarter Sessions for parts of Kesteven, 1674-95*, Lincs Rec. Soc., XXV, 1928, XXVI, 1929.

Merioneth   K. Williams-Jones, *Calendar of the Merioneth Quarter Sessions Rolls, 1733-65*, Gwynedd Archives Service, 1979.

Middlesex   J. Cameron, 'Middlesex Quarter Sessions Records', *Genealogists' Magazine,* X/1, 1947; E.G. Dowdell, *A Hundred Years of Quarter Sessions; the Government of Middlesex from 1660-1760*, C.U.P., 1932; W.J. Hardy, 'Middlesex County Records', Extracts from Reports to Standing Joint Committee, 1902-8; W.J. Hardy and W. le Hardy, 'Middlesex County Records', Reports to Standing Joint Committee, 1902-28; C.D.P. Nicholson, 'Middlesex Sessions Records; Plantation Indentures, Some Early Emigrants to America', *Genealogists' Magazine*, 12, no.1, 1955; J.C. Jeaffreson, *Middlesex County Records:* 1, 'Indictments, Coroners' Inquests Post Mortem and Recognisances from 3 Edward VI to 1603', Middlesex County Records Society, 1886; 2, 'Indictments, Recognisances, Coroners' Inquisitions post Mortem, Orders and Memoranda, temp. James I', Middlesex County Records Society, 1887; 3, 'Indictments, Recognisances, Coroners' Inquisitions post Mortem, Orders and Memoranda and Certificates of Convictions of Conventiclers, temp. Charles I to 18 Charles II', Middlesex County Records Society, 1888; 4, 'Indictments, Recognisances, Coroners' Inquests post Mortem, Orders, Memoranda and Certificates of Conviction of Conventiclers, 19 Charles II to 4 James II', Middlesex County Records Society, 1892; W.J. Hardy, *Calendars of Sessions Books, 1689-1709*, London, 1905; W. le Hardy, *Calendar to the Middlesex Sessions Records*, 1 (1612-14), London, 1935; 2 (1614-15), London, 1936; 3, (1615-16), London, 1937; 4 (1616-18), London, 1941.

Monmouthshire   None of the records of the Monmouthshire Quarter Sessions has been published. Detailed lists of these Records have been prepared and are available in the C.R.O. for use by searchers. Full details of these records appear in the *Guide to Monmouthshire Record Office*, Monmouthshire Archives Committee, Newport, 1959.

Norfolk   D.E. Howell-James, *Quarter Sessions Order Book, 1650- 57*, Norfolk Rec. Soc., 1955; A. Hassall Smith, *County and Court: Government and Politics in Norfolk, 1558-1603*, Oxford, Clarendon Press, 1969.

Northamptonshire   J. Wake and S. A. Peyton, *Quarter Sessions Records of the County of Northampton, 1630; 1657; 1657-8*, Northants Rec. Soc. Pub., I, 1924 (texts with introduction); The original Rolls, Minute Books, Account Books, etc. continue from 1658 to date. There were also separate Sessions for the Soke of Peterborough, of which those of 1699-1710 (Rolls) and 1756-87, and 1795-1912 (Record Books) are preserved in the C.R.O.; M. Gollancz, *Rolls of Northamptonshire Sessions of the Peace (Supervisors 1314-16 and Keepers 1320)*, Pubns. NRS, 11, 1940.

Northumberland   County Record Office, *The Northumberland Record Office*, Northumberland C.C., 1970.

Nottinghamshire   H. Hampton Copnall, *Nottingham County Records of the Seventeenth Century*, Nottm., 1915 (extracts with commentary); K. Tweedale Meaby, *Nottinghamshire County Records of the Eighteenth Century*, Nottm., 1947 (extracts with commentary) (Originals at the Nottinghamshire Archives date from the Minute Books of 1603); K.T. Beaby, *Records of the Borough of Nottingham*, 9 vols., 1888-1956.

Oxfordshire   M.S. Gretton, *Oxfordshire J.P.s in the Seventeenth Century*, ORS, XVI, 1934; H.M. Walton, 'Quarter Sessions Records in Oxfordshire and their use for the genealogist', *Oxf. Family Historian*, 2, IV, 1981; F.D. Price, *The Wigginton Constables' Book, 1691-1836*, Phillimore, 1971.

Shropshire   *Abstracts of Orders and Rolls of Shropshire Quarter Sessions*, Shrops C.C. pub. nos.2-7, 9-17. Records covered date from 1638. Many earlier records were destroyed by fire in 1880. Published *c.*1908 (n.d.); *A Guide to the Shropshire Records*, Salop C.C., 1952.

Somersetshire   *Interim Handlist of Somerset Quarter Sessions Documents and other Official Records preserved in the Somerset Record Office*, Somerset C.C., Records Committee (now out of print; one loan copy available to individual students for a limited period); E.H. Bates Harbin, *Quarter Sessions Records for the County of Somerset, James I, 1607-25*, Som. Rec. Soc., XXIII, 1907; E.H. Bates Harbin, *Do. . . Charles I, 1625-39*, Som. Rec. Soc., XXIV, 1908; E.H. Bates Harbin, *Do . . . Commonwealth, 1646-60*, Som. Rec. Soc., XXVIII, 1912; M.C.B. Dawes, *Do . . . Restoration, 1666-77*, Som. Rec. Soc., XXXIV, 1919; S.W. Bates Harbin, *Somerset Enrolled Deeds*, Som. Rec. Soc., LI, 1936; T.G. Barnes, *Somerset Assize Orders, 1629-40*, Som. Rec. Soc., LXV, 1959.

Staffordshire   *The Staffordshire Quarter Sessions Rolls:* I (1581-9), 1929; II (1590-3), 1930; III (1594-7), 1932; IV (1598-1602), 1935; V (1603-6), 1940; VI (1606-9), 1948-9. (Vols.I-V were edited by S.A.H. Burne and VI by D.H.G. Salt). All six volumes were published by the Staffordshire Record Society (William Salt Arch. Soc. until 1936). A list of the original Quarter Sessions records from the mid-16th century onwards is available at the County Record Office, whilst transcripts of the rolls up to 1635 are available at the William Salt Library.

Suffolk   'Minute and Order Books, 1639-1872', are on microfilm (11 reels) and can be purchased through E.P. Microforms Ltd.

Surrey   H. Jenkinson and D.L. Powell, *Surrey County Records, Quarter Sessions, 1659-66,* vols.V-VIII, Surrey C.C., 1931-8; Typed Calendars to 1688 are available at the C.R.O.; D.L. Powell and H. Jenkinson, *Surrey Quarter Sessions Records, 1659-61; 1661-3 and 1663-6,* SuRS, nos. XXXV, 13, 1934; XXXVI, 14, 1935; XXXIX, 16, 1938.

Sussex   B.C. Redwood, *Quarter Sessions Order Book, 1642-9,* Sussex Rec. Pub. no.3, E. and W. Sussex C.C., 1954; F.W. Steer, *A Descriptive Catalogue of the Quarter Sessions Records in the Custody of the County Councils of East and West Sussex,* Suss. Rec. Pubn. no.2, 1952; C. Brent *et al., Sussex in the Sixteenth and Seventeenth Centuries, a Bibliography,* Centre for Continuing Education, University of Sussex, Occasional Papers, no.2, 1980; M. Reed, 'The keeping of Sessions of the Peace in the borough of Hastings', *SAC,* no.100, 1962.

Warwickshire   S.C. Ratcliff and H.C. Johnson, *Warwick County Records,* .I-VIII, Warwick C.C., 1935-47; E.G. Kimball, *Rolls of the Warwickshire and Coventry Sessions of the Peace, 1377-97,* Dugdale Soc., XVI, 1939; N.W. Alcock, *Stoneleigh Villagers, 1597-1650,* University of Warwick, 1975; F.W. Markwell, *Tracing your Ancestors in Warwickshire,* Birm. & Mids. Soc. H.G., 1981; R.H. Hall, *Parish Government in Northfield,* Northfield Conservation; E.G. Kimball, *Rolls of Warwickshire and Coventry Sessions of the Peace, 1377-1397,* Dugdale Soc., 16, 1939; N.W. Alcock, *Stoneleigh Villagers, 1597-1650,* University of Warwick, 1975; R.H. Hall, *Parish Government in Northfield,* Northfield Conservation Group, 1975.

Wiltshire   M.G. Rathbone, *Guide to the Records in the Custody of the Clerk of the Peace for Wiltshire,* Part I, 1959, Part II, 1961, Wilts C.C.; H. Cunnington, *Records of the County of Wilts,* Devizes, 1932 (extracts); H.C. Johnson, 'Wiltshire County Records: Minutes of Proceedings in sessions 1563 and 1574-92', *WANHS,* Recs. Branch, IV, 1949; J.P.M. Fowle, *Wiltshire Quarter Sessions and Assizes, 1736,* Wilts. Rec. Soc., XI, 1955; R.W. Merriman, 'Extracts from the records of the Wiltshire Quarter Sessions', *WANHM,* XX-XXII, 1883-5.

Yorkshire   J.C. Atkinson, *Quarter Sessions Records (N. Riding), 1605-1791,* 9 vols., N. Riding Rec. Soc., 1884-92; J. Lister, *W. Riding Sessions Records, 1598-1642,* 2 vols., Yorks Arch. Soc. Rec. Ser., III, 1888; LIV, 1915; B.J. Barber, *Guide to the Quarter Sessions Records of the West Riding of Yorkshire, 1637-1971, and other official records,* W. Yorks. Archive Service, 1984.

Original Documents to be found at:

County Record Offices.

Probate Records: Inventories and Wills

The Documents

Domestic Inventories. During the Elizabethan, Stuart and Hanoverian periods, and indeed to 1859, probate of a will required[4] that a detailed inventory of the 'goods, chattels and cattle' of the deceased be produced. These inventories were made, or 'appraised', by reputable neighbours, who were considered to be competent and qualified to assess the value of the goods. In fact, these assessors were often barely literate, and in most cases they under-valued the property quite recklessly. Although there are other common errors, the inventory being often incomplete and wrongly totalled, these documents are most fascinating sources for the

---

[4] Statute 21, Henry VIII, c.5 (1529).

domestic history of the period. They deal with the households of gentry and bourgeois, yeoman farmer and pauper, and are in fact invaluable in portraying the smaller house and its contents, about which so little is otherwise known. They may list, with all usual furnishings, occasional jewellery and plate, full descriptions of all clothing in the chests, the implements of the dairy, still-room, kitchen, barns, stables and workshops. They can also provide information on the tools, stock and techniques of farming and other crafts. The number of rooms in the house is sometimes given, with the contents of each, to the last spoon or candle-stick. These inventories are indispensable for a study of domestic crafts, history of furniture, clothing, agriculture, and general standard of living during a critical transition period. They can also be usefully compared with the equally detailed contents of farm sale catalogues of the 19th and 20th centuries to show changes in standards of living. Most inventories are written on loose sheets of paper, although the earlier examples may be found on lengthy rolls of vellum. The latter may extend to a narrow roll many feet in length, but more usually a complete inventory is contained in a page or two, each about a foot long. The inventory is usually found attached to the relevant will, or may be housed in a separate collection, or found loose amongst other wills.

Wills. The will which a probate inventory accompanies is, legally, the more important; for the local historian each provides a different, though equally important, type of information. Inventories give us a picture of the 17th-century household, which is at first sight a superficial one, though its contents can be analysed, and significant facts discovered; for the more complex questions of family life and relationships, the wills must be consulted. These documents are obviously of primary importance to the genealogist and the family historian. Here we find the names of widows and children, the names of 'in-laws' and more distant relatives, so that the wills combine with the evidence of parish registers, where they survive for the early centuries, or supplement their absence. Often it is the information discovered in local wills which provides us with clues to follow up in the registers, or tells us in which years of the register we should search; for instance, reference to relatives and marriage connections in another parish will lead us directly to another parish chest. Other important clues to a family's life and business are found in the particulars of lands and property bequeathed; often the site of a man's house, and the position of his lands amongst the village fields is explained. The will often supplies details of a tradesman's stock-in-trade, his debts, and information about outstanding orders, commitments to suppliers of materials and to customers, and other business arrangements, which we would not expect to find in the inventory's brief entries of the contents of shop and working premises. Just as the inventory sets the scene, and lists the inanimate contents of the 17th-century home, so the will provides the house with a family, albeit a bereaved one.

We shall often discover the more rewarding possibilities of studying a *group* of different but associated groups of documents together, rather than confining our attention to one type only. In the case of the combination of wills, inventories and administrations, we have only recently discovered the possibility of another item in the set, the previously neglected probate accounts.[5] It must be admitted that there is always a tendency for an enthusiast to concentrate his attention on the most attractive documents in a set; in the case of probate records, these were once the inventories. In the 1950s and '60s, the sheer novelty of these homely lists, with their wealth of domestic detail and simple format, caused an inevitable preoccupation with

---

[5] C. Gittings, 'Probate Accounts, a neglected source', *The Local Historian*, 21, no.2, May 1991.

TRANSCRIPT

1 ...	A true Inventory of all the goodes and cattels that were John	
	Walderns at the tyme of his deathe praysed by William Walderne	
	Thomas Smythe and John Westwod the xvj th. of September ann. domni. 1574.	
	In primis one yoke of oxen	iiij li.
5 ...	Item, one yoke of Steres	liijs. iiijd.
	Item, one cowe	xxxs.
	Item, yerelyng calf	xs.
	Item, one horse	xxs.
	Item, xl ti. shepe	iij li. vjs. viijd.
10 ...	Item, vj swyne	xvjs.
	Item, Item, corne	xvjs.
	Item, heye	xxs.
	Item, wayne tombrels, harrows, yokes and towes and all	
	all that belongeth thereto	liiis.
15 ...	Item, a onfeld	xls.
	Item, a pere of belowes	xxs.
	Item, hambers, tonges and a tewyrne	xxs.
	Item, ii fetherbedds, ii flockbedds and iiij bolsters	xls.
	Item, v pere of blankets	xxxs.
20 ...	Item, xii canvesses	xxvjs. viijd.
	Item, iii coveryngs	xxs.
	Item, paynted clothes, coysshens and pyllowes	xxjs. ..d.
	Item, iiij pere of flaxen shetes	xxs. ..d.
	Item, iiij pere of hempen shetes	xxs.
25 ...	Item, vj pere of hurden shetes	xviijs.
	Item, bordes clothes	xxiijs. iiijd.
	Item, towels, napkyns and pelowe beres	xxxiiijs.
	Item, a fetherbedde case	vjs.
	Item, all other lynnen stuffe	xs.
30 ...	Item, bestedds coffers and presses	xiijs. iiijd.
	Item, yrne stuffe	xs.
	Item, wole	xs.
	Item, pottes, pannes cathornes and chafornes	iij li. vjs. viijd.
	Item, pewter and maslyn	xxxs.
35 ...	Item, a cubborde	iijs. iiijd.
	Item, bagges & wynowyng shete	vjs. iiijd.
	Item, pyntes, payles and all trene vessels	xijs.
	Item, bordes, formes and stoles	vjs.
	Item, wheles and cardes	ijs.
40 ...	Item, pothokes, pothangles, fyreshovels, tonges	
	and a pere of hande belowes	ijs.
	Item, broches, cobberds, brandyrne axes and bylles	vjs.
	Item, hens and gese	vs.
	Item, his apparell	xxs.
45 ...	Item, ynens and garlycke	iijs.

Summa. lix li. ixs. vijd.

Plate XIII. Inventory of the Goods of John Walderne, Chaddesley Corbett, 1574.
(Worcester Record Office Ref: 008.7.1574/84)
Actual size: 15.25 x 37cm

008·7 84
1574

84

A true Inventorie of all the goodes & cattels that were John
walker at the tyme of his death praysed by willm walker
Thomas smythe & John westwad the xxj of September a° dni 1574

In primis one yoke of oxen —————————————————— iij li
Item one yoke of steeres ———————————————————— liij s iiij d
Item one cowe ———————————————————————————— xxx s
Item yereling calfe ———————————————————————— x s
Item one hogg ————————————————————————————— xx s
Item xlti shepe ——————————————————————————— iij li xvj s viij d
Item vj stayrs ——————————————————————————— xvj s
Item corne ———————————————————————————————— xxvj li
Item haye ————————————————————————————————— x s
Item wayne tombrell garromes yokes & teames & all
all that belongeth therto —————————————————— liij s iiij d
Item a orfelld ————————————————————————————— x s
Item a peir of bellowes ——————————————————— x s
Item hambers tonges & a terymre ————————————— x s
Item ij fetherbedde ij flockbedde & iij bolster —— xl s
Item v peir of blankets ——————————————————— xvj s
Item xij candessess ———————————————————————— xxxij s iiij d
Item ij coverynge ——————————————————————— xvj s
Item paynted clothes cosshens & pyllowes ———— xx s
Item iiij peir of flaxen shetes ——————————————— xxx s
Item iiij peir of hempen shetes ——————————————— xx s
Item vj peir of harden shetes —————————————— xviij s
Item bordes clothes ———————————————————————— xxviij s iiij d
Item towels napkyns & pelowe bears —————————— xxxiiij s
Item a fetherbedde cast ——————————————————— vj s
Item all other lynnen stuffe ——————————————— vj s
Item bestodde coffers & presses —————————————— xviij s iiij d
Item yron stuffe ——————————————————————————— vj s
Item wole ————————————————————————————————— xx s
Item potts pannes caldornes & chafornes ———— iij li xij s iiij d
Item pewter & masslyn ——————————————————————— xx s
Item a cubbord ———————————————————————————— x s
Item bagges & wynnowyng sheve —————————————— iij s iiij d
Item pynnes payles & all treene vessell ———— xij s iiij d
Item bordes formes & stoles ————————————————— xij s
Item wheles & cardes ———————————————————————— ij s
Item potthoks pothangeles presshobels tonges
and a peir of hande bellowes —————————————— iij s
Item broches cobborde brandyren a gredyren & bytell — vj s
Item hens & geese ————————————————————————— v s
Item his apparell ———————————————————————— xxx s
Item ynons & garlyke ——————————————————————— x s

Sm̄ lxx li xv s iiij d

inventories, even at the expense of the more extensive wills and less exciting administrations. The result was a long series of publications as satisfying as the early treasure trove of F.W. Steer's *Farm and Cottage Inventories of Mid-Essex* in 1950. Nowadays, the trend of newcomers to this subject is, as in other cases like enclosures, to concentrate more closely upon the circumstances of the people behind a set of documents rather than upon the things which the records portray. This approach makes a study of probate accounts very attractive indeed.

Surviving in their thousands (10-20,000 in Kent CRO for example), these documents record executors' accounts for the the cost of administering the estate of the deceased, usually in the case of one who had died intestate. The executor is often the widow, a daughter or a son. Each document begins with a common form; for example in 1685 we find: 'The account of John Bach, the sonne and Administrator of all and singular the Goods, Chattels and Creditors of John Bach, late whilst he lived of Chaddesley Corbett in the county and diocese of Worcester, intestate, made by him of and upon his Administration in the provisions as followeth, viz:'

The account is then divided into two parts, charges and discharges. The first charge is always a valuation of the estate, with reference to an inventory deposited in the Registry of Worcester but not traceable in the CRO or Fry's Indexes (qv). John Bach's estate was valued at £134 06s. 02d. The discharge then begins with funeral expenses (£15) and ends with the costs of administration and drafting of the accounts. Between these two entries John Bach's estate accounts only for his debts, £205 10s. 0d. in all. These include a mortgage of £70 due to William Cole of Belbroughton and seven bonds. £52 10s. was due to William Smith of Clent, £26 to John Holder of Chaddesley Corbett, £20 to Mr. Seager of Bewdley, £11 to Mr. Stephens of Bromsgrove, £10 to Mr. Insall and £6 to William Johnson, both of Chaddesley and £10 to Richard Farmer of St John's in Bedwardine. With a negative equity of £78 13s. 10d. it is difficult to know what happened to resolve John Bach's estate; the accounts do not say.

The possibilities of using this sort of evidence to draw a net of local financial arrangements in a pre-banking age are obviously immense and cry out for access to a computer. In many cases debts are more informative than mere reference to 'bonds' and will offer valuable information on tradesmen's investments and running costs. We learn for instance in the account of John Blakeway, yeoman of Chaddesley in 1752, that his estate owed to John Elcox £1 10s. as two years' interest on a loan of £15, that is at five per cent. Anne Bacon of Chaddesley, administering the estate of her late husband, Charles in 1682, lists, as his debts: to Mr. Trowbridge for Iron, £18; to Mr. Oristran of Swinford, for steele £4, and to Geo. Barnett of Chaddesley Corbett, for grinding scythes £4. Many other intestates are listed by occupations, such as mercers, scythesmiths, nailers and innkeepers.

There is also a great deal more detail of social custom in the accounts. Other typical charges include, in John Blakeway's case, costs of cake (£1 10s.), gloves (£3), cyphers (£1 10s.) and wine (10s.) at his funeral—far more expense than his shroud (8s. 6d.) and coffin (18s.) He also gave £1 10s. to the poor on that occasion. He also owed his serving man 20s. in wages, £1 15s. in tithes and £1 2s. in land tax. A payment of £9 10s. as *Herriotts* is interesting evidence of the survival of ancient manorial custom as late as 1727. A search of these accounts may disclose details of a final illness and medical treatment or details of sudden death by accident or violence. Special deathbed requests and bequests are noted; also payment for extra-large coffins for the obese and overtime for a sexton digging in a frost-bound graveyard. There may also be information on provision for orphans, their apprenticeship and education, the cost of tombs and memorials. Clare Gittings's article has even more fascinating details: of payments to three soldiers to dig for a dead man's buried savings; the rewarding of a miller who retrieved the body from his millpool with a drowned man's suit of clothes and murderers brought to trial at the widow's expense. She also points out the importance of information offered about the role of the poor in sickness and death, with payments as nurses, for laying out the corpse, cleaning the house, acting as messengers or cooking the funeral meal. The poor, she says, were always at hand to be used, or as objects of charity.

Searchers for probate acounts in Worcestershire Record Office are fortunate in finding a ready-made index there. The accounts are not boxed with wills and administrations, nor are they indexed by Fry or stored on microfilm. They are nevertheless easily found by reference to a separate typescript index compiled by Mrs. Nesta Evans of the University of Cambridge, Faculty of History in 1992. Dating from the 16th to 18th centuries, the accounts are listed alphabetically by surname, with date, place and occupation wherever this is given. The typescript is indexed by 38 occupations, and place-names, which include accounts from Gloucestershire (2), Herefordshire (3), Shropshire (3), Staffordshire (8), Warwickshire (119) and Worcestershire (422).

In a different context, a closer attention to the wills of 407 women testators from Leeds and Hull between 1520 and 1650[6] explodes two prevalent myths: that is, that middle- and lower-class women were 'invisible' in Tudor and Stuart times and that only the rich made wills. More than this, however, the focus of attention on northern women of all sorts, rich and poor, old and young, single and widowed, offers a different perspective on probate records, other than our earlier preoccupation with mere patriarchal property. It persuades us to consider what were the social and economic conditions of widows and orphans, the relative independence of girls with child portions or widows with property from first, second and even third marriages and earlier commitments to the children of those unions. Some of these wills deal with single unmarried women as workers or prosperous business owners. It also reveals graphic detail of deathbed bequests to midwives and nurses, the extension of family arangements to care for orphans and grandchildren and women's attitudes to religious charities and education which amounts in some cases to a rudimentary system of poor relief. This is in fact an excellent example of the wider sociological view which recently arises from a more politically correct searching of familiar documents.

As the example shows (Plate XIII), these documents are written in English; at first sight the unfamiliar 'secretary' hand of the 17th century looks more difficult to read than it proves to be. Certain individual letters, especially *s, c, r, e, sh, th, h*, and several capitals hinder the reader, and the difficulties are increased by individual idiosyncracies of hand-writing from document to document. The only solution is familiarity through constant study of the documents, and it takes surprisingly little regular practice to learn to read them without difficulty, apart from the constant element of surprise at highly original phonetic spelling, e.g. *quishins, wolle, collys, freinpon,* for cushions, wool, coals and frying-pan. The last obstacle lies in words which, painfully deciphered, fail to hold any meaning for the uninitiated, e.g. *swingletrees, shopickes, twilleys* and *cratches.* Most of these can be traced in the larger dictionaries, or in special glossaries of obsolete and dialect words. It has been found that older students can master these hands after a few lessons and frequent practice; even older secondary modern schoolchildren have found enjoyment in the attempt, with a good deal of success.

---

6 'Northern Women in the Early Modern period; The female testators of Hull and Leeds, 1520-1650', *Yorkshire Archaeological Journal,* 59, 1987.

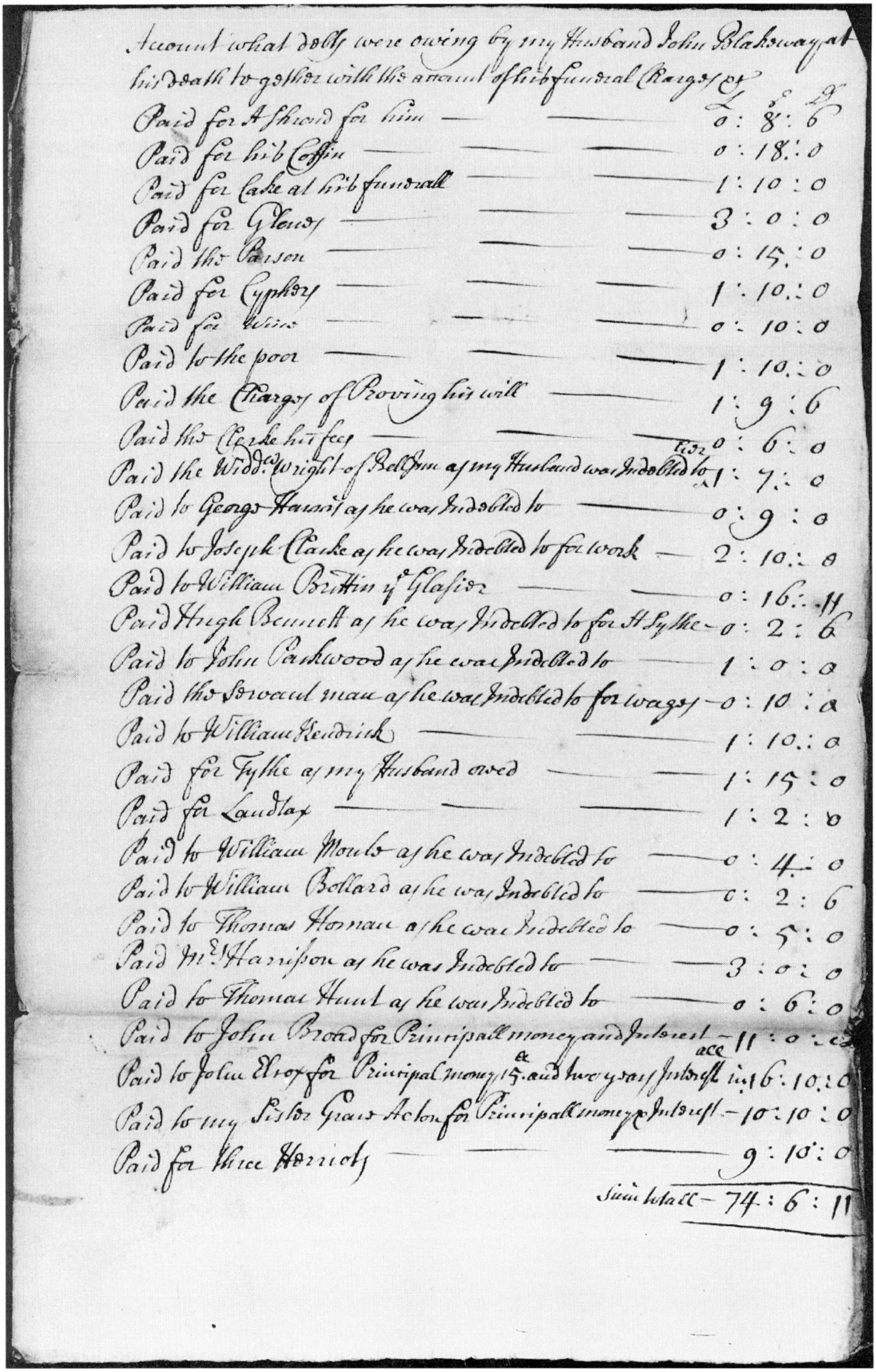

Account what debts were owing by my Husband John Blakeway at
his death together with the amount of his funeral Charges &c

	£	s	d
Paid for A Shroud for him	0	8	6
Paid for his Coffin	0	18	0
Paid for Cake at his funerall	1	10	0
Paid for Gloves	3	0	0
Paid the Parson	0	15	0
Paid for Cyphers	1	10	0
Paid for Wine	0	10	0
Paid to the poor	1	10	0
Paid the Charges of Proving his will	1	9	6
Paid the Clarke his fees	0	6	0
Paid the Widd: Wright of Bellam as my Husband was Indebted to	1	7	0
Paid to George Hawns as he was Indebted to	0	9	0
Paid to Joseph Clarke as he was Indebted to for work	2	10	0
Paid to William Brittin ye Glasier	0	16	11
Paid Hugh Bennett as he was Indebted to for A Sythe	0	2	6
Paid to John Packwood as he was Indebted to	1	0	0
Paid the Servant man as he was Indebted to for wages	0	10	0
Paid to William Kendrick	1	10	0
Paid for Tythe as my Husband owed	1	15	0
Paid for Landtax	1	2	0
Paid to William Moule as he was Indebted to	0	4	0
Paid to William Bollard as he was Indebted to	0	2	6
Paid to Thomas Hornan as he was Indebted to	0	5	0
Paid Mr Harrison as he was Indebted to	3	0	0
Paid to Thomas Hunt as he was Indebted to	0	6	0
Paid to John Broad for Principall money and Interest	11	0	0
Paid to John Elroy for Principal money 15 and two years Interest	16	10	0
Paid to my Sister Grace Acton for Principall money & Interest	10	10	0
Paid for three Herriots	9	10	0
Sum totall	74	6	11

Plate XIV
Probate Account of John Blakeway of Chaddesley Corbett, 1752.
Printed by permission of Worcestershire Record Office.
Ref: 008.7 BA 3585/829/4. Actual size: 32.5 x 21.1cm

Any series or class of records which offers a mass of minute detail such as personal names, working occupations, field names, prices, wages and other costs, furniture, cattle, etc., especially in the intensive form of lists, registers and tables, lends itself very aptly to the compilation of a computer database. Although the preparation of any base from a significantly large sample is time consuming, the completed programme creates the possibility of swift and flexible analysis and cross-reference. Several useful commercial software packages are available for adaptation to any type of documentary series. The feasibility of sorting and setting an otherwise unmanageable mass of material facilitates the testing of many more hypotheses than a manual searcher could envisage. The modern magic of 'wild card' and 'sounds like' searches may also offer a remarkable new keyboard technique for solving problems of illegible or inconsistent entries.

Probate inventories, like parish registers and the national census, lend themselves particularly well to database analysis. The possibility has been admirably demonstrated, with simple instructions for the computer-barely-literate student, by Janet Spavold and members of the South Derbyshire Local History Research Group ('Analysing Wills and Inventories: Church Gresley, Derbyshire 1535-1700', *The Local Historian*, 26, 2, 1996). The project was intended for the guidance of teachers with children in schools but is applicable to any other research purpose. A complete series of 214 inventories from 1535-1700 from the Diocesan Archives at Lichfield was analysed with some interesting results: 'Details were obtained in this way about timepieces (only two, an hour-glass and a gold watch), glass windows, the rise and fall of painted cloths as room hangings (1580-1640s), new fashions in clothing (one girl has a side-saddle habit within a year of this fashion's introduction to London by ladies at Court), paintings, books and chamber pots (so rare we classified them as luxuries!), the operation of a financial market (through interest rates and the purchase of an annuity) and many other subjects such as women's employment in textile preparation in the home and evidence of religious change in the phraseology of testators.' Modestly, the director of the project acknowledges, with refreshing candour, that: 'The group did not all take to computers and some preferred to keep to paper and pencil methods throughout, though everybody appreciated the extensions to our researches which the database made possible.' There is, it seems, hope for us all, even poor Ned Ludd!

FURTHER READING

O. Ashmore and J.J. Bagley, 'Inventories as a Source of Local History', four articles in *Amateur Historian*, beginning in 4, no.4, 1959

A.K. Biggs, *A step-by-step guide to wills and probate*, 1991

J. Bower, *Probate Accounts*, Historical Association's Short Guides to Records, no.34, 1995

A.J. Camp (revision of B.G. Bouwens and H. Thacker), *Wills and their Whereabouts*, 1951

J. Cox, *Wills, Probate and Death Duty Records*, FFHS, 1993

N. and J. Cox, 'Probate Inventories, the legal background', Parts 1 and 2, *The Local Historian*, 16, nos.3 and 4, 1984; and: 'Valuation in probate inventories', Parts 1 and 2, *The Local Historian*, 16, no.4, 1985 and 17, no.2, May 1986

J. Gibson, *Probate Jurisdictions: Where to Look for Wills*, FFHSS, 4th edition, 1994; *Wills and Where to Find Them*, Phillimore, 1974; and: *Simplified Guide to Probate Jurisdictions*, FFHS, 2nd edition, 1982

C. Gittings, 'Probate Accounts, a neglected source', *The Local Historian*, 22, no.2, May 1991

J.H. Harvey, *Sources for the History of Houses*, Archives for the User, no.3, British Records Association, 1974

B.C. Jones, 'Inventories of Goods and Chattels', *Amateur Historian*, 2, no.3, 1954

E. McLaughlin, *Wills before 1858*, FFHS, 1985

J.S. Moore, 'The Making of Probate Inventories', *The Local Historian*, 12, no.1,1976; and: *The Goods and Chattels of our Forefathers*, Phillimore, 1976

G. Morgan, 'Welsh names in Welsh wills', *The Local Historian*, 25, no.3, August 1995

M. Overton, *A Bibliography of British Probate Inventories*, Department of Geography, University of Newcastle-upon-Tyne, 1983

S. Porter, 'The Making of Probate Inventories', *The Local Historian*, 12, no.1, 1976

F.W. Steer, *Farm and Cottage Inventories of Mid-Essex*, Phillimore, 1969; and: 'Short Guides to Records No:3 Probate Inventories', *History*, no.47, 1962

H. Thacker, 'Wills and other Probate Records', *Amateur Historian*, 9, 1953

B. Trinder and J. Cox, *Yeomen and Colliers in Telford*, Phillimore, 1980

INDEXES FOR WORCESTERSHIRE

The County Record Office holds different editions of these indexes at Shire Hall (1) and St. Helen's Church (2):

(1) Edward Alex Fry, *Calendar of Wills and Administrations in the Consistory Court of the Bishop of Worcester 1451-1600*, XXXI, 1904, and *1601-1652*, xxxix, 1910 (London, British Record Society [Index Library]); (2) E.A. Fry, *Index of Worcestershire Wills 1451-1680*, Worcestershire Historical Society, 1904.

Also at Shire Hall, we find alphabetical volumes in bound typescript of Wills for 1601-1690; 1700-1749; 1750-1799; 1800-1858 and 1859-1928. See also:

K.G. Collyer, *An Alphabetical Index of Miscellaneous Probate Inventories*, typescript, 1988; and: W.E. English, *An Index to Occupations in Worcestershire Wills 1451-1652*, typescript by reference to Fry's Calendar, n.d.

ORIGINAL DOCUMENTS TO BE FOUND AT:

Inventories will usually be found either at a County Record Office, or at the local Probate Office. These Worcestershire examples were originally at Birmingham Probate Office, but have been transferred to Worcester Record Office. To trace other local examples see B.G. Bouwens and H. Thacker, *Wills and Their Whereabouts* (Society of Genealogists, 1951).

There are also many Worcestershire Inventories at the Birmingham Reference Library. These include, for example:

Altch Lench	Eldersfield	North Piddle
Beaudesert (Wa.)	Evesham	Pershore
Bedwardine	Feckenham	Rushley
Belbroughton	Frankley	Stoke Prior
Bromsgrove	Hampton Lovett	Stourbridge
Castlemorton	Hunnington	Strensham
Chaddesley Corbett	Ilmington (Gl.)	Studley (Wa.)
Cropthorne	Kidderminster	Whiteladies Aston
Droitwich	Kings Norton	Worcester

Houses Illustrated by Inventories[7]

The following examples of domestic inventories are of particular value in that they not only list the furniture and chattels of the deceased, but also specify the rooms of the houses in which they were found. Comparative studies of such inventories from the 16th to the 18th centuries can teach us a great deal about changes in the design, size and shape of houses, both large and small, during the period. In the following cases, an architect has used the information from the inventories to make a conjectural reconstruction of the possible shape and lay-out of the houses described. Whilst these cannot pretend to be exact, as there could be numerous similar combinations of each set of rooms, such reconstruction is invaluable in helping us to bring the documents to life; in rare and fortunate cases a correct interpretation of an inventory may help us to identify a particular house which still stands today.

Conjectural drawings are of course unnecessary, if a particular surviving house can be certainly identified with a 'named-room' Inventory, but exact identification is by no means an easy matter. The most direct method would be to discover the names of previous owners from the earliest title-deeds of the house, and endeavour to discover the same names in the Index to local Inventories. Title deeds are, however, not always easily accessible, and contemporary references to an 'address' in other types of early documents are comparatively rare (but see Hearth Tax exceptions, page 183). One alternative is to work from an estate map which names the occupiers of houses shown (see Chaddesley Map of 1697, Plate VII), and to search for these names amongst the inventories. There are four major obstacles here; firstly, few villages will in fact provide 17th-century maps which name the householders; secondly, not all the occupiers' names will produce an inventory of any sort; thirdly, not all inventories unearthed will name the rooms of the house, and, finally, recent demolition may have removed all trace of the house itself from the ground. From the Warwick map of Chaddesley, for example, of the 12 householders named, only two names yielded inventories 'with rooms', for Mrs Aston's 'two tenements which contain two large bays and two little bays, tyled ...', an Inventory of 12 rooms, and for Richard Lamb's 'tenement containing three large bays ...', an Inventory of 13 rooms. These proved to be the only two of the few houses shown on the map which have been demolished since 1697. William Kindon's home still stands at Bluntingdon Farm—the tie beam is marked 'W.K. 1680'; there are two Kindon inventories, both for 1607, but neither gives details of rooms in the house. This means that it is impossible to provide a contemporary inventory for any surviving house in Chaddesley, at least by this method. Recent work on John Doharty's 18th-century (1744) copy of John Blagrave's *Map of Feckenham Forest and Manor*, made in 1591, is proving much more rewarding. The original of this map is at the British Library (P. 12609.MI.6b i [12]) and a photocopy is held at Worcester Record Office (f.989.9: 90.BA: 978) (see R.H. Hilton's *Swanimote Rolls of Feckenham Forest* in Worcestershire Historical Society's *Miscellany I*, 1960). Three houses shown on this map have already been definitely identified on ground, map and inventory. The house of Henry Bolte can be identified as Lower Grinsty Farm (*O.S. ref: 023657*), and is provided with a seven-room Inventory of 1617; Joshua Hanbury's house, with a five-room Inventory of 1598, still stands (*O.S. ref: 025648*); and John Bonde's home, a three-room hall-house, with an Inventory of 1599, also survives. Worcester Record Office also has early estate maps, complete with householders' names, for Claines, Powick and Grafton Flyford, which will probably lead to more Inventories of surviving houses in those villages.

---

[7] For a full and exciting treatment of this subject at length see M.W. Barley, *The English Farmhouse and Cottage* (Routledge and Kegan Paul, 1961). This is the first major work to deal fully with the development of the smaller house in England, with full references to regional differences in structure. Dealing very fully with the use of documents as an aid to architectural study, it gives very clear and much-welcomed assistance on the application of a study of Inventories, Glebe Terriers and Estate Maps, etc. to the study of vernacular buildings.

William Wilkes, 1608

A true inventory of all the goods, chattels and debts of William Wilkes of Chadsley in the Diocese of Worcester, gentleman, deceased; taken and praysed by Richard Courtald Smith, Ralf Let, Nicholas Knight and William Dees, the eighteenth day of July in the year of the reign of our lorde James, King of England, France and Ireland the sixth, and Scotland one and forty, anno domini 1608.

Imprimis, *In the Hawle*, one long table with a frame and two forms thereto belonging, one square table with a frame and 4 joined stools thereto belonging, one low joined stool, 2 chairs and 7 cushions, 20 yards of waynescote, one waynescote cubbarde, one gun, one horslock, one pair of bellows, 2 andirons, one fireshovell, one pair of tongs, 3 benches, links and pothooks and one spinning wheel. £4 3s. 10d.

Item, *In the Parlour*, one long table with a frame, 3 joined stools and 2 benches thereto belonging, one waynescote press, one joined bed and curtains and 3 iron rods to hang them on, one carpet for the forseyd table, one fetherbed, 2 fustyan pillows, 2 blankets and one bybell. One bolster, one coverlet. £8 2s. 2d.

Item, *In the Chamber over the Parlour*, one joined bedstead, one flockbed, 3 blankets and 2 bolsters. 52s. 0d.

Item, *In the Kitchen*, one tablecord, one wetting vat, one bread skeele, one old salting trough, one kilden herecloth, one salting cup. 27s. 0d.

Item, *In the Buttery Entry*, 2 benches, 2 shelves, 3 pails, glasses, cups, dishes, spoons, and such implements. 25s. 0d.

Item, *In the Buttery*, one table with a frame, 3 benches, 4 shelves, 5 barrels and one bruing-loome. One hanging save. 44s. 6d.

Item, *In the Deyhouse*, one great cawthern, 2 lesser cawtherns, 1 pot, 1 pan, 1 broche, 1 pair of cobbards and 2 dripping pans, 2 dabnets, 1 frying pan, 1 skimmer, 2 chafing dishes, 1 cheese press, 3 benches, 1 churn, 2 cheese cowles, 3 skeeles, 1 little powdering tub, some Wedsbury brass searches for meal, and some small implements. £4 18s. 0d.

Item, *In the Chamber over the Hall*, 1 joined trundle bed, 1 press of board, 3 coffers, 1 joined desk, 1 featherbed, 2 fustyan pillows, 1 coverlet, 1 twiggen chair, 5 curtaynes, with 3 iron rods to hang them on, 6 payres of flaxen sheets and 8 payres of hurden sheets, 2 payres of hemten sheets, 8 flaxen pillow beres, 1 flaxen tablecloth, 1 hemten tablecloth, 5 hurden tablecloths, 2 dossen of flaxen tablenapkins, 1 dossen of hemten table napkins, 7 hande towels, 22 ells of new hemten cloth, 6 yards and half of new cloth for bed tycks. £29 1s. 0d.

Item, *In the Maydes Chamber*, 2 bedsteads, 2 flockbeds, 4 featherbolsters, 2 coverlets, 3 blankets, 1 coarse coverlet, 1 shelf. £4 0s. 0d.

Item, *In the Chamber over the Entry*, wool yarn and hurds, and certeyn lycor. £3 5s. 0d.

Item, *In the Cheese Chamber*, 1 cheese vat, 5 bordes, 1 plank, 100 cheeses, weights and other implements with cheesevats. £5 2s. 0d.

Item, *In the Garner*, certeyn mault. 26s. 0d.

Item, 2 hogges of bacon. 32s. 0d.

Item, 13 kine and 1 bull, 4 young beasts, 6 weaning calves, 16 sheep and 4 lambs. £46 13s. 4d.

Item, 2 sowes, 4 weaned pigs, geese, ducks and hens. 51s. 0d.

Item, 1 mare, 3 colts. £8 0s. 0d.

Item, barley and oats on the ground, and certayne fire wood. £5 10s. 0d.

Item, one dossen of platters, 10 sawsers, 1 pewter bason, 2 pewter chamber pots, 3 brasen candlesticks, 4 counter dishes, 1 double pewter salt, 1 single pewter salt, 2 pewter drinking cups. 27s. 0d.

Item, 8 silver spoons and 4 pewter pans. 40s. 0d.

Item, his apparrell. £3 0s. 0d.

Debts owing: Item, due at Michaelmas, a debt to be paid by Thomas Bradnocke. 40s. 0d.

Sum Tot: £133 6s. 6d.

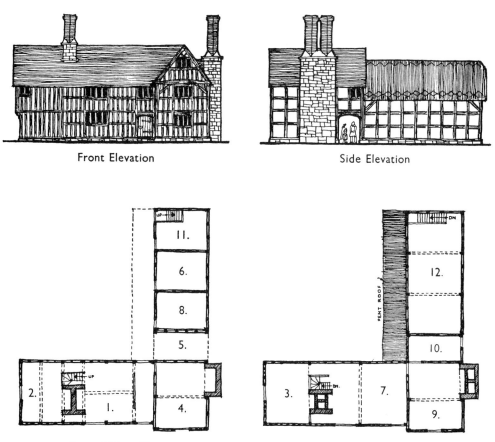

Front Elevation

Side Elevation

Ground Floor Plan

First Floor Plan

Inventory of William Wilkes (1608) :—

1. Hall
2. Parlour
3. Chamber over parlour
4. Kitchen
5. Buttery entry
6. Dayhouse (dairy?)

7. Chamber over hall
8. Buttery
9. Maid's chamber
10. Chamber over entry
11. Cheese Chamber
12. Garner (granary?)

The style of the house is c.1590. Buttery, dairy and cheese chamber are shown as occupying the ground floor of a wing at the rear of the house, with granary in the roof space above these rooms. The buttery one would expect to find in the main part of the house, but no chamber is mentioned in the inventory as "over the buttery". It is also strange that there is no cellar.

Fig. 2. William Wilkes's House, 1608

Richard Smith, 1608

A note of a True inventorie taken the xxvjth day of Januarie of the goods and cattels of Richard Smith of Draiton in the parish of Chadsley Corbett late deceased by Mr ffrauncis Smith and Thomas Smith the elder in the year of our Lord God 1608, as followeth.

Imprimis his purse, girdle and wearing clothes.	£3		
Item, iiij oxen the price.	£14		
Item, iij kyne and on heyfer the price.	£7	6s.	
Item, xlix shepe the price.	£8		
Item, on mare and on nagge.	£5		
Item, x acres of Rye the price.	£10		
Item, corne in the barne of all sorts.	£6	13s.	4d.
Item, hay in the barne, to say fyve lode.	£3	6s.	8d.
Item, on wayne, on tumbrell, a oxharrow, a peare of small harrows with spades shovells nagers a mattock axes bylls wth. other husbandry tooles.	£3		
Item, iiij yocks iij towes a cloviron with apin of Iron a horshock ij plowes ij peare of Irons to them.		18s.	0d.
Item, ij ladders xij hurdells iiij axetrees viij throkes ij plowbeames.		10s.	0d.
Item, iij tonne of Iron.	£27	10s.	0d.
Item, on barrell of Saell.	£23	0s.	0d.
Item, iiij burdeyne of saell.		40s.	0d.
Item, all the shoppe tooles.	£10	0s.	0d.
Item, cooles.	£3	0s.	0d.
Item, charcke coalles.		10s.	0d.
Item, plancks & tymber & wood of all sorts.		40s.	0d.
Item, *In the Hall* a table bord on a frame wth. on joynd cubbord iiij chayers wth. fformes & benches ij shelves wth. peynted clothes wth. a shelf called a mattle tree wth. v cossyns.		32s.	6d.
Item, x peawter platters.		15s.	0d.
Item, viij pottingers; iiij sawsers vij counterfett dyshes iiij peawter candle sticks three salts on peawter pott, on peawter cupp a maslin bason a chafyngdishe.		13s.	0d.
Item, xvj flitchyngs of beaffe in the Roffe.	£4		
Item, vj flitchyngs of Backon.		20s.	0d.
Item, butter and Chease.	£3		
Item, *In the Seller next to the hyewaye.* five coffers iij shelves iij barrells.		6s.	0d.
Item, on joynd bedd wth. a joynd Trocle bedd.		13s.	4d.
Item, on fetherbedd and a flockebedd, ij bowsters ij pillowes ij plancketts & a canvasse ij coverletts & a carpett cloth wth. another bedd upon the troclebedd.	£3		
Item, a xi yard of woollen clothe.		22s.	0d.
Item, iiij yard of fflannell.		4s.	0d.
Item, *In the Chamber over the Hall.* On joynd bedd wth. a trocle bedd.		15s.	0d.
Item, ij fetherbeds ij bowsters ij pillowes & a flockbed case with a blankett and a coverlett.		45s.	0d.
Item, on flockebedd ij bowsters & a pillowe ij canvasses and a binerlett.			
& also peyneted clothes in the same chamber.		20s.	0d.
Item, iij peares of flaxen sheates and viij peare of hemten sheetes & xiij table napkins iij pillowes beares iij towelles on wrought with blew iij bord clothes of flaxen ij borde clothes of hemten & on of noggen.	£5	10s.	8d.
Item, *In the Chamber Next the Kitchin.* ij peare of beddstedds wth. ij flockbeds iiij bowsters iiij canvasses.		20s.	0d.
Item, a hackney saddle wth. a Iron grate.		4s.	0d.
Item, *In the Buttery.* iiij shelffes iiij barrells ij pynts iij skeeles iiij chesfatts a meele seve a costrell vij earthen vessells iij wooden platters.		10s.	0d.
Item, *In the Darckhowse.* A churne, iij barrells a grediron, a little paylle a bottle a little			

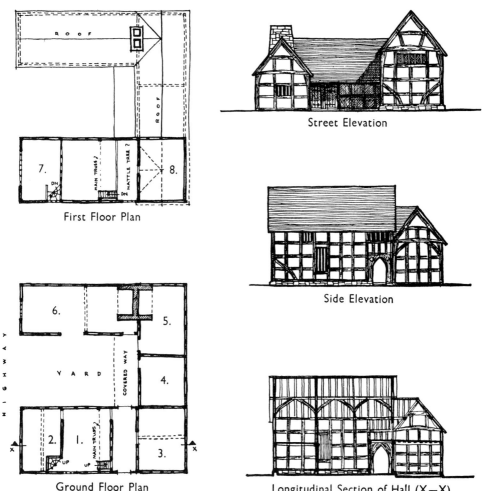

First Floor Plan

Street Elevation

Side Elevation

Ground Floor Plan

Longitudinal Section of Hall (X—X)

Inventory of Richard Smith (1608) :—

1. Hall (with shelf called "Mattle Tree"—possibly gallery over screen's passage)
2. Cellar next the Highway (shown at street level)
3. Buttery
4. Chamber next the Kitchen
5. Kitchen
6. Workshop
7. Chamber over the Hall (shown as overlooking the Hall—otherwise the plan is impossible)
8. Darkhouse (shown as room in roof space accessible from the gallery)

Fig. 3. Richard Smith's House, 1608

ladder, fyve knitchen of hempe and on ston of woll.	13s.	0d.
Item, on weetyng fatt ij barrells iiij peynts vj payells iiij meelles on skelle on here seve.	14s.	0d.
Item, a knedynge Trowe wth. a coveringe a heare cloth a little ladder a little trowe and a swolle.	3s.	4d.
Item, vj cothernes ij pannes and a brondard.	20s.	0d.
Item, iij potts, iiij posnetts a skellett & a skymmer.	40s.	0d.
Item, a cleansyng seve a can wth. ij platters & ij pottingers wth. dishes & trenchers & spones.	3s.	0d.
Item, v shwyne.	20s.	0d.
Item, broches & cobbards potthookes & hanglesses a peare of ballis a peare of fire tongs.	8s. 8s.	0d. 0d.
A spice morter with a pessle of brass		
Item, henns geese and duckes.		
Item, ij spynnyng wheells with a strick a malt scve a wheppe & on peare of bootes a pack saddle a pack ij bridles and gyrthes.	5s.	0d.
Item, ix peare of hurden sheates.	40s.	0d.
Item, vij bagges a sword and a dagger.	20s.	0d.
Item, lynnen yarne.	13s.	4d.

The wholle Som is £177 2s. 10d.

William Leyte, 1615

A note of a true Inventory taken on the 14th. day of October, 1615, upon the goods and cattell of William Leyte, late deceased in the parish of Chadsley Corbett, by Phillip Mannepse, Thomas Taylor, Griffin Hughes and Roger Purshall, as followeth.

Imprimis, his purse, girdell and wearing apparrell.	......	
Item, *In the Hall*, 4 brass pots, 1 dabnett, 2 pannes.	......	
Item, 7 cothernes, 2 skimmers, 22 peeces of pewter, 5 sawsers, 2 cownterfytt dyshes, 2 pewter pots, 2 pewter candlesticks, 3 salts, one pewter cup.	£3 0s.	0d.
Item, 3 brasen candlesticks.	......	
Item, one table borde, one forme, 5 stolles, one cubbard and one painted cloth.	12s.	0d.
Item, 3 payles, with dishes and spones and other treen ware.	2s.	0d.
Item, one pair of bellis, one pair of tongs, one fyer shovell, one pott hanglesse with 2 hooks and one Andiron and 2 shelves.	3s.	8d.
Item, *In the Rome above the Hall*, one wetting vat, one meele trough, 2 peynts, 3 barrels, one churne, 3 mele syves, 2 great wheels, 2 little wheels and all other Trumberye.	10s.	0d.
Item, *In the Solar over the Hall*, 6 stryke of Rye in bagges, 1 stryke of Otes, 1 stryke of malte.	3s.	0d.
Item, 3li. of Wooll, 4 slyppes of yarne, 1 stryck, 2 maltsyves, 4 basketts, 1 hobber, 2 mattocks, 2 broches, 2 peare of cobbards with all other Trumperies.	26s.	0d.
Item, *In the Seller beneath the Hall*, 4 peare of hemten sheets, 3 tablecloths, 1 dyssen of table napkins, 3 towells and 11 spones, with a coffer in which they lyve.	53s.	4d.
One peare of waferne irons, 3 hachells, 1 peare of combes, 1 standing bed with a presse, 1 fetherbed, one flockbed, 2 canvasses, 2 bolsters, 2 pillowes, 3 bedhyllings, 2 quissins with all peanted cloths, and apples and peares.	30s.	0d.
Item, *In the North Chamber beneath the Hall*, one standing bed with the apurtenances.	10s.	0d.
Item, *In thother Chamber beneath the Hall*, 2 standing beds, 1 course fetherbed and a flockbed, 2 plancketts, 1 canvas, 1 bedhylling, 3 bowlsters, with peynted cloths in the same chamber.	20s.	0d.
3 coffers, 2 forms, 3 shelves, 5 peare of noggen sheates, one towell, with certayne hempe and flaxe ready dressed.	40s.	0d.
Item, corne *In the Barne*, to say Rye and Barley, hay and straw, Soyelle or mucke.	£3 16s.	7d.
Item, one wayne, a broken tumbrell with a plow and one pair of harrows, with all other instruments belonging to husbandrie.	13s.	4d.

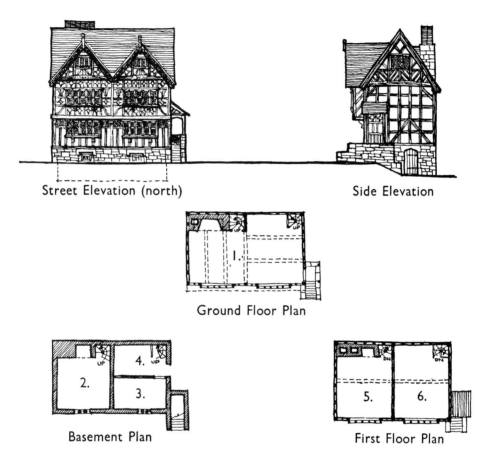

Street Elevation (north)   Side Elevation

Ground Floor Plan

Basement Plan   First Floor Plan

Inventory of William Leyte (1615) :—

1. Hall
2. Cellar beneath the Hall
3. North Chamber beneath the Hall
4. The other Chamber beneath the Hall
5. The Solar over the Hall
6. Room above the Hall

Drawn as a late Elizabethan two-bay town house with the cellar floor four or five feet below street level.

Fig. 4. William Leyte's House, 1615

Item, *In the Staple*, one trowgh, 1 slede, 1 tewtowe, with rough flax poolles overhead, with a Rowle and other moveable stuffs. 15s. 0d.

Item, *In the Barne*, 2 ladders and other moveable stuffe. 5d. 0d.

Item, 21 shepe, 2 calves and beese. £4 3s. 4d.

Item, 2 swyne, 2 weaning piggs, with hens and geese. 21s. 8d.

Item, wood and things forgotten. 2s. 0d.

(Sum total omitted.)

Francis Smith, 1617-18

The Inventorye of all and singular the goodes and cattells and chattells and debts of Francis Smith of Hillpool in the parish of Chadeslie Corbett and Countie of Worcester, Gentleman, deceased, taken and prized by George Holden, Gentleman, John Raybold and Thomas Taylor, Yeoman, the eleventh day of February, Anno Dmni. 1617.

Imprimis, his purse, girdle and apparrell. £10 0s. 0d.

Suma: £10 0s. 0d.

In the Chamber over the Inward Chamber.

Item, one joined Bedstede with the curtaines, 2 fetherbeds, 3 boulsters, one pair of blankets, one dubble canvas and a green coverlett. £5 0s. 0d.

Item, one greate cheste. 5s. 0d.

Item, one truckle bedstede. 3s. 4d.

Suma: £5 8s. 4d.

In the Chamber over the Parlour.

Item, one joyned bedstede with curteynes, 2 fetherbeds, 3 boulsters, one pillow, blanketts one pair, a double canvas and a coverlett. £6 0s. 0d.

Item, one truckell bedd. 3s. 4d.

Item, 4 chests with a Presse. £1 16s. 8d.

Suma: £8 0s. 0d.

In the Inner Chamber by the Hall.

Item, one joyned bed with curteynes, one fetherbed, 2 boulsters, one blankett, one double canvas and a coverlett. £3 0s. 0d.

Item, one presse, one coffer, one little table borde with a forme. £1 0s. 0d.

Suma: £4 0s. 0d.

In the Parlour.

Item, one bedstead with curteynes, 2 fetherbeds, one boulster, 2 pillowes, 3 blanketts and a coverlett. £6 0s. 0d.

Item, one truckle bedstead with a fetherbed, one boulster, 2 blanketts and a coverlett. £2 0s. 0d.

Item, one presse. £1 10s. 0d.

Item, one table board, one coffer and a warming pan. 10s. 0d.

Suma: £10 0s. 0d.

In the Hall.

Item, 3 tableboards, one cupboard table, 2 forms, 6 joyned stools, 3 chayres. £1 10s. 0d.

Item, Silver spones. £4 0s. 0d.

Item, 3 Carpetts, 7 Cushions. 16s. 0d.

Suma: £6 6s. 0d.

In the Chamber over the Hall.

Item, Cheeses and Butter, £4. Wool, £1. Hemp, flax and yarn, £1. Whisketts, kipes and other implements in that Rome, £1. In all in that Rome. £7 0s. 0d.

Suma: £7 0s. 0d.

In the Porch Chamber.

Item, one fetherbed, one bolster, a canvas and coverlett with the bedstede. £1 0s. 0d.

Item, malt in the house. £1 13s. 0d.

Item, beef and bacon. £5 0s. 0d.

Suma: £7 13s. 4d.

North Elevation

South Elevation

(Inventory of Francis Smith (1618):—

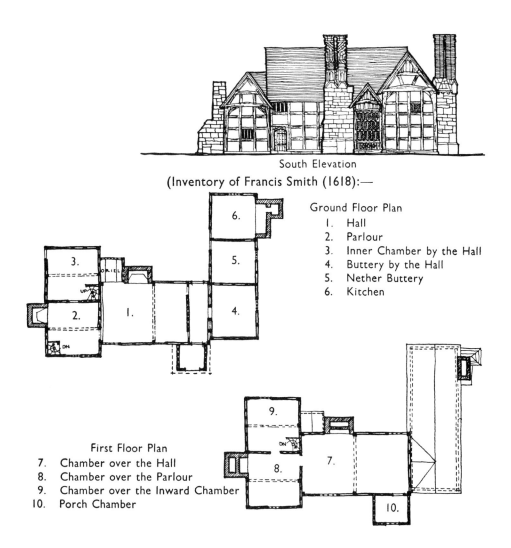

Ground Floor Plan
1. Hall
2. Parlour
3. Inner Chamber by the Hall
4. Buttery by the Hall
5. Nether Buttery
6. Kitchen

First Floor Plan
7. Chamber over the Hall
8. Chamber over the Parlour
9. Chamber over the Inward Chamber
10. Porch Chamber

Drawn as an early fifteenth century manor house with a bower opening off the south side of the Hall. The only later addition presumed to have taken place is the insertion of the first floor over the Hall.

Fig. 5. Francis Smith's House, 1618

In the Kitchen.

Item, brass potts, 3 pans, 32 kettles, a scummer and other brass.	£6	0s.	0d.
Item, 3 cressets, 4 broches.	£1	0s.	0d.
Item, Treen ware in the Kitchen and *Nether Buttery*.	£1	0s.	0d.
Item, *In the Seller*, Treen ware.	£1	10s.	0d.
Item, cobirons, a great fyer shovell and tongs with pothooks and Sayes.		13s.	4d.
Suma:	£10	13s.	4d.

In the Buttery by the Hall.

Item, linnens, as sheets, table cloths, napkins, towells and other linnens.	£15	0s.	0d.
Item, pewter of all sorts.	£4	0s.	0d.
Item, dishes, trenchers, spinning wheels and all other odd things not named.	£2	0s.	0d.
Suma:	£175	0s.	0d.
Item, 4 oxen.	£18	0s.	0d.
Item, 8 kine.	£21	6s.	8d.
Item, 6 young bease of 2 yere old.	£10	0s.	0d.
Item, 4 year-old bease.	£3	3s.	4d.
Item, 2 horses.	£6	0s.	0d.
Item, Sheepe of all sorts, 194.	£60	0s.	0d.
Item, Corne in the barne.	£20	0s.	0d.
Item, Corne in the grounde.	£30	0s.	0d.
Item, Haye in the barne.	£6	0s.	0d.
Suma:	£175	0s.	0d.
Item, Husbandry implements - 1 wayne, 2 Tumbrells, 2 pair of harrows, 4 Yokes, 2 ploughs, 3 chaines, 1 sleede and bridles.	£5	10s.	0d.
Item, spades, shovells, Axes, bills and mattocks.	£1	0s.	0d.
Item, Ladders, Hurdles, Cratches and Plowe Timber.	£1	0s.	0d.
Suma:	£7	5s.	0d.
Item, 6 swine.	£2	0s.	0d.
Item, Powltry of all sorts.	£1	0s.	0d.
Suma:	£3	10s.	0d.
Summa Totalis huius Inventary:	£275	6s.	0d.

Debts owing to the deceased:

Item, John Smale.	£5	10s.	0d.
Item, Thomas Heath.	£3	2s.	0d.
Item, John Bache.	£1	1s.	8d.
Josyas Hunt.	£1	7s.	10d.
Joane Bennett.	£1	13s.	4d.
Skiler and Hicmans.	£7	0s.	0d.
Item, Mr Barrett.	£6	2s.	0d.
Ducke.		16s.	0d.
Joane Barnett.	£1	2s.	0d.
John Burford.		17s.	6d.
Item, Roger Ellis.		17s.	6d.
Suma:	£29	10s.	8d.

H. George Holden, his mark.
John Raybold.
Thomas Taylor.

Margerie Booth, 1621

A true inventory . . . [illegible] . . .

Imprimis, purse, girdle and knives.	3s.	6d.
Item, one gowne, 1 petticoate and one wasecote.	24s.	od.
Item, 2 hatts.	8s.	6d.
Item, 3 stuffe aprons, 1 silk girdle, and a pair of gloves.	3s.	8d.
Item, 3 old petticoates, 2 pair of stockings, 2 pair of shoes.	11s.	od.
Item, Smocks, Partletts,[8] with all her wearing linen.	20s.	od.
Item, 3 pair of flaxen sheets.	27s.	od.
Item, 7 pair of hurden sheets.	22s.	4d.
And one sheet.	3s.	od.
Item, 3 flockbeds.	4s.	6d.
Item, 4 towells.	15s.	od.
Item, 4 tablecloths.	11s.	od.
Item, half a dossen of table napkins.	4s.	od.
Summa:	£7 17s.	6d.

In the Chamber over the Parlour.

Item, one join bedstead, 3 coffers, 1 boxe, one half bedstead, 1 square table, 1 other table, and trestles, 1 form, 1 stoole.	17s.	od.
Item, 2 fetherbeds, 2 flockbeds, 2 bolsters, 5 pillowes.	£2 18s.	od.
Item, 3 cushions.		18d.
Item, 2 fayre coverletts, one olde coverlett, 2 rugges, 3 canvasses.	£2 12s.	od.
Summa:	£6 10s.	6d.

In the Parlour.

Item, one joined bedstead, 1 cupboorde, 1 table and tressells, 1 bench, 2 formes, 1 coffer.	16s.	6d.
Item, 1 fetherbed, 3 bolsters, 1 coverlet.	30s.	od.
Summa:	£2 6s.	od.

In the Hall.

Item, all the pewter and platters, sawsers, candlesticks, salts, potts.	£1 1s.	od.
Item, one cupbord, 1 frame of a table boord, 2 formes, 1 chayre, 1 stoole, 1 plank, 2 skeeles, 1 payle, 1 gawne, 1 barrell, 1 piggin.	16s.	6d.
Item, paynted clothes.	2s.	6d.
Item, one fier grate, one payre of tongs, one fyershovell, 1 payre of pothangers, and links, 1 iron peale, 1 broach, and one payre of cobbards, 1 branderd, 1 axe, 1 shoppicke, 1 chopping knife, 1 colehammer, 1 drypping panne, 1 frying panne, 1 payer of flax combes, and 2 sides of bacon.	26s.	od.
Summa:	£3 6s.	od.

In the Chamber over the Buttery.

Item, 3 strikes of meslin corn.	3s.	6d.
Item, 9 knitchins of hempe.	8s.	od.
Item, 5 bagges.	6s.	od.
Item, 2 kneeding tubbs, 1 strike, 2 dry vessells, 1 churne, 2 little wheels, 1 payre of cordes and 1 hatchell, 2 sieves, 3 rakes, and other trumperie.	5s.	od.
Summa:	£1 2s.	6d.

In the Buttery.

Item, all the brass.	£3 6s.	8d.
Item, 7 barrells, 2 ealing vessells, 1 pynte, dishes, trenchers and other small necessaryes.	18s.	od.
Summa:	£4 4s.	8d.

In the Outhouse, or Barne.

Item, wood and cole.	12s.	od.
Item, 2 ladders, 1 tutowe, 1 boord, 1 peece of tymber, 1 fourme, 2 stooles, 1 clensing seve, 1 hoope, 2 tubbes and other trumperie.	4s.	od.

[8] *Partlett:* 16th-17th century 'fill-in' for low decolletage, made with a high collar from *c.*1530. See Glossary (p.123). For this and many unfamiliar names for garments and their colours and materials found in these inventories, see C.W. and P.E. Cunnington, *Dictionary of English Costume (900-1900),* A. and C. Black, 1960.

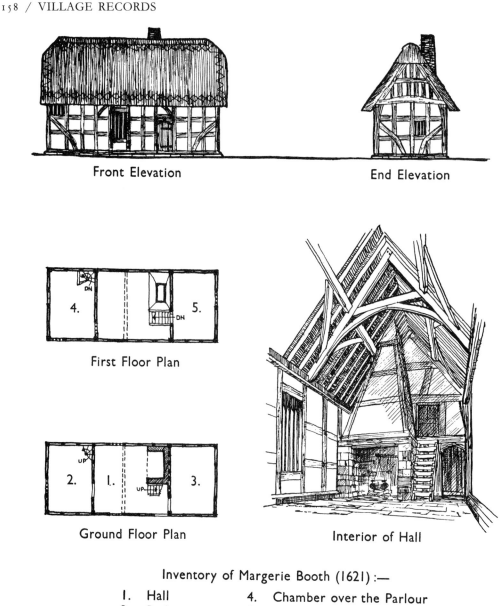

Front Elevation

End Elevation

First Floor Plan

4.

5.

Ground Floor Plan

2. 1. 3.

Interior of Hall

Inventory of Margerie Booth (1621) :—

1. Hall
2. Parlour
3. Buttery

4. Chamber over the Parlour
5. Chamber over the Buttery

This is the typical three-bay house of the fifteenth and sixteenth centuries—possibly even earlier—showing an open truss near the upper end of the Hall. The fireplace and hood—oak framed with wattle and daub panels, characteristic of early flues in these smaller halls—would have been inserted around 1600. The means of access to the room over the buttery is also in keeping with the smaller type of hall.

Fig. 6. Margerie Booth's House, 1621

Item, 2 sowes and 2 pigges.		30s.	od.
Item, hempe growing.		20s.	od.
	Summa: £3	6s.	od.
	Summa tot.: £29	6s.	od.

Evan Norrice oweth.	......	
Widow Sankye.	3......	
Sylvester Styre.	12......	
Richard Styre.		12d.
John Gressam.		5s.
Summa:	15s.	4d.

Most of the Inventories so far transcribed list the possessions of folk engaged in farming—as indeed were the majority of 16th- and 17th-century Englishmen. Let us now examine the household possessions of people in other walks of life.

INVENTORIES FROM VARIOUS LEVELS OF SOCIETY

AN ELIZABETHAN GENTLEMAN   **Sir Edward Littleton, 1586**

Jewels of Gold and Silver and other Riches.

Imprimis, one chayne of gold of ffortye ounces, with two pictures in the same, being in valuc in gold worth.	£520	os.	od.
Item, one fayre flatte linke chayne of gold, value.	£20	os.	od.
Item, one payre of flagen braceletts of gold, with pictures in the same, value.	£4	os.	od.
Item, one flatte linked girdle of gold, value.	£4	os.	od.
Item, one border of gold for a French hood, value.	......		
Item, 19 buttons of gold for a cape, which come to.	£7	os.	od.
Item, 60 buttons of gold for a Jerkin, value.	£14	os.	od.
Item, one jewell with a unicorn horne sett in gold, with a stone, value	£10	os.	od.
Item, one carkenett of gold with pearls and stones.	£5	os.	od.
Item, one tablett of gold, valued at.	£3	os.	os.
Item, one tablett of gold, with a red cross, valued at.		50s.	od.
Item, a little black tablett enamelled with gold, valued at.		40s.	od.
Item, two brooches of gold, in one of which is conteyned the history of King Solomon, and in the other of which is conteyned the history of Abraham.	£6	os.	od.
Item, one gold signet ring, valued at.	£3	os.	od.
Item, one gold ring with a great ruby in it.	......		

[*Unfortunately, none of the remaining items is valued.*]

Item, one gold ring, with 5 Turkeys in it.
Item, one gold ring, with one Turkey in it.
Item, one gold ring with a red stone graven.
Item, 10 gold rings, enamelled and playne.
Item, one gold ring with grimmals fastened together.
Item, one gold thimble and a horne with 3 tipps of silver.
Item, 20 dozen of silver buttons.
Item, two silver salts with a cover.
Item, 3 silver cuppes with a cover.
Item, 2 silver boles and one dozen of silver spoons.
Item, silver harness and clasps for the covering of a book.

Apparell for my Body.

Imprimis, two fyne cloaks of black clothe, garded with 6 yardes of velvet laid on it with lacing.
Item, a black damask cloake garded with 3 yardes of velvet and faced with vulver.

Item, a silk grograyne cloake, with 5 yardes of velvet.
Item, one long gowne of riche Taffitye layde over with lillin, one lacing lyned with bayes and faced with black.
Item, one long gowne of purple charnelett layd over with parchment lacing, lyned with bayes and faced with black conye.
Item, 3 velvet jerkins, one bonse jerkin.
Item, 2 black sattin doubletts.
Item, one yellow millian fustian doublett.
Item, one blacke Dutche fustian doublett.
Item, 6 payre of velvet French hose.
Item, one payre of black satin velvet Venetian drawers.
Item, one payre of russett chamlett Venetian hose.
Item, one payre of Venetian moulds of black.
Item, one payre of bonse lether hose, layd on with lacynge.
Item, 3 payre of carsie French drawers for French hose.
Item, 5 payre of black worsted stockings.
Item, 2 payre more of worsted stockings, one payre white and the other russett.
Item, one Tiffany girdle alyde over with lace.
Item, two velvet capes with feathers.
Item, one satin guise with three felt hats.
Item, six shirts with six bands.
Item, 8 bands with 20 payre of ruffles to the same.
Item, one dozen of fine white handkerchers.
Item, 5 head kerchiefs, 2 wrought with silk and the others with thread.
Item, one payre of velvet pantables.
Item, four payre of Spanish leather shoes.
Item, three payre of leather pantables.
Item, two payre of winter boots and two payre of summer boots.
Item, one long brown rugge gown.[9]

Woman's Apparrell.
Imprimis, one wrought gown of velvet taffitye, layde over with silver lace.
Item, one white satin kirtle, layde over with silver lace and fringed with silke and silver lined with white sarsnett.[10]
Item, white satin sleeves layd with silver lace and lyned with sarsnett.
Item, a crimson taffitye petticoat, layd with 7 yards of velvet and laced.
Item, 2 satin suggerie velvet kirtles.
Item, two kirtles of wrought velvet.
Item, 1 kirtle of wrought velvet unshorn.
Item, one black satin kirtle wrought with velvet and embroidered.
Item, one kirtle of Tawnye satin layde over with velvet and lace.
Item, one scarlett petticoat with a Taffitye bodye, layd over with velvet garded with a diamond work and laced.
Item, 3 placketts for three gowns.
Item, one payre of velvet sleeves.
Item, one French hood, with all the furniture.
Item, a velvet cape edged with silk and spangs of gold.
Item, one purse of gold and silver and silk.
Item, a payre of knyfes with chape and locker of silver gilted.
Item, two looking glasses for a gentlewoman.
Item, 3 gorgettes of silk and nett work for a gentlewoman.
Item, one payre of silk sleeves wrought witht the needle.
Item, a payre of sleeves of network and a gorgette for the same.
Item, 2 payre of velvet shoes, two payre of Spanish leather shoes.

[9] *Nerissa:* What say you then to Falconbridge, the young baron of England?
Portia: ...How oddly he is suited! I think he bought his doublet in Italy, his round hose in France, his bonnet in Germany, and his behaveiour everywhere. (*The Merchant of Venice,* I.2.).
[10] See also *Much Ado About Nothing,* III.4 (Hero dressing for her wedding) and *The Taming of the Shrew,* IV.3.

My Armorye.

Imprimis, one black armour of prouse, to serve one horse, black and one soule edged with black silke and gold and quilted with satin of Bruges.

Item, one white dilmulance armour.

Item, 2 penny platt coats and 2 privy coats.

Item, 2 skulls and 2 murrins.

Item, one large black armour of prouse edged with black fringe and quilted with leather.

Item, one penny platt coatte and a headpiece for the same.

Item, 4 sackes and 2 privie coatts to wear under armour.

Item, a sleeve laid with armour male, and a pair of hose layd with male, and 2 cases for hand gunes.

Item, 3 hand gunes and a case of daggers.

Item, 3 horn flaske boxes to carry powder in.

Item, a sword and a dagger, a rapier and a dagger, an arming sword and a dagger, 3 bucklers and 2 sword girdles of velvet and leathers.

Item, 3 forest billes, 3 bowes of Ewe, 9 score arrowes and shafts and one chubb.

Item, a wooden quiver of joined work and a quiver to put in arrowes.

Horses with their Furniture.

Imprimis, one baye trotting gelding.

Item, one dun ambling gelding.

Item, one black trotynge mare and a colt.

Item, one baye storid horse.

Item, two bright baye geldings.

Item, my best whyte ambling nagge.

Item, one black ambling nagge and a colt.

Item, my two scothe saddles dressed with cloth and embroidered with velvet.

Item, one bonse saddle and 3 scothe saddles.

Item, bridles, stirropes, gerthes for all my saddles, saving one, with all the furniture belonging to the same saddles.

Item, 3 saddle clothes, 3 sursingles and collars for them.

Item, two horse combs and one mane comb.

Chests and Coffers.

Imprimis, *In my Chamber*, a fyelde bedstead with a canopy of red Taffity and testers of the same, fringed with silk and five curtynes of red Taffity and one coverlet of tapestrye.

Item, one featherbed, 2 bolsters and 2 pillows, a truckle sheet to lay under a bed, a matte, 3 white blankets and a covering, a cupboard with a greene cupboard cloth, one stole and one close stole with six bedstaves.

Item, *In the Chamber over the Hall*, 2 besteads, with a branch buckram canopye and gilt belles with curtynes, a matte and fether bed, one bolster, 2 pillowes, 3 white blanketts, a blew Irish rugge coverlett, 6 bedstaves, 2 stoles, 2 cushions of buckram, a cupboard with a green cupboard cloth, a payre of handirons, a fireshovel and a payre of tonges.

Item, *In the Greene Chamber Next unto it.* A grene fyelde bed of walnutt tree, with a canopy of greene Saye, 5 curtyns with gilt belles, a green Irish rugg coverlett, a matte, a featherbedd, one bolster, 2 pillowes, 3 white blanketts, a cubard with a greene cubarde clothe, one stole, one cushion of greene, 6 bedstaves, a payre of landirons, a fyer shovel and a payre of tonges.

Item, *In the Chamber Next unto the Parlour*, a fyelde bedstede with a canopy of branch buckram and curtyns of the same and gilt pannells, a fetherbed, a bolster, 2 pillowes, 2 white blanketts, a coverlet of tapestrye work, 6 bedstaves, a matte, a cubarde with a grene cubarde clothe, 2 stoles, 1 branch buckram cushion, a payre of landirons, a fyer shovell and a payre of tonges.

Item, *In My Cozen Amphilis's Chamber*, a bestead, a matte, a fetherbed, one bolster, one pillowe, 2 blanketts, a coverlet white rugg, a cubard, one stole, 6 bedstaves.

Item, *In John Martin's Chamber*, a bedstead, a matte, a fetherbed, one bolster, 2 blanketts, an ordinary coverlett of tapestrye work, a cubarde.

Item, *In the Mayd's Chamber over it*, a bedstead, a matte, a flockbed, 2 bolsters, 2 blanketts, a green coverlet and a tawny Irish mantle, 2 basketts with 4 jacks, a dozen of boles, a trunke and a warming pan.

Item, *In the Chamber over the Parlour*, a bedstead, a truckle bed, a matte, a flocke bed, one bolster, 2 blanketts, one coverlet, red and yellow, a cubarde.

Item, *In the Stable*, a bedstead, a mattress, a bolster, a double twillye sheete, a white and a black coverlett and an old green blankett.

Furnituyre for the Parlour.

Imprimis, a table board to draw out at both ends, one forme, one bench, 2 stoles at both ends of the table, 6 joined stoles, 2 cubardes, 2 chests to play withall, a green carpett for the table with two green cubarde cloths for the cubarde, a payre of andirons, a fyer shovell, a payre of tonges and a fyer forke, one payre of tables.

Item, *In the Hall*, 2 table bordes and 2 formes.

Item, *In the Parlour and the Kitchen*, a table board, 2 cubardes and 3 grene cubarde clothes, 4 grene cushions, 8 stoles, a forme, a payre of andirons, a fyer shovell and a payre of tonges, one payre of tables.

In the Stud, Imprimis, one cubarde with a grene cubarde cloth, one joyned stole, 30 books and one box.
Item, 10 pictures covered with grene sarsnett.

The Cattle.

Imprimis, 6 draught oxen.
Item, 17 milch kine and a bull.
Item, 2 three-year-old heyfers.
Item, 9 two-year-old, and 4 of them be steers.
Item, 8 yearlings, 3 of them be steers and one bull.
Item, 8 wayning calves, 5 be steers and one bull.
Item, of old wether sheep, 3 score and 19.
Item, of old Ewes, 6 score and 15.
Item, of wether lambs 18.
Item, of Ram lambs, 3.
Item, of Ewe lambs, 42.
Item, of Swyne, 13.

Pullayne Poultry.

Imprimis, a Turkeycocke and 2 Turkey hennes.
Item, 4 cockerells or capons.
Item, 16 hens, 2 ganders and 6 dux.

Brass and Pewter.

Imprimis, 4 brasse potts, 2 great and 2 little.
3 brasse panns and 2 brasse plates to hang in the Hall.
Item, one little caldron and one little dabnett.
Item, one chaferne of brasse.
Item, one morter and one pestell of brasse.
Item, one chaffering dish.
Item, one brazen washer.
Item, 3 basons and 3 ewers of pewter.
Item, 8 candlesticks of pewter.
Item, 3 plate candlesticks to hang.
Item, 4 great swan dishes.
Item, 20 great platter dishes.
Item, 24 great porringer dishes.
Item, 12 pottage dishes.
Item, 7 counterfett dishes for pottage.

Item, 13 fruyte dishes of one sorte.
Item, 17 small sawcers.
Item, 2 playne platters, to sett under pies.
Item, 8 livery potts and one pint pott.
Item, 1 possett cupp and one bason bole.
Item, 13 spones and one salt cellar of copper.
Item, 1 salt cellar of pewter.
Item, 6 flower potts and 4 chamber potts.
Item, 2 quarte bottles of pewter.
Item, 1 pewter turning dish.
Item, one pewter pan and one brass pann for two close stools.
Item, 2 black drinking jacks of leather.
Item, 2 stone cruses and 8 black cuppes.
Item, 4 drinking glasses.

Kitchen Stuffe.
Imprimis, 1 Iron Jacke to turne spits with, 2 cheynes and one great corde to turn spitts withall.
Item, one great cubbard for the spitt.
Item, 3 spitts and 2 fyer forke.
Item, one frying pan and 2 girde irons.
Item, 2 pott gales and 2 payre of pothooks.
Item, 1 ladle of brasse and a chappyng knife.
Item, 1 flesh hooke and a skimmer, 1 threading knife.
Item, 2 little basting ladles of brass.
Item, a payre of bellowes and 2 dressing bordes.

Grynen Stuffe.
Imprimis, one cheese coule and one other coule.
Item, 2 great powdering tubbs, close.
Item, 2 close books of six gallons a payre to put salt butter in, one borde in the Kitchen.
Item, one piggin, one churne and one kinnell.
Item, one cheese press and 9 cheese vats, one suter.
Item, one great salting bole, one turning dish.
Item, 2 wooden platters and two costrells.
Item, 10 barrells, 4 lomes, 1 turnell.
Item, 1 great wetting vessel and peales.
Item, 1 vergis barrell and half a strike.
Item, 1 rope with a bucket for the well.
Item, 6 dozen of square trenchers.
Item, 3 dozen of round trenchers.
Item, 1 dozen of fyne round trenchers, wrought with limned work.
Item, 4 basketts and 1 mantle seve.
Item, one salt boxe and one cheese cratch.
Item, one dozen of wooden dishes and a case of wooden knifes.
Item, 7 milke pans and 20 earthen.
Item, a heare cloth for the kilne.
Item, 4 sacks to put corne in.
Item, one great spinning wheele and a little spinning wheele, 1 embroidering frame.
Item, 2 hoggsheads and one yelding vessell.
Item, a rele and yarnells to wind one.

Napperie Ware.
Imprimis, 2 long table cloths.
Item, 2 long table cloths of flaxen.

Item, 10 borde cloths of flaxen.
Item, 9 flaxen pillowe beres.
Item, 2 hempen cubarde cloths.
Item, 8 payre of hempen sheets.
Item, 7 shorte towelles of hemp.
Item, 6 payre of hurdon sheets.
Item, 2 long towelles of flaxen.
Item, 1 long towelle of hempe.
Item, 7 diaper napkins.
Item, 31 napkins of hempe.
Item, 21 fyne napkins of flaxen.
Item, 4 payre of noggen sheets.
Item, 3 wolletts, 1 surplese and a kerchief.

Other Furniture for the House.
Imprimis, one long cushion of crimson satin, embroidered with my armes and the armes of my ladye wife.
Item, 3 long cushons of crimson velvet.
Item, one long cushon of crimson satin.
Item, one long cushon blewe and red with stripes of gold silke.
Item, 6 square cushons wrought with needlework.
Item, a velvet case embroidered with gold.
Item, 1 vestment of crimson velvet embroidered with gold and silk.
Item, 1 silk sarsnett vestment and 1 fustyan vestment.
Item, 3 banner stremes.
Item, 2 peces of grene and yellow saye.
Item, 1 old tester for a bed, red and grene.
Item, 2 lethers for a horse litter and 1 foot stole.
Item, 2 skynes of parchments and cordes for a drum.
Item, 1 little lock for a presse with a hinge.
Item, 1 mysrole and a payre of pastens.
Item, 1 payre of ballance with 2 pounds waytes for the same.

Husbandry Stuffe.
Imprimis, 1 Iron bound wayne and 2 bodies.
Item, 2 tumrells and 1 tumrell chest more.
Item, 6 yorkes, 2 copyorkes and 5 cheynes.
Item, 2 copsells and copsell pins for the wayne.
Item, 2 plowes with 2 payre of irons.
Item, 1 copsell for a plowe and 2 harrowes.
Item, 1 mattocke, 6 spades and 1 pick.
Item, 2 axes and 2 billes for hedging.
Item, 2 small nawger and 1 bigge nawger.
Item, 1 chisell and 1 hatchett.
Item, 4 togwithes of iron and 3 iron wedges.
Item, 2 marking irons for sheep.
Item, 2 picke evells and a mucke evell.
Item, 1 hammer and a payre of pincers.
Item, 1 blocke sawe, a handsawe and a little sawe.
Item, 1 whimble bitte and a payre of sheetes.

A KIDDERMINSTER SEMPSTRESS.	**Alice Stinten, 1668**		
Imprimis, her wearing apparrell.	£5	9s.	0d.
Item, Rings and plate.	£1	0s.	0d.
Item one fetherbed and bolster, with curteynes, vallance, blanketts and covrlett.	£4	9s.	0d.

Item, 4 payer of blanketts.	£1	4s.	0d.
Item, one low bedstead, 2 chests, 6 cushions, and 1 looking glass.		16s.	0d.
Item, brass and pewter, fireshovell and toungs and 4 chayres.	£1	16s.	6d.
Item, ware of severall sortes ready made, as bands, cuffs, whisks and other semstrey ware.	£13	13s.	4d.
Item, cloth in the house of all sorts, as Holland, Lawne, Cambric and Callico.	£61	18s.	0d.
Item, Indian Silk, Taffity, Lace Tape, Twist, and other things belonging to her trade.	£3	10s.	0d.
Item, her Debts, of whereof some are desperate.	£3	0s.	0d.
Item, All other things, forgotten or not mentioned about the house or belonging to her trade.	£1	0s.	0d.
Summer Totalis:	£99	1s.	10d.

A KIDDERMINSTER CLOTHIER. Edward Bayneham, 1668

Imprimis, *In the Hall of His Dwelling House*, One joyned table with a frame thereto belonging, one joyned forme, 5 chayres, 1 joyned stool, one iron grate with cheeks, one fyer shovell, 2 pairs of tongs, one pair bellowes, valued to be worth.	£1	9s.	0d.
Item, *In the Parlour*, One round table, one joyned chayre, 10 joyned stools, 2 carpetts, 1 joyned bedstead with the bedding thereto belonging, curtains and vallances, one joyned press, one iron grate.	£5	14s.	0d.
Item, *In the Chamber Over the Parlour*, One joyned table with frame, 2 joyned stools, one joyned chest, one joyned press, one joyned bedstead with the bedding, curtains and all thereunto belonging.	£5	8s.	6d.
Item, *In the Chamber Over the Kitchen*, One round table, 3 carpetts, one trunke, one chest, 2 Coffers, 2 half-headed bedsteads and furniture thereto belonging.	£2	10s.	0d.
Chamber Over the Buttery.			
One chest, one beam and scales, with weights thereunto belonging, one kneading skeele, one small coffer.		8s.	0d.
In the Kitchen.			
One furnace, one brewing vat, 6 skeeles, one brewing vessell.	£2	4s.	0d.
In the Buttery.			
One small table with frame, one carpett, 3 stools, 9 hogsheads, 3 skeeles, 1 bowl, one tin dish.	£2	14s.	0d.
3 hogsheads of beer.	£2	10s.	0d.
One silver bowl, 2 small silver dishes.	£2	14s.	0d.
8 small flagons, 4 pewter candlesticks and other pewter dishes.	£2	14s.	0d.
2 brass pots, one iron pot, 4 kettles, one brass pan, one warming pan, 3 pewter chamber pots, one dripping pan and basting ladle.	£3	6s.	0d.
In Another Upper Chamber.			
3 flaxen sheets, 2 pair hempen sheets, 2 pair hurden sheets, 5 pillow beres, 2 dozen napkins, 5 table cloths, one long towell, 4 hand towells.	£1	4s.	0d.
Wearing Apparrall.	£1	1s.	0d.
In the Shop, One warping bar and some other small implements that cannot well be enumerated.		19s.	0d.
	£22	4s.	0d.

AN EVESHAM JOINER. Edward Bickerton, 1668

Imprimis, his wearing apparell.	£5	0s.	0d.
Item Timber in his house and abroad.	£63	8s.	6d.
Item, *In the Kitchen*, Brass and Pewter, with one furnace, at	£6	13s.	4d.
One joined cubard, one table, 4 joined stools, four chairs.	£1	10s.	0d.
Item, one Jacke, one Gunne, 2 Spitts, fire shovell and tongs, one lanthern, 2 dripping panns.		19s.	6d.
Item, *In the Hall*, One joined cupboard, one table and stools, 5 bedposts.	£1	6s	0d.
Item, *In the Chamber Over the Hall*, one joined Bedstead, one Tester bed with the furniture			

thereto belonging, one trundell bed with a flock bed and furniture thereto belonging. 2 trunckes, one forme and a warming pan. £4 13s. 4d.

Item, *In the Chambers Over the Kitchen*, Two bedsteads, one fetherbed with the furniture belonging to them both. 6s. 8d.

Item, one table, one little cubbard. £1 13s. 4d.

Item, one box of linning, *In the Top Loft*. £1 13s. 4d.

Item, *In the Brew House*, One Malt Mill, two stools, with other brewing vessells. £1 13s. 4d.

Item, *In the Cellar*, Two hogsheads of Beare. £2 0s. 0d.

Item, one hogshead and 7 half hogsheads. £1 0s. 0d.

Item, all his working tools. £5 0s. 0d.

£101 6s. 0d.

A POOR CORDWAINER OF BEDWARDINE. **William Nicholls, 1668**

Imprimis, one standing bedstead. 6s. 0d.

Item, one half-headed bedstead. 2s. 6d.

Item, 3 old flockbeds. 10s. 0d.

Item, an old flock bolster and four old blankets. 1s. 6d.

Item, one little chest and 2 coffers and one little cuberd. 4s. 6d.

Item, 1 washing stool and one Segg chayre and one Segg stool. 1s. 0d.

Item, one table bord, 2 barrells, fire shovell and tongs. 6s. 0d.

Item, 1 fire bar, with other implements in the house and Shop. 2s. 6d.

£1 14s. 0d.

BOOKS IN INVENTORIES

References in books amongst the deceased's property are quite frequent in Worcestershire inventories. Usually, however, only one or two books, or a single Bible, are mentioned, 'Two Bibels and other books, £1' (Jane Grove, 1668); 'Three Bibles with other books' (John Butler, 1644/4); 'One small Bible, with other small books, 10s.' (John Smith, 1620/152); 'Item, for a Bible, 4s. 0d.' (Thomas Smith, 1639/120) and many other similar entries. Usually, if several books are mentioned, they are not listed, but merely entered as one lot. Amongst the goods of Avery Edkins, a musician of Worcester, are found 'His books, ballades and Instruments' (1607/15); Robert Riley, bookbinder of Evesham, had amongst his household goods, in 1616,

'Imprimis all his bookes, papers & penninkhornes as they were bought in London.£19 7s.
Item, seaven dozen of ould small bookes, at 20s.
Item, 6 dozen of horne books, 4d.'

William Bennet of Bromsgrove, gentleman, owned, in 1644:

'Item, one Bible and other Books of divinitie, The Statutes at Lardge[11] and all other his law books, and the ioyned worke about the study.'

It is fairly common to find entries of a few books, not only in the case of professional men ('Item, hys books 26s. 8d.', Roger Colburne, schoolmaster, 1559/328a), but also amongst the possessions of 17th-century yeomen farmers, 'Item, all the books, 19s. 0d.' appears in the inventory of Thomas Moore, yeoman, in 1644 (1644/88); 'Item, one Bible and a few small bookes, 10s. 0d.' (John Oldnall, yeoman, 1644/94). Bibles apart, however, private collections of books are rare and small in number; they are usually devotional works, or books connected with the profession of the owner, as 'Item, the testator's books, £15' (William Cotterell, clerk, 1644/30). The following inventory is thus a rare and exciting find. Unfortunately no indication

---

[11] 'Statutes at Large', i.e. 'Statutes in Force', all Statutes then on the Statute Book.

of the owner's occupation is given, but his library is inventoried book by book, to a total of 57 volumes, with authors and titles given. This is the library of one who must have been a bibliophile and scholar - many of the editions were acquired shortly before his death. Both Catholic and Protestant doctrine are represented in the many religious books; there are several books on mathematics, astrology and surveying, a book of music, a book of common law, and a very recent publication of *The Comedy of Midas* by John Lyly (1592). With these are some of the major classics of Roman literature, and of the Fathers of the Church. The entire collection is listed as follows: (In each case where a Continental or English publication of any of these works is known to have existed in 1594, the full title, author's name and date of publication is given in italics on the following line[12]):

Richard Evans, Bredon, 1594[13]

An Inventorye of the goods of Richard Evans of Breedon deceased, taken and prised by Christopher Elgar and Geffreye Homfreis the 23rd daye of Marche, Ao. R. Regine Elizabeth, etc. 36th.

Aquinas works 3 volumes.   6s. od.
(*'Summa Theologica': 3 parts. Haganaw. 1512.*)

A psalme booke, Latin.   6d.

Scotreti, Mathematica.   12d.
(*Abraham Scultetus: 'Sphericorum libri tres', Heidelberg, 1595.*)

Rarisorianum Calend: 6d.
(*Possibly 'Calendarium Gregorianum perpetuum'. 1583*)

Sermon. Bernadi.   12d.
(*St Bernard of Clairvaux: 'Sermons de tempore et de sanctis'. 1475 &c. or 'Sermones super Cantica Canticorum'. 1481 &c.*)

Clari Horolog'   6d.

Marlorati loci Comm.   2s. od.
(*Augustin Marlorat: 'Enchiridion locorum communium.' London. 1591*)

Firier, Mathemat.   6d.
(*Ludivico Ferrara 6 'Cartelli' in a mathematical controversy with N. Tartaglia. 1547-8.*)

Theorema Arithm: 3d.

Sermon.   2d.

A Testament Englishe.   12d.

Alboharon, Astrology.   16d.
(*Albohazen Haly: 'Libri de iudiciis astrorum' Basle. 1551, 1571.*)

Tullies Epistles.   3d.
(*M. Tullius Cicero: 'Epistolae Familiares'. H. Bynneman, Printer 1571 &c.*)

Purbachi Theorema.   12d.
(*Georgius Peurbachius: 'Theorica novae planetarum'. Many editions from 1482.*)

Hugo de prato in evan.   2d.
(*Hugo de prato Florido: 'Sermones dominicales super Evangelia et Ep;istolas'. Many editions from 1475.*)

Flores Biblie.   3d.

(*'Flores Bibliorum, sine Loci communes, excerpti a F. Thomas Hybarnico (Palmer)'. Antwerp. 1567. 1568.*)

Livie Decad.   4d.
(*T. Livius: 'Decades tres cum dimidia' Basle. 1535.*)

Ovid, de fasto.   2d.
(*Naso Publius Ovidus: 'Fasti'. 1477 &c.*)

Chrisostom in epist paul ad rom: 3d.
(*St John Chrysostom: 'Homiliae in Pauli Epistolas' 1529.*)

Munster de rud: mathemat.   10d.
(*Sebastian Munster: 'Rudimenta Mathematica'. 1551.*)

Arolastus bis.   4d.
(*Possibly Alexander Ariostus: 'Tabula in tractatum usurarum'. 1486. Enchiridion, Venice, 1513. Paris, 1514, 1520.*)

Summa Angelica.   4d.
(*Angelus de Clavasio: 'Summa Angelica'. Strasbourg, 1513. Basle, 1515.*)

Groper de Sacr: 4d.
(*Johann Gropper: 'De veritate corporis et sanguinis Christi in Eucharistia'. Cologne, 1560.*)

Sulpicinis gramer.
(*Joannes Sulpicius: 'Grammatice Sulpiciana'. Paris, 1503, 1514.*)

Aurelinis prudentis.   6d.
(*Probably the works of the early Christian poet and hymn-writer, Clemens Prudentius Aurelius. His works were reprinted at Antwerp, 1564.*)

Ringlbirg: opera.   12d.
(*Joachimus Fortius Ringelbergius: 'Opera ... quae ... enumerantur'. London, 1531.*)

Firier pars altera.   8d.
(*Ludovico Ferraro: see above.*)

Tho: Moore. &c.   5d.
(*Sir Thomas More: probably 'The works'. London, 1557.*)

[12] For all the bibliographical detail above, both the research and the notes, I am indebted to the Librarian, Department of Printed Books, Bodleian Library, Oxford, and to the Librarian, Institute of Education Library, University of Birmingham. I have reproduced their notes on the titles and authors verbatim. In endeavouring to trace books listed in Domestic Inventories, reference should be made to A. W. Pollard and G. R. Redgrave's *Short Title Catalogue of English Books, 1475-1640* (Bibliographical Society, London, 1950), which, however, does not list the many books published on the Continent. These may be identified in the British Library General Catalogue.

[13] W.R.O. 008.7.1594/28m.

Copia vergorum. 3d.

Points upon the Sacram: 3d.

(John Poynet: 'Dialecticon de veritate corporis Christi in Eucharistia'. 1557. or 'A Notable Sermon concerning the Lord's Supper'. 1550.)

Damadis de gaule. 2d.

(The popular romance of 'Amadis de Gaul', originally written in Spanish and published in 4 Books, 1508. It was extended and translated into French, English and other languages. Numerous editions appeared in the 16th Century; the first English translation, by T. Paynell, was printed in 1567.)

Textoris Epith. 2d.

(Ravisius Textor: 'Epithetorum opus'. Paris. 1580)

An Hebrue gramer. 2d.

Eusebie in Evan. 3d.

(Eusebius: 'Evangelicae demonstrationis'. Cologne. 1542)

Gemme frisius mathemat. 4d.

(Gemma Reinerius Frisius: 'Arithmeticae practicae methodus facilis'. Wittenberg, 1550. Antwerp, 1552)

Booke of Common Lawe. 2d.

Horolog sapientie. 3d.

(Horolog sapientiae' Cologne, 1503.)

Melanch' rathoricke. 2d.

(Phillip Malanchthon: 'De Rhetorica, Libri tres', Wittenberg, 1519. Cologne, 1523. or 'Institutiones Rhetoricae'. Haganau, 1521. Wittenberg, 1532.)

Isop: fabul: 2d.

(Aesop's 'Fables'. Printed by Caxton in 1484, many subsequent editions during the 16th century to 1591.)

Cornelius. 2d.

(Probably Cornelius Nepos: 'Vitae excellentium imperatorum'. Numerous editions from 1471.)

Horace. 2d.

(There were numerous editions of Horace before 1594. The first English translation was printed in 1567.)

Virgills Eglogs Englishe. 2d.

(Many 16th-century editions.)

A booke of pricksonne. 4d.

(i.e. 'Prick-song': Music sung from notes written, or 'pricked'; vocal music or descant.)

Erasm: de conscribend: Epist. 2d.

(Desiderius Erasmus: 'Libellus de Conscribendis Epistolis'. Cambridge, 1519)

Gemme frisii de orbis division. 4d.

(Gemma Reinerius Frisius: 'De orbis divisione et insulis'. 1576.)

Guilielmus parisiensis. 4d.

(Guillelmus Pariensis: 'Sacorum Evangeliorum ac Epistolarum expositiones'. Many editions from 1473.)

Institutio: Imperial: 4d.

('Institutiones Imperiales'. Louvain, 1554.)

Diarosio: Maticion. 2d.

Castaliari dialog: 2d.

(Count Baldassare Castiglione: 'Dialogue, 'Il Corregiano', 'The Courtyer', ... done into Englysh by Sir Thomas Hoby'. 1561.)

Tulli ad herrenium. 4d.

(M. Tullius Cicero: 'Rhetorica ad Herennium'. 1470 &c.)

Valleri. Elegentia. 8d.

(Laurentius Valla: 'De linguae Latinae elegentia'. Many editoins from 1471 to 1549.)

Other little books. 2d.

Three gownes & other apparell. 40s. 0d.

Per me Chrispoher Elgar.
Per me Galfridus Humffreys.

An Astrolabe of wood, Insturments of Iron, wood and brasse and yelowe tynne, a chaine of wyer to measure grownd, paper & such trifles. 12d.

A Deske. 6d.

A rapier & an ould ruffe band. More bookes viz. Passion Planetar'. Mathematicall Juell. *(John Blagrave: 'The Mathematical Jewel'. London. 1585)*

Use of the Globe. *(Thomas Hood: 'The Use of the Celestial Globe'. 1590; or 'The Use of both the globes, celestial and terrestial'. London. 1592.)* Survey of Land. *(John Fitzherbert: 'The Boke of Surveying.' London, 1523 and later editions.)* The comedie of midas. *(John Lyly: 'Midas, a Comedy in Five Acts'.)*

2 paper bookes, other bookes & papers. 2s. 0d.

Summa: £3 11s. 0d.

GLOSSARY OF SOME UNUSUAL WORDS FOUND IN INVENTORIES

It was an unexpected pleasure to discover an interesting article in *The Local Historian*,[14] devoted entirely to this chapter of *Village Records*. Written by no less an authority than the Deputy Chief Editor of the *Oxford English Dictionary*, this focuses attention on the actual *vocabulary* of the inventories, which the author reveals, is a neglected aspect of their study. 'It is easy to overlook the language in which a document is couched ... it must not be forgotten that probate inventories are texts, and like other texts, they require to be understood in their entirety'. The article analyses and classifies different groups of words and phrases listed in our next glossary. We

---

[14] Edmund Weiner, 'Local History and lexicography', *The Local Historian*, 24, no.3. August 1994, pp.164-173.

find that over a hundred of these turn out at least to modify the *OED*'s documentation, and in many cases fall entirely outside it. Some words, like *bonse* cannot be connected with any known word in the *OED*; some like *warping-bar* are recorded in the *OED*, but not for as early a date as in Edward Bayneham's clothier's shop (1668); other phrases like *to say* (1608 and 1615) are not recorded elsewhere at such a late date. Some of our inventories' words actually *improve* upon the *OED*'s documentation, as with *throck* (Richard Smith, 1608). First recorded *c.*A.D.1,000, naming a share-beam or plough-head, 'this word does not reappear in English until 1649. Our inventory occurrence helps to fill this enormous gap.'

Pleasure apart, the real impact of this article, as in so many other recent re-interpretations of familiar local field, is to appreciate once again how much a different specialism or viewpoint adds to and re-orientates our narrower view of what, in 1962, we thought was a document's most important content. At first sight it seems adequate to assume that the furniture, utensils, tools and and farmyard tackle were the main, if not the only significant content of an inventory. But, as Weiner says: 'An overall picture of the contents of an inventory, or a statistical summary of its constituent parts, may be sufficient for many historical purposes, but ... the full value of each inventory is only obtained when everything in it has been understood and taken into account'.

The set of titles which follow, of those dictionaries of dialect which helped to decipher so many of these archaic words, make it clear that one was already aware of the possible limitations of standard works such as the *OED*. All these apart, as the original acknowledgment on page xxiv makes plain, the spoken words of the late Charlie Amies, last of the Chaddesley ploughmen, were the readiest and most reliable source of the lexicography of local history. Charlie assumed that everyone still knew ('of *course* you do, lad!') what a *throck* or a *swingletree* is. I wish that he could have seen Edmund Weiner's article and realised how important this was.

For help in understanding archaic and provincial words, the student should refer to: J. Wright, *Dictionary of Dialect*, O.U.P., 1905; J. O. Halliwell, *Dictionary of Archaic and Provincial Words*, Routledge, 1924. Also to regional publications, e.g. J. Salisbury, *A Glossary of Words and Phrases used in S.E. Worcestershire*, London, 1893; Mrs. Chamberlain, *A Glossary of West Worcestershire Words*, London, 1882.

Alum-trough, used in tanning.
Andirons, iron trivets for supporting burning wood in a fireplace. See also brandard.
Aquavitie, spirits.
Axe-tree, axle-tree; fixed bar under a cart, on which the wheels rotate.
Back-stool, stool with a back; a 'single' chair.
Backsword, bar of wood fixed to the back of a cart to prevent the 'bed' over-tilting when unloaded. Also a single-stick or staff, used for fencing.
Band, i.e. 'bond'; a loan or agreement.
Bandcloth, linen collar.
Barlines, traces.
Beares, Beres, 'pillow beares'; pillow-cases.
Bease, beasts or cattle.
Bed-hillings, bed-healings, bed coverings.
Ben, hardware.
Bend, bene, half a 'butt', or hide of sole-leather.
Betwell, wicker strainer used in brewing.
Bickern, Beakiron, cooper's anvil.

Bin, apparently a Midland plural for 'bees'.

Bodies, i.e. 'bodice'.

Bolting, a bundle of straw, usually 12 or 24 lbs. 'Bolting' was also the process of sifting meal or flour, as in 'bolting-sieve' and 'bolting-house'.

Brake, toothed instrument for dressing flax or hemp.

Broche, a spit; a spindle or reel for yarn.

Brondard, Brandard, gridiron or grill; andiron, or iron bar to support burning brands; a trivet.

Brumhook, broom-hook.

Butt, a beer-barrel of 108 gallons, or a hide of sole-leather.

Canvas, cloth made from hemp or coarse tow.

Carsey, coarse woollen cloth, usually ribbed.

Cawtherne, a cauldron.

Chaffe bed, straw mattress.

Chamlet, Camlet, a rich cloth.

Chapping-knife, i.e. 'chopping'-knife.

Cheeks, i.e. of a grate, the iron side-pieces.

Cheese-brigs, Cheese-ladder, crossed bars of wood, resting across the cream-pan to support the skimming bowl.

Cheese cowle, cheese tub.

Cheese-crack, cheese cratch, i.e. 'rack' or 'lather'; rack for setting newly made cheese to dry.

Cheese-ring, i.e. 'wring(er)'; a cheese press. 'Cheese' was also used as a name for the apple pulp arranged in a press ready to be 'wrung' out as cider; thus, possibly, a cider-press; see 'crab-ring'.

Cheeving-bit, a lynch pin.

Chewtawe, see *Tutoe*.

Clansbucke, closebuck, 'buck' is laundry, thus a 'cleansing' or 'clothes'-buck was a laundry tub or basket.

Clansing-sieve, i.e. 'cleansing'; a hair sieve for meal.

Close-stool, a commode; indoor sanitation. See also 'powe-potts'.

Clossbowke, a bucket with a lid.

Clove-iron, iron at end of a plough-beam, to which traces are attached. 'Clove' or 'clovie' is a nail or spike.

Cob, a sower's seed-box, hopper or basket.

Cobbards, always found with spits, e.g. 'broch and cobbards' is very common; cobbards were the 'cob-irons' or rests upon which a spit was held.

Cobbert, cupboard.

Cob-irons, andirons, or the rests that support a spit.

Copsell, Copsal, piece of iron at front end of a plough.

Cordwood, firewood.

Costrell, cosrell, a drinking-cup, flagon or bottle, made of leather, wood or earthenware, usually flat, with lugs for hanging or carrying. Used by harvesters.

Counterfeit, countfelt, plate; plated silver.

Court-cupboard, cabinet or sideboard with shelves for displaying plate.

Cowle, tub, vat or cask.

Crab-ring, cider press.

Cratch, a rack or manger for feeding animals out of doors. Also a cradle; a wooden dish.

Creache, a wicker basket.

Creeper, an andiron.

Cresset, a hanging lamp or brazier; kitchen utensil for setting a pot over the fire. A brazier.

Culking-iron, i.e. 'caulking-iron'; chisel for caulking or sealing the seams of wooden vessels.

Dassells, a saddle.

Deyhouse, dairy.

Dormants, fixed ends of a 'joined' table.

Dredge, mixed corn; oats with barley.

Falling bands, collars, neckerchiefs.

Falling-table, gate-legged table.

Fatt, i.e. 'vat'.

Fellies, curved sectors of the circumference of a wheel.

Ferret, silk ribbon.

Firkin, half a hundredweight of butter.

Fitches, vetches.

Flasket, clothes basket.

Flockbed and Featherbed, large cover filled with flock or feathers and used as a mattress or quilt.

Frame, the 'frame' or trestles of an 'unjoined' table.

Frise, thick woollen cloth, used for cloaks and outer garments.

Fustian, stout cloth of cotton and flax mixed.

Gales, metal bars with hooks for hanging cooking pots.

Garner, granary.

Gawne, a gallon pail, small tub or lading vessel, usually with one stave lengthened to form a handle. A 'gawne' of butter is 12 lbs.

Grindle-stone, i.e. 'grind'-stone.

Grogern, Grograin, coarse fabric of silk and wool.

Haircloth, woven from horsehair, used for sieves and, occasionally, upholstery.

Hard corn, general name for wheat or rye.

Harness, 'body-harness' was armour; horse harness was more usually called 'gears'.

Hatchell, the process of separating the fibres of flax or hemp from the plant. Also the instrument with long iron teeth, for cleaning flax or hemp from the coarse 'tow'. See also 'tew-tows'.

Hearecloth, i.e. 'hair'-cloth; hair sieve, or meal sieve of fine transparent cloth for sifting meal. Also, a horsehair cloth which holds malt in the kiln.

Hogshead, 54 gallons.

Holland, linen imported from the Netherlands.

Hopper-gawne, seed-basket.

Horse-geares, harness.

Horsehocke, Horse-hook, iron hook for attaching to timber or a sled to be pulled by horses.

Hurden, made of hurds, tow, or oakum. Coarse canvas.

Hurds, the refuse or coarse part of hemp, flax or wool.

Hutch, a small light chest for clothes.

Jack, a leather beef flask or small cask.

Joined, e.g. 'joined' tables and beds; as distinct from trestle tables and truckle beds.

Joined bed with curtains, a 'four-poster'.

Keel, shallow tub in which milk is set to cool.

Keep, a safe, meat-safe.

Kilden, Keeling, process of cooling milk for cheese.

Kilderkin, 18 gals.

Kimmel, scalding-tubs.

Kipe, an osier basket.

Knitchen, Knitch, Knitchet, Kinchin, a small bundle; commonly used in reference to measures of flax.

Lather, ladder.

Lead, a measure of cheese; 56 lb.

Lidds, shutters.

Livery cupboard, a hanging or standing cupboard with a shelf, used to hold food and drink.

Male, travelling bag.

Malt-mill, mill for grinding malt before brewing.

Marmett, boiling pot.

Maslin, a kind of brass or alloy.

Maslin corn, mixed grain, especially rye with wheat.

Mattle-tree, Mantle tree, beam or lintel behind the fireplace, hence 'mantel-shelf'.

Maund, a basket.

Maundrell, miner's pick-axe.

Misken, a dunghill; more recently an outdoor lavatory.

Mout or mould, probably a cheese mould; also padding for clothes.

Mule chest, small chest with drawers.

Muncke corn, beer-corn or barley; mixed corn, hence possibly 'Munckland-mill'.

Murrey, mulberry coloured; dark red.

Nager, Nauger, i.e. 'an-auger'.

Nave, the hub of a wheel.

Noggen, made of nogs or hemp; hence thick or rough.

Pad pannel, piece of cloth or pad, serving as a saddle.

Pantables, slippers; c.f. the French 'pantoufles'.

Parger, a plastering tool or trowel.

Partlett, a woman's neckerchief or ruffled collar for the neck and shoulders.

Pascers, a wood-drill.

Pattel staff, Paddle staff, a staff with a small spike, or blade at the end, with a long handle, used as a walking-stick, and for cutting up weeds and thistles whilst walking the fields.

Peale, baker's long-handled implement for placing and removing bread in the oven.

Piggin, a little earthen jar, pitcher or pot; also a small wooden pail.

Pilling iron, a bark-stripping knife.

Pillow-beares, pillow-cases.

Pinson, pincers.

Plough-beams, horizontal projection from a plough, by which it is drawn.

Pocket, a measure of hops; 1¼ cwt.

Polder-meat, i.e. a 'powdering'-tub, in which meat was salted down.

Porringer, Pottinger, Pottager, a small dish with upright sides.

Posnett, a little basin or porringer; or a cooking-pot on short legs, or with a long handle, for standing in the fire.

Pothangles, pot-hooks or pothangers; large hooks secured in the chimney, or on a crane, to support pots over the fire; or an iron bar for lifting lids.

Press-cupboard, a wardrobe.

Pullen, poultry.

Purgatory, ash receptacle in fireplace.

Raves, racks to extend the height of a cartload.

Rave-pins, pins for fixing such racks to a cart.

Rough, raw, e.g. 'meat in the rough'.

Sarsnett, 'Saracen cloth'; fine thin silk stuff.

Sawsers, small dish or pan, sauce dish.

Scothe, a 'dragstaff', or pole pivoted on the rear axle of a cart, trailing on the ground behind to prevent running back on a hill.

Searche, a fine sieve or strainer.

Segg, made of sedge, as a rush-bottomed chair.

Setters, dibbers for 'setting' seeds.

Shacadown, shoddy cloth.

Shopicke, a two-tined fork or sheaf-pike.

Skeele, a pail.

Sleed, sledge for carrying goods.

Slick-trough, a blacksmith's cooling trough.

Slip, a skein or quantity of yarn.

Spence, the buttery or larder.

Stalls, hives of bees.

Stiddy, anvil.

Strakes, Stroke, iron hoops or tyres of a wagon-wheel.

Swingletree, a cross-bar, pivoted at the centre, to which traces are fastened to a plough or cart. Part of a flail.

Syboles, shallots or onions.

Table-board, the board of a trestle table.

Teg, yearling sheep.

Thrave, threne, measure of straw of 24 'boltings', i.e. about 2¼ cwt.

Thrumcloth, cloth made from 'thrums' or waste ends of yarn; tufted or fringed.

Tilder, i.e. 'tilter'; a wedge place behind or under a barrel to tilt it.

Towes, chains or ropes.

Trap-rails, trap-reels, wheels for skeining and measuring yarn.

Treen, wooden.

Trepit, trivet.

Trouse bill, hedger's hatchet.

Tunnel, a funnel.

Tun-pail, a large pail, with a tube at the bottom, by means of which casks were filled.

Turnover, a shawl.

Tutoe, Tutoo, tew-tow, a tow-rope or chain; or an instrument for beating or 'towing' hemp; a hatchell.

Twilleys, woollen material.

Twinter, two-year old sheep.

Vallance, Valiants, short curtain for a bed, either at the canopy (a 'tester-valance'), or around the lower frame (a 'base-valance').

Voide, large basket.

Waferne irons, i.e. 'wafering-irons', thin blades or tongs which hold the paste to the fire for making wafers; a sort of waffle-iron.

Warping-bar, in a loom, the bar used to separate the warp; in rope-making, a brace for twisting the yarn into rope.

Washing-stock, bench on which laundry was laid to be beaten.

Waye, Weigh, a measure of cheese; 330 lb.

Whimble-bit, a drill or gimlet.

Whisk, small broom or besom; or a cooper's plane; or a woman's 'band' or neckerchief, as in 'falling-whisk'.

Whiskett, a straw basket, especially for feeding cattle; a nose-bag.

Whitch, chest or coffer.

Wort-sive, brewing sieve.

Wort-tub, brewing vessels.

Yarn-blades, Yorning blades, yarn cleaners; a fork or pair of blades, set close together to remove burls or unevenness from yarn passing between them.

Yorn, iron, or yarn.

OCCUPATIONS NAMED IN WORCESTERHIRE INVENTORIES[15]

The two volumes of the *Index to Worcestershire Wills and Inventories*, prepared for the Worcestershire Historical Society by E.A. Fry, list approximately 30,000 documents. Volume I comprises the *Index* to almost 20,000 Wills, Inventories and Marriage Bonds for the years 1451-1600; before 1550, however, the documents are scanty, a mere 600 or so. Thus I may be more properly considered to cover the 50 years 1550-1600, and II a similar period of 50 years, from 1601-50. The first volume, however, makes reference to twice as many documents, approximately 20,000 as compared with 10,000 in II. In each volume, though, a similar total number of inventories contains references to the trade or occupation of persons concerned in the documents, between 4,000-4,500 in each case. These trades have been analysed as follows:

		Vol.I	(%)	Vol.II	(%)	Total	(%)
I.	Gentry so titled:	393	9	252	6	645	7½
II.	Churchmen:	371	8½	149	3	520	6
III.	Farmers and Farm Workers:	2539	60	2980	67	5519	63
IV.	Crafts and industry:	609	14	737	17	1346	15½
V.	Distribution Trades, Food, Clothing, etc.:	331	8	291	6½	622	7½
VI.	Miscellaneous, Services, etc.:	35	½	28	½	63	½

15 See Fig. 11, p. 233.

The last three classes of occupations can be further analysed as follows:

IV. Crafts and Industry. 609 (14%) 737 (17%)

Cloth Manufacture: 221 (5½%) 304 (7%)

Cappers	4	3	Journeymen		
Cardmakers	3	1	Weavers	0	1
Clothiers	36	72	Silkweavers	2	0
Clothmakers	0	2	Skeyners	1	0
Clothworkers	1	6	Spinsters	20	34
Coverlet Weavers	0	2	Tuckers	3	2
Drapers	26	5	Walkers	28	18
Dyers	10	10	Weavers	75	142
Embroiderers	1	0	Woolcombers	1	0
Feltmakers	1	1	Wooldrivers	1	0
Fullers	5	2	Woolwinders	3	3

Iron Trades 133 (3%) 146 (3½%)

Bellfounders	1	0	Nailers	24	34
Blacksmiths	16	59	Scythegrinders	4	6
Bladesmiths	1	0	Scysesmiths	19	18
Cutlers	6	4	Smiths	57	19
Grinders	1	2	Tinkers	2	0
Hammermen	1	0	Wiredrawers	1	4

Leatherworkers 109 (2½%) 95 (2%)

Cordwainers	7	3	Skinners	3	3
Curriers	3	2	Tanners	55	37
Glovers	26	39	Whitawyers	1	3
Saddlers	14	8			

Building Trades 63 (1%) 109 (2½%)

Bricklayers	2	2	Plasterers	0	1
Brickmakers	0	4	Sawyers	1	0
Carpenters	35	61	Thatchers	0	1
Glaziers	5	6	Tilemakers	5	2
Joiners	3	14	Tilers	2	3
Masons	5	10	Timbermen	5	5

Miscellaneous Crafts 83 (2%) 83 (2%)

Bedders	1	0	Locksmiths	1	7
Bolstermakers	1	0	Lorimers	1	0
Bookbinders	0	1	Millwrights	1	3
Bowyers	2	0	Pewterers	8	4
Bucklemakers	0	2	Ploughmakers	8	4
Chandlers	6	9	Potters	2	0
Coopers	9	15	Ropers	4	5
Fletchers	4	1	Sievemakers	1	2
Furriers	0	1	Stringers	1	1
Goldsmiths	3	0	Turners	6	1
Gunmakers	1	3	Wheelwrights	28	23
Horners	1	0			

V. Distribution Trades, Food, Clothing, etc. 331 (8%) 291 (6½%)

Apothecaries	2	0	Hosiers	3	0
Bakers	35	26	Innkeepers	7	6
Brewers	18	17	Maltmakers	1	5
Butchers	44	38	Mercers	35	11
Chapmen	2	7	Milliners	19	21
Cobblers	0	1	Pointmakers	0	1
Fishermen	14	7	Shoemakers	52	42
Fishmongers	6	6	Tailors	80	84
Grocers	1	1	Victuallers	4	10
Haberdashers	7	3	Vintners	1	4
Hatters	0	1			

VI. Miscellaneous, Services, etc. 35 (½%) 28 (½%)

Boatmen	1	0	Painters	3	2
Carriers	4	7	Potcarriers	1	0
Cooks	2	4	Schoolmasters	1	1
Doctors	1	0	Scribes	1	0
Drivers	0	1	Servants	13	2
Maidservants	1	6	Soldiers	1	1
Mariners	1	0	Trowmen	1	0
Men-at-Arms	1	0	Watermen	2	1
Musicians	0	2	Workmen	1	0
Ostlers	0	1			

These figures cannot be held to be true statistics, they merely indicate certain trends and distribution of trades. In connection with these, see K. McP. Buchanan's 'Studies in the Localisation of 17th Century Worcestershire Industries, 1600-50', *Worcs. Arch. Soc.*, vols. XVII-XIX, 1940-2. See also the chapters on county industrial history in various Victoria County Histories, e.g. 'Industries' chapter in *V.C.H. Worcestershire*, 2.

AVERAGE PRICES FROM CHADDESLEY INVENTORIES AND QUARTER SESSION PAPERS (1601-52)

Farm Stock and Crops

Oxen	£3 to £4 each.	lambs	1s. 6d. each.
Kine	£2 to £3 each.	Swine	3s. 0d. each.
Cows	£2 to £3 each.	stores	5s. to 7s. each.
'Beasts' 2 year-olds	£1 15s. 0d. each.	Pigs	3s. to 6s. each
4 year-olds	£3 15s. 0d. each.	Horses	£3 each, or ranging
'little'	15s. 0d. each		from £1 to £34.
'young'	£2 10s. 0d. each	Mares	£1 10s. to £3 each.
Calves yearlings	13s. 0d. each.	Geldings	£3 10s. each
weanings	4s. 0d. each.	Hens	4d. to 6d. each
Heifers	£1 10s. 0d. each.	Capons	16d. each.
Sheep January	3s. to 7s. each.	Chickens	1d. each
February	6s. each.	Geese	10d. each, ranging
April	2s. 6d. each.		from 6d. to 2s.
July	3s. 0d. each.	Turkeys	4d. to 1s. each

Hay	per load	10s. to 15s.
Oats	per acre	13s. 4d.
	per strike	3s. 0d.
Rye	per acres	16s. to £1 10s.
Pulse	per acre	10s.
Pease	per peck	16d.
Vetches	per acre	6s. 8d.
Malt	per strike	1s. 8d.
Dredge and peas	per strike	4s. 4d.
	per acre	10s. 0d.
Wheat and rye	per strike	2s. 0d.
	per acre	11s. 8d.
Wheat meal	per bushel	4s. 0d.

Barley	per acre	£1 0s. 0d.
	per strike	5s. 6d.
Maslin corn	per strike	1s. 3d.
Hemp	per knitchin	1s. 0d.
Flax	per pound	6d.
Wool	per stone	8s. to 16s.
Corn	'Hard'	13s. 4d. per acre.
	'Lent'	10s. per acre.
	Unthreshed	8s. per strike.
Bees	per stall	2s. 3d. to 3s.
Cheeses	each	6d.4d.
	per pound	2d.

Clothing

Smock	10d. to 18d.
Ruff Band	4s.
Hempen Shirt	16d.
Pair of sleeves	2s.
Shirt	1s.
Gown	£2 10s.
Apron	8d.
Breeches	5d. to 10s.

Napkins	1d. to 4d. each.
Flannel petticoat	5s.
Table cloth	10d.
Woollen waistocat	6d.
Woollen yarn	1s. to 2s. per lb.
Pair stockings	20d.
Woollen cloth	7s. 0d. a yard.

Household Goods

Pewter pots	5s. 0d.
Candlesticks	20d.
Lantern	1s.
Silver spoons	5s. to 10s.
Cushions	3s. to 5s. 6d.
Earthen jugs	2d.
Frying pan	3d.
Shovel	1s.

Pewter	6d. per lb.
A Bible	4s. and 5s.
Spinning wheels	2s.
Carpets (worn)	5s. to 10s.
Hand gun	3s.
Brass Pot	10d.
Silver bowl	£2 10s.

COUNTY GAZETTEER OF COLLECTIONS OF INVENTORIES

(listed chronologically under county by publication date within author groups)

Bedfordshire F.A. Blaydes, *Genealogia Bedfordiensis, 1538-1700*, privately published, London, 1890; F.A. Page Turner, *Bedfordshire wills and administrations, 1379-1627, proved at Lambeth Palace and in the archdeaconry of Huntingdon*, Pubns. BHRS, 2, 1914; J.H. Blundell, *Inventory of Toddington Manor House, 1644*, BHRS, 1924; F.G. Emmison, *Jacobean Household Inventories, 1606-20*, BHRS, 20, 1938; C.E. Freeman, *Elizabethan Inventories, 1562-91*, BHRS, 32, 1952; P. Bell, *Bedfordshire Wills, 1480-1519*, BHRS, 45, 1966; M. McGregor, *Bedfordshire wills proved in the Prerogative Court of Canterbury*, Pubns. BHRS, 58, 1979; J. Stuart and P. Wells (eds.), *Index of Bedfordshire Probate Records 1484-1858*, British Records Society, 1993; J. Collett-White, *Inventories of Bedfordshire Country Houses 1714-1830*, BHRS, 1995; H. Jenkinson and G.H. Fowler, *Some Bedfordshire wills at Lambeth, 1387-1570, and Lincoln, 1319-1533*, Pubns. BHRS, 14, 1931.

Berkshire *The Unton Inventories, relating to Wadley and Faringdon*, Berks Ashmolean Soc., 1841; J.S. Howse, *An Index of the Probate Records of the Court of the Archdeacon of Berkshire*, 2: *1653-1610*, British Record Society and Phillimore, 1975 (for 1: *1508-1652*, see W.P.W. Phillimore: *Index of Probate Records*, British Record Society, 1893); 'Inventory and accounts of the executors of the will of John Williams, an innkeeper of Farnham', *Farnham & District Museum Society Newsletter*, 9, no.11, September 1992; G.F.T.

Sherwood, 'Early Berkshire wills', *BBOASJ*, 2, 3, and n.s., 1, 3, 5, 6, 7 and 20, 1892-1914/15.

Buckinghamshire   A.L. Browne, 'Wills of Buckinghamshire clergy in the sixteenth century', *Records of Bucks.*, 13, 1936; A.V. Woodman, 'A Seventeenth-Century Inventory at Crafton', *Records of Bucks*, XIV, 1941-6; and: 'The Inventory of a 16th Century Parson', *Records of Bucks*, XV, 1947-52; J. Cornwall, 'John Carter of Denham, Yeoman', *Records of Bucks*, XVI, 1953; E.M. Elvey, *The Courts of the Archdeaconry of Buckingham, 1483-1523*, Pubns. BRS, 19, 1975; M. Reed, *Buckinghamshire Probate Inventories 1661-1714*, BRS, XXIV, 1988.

Cambridgeshire   W.M. Palmer, 'College dons, country clergy and university coachmen' (from probate records at Peterborough), *CAS*, 16, 1911; C.A. Thurley, *Index to the Probate Records of the Court of the Archdeaconry of Ely, 1537-1837*, Brit. Rec. Soc., 88, Phillimore, 1975; M. Farrar, *Genealogical Sources in Cambridgeshire*, Cambs. CRO, 1979.

Carmarthenshire   A.W. Matthews, 'Carmarthenshire wills, 1480-1604', *CASFC*, o.s. 7, 1911-12; 'Inventory of the goods of Sir Henry Vaughan the younger (d.1676)', *CASFC*, 20, 1926-7.

Cheshire   G.J. Piccope, *Lancashire and Cheshire Wills and Inventories*, Chetham Soc., o.s., 1857, 1860, 1861; J.P. Earwaker (LPRS unless otherwise stated), *Index to Wills and Inventories at the Court of Probate, Chester, 1545-1620*, 1879; *Index to Wills and Inventories formerly at Chester, 1621-50*, 1881; *1660-80*, 15, 1887; *1681-1700*, 8, 1888; *1701-20*, 20, 1889; *1721-40*, 22, 1890; *1741-60*, 25, 1892; *1572-1696*, Chetham Soc., n.s., 1893; W. Fergusson Irvine, *Collection of Lancashire and Cheshire Wills, 1301-1752*, LCRS, 1896; *Index to Wills, Inventories, etc. at the Diocesan Registry, Chester, 1485-1620*, LCRS, 1896; *An Index to the Wills and Inventories formerly preserved at the probate registry at Chester, 1590-1665*, LCRS, V, 1905; J.P. Rylands, *Lancashire and Cheshire Wills and Inventories, 1563-1807*, Chetham Soc., n.s., 1897; W.H. Price, *Index to Wills, Inventories, etc. at the Diocesan Registry, Chester, 1621-1700*, LCRS, 1902; *Index to Wills and Inventories formerly at Chester, 1781-1790-1800*, LCRS, 1902; 'Calendar of Wills, Inventories, etc. formerly preserved in the Diocesan Registry of Chester, 1701-1800', *LCRS Misc.*, V, 1905; R. Dickinson, *An Index to the Wills and Administrations formerly preserved in the Probate Registry of Chester, for 1821-25*, LCRS Publications, 107, 1961; *An Index to Wills and Administrations . . . Chester, 1826-1830*, Record Society of Lancashire and Cheshire, 113, Phillimore, 1972; R. and F. Dickinson, *An Index to the Wills and Administrations . . . Chester, 1831-1833*, Record Society of Lancashire and Cheshire, 118, 1978.

Cornwall   R.M. Glencross, *Calendar of wills etc. relating to Cornwall and Devon*, Part 1 1569-1699, 56, 1929; Part 2 1700-99, 59, 1932, British Rec. Soc., Index Library; *Index to Cornish Probate Records, 1600-49* (in five parts), Cornwall CRO, 1988; Cornwall County Record Office, *Index to Cornish Probate Records 1600-1649*, n.d.; E.A. Fry, *Calendars of wills and administrations relating to the counties of Devon and Cornwall, preserved in the probate registry of Exeter*, 1, 1540-1799; 2, 1532-1800, British Rec. Soc., Index Library.

Cumberland   See *Yorkshire* below, Publications of the Surtees Society: *North country wills*, published 1908-12; J.V. Harrison, 'Five Bewcastle Wills, 1587-1617', *Cumberland and Westmorland Antiquarian and Archaeological Soc. Trans.*, 67, 1967; W.G. Collingwood, 'Inventory of Mistress Fleming of Skirwith, 1639', *CWAAS*, 28, 19–.

Derbyshire   S.O. Addy, 'Wills (15th and 16th centuries) at Somerset House relating to Derbyshire', *DANHSJ*, 45, 1923; W.G. Clark-Maxwell, 'Inventory of the contents of Markeaton Hall, 1545', *DANHSJ*, n.s., 51, 1930; J.M. Bestall and D.V. Fowkes, *Chesterfield Wills and Inventories, 1521-1604*, Derbyshire Record Office, Derbyshire Record Society, 1, 1977; J. Spavold, 'Using a Relational Database: The example of Church Gresley (Derbs.) Inventories', *The Local Historian*, 26, no.2, May 1996; H. Lawrance, 'Will of Lionel Tylney, lead-miner and merchant, 1653', *DANHSJ*, n.s., 5, 1931.

Devonshire   E.A. Fry, *Calendars of wills and administrations relating to the counties of Devon and Cornwall, preserved in the probate registry of Exeter: 1, 1540-1799; 2, 1532-1800*, British Rec. Soc., Index Library, 35 and 46, 1908-14; R.M. Glencross, *Calendar of wills etc. relating to Cornwall and Devon: 1, 1569-1699; 2, 1700-99*, British Rec. Soc., Index Library, 56 and 59, 1929-32; M. Cash, *Devonshire inventories of the 16th and 17th centuries*, DCRS, 35, n.s., XI, 1966; E.A. Donaldson, 'Inventory of the goods and chattels of Richard Bevys, late mayor of Exeter, 1603', *DASLA*, 31, 1899.

Dorset   G.S. Fry, *Calendar of wills and administrations relating to Dorset*, British Record Soc., Index Library, 53, 1922; L.A. Cooper, *Two Seventeenth Century Dorset Inventories (Wimborne)*, Dorset Record Society, 1974; R. Machin, *Probate Inventories and Manorial Excerpts of Chetnole, Leigh and Yetminster*, University of Bristol, 1976; J.H. Bettey and D.S. Wilde, 'The Probate Inventories of Dorset Farmers, 1573-1670', *The*

Local Historian, 12, no.5, 1977, p.228; N.M. Richardson, 'A Dorset inventory of 1627 (William Edmonds, alias Younge, yeoman', *DNHAS*, 35, 1914.

Durham Publications of the Surtees Society: *Wills and Inventories … of the Northern Counties etc.*, published 1835-1929, including: J.C. Hodgson and H.M. Wood, *Wills and inventories from the registry at Durham*, Pubns. Surtees Soc., 112 and 142, 1906-29; B. Crosby, 'A Seventeenth Century Durham Inventory', *Musical Times*, no.118, 1978; See also: *Yorkshire*.

Essex Essex Record Office Publications: no.8, F.W. Steer, *Farm and Cottage Inventories of Mid-Essex, 1634-1749*, 1950; no.22, F.G. Emmison, *Ingatestone Hall in 1600*, 1954; *Essex Arch. Soc.*, 10, 1907: R.C. Fowler, 'Essex Monastic Inventories'; 'Archaeological Notes: A Domestic Inventory'; Rev. E.G. Norris, 'A Seventeenth-Century Inventory', *Essex Review*, 15, 1906; 'Two Interiors: Toppingho Hall and Hatfield Peverel, in the 16th and 17th Centuries', *Essex Review*, 53, 1944; R.C. Fowler, 'Essex monastic inventories', *EAS*, n.s., 10, 1909; J.F. Nichols, 'Milton Hall extent of 1309 and an inventory of 1278', *Southend-on-Sea Antiq. & Hist. Soc.*, 1, 1921; G.M. Benton, 'Essex wills (1292-1559) at Canterbury', *EAS*, n.s., 21, 1934; A.C. Edwards, 'Sir John Petre and his household, 1576-7', *Essex Review*, 1954; F.G. Emmison, *Wills at Chelmsford (from Essex and East Hertfordshire, 2: 1620-1720)*, British Record Society, 1961; F.W. Steer, *Farm and Cottage Inventories*, Phillimore, 1969; *Wills at Chelmsford, 3: 1721-1858*, British Record Society, 1969; *Elizabethan Life: Wills of Essex Gentry and Merchants*, Essex County Council, 1975; D. Cressey, 'Death and the social order', Funerary preferences of Elizabethan gentlemen, based on wills in Essex, *Continuity and Change*, 5, May 1990; Essex Life, Home, Work and Land, from Essex Wills etc. (Essex Record Office 1991, re-print of 1976 edition) and: Essex Wills …: The Commissary Court 1558-1569 (Essex Record Office, 1993); and: Essex Wills …: The Commissary Court 1569-78 (Essex Record Office, 1994); W.H. St J. Hope, 'The last testament and inventory of John de Vere, 13th Earl of Oxford (d. 1513)', Procs. Soc. Antiqs. London, *Archaeologia*, 66, 1914-15; G. Rickword, 'An early Georgian inventory (of Isaac Rebow, 1735)', *EAS*, n.s., 14, 19..; J.H. Round, 'Two great Vere documents; the will of John de Vere, 13th Earl of Oxford (d. 1513), with an inventory of his goods', *EAS*, n.s., 14, 19..; The *Essex Wills* series, in progress, now has seven volumes: 1: 1558-1565; 2: 1565-1571; 3: 1571-1577; 4: 1577-1584; 5: 1584-1591; 6: 1591-1597; 7: 1597-1603, (ed. F.G. Emmison *et al.*, Essex Record Office. When completed, this series will comprise more than 12,000 wills).

Gloucestershire Probate inventories and wills are now in the Gloucestershire Record Office. The wills run from the formation of the diocese in 1541 to 1858, when the civil Probate Registry was established. The inventories have mostly been separated from the wills, but few survive before 1683. The wills are listed in *A calendar of wills proved in the Consistory Court of Gloucester, 1541-1800* (British Records Society, Index Library, XII and XXXIV). *Gloucester wills and administrations, 1801-1858* has also been published by the British Records Society (microfiche series 4, 1996). An unpublished list of inventories is available at Gloucestershire Record Office; E.A. Fry and W.P.W. Phillimore, *Calendar of wills proved in the consistory courts of the bishop of Gloucester: 1, 1541-1650; 2, 1660-1800*, British Rec. Soc., Index Library, vols.19, 1895, and 34, 1907; P. McGrath, *Merchants and Merchandise in Seventeenth-Century Bristol*, Bristol Rec. Soc., 1955; M.G. Dickinson, *Wills proved in the Gloucestershire Peculiar Courts*, Gloucester City Library, 1960; P. McGrath and M.E. Williams, *Bristol Wills, 1546-1593*, University of Bristol, 1975; J.S. Moore, *The Goods and Chattels of our Forefathers (Frampton Cotterell, Iron Acton, Westerleigh, Stoke Gifford and Winterbourne)*, Phillimore, 1976; and: *Clifton and Westbury Probate Inventories, 1609-1761*, Avon Loc. Hist. Assoc., 1981; *Gloucestershire Family History*, Glos. C.R.O., 1982; L.J.U. Way, 'Inventory of the goods of John White of Brystowe, 1559', *BGAS*, 43, 1921.

Hampshire A.J. Willis, *Wills, Administration, Inventories in the Winchester Diocesan Records*, Phillimore, 1968; J.L. Whitehead and E.R. Rubey, 'Inventory of the goods and chattels of Sir Richard Worsley of Appuldurcombe, 1566', *HFCAS*, 5, 1905-6.

Herefordshire F.C. Morgan, 'A Herefordshire Bookseller's Catalogue of 1695', *Woolhope Nats. Field Club*, 31, I, 1942; and: 'A Herefordshire mercer's inventory of 1689, *Woolhope Nats. Field Club*, 31, III, 1944; and: 'Inventories of a Herefordshire saddler's shop in 1692 and 1696', *Woolhope Nats. Field Club*, 31, IV, 1945; J.W. Tonkin, 'The Goods and Chattels of our Forefathers 1660-1760', *Woolhope Nats. Field Club*, 45, 1985; J. and M. West, 'Seventeenth-century homes' in *A History of Herefordshire* (chapter XV), Phillimore, 1985; M.A. Faraday and E.J.L. Coles, *Calendar of probate and administrative acts 1407-1541 and abstracts of wills 1541-1581 in the Court Books of the Bishop of Hereford*, British Records Society, 1989.

Hertfordshire F.G. Emmison, *Wills at Chelmsford (from Essex and East Hertfordshire)*, 2: *1620-1720*, British Record Society, 1961; L.M. Munby, *Life and death in Kings Langley. Wills and Inventories 1498-1659*, Kings Langley Loc. Hist. & Mus. Soc., 1981; *All My Worldly Goods: An Insight into Family Life from Inventories, 1447-1742*, Bricket Wood Society, 1991; S. Flood, *St. Albans Wills 1471-1500*, Hertfordshire Record Society, 1994.

Huntingdonshire W.M. Noble, *Calendar of Huntingdonshire wills 1479-1652*, British Rec. Soc., Index Library, 42, 1911; J.A. Humphries, 'Index of wills proved in the peculiar courts ... in the county of Huntingdonshire, with bonds and inventories ... all now preserved in the Probate Registry at Peterborough', *CHAS*, 6, 1947.

Kent L.B. Larking, 'The Inventory of Juliana de Leyborne, Countess of Huntingdon, 1367', *AC*, I, 1858 (transcript); Canon Scott Robertson, 'Inventory of Beds, Tapestry and Linen at Leeds Castle, 1532', *AC*, XV, 1883 (transcript); and: 'Cobham Hall, an Inventory of Furniture and Pictures in 1672', *AC*, XVII, 1887 (transcript); A. Hussey, 'Faversham Household Inventory, 1609', *AC*, XXVII, 1905; and: 'Milton (near Sittingbourne) wills', *AC*, 45-7, 1933-5; and: 'Hythe wills', *AC*, 49 and 50, 1938-9; An Inventory of an Innkeeper's possessions in 1685', 'W.P.D.S.' *AC*, XLVI, 1934; C. Eveleigh Woodruff, 'Some early Kentish wills', *AC*, 46, 1934; L. Sherwood, 'Seventeenth and Eighteenth Century Inventories', *AC*, LXI, 1948; R. Keen, 'Inventory of Richard Hooker, 1601', *AC*, LXX, 1956; M. Fitch, *Index to Administrations in the Prerogative Court of Canterbury, now preserved in Somerset House*, 4: *1596-1608*, British Record Society, 1964; *Probate Records of the Church of England: Canterbury Province Prerogative Court, 1642-1722*, List and Index Society, 161, London, 1979; J.S.W. Gibson, 'Inventories in the Prerogative Court of Canterbury', *The Local Historian*, no.4, 1980, p.222.

Lancashire J. Harland, *House and farm accounts of the Shuttleworths of Gawthorpe Hall, 1582-1621*, Chetham Soc., 35, 41, 43 and 46, 1856-58; J.G. Piccope, *Lancashire and Cheshire Wills and Inventories*, Chetham Soc., XXXIII, 1857; LI, 1860; LIV, 1861; J.P. Earwaker, *Lancashire and Cheshire Wills and Inventories*, Chetham Soc., III, 1884; XXVIII, 1893; XXXIV, XXXVII, 1897; R. Dickinson, *An Index to the Wills and Administrations formerly preserved at the Probate Registry at Chester, for 1821-5*, LCAS Publications, 107, 1961; J. Banks and E. Kerridge, 'The Probate Inventory of James Bankes, 1617', *The early records of the Bankes family at Winstanley*, Chetham Soc., 1973; C.B. Phillips and J.H. Smith, *Stockport Probate Records*, LCRS, 131, 1992.

Leicestershire H. Hartopp, *Calendars of wills and administrations relating to Leicestershire, 1495-1649 (includes peculiars of Rothley, Groby and Evington)*; and: *Index to wills etc. ... 1660-1750 (includes peculiars of Rothley and Rutland)*, British Rec. Soc., Index Library, 27, 1902; W.G. Hoskins, 'The Leicestershire farmer in the sixteenth century', *LeAS*, 22, 1944-5; F.A. Greenhill, 'Seven Leicestershire wills (Newhall, Thurlaston, 1506; Westcotes, 1546; Long Walton, 1577; Leicester, 1589 and 1617; Kirkby Mallory, 1595; and Stoughton, 1633)', *LeAHS*, no.38, 1962-3; F.E. Skellington, 'Enclosed in Clay: a study in Leicestershire wills', *LeAHS*, no.42, 1966-7; G.C. Astill, 'An early inventory of a Leicestershire Knight: Sir Edmund Appleby of Appleby Magna', *Midland History*, no.2, 1974; See also: *Rutland*.

Lincolnshire C.W. Foster, *Calendars of Lincoln wills: 1, 1320-1600; 2, 1601-52; 3, 1540-1659; 4, Miscellaneous wills and administrations*, British Rec. Soc. Index Library, 28, 41, 52 and 57, 1902-30; C.W. Foster, *Lincoln Wills* (1271-1526), 1914; (1505-30), 1918; (1530-2), 1930, Lincs Rec. Soc.; M.W. Barley, 'The Lincolnshire Village and its Buildings', *The Lincolnshire Historian*, no.7, 1951; and: 'Farmhouses and Cottages, 1550-1725', *Economic History Review*, VII, no.3; 'Craftsmen and Shopkeepers in the Sixteenth and Seventeenth centuries', *Lincolnshire Historian*, 2, no.9, 1962; S. Needham, *A Glossary for Yorkshire and North Lincolnshire probate inventories*, Un. of Hull, Dept. Adult Edn., 'Studies in Regional and Local History', no. 3, 1984; S. Coppell, 'Will-making on the deathbed (in Leventon and Grantham)', *Local Population Studies*, 40, Spring 1988; See also *Yorkshire*.

London & Middlesex R.R. Sharpe, *Calendar of wills proved and enrolled in the court of Hustings*, 2 vols., London, 1889-90; G.D. Ramsay, *John Isham, mercer and Merchant Adventurer: Two account books of a London merchant in the reign of Elizabeth I*, Northants. Records Soc., 21, 1960-1; F.J. Furnivall, *The Fifty Earliest Wills in the Court of Probate, London, 1387-1439*, Early English Text Society Publications, original series, no.78 (reprint of the first edition of 1772), O.U.P., 1964; I. Darlington, *London Consistory Court Wills, 1492-1547*, London Records Society, 3, 1967; L.S. Snell, 'The Edwardian Inventories of Middlesex', *LMAS Trans.*, nos.26, 27 and 29, 1975, 1976 and 1978; M. Fitch, *Probate Records of the Court of the Archdeacon of London, 1363-1649*, British Record Society, Phillimore, 1979.

Merioneth T.P. Ellis, 'Merioneth notes' (includes a Hen Gwrt inventory of 1696), *Y Cymmrodor*, 38, 1924.

Montgomery W.A. Griffiths, 'Early Montgomeryshire wills at St Asaph's and Somerset House, relating to the parishes of Llandysilio, Llandrinio and Guilsfield (16th-18th centuries)', *Powys-Land Club Colls.*, 37, 1915.

Norfolk J. Bulwer, *An Inventory and Valuation of the Goods and Chattels of Charles Wyndham of Stokesby, 1668*, Norfolk Arch. Soc., V, 1859; L.G. Bolingbroke, *Two Elizabethan Inventories*, Norfolk Arch. Soc., XV, 1902; F.R. Beecheno, *The Sucklings House at Norwich*, Norfolk Arch. Soc., XX, 1917; T.F. Barton, M.A. Farrow and L.A. Bedingfeld, *Index of Wills proved in the Consistory Court of Norwich, 1751-1818*, Norfolk Record Society Publications, no.38, 1969; P. Palgrave-Moore, *An Index of Wills proved in the Norfolk Archdeaconry Court, 1560-1604*, Norfolk and Norwich Genealogical Society, 10, 1978; C. Frostick, *Index of wills proved in the Consistory Court of Norwich, 1819-57, now in the CRO*, Norfolk Rec. Soc., 47, 1980-2; J. Wilson, *Wymondham inventories, 1590-1641*, Creative History from E. Anglian sources, no.1, 1983; U. Priestley and A. Fenner, *Shops and Shopkeepers in Norwich, 1660-1730*, Centre of East Anglian Studies, 1985; M. and G. Nobb, *In and Around Yaxham, Norfolk: Places and people from their Wills, 1432-1774, and other sources*, 1991; H.L. Bradfer-Lawrence, 'Inventory of the goods of Sir Roger Townshend at his house at Stiffkey, 1636/7', *Norfolk Archaeology*, 23, 1927-9.

Northamptonshire 'Inventory of Alice Elmes, 1607', *Northants Nat. Hist. Soc. J.*, XXVIII, 1935; P.A. Kennedy, 'Inventory of Henry de Vere, 1493', *Northants Past and Present*, II, no.1, 1954; P.I. King, *Guide to the Northampton and Rutland Probate Records*, Northamptonshire Record Office, 1964.

Northumberland Publications of the Surtees Society: *Wills and Inventories … of the Northern Counties etc.*, 1835-1929; J.V. Harrison, 'Kirkhaugh Wills', *Archaeologia Aeliana*, no.43, 1965; *See under 'Yorkshire' below*.

Nottinghamshire *Wills and Inventories … of the Northern Counties etc.*, published 1835-1929; P.A. Kennedy, *Nottinghamshire household inventories, 1512-66/8 (from the peculiar court of Southwell)*, Thoroton Soc., 22, 1963; E. Perkins, *Village life from wills and inventories; Clayworth parish, Notts., 1670-1710*, Centre for Loc. Hist., Un. Notts., 1981; References to wills and admons. from the Archdeaconry of Nottingham are included in Indexes to the probate records (1389-1688) of the Prerogative Court of York, published by the Yorks. Arch. Soc. (Record Series) in volumes dated from 1888-1934. There is also a printed index to Notts. wills and admons only (extracted from these volumes), 1568-1619 (J.S.W. Gibson, *Simplified Guide*); J.W. Clay, *North country wills, being abstracts of wills relating to the counties of York, Nottingham, Cumberland and Westmorland at Somerset House and Lambeth Palace. 1: 1383-1558; 2: 1558-1604*, Pubns. Surtees Soc., 116 (1908) and 121 (1912); See, under *Yorkshire* below: Publications of the Surtees Society.

Oxfordshire M.A. Havinden, *Household and farm inventories in Oxfordshire, 1550-90*, ORS, 44, 1965; E.R. Brinkworth and J.S.W. Gibson, *Banbury Wills and Inventories: Pt. 1, 1591-1620; Pt. 2, 1621-50*, Banbury Hist. Soc., vols. 13, 1975, and 14, 1976; F.J. Denzey, *Chilton's Chattels, 1551-1725*, Oxford, 1977.

Radnorshire D.S. Davis, 'Radnorshire wills, 1383-1656', *Radn. Soc.*, 3, 1933.

Rutland H. Hartopp, *Index to wills etc. in … the Rutland peculiars of Caldecott, Ketton, Tixover and Liddington prior to 1821*, British Rec. Soc., Index Library, 51, 1920.

Shropshire J.B. Oldham, 'A 16th century Shrewsbury school inventory', *SANHS*, 47, 1933; 'Shrewsbury Drapers' Inventories', 1653-4, *ShAS*, LII, 1947-8; B. Trinder and J. Cox (eds.), *Yeomen and Colliers in Telford: Probate Inventories for Dawley, Lilleshall, Wellington and Wrockwardine, 1660-1750*, Phillimore, 1980.

Somersetshire F.W. Weaver, *Somerset Mediaeval Wills* (1383-1500), 1901; (1501-30), 1903; (1531-58), 1905, Som. Rec. Soc.; E.A. Fry, *Calendar of wills and administrations in the court of the archdeaconry of Taunton: Pts. 1 and 2, 1537-1799; Pt. 3, Administrations 1596-1799; Pt. 4, Peculiar of Ilminster 1690-1857*, British Rec. Soc., Index Library, 45, 1912, and 45a, 1921; S.W. Rawlins and I. Jones, *Somerset wills from Exeter, 1529-1600*, Som. Rec. Soc., 62, 1952.

South Glamorgan M. Griffiths, *Penmark and Pothkerry families and farms in the seventeenth century Vale of Glamorgan*, University of Cardiff, 1979.

Staffordshire J.S. Roper, *Sedgley Probate Inventories, 1614-1787* (by courtesy of A. Wilson, F.L.A., Borough Librarian and Curator, Dudley, 1960); D.G. Vaisey, *Probate inventories of Lichfield and district, 1568-1680*, Staffs. Records Soc., 1969; *Probate Inventories of Tamworth*, Staffordshire County Council, Education Committee, 1978.

Suffolk S. Tymms, *Wills and Inventories from the Registers of the commissary of Bury St Edmunds, 1370-1650*, Camden Soc., O.S., 49, 1850; V.B. Redstone, 'Calendar of pre-Reformation wills etc. registered at the probate office, Bury St Edmunds', *SIANH*, 12, 1902; and: 'Early Suffolk wills enrolled at Ipswich, 1284-1660', *SIANH*, 16, 1910; C. Partridge, 'Tabular lists from Redstone's Calendar of Bury wills',

SIANH, 13, 1908; C.W.S. Randall Cloke and T.W. Oswald-Hicks, *A Calendar of Suffolk wills, 1384-1604*, Eng. Mon. Inscriptions Soc., 1913; H.W.B. Wayman, *Abstracts of Suffolk wills, 1383-1604*, Eng. Mon. Inscriptions Soc., 2, 1914; J.T. Munday, *Simeon Styward's Substance, 1566*; and: 'Lakenheath to 1550: Thirty testaments', *Lakenheath Records*, nos.3 and 5, 1960-70; P. May, *Newmarket inventories, 1662-1715*, Newmarket, 1976; S. Colman, 'Post-medieval houses in Suffolk: some evidence from probate inventories and Hearth Tax returns', *Suffolk Institute of Archaeological and Historical Procs.*, no.34, 1979; W.R. and R.K. Sergeant, *Index of probate records of the Archdeacon of Suffolk at Ipswich, 1444-1700*, British Record Society, 1980; M. Reed, *The Ipswich Probate Inventories, 1583-1631*, Pubns. Suff. Rec. Soc., 22, 1981; N. Evans, *Wills of the Archdeaconry of Sudbury 1630-1635*, Suffolk Record Society, XXIX, 1987; M. Allen, *Wills of the Archdeaconry of Suffolk 1625-1626*, Suffolk Record Society/Boydell Press, 1995.

Surrey   G. Clinch, 'Inventory of a Surrey farmer, John Potter of Thorpe', *SAS Colls.*, 23, 1910; K.Y. Heselton, *Sunbury household effects, 1673-1724*, Sunbury and Shepperton Local History Society, no.3, 1977; J. Holman and M. Herridge, *An Index of Surrey Probate Inventories of the 16th to 19th centuries*, Domestic Buildings Research Group, Surrey, 1986; 'The Will of Richard Stubbington, clothier, 1527', Farnham & District Museum Society, Quarterly Newsletter, 9 no.3, September 1990; 'A Beddington Inventory of furniture, 16th century', *SAS Colls.*, 31.

Sussex   W.H. Hall, *Calendar of wills and administrations in the archdeaconry court of Lewes in the Bishopric of Chichester (with peculiars of South Malling and Battle), from temp. Henry VIII to the Commonwealth*, British Rec. Soc., Index Library, 24, 1901; R. Garraway Rice, 'The household goods etc. of Sir John Gage of West Firle, 1556', *SAC*, 45, 1902; and: 'Index to some wills proved and administrations granted in the peculiar of the deanery of South Malling (1560-7) and an index to 216 other 16th-century Sussex wills', *SAC*, 50, 1907; P.S. Goodman, 'Two Sussex inventories' (James Stilwell, 1677, and Elizabeth Capron, 1747), *SAC*, 51, 1908; H.M. Whitley, 'An inventory of the goods and chattels of William Shelley of Michelgrove, 1585', *SAC*, 55, 1912; E.A. Fry, *Calendar of wills in the consistory court of Chichester, 1482-1800*, British Rec. Soc., Index Library, 49, 1915; F. Harrison, 'A Bepton farmer's goods, 1577', *SASN&Q*, 1, 1926; R.G. Rice and W.H. Godfrey, *Transcript of Sussex wills ... to 1560*, 4 vols., Sussex Rec. Soc., 41-3 and 45, 1935-41; G.H. Kenyon, 'Kirdford Inventories, 1611-1776' (with particular reference to Weald clay farming), *SAC*, XCIII, 1955; 'Documents relating to Uckfield and Framfield (including an inventory of the goods of Edward Russell, 1653', *SAC*, 3, 1850; 'Inventory of a Warnham farmer's goods, 1670', *SASN&Q*, 2.

Warwickshire   'Inventory of the goods of Sir Charles Hales of Newland, Coventry, 1618', *Midland Rec. Soc.*, 5, 1902; R. Holt, J. Ingram and J. Jarman, *Birmingham Wills and Inventories*, University of Birmingham, 1985.

Westmorland   *See, under 'Yorkshire' below:* Publications of the Surtees Society: *Wills and Inventories ... of the Northern Counties etc.*, published 1835-1929.

Wiltshire   T.E. Vernon, 'Anne, Lady Beauchamp's inventory at Edington, 1665', *WANHM*, 58, 1963; and: 'Inventory of Sir Henry Sharrington: The contents of Lacock House in 1575', *WANHM*, 63, 1968; C.R. Everett, 'Wiltshire wills preserved in the diocesan records', *WANHM*, 45, 1930-2 (Almost all the wills listed by Everett came to the CRO in 1958. He also listed other Salisbury diocesan wills for Berkshire, Dorset and Uscombe in Devon, in the *Genealogists Magazine*. The CRO holds more than 100,000 probate records from 1540-1858); W. Smith, 'Two medieval Salisbury wills', *Soc. of Archivists Journal*, 10 July 1989.

Worcestershire   E.A. Fry, *Calendar of wills and administrations in the consistory court of the Bishop of Worcester: 1, 1451-1600; 2, 1601-52*, British Rec. Soc., Index Library, Vols. 31 and 39, 1904-10; E.A.B. Barnard, 'Will and inventory of Philip Hawford, pseudo-abbot of Evesham and Dean of Worcester, 1553-7, *WAS*, n.s., 5, 1928; J.S. Roper, *Dudley probate inventories, 1544-1603; 1605-1685; and 1601-1650*, Dudley Public Libraries, 1954, 1966, and 1968; A.D. Dyer, 'Probate inventories of Worcestershire tradesmen, 1545-1614', *Worc. Hist. Soc. (Miscellany)*, 48, 1967; J.A. Yelling, 'The combination of and rotation of crops in East Worcestershire, 1540-1660', *Agr. Hist. Rev.*, 17, 1969; and: 'Probate Inventories in the geography of livestock farming: a study of East Worcestershire, 1540-1750', *Inst. Br. Geog.*, 51, 1970; J.A. Johnston, 'The Vale of Evesham 1702-8; the evidence from probate inventories and wills', *Vale of Evesham Hist. Soc. Research Papers*, 4, 1973; *Bewdley in its Golden Age; Life in Bewdley 1660-1740*, Bewdley Historical Research Group, 1991.

Yorkshire and the North   J. Raine, *Wills and Inventories illustrative of the manners, history, language, statistics,* *etc. of the Northern Counties of England from the Eleventh Century to 1581*, Surtees Soc., 5 vols., 1835-1929; and: *Testamenta Eboracensia; a selection of Wills from the Registry at York* (6 vols.), Surtees Soc., 1836-1902; and: *Wills and Inventories from the Registry of the Archdeaconry of Richmond, 1442-1579*, Surtees Soc., 1853; F. Collins, *Wills and administrations from the Knaresborough court rolls: 1, 1507-1607; 2, 1607-68*, Surtees Soc., 104 and 110, 1902-5; J.W. Clay, *North country wills; being abstracts of wills relating to the counties of York, Notts., Northumberland, Cumberland and Westmorland at Somerset House and Lambeth Palace: 1, 1383-1558; 2, 1558-1604*, Surtees Soc., 116 and 121, 1908-12; 'The estate and inventory of James Ashworth of Ibbotroyd, 1699', *Papers of Halifax Antiq. Soc.*, 1911; W.B. Crump, 'The Yeoman Clothier of the Seventeenth Century; His house and loom-shop', *The Bradford Antiquary*, n.s., V, 1932; E.W. Crossley, 'Two Seventeenth-Century Inventories', *Yorks Arch. J.*, XXXIX, 1939; G.E. Kirk, 'Wills, Inventories and bonds of the Manor Court of Temple Newsham, 1612-1701', *Thoresby Soc. Misc.*, 1935; and: *Some Documents of Barnoldswick Manor court of Probate, 1660-1794*, YAS, 1953; A. Lonsdale, *A note on Leeds wills, 1539-1561*, Thoresby Soc. Pubs., 50, 1954; 'Wills and admons. etc.: Listings taken from the Calendar of the old Diocese of York and the Diocese of Lincoln, with certain additions from Durham', *Family History*, no.2, 1963; H. Thwaite, *Abstract of Abbotside wills, 1552-1688*, YAS Records series, no.130, 1968; P.C.D. Brears, *Yorkshire probate inventories, 1542-1642*, YAS Records series, 134, 1972; A. Rycraft, *Sixteenth and Seventeenth Century Wills, Inventories and other Probate Documents*, Borthwick Wallet no:4, Borthwick Institute, York, 1973; R. Fieldhouse, 'Social structure from Tudor lay subsidies and probate inventories: A case study from Richmond', *Local Population Studies*, no.12, 1974; S. Needham, *A Glossary for Yorkshire and north Lincolnshire probate inventories*, University of Hull, Dept. Adult Edn., 'Studies in Regional and Local History', no.3, 1984; D.M. Smith, *Medieval Latin Documents, series 2: Probate Records*, Borthwick Wallet no.7, Borthwick Institute, York, 1984; E. Hall, *Michael Warton of Beverley, an Inventory of his possessions*, University of Hull Department of Adult and Continuing Education, 1986; N. Vickers, *The Probate Inventories of Whitby, North Yorkshire, 1700-1800*, KAF Brewin Books, 1986; R.W. Ambler and B. & L.Watkinson, *Farmers and Fishermen: the Probate Inventories of the Ancient Parish of Clee, South Humberside 1536-1742*, University of Hull, 1987; P. Brears, *Traditional Food in Yorkshire*, John Donald, 1987 (Evidence from probate inventories of cooking utensils and groceries in shops; chiefly 19th century); C. Cross, 'Northern women in the early modern period; female testators of Hull and Leeds 1520-1650', *Yorks. Arch. Journal*, 59, 1987; E.W. Crossley, 'A Temple Newsam inventory, 1565', *Yorks. Arch. Journal*, 25, 1918-20; W.B. Crump, *The yeoman-clothier of the 17th century, his home and his loom-shop. A study of the probate inventories in Bradford*, Local Record series, 1, Bradford Hist. & Antiq. Soc.

HEARTH TAX RETURNS

THE DOCUMENT

The records of an extremely unpopular and short-lived tax provide us with some of our most important information for the study of the people and homes of an English village in the 17th century. In 1662 the so-called 'Cavalier Parliament' endeavoured, by the Act 13-14 Charles II, c.10, to raise an annual tax which, together with other fiscal measures, would augment the income of the Restoration monarchy by an estimated £1,200,000 per annum. Evey householder who was 'Rated or Rateable to Church and poor', that is, anyone who owned property worth 20s. a year or more, and was not otherwise exempt by poverty, the receipt of alms or relief, was liable to an annual payment of 2s. for every fireplace or stove in his house. There had been an ancient precedent for 'chimney money' in England since Norman times, but the new measure came, nevertheless, as a distinct shock to the English taxpayer of the 17th century. Returns were to be made to the Justices by the village constables and tithing-men, listing those householders who were liable to payment of Hearth Tax, with a statement of the number of fire-places in each man's house. This return was to be delivered by the constable to the Justices at Quarter Sessions, to be enrolled by the Clerk of the Peace, and a duplicate sent to the Exchequer. If the constable was not satisfied with a householder's statement, he was empowered to search the house and count the hearths.

Such direct taxation, involving as it did intrusion into the home (intrusion which might reveal all sorts of unlicensed and otherwise illegal activity), was heartily disliked and thoroughly resisted. Moreover, the financial needs of Charles II's government were associated by many sections of society with foreign and religious policies which were, to them, highly suspect. The English people could still react violently to the issues of the Civil War and Commonwealth, and the unpopularity of the Hearth Tax resulted in passive non-payment, a good deal of evasion and false returns, and even, in Bristol and London, in active rioting. The existing local machinery of assessment and collection quickly proved itself to be so unreliable that only a fraction of the estimated amount, between £170,000 to £700,000 a year, was ever collected. Repeated measures were taken to re-organise the collection of the Tax; Receivers-General were twice appointed by the Treasury, in 1664 and 1669; the collection was twice farmed out by contract, in 1666 and 1674; in 1684 a special Commission was appointed to undertake all collection. In 1689 the attempt was abandoned altogether, and the statute repealed. Like so many taxation returns, the documents of the Hearth Tax must be regarded as very unreliable sources of information about the condition and wealth of English society. Even so, if used with caution, and particularly if their study is combined with an investigation of probate inventories, they can provide much fascinating additional detail to supplement the evidence of the latter. Any endeavour to identify a 17th-century house, or reconstruct its plan from documentary evidence (see pp.147-158), must depend to a very large extent for its success upon the correct positioning of the chimney stack. Thus, when using the inventories for this purpose, a careful check must always be made of references to fire-irons and equipment for the hearth, in order to discover which rooms adjoin the stack. Hearth Tax returns provide invaluable additional information on the number of hearths which should be included in the plans of those houses whose goods have been found amongst contemporary inventories.

The documents, as the illustration shows, supply no information other than a list of names of those assessed in any parish, occasionally in ruled columns, but seldom in any particular order, with a column of 'fyerhearthes' alongside the names. No particulars of the householders' occupations are given, though a few cases in each list will usually be distinguished by a title (Mr, Esq., Gent., Senior, Junior, clerk, widow are the most frequent styles). Very infrequently a name will be given to the house itself, e.g.:

Sir John Lumford, Knight, in Glashampton House.	14.
Also in Bull Hill House for him.	3.
John Portman at the Poolehouse.	4.
(*W.R.O. Astley, Worcs. 1662/166.*)	4.

This is invaluable information for identifying a family with a particular house which may survive today, difficult in view of the general absence of addresses in pre-postal times, almost impossible if deeds and early large-scale maps are not available. Occasionally a return gives a list of names on which each statement has been endorsed by the householder:

Roger Osland hath two hearths. Roger Oslands mark. R.
(*W.R.O. Little Kyre. 1662/166.*)

Sufficient numbers of such endorsements would give a valuable indication of the extent of literacy in a 17th-century parish, but this does not appear to be the required custom by any means. In some returns the constable includes particulars of those in his village who are exempt, as well as those who are taxable; the entries 'voyd', 'new-built' and 'unpaid' are fairly common. At the end of the return we find the constable's signature and a certificate thus:

'Item, there are noe persons in this parish Rated or Rateable to Church and Poore that refuse or to my knowledge neglect to give an account of all their fyerhearthes.'
'Item, we have no stoves. George Adams, Constable.'

The monotonous repetition of this reassuring formula, in the Worcestershire examples at least, would lead one to suppose that the tax was received with equanimity. However, there are occasional examples which tell another story. Attached to the return for Clifton-on-Teme for 1662 is a tiny scrap of paper which reads:

'We have made a true and deligent search with 5 men at Mr George Caldwells and we found 14 hearths which is a true and just return by me. William Ambler, Constable.
Thos. Terry, Tythingman.'

Among the first names on the Clifton list we find:

'George Caldwell Gent. 2.'

but this figure has been heavily scratched out, and replaced by an emphatic 14. One wonders how Mr. Caldwell, Gent. explained away the existence of 12 fireplaces which he had never noticed in his own house. Whatever his excuse, he evidently maintained his position in a determined fashion, for on the reverse of the return is the usual Constable's certificate, with a very welcome difference:

'There are non that refuse to give an accompte of theyr fyerhearthes but only Mr Caldwell. Hee will pay but for tow.'

The returns, to be found in County Record Offices amongst the Quarter Sessions papers, are typical 17th-century parish officials' efforts, as far as legibility and form are concerned (see sections on Quarter Sessions papers and inventories). In other words they are liable to the same personal idiosyncracies of the writers, which may occasionally yield information which was never required by law. In some counties it may require a diligent search to unearth the returns. *County Records*, pp.28-31, tabulates (Section 6a) the earliest date of surviving Hearth Tax lists in County Record Offices. Where a local historian has difficulty in tracing returns at his County Record Office, the Public Record Office may be able to supply the deficiency from the Exchequer Duplicates. These membranes are, however, extremely bulky, and it may prove equally difficult to trace a particular parish, without a personal search, among the hundreds of returns for any one county. These duplicates are neater and more formal than the parish constables' returns to Quarter Sessions and are extremely legible. This then, is yet another village record which can take us directly, as it took the village constable, into the house of the 17th-century yeoman.

Plate XV
Exchequer Duplicate of Chaddesley Corbett Hearth Tax Return, 1666
(P.R.O. Exchequer K.R.E./179/260/5.) Actual size: 19 x 30.5cm

Chadsley corbet

Name		
Thomas Moore	02	burnt
Henry Dallway	01	
Gilbert Brooke	01	
Thomas Brooke	01	burnt
Francis Stott	02	
Elizabeth Iount wick	03	
Richard Lambe	02	
William Ellins	01	burnt
Thomas Rayhone	01	
John Hitchcocks	01	
Edward Price	01	
Humfrey Potter	02	
Mr Broxton it	06	
Oliver Gynings	01	
John Best	03	
Lady Mary Yate	25	
Mr Harrott	07	
John Brooke	01	
Mary Raybone	01	burnt
Valentine Lambe	07	
Widow Enjell	02	
John Baylies	01	
John Disoll	01	all 4 burnt
Willm Stainsfield	01	
Widow Heyles	01	
Will: Coote	01	
Humfrey Newnam	01	
Edward Jones	02	
Willm Newnam	05	
Thomas Braytocke	01	
Stephen Death	03	
Charles Webb	03	
John Taylor	04	
Willm Wright	02	
Griffin Hughes	01	
Thomas Taylor	02	

FURTHER READING

J.V. Beckett, 'Local Taxation in England from the Sixteenth Century to the Nineteenth Century', *The Local Historian*, 12, no.1, 1976

D. Foster, 'The Hearth Tax and Settlement Studies', *The Local Historian*, 11, no.7, 1975

J.S.W. Gibson, *The Hearth Tax and other Later Stuart Tax Lists and the Association Oath Lists*, Federation of Family History Societies, 2nd edition, 1996, gives a valuable introduction and lists of original assessments and returns, including counties and their separate towns.

J. Holwell, 'Hearth Tax Returns', *History*, no.49, 1964

J.F. Mitchell, 'Hearth Tax and Poll Tax', *Scottish Genealogist*, no.11, 1964

J. Patten, 'The Hearth Taxes, 1622-1689', *Local Population Studies*, no.7, 1972

R.S. Schofield, 'Estimates of Population Size: The Hearth Tax', *Local Population Studies*, no.1, 1968

J. Thirsk, 'Sources of Information on Population, 1500-1760', *Amateur Historian*, 4, nos.4 and 5, 1959

Various papers: *The Hearth Tax - Problems and Possibilities*, Institute of Hist.Research, 1983

COUNTY LIST OF HEARTH TAX RETURNS

(listed alphabetically by author within each county)

Bedfordshire   L.M. Marshall, *The Rural Population of Bedfordshire, 1671-1921*, BHRS, 16, 1934.

Berkshire   J.E. Little, *Hearth tax for the parishes of Uffington, Baulking, Woolstone, Kingston Lisle and Fawler, 1663*, Faringdon, 1968.

Caernarvonshire   Originals for 1662 at C.R.O.

Cambridgeshire   'Cambridge University and Borough Hearth Tax Assessments, 1662-74', *V.C.H.: Cambridgeshire*, III, 1959; Cunningham, 'Hearthe Tax for Cambridge, 1664 and 1674', *Camb. Ant. Soc.*, LXVIII, 1917; J. Hurst, 'Family History from records of property: Hearth tax', *JCFHS*, 2/5, 1980; and: 'Some Seventeenth century inhabitants of S. W. Cambridgeshire', *JCFHS*, 3/2, 1981; W.M. Palmer, *Cambridgeshire Subsidy Rolls, 1250-1695*, Norwich, 1912; E. Powell, 'Notes on the Hearth Taxes for Cambridge 1664 and 1674', *CAS*, xx, 1920; H.M. Spufford, 'The Significance of the Cambridge Hearth Tax', *CAS*, 55, 1961.

Carmarthenshire   Carmarthen Hearth Tax, 1670, *CASFC*, 8, 1911.

Cheshire   F.C. Beazley, *Chester Hearth Tax Returns, 1664-5*, 1906; M.N. Jackson, 'Hearth Tax Assessments of Lymm', *N. Ches. FHS.*, 5/2, 1978; G.O. Lawton, *Northwich Hundred: Poll Tax 1660 and Hearth*, LCRS, 119, 1979.

Cornwall   *Hearth Tax Roll for Parish of Constantine, 1664*, DCRS, 1910; B. Mayne and W.H. Shadwell, *Subsidy Rolls, Muster and hearth tax rolls and probate calendars of the parish of St Constantine (Kerrier), Cornwall*, Pubns. DCRS, IX, 1910; T.L. Stoate, *Direct Taxation in Cornwall in the reign of Charles II*, 1981.

Cumberland   J.V. Beckett, 'Local custom and the "New Taxation" in the seventeenth and eighteenth centuries: the example of Cumberland', *Northern History*, 12, 1976.

Denbighshire   W.A. Morris, 'Hearth Tax Assessment for Isaled Commote', *Hel Achau* (FHS Clwyd) 13, 1984.

Derbyshire   D.G. Edwards, *Derbyshire Hearth Tax Assessments, 1662-70*, Derbs. Rec. Soc., VII, 1982; R.E. Chester Waters (intro.), 'Marriage Tax, Melbourne 1695', *DANHSJ*, VII, 1885.

Devonshire   W.G. Hoskins, *Exeter in the seventeenth century: Tax and Rate assessments*, DCRS, n.s., 3, 1957; T.L. Stoate, *Devon Hearth Tax Returns, 1674*, 1982.

Dorset   C.A.F. Meekings, *Hearth Tax Returns, 1662-4*, DNHAS, 1951; F.J. Pope, *SDNQ*, V, 1897.

Dumfries and Galloway   D. Adamson, 'The Hearth Tax for Dumfriesshire', *Dumfriesshire and Galloway Natural History Soc.*, no.49, 1972.

Durham   'The Hearth Tax', *J. Northd. & Durham FHS*, 3/3, 1978.

Essex   Originals from 1662 (see *Guide to Essex Record Office*, Pt. I, 1946, pp.47-8); Analysis of Returns for Ongar Hundred, *V.C.H.: Essex*, IV, 1956.

Glamorgan   E. Parkinson, *Glamorgan Hearth Tax Assessment of 1670*, South Wales Record Society, 1994.

Gloucestershire   J.S.W. Gibson, 'The Hearth Tax in Bristol'; and: 'Bristol Tax Assessments in the later Stuart period (1660-1715)', *J. B. & Avon FHS*, 36 and 37, Summer and Autumn 1984; E. Ralph and M. Williams, *The Inhabitants of Bristol in 1696*, Bristol Records Soc., no.25, 1968; Photocopy of Gloucestershire Enrolment for 1671 is at C.R.O.

Hampshire   E. Hughes and P. White, *The Hampshire Hearth Tax Assessment of 1665 with the Southampton Assessments for 1662 and 1670*, Hampshire Records Series, 11, 1991.

Herefordshire   M.A. Faraday, *Hereford Militia Assessments of 1663*, Camden Soc. (fourth series), 10, 1972; and: *The Hearth Tax in Herefordshire*, Woolhope Naturalists' Field Club, no.41, 1973.

Isle of Wight   P.D.D. Russell, *Hearth Tax Returns for the Isle of Wight*, I.O.W. CRO, 1981.

Kent   'Archaeological Notes for Thanet', *AC*, XII, 1878; E.R. Green, *Hearth Tax Returns 1664 (Gravesend, Mitton, Northfleet and Southfleet)*, 1984; Originals for 1664-8 at C.R.O.

Lancashire   W.F. Irvine, 'Lancashire hearth taxes 1662', *HSLC*, LII, 1900 (1902); J. Tait, *Taxation in Salford Hundred, 1524-1802*, Chetham Soc., n.s., 83, 1924; G.J. Wilson, 'The Land Tax and West Derby Hundred, 1780-1831', *HSLC*, 129, 1979-80; Originals for Salford Hundred, 1664, at C.R.O.

Leicestershire   G.F. Farnham, 'The Hearth Tax of 1666', in *Leicestershire Medieval Village Notes*, 6 vols., 1920.

Lincolnshire   Typescript copy, with index of persons of Returns for parts of Kesteven 1677 and 1683, and Lincoln City Return of 1662 are in C.R.O.

London and Middlesex   K.J. Allison, *Ealing in the Seventeenth Century*, Ealing Loc. Hist. Soc., Members' Paper no.4, 1963; D.V. Glass (intro.), *London Inhabitants within the Walls 1695*, London Rec. Soc., II, 1966; G. Glazebrook, 'The Harrow Hearth Tax 1674', *Middx. & Herts. N. & Qs.*, XIV, 1898; P.E. Jones and R. Smith, *Guide to the Records at the Guildhall*, 1951; *London Rate Assessments and Inhabitants' Lists in Guildhall Library and the Corporation of London Record Office*, 1968; H.A. Randall, Hearth Tax for Staines 1664, *Staines Loc. Hist. J.*, 6, 1972; *A Supplement to the London Inhabitants' List of 1695*, Guildhall Studies in London History, II/2 and 3, 1976.

Merioneth   'The History of the Hearth Tax, 1662-88', *J. of Merioneth Hist. & Rec. Soc.*, Pt. I, 1953; O. Parry, *The Hearth Tax of 1662 in Merioneth*, Mer. Hist. & Rec. Soc., 2/1, 1953-6.

Middlesex   Originals from 1664 at C.R.O.

Norfolk   M.S. Frankel and P.J. Seaman, 'Norfolk Hearth Tax Assessments 1664', *Norf. Genealogy*, XV, 1983; P. Seaman, *The Norfolk Ancestor, II, parts 2, 3, 5, 6 and 9*, 1980-2; P. Seaman (ed.), *Norfolk Hearth Tax Assessment 1664*, Norfolk & Norwich Genealogical Society, 1983.

Northamptonshire   The Record Office holds microfilms of the Hearth Tax returns for the period 1662-1674, but the originals are in such poor condition that the films are difficult to read.

Northumberland   D.W. Smith, 'Northumberland Hearth Tax 1664', *J. Northd. & Durham FHS*, 8/3, 9/1, 2 and 4, 10/1, 1983-7; R. Wesford, 'Newcastle Householders in 1665; Assessment of Hearth Tax', *Arch. Aliana*, s. 3, 7, 1911.

Nottinghamshire   J. Potter Briscoe, 'Hearth Tax of 1674', in *Chapters of Nottingham History*, 1908; G. Marshall, *Nottinghamshire Subsidies 1895*, re-issued by W.F. Webster in *J. Notts. FHS*, Recs. Sers. 24, I and II, 1983; W.F. Webster, *Nottinghamshire Hearth Tax 1664-1674*, Thoroton Soc. Rec. Series, XXXVIII, 1988.

Oxfordshire   J. Geere, *An Index to the Oxfordshire Hearth Tax of 1665*, Oxfordshire Family History Society, 1985; H.E. Salter, *Hearth Tax for Oxford City, 1665*, Oxford Hist. Soc., 75, 1920; M.M.B. Weinstock, *Hearth Tax for Oxfordshire, 1665*, ORS, 21, 1940.

Pembrokeshire   'Pembrokeshire Hearths in 1670', *W. Wales Historical Records*, IX, 1923.

Rutland   J. Bourne and A. Goode, *The Rutland Hearth Tax*, Rutland Record Society, 1991.

Shropshire   J. Capewell, *The Late 17th Century Tax Lists of the Borough of Shrewsbury and its Liberties*, Shrops. FHS, 5/2, 1984; M. A. Faraday, 'The Ludlow Poll Tax Return of 1667 , *ShAS*, no.59, 1972; W. Watkins-Pitchford, *Hearth Tax Roll for 1672*, ShAS, 1949.

Somersetshire   E. Dwelly, 'Somerset Hearth Tax for 1664-5', in *National Records, I, Directory of Somerset*, 1916; R. Holworthy, *Hearth Tax for Somerset*, Dwelly's National Records, I, Fleet, Hampshire, 1916.

Staffordshire   A.H. Chatwin, 'Bushbury Hearth Tax 1665', in *Bushbury Parish and People*, 1983; R. Milner, 'Cheddleton Hearth Tax, 1666', in *Cheddleton, a village history*, Cheddleton Hist. & Arch. Soc., 1983; Staffs Rec. Soc. Collections for a History of Staffordshire, Wm. Salt Arch. Soc., 1921; 1923; 1925; 1927; 1936.

Suffolk   S. Colman, 'The Hearth Tax Returns for the Hundred of Blackbourne, 1662', *Suffolk Institute of Archaeological Procs.*, no.32, 1971; S.H.A. Hervey, 'Suffolk in 1674', *Suffolk Green Books*, no.11, 13, 1905.

Surrey   C.A.F. Meekings, *The Surrey Hearth Tax, 1664*, Surrey Rec. Soc., XVII, 1940; C. Webb, *Calendar of the Surrey Portion of the Free and Voluntary Present to Charles II, 1661-2*, W. Surrey FHS, Rec. Sers., 2, 1982.

Sussex   M.J. Burchall, *Sussex Hearth Tax Assessments 1662*, Suss. Gen. Centre., Occ. Papers 3 and 4, 1980; W.D. Cooper, 'Hearth Tax of Chichester 1670', *SAC*, 24, 1872.

Warwickshire   R.M. Lea, *The Quarters of Sutton: A List of the Householders of Sutton Coldfield, Warwickshire, 1663-74, based on the Hearth Tax returns*, University of Birmingham, Extra-Mural Studies, 1981; M. Walker, 'Hearth Tax Returns', *Warwicks County Records*, I, 1957. Originals from 1662 are at C.R.O.; D.B. Woodfield, 'Hearth Tax of Tysoe 1662 and 1671', in *The Parish Registers of Tysoe*, 1976.

Westmorland   E. Conder, 'Hearth Tax return 22 Chas II, Kendal Barony', *CWAAS*, n.s., 19, 1919; J.F. Curwen, *The Later Records relating to Westmorland*, 1932; W. Farrer and J.F. Curwen, 'Hearth Tax of Westmorland 1670', in *Records Relating to the Barony of Kendale*, vols.1 and 2, 1923 and 1924.

Wiltshire   C.D. Ramsay, *Two Seventeenth century Taxation lists*, Wilts. Archaeological and Natural History Soc. (Records Branch), 10, 1954.

Worcestershire   C.A.F. Meekings, S. Porter and I. Roy, *The Hearth Tax Collectors' Book for Worcester, 1678-80*, Worcs. Hist. Soc., n.s., II, 1983; Originals from 1662 at C.R.O., with contemporary MS. Index.

Yorkshire   J.A. Bottomley and D. Petyt, 'The Hearth Tax Returns of 1672 for the Wakefield Metropolitan District', *Wakefield Hist. J.*, 5, 1978; C. Clegg, 'Hearth and window taxes' (includes returns for Halifax and Southowram, 1664-5 and Halifax, 1666), *Halifax Antiq. Soc.*, 1913; R. Fieldhouse, 'The Hearth Tax and other Records' (Hearth Tax for Downholme and Walburn 1673), in *Group Projects in Local History* (ed. A. Rogers), 1977; G.C.F. Forster, 'York in the Seventeenth Century', in *VCH City of York*, 1961; J. Stansfield, 'Return of the HearthTax for the Wapentake of Skyrack 1672', Thoresby Soc., *Miscellanea*, 2, part III, 1891; J. Wardell, 'Hearth Tax of Leeds 1663', in *The Municipal History of the Borough of Leeds*, 1846.

ORIGINAL DOCUMENTS TO BE FOUND AT:

County Record Offices.
Public Record Office.

CHAPTER V

The Eighteenth and Nineteenth Centuries

✧

During the past two centuries the final phases of the development of the English countryside as we see it today have been recorded. In 1700 a structure based upon oligarchical complacency and *laissez-faire* was soon to be shattered by widespread industrial and social revolution. Political change continued gradually, to culminate in the supremacy of sovereign parliamentary government and a widening franchise. In English economic life, industrial and agrarian change was accomplished, at first by haphazard private arrangements, authorised, but barely supervised, by central authority. Thus the governing class of 18th-century England sought to effect their changes conservatively, and according to the tenets of self-interest and class-conscious compromise, tempered only rarely by philanthropy and humanitarianism. Nineteenth-century warfare and international rivalry, the demands of a reformed parliament, the needs of newly-enfranchised industrialist and artisans, even industrial prosperity itself, all created the need for a bureaucratic and utilitarian state. In this increasingly industrial and urban age, neither the autonomy of the parish, nor the vested interest of a single landed class could long survive. Intercourse between town and country, promoted by the demands of new urban industries and markets, was made possible by the intercommunication of new roads and railways. Parliamentary enclosures had already laid down the familiar pattern of the fields and hedges of our modern rural scene. More subtly achieved, but equally permanent, were the social changes. County councils, Non-conformist chapels, the board schools, newspapers, village post offices and railway stations, all these combined to isolate the squire, the vestry meeting, the rural craftsmen, the very village green, and make them anachronisms, remaining today only to remind us of a past society. Only the farmer remains, mechanised and commercial it is true, yet still closely in touch with the basic agrarian processes evolved by his medieval, Tudor and Hanoverian forefathers, perpetuating the true reason for the village's existence. Elsewhere, 19th-century village history is a record of mobility, standardisation, and conformity with national institutions and the urban way of life.

A few of the documents which record these changes are included in this chapter. They cannot attempt to do more than indicate and suggest the vastness of the field of documents which reveal our more recent past to the local historian.

ENCLOSURE AWARDS AND MAPS

THE DOCUMENTS

These documents record the local administration of the Parliamentary Enclosure movement which assisted the agrarian revolution of the late 18th and early 19th centuries. This great re-allocation of common land, which completed the pattern of the enclosed countryside familiar to us today, must not be confused with the 'ancient enclosures' of medieval and Tudor times. Enclosure was effected by a local committee of substantial men, authorised by Act of Parliament, who employed surveyors to divide and re-allocate the commons and heath-land remaining in the village, and, in such cases where these still survived, the open arable fields of the medieval 'three-field system'. Parishes which had been more gradually enclosed, by private arrangement over the course of several centuries, have therefore no awards, or, at most, reveal a redistribution of small remaining portions of commons and waste-land. Others may record the enclosure of a whole parish, with its open fields and commons; in a few fortunate cases the map may show the pre-enclosure state of the great open fields, still divided into 'strips', with each tenant's name entered. These documents are thus incomparable for the light which they may throw upon the extent and nature of enclosures in a county, and its progress down to the early 19th century. They 'constitute a topographical and economic record which can only be compared with Domesday Book in importance'.[1]

The awards are full of information about field names and boundaries, land use, extent of glebe lands, roads and foot-paths, and the endowments of local schools and charities; they also provide us with very full details of the farm units of individual families. They are some of the most reliable, and most easily accessible, local records, clearly legible, with fine large-scale maps. Two copies were required, both of which frequently survive, one in the custody of the enclosed parish, another at the County Record Office. 'They form the best—in many cases the only—source of accurate information as to the distribution of land ownership in the villages of a century and a half ago.'[2]

It is a common complaint from County Archivists that students too often request source material for 'a History of Enclosure' in their county. It must be remembered that the enclosure movement was a long and gradual process over many centuries, with three main periods of accelerated change. These occur in the 13th century, during a wide-spread agricultural boom period; in the 16th century, with increasing investment in sheep-farming; and from the 18th to the 19th centuries, with agricultural response to the growing demands of the new urban food-markets. The sources for the two earlier periods of enclosure are much more complex, and more difficult to seek out (but see the occasional slight references in the medieval court rolls and 17th-century Quarter Sessions papers given above). The 'assarts', 'purprestures' and 'encroachments' of medieval enclosure can only be studied from the printed records; the 16th-century documents are almost as complex; only the 18th-century enclosure awards and plans

---

Plate XVI
Final page of Enclosure Award of Chaddesley Corbett, 1799
(Worcs. Record Office. Ref: S. 652. BA. 528/I.) Actual size: 73.5 x 73.5cm

[1] Emmison and Gray, *County Records*, p. 12. See also p. 17.
[2] W.E. Tate, *The Parish Chest*, Ch. V, p. 269.

afford much real scope to the beginner. It would be reasonable to expect a student to make a study of one of these periods, *in a closely limited area*, but certainly no more.

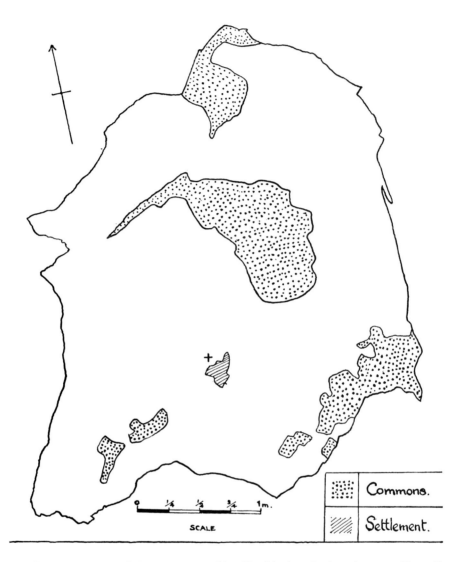

⣿⣿⣿	Commons.
▨▨▨	Settlement.

SCALE

Fig. 7. Map shewing extent of Common Land in Chaddesley Corbett in 1740. Data discovered by reference to a Throckmorton Estate Map (1745), and Enclosure Award (1799).

FURTHER READING

First read: R.C.Russell, 'Parliamentary enclosure and the documents for its study' in: Landscape and Documents, edited by A. Rogers and T. Rowley, National Council for Social Services, 1974

R.C.Allen, *Enclosure and the Yeoman*, Clarendon, 1992

M. Aurousseau, 'Neglected aspects of the enclosure movements', *Economic History Review*, 1, 1926

R. Burt and J.M. Archer, *Enclosure Acts, sexuality, property and culture in early modern England*, Ithaca-London-
    Cornell U.P., 1994
J. Chapman, 'The extent and nature of Parliamentary Enclosure', *Agricultural History Review* 35, 1987
and: 'Parliamentary enclosure, saviour of agriculture, destroyer of landscapes', *Geographic Magazine*, February
    1989
and: 'A guide to Parliamentary Enclosures in Wales', University of Wales Press, 1992
J.T. Coppock, 'Changes in Farm and Field Boundaries', *Amateur Historian*, 3, no.7, 1958
J. Field, *English Field Names, a Dictionary*, Alan Sutton, 1989
T. Bedford Franklin, 'Enclosures in the Nineteenth Century', *Amateur Historian*, 1, no.6, 1953
W.G. Hoskins, *The Medieval Peasant. Sample studies of process and consequences of enclosure*, 1957
E.M. Leonard, 'Inclosure of common fields in the seventeenth century', *R.Hist.Soc.*, n.s., 19, 1905
R. and N. Muir, *Hedgerows, their History and Wild Life*, Michael Joseph, 1987
F.W. Munslow, 'Field Names', *Amateur Historian*, 2, no.12, 1956
J.M. Neeson, *Commons, Common Rights, Enclosure and Social Change in England 1700-1820*, Cambridge University
    Press, 1996. This book is a 'social history of the smallest landholders and users of commons in the
    18th and 19th century English villages'.
F.A. Sharman, 'An introduction to Enclosure Acts', *Journal of Legal History*, 10, May 1989
G. Slater, 'The enclosure of common fields considered geographically', *Royal Geog. Soc. Journal*, 29, 1859
W.E. Tate, 'Opposition to Parliamentary Enclosure in eighteenth century England', *Agricultural History
    Review*, 19, 1945
G.H. Tupling, 'Searching the Parish Records, 6: Terriers, Tithe and Enclosure Awards', *Amateur Historian*,
    1, no.12, 1954
M. Turner, E*nclosure, its Historical Geography and Economic History*, 1980
J.R.Walton, 'On estimating the extent of parliamentary enclosure', *Agricultural History Review*, 38, 1990

ORIGINAL DOCUMENTS TO BE FOUND AT:

County Record Offices.

Individual parish chests.

As there were two copies, if both have survived, it may be that both are now deposited at C.R.O. On the other hand, one copy may well have strayed into private hands. (There are several Worcestershire strays, for example, in Birmingham Reference Library.)

HANDLISTS

See County List for counties which have produced a handlist of awards.

For the availability of originals in any County Record Office, see Emmison and Gray, *County Records*, App. II.

For Worcestershire awards and plans, see typescript handlist available at the County Record Office.

The Victoria County Histories record, in each parish survey, the date of the enclosure of its fields and commons.

WORCESTERSHIRE ENCLOSURE AWARDS AND PLANS

See W.E. Tate, *Worcestershire Enclosure Acts and Awards*, Worcs Arch. Soc., n.s., XXI, 1944.

A typical county list of enclosure awards to be found in the County Record Office is arranged below in chronological order. The information is taken from the typescript handlist supplied by the Record Office. Most of the awards have a map as well, except those marked *; one of them, Leigh, consists only of a map.

Blockley (Aston Magna)	*	1735	Abbots Morton	1803
Alderminster (War)	*	1736	Belbroughton	* 1803
Pershore (Holy Cross)	*	1762	Pershore (Drakes Broughton)	* 1803
Childswickham	*	1763	Lindridge	* 1803
Stone	*	1763	Little Comberton	* 1806
Pirton	*	1763	Queenhill	1807
Bretforton	*	1765	Wick	* 1807
Norton and Lenchwick	*	1766	Crowle	1808
Hill and Croome	*	1771	Broughton Hackett	1808
Naunton Beauchamp	*	1771	Aldington	1808
Redditch (Common, etc.)	*	1771	Holt	* 1810
Feckenham (Beanhall Fds.)	*	1771	Bredon	1811
Broadway		1771	Pershore	1812
Stoke Prior	*	1772	Rushock	1812
Throckmorton	*	1772	Holdfast	* 1812
Kemerton	*	1772	Tibberton	1813
Bentley Pauncefoot	*	1772	Sedgeberrow	1813
Hadzor	*	1773	Eckington	1813
Churchill (Hagley)	*	1774	Bromsgrove (Bonehill)	1813
Kings Norton	*	1774	Astley	1814
Birlingham		1774	Pebworth	1814
Defford	*	1775	Overbury	* 1815
Kidderminster (Foreign)		1775	Badsey	* 1815
Upton Snodsbury		1775	Bredon's Norton	1815
Bricklehampton	*	1775	Shipston-on-Stour	* 1815
Charlton	*	1775	Hallow	* 1816
Severn Stoke	*	1775	Strensham	1817
Cleeve Prior	*	1776	Salwarpe	1817
Leigh [Map only]		1776	Inkberrow	1818
Pinvin	*	1776	Flyford Flavell	1819
Evesham (Gt. and Little Hampton)	*	1777	Great Comberton	1820
Cow Honeybourne		1778	Abberley	1821
Wolverley		1778	Hartlebury	1821
Broome	*	1780	Lindridge	1823
Cropthorne	*	1780	Ombersley	1827
Himbleton	*	1780	North Piddle	1830
Grafton Flyford	*	1780	Lower Mitton	1830
Stourbridge (Old Swinford)	*	1782	Hagley	1831
Kington	*	1782	Cofton Hackett	1831
Dudley	*	1783	Feckenham	1832
Church Lench	*	1783	Hill and Moor	1833
Hanbury		1783	Norton-juxta-Kempsey	1840
Harvington (Evesham)	*	1787	Peopleton	1841
Lower Clent	*	1788	Wyre Piddle	1841
Fladbury		1789	Pendock	1843
Dormston	*	1791	Birtsmorton	1845
Bromsgrove (Chadwick)		1795	Castlemorton	1845
Evesham (Bengeworth)	*	1795	Eldersfield	1845
Bishampton	*	1797	Longdon	1845
Hanley Castle		1797	Bredicot	1846
Chaddesley Corbett	*	1799	Yardley (War)	1847
Bromsgrove Manor	*	1802	Areley Kings	1848

Welland	1852	Alfrick	1870
Norton-juxta-Kempsey	1854	Hanley	1871
Bromsgrove (Woodcote)	1855	Longdon Marshes	1872
Berrow	1860	Elmley Lovett	1874
Upton-on-Severn	1863	Elmbridge	1874
Eldersfield	1865	Clent Hill	1881
Tenbury	1868		

County Gazetteer of Enclosure Awards

The most complete summary of all enclosure awards will be found in: W.E. Tate, *Domesday of Enclosure Acts and Awards*, University of Reading, 1978. This book tabulates, county by county, for every village in which enclosure took place: the date of each Act, the name of the place, the area and acreage of the enclosure and the date of the Award. Tables are also divided into lists of places enclosed by private Act and those with arable enclosures. Tate's *Domesday* includes every county in the following gazetteer with the exceptions of Cardiganshire, Glamorgan and Montgomeryshire.

Because the process of Parliamentary enclosure was carried out by a long series of individual Acts of Parliament for each village, these 'private' or 'local' Acts can be found and identified by reference to reference library copies of: G. Bramwell, *Index to the Private Acts, 1727-1834*, 1835; T. Vardon, *Index to the Private Acts, 1798-1839*, 1840 and *Index to Local and Personal Acts, 1801-1949*, HMSO, 1949. Any local Act traced in any of these indexes can be found in full in the printed volumes of *Statutes at Large* (collected by regnal years and available in most large libraries).

As mentioned above, where a Victoria County History exists for a county, each parish history will usually give the date of its enclosure, if this was accomplished by Act of Parliament. Several counties have also published handlists of all the awards for the county, as follows:

Bedfordshire *Guide to the Bedfordshire Record Office*, Beds C.C., 1957 (contains a list of 100 parishes enclosed 1742-1891, giving the acreage affected); G.H. Fowler, *Four pre-enclosure village maps (strip-map of Oakley Reynes, 1795; Renhold, 1781; Apsley Guise, 1745-61; Eversholt, 1764; Houghton Regis, 1762*, Pubns. BHRS, Quarto memoirs, 2, 1936; A. Cassons, 'Early Enclosures in Beeston', *Thoroton Soc.*, 62, 1959.

Berkshire P. Walne, *A Catalogue of Inclosure Maps in the Berkshire Record Office*, 1954 (this is kept up-to-date in the C.R.O. card index); M. Dumbleton, *Easthampstead enclosure, 1827*, 1991; E.W. Dormer, 'The ancient common fields and common meadows of Earley', *Berks. Arch. Soc. J.*, 31, 1927; E.W. Dormer, 'A Berkshire enclosure by mutual consent (in the manor of Bulmershe) 1794', *Berks. Arch. Soc. J.*, 36, 1933.

Buckinghamshire W.E. Tate, *A Handlist of Buckinghamshire Enclosure Acts and Awards*, Bucks C.C., 1946; G. Eland, 'Inclosure of Drayton Parslow' (Minute Book of the Commissioners), *Records of Bucks*, XI, 1920-6; J.E. Davis, 'Eighteenth-Century Minute Book' (Enclosure Minutes for Hartwell and Stone, 1776-7; Weston Turville, 1798-1800), *Records of Bucks*, XV, 1947-52; M. and K. Morley, *The Great Upheaval. An account of the Enclosure of Wingrave and Rowsham in 1798, with a Field Map of both places in the early 19th century*, 1994, from 121 Winslow Road, Wingrave, Bucks., HP22 4QB; L. Rigby, *The History of Stoke common, 1810-22*, Stoke Poges, 1975; M.E. Turner, *Land Shortage as a Prelude to Parliamentary Enclosure: the example of Buckinghamshire*, University of Sheffield, 1975; and: 'Parliamentary Enclosure and Land Ownership Changes in Buckinghamshire', *Econ. Hist. Rev.*, no.28, 1975.

Cambridgeshire H. Rogers, *Bottisham Enclosed, 1801*, Staine Hundred Local Historical Society, 1992; W.M. Palmer, 'Enclosures at Ely, Downham and Littleport, 1548', *CHAS*, 5, 1937; J.M. Gray, 'Proposals for the Enclosure of Coldham Common in 1666 and 1667', *CAS*, 53, 1960; M. Spufford, *A Cambridgeshire*

Community (Chippenham) from settlement to enclosure, Leics. University Press, 1965.

Cheshire   P. Thompson, L. McKenna and J. Mackillop, *Ploughlands and pastures; agrarian history in four Cheshire townships (Peckforton, Haughton, Bunbury and Huxley)*, Libraries, Museums and County Planning Department, Cheshire Monographs, no.4, 1982; C.S. Davies, *The Agricultural History of Cheshire, 1750-1850*, Chetham Soc. and Manchester University Press, 1961; W. Hanson, 'Commons Enclosures in Lancashire and Cheshire in the eighteenth century', *LCAS*, 6, 1888.

Cumbria   R.L. Belhouse, 'The Aughertree Fell Enclosure', *CWAAS*, no.67, 1967; G.C. Elliott, 'The Enclosure of Aspatria', *CWAAS*, 60, 1960; and: 'The system of cultivation and evidence of enclosure in the Cumberland open fields in the sixteenth century', *CWAAS*, 59, 1960.

Derbyshire   J. Spavold, *At the sign of The Bull's Head* (a history of Hartshorne and its enclosure), South Derbyshire Local History Research Group, 1984; *Enclosure Maps in the Derbyshire Record Office*, Derbyshire County Council, 1992; Derbyshire Record Office, *Enclosure in Derbyshire: An Archive Teaching Unit*, Derbs. C.C., 1976; N. Kirkham, *The boundary of Sheldon*, Peakland Archaeological Soc. Bulletin, no.19, 1963.

Devonshire   H.S.A. Fox, 'The Chronology of Enclosure and Economic Development in medieval Devon', *Econ. Hist. Rev.*, no.28, 1975.

Dorset   G.B. Endicott, 'The Progress of Enclosures in Dorset in the 18th and part of the 19th Centuries', typescript thesis at C.R.O. Oxford, n.d.; Enclosure Records are listed in A.C. Cox, *Index to the Dorset County Records*, 1938; B. Kerr, 'Dorset Field names and the Agricultural Revolution', *DNHAS*, 1967.

Durham   T. Westgarth, *Washington Common Enclosures, 1762-3*, Northern notes, IV, 1974.

Dyfed   A.E. Davies, 'Enclosures in Cardiganshire', *Ceredigion*, no.8, 1976.

Essex   F.G. Emmison, *Catalogue of Maps in Essex Record Office; First Supplement*, Essex C.C., 1952; P. Thompson, 'The Willingales of Loughton; to whom do we owe Epping Forest?', *Essex Field Club, Essex Naturalist*, 21, 1915; M. Deacon, *Great Chesterford; A common-field parish in Essex,* 1984; W. Chapman Walker, 'Essex field names', *EAS*, n.s., 5, 5-10, 1895-1906.

Glamorgan   T. Jones, 'An interesting eighteenth century document (enclosed lands belonging to the borough of Aberfan in 1788)', *Aberfan & Margam District Hist. Soc.*, 2, 1929.

Gloucestershire   W.E. Tate, *Gloucestershire Enclosure Acts and Awards*, BGAS, LXIV, 1943; See also, MS. Index of Awards, from 1727, at the C.R.O.; E.C. Scobell, 'Common fields at Upton St Leonard's and the recent enclosure of 1897', *Cotteswold Nats. Field Club*, 13, 1899; B. Smith and E. Ralph, 'Gloucestershire Farmers' (refers to enclosure of Aston Blank, with maps), in *A History of Bristol and Gloucestershire*, Phillimore, 1996; E.M. Chifford, 'An Enclosure on Crickley Hill', *BGAS*, no.83, 1964; C. Erlington, 'Open Fields and Enclosures in the Cotswolds', *Cotteswold Naturalists' Field Club*, no.34, 1962-3; J.H.S. Johnson and B.S. Smith, *Inclosure in Gloucestershire, 1735-1886*, Glos. Record Office, 1976.

Hampshire   J.E.H. Spaul: *Enclosure Award for Andover, 1785*, Andover Local History Committee, 1970.

Herefordshire   M. Tonkin, 'The Wigmore Enclosure Act and Award 1810-1828', *Woolhope Nat. Field Club*, 1984; J. and M. West, 'The enclosure of the (Herefordshire) Fields', (gives distribution map of enclosures and Enclosure Map of Ullingswick, 1856), in *A History of Herefordshire*, Phillimore, 1985; W.K. Parker, 'Opposition to Parliamentary enclosure in Herefordshire 1793-1815', *Woolhope Nats. Field Club*, 44, I, 1982; W.E. Tate, 'A Handlist of Herefordshire Enclosure Acts and Awards', *Woolhope Nats. Field Club*, 30, 1941; C. Watkins, 'The Parliamentary enclosure of Much Marcle', *Woolhope Nats. Field Club*, 43, III, 1981.

Hertfordshire   W.E. Tate, 'A Handlist of Hertfordshire Enclosure Acts and Awards', Part 16 of 'A Handlist of English Enclosure Acts and Awards', *EHAS*, XII, Part I, 1946; C.W. Cook, 'The Cheshunt inclosure award, 1804', *EHAS*, 2, 1902.

Huntingdonshire   G.H. Findlay, *Guide to the Huntingdonshire Record Office*, Hunts. C.C., 1958.

Kent   W.E. Tate, 'A Handlist of English Enclosure Acts and Awards', Part 17, 'Kent', *AC*, 56, 1943; A.M. Everitt, 'The making of the agrarian landscape of Kent', *AC*, 92, 1976; A.R.H. Baker, 'Some fields and farms in mid-Kent', *AC*, 80, 1965; and: 'The Field System of an east-Kent parish (Deal)', *AC*, 78, 1963.

Lancashire   W.E. Tate, *Handlist of Lancashire Enclosure Acts and Awards*, Lancs C.C., 1946; R. Sharpe France, *Handlist of Acts of Parliament relating to Lancashire*, Lancs C.C. Record Publication no.3, 1950; A.P. Coney, 'Aughton Enclosure in the 18th and 19th century; the struggle for superiority', *HSLC*, 136, 1986; A. Harris, 'A note on common fields in N. Lancashire', *HSLC*, 119, 1967; I. Leach, 'The Wavertree enclosure act, 1768', *HSLC*, 83, 1932; H. Wicklan, *Worsley in the eighteenth century; a study of* *a Lancashire landscape*, 1984; T.W. Fletcher, 'The Agrarian Revolution in arable Lancashire', *LCAS*, 72, 1962; See also: *Cheshire*.

Leicestershire   See *VCH: Leicestershire*, II, App. II, O.U.P., 1954; M.W. Beresford, 'The Minute Book of a Leicestershire enclosure', *LeAS*, 23, II, 1947; and: 'Glebe terriers and open fields in Leicestershire', *LeAS*, 24, 1948; H.G. Hunt, 'The Chronology of Parliamentary Enclosures in Leicestershire', *Econ. Hist. Rev.*, 10, no.2, 1960; T.H. Worth, *The Anstey Enclosures, 1761*, Anstey, 1978.

Lincolnshire   *The Enclosures of Barton-on-Humber (1793-6) and Hibaldstow, 1796-1803*, Barton W.E.A., 1962; E. Gillett, R.C.Russell and E. Trevitt, *The Enclosures of Scartho 1795-1798 and Grimsby 1827-1840*, Grimsby Public Libraries and Museum, 1970; R.C.Russell, *The Enclosures of Market Rasen 1779-1781 and of Wrawby cum Brigg 1800-1805*, Market Rasen WEA, 1969; and: *The Enclosures of Scawby 1770-1771, Kirton in Lindsey 1793-1801, and Hibaldstow 1796- 1803*, Barton on Humber WEA, 1970; and: 'The enclosures of Bottesford and Yaddlethorpe 1794-1797, Messingham 1798-1804 and Ashby 1801-09', *Journal of Scunthorpe Museum Society*, 1, no.1, 1964; and: *Revolution in North Thoresby: the Enclosure of the parish by Act of Parliament, 1836-46*, North Thoresby, W.E.A., 1976; and: 'Parliamentary enclosure and the documents for its study', *Landscape and Documents*, edited by A. Rogers and T. Rowley, National Council for Social Services, 1974, has references, maps, costs etc. for: Barnetby le Wold (1766-1768), Barrow on Humber (1797-1803), Fulstow (1801), Goxhill (1773-1775), Hibaldstow (1796-1803), Kirmington (1777-78), Kirton Lindsey (1793-1801), Louth (1801), North Kelsey (1795), North Thoresby (1801), Scotter (1705), Scunthorpe and Frodingham (1812), Tetney (1779), Ulceby (1801) and Wrawby cum Brigg (1800-1805); E. and R. Russell, *Parliamentary Enclosure and New Lincolnshire Landscapes*, Lincolnshire County Council Record Series, 1987; and: *Old and New Landscapes in the Howcastle Area*, Lincolnshire County Council, Lincolnshire History series no.7, 1985; H. Buckle, *The Agricultural Revolution in Humberside*, Humberside College of Higher Education, 1986; D.R. Mills, 'Enclosure in Kesteven', *Amateur Historian*, 7, no.2, 1959; S.A. Johnson, *Some aspects of Enclosure and changing agricultural landscapes in Lindsey, from the sixteenth to the nineteenth centuries*, Lincs. Architectural and Archaeological Soc. Report, no.9, 1962; D.R. Mills, 'Enclosure in Kesteven', *Agricultural History Review*, no.7, 1959.

London & Middlesex   J. Hardy, 'Enclosure Awards for Middlesex and Herts', *Middlesex and Herts Notes and Queries*, 1, 1895; W.E. Tate, 'Enclosure Acts and Awards of the County of Middlesex', *LMAS*, n.s., 9, 1948; L.E. Morris, 'The Enclosure of the Ruislip Commons, 1769 and 1804', *J. Ruislip Nat. Hist. Soc.*, no.1, 1951; P. Carter, 'Poor relief strategies—women, children and enclosure in Hanwell 1780-1816', *The Local Historian*, 25, no.3, August 1995; N. Trimble, *Sunbury Enclosure 1800*, Sunbury and Shepperton Local History Society, 1989; B. Hammond, 'Two towns' enclosures (Sheffield and Lambeth, late 18th and early 19th centuries)', *Econ. Hist.*, 2, 1933; M. Baptist, 'Eighteenth Century maps and estate plans of Bromley, Beckenham and Penge', *AC*, 81, 1967; D.O. Pam, *The fight for common rights in Enfield and Edmonton, 1400-1600*, Edmonton Hundred Historical Soc. occasional papers, n.s., no.27, 1974.

Monmouthshire   There are only 12 awards for Monmouth. None of these has been published, all but one can be seen at the C.R.O.

Montgomeryshire   I.E. Jones, *The Arwystli Enclosures 1816-1828*, University of Birmingham Department of Geography, Occasional Paper no.18, 1985; E.G. Bowen, 'Map of the Trehelig common fields', *Powys-Land Club Colls.*, 41, 1930; 'The manors of Street Marshal, Tyr y mynech and Deytheur enclosure act, 1788', *Powys-Land Club Colls.*, 34, 1907; W.T. Rees Price, *Enclosure and field patterns in the Banwy valley*, Montgomeryshire Collections, no.57, 1961; J.G. Thomas, *Distribution of commons in part of Arwystli at the time of enclosure*, Montgomeryshire Collections, no.54, 1957.

Northamptonshire   The CRO has a card index of enclosures … arranged by parishes, which contains references not only to awards and plans but also to other associated documents; W.E. Tate, 'The Inclosure Movement in Northamptonshire', *Northants Past and Present*, I, no.2, Northants Record Soc. Pub., 1949; J.W. Anscomb, 'Parliamentary enclosure in Northamptonshire, processes and procedures', *Northamptonshire Past & Present*, 7, 1988/9; and: 'An eighteenth century inclosure and football-play at West Haddon', *Northants. Past and Present*, no.4, 1968-9; J.R. Lowerson, 'Enclosure and farm holdings in Brackley, 1829-1851', *Northants. Past and Present*, no.3, 1978; S. Ranson, 'Finedon Enclosures, 1804-8', *Northants. Past and Present*, no.6, 1965-6.

Northumberland   R.A. Butlin, 'Enclosure and improvement in Northumberland in the sixteenth century', *Archaeologia Aeliana*, 45, 1967; G.W. Ridley, 'Enclosure and division of certain wastes and commons in the manor of Hexham', *Archaeologia Aeliana*, 11, 1974.

Nottinghamshire   W.E. Tate, *Parliamentary Land Enclosures in the County of Nottingham, 1743-1868*, TSRS, V, 1935; and: *Parliamentary Enclosure in Nottinghamshire*, Thoroton Society, 1935; and: 'The eighteenth century enclosures of the townships of Bonington St Michael's and Sutton St Anne's', *Thoroton Soc.*, 34, 1931; P. Lyth, *Farms and fields of Southwell; a study of enclosures*, Un. Notts. Centre for Local History, 1984; M.I. Thomis, 'The Politics of the Nottingham Enclosure', *Thoroton Soc. Trans.*, no.71, 1967.

Oxfordshire   P. Vinogradoff, 'An illustration of the continuity of the open field system', reprinted as 'By-laws of an Oxfordshire manor (Great Tew)', *Quarterly Journ. Econ.*, 22, 1907; G.N. Clark, *Open Fields and Inclosure at Marston*, Oxford, 1924; W.E. Tate, 'Members of Parliament and their personal relations to enclosures, a study with particular reference to Oxfordshire enclosures, 1757-1843', *Agr. Hist.*, 23, published by the Agr. Hist. Soc. of Chicago, 1949; W.E. Tate, 'Oxfordshire enclosure commissioners, 1737-1856', *Journ. Mod. Hist.*, 23, II, 1951; A. Ballard, 'Notes on the open fields of Oxfordshire', *Rept. OAS*, 1908; A. Ballard, 'The management of open fields (in Chipping Norton and Steeple Aston)', *Rept. OAS*, 1913; J.L.G. Mowat, *Sixteen old maps of properties in Oxfordshire (with one in Berkshire) ... illustrating the open-field system*, Oxford, 1888; C.E. Prior, 'Charlton-on-Otmoor open fields', *OAS*, 51, 1907; A. Ballard, 'The open fields of Fritwell', *Rept. OAS*, 1907; B. Reaney, *The Class Structure in nineteenth century Oxfordshire: Otmoor, 1830-35*, Ruskin College, Oxford: History Workshop pamphlets, no.3, 1970; A. Lambert, 'The agriculture of Oxfordshire at the end of the eighteenth century', *Agricultural History Review*, no.29, 1955.

Rutland   W.E. Tate, *Domesday of English Enclosure Acts and Awards*, University of Reading, 1978, pp.221-2.

Shropshire   W.E. Tate, 'The Enclosure Movement in Shropshire', *ShAS*, LII, 1947-8; *Commissioners' Awards for Inclosing Lands, 1773-1891*, list published by Shrops C.C.; Consult Index to A.W. Ward, *Shropshire Records*, Shrops C.C., 1952, for reference to all originals held at C.R.O.; G.C. Baugh (ed.), 'A History of Shropshire, IV: Agriculture', *Victoria County History of Shropshire*, O.U.P. for the Institute of Historical Research; M.C. Hill, 'The demesne and the waste; a study of medieval enclosure in the manor of High Ercall, 1086-1399', *ShAS*, 62, 1980.

Somerset   W.E. Tate, *Somerset Enclosure Acts and Awards*, SANHS, 1948.

Staffordshire   H.R. Thomas, *The Enclosure of Open Fields and Commons in Staffordshire*, Staffs Rec. Soc. (Wm. Salt Arch. Soc.), 3rd Ser., 1933; W.E. Tate, *A Handlist of English Enclosure Acts and Awards: Staffordshire*, Staffs Rec. Soc., 1942; R.E. Hebden, 'The development of the settlement pattern and farming in the Shenstone area, prior to the general enclosure movement', *Lich. & S. Staffs. Arch. & Nat. Hist. Soc.*, 3, 1961-2; *VCH*, VI, contains articles on agriculture, with particular reference to enclosures, O.U.P., 1979; E.M. Yates, 'Enclosure and the rise of grassland and farming in Staffordshire', *North Staffs. Journal of Field Studies*, no.14, 1974.

Suffolk   W.E. Tate, *Handlist of Suffolk Enclosure Acts and Awards*, offprints from *Suff. Inst. Arch.*, XXV, Pt. 3, 1951; R. Downing, 'The field-names of some Suffolk parishes', *The Local Historian*, 17, no.5, February 1987; The Bury St. Edmunds and West Suffolk Record Office holds a card-index to all known West Suffolk enclosure awards, maps and related papers.

Surrey   W.E. Tate, *Handlist of Enclosure Awards, Surrey*, SAS, XLVIII, 1943; J.G.W. Lewarne, 'Fetcham Enclosure Award, 1813', *Leatherhead and District Local History Soc.*, no.3, 1967.

Sussex   W.E. Tate, *Handlist of Sussex Inclosure Acts and Awards*, Sussex C.C. & Sussex Arch. Soc., 1950; C.H. Goodman, *Tarring inclosure award, 1811*, Worthing Arch. Soc., 8th Annual Report, 1930; J. Chapman, 'The unofficial enclosure proceedings: a study of the Horsham, Sussex enclosure 1812-13', *SAC*, 120, 1982; and: 'The Parliamentary Enclosures of West Sussex', *Southern History*, no.2, 1980; and: 'Land purchases at enclosure; evidence from West Sussex', *The Local Historian*, 12, no.7, 1977.

Wales   J. Chapman, 'The late Parliamentary enclosures of South Wales', *Agricultural History Review*, 39, 1991.

Warwickshire   J.M. Martin, 'The small landowners and parliamentary enclosure in Warwickshire', *Econ. Hist. Rev.*, 32, 1979; M.W. Beresford, 'The economic individualism of Sutton Coldfield', *BAS*, 64, 1941-2; W.E. Tate, 'Enclosure Acts and Awards relating to Warwickshire', *BAS*, 64, 1941-2; B. Walker, 'Local enclosures', *Birm. & Midland Inst.* (Birm. Arch. Soc.), 41, 1915; A. Gooder, *Plague and Enclosure: a Warwickshire village (Clifton Dunsmore) in the seventeenth century*, Historical Association, Coventry and N. Warwickshire History Pamphlets, no.2, 1965; J.M. Martin, 'The cost of Parliamentary enclosure in Warwickshire', *University of Birmingham Historical Journal*, no.9, 1964; and: 'The Parliamentary Enclosure movement and rural society in Warwickshire', *Agricultural History Review*, no.15, 1967.

Westmorland   W.E. Tate, *Domesday of English Enclosure Acts and Awards*, University of Reading, 1978, pp.264-9.

Wiltshire   W.E. Tate, 'A Handlist of Wiltshire Enclosure Acts and Awards', *Wilts Arch. Soc. Magazine*, LI, 1947; See also Historical MSS. Commission Report no.55, 1, 1901-14, for list of all Enclosure Awards before 1800; J.R. Ellis, 'Parliamentary enclosure in Wiltshire by Public General Acts', *Wilts. Arch. Mag.*, no.72, III, 1980; J.R. Ellis, 'The Parliamentary enclosures of Aldbourne, Wilts.', *Archaeological Soc. Magazine*, no.68, 1973; R.E. Sandell, *Abstracts of Wiltshire Enclosure Awards and Agreements*, Wilts. Record Society, 25, 1971.

Worcestershire   W.E. Tate, *Domesday of English Enclosure Acts and Awards*, University of Reading, 1978, pp.279-84.

Yorkshire   R.A. Bellingham, 'Mr. Powell's Enclosure Award (of Pocklington 1759) and the computer', *The Local Historian*, 25, no.2, May 1995; H. Buckle, *The Agricultural Revolution in Humberside*, Humberside College of Higher Education, 1986; B. English, *Yorkshire Enclosure Awards*, University of Hull, 1985; J. Crowther, *Enclosure Commissioners and Surveyors of the East Riding*, East Yorkshire Local History Society, 1986; B. Hammond, 'Two towns' enclosures (Sheffield and Lambeth, late 18th and early 19th centuries)', *Econ. Hist. (Econ. Journal)*, 2, 1933; Enclosure Awards for the East Riding, the North Riding, the West Riding and Ainsty of York are tabulated in: W.E. Tate, *Domesday of English Enclosure Acts and Awards*, University of Reading, 1978, pp.285-320; M. Harvey, 'Regular fields and tenurial arrangements in Holderness, Yorkshire', *J. Hist. Geog.*, 6, 1, 1980; B. Loughborough, 'An account of a Yorkshire enclosure Staxton, 1803', *Agricultural History Review*, no.13, 1965; B.A. English, *A Handlist of West Riding Enclosure Awards*, National Register of Archives, W. Riding (Northern section) Committee, 1965; North Yorkshire County Record Office publishes *Guide No.2: Parish registers, census returns, land tax assessments, tithe apportionments and enclosure awards in the record office*; also *Guide No.4: Enclosure awards in the record office (a detailed list)*.

LAND TAX AND TITHE RECORDS

THE DOCUMENTS

Land Tax Assessments. Land tax takes its place, with poll taxes and tithes, as one of the notoriously unpopular historic English taxes. It was first levied in 1692, on freehold and leasehold as well as on offices and other property, including shops, carriages, waggons and servants. It was later confined entirely to land, as so varied an assessment proved too difficult to maintain. Throughout the 18th century the rate of tax fluctuated between 1s. and 4s. in the pound, based upon the annual value, not the acreage, of land, but in 1798 the tax was fixed 'perpetually' at a rate of 4s. in the pound. Provision was made for landowners to redeem their annual tax with a lump sum which 'exonerated' them from further payments. Land Tax assessments assumed a further, political importance in 1779, when they were used as the record of qualification to vote in parliamentary elections; they continued to be so used, until the Reform Act of 1832 provided for a separate register of electors. Returns of the total valuation of a parish's lands were made by local assessors, who were nominated by special Commissioners appointed for the purpose, usually the Justices of the Peace acting as *ex officio* Commissioners. A copy of the assessment was displayed on the church door, to give an opportunity for appeal; these copies will occasionally be found in the parish chest. The amended assessment was sent to the Clerk of the Peace who enrolled it for electoral purposes; these copies found their way into the Quarter Sessions papers, though later returns have usually been filed separately.

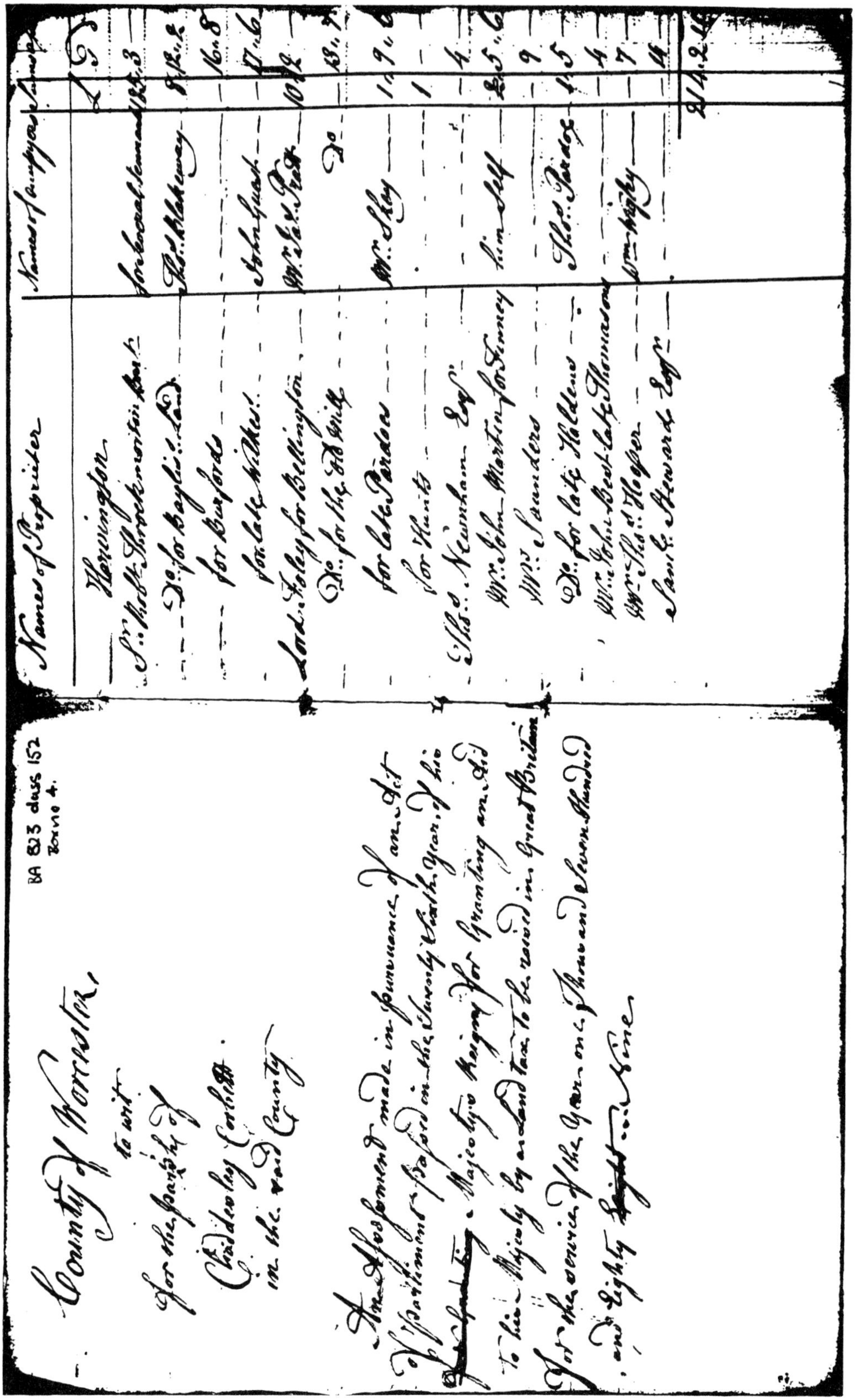
County of Worcester, to wit

for the Parish of Chaddesley Corbett in the said County

An Assessment made in pursuance of an Act of Parliament passed in the Twenty Sixth Year of his present Majesty's Reign for granting an aid to his Majesty by a Land tax to be raised in Great Britain for the service of the Year one thousand seven hundred and Eighty Nine

Names of Proprietor	Names of Occupiers	Sums Assessed £ s d
Harvington		
Sir Robt. Throckmorton Bart.	For several tenants	183.3
Do. for Bayliss Land	Thos. Blakeway	8.12.8
for Burfords		16.8
for late Wilkes	John Guest	17.6
Lord Foley for Bellington	Wm. [illegible]	10.2
Do. for the Smith	Do.	13.7
for late Pardoes	Wm. Skey	1.9.6
for Hunts		1
Thos. Newnham Esqr.		4
Mr. John Martin for Finney	Himself	25.6
Mrs. Saunders		9
Do. for late Holdens	Thos. Pardoe	1.5
Mr. John Best late Thomasons		4
Mrs. Thos. Hooper	Com. Highy	7
Saml. Steward Esqr.		11
		214.2

Fig. 8. Chaddesley Corbett Land Tax Assessment, 1789.

Each parish was assessed to produce a certain total quota of tax; the rate which would provide the quota from the village's assessment was fixed by the local assessors. Thus a parish's quota tended to remain fixed, in spite of considerable changes in real value over periods of years. The machinery of 1798 was amended by Lloyd George, in his 1909 Budget, and down to 1949 each parish produced its quota of Land Tax by means of a rate which was not to be less than 1d., and not to exceed 1s. in the pound. In practice this meant that the richer parishes produced an annual surplus, even at the minimum rate, and this fund could be paid in exoneration of all further tax. Land Tax was not levied from agricultural land alone, but could be demanded from owners of houses which had been built on land previously assessed. The Finance Act of 1949 stabilised the rates and valuations on the basis of those paid for 1948-9, with a further provision that all Land Tax must henceforth be compulsorily redeemed at the death of the owner or on transfer of land by sale; the rate of redemption was fixed at 25 times the land's annual charge. Thus Land Tax became a diminishing return and was finally abolished in 1963. Revenue raised in 1958-9 was £245,519 for the United Kingdom as a whole; local Land Tax Commissioners were still appointed and their powers were considerable; but assessment and supervision were increasingly supervised by H.M. Inspectors of Taxes. Since 1963 farmers are liable like other landlords, for Property Tax, Schedule A, but this levied on rents received, not on main property. They are, in fact, now taxed as the rest of the nation is taxed and—possibly—have no further historic ground for complaint.

A box of Land Tax assessments taken from the shelves of a county's Archives, where they will usually be grouped in separate consecutive years, will contain a mass of returns, parish by parish. These will usually be written on separate sheets of paper, varying in size from small scraps to foolscap size and larger, folded neatly, with the parish's name on the outside; some parishes provided a small exercise book for the purpose. Often the returns have been entered into a ledger, one for each hundred, the parishes arranged alphabetically, and the landowners' names also entered in alphabetical order in ruled columns, with a printed heading for each return, citing the Act of Parliament. The local assessors' returns are headed, e.g. 'An assessment made the 2nd day of May, 1781 by William Bowkett and Thos. Andres, assessors of the Land Tax of the parish of Hanley William in the county of Worcestershire, for raising a sum of £35 12s. upon the said parish for the said year'. There follows a list of names of landowners, occupiers of their land, rateable value, and amount assessed. In some cases the name of the property is mentioned, and occasionally its use, as 'garden', 'cherry orchard', 'cottage and close', 'tithe', 'Black Swan', 'mills', 'house and stalls', etc. Sometimes 'sums exonerated' are entered in a separate column from 'sums not exonerated'. The larger parishes' returns are usually sub-divided into quarters, or yields.

So widespread and continuous were the Land Tax assessments for every parish, that they are an essential document for supplying detailed information about the ownership and occupation of land during the 19th century. They should certainly be used to supplement the information given in the records of enclosure and tithe. Their very continuity is extremely important, as is their almost complete coverage of parishes over the whole country.

A list of dates from which the Land Tax assessments continue in each County Record Office is tabulated in *County Records* (Section 6*b*, pp. 28-31).

Tithe Awards and Plans. From A.D. 787 (King Offa) compulsory tithes (one-tenth of all produce) were exacted from the laity by the Church. Tithes were of three kinds, 'predial' (on agricultural crops), 'mixed' (on the increase of farm stock), and 'personal' (from mills and fisheries, etc.). The Reformation saw the transfer of a large proportion of this revenue into the hands of lay rectors, although the greater part remained in the hands of local parish clergy. Continued secular resistance to tithes, and obstruction of their payment, came to a head during the agrarian revolution of the 18th and 19th centuries, as farmers' improvements and investment in their land and its stock continually involved them in increased tithe commitments. In some districts, payments of a money rent from titheable lands had already been substituted for the more inconvenient payments in kind. Parliamentary enclosure, too, had more recently offered a solution to the problem, by allocating a parcel of enclosed land to the tithe-owner in full settlement of the landowners' obligations.

From 1836 to 1860 the basis of tithe payment was changed. The Tithe Commutation Act of 1836 and subsequent amending Acts resulted in the appointment of three Tithe Commissioners to review rates of payment in thousands of parishes and townships all over England and Wales. Landowners were invited to come to a voluntary agreement with their tithe-owners, substituting a new rent charge for payments in kind or other ancient dues; this charge was to be based upon an annual assessment, index-linked to agricultural prices. If no agreement could be reached at local meetings a compulsory award would be imposed; some disputes continued into the 1880s. The parish or township was surveyed and mapped to show tithable areas and landowners' commitments were tabulated in a manuscript apportionment or award. Tithe files at the PRO also contain much useful information on regional agricultural methods and production.

Three copies of each tithe map and apportionment were made; the maps vary in scale from three to 12 chains to the inch, the majority being drawn to 3-6 chains, otherwise the documents are almost identical in format. Commissioners' copies are those now housed at the PRO amongst Inland Revenue (IR) papers; the set which is sometimes referred to as the Bishop's copies were sent to the County Record or Diocesan Record Offices and parish copies should also have found their way from the parish chest to the county Record Office which may, as at Worcester, be identical with the diocesan archives. The first two sets will usually be more complete than lists of surviving parish copies, so that searchers should not be put off by initial failure to find a local award in only one repository. Some CROs, as at Worcester, may have obtained microfilm sets of the Commissioners' copies from the PRO to complete their parish collection. The PRO cannot be expected to check their indexes on the searcher's behalf, research must be carried out in person. County Record Offices are usually more accessible.

These documents are thus available for thousands of parishes, comprising a record of 19th-century agricultural life which is of the utmost importance, comparable in extent with more recent land-use surveys. The large-scale maps show the fields of the parish, numbered for easy reference to a great companion Schedule and Index. The latter is usually ruled in

---

Plate XVII. Portion of Tithe Map, Chaddesley Corbett, 1839
Actual size (full page): 138 x 152.5cm. Scale: 6 chains : 1 in. (a chain was 22 yards)
Actual size of extract: 23 x 26.5cm. Scale: 9 ins. : 1 mile
(Worcs. Record Office Ref: S. 760/178. BA. 1572.)

columns, which specify, for each numbered field, its owner, occupier, field-name and description (whether arable, meadow, wood, pasture or premises), its state of cultivation, and its exact acreage. These entries are arranged, owner by owner, each complete, wherever his fields lie in the parish. A preliminary Schedule states the whole area of the parish, and the total subject to tithes, divided into total areas of arable, meadow, pasture and woodland. The land-use column also classifies each field as either arable, meadow, pasture or woodland, also including houses, out-houses, workshops, shops, gardens and orchards. As a record preserving the field names alone, the survey is invaluable; the land-use data provides a comprehensive statement of the state of 19th-century agriculture.

Tithes were a lively topic of conversation with modern farmers in 1962. A Chaddesley farmer recalls how, as a boy in Herefordshire, he attended a meeting of the Tithe Payers' Association. This body, substantially, though not entirely, backed by Nonconformist opposition to Church of England taxes, was raised in the eastern counties, but in 1930 bade fair to set the Marches alight, with a banner bearing the following medieval legend:

'Lord, save us from this craving priest,
Who steals our crops and seize our beast.'

A Tithe Act of 1936 cancelled all future charges by payment of lump sums or annuities to be paid over 60 years. Thus, tithes finally expired in 1996.

A Catalogue of County Tithe Awards and Plans

The most comprehensive new resource available to help students search this field is now Roger J.P. Kain and Richard R. Oliver's *The Tithe Maps of England and Wales (A cartographic analysis and county-by-county catalogue)*, C.U.P., 1995 at £135.00, available on inter-library loan, as very few local libraries or archives will have bought this expensive book. This massive catalogue of 14,678 tithe districts in 55 English and Welsh counties refers to the Public Record Office's classification of tithe apportionment (PRO IR 29) and of tithe maps (PRO IR 30). Each county's tithe districts are listed numerically-alphabetically with reference to a county map (3-13 mile: 1 inch) which shows districts by number but not by name. County Record Offices will supply a county map of named ancient parishes to match this outline. Kain and Oliver's map identifies (shaded) tithable and (blank) tithe-free districts but large un-tithed areas, as for example in Huntingdon, Leicestershire and Northamptonshire, do not show individual parish boundaries.

Each county survey begins with a concise statement of the number of tithe districts and their total acreage, the number and acreage of tithe commutations, and their division into voluntary agreements and compulsory tithe awards. This is followed by a brief introduction to the nature and progress of commutation within the county. Names of local tithe agents, map-makers, assistant commissioners and valuers are tabulated.

Entries in the main catalogue identify each tithe district by its PRO county and district numbers (eg. 32/207 is Tettenhall in Staffordshire), the name of the tithe district as parish or township and a six-figure National Grid map reference to its centre. Information in each entry includes: date of apportionment and acreage covered, scale of the tithe map as chains to the inch, the map-maker's name and address, where known, and a brief description of the main agrarian features of the district. Special mention is made of any important agricultural, topographical or industrial features. These include communications, such as turnpike roads, canals, railways and ferries, industrial brick kilns, factories, mills, stone pits, quarries, forges and furnaces, and the occasional castle, folly or tumulus. Reference is sometimes made to pre-enclosure boundaries and field names or survival of un-enclosed fields. Details of decorative or colourful embellishment are also mentioned.

This catalogue is an incomparable source of reference, best used first to confirm the existence and basic details of a village's tithe award. Once these are verified, it is advisable to check the local diocesan and county archives to discover the whereabouts of any copy which is nearer to home. If this cannot be found, we can fall back on the more complete PRO collection. It should also be borne in mind, as the Worcestershire list (below) shows, that 19th-century county boundaries may have changed, necessitating a search for borderline parishes in neighbouring counties. If the searcher seeks a particular house or fields the first attempts may also be confounded by a similar change in the ancient parish boundary.

WORCESTERSHIRE TITHE AWARDS AND PLANS

Kain and Oliver's *Catalogue* for Worcestershire (PRO IR29 and IR30 39/1-153) lists 208 tithe districts, extending over 478,528 acres. From 1837 (Hagley) to 1841 (Cutsdean) 153 tithe commutations are listed for the county, of which 82 were voluntary agreements and 71 were compulsory tithe awards. Only 54 districts were entirely subject to tithe, many more landowners were tithe-free by virtue of earlier enclosure arrangements and other exemption. The Worcestershire list comprises the county as it was in the 1840s; awards for parishes which were then in neighbouring counties are entered elsewhere. The record of land-use for the county is said to be 'poor' and industrial workings are recorded in only seven per cent of the county's maps; these include quarries, forges, brine pits, chemical and brickworks and mills for spinning, paper manufacture and snuff making; on some maps canals are mapped in detail. Unusual details include a police station at Bredicote, a maypole at Kings Norton, a folly at Orleton and a ferryman's picture at Offerton.

The County Record Office keeps an accessions handbook or *List of Worcestershire Tithe Apportionments and Plans* which are available there. This records full details of accession numbers and identifies Parish and Diocesan copies; both sets survive for many parishes. The *List* includes several districts which were taken in from neighbouring counties after 1836. These will be found in Kain and Oliver's *Catalogue* under Shropshire (29), mostly townships like Romsley and Lapal in Halesowen; in Staffordshire (32), Gloucestershire (13), Herefordshire (14) and Warwickshire (36), as well as a few which have reverted to bordering counties, especially Gloucestershire and the West Midlands, as a result of later boundary changes. The CRO also keeps an *Inventory (Acc.10603)* of almost all the county's apportionments and plans which have been obtained from the PRO on microfilm. These are kept at the Record Office at Shire Hall, on the outskirts of Worcester; originals are held in the more ancient St Helens repository in the city. Thus, for many Worcestershire parishes, three copies of apportionments and plans exist, including the Public Record Office microfilms. The following up-to-date list of Worcestershire tithe apportionments and plans correlates the availability of these records, locally and nationally. Note that the following list refers only to Apportionments and Plans; the

CRO *List* also includes 'associated papers' concerned with tithes, including some papers for villages with no Awards or Plans.

The entry for each place (a parish unless otherwise described) is numbered as in the PRO *Catalogue*. This reference number is followed by initial letters which indicate the CRO's holdings of microfilm (M), Diocesan copies (D) and/or Parish copies (P). Entries (*in brackets*) indicate parishes where tithe commutation had been arranged with enclosure. A very few anomalies will be found (for example at Pensax), where the PRO appear to omit an entry and a few more where no microfilm copy is available at the CRO. At least one type of copy can be found in every case, as follows:

PRO	CRO	Name of tithe district
39/1	M D P	Abberley
39/2	M D	Abberton
39/3	M D P	Abbots Lench (hamlet in parish of Fladbury, now in Church Lench
Enc		(*Abbots Morton*)
39/4	M	Acton Beauchamp
39/5	M	Alderminster, now in Warwickshire
Enc		(*Aldington*)
39/6	M D P	Alfrick (hamlet in parish of Suckley)
39/7	M D P	Alvechurch
-	P	Amblecote (now in Stourbridge, West Midlands)
39/9	M D	Areley Kings (or Kings Areley, in Stourport-on-Severn)
39/10	M D	Astley (Ashton-under-Hill)
39/11	M	Aston (hamlet in parish of Blockley, now in Gloucestershire; Diocesan AP has been transferred to Gloucester Diocesan Registry)
39/12	M D P	Atch Lench (hamlet in parish of Church Lench)
Enc		(*Badsey*)
Enc		(*Bayton*)
39/14	M D P	Belbroughton (or Bellbroughton)
Enc		(*Bengeworth, see Evesham*)
39/15	M D P	Beoley
39/16	M	Berrington (township in parish of Tenbury, now in Salop.)
39/17	M	Berrow
39/18	M D P	Bewdley (hamlet in parish of Ribbesford)
39/19	M D P	Birlingham (township in parish of Nafford)
39/20	M D	Birtsmorton
Enc		(*Bishampton*)
39/21	M	Blockley (hamlet in parish of Blockley now in Gloucestershire Diocesan AP has been transferred to Gloucester Diocesan Registry)
39/22	M	Bockleton (mostly in Herefordshire, H&W)
39/23	M D P	Bredicot (or Bredicote)
Enc		(*Bredon*)
Enc		(*Bredon's Norton*)
Enc		(*Bretforton*)
Enc		(*Bricklehampton*)
39/24	M D P	Broadwas
Enc		(*Broadway*)
39/25	M D P	Bromsgrove
29/54	D P	Broome
Enc		(*Broughton Hackett*)
Enc		(*Bushley*)
-	D	Cakemore (township in the parish of Halesowen, West Midlands)

39/26	M D P	Castlemorton
39/27	M	Chaceley, now in Gloucestershire; Diocesan AP has been transferred to Gloucester Diocesan Registry
39/28	M D P	Chaddesley Corbett
Enc		(*Charlton*)
Enc		(*Childs Wickham*)
Enc		(*Churchill, near Worcester*)
39/29	M D	Church Honeybourne (or Honeybourne)
39/30	M D P	Church Lench (township in parish of Church Lench)
39/31	M D P	Churchill and Blakedown
39/32	M D P	Claines (see North Claines)
Enc		(*Cleeve Prior*)
32/67	M D	Clent (*also Enc*)
39/33	M D P	Clifton-upon-Teme
39/34	M D P	Cofton (or Coston) Hackett
-	M D P	Comberton (see Kidderminster)
39/35	M D	Cotheridge
Enc		(*Cow Honeybourne*)
39/36	M D	Cradley (township in parish of Halesowen, West Midlands)
39/37	M D	Croome D'Abitot
39/38	M D	Cropthorne
Enc		(*Crowle*)
39/39	M	Cutsdean (or Cutsden; hamlet in parish of Bredon now in Gloucestershire; Diocesan AP has been transferred to Gloucester Diocesan Registry)
39/40	M	Daylesford (now in Gloucestershire; Diocesan AP has been transferred to the Bodleian Library in Oxford)
37/41	M D P	Defford (chapelry in parish of Pershore)
39/42	M	Ditchford (hamlet in parish of Blockley now in Gloucestershire; Diocesan AP has been transferred to Gloucester Diocesan Registry)
39/43	M D	Doddenham (or Dodenham)
39/44	M D	Dodderhill
Enc		(*Dormston*)
39/45	M	Dorn (hamlet in parish of Blockley now in Gloucestershire; Diocesan AP has been transferred to Gloucester Diocesan Registry)
39/46	M D P	Doverdale (P) in Ombersley
29/110	D	Dowles (see Bewdley)
39/47	M D P	Droitwich (St Andrew parish)
39/48	M D P	Droitwich (St Nicholas parish)
39/49	M D P	Droitwich (St Peter parish)
Enc		(*Dudley*) *now West Midlands*
39/50	M D P	Earls Croome
39/51	M D P	Eastham
Enc		(*Eckington*)
39/52	M	Edvin (or Edwin) Loach, now in Herefordshire
39/53	M D P	Eldersfield
39/54	M D	Elmbridge (chapelry in parish of Dodderhill)
39/55	M D P	Elmley Castle
39/56	M D P	Elmley Lovet (or Lovett)
39/57	M	Evenlode (now in Gloucestershire; Diocesan AP has been transferred to Gloucester Diocesan Registry)
-	P	Evesham: Bengeworth (Enc); Hampton (P); St Lawrence (P)
39/58	M D	Feckenham (see Redditch)
Enc		(*Fladbury*)
Enc		(*Flyford Flavell*)

39/75	M D P	Foreign of Kidderminster (see Hurcott and Comberton)
39/136	M	Foreign of Tenbury (township in parish of Tenbury)
39/59	M D	Frankley
Enc		(*Grafton Flyford*)
Enc		(*Grafton Manor*)
Enc		(*Great Comberton*)
39/149	M D	Great Witley
39/60	M D P	Grimley, with Holt (*also Enc*)
Enc		(*Hadsor or Hadzor*)
39/61	M D	Hagley
29/140	D	Halesowen: now in West Midlands (see also: Cakemore, Cradley, Hasbury, Hawne, Hill, Illey, Lapal, Oldbury, Ridgacre, Warley Salop and Warley Wigorn)
39/62	M D P	Hallow
39/63	M D	Hampton Lovet (or Lovett) (*also Enc*)
39/64	M D P	Hanbury
Enc		(*Hanley Castle*)
39/65	M D	Hanley Child (chapelry in parish of Eastham)
39/66	M D P	Hanley William
39/67	M D P	Hartlebury (fragile, see photocopy f926.382)
Enc		(*Harvington*)
29/148	D	Hasbury (township in the parish of Halesowen, West Midlands)
29/151	D	Hawne (township in the parish of Halesowen, West Midlands)
29/158	D	Hill (or The Hill)
Enc		(*Hill and Moor*)
39/68	M D P	Hill Croome
39/69	M D	Hillhampton (hamlet in parish of Martley)
Enc		(*Himbleton*)
39/70	M D	Hindlip
13/108	D P	Hinton-on-the-Green
Enc		(*Holdfast*)
39/71	M D	Holt (with Little Witley; parochial chapelry)
29/172	D P	Hunnington
39/72	M D P	Hurcott and Comberton (part of Kidderminster Foreign parish)
29/174	D	Illey (township in the parish of Halesowen)
39/73	M D P	Inkberrow
36/82	D	Ipsley (see Redditch)
39/74	M D P	Kempsey
39/75	M D P	Kidderminster Borough (D P), Hurcott and Comberton (D P)
39/80	M D P	Kidderminster, lands west of R. Stour
39/76	M	Kings Norton, now in Birmingham
39/77	M D	Kington
-	D P	Knighton-on-Teme (hamlet in parish of Lindridge; includes (P) plan of Pensax
39/78	M D P	Knightwick
39/79	M D	Kyre Wyard (or Kyre)
19/158	D	Lapal (or Lapall) township in the parish of Halesowen, West Midlands
39/81	M D P	Leigh (fragile)
39/82	M D P	Lindridge (includes (P) plan of Pensax)
Enc		(*Little Comberton*)
39/89	M D	Little Malvern
Enc		(*Littleton, North and Middle*)
39/84	M D	Longdon
39/94	M D	Lower Mitton (hamlet in parish of Kidderminster/Stourport-on-Severn

39/117	M D	Lower Sapey (or Sapey Pitchard)
39/85	M D P	Lulsley (hamlet in parish of Suckley)
39/86	M D	Lutley (or Luttley) township in the parish of Halesowen, West Midlands
Enc		(*Lye and Wollascote, see Stourbridge, West Midlands*)
39/87	M D	Madresfield
39/88	M D P	Malvern (Great Malvern except Newland)
39/90	M D P	Mamble
39/91	M D P	Martin Hussingtree
39/92	M D	Martley (except Hillhampton)
39/93	M	Mathon, now in Herefordshire H&W; AP has been transferred to Hereford
Enc		(*Naunton Beauchamp*)
39/95	M	Newbold-upon-Stour
39/96	M D	Newland (hamlet in parish of Great Malvern)
39/32	M D P	North Claines
39/97	M	Northfield, now in Birmingham
Enc		(*North Piddle*)
39/98	M	Northwick (hamlet in parish of Blockley; now in Gloucestershire; Diocesan AP has been transferred to Gloucester Diocesan Registry)
9/99	M D	Norton and Lenchwick
39/100	M D P	Norton juxta Kempsey
39/101	M D P	Oddingley
39/102	M D	Offenham
39/103	M	Old berrow/Oldborough, now in Warwickshire
29/242	D	Oldbury (township in the parish of Halesowen, West Midlands)
Enc		(*Old Swinford in Stourbridge, West Midlands*)
39/104	M D P	Ombersley
39/105	M	Orleton (hamlet in parish of Eastham; see Stanford with Orleton)
Enc		(*Overbury*)
Enc		(*Pebworth*)
39/106	M D	Pedmore (now in Stourbridge, West Midlands)
39/107	M D PL	Pendock (including plan of Berrow)
-	D P	Pensax (hamlet in the parish of Lindridge)
39/108	M D P	Peopleton
39/8 M	M D P	Pershore (St Andrew chapelry)
39/109	M D	Pershore (Holy Cross parish)
Enc		(*Pinvin*)
39/111	M D	Pirton
39/112	M D P	Powick
Enc		(*Queenhill*)
39/113	M	Redmarley D'Abitot, now in Gloucestershire; Diocesan AP has been transferred to Gloucester Diocesan Registry)
39/114	M D	Ribbesford
29/267	D P	Ridgacre (township in the parish of Halesowen, West Midlands)
Enc		(*Ripple*)
14/183	D	Rochford
39/115	M D P	Rock
29/271	D P	Romsley (township in the parish of Halesowen, West Midlands)
Enc		(*Rous Lench*)
39/116	M D	Rushock
39/13	M D	St John in Bedwardine (in Worcester city)
Enc		(*Salwarpe*)
Enc		(*Sedgberrow or Sedgeberrow*)
39/118	M D	Severn Stoke
39/119	M D P	Shelsley Beauchamp
39/120	M	Shelsley Walsh
39/121	M D P	Sheriffs Lench (hamlet in parish of Church Lench)

39/122	M	Shipston-upon-Stour, now in Warwickshire
39/123	M D P	Shrawley
39/83	M D	South Littleton
39/124	M D	Spetchley
39/125	M D	Stanford (Stanford on Teme and Stanford with Orleton)
39/126	M	Staunton, now in Gloucestershire; Diocesan AP has been transferred to Gloucester Diocesan Registry)
39/127	M D	Stock and Bradley (Bradley Green; chapelry in parish of Fladbury)
39/128	M D	Stockton-on-Teme or Stockton
39/129	M D P	Stoke Prior
39/130	M D	Stone
39/131	M D	Stoulton
Enc		(*Strensham*)
39/132	M D P	Suckley (except Alfrick and Lulsley)
39/133	M	Sutton (hamlet in parish of Tenbury)
39/134	M D P	Tardebigge (or Tardebigg; hamlet in Tutnall and Cobley, with Webheath in Redditch)
39/135	M	Tenbury (township: Tenbury Wells)
Enc		(*Throckmorton*)
Enc		(*Tibberton*)
39/137	M	Tidmington, now in Warwickshire
39/138	M	Tredington, now in Warwickshire
32/9	D P	Upper Arley
39/140	M D P	Upton Snodsbury
39/139	M D P	Upton-upon-Severn
39/141	M D P	Upton Warren
29/242	D	Warley Salop (township in the parish of Halesowen, see Oldbury)
39/142	M D	Warley Wigorn (township in parish of Halesowen, see Oldbury)
39/143	M D	Warndon
39/144	M D P	Welland (except land in dispute with Little Malvern)
39/145	M D P	White Ladies Aston
39/146	M D P	Whittington (chapelry in parish of St Peter the Great, Worcester)
39/147	M D P	Wichenford
Enc		(*Wick*)
39/148	M D	Wickhamford
39/150	M D P	Wolverley (parts in Wolverley and Cookley)
39/151	M D P	Worcester (St Clement's parish)
39/13	M D	Worcester (St John in Bedwardine)
39/152	M D	Worcester (St Martin parish)
39/153	M D	Worcester (St Peter the Great, County parish)
39/110	M D	Wyre Piddle (hamlet in parish of Fladbury)
Enc		(*Yardley*) now in West Midlands

TITHE COMMUTATION IN CHADDESLEY CORBETT

'39/28 Chaddesley Corbett (parish) SO892750

Apt. 17.07.1839 3914a (5914) Map 1838 6 chains litho (Standige) foot bridleway, waterbodies, wood, building names, road names, school, vicarage, Catholic chapel, mills, spinning mills, forge' (Kain and Oliver, *op.cit.*, p.566).

The data below are abstracted from this Tithe Award. Names in block capitals are landowners; names in small print the occupiers. **A**: arable; **P**: pasture; **W**: woodland; **H B G**: house, buildings, gardens; **Sh**: shop. Numbered fields are arranged consecutively; in the Awards they are arranged under landowners, wherever they lie, making search for a particular field more difficult. Those marked with an asterisk will be found on the illustrated page of the Award (Plate XVIII).

Description of the Fields and Tenements Shown in the Portion of Chaddesley Corbett's Tithe Map as Illustrated in Plate XVIII

*1.	REV. G.H. PIERCY (OLD GLEBE)	Rev. G.H. Piercy	Churchyard	-
2.	SIR CHARLES THROCKMORTON	James Blakeway	Orchard	A
3.	SIR CHARLES THROCKMORTON	James Blakeway	H B G	-
4.	SIR CHARLES THROCKMORTON	James Blakeway	'Dial Park'	P
5.	TRUSTEES CHADDESLEY CHARITY	Trustees	School House	-
6.	THOMAS COLLIS	Thomas Depper	Bell Inn and Yard	-
7.	CORPORATION OF WARWICK	Daniel Perry	H Sh G	-
8.	CORPORATION OF WARWICK	John Bough	H G	-
8a.	CORPORATION OF WARWICK	Samuel Potter	Sh	-
9.	CORPORATION OF WARWICK	John Broad	H G	-
10.	CORPORATION OF WARWICK	William Jackson	H G	-
11.	CORPORATION OF WARWICK	Elizabeth Bate	G	-
12.	CORPORATION OF WARWICK	Thomas Bate	H B G	-
13.	CORPORATION OF WARWICK	Thomas Bate	'The Paddock'	A
14.	JAMES BLAKEWAY	John Stringer		
		William Taylor	2 Cottages. Gs.	-
15.	WILLIAM PERRINS	George Drew	G	-
16.	CORPORATION OF WARWICK	Thomas Bate	Workhouse Piece	P
17.	REV. G.H. PIERCY	Samuel Bough		
		Sarah Tutsall		
		John Lowe		
		James Yates	4 Hs & Gs	-
18.	CHARLES BLAKEWAY	Thomas Chance		
		Thomas Potter		
		John Gubbs		
		Charles Tongue	4 Hs & Gs	-
19.	CHARLES BLAKEWAY	George Drew	H G	-
20.	SAMUEL GILES	Richard Gold		
		John Manus	2 Hs & Gs	-
21.	ELIZABETH BATE	Herself	Malthouse	-
		Samuel Potter	H G	-
22.	ANN POOL	Richard Gold		
		Elizabeth Wright		
		Samuel Payliss		
		Thomas Humphries	4 Hs & Gs	-
23.	ANN POOL	Herself		
		Thomas Taylor	2 Hs & Gs	-
24.	ANN POOL	Void	H G	-
25.	CORPORATION OF WARWICK	Thomas Pope	H G	-
25a.	CORPORATION OF WARWICK	Mary Foxhall	H G	-
25b.	CORPORATION OF WARWICK	William Walker	H	-
25e.	CORPORATION OF WARWICK	William Depper	H G	-
25f.	CORPORATION OF WARWICK	John Brook	H G	-
25c.	REV. G.H. PIERCY	John Wigley	H G	-

No. 4.—London : Printed and Published by Authority by G. ROUTLEDGE, 11. Ryder's Court, Leicester Square.

LANDOWNERS	OCCUPIERS	Numbers referring to the Plan	NAME AND DESCRIPTION of LANDS AND PREMISES	STATE of CULTIVATION	QUANTITIES in STATUTE MEASURE			Amount of Rent-Charge apportioned upon the several Lands, and Payable to the Impropriator.			REMARKS
					a.	r.	p.	£	s.	d.	
			Brought forward		22	3	14				
Percy, The Reverend George Henry, (In Old Gate) (Continued)	James Hathaway (Continued)	44	Pit Close	Arable	8	2	24				Tithe Free
		46	The Nine Acres	Arable	8	3	16				
		64	The Five Acres	Arable	5	.	1				
		67	Pea Moor	Arable	6	2	24				
					52	.	11				
Percy, Reverend George Henry	Himself	1	Church Yard	Pasture	1	3	1				
		29	Vicarage House and Yards		1	.	31				
		113	The Space Meadow	Pasture	4	.	21				
					7	.	13				
	George Durant	35	House and Garden		1	3	.				
	John Broad	35a	Garden		.	2	23				
	Elizabeth Bate	154	Pool Meadow	Pasture	3	2	32				
		156	Homestead		1	1	14		1	6	
		157	Barn Close	Arable	3	1	30		13	6	
		163	Three Cornered Field	Arable	2	1	36		18	6	
		169	The Four Acres	Arable	3	1	31				
		184	Upper Meadow	Pasture	2	.	1				
		196	Sandy Bank piece	Arable	6	2	2	1	14	.	
		198	Brier Hill Field	Arable	3	3	5	1	1	.	
					25	.	14	5	4	6	
	Thomas Darby	155	House and Garden		.	1	25				
	Thomas Wills	291	The Quarry Field	Arable	7	2	32	1	13	6	
	John Higgs	319	Pick Field	Arable	8	.	9		16	6	
		321	Church Lane	Arable	3	.	16		13	6	
		324	Haywood Field	Arable	3	2	10				

25d.	MOSES WILLIAMS	Edward Jackson	H G	-
25g.	ELIZABETH WILLIAMS	Mary Jackson	'Talbot Inn', Yard, G	-
25h.	WILLIAM PERRINS	Sarah Evans	H G	-
25hh.	WILLIAM PERRINS	Thomas Depper	Malthouse & Yard	-
26.	SIR CHARLES THROCKMORTON	Samuel Hodgkiss		
		John Richards	2 Hs & Gs	-
27.	TRUSTEES CHADDESLEY CHARITY	Daniel Walters		
		Moses Perks	2 Hs & Gs	-
28.	SIR CHARLES THROCKMORTON	Theresa Emery	H G	-
28a.	TRUSTEES CHADDESLEY CHARITY	Hannah Crane		
		Jas Steadman	3 Hs & Gs	
		Thos. Tombs		
28b.	SIR CHARLES THROCKMORTON	Esther Maiden		
		Edward Heath	3 Hs & Gs	-
		John Steadman	3 Hs & Gs	
28c.	SIR CHARLES THROCKMORTON	Joseph Cartwright	H	-
28d.	CORPORATION OF WARWICK	Joseph Cartwright	G	-
*29.	REV. G.H. PIERCY	Himself	Vicarage, Ho. G	-
30.	CORPORATION OF WARWICK	Ann Mary Hill	Rickyard	-
31.	CORPORATION OF WARWICK	Ann Mary Hill	Orchard	P
32.	CORPORATION OF WARWICK	Ann Mary Hill	Barn & Yard	-
33.	SIR CHARLES THROCKMORTON	Ann Mary Hill	H G B	-
34.	REV. G.H. PIERCY (OLD GLEBE)	Ann Mary Hill	'Little Fd.'	A
*35.	REV. G.H. PIERCY (OLD GLEBE)	George Durrant	H G	-
*35a.	REV. G.H. PIERCY (OLD GLEBE)	John Broad	G	-
36.	REV. G.H. PIERCY (OLD GLEBE)	James Blakeway	'Big Field'	A
37.	CHARLES BLAKEWAY	Himself	'Weavers Close'	P
38.	REV. G.H. PIERCY (OLD GLEBE)	James Blakeway	'The Two Acres'	A
39.	REV. G.H. PIERCY (OLD GLEBE)	James Blakeway	Barn, Rickyard	-
40.	REV. G.H. PIERCY (OLD GLEBE)	James Blakeway	'Ten Acres'	A
41.	REV. G.H. PIERCY (OLD GLEBE)	James Blakeway	'Vicarage Meadow'	P
42.	REV. G.H. PIERCY (OLD GLEBE)	James Blakeway	'Rough Meadow'	W
43.	REV. G.H. PIERCY (OLD GLEBE)	James Blakeway	'Four Acres'	A
*44.	REV. G.H. PIERCY (OLD GLEBE)	James Blakeway	'Pit Close'	A
45.	REV. G.H. PIERCY (OLD GLEBE)	Ann Mary Hill	'Four Acres'	A
46.	REV. G.H. PIERCY (OLD GLEBE)	Ann Mary Hill	'Five Acres'	A
47.	REV. G.H. PIERCY (OLD GLEBE)	Ann Mary Hill	'Upper Square Meadow'	A
*48.	REV. G.H. PIERCY (OLD GLEBE)	Himself	'Square Meadow'	P
49.	SIR CHARLES THROCKMORTON	Ann Mary Hill	'Seven Acres'	A
50.	SIR CHARLES THROCKMORTON	Ann Mary Hill	'Old Grove'	P
51.	SIR CHARLES THROCKMORTON	Ann Mary Hill	'Horse Croft'	P
52.	REV. G.H. PIERCY	Himself	'Hughes Croft'	P
53.	WILLIAM NEWEY	John Wright	H G	-
54.	WILLIAM NEWEY	Sarah Purcell		
		Thomas Highley		
		Matthew Merriman		

Plate XVIII. Page from Chaddesley Corbett Tithe Award, 1839
Actual size (full page): 56 x 48cm. Actual size of extract: 56 x 31.75cm
(Worcs. Record Office Ref: S. 760/178. BA. 1572.)

		George Butcher		
		William Merriman	6 Hs & Gs	-
55.	SIR CHARLES THROCKMORTON	Ann Mary Hill	'Jolly's Pit'	P
56.	SIR CHARLES THROCKMORTON	Ann Mary Hill	'Horse Croft Meadow'	P
57.	SIR CHARLES THROCKMORTON	Ann Mary Hill	'The Old Rye Grass'	A
58.	SIR CHARLES THROCKMORTON	Ann Mary Hill	'The Long Hill'	A
59.	SIR CHARLES THROCKMORTON	Ann Mary Hill	'Blakeway Pieces'	A
60.	SIR CHARLES THROCKMORTON	Ann Mary Hill	'The Little Hill'	A
61.	SIR CHARLES THROCKMORTON	Ann Mary Hill	'Pit Close'	A
62.	SIR CHARLES THROCKMORTON	Ann Mary Hill	'Underhill Meadow'	P
63.	SIR CHARLES THROCKMORTON	Ann Mary Hill	'Six Acres'	P
64.	SIR CHARLES THROCKMORTON	Ann Mary Hill	'Lower Ox Leasow'	A
*65.	REV. G.H. PIERCY	James Blakeway	'Nine Acres'	A
*66.	REV. G.H. PIERCY	James Blakeway	'Five Acres'	A
*67.	REV. G.H. PIERCY	James Blakeway	'Pew Moor'	A
68.	JOHN PAGE	John Turner	'Chaddesley Meadow'	P
69.	JOHN PAGE	John Turner	'Lane Croft'	A
70.	SIR CHARLES THROCKMORTON	John Nicholls	'Lane Croft'	A
71.	JOHN PAGE	John Turner	'Long Lands'	A
72.	JOHN PAGE	John Turner	'Smooth Leasow'	A
73.	SIR CHARLES THROCKMORTON	Ann Mary Hill	'Mannings Close'	A
74.	SIR CHARLES THROCKMORTON	Ann Mary Hill	'Upper Ox Leasow'	A
75.	SIR CHARLES THROCKMORTON	Ann Mary Hill	'Lower Wheat Field'	A
76.	SIR CHARLES THROCKMORTON	Ann Mary Hill	'Upper Wheat Field'	A
77.	SIR CHARLES THROCKMORTON	Ann Mary Hill	'Tagbourne Meadow'	P
78.	SIR CHARLES THROCKMORTON	Ann Mary Hill	Tagbourne Barn & Cottage	-
79.	SIR CHARLES THROCKMORTON	Ann Mary Hill	'Big Tagbourne'	A
80.	SIR CHARLES THROCKMORTON	Himself	'Tagbourne Coppice'	W
81.	.SIR CHARLES THROCKMORTON	Henry Ludlow	Garden	-
82.	SIR CHARLES THROCKMORTON	Henry Ludlow	Garden	-
83.	SIR CHARLES THROCKMORTON	Ann Mary Hill	'Outwood Meadow'	P
84.	SIR CHARLES THROCKMORTON	Ann Mary Hill	'Little Meadow'	P
85.	SIR CHARLES THROCKMORTON	Ann Mary Hill	'Outwood Piece'	A
86.	SIR CHARLES THROCKMORTON	Henry Ludlow	House & Garden	-
87.	THOMAS BAKER	Himself	Garden	-
88.	REV. THOMAS NEWPORT	Mary Gabb	'Pleck'	A
89.	SIR CHARLES THROCKMORTON	Himself	'Bayliss's Close'	A
90.	SIR CHARLES THROCKMORTON	Francis Lilley	'Roundabout'	P
91.	SIR CHARLES THROCKMORTON	William Jackson		
		Thomas Bate	Pool	-
92.	SIR CHARLES THROCKMORTON	Francis Lilley	Orchard	P
93.	SIR CHARLES THROCKMORTON	Thomas Richardson	House & Garden	-
94.	SIR CHARLES THROCKMORTON	Francis Lilley	Orchard	P
95.	REV. THOMAS NEWPORT	Mary Gabb	'Part of Marley's Piece'	A
96.	REV. THOMAS NEWPORT	Mary Gabb	'Chaddesley Meadow'	P
97.	REV. THOMAS NEWPORT	Mary Gabb	'Little Gain'	A
98.	SIR CHARLES THROCKMORTON	Himself	'Chaddesley Woods'	W
99.	SIR CHARLES THROCKMORTON	Himself	'Stanery Hill Coppice'	W
100.	SIR CHARLES THROCKMORTON	William Ingram	'Pleck'	P
101.	SIR CHARLES THROCKMORTON	Himself	'Coppice'	W
102.	SIR CHARLES THROCKMORTON	Thomas Hemming	House & Garden	-
103.	SIR CHARLES THROCKMORTON	Joseph Small	House & Garden	-

104.	SIR CHARLES THROCKMORTON	Joseph Small	'The Meadow'	P
105.	SIR CHARLES THROCKMORTON	John Timmings	'Little Pleck'	P
106.	SIR CHARLES THROCKMORTON	Samuel Ayres	'Blake Meadow'	P
107.	SIR CHARLES THROCKMORTON	Samuel Ayres	'Blake Meadow'	P
108.	SIR CHARLES THROCKMORTON	Himself	'Coal Pit Coppice'	W
109.	THOMAS WILKES	Himself	'Further Astwood Hill Meadow'	P
110.	THOMAS WILKES	Himself	'Astwood Hill Meadow'	P
111.	THOMAS WILKES	William Crump	Cottage and Gardens	-
112.	JOHN TIMMINS	Himself	'The Ham'	P
113.	SIR CHARLES THROCKMORTON	Himself	'Astwood Hill'	W
114.	SIR CHARLES THROCKMORTON	Himself	'Coppice'	W
115.	THOMAS WILKES	Himself	'Pleck'	P
116.	THOMAS WILKES	Himself	'Rough'	W
117.	THOMAS WILKES	Himself	'Owls All'	P
118.	SIR CHARLES THROCKMORTON	John Nicholls	'Rough'	W
119.	SIR CHARLES THROCKMORTON	John Nicholls	'Four Acres'	A
120.	SIR CHARLES THROCKMORTON	John Nicholls	'Upper Stale Reddings'	A
121.	SIR CHARLES THROCKMORTON	John Nicholls	'Hither Stale Reddings'	A
122.	SIR CHARLES THROCKMORTON	John Nicholls	'Rough'	W
123.	JOHN PAGE	John Turner	'The Coppy Hole'	A
124.	JOHN PAGE	John Turner	'Stall Reddings'	A
125.	JOHN PAGE	John Turner	'Little Roe Bacon'	A
125a.	JOHN PAGE	John Turner	'Pool Coppice'	W
126.	JOHN PAGE	John Turner	'Dingle'	W
127.	JOHN PAGE	John Turner	'Big Roe Bacon'	A
128.	JOHN PAGE	John Turner	'Lower Orchard'	P
129.	JOHN PAGE	John Turner	'Thistley Field'	A
130.	JOHN PAGE	John Turner	'Perry Mill Field'	A
131.	JOHN PAGE	John Turner	House, Building, Garden	-
132.	JOHN PAGE	John Turner	Garden & Orchard	-
133.	JOHN PAGE	John Turner	Orchard	P
134.	JOHN PAGE	John Turner	'Barn Field'	A
135.	JOHN PAGE	John Turner	'Big Meadow'	P
136.	JOHN PAGE	John Turner	'Brook Close'	A
137.	SIR CHARLES THROCKMORTON	John Nicholls	'Upper Brook Close'	A
138.	JOHN PAGE	John Turner	Coppice & Foredrive	-
139.	SIR CHARLES THROCKMORTON	John Nicholls	'Lower Brook Close'	P
140.	SIR CHARLES THROCKMORTON	John Nicholls	'Orchard'	P
141.	SIR CHARLES THROCKMORTON	John Nicholls	'Long Land'	P
142.	SIR CHARLES THROCKMORTON	John Nicholls	'The Meadow'	P
143.	SIR CHARLES THROCKMORTON	John Nicholls	'Calves Close'	P
144.	SIR CHARLES THROCKMORTON	John Nicholls	'Swancote House, etc'	-
145.	SIR CHARLES THROCKMORTON	John Nicholls	'Barn Close'	P
146.	SIR CHARLES THROCKMORTON	John Nicholls	'Hunts Close'	P
150.	MARTHA GILES	Joseph Blakeway	'Floodgate Field'	A
151.	MARTHA GILES	Joseph Blakeway	'St John's Field'	A
152.	MARTHA GILES	Joseph Blakeway	'Chaddesley Meadow'	P
153.	MARTHA GILES	Joseph Blakeway	'Dockey Piece'	A
*154.	REV. G.H. PIERCY	Elizabeth Bate	'Pool Meadow'	P
*155.	REV. G.H. PIERCY	Thomas Danby	House and Garden	-
*156.	REV. G.H. PIERCY	Elizabeth Bate	'Homestead'	-
*157.	REV. G.H. PIERCY	Elizabeth Bate	'Barn Close'	A

*158.	REV. G.H. PIERCY	Elizabeth Bate	'Three-Cornered Field'	A
*159.	REV. G.H. PIERCY	Elizabeth Bate	'The Four Acres'	A
*160.	REV. G.H. PIERCY	Elizabeth Bate	'Upper Meadow'	P
161.	MARTHA GILES	Joseph Blakeway	'Goose Acre'	A
162.	MARTHA GILES	Joseph Blakeway	'Long Meadow'	P
163.	CORPORATION OF WARWICK	Samuel Ayres	G	-
164.	CORPORATION OF WARWICK	Samuel Ayres	'Chaddesley Meadow'	P
165.	CORPORATION OF WARWICK	Samuel Ayres	'Brier Hill'	A
166.	CORPORATION OF WARWICK	Samuel Ayres	H G B	-
167.	CORPORATION OF WARWICK	Samuel Ayres	'Cow Pasture'	P
168.	MARTHA GILES	Joseph Blakeway	'Lawn'	P
169.	MARTHA GILES	Joseph Blakeway	H G B	-
170.	ELIZABETH BLAKEWAY	Henry Gwin	H G	-
171.	ELIZABETH BLAKEWAY	James Clark	H G	-
172.	ELIZABETH BLAKEWAY	Thomas Skinner	H G	-
173.	MARTHA GILES	Joseph Blakeway	'Rick Yard Field'	A
174.	MARTHA GILES	Joseph Blakeway	'Garden Field'	A
586.	THOMAS POOL	Thomas Lea	'Near Field'	A
587.	THOMAS POOL	Thomas Lea	H Barn & G	-
588.	CORPORATION OF WARWICK	Samuel Ayres	'Stony Field'	A
589.	CORPORATION OF WARWICK	Elizabeth Bate	'Robin Hood's Oak'	A
590.	ANN POOL	Herself	'Robin Hood's Oak'	A
591.	CHARLES D'OYLEY	Charles Blakeway	'Stony Field'	A
592.	CHARLES D'OYLEY	Charles Blakeway	'Sling'	P
593.	CORPORATION OF WARWICK	Samuel Ayres	'New House Piece'	A
594.	CORPORATION OF WARWICK	Samuel Ayres	'Beauty Bank Piece'	A
*595.	REV. G.H. PIERCY	Elizabeth Bate	'Beauty Bank Piece'	A
596.	ROBERT BRAZIER	John Keatley		
		Phoebe Keatley		
		James Madin	3 Cottages & Gs	
597.	MARY BACON	Abel Kings	Cottage & G	-
*598.	REV. G.H. PIERCY	Elizabeth Bate	'Brier Hill Field'	A
599.	WILLIAM PERRINS	Thomas Depper	'Perrins Meadow'	P
600.	WILLIAM PERRINS	Thomas Depper	G	-
601.	SIR CHAS. THROCKMORTON	James Blakeway	'Upper Park'	P
602.	SIR CHAS. THROCKMORTON	James Blakeway	'Potters park'	A
602a.	ROBERT BRAZIER	John Bland	H G	-
603.	SIR CHAS. THROCKMORTON	James Blakeway	'Upper Long Park'	A
604.	SIR CHAS. THROCKMORTON	James Blakeway	'Lower Long Park'	A
605.	SIR CHAS. THROCKMORTON	James Blakeway	'Lower Park'	P
606.	SIR CHAS. THROCKMORTON	James Blakeway	'Pool Meadow'	P
607.	SIR CHAS. THROCKMORTON	James Blakeway	Pool	-
608.	SIR CHAS. THROCKMORTON	James Blakeway	Rough	-
609.	SIR CHAS. THROCKMORTON	James Blakeway	'Picklewell Park'	A
871.	SIR CHAS. THROCKMORTON	James Blakeway	'Two Acres'	A
872.	WIDOW'S CHARITY	Sarah Clements	5 Houses & Gs	
		Jane Perry	*(These are the 'Delabere' Almshouses*	
		Mary Bird	*built 1637 by Margaret Delabere for 5*	
		Sarah Guise	*poor widows, still standing)*	
		Hannah Owen		
873.	JOHN GREGORY WATKINS	Nancy Hall	'Duffins lane Piece'	A
874.	JOHN GREGORY WATKINS	Nancy Hall	Cottage & G	-

875.	JAMES BLAKEWAY	Himself	'Almshouse Piece'	A
876.	SIR CHARLES THROCKMORTON	James Blakeway	'Pear Tree Piece'	A
877.	SIR CHARLES THROCKMORTON	James Blakeway	'Six Acres'	A
878.	SIR CHARLES THROCKMORTON	James Blakeway	'Five Acres'	A
879.	JAMES BLAKEWAY	Himself	'Earsall'	A
880.	JAMES BLAKEWAY	Himself	'Coopers Piece'	A
881.	JAMES BLAKEWAY	Himself	H G B Rickyard	-
882.	JAMES BLAKEWAY	Himself	'Barn Close'	P
883.	JAMES BLAKEWAY	Himself	'Roundings Hill'	A
884.	JAMES BLAKEWAY	Himself	'Pool Close'	A
885.	JAMES BLAKEWAY	Himself	'Crab Tree Field'	A
886.	JAMES BLAKEWAY	Himself	'Hop Meadow'	P
887.	JAMES BLAKEWAY	Himself	'Low Meadow'	P
888.	JAMES BLAKEWAY	Himself	'Three Acres'	A

This represents, of course, only a fraction of the survey made for the Commutation of Tithes in 1839. The entire award gives the area of the whole parish, as 5,914 acres. Of these, 5,054 acres were said to be subject to tithes, 3,698 acres as arable land, 1,356 acres as meadow or pasture. There were also 261 acres of woodland, according to the award, which were exempt from tithe. This tithable land is all contained in the Survey, which lists 1,280 units of land, tenements and messuages. The final assessment of the Commissioner was that Chaddesley Corbett was to be assessed at a gross rent charge of £765 8s. per annum, valued at

726.78932 bushels of Wheat @ 7s. 0¼d. per bushel

1289.0943 bushels of Barley @ 3s. 11½d. per bushel, or

1855.51516 bushels of Oats @ 2s. 9d. per bushel.

A Numerical Key to the Tithe Award of Chaddesley Corbett 1839 was compiled by W.E. English in 1977.

FURTHER READING

E. Davies, 'The small landowner, 1780-1832, in the light of the land-tax assessments', *Econ. Hist. Review*, 1, 1927

E.J.Evans, *Tithes, Maps, Apportionments and the 1836 Act*, BALH, 1993

N. Evans, 'Tithe Books as a Source for the Local Historian', *The Local Historian*, 14, no.1, 1980

J. Gibson and D. Mills, *Land Tax Assessments c.1690-c.1950*, FFHS, 1984

J.B. Harley, 'Enclosure and Tithe Maps', *The Local Historian*, 7, no.8, 1967

R.J.P. Kain, *An Atlas and Index of the Tithe Files of mid-19th century England and Wales*, C.U.P., 1986; and: 'Tithe Surveys and the Study of Land Occupation', *The Local Historian*, 12, no.2, 1976; 'Compiling an Atlas of Agriculture in England and Wales, using Tithe Surveys', *Geographical Journal*, 145, 1979

R. Kain and H. Prince, *The Tithe Surveys of England and Wales*, C.U.P., 1985

J.M. Martin, 'Landownership and the Land Tax returns', *Agr. Hist. Rev.*, 14, 1966

G.E. Mingay, 'The Land Tax and the small landowner', *Econ. Hist. Review*, 17, 1964

H.C. Prince, 'The Tithe Surveys of the mid-Nineteenth Century', *Agricultural History Review*, 7, 1959

G.H. Tupling, 'Searching the Parish Records 6: Tithe and Enclosure Awards', *Amateur Historian*, 1, no.12, 1954

A. Wareham, 'Tithes in Country Life', *History Today*, no.22, 1972

R. Workman, 'Analysing a tithe map in depth', *The Local Historian*, 14, no.5, 1981

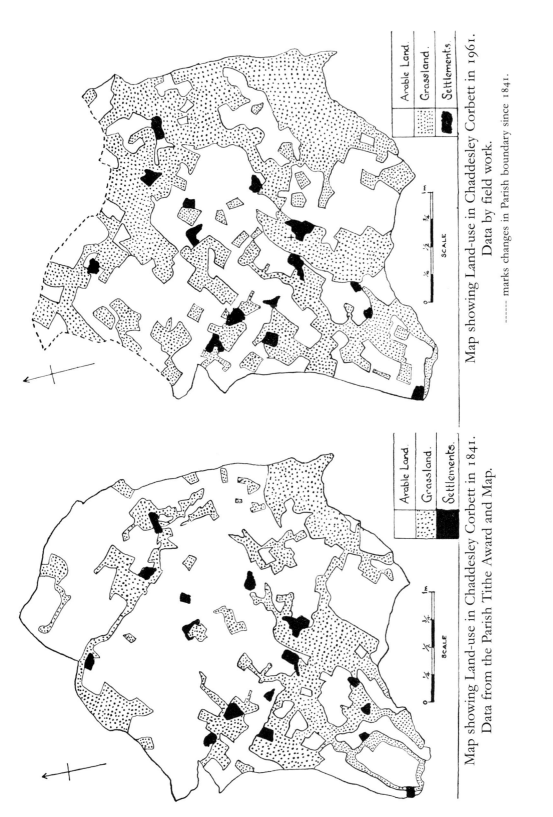

Arable Land.
Grassland.
Settlements.

Map showing Land-use in Chaddesley Corbett in 1961.
Data by field work.

------ marks changes in Parish boundary since 1841.

SCALE

Arable Land.
Grassland.
Settlements.

Map showing Land-use in Chaddesley Corbett in 1841.
Data from the Parish Tithe Award and Map.

SCALE

Fig. 9. Comparative Land-Use Maps; Chaddesley Corbett in 1841 and 1961.

Availability of Collections, printed and Originals, of Tithe and Land Tax Documents

The most comprehensive addition to this field is now: Roger Kain and Richard Oliver, *The Tithe Maps of England and Wales (A cartographical analysis and county by county catalogue*, C.U.P., 1995. Possibly a more accessible local source of information for any county is the printed *Guide to the County Archives*, to which further reference must be made. Further information can also be supplied for any area by the Tithe Redemption Commission, Finsbury Square, London. See also the list of original Land Tax returns (earliest documents) for each county in *County Records*. The following very limited list may be of some assistance to students in the few counties for which definite information is readily available.

The List and Index Society, Public Record Office, Chancery Lane, London WC1A 2LR, publishes, at £13.00 for its members (@ £5.00 per annum) and at £19.50 for nonmembers, the following three Indexes to lists of nearly 12,000 parishes' Tithe Files, arranged alphabetically by county. The Society's stock-list for 1965-1995 advises that 'it is likely that many of the titles advertised here will go out of print during 1995' and will be sold on a 'first come, first served basis'; the up-to-date stocklist does not include out-of-print titles. A reliable reference library, however, will probably hold copies; Birmingham, for example, as a subscriber to the Society, has every volume published since 1 in 1965, including:

219   Tithe Files (IR18), Beds.-Leics. (1836-1870)
225   Tithe Files (IR18), Lincs.-Southampton (1836-1870)
226   Tithe Files (IR18), Staffs.-Yorkshire and the Welsh counties (*no dates given*)

(listed chronologically by publication date within each county)

Bedfordshire   E.O. Payne, *Property in Land in South Bedfordshire*, Beds Rec. Soc., 15, 1933.

Berkshire   There is an internal typescript index at the C.R.O., but no published handlist. Originals previously at the Bodleian Library have now been removed to the C.R.O. and the Tithe Redemption series are now at the P.R.O.; A.H. Cooke, 'Windsor tithes in the sixteenth and seventeenth centuries', *BBOAJ*, n.s., 31, 1923; M. Dumbleton, *Easthampstead tithe apportionment, 1841*, 1991.

Caernarvonshire   I.E. Davies, 'The tithe map of Dwygyfylchi', *Arch. Cambr.*, 7th sers., 3, 1923; E. Evans, 'The Tithe Schedule for the Parish of Dolbermau', *Caern. Hist. Soc.*, 12, 1952; and: 'Tithe Schedule for Boduan', *Caern. Hist. Soc.*, 17, 1956.

Carmarthenshire   T.W. Barker, 'Carmarthenshire tithe', *CASFC*, 2, 1906.

Cheshire   R.J.P. Kain and H.M.E. Holt, 'Farming in Cheshire c.1840, some evidence from the tithe files', *LCAS*, 82, 1983.

Cumberland   J.H. Colligan, 'A tithe dispute between the rector of Graystoke and his parishioners, 1672-4', *CWAAS*, n.s., 9, 1909; R.F. Dickinson, 'Tithing customs in West Cumberland in the eighteenth century', *CWAAS*, n.s., 60, 1960; E.J. Evans, 'A nineteenth century tithe dispute and its significance: the case of Kendal', *CWAAS*, no.74, 1974.

Derbyshire   S.O. Addy, 'Bakewell Easter roll of tithe payments, 1348', *DANHSJ*, 36, 19–.

Devonshire   W.P.S. Bingham, 'Tithe "modus" for the parish of Kenton, 1606', *DASLA*, 33, 1901; R. Lethbridge, 'Tithe commutation in Exbourne in the seventeenth century', *DASLA*, 44, 1911; W.A. Roberts, *Stokenham, South Devon, tithe map, 1841-60*, 1984; R.M. Guyver (facsimile reproductions of): *East Budleigh Tithe Map, 1843* (Sir Walter Raleigh Edition, with field names), TMP, 1984; and: *Wembury Parish Tithe Map, 1840* (Major Edmund Lockyer, W. Australia Edition, with field names), TMP, 1984; and: *Wembury Historical Information: 1841 Parish Census and 1840 Tithe Apportionment*, TMP, 1987; and: *Plympton St Maurice Tithe Map, 1843* (Joshua Reynolds edition), TMP, 1986; and: *Plymstock Tithe Map, 1843*, TMP, 1987; and: *The Wembury Project*, TMP, 1987.

Dorset   W. Sharpe, *The Hard Case of a Country Vicar in respect of Small Tythe*, 1776; C.D. Drew, 'Small Tithes of Hampreston', *SDNQ*, xx; B. Kerr, 'Dorset Fields and their names', *DNHAS*, 89, 1968.

Durham   M. Still, 'Using the Tithe files, a County Durham study', *The Local Historian*, 17, no.4, November 1986.

Gloucestershire   Tithe maps and apportionments for Gloucester diocese are deposited at Gloucestershire Record Office. These include the diocesan copies and many of the parish copies. They are listed in *Handlist of the contents of the Gloucestershire Record Office*, GCC, 1995.

Hampshire   F.J. Baigent (ed.), *A Collection of Records and Documents relating to the Hundred and Manor of Crondal in the County of Southampton*, Part 1 (includes records of a tithe dispute in Yateley in 1605), Hampshire Record Society Publications, 3, 1891; W.S. Sykes, 'A list of principal inhabitants of Milford, 1680-90' (taken from tithe account; some traced down to 1800), *Milford-on-Sea Rec. Soc. Occ. Mag.*, 2, 1914; and: 'Milford tithe award and map of 1840', *Milford-on-Sea Rec. Soc. Occ. Mag.*, 3, 1923.

Herefordshire   J. Lloyd, 'Old Herefordshire rectories and tithes', *Woolhope Nats. Field Club*, 1902.

Hertfordshire   A.M. Carpenter, 'The value of Tithe surveys to the study of land ownership and occupancy in the mid-nineteenth century, with special reference to South Hertfordshire', *Hertfordshire Past and Present*, no.7, 1967; Original tithe maps and awards are in the C.R.O., covering most Hertfordshire parishes with the exception of those in the Diocese of London.

Kent   R.J.P. Kain, 'The Tithe Commutation Surveys', *AC*, 89, 1974; The C.R.O. houses tithe awards and maps for parishes in the Rochester diocese.

Lancashire   J. Tait, *Taxation in Salford Hundred, 1524-1802*, Chetham Soc., n.s., 83, 1924 (includes Land Tax 1780-1802); W.H. Chippindall, *A History of the Parish of Tunstall*, Chetham Soc., n.s., 104, 1940 (includes tithe award of 1851); *Crosby; Local maps and documents*, Crosby Public Libraries, 1967; J. Langton, *Geographical change and industrial revolution; coal-mining in south-west Lancashire, 1590-1799*, Appendix 4, CUP, 1979; G.J. Wilson, 'The land tax and West Derby Hundred, 1780-1831', *HSLC*, 129, 1980; N.J. Morgan, 'Lancashire Quakers and the Tithe 1660-1730', *John Rylands Library Bulletin*, 70, Autumn 1988; A. Cotham, 'An Altcar tithe dispute in the fourteenth century', *HSLC*, 82, 1930.

Leicestershire   *Leicestershire Tithe Records*, Leics. Record Office, 1959.

Lincolnshire   D.B. Grigg, 'The Land Tax Returns in Lincolnshire', *Agricultural History Review*, no.11, 1963.

Monmouthshire   Monmouthshire's county archives, previously at Newport, are now housed in the new town (1949) of Cwmbran, Gwent. (The ancient diocese of Monmouth was Llandaff.) Those tithe maps held at the CRO are listed in the CRO's publication: *The History of Houses, Guide to Records*, no.4, *c.*1981.

Montgomery   D.R.T. , 'Welshpool tithe commutations, 1840', *Powys-Land Club Colls.*, 34, 1907.

Northamptonshire   E. King, 'Daventry Tithing Book', in *Northants. Miscellany*, Pubns. Northants. Rec. Soc., 32, 1982; MS. index to all tithe maps (Diocesan copies), 1837-57, is available at the C.R.O., where there is a full set of original maps.

Nottinghamshire   Nottinghamshire Archives has tithe awards for 103 parishes for the years 1837-50; altered apportionment of tithes for 28 parishes, 1855-1930; awards of exchange for 29 parishes, 1849-93; certificates of redemption for 8 parishes, 1880-93, and certificates of capital value for nine parishes, 1889.

Pembrokeshire   B. Charles, 'The Vicarage and Tithes of Nevern, in Pembrokeshire', *Hist. Soc. of the Church in Wales Journal*, 1, 1947; F. Jones, 'The Mathry Tithe Suit 1754', *Hist. Soc. of the Church in Wales Journal*, 2, 1950; P. Horn, *The Tithe War in Pembrokeshire*, 1983.

Radnorshire   'Nantmel tithe, 1719', *Radn. Soc.*, 3, 1933.

Shropshire   W.G.D. Fletcher, 'Two Exchequer suits respecting tithes of the rectory of Shifnal, 1585', *ShANHS*, 3rd sers., 3, 1903.

Somersetshire   Nothing has been printed on tithes for Somerset. Diocesan copies are held almost complete for the whole diocese. Consult J.E. King, *Somerset Parochial Documents*, Taunton, 1938, to trace individual tithe awards in local parish chests.

Staffordshire   *A Terryar for Audley parish for 1708, and the manner of tytheing with the vicar*, Staffs Rec. Soc., 68, 1947; R.E. Hebden, 'The tithe maps (1840-1) of Aldridge, Great Barr and Shenstone', *Lich. & S. Staffs. Arch. & Hist. Soc.*, 5, 1963-4.

Suffolk   Original tithe maps and awards for parishes within the Archdeaconry of Suffolk are available in Suffolk Record Office, Ipswich and those parishes within the Archdeaconry of Sudbury are at the Suffolk Record Office, Bury St Edmunds. Photographic copies of tithe maps and awards for the

Suffolk parishes falling within the Deanery of Lothingland are at the Suffolk Record Office, Lowestoft (originals at Norfolk Record Office). Typescript catalogues are available.

Surrey   Diocesan copies of tithe awards are deposited at the C.R.O.

Sussex   F.W. Steer, *Catalogue of Sussex estate and tithe award maps*, SRS, 61, 1962.

Wales   R.M. Roberts, *Rhyfel y degwm* or *The Tithe War*, translated from the Welsh by G.M. Morris, O.U.P., 1989.

Wiltshire   S.W. Shaw, 'Notes on Purton tithe books, 1726 and 1788', *WANHM*, 43, 1926; R.E. Sandell, 'Abstracts of Wiltshire Tithe Apportionments', *Wilts. Rec. Soc.*, 30, 1975.

Westmorland   J. Rawlinson Ford (ed.), *The Beetham Repository, 1770*, CWAAS Tract Ser., 7, 1906.

Yorkshire   W.E. Preston, 'The Tithes of Farnley; an eighteenth-century dispute', *Thoresby Soc., Miscellanea*, x, 1935; J.S. Purvis, *Select sixteenth-century causes in Tithe, from Yorkshire Diocesan Registry*, YAS, 114, 1949; R.W. Unwin, *Search Guide to the English Land Tax*, West Yorkshire CRO, 1982; North Yorkshire County Record Office publishes *Guide No.2: Parish registers, census returns, land tax assessments, tithe apportionments and enclosure awards in the record office*.

TURNPIKE TRUST RECORDS

THE DOCUMENTS

From medieval times until the 18th century, the work and expense involved in maintaining and repairing roads was levied from the inhabitants of each village through which such roads passed. These duties were enforced by Common Law, and responsibility for supervision of this local unpaid labour was undertaken at different times by various authorities, each with indifferent success. Until Tudor times these local organisers were the medieval corporate units—the Church, the manorial court, the gilds and borough corporations. From these very earliest times, the history of road maintenance is a record of half-hearted and unskilled effort, and of complaints by travellers of disrepair and neglect which made travel slow and hazardous. Tudor government, in accordance with its policy of paternal supervision of the national social and economic well-being, attempted to reorganise local labour and its supervision, by statute. An Act of 1555 made provision for each parish to administer and regularise its methods of highway maintenance, and authorised the appointments of parish surveyors, descendants of the medieval 'way-wardens', who were to exact an annual four days' labour and cartage service from local landowners and householders. This 'statute labour' was supervised by the J.P.s at Quarter Sessions, an aspect of the Justices' work which has been illustrated in a previous document (p.132). From the end of the 17th century, a parish rate was levied to provide hired labour in place of unpaid service. This basic idea of the local inhabitants' responsibility, organised by parochial officials, remained in force until the 19th century, when the Local Government Act of 1894 finally removed all remaining parish authority to the new district councils.

In spite of these provisions, the state of the roads continued to deteriorate; Wesley wrote of an Essex road in 1749, 'the ruts were so deep and uneven that the horses could scarce stand, and the chaise was continually in danger of overturning'. Such comments are commonplace in the diaries and correspondence of the 18th century; in 1770, such was Arthur Young's complaint of the Preston road:

> Let me most seriously caution all travellers who may accidently purpose to travel this terrible country, to avoid it as they would the Devil, for a thousand to one but they break their necks and their limbs by overthrows or breakings-down. They will here meet with ruts which I actually

measured four feet deep and floating with mud only from the wet Summer; what, therefore, will it be after a winter? The only mending it in places receives is the tumbling in some loose stones which serve no other purpose but jolting a carriage in the most intolerable manner.

Between Kensington and London was 'an impassable sea of mud', and the mere 40 miles from Windsor to Petworth involved 14 hours' travel, 'whilst almost every mile was signalised by the overturn of a carriage or its temporary swamping in the mire'. Such conditions were a constant hindrance to trade and industry, involving expense, delay and damage which inhabited commercial intercourse. Just as enclosure was, in many regions, to be an essential prelude to any agrarian revolution, so industrial development was conditional upon improved transport and communications. The remedy was first sought during the 18th century with the simultaneous development of canal transport and the improvement of road surfaces for faster traffic. The latter improvement was effected largely by privately-vested Turnpike Trusts, authorised by local acts of Parliament to recoup their expenses by the levying of tolls upon road users. This idea had been legalised, as early as 1663, for the maintenance of a stretch of Cambridgeshire road. During the period *c*.1700-1830 hundreds of such private enterprises grew up all over England. Many parishes were prepared to relinquish their responsibilities to a local trust, and indeed to supplement its revenue from the parish rate. A general Turnpike Act of 1773 intensified this development, and although many trusts were haphazardly organised, a widespread improvement was in fact the result. Meanwhile, some parishes attempted further reorganisation and consolidation of the older parochial system; the Highway Acts of 1835 and 1862 authorised the combination of groups of parishes into 'Highway Boards', whose Minutes are often found deposited at County Record Offices.

Turnpike revenues made possible the employment of expert professional surveyors and road engineers, like Telford, Metcalf and Macadam, whose new methods of surfacing and drainage revolutionised the English roads system. In spite of the stimulus to trade and traffic which resulted, the golden age of fast Mails and 'Flyers' was short-lived. The development of railways in the 1870s caused a widespread decline in road-use, and the trusts were inexorably driven out of business. In 1888 the upkeep of the 'disturnpiked', or 'Main', roads was transferred to the county councils, and a subsequent Act of 1894 completed the transfer of remaining 'parochial' roads to the district councils.

The records of the business of road maintenance by Turnpike Trusts often survive in large numbers at County Record Offices, where they have been deposited from unofficial

---

Plate XIX
(i) Bromsgrove to Worcester Turnpike Map, 1823 (northern half).
Actual size: 45.75 x 68.5cm at 4 in. : 1 mile.
Scale of extract shewn: 1½ inches: 1 mile.
(Worcs. Record Office Ref: 614/BA. 1006.)
(ii) Corresponding extract from Ordnance Survey Sheet 130.
7th Series, 1954 at 1 in. : 1 Statute Mile. Reproduced with the sanction of the Controller of H.M. Stationery Office (*Crown Copyright Reserved*). Actual size: 16 x 7cm at 1½ in. : 1 mile.

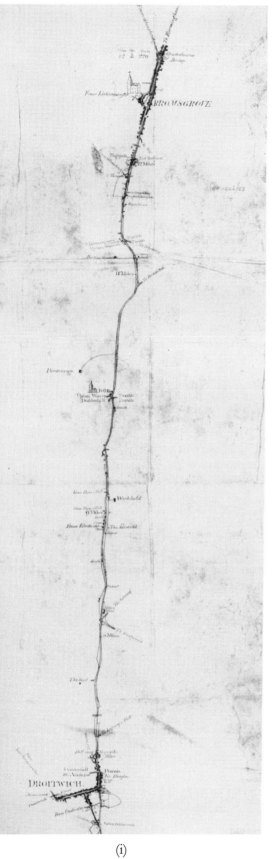

(i)   (ii)

sources. Typical documents include the order and minute books, maps and plans of projected improvements, plans and elevations of toll-houses, statements of expenses, payments for materials and labour, agreements with parishes, letters setting down standards to be observed, regulations of number and weight of traffic, and details of tolls to be charged. The records occasionally include individual toll-house keepers' day books, which give exact details of traffic passing a certain point throughout several years. These are, in fact, very practical documents, with a good deal of visual attraction, and containing a great deal of worthwhile, often amusing, detail of travel at the beginning of the 19th century. Used in conjunction with the contemporary directories (page 227-8), and with the works of Regency and Victorian diarists and letter-writers, they provide a picture of 19th-century life which is indispensable.

When considering the turnpike records as a source of social history, we should pause also to take note of another source of large-scale plans and topographical detail. These are the schemes and projects for the other transport and 'public utilities', with which the turnpike records are often acceded and stored in a Record Office. The most numerous of these are the plans for canal and railway development, taking over from the Turnpike Trusts as a source of even more detailed plans and maps, and recording new and drastic changes to the English landscape. Important, too, are the schemes for much-needed improvements in town water supplies, and projects for 'the better lighting, paving and watching' of these towns. Throughout the 19th century, the Clerks of the Peace were amassing vast quantities of such plans, deposited at first by local companies, trusts and contractors; later deposits, after the 'Adoptive Acts' of 1833 and after, and the Local Government Acts of 1888 and 1894, were made increasingly by local councils.

These records provide the topographer with a mass of really large-scale plans, from which changes in landscape, buildings, industrial and urban growth can be examined in close detail. The plans are on a very large scale, usually 4 in. to the mile, in some cases as large as 16 in. or 25 in. to the mile, with sections through the transects mapped scaled to 15 ft. to the inch. The surveying is of a high degree of accuracy, and the maps themselves are most attractively coloured and finished. Property on, or along, the site of such a scheme, whether for provision of a reservoir, a canal, railway, or road is carefully numbered. The plans should be accompanied by a book of reference to the numbered properties; this gives the names of owners, leaseholders and occupiers, arranged in parishes along the route. Frequently the description, or use, of the land through which 'the project' passes, is given, e.g. 'road through arable', 'gardens', 'town-houses', etc. For the study of industrial topography and archaeology of workshop and factory sites of the Industrial Revolution, the plans of developments in the Black Country and other industrial areas are particularly important at this time. The canals and railroads pass through, and record the positions of, the sites of wharves, docks, locks, brass-houses, brick-kilns, collieries, nail-warehouses, boat-yards, coach-factories, glasshouses, steam-engine houses, in fact the whole panorama of the 19th-century Black Country. Changes in street and lane names can be checked from these records, as well as minute changes in industrial sites and ownership. These are, in fact, sources of primary importance in the study of 19th-century topography, landscape, industry, and the physical growth of new towns. Most Record Offices will have an inventory, or handlist, of all deposited plans, sections and books of reference for public schemes.

FURTHER READING

W. Addison, *The Old Roads of England*, Batsford, 1980

W. Albert, *The Turnpike Road System in England, 1663-1840*, Cambridge, 1972; and: 'Public Opposition to Turnpike Trusts in the Early Eighteenth Century', *Journal of Transport History*, 5, 1979

A. Birch, *Directory of Stagecoach Services*, David & Charles, 1969

J. Copeland, *Roads and their Traffic, 1750-1859*, David & Charles, 1968

A. Cossons, 'Misconceptions about Turnpikes', *Amateur Historian*, 5, no.2, 1962

B.F. Duckham, 'Short Guides to Records 18: Turnpike Records', *History*, no.53, 1968

H.G. Fordham, *Roads of England and Wales and the Turnpike System*, 1912; and: *Road-books and Itineraries of Great Britain 1570-1850*, CUP, 1924

M.J. Freeman, 'Road transport in the English Industrial Revoltion, an interim re-assessment', *Journal Hist. Geog.*, 6 (i), 1980

E.C.W. French, 'Turnpike Trusts', *Amateur Historian*, 2, no.1, 1954

G.E. Fussell, *Exploration of England: A Select Bibliography of Travel and Topography, 1570- 1815*, 1935

E. Pawson, *Transport and Economy, the Turnpike Roads of Eighteenth century Britain*, London, 1977; and: 'The Turnpike Trusts of the Eighteenth Century; a Study of Innovation and Diffusion', *University of Oxford School of Geography Research Papers*, no.14, 1975

G. Pennethorne, 'Payment on the Road', *Amateur Historian*, 1, no.4, 1953

J.M. Thomas, *Roads before the Railways*, Evans Bros., 1970

G.L. Turnbull, 'Provincial road-carrying in England in the eighteenth century', *Journal of Transport History*, n.s., 4, 1977

PRINTED MATERIAL FOR LOCAL TURNPIKE STUDIES

It appears that much less has been published from these original records than for any of the others. On the other hand, the originals themselves can usually be found easily, as every Record Office Guide contains full information of all deposited turnpike records. A few counties have other published material, as follows:

(Listed chronologically by publication date)

Bedfordshire   P. Smith, *The Turnpike Age*, Luton Museum and Art Gallery, 1970.

Berkshire   A.T. Heelas, 'The Windsor Forest turnpike', *Berks. Arch. J.*, 37, 1933.

Caernarvonshire   I.E. Davies, 'The old turnpike road, Penmaenmawr', *Llandudno, Colwyn Bay and District Field Club*, 16, 1932.

Cornwall   *Turnpikes, Canals and Ferries*, Cornwall Record Office Handlist no.5, 1982.

Derbyshire   A.P. Munsford and D.V. Fowkes, *Derbyshire Turnpikes, 1724-1883*, Darlington Corporation, 1971.

Devonshire   L. Sheldon, 'Devon toll-houses', *DASLA*, 65, 1933; E.P. Bund, 'Okehampton Turnpikes', *DASLA*, 68, 1936; A.B. George, 'Exeter Turnpike Trust, 1820-35', *Devon Historian*, no.45, October 1992; M.C. Lowe, 'Toll Houses of the Exeter Turnpike Trust', *Devonshire Association*, 124, 1992.

Dorset   J. Harvey, *Alphabetical List of the Cities and Towns of England and Wales, with their County, Distances and Number of Stages from Weymouth*, Weymouth, 1839; C.H. Mayo, 'Communications between London and Dorset, 1772', *Dorset N. & Q.*, v, 1896-7; and: 'Westhill Road, Sherborne', *Dorset N. & Q.*, XII, 1903-4; and: 'Blandford and Poole Turnpike Road, and the Vale of Blackmore Turnpike Roads', *Dorset N. & Q.*, XV, 1906-7; 'Maiden Newton Turnpike', *Dorset N. & Q.*, XXII, 1914-15; E.K. le Fleming, 'Records of the Turnpike Trustees of the Poole, Wimborne and Cranborne Trust', *DNHAFC*, XLVIII, 1927; R.D'Oyley Good, *The Old Roads of Dorset*, Bournemouth, 1966; J. Cross, 'Wimborne and Puddletown Turnpike'.

Essex   C. Cochrane, *The Lost Roads of Essex*, David and Charles, 1969; K.C. Newton, *A History of the Highways and Byways of Essex*, Essex Record Office, 1969.

Gloucestershire   B. Smith and E. Ralph, 'Roads and Travellers', in *A History of Bristol and Gloucestershire*, Phillimore, 1996.

Hampshire   C.F.C. Hawkes, *Old Roads of Central Hampshire*, Hants. Field Club, IX, Part 3, 1925; M.J.

Freeman, 'The stage-coach system of South Hampshire', *J. Hist. Geog.*, 1, 1975; and: 'The carrier system of South Hampshire', *J. Transport Hist.*, n.s., 4, 1977; J.E.H. Spaul, *Turnpikes near Andover, 1775-1882*, Andover Local Archives Committee, 1977.

Herefordshire J. and M. West, 'Canals, Turnpikes and Stage Coaches', in *A History of Herefordshire*, Phillimore, 1985.

Hertfordshire F.H. Maud, *The Hockerill Highway*, Colchester, 1957; H.C.F. Lansberry, 'James McAdam and the St. Albans Turnpike Trust', *Journal of Transport History*, 7, 1965; *Hertfordshire Turnpike Roads*, Hertfordshire County Record Office, 1970.

Huntingdonshire R. Young, 'Following the Stage-coaches (Huntingdonshire)', *The Local Historian*, 14, no.6, 1981.

Kent F.C. Elliston Erwood, 'The Biddenden and Boundgate Turnpike Road, 1766-1883', *AC*, LXXI, 1957; E. Melling, *Kentish Source Book, Some Roads and Bridges*, Kent C.C., 1959; T.P. Smith, 'The pattern of coaching services in Kent in 1836', *AC*, 98, 1982-3.

Lancashire W. Harrison, 'The history of a turnpike Trust (Manchester and Wilmslow)', *LCAS*, 34, 1916; J.R. Ashworth, 'The highway through Rochdale and its coaches', *Rochdale Litt. & Sc. Soc.*, 13, 1917-19; A.P. Wadsworth, 'Rochdale's main roads; the history of turnpikes', *Rochdale Litt. & Sc. Soc.*, 13, 1917-19; A.H. Arckle, 'Early Liverpool coaching', *HSLC*, 73, 1921; F.A. Bailey, *The Minutes of the Trustees of the Turnpike Roads from Liverpool to Prescot, Warrington and Ashton in Makerfield*, LCRS, 88, 1936; 89, 1937; Liverpool Teachers' Archive Study Group, *The Liverpool-Prescot Turnpike Trust, 1725-1861*, Education Committee, 1965; W. Harrison, 'The Development of the Turnpike System in Lancashire; and: Turnpike Roads in Lancashire and Cheshire', *LCAS*, IV and X.

Leicestershire P. Russell, *A Leicestershire Road, Harborough to Loughborough*, Leicester, 1934.

London & Middlesex 'Hammersmith and Brentford Turnpikes; Report of a Committee of Trustees … appointed 15th Feb. 1800, to make a Survey of the Roads under the control of the said Trust', Strahan, printer, 1800; 'Isleworth Turnpike Trust', printed by order of the Board of Trustees, 1814, Norbury, 1815; 'A Return of the Aggregate Length of Turnpike Roads in the County of Middlesex, etc.', ordered by the House of Commons to be printed, *Accounts & Papers*, 46, 1849; W.B. Passmore, 'The Great North Road, Whetstone Turnpike Trust', *Middx. & Herts Notes & Queries*, 4, 1898; T.F. Ordish, 'History of Metropolitan Roads', *London Topographical Record*, 8, 1913; G.H.A. White, 'Coaching notes; with some memories of old days on the Woolwich coach', *J.R. Artillery Inst.*, 50, 1924; M. Searle, *Turnpikes and Toll-Bars*, 2 vols., Hutchinson, 1930 (see I); D.G. Denoon, 'Hendon Highways; Their Development and Administration', *Mill Hill Hist. Soc.*, no.2, 1936; D.O. Pam, *The Stamford Hill-Green Lanes Turnpike Trust*, Edmonton Hundred Historical Society, 1965; A.C.B. Urwin, *The Isleworth, Twickenham and Teddington Turnpike, 1767-1872*, Borough of Twickenham Local History Society, no.8, 1965; and: *The Hampton-Staines Turnpike, 1733-1859*, Borough of Twickenham Local History Society, no.11, 1968; W.G.S. Tonkin, *The Lea Bridge Turnpike and Wragge Stage Coaches*, Walthamstow Antiquarian Society, n.s., no.14, 1974; S. Margetson, 'Pay Up or Turn Back! The Age of Turnpikes in London', *Country Life*, no.164, November 1978.

Montgomery J.B. Williams, 'The roads of old Montgomeryshire', *Powys-Land Club*, 41, 1930.

Norfolk R.F.E. Ferrier, 'The toll house at Great Yarmouth', *J. Brit. Arch. Soc.*, 31, 1923; 'A Survey of Norfolk Turnpikes', *Norfolk Arch.*, XXX, 1947-52.

Northamptonshire A. Cossons, 'The Turnpike Roads of Northamptonshire', Northants Rec. Soc. Pub., *Northants Past and Present*, 1, no.3, 1950; K.F. Brown, *Northamptonshire Turnpike Roads and Milestones*, Northants. Record Office, 1972.

Northumberland D.R. Brenchley and C. Shrimpton, *Travel in the Turnpike Age, 1750-1850: An Archive Teaching Unit*, Un. Newcastle, Edn. Dept., 1968.

Nottinghamshire A. Cossons, *The Turnpike Roads of Nottinghamshire*, Historical Association Leaflet, no.97, 1934; P. Stevenson, *The Nottingham and Ilkestone Turnpike Trust, 1764-1874 and the Declining Years, 1846-1883*, Ilkestone and District Local History Society Papers, no.4, 1972; A. Cossons, *Coaching Days: The Turnpike Roads of Nottinghamshire*, Notts. C.C., 1994.

Oxfordshire W. Bayzand, 'Coaching in and out of Oxford, 1820-40', *Ox. Hist. Soc. Collect.*, 4th ser., 1905.

Powys R.T. Pritchard, *Montgomeryshire Turnpike Trusts*, Montgomeryshire Collections, no.57, 1961.

Somersetshire G.J. Grey, 'The romance of the old turnpike roads', *SANHS*, 1929-33; A Survey of Somersetshire Turnpike Trusts and their surviving records is in preparation in the county.

Staffordshire   A. Longton Thomas, *Geographical Aspects of the Development of Transport and communications ...
during the Eighteenth Century*, Staffs Rec. Soc. (Wm. Salt Arch. Soc.), Part I, 1934; Staffordshire Education
Department, *Staffordshire Roads, 1700-1840*, Staffordshire County Council, 1968; S.A. Burne, 'The coaching
age in Staffordshire', *N. Staff. F. C.*, 56, 1921-2.

Suffolk   Original documents for the following turnpikes are in the Ipswich and E. Suffolk Record
Office: Ipswich to Helmingham and Debenham and Hemingstone to Otley Bottom; Ipswich to South
Town (Great Yarmouth) and Bungay; Little Yarmouth; Aldeburgh; Stratford St Mary.

Surrey   F.M.H. Harper, *Chessington's Eighteenth and Nineteenth Century Papers and Documents*, New Malden,
1974.

Sussex   I.D. Margary, *Traffic Routes in Sussex, 1724*, SAC, no.109, 1971.

Warwickshire   A. Cossons, 'Warwickshire Turnpikes', *BAS*, 64, 1941-2.

Yorkshire   C. Clegg, 'Turnpikes and toll bars', *Papers Halifax Antiq. Soc.*, 1915; C. Clegg, 'Coaching days'
(An account of the London to Yorkshire stagecoaches in the early 19th century), *Papers Halifax Antiq.
Soc.*, 1923; K.A. MacMahon, *Roads and Turnpikes in East Yorkshire*, East Yorkshire Historical Society,
1964; The North Yorkshire County Record Office offers: J. Perry, *York-Oswaldkirk Turnpike Trust 1761-
1881*, a minute book; also: *The Diary and Turnpike Papers of Alexander Fothergill, the surveyor of the northern
portion of the Richmond-Lancaster road, 1751-1775*. These papers illustrate 18th-century life in the dales,
particularly in relation to the Quakers, and include lists of householders in the parishes through which
the road passed.

COMMERCIAL DIRECTORIES

THE DOCUMENT

Anyone who has used his local library's reference and reading room may on occasion have
referred to its selection of local and other directories. If so, the information sought will
probably have been concerned with postal addresses, or postal services in that town or another—
distributors of circulars address countless envelopes to householders listed in these volumes.
Most libraries keep up-to-date copies of the leading national directories, usually England. In
spite of the fact that these reference books are so familiar, few students realise their significance
as sources of social and economic history. Directories have a long and continuous history of
their own, particularly during the last 200 years, though some historians trace their origins back
to the employment exchanges organised by some medieval nunneries.

Directories, in the true sense, are a product of the Industrial Revolution, reaching their
full development as accessories to trade and the distribution of goods. It is true that other
specialised forms appear at different times, such as pictorial, cultural and police directories, but
their primary purpose was commercial. With the expansion of foreign trade, the growth of
industrial towns, and the development of wider markets for goods and services, information
was needed by producers and consumers alike which would bring manufacturer, retailer and
customer into contact. Factories needed to know of the whereabouts of supplies of materials,
wholesalers required information as to regional retailers and distributors. In order to supply
their widening markets, manufacturers depended upon details of regional transport services
by road and water; with the development of the postal service in the 19th century, knowledge
of local post office arrangements became important.

From *c.*1760, therefore, commercial directories were produced in increasing numbers all
over England to meet these needs. The earlier versions of the late 18th century have rarely
survived to the present day, but the later editions, from *c.*1800, are easily found in most large

reference libraries. From *c.*1820, great national enterprises were undertaken by publishers, like Pigot & Co., who employed investigators and agents all over England to supply their material.

In its simplest, earliest form, the directory contained brief lists of the chief inhabitants of all the villages and towns of a county, arranged alphabetically, giving each man's occupation. In this simple form, though not in intention, the directories are reminiscent of the medieval Lay Subsidy Rolls, and, like the Subsidy Rolls, their lists do not pretend to contain the total population of any place; only the more substantial tradesmen and professional classes are included. These lists of names of consumers and suppliers were the vital basic information required of the directories, but as their use became widespread other types of information were added. Firstly, details of inns, and of coaching services, arrivals of mails and stage wagons, or barge transport were given. As intercourse between town and countryside was stimulated by railway traffic, holiday resorts and shopping centres needed to advertise their cultural and commercial advantages to travellers. Thus directories began not only to include further details of the shops, booksellers and services of a place, with some very informative pictorial advertisements, but finally added historical and other information of a more general interest.

By the mid-19th century, the directory had assumed the pattern which is still basically the same today. For any town or village, the information given was as follows: firstly, the position of the place in relation to neighbouring towns and its distance from them; then followed architectural and historical data about the Church, its fabric, the living, and its glebe land and tithe-owners. Brief historical notes on the origins of the place became very popular, though these were usually derived from the simplest local histories, and were much plagiarised, and there was usually a disproportionate amount of detail on local charities and endowments. The names of the lord of the manor and principal landowners were given special prominence, and the chief industries which employed the inhabitants were named. The nature of the soil, its chief crops, and other details of geology and natural history were occasionally given, and there were statistics of the area, rateable value and total population at the last census. There was, from an early date, information as to local officials and services, such as the details of post offices, insurance agents, doctors and Medical Officers, Veterinary Surgeons, Tax Collectors and Poor-Rate Overseers. There was usually much evidence of the early schools and their teachers; over the years the former included National Schools, School Boards, Catholic and Church of England Schools, private Academies and the Free and endowed establishments of various denominations. Then followed the list of chief inhabitants, which was the directory's *raison d'être*; this began with 'Gentry and Clergy' or 'Private Residents', followed by the 'Commercial' classes, alphabetically arranged, or divided into their trades.

It will perhaps give some idea of the extent and scope of this field of local information if reference is made to a typical county list, prepared by the Worcestershire Record Office during 1959. This consolidates information 'of Worcestershire Directories held in repositories in or near Worcestershire'; it draws upon ten Midland public libraries, and lists 452 copies of county directories, dating from 1783-1959.

It is evident that these volumes are an outstanding source of information about the social and commercial life of a county during the past 200 years. They provide us with evidence of the rise and decline of various crafts and trades during the whole period of industrial revolution. They also supply some information as to the growth, change and mobility of population, and although the additional information given is quite incidental, it is occasionally such as to be not

𝔚orcestershire CHADDESLEY-CORBETT, &c. Pigot & Co.'s

from Stourbridge, and 6 N. W. from Bromsgrove. It is a respectable and flourishing little place, and besides those trades generally found in a village, there is a considerable manufactory for scythes, hay knives, &c. belonging to the Messrs. Waldron, and malt is made here to a limited extent. A sheriff's court, for the recovery of small debts, is held on the third Wednesday in every month. The church, which is dedicated to the Holy Trinity, has, within these few years, received an additional number of sittings, by means of a grant from the incorporated society for enlarging churches and chapels, and been otherwise improved; and it is now a spacious and handsome structure, with a lofty spire: the living is a rectory, in the patronage of the president and fellows of St. John's College, Oxford: the Rev. G. F. Blakiston is the present incumbent. An endowed charity school is in the village. Fairs are held on the last Monday in April, and the Monday before St. Luke's day. The parish contained, at the last census (1831), 1,489 inhabitants.

GENTRY AND CLERGY.
Blakiston Rev. George Frank, Rectory, Belbroughton
Brownlow Rev. John, Chaddesley-Corbett   [Corbett
Piercy Rev. Geo. Hen. Chaddesley-
Russell Mrs. Sion house
Stephenson — esq. Brokencote hall
Warren Thos. esq. Brokencote house
Wylde Rev. John, Belbroughton

ACADEMIES & SCHOOLS.
CHARITY SCHOOL, Belbroughton—
William Ganderton, master
CHARITY SCHOOL, Chaddesley-Corbett—John Wigley, head master; Edmund Taylor, second master
Morris the Misses (day) Belbroughtn
Parkes Ann (day) Belbroughton
Rawlinson Louisa (day) Belbroughtn

BLACKSMITHS.
Davis Thomas, Belbroughton
Goodyear William, Belbroughton
Loines Benjamin, Fairfield
Perry John, Chaddesley Corbett
Price William, Belbroughton
Wright Thomas, Chaddesley-Corbett

BOOT & SHOE MAKERS.
Cole Joseph, Belbroughton
Davis John, Fairfield
Drew George, Chaddesley-Corbett
Duce William, Belbroughton
Maiden Eli, Belbroughton
Pardoe William, Belbroughton
Ruston William, Belbroughton
Taylor John, Belbroughton
Tolley William, Belbroughton
Tranter Joseph, Belbroughton

BUTCHERS.
Fox Taylor, Belbroughton
Giles Benjamin. Chaddesley-Corbett
Price Joseph, Belbroughton
Small Joseph, Fairfield
Spilsbury Thomas, Belbroughton

CARPENTERS.
Broad Charles, Belbroughton
Broad John, Chaddesley-Corbett
Bourn Edward, Belbroughton
Dunn John, Belbroughton
Dunn William, Belbroughton

GROCERS & DEALERS IN SUNDRIES.
Bate John, Chaddesley-Corbett
Brook John, Chaddesley-Corbett
Canadine Abraham, Belbroughton
Depper Thos. Chaddesley-Corbett
Gollins Samuel, Belbroughton
Jones Charles, Chaddesley-Corbett
Lacy James (& miller) Belbroughton
Lees Edward, Fairfield
Small Joseph, Fairfield

MALTSTERS.
Bate John, Chaddesley-Corbett
Fazey John (& corn dealer) Fairfield
Lilley William, Belbroughton
Parkes William, Belbroughton
Perrins John, Chaddesley-Corbett
Wiggin John, Belbroughton

PLUMBERS & GLAZIERS.
Goode Geo. (& draper) Belbroughton
Jackson Wm. Chaddesley-Corbett

SCYTHE MANUFACTURERS.
Waldron Thomas and William, Belbroughton

STONE MASONS.
Bate John, Belbroughton
Hill William, Fairfield
Taylor Thos. Chaddesley-Corbett

SURGEONS.
Jackson Edwd. Chaddesley-Corbett
Lees Thomas, Bluntington house

TAILORS.
Bough John and Son, Chaddesley-Corbett
Fox John, Belbroughton
Manning Thomas, Fairfield
Osborne Richard, Belbroughton

TAVERNS & PUBLIC HOUSES.
Queen's Head, John Kingdon, Belbroughton   [Corbett
Swan, William Tandy, Chaddesley-
Swan, Daniel Weaver, Fairfield
Talbot, Adam Jackson, Chaddesley-Corbett   [broughton
Talbot, Thomas Spilsbury, Bel-

WHEELWRIGHTS.
Gollins Samuel, Belbroughton
Lilly William, Fairfield
Smith John, Fairfield

Miscellaneous.
Bate Thos. retailer of beer, Belbroughton
Depper Thomas, retailer of beer, Chaddesley-Corbett   [ton
Downing Francis, millwright, Belbrough-
Grove Thomas, retailer of beer, Fairfield
Hodgkins Samuel, retailer of beer, Chaddesley-Corbett
Leek Peter, saddler, Belbroughton
Mills John, retailer of beer, Fairfield
Osborn Daniel, parish clerk, Belbroughton
Potter Saml. cooper, Chaddesley-Corbett
Rogers John, hair dresser, Chaddesley-Corbett   [broughton
Whitaker Elizabeth, milliner, &c. Bel-

DROITWICH

IS a borough and market town, having exclusive jurisdiction, locally in the upper division of the hundred of Halfshire; 118 miles N. W. from London, about 7 N. E. by N. from Worcester, and 14 W. by N. from Alcester; pleasantly situate on the river Salwarp, and on the road leading from Birmingham to Worcester, and the fashionable watering place of Malvern; from which circumstance of thoroughfare the town is materially benefitted: for the accommodation of travellers an excellent commercial and posting Inn, the 'George and Foley Arms,' is established. This place was anciently denominated *Wich* or *Wiche*, from the wiches or salt springs with which the neighbourhood abounds; and the prefix *Droit* (right or legal) is conjectured to refer to some exclusive privilege for the manufacture of salt, obtained by the inhabitants. This branch has been traced to have existed here before the Norman conquest, and to this day it constitutes the staple of the place: of the other trades, malting and tanning, together with mills for grinding corn, may be mentioned as the principal ones. The town was originally incorporated by Charter from John, but that by which it is now governed was granted by James I, in the 22nd of his reign: the corporate body consists of two bailiffs, a recorder, two justices, a town clerk, burgesses, &c. A court of record is held every Thursday, before the bailiffs and town clerk, for the recovery of debts under £10, and sessions quarterly, by the bailiffs, recorder, &c. The borough returned two burgesses to the parliaments of Edward I, and to those held in the 2nd and 4th of Edward II, from which period the privilege ceased until its renewal in 1554. The Reform Bill deprived the borough of one of its members; the gentleman returned at the general election in January, 1835, was John Barnaby, of Brockhampton, in the county of Hereford, Esq. The bailiffs are the returning officers. The limits of the borough, as defined by the new *Boundary Act* (an appendage to the Reform Bill,) comprise the old borough of Droitwich, and certain contiguous parishes and places are added thereto: the same act ordains that the election of knights of the shire, to represent the eastern division of the county in parliament, shall take place in this borough.

The old borough comprised the greater part of the united parishes of St. Andrew and St. Mary de Witton, those of St. Peter de Witton and St. Nicholas, and a small portion of that of St. Augustine de Wich, or Dodderhill. The church of St. Andrew, which was re-built after being destroyed by fire in 1293, is of several styles of architecture; the southern entrance, which formed part of the more ancient church, appears to be Saxon; the living is a discharged rectory, in the patronage of the crown, and incumbency of the Rev. John Topham. St. Peter's church has a tower, in the later English style, and some fine decorated windows. The living is a discharged vicarage, in the gift of Earl Somers, and incumbency of the Rev. J. R. Ingram. The church of St. Nicholas was greatly damaged during the parliamentary war, and only about half the tower remains: the living is a rectory, in the gift of the crown. The other places of worship are a chapel of ease, and one each for independents and Wesleyan methodists. The principal charities are a hospital for thirty-eight aged men and women, founded by Henry Coventry; in 1686, and a charity school for forty boys and forty girls, who are educated and clothed, and, on leaving school, apprenticed. The neighbourhood of this town is very

632

Fig. 10. Page from *Pigot's Commercial Directory*, 1835.

easily found elsewhere. As to their reliability, this needs careful and discriminating attention. Before the establishment of the great national directory-publishing companies, such as Pigot and Kelly, there was a great deal of hasty compilation of small directories for quick sale, many of a transitory nature. This resulted in a good deal of inaccuracy, and particularly in extensive pirating of earlier, out-of-date editions. The careful student will soon notice startling discrepancies among several earlier versions, which often take no account of the mobility and change which was such an important feature of the economic life of the day. Furthermore, even reliable firms often found that amassing and editing their material imposed an inevitable delay on publication, during which time certain information might already have become out of date. Used with care, however, the more reliable directories, that is those which have employed skilled local agents and published a series of editions over many years, offer a fascinating insight into village life over the past three or four generations.

FURTHER READING

N. Davies, J.A. Griggs and D.Herbert, 'Directories, Rate Books and the Commercial Structure of Towns', *Geography*, 53, 1968

C.R. Lewis, 'Trade Directories, a Data Source in Urban Analysis', *National Library of Wales Journal*, no.19, 1975

D. Page, 'Sources for Urban History 8: Commercial Directories and Market Towns', *The Local Historian*, 11, no.2, 1974

G. Shaw, 'The Content and Reliability of Nineteenth Century Trade Directories', *The Local Historian*, 13, no.4, 1978

G. Shaw and A. Tipper, *British Directories: A Bibliography and Guide to Directories Published in England and Wales, 1850-1950 and in Scotland 1773-1950*, Leicester University Press, 1989

G. Timmins, 'Measuring Industrial growth from Trade Directories', *The Local Historian*, 13, no.6, 1979

J.R.Walton, 'Trades and professions in late 18th century England; Assessing the evidence of Directories', *The Local Historian*, 17, no.6, May 1987

WORCESTERSHIRE ORIGINALS FOUND AT:

The Consolidated Chronological List of Worcestershire Directories held in repositories in or near Worcester, first issued by the County Record Office in 1959 is still available for reference (453 BA 11,560) but copies are not available to be taken away. Inevitably that list is now out-of-date in many respects and indeed local government re-organisation in 1974 may also have affected the locations of some of the Worcestershire libraries and places listed. More up-to-date is the elegant publication: Margaret Tohill, *Genealogical Resources in Worcestershire, No.2 Trade Directories and Almanacks*, available from the Record Office. This is a handlist of those publications, both in their original form and on microfilm, held at the Worcestershire branches of Hereford and Worcester Record Office and some Worcestershire public libraries, including Droitwich, Evesham, Kidderminster, Malvern, Pershore, Redditch, Rubery, Stourport, Upton on Severn and Worcester.

As well as directories of Worcestershire place, the guide lists other counties' directories housed in Worcestershire libraries. These include: Berkshire, Cornwall, Derbyshire, Devon, Dorset, Gloucestershire, Herefordshire, Leicestershire, Lincolnshire, London, Monmouthshire, Northamptonshire, Nottinghamshire, Oxfordshire, Rutland, Shropshire, Somerset, Staffordshire, Warwickshire, Yorkshire and Wales. Under Worcestershire itself more than 600 directories, dated from 1788 to 1986-7, are listed for the county itself and 30 other Worcestershire or *quondam* Worcestershire place-names (Kidderminster, Malvern, Stourport, Tenbury, etc.). Post re-organisation changes of county (or in the case of Halesowen pre-1844 and post-1974) for places like Cradley, Shipston-on-Stour, Stourbridge, etc. are cross-referenced to their new locations. The libraries in which each volume is held are indicated and there are indexes of publishers and place-names.

The few Worcestershire directories listed below are included to indicate a typical range available locally. It does not pretend to be all-inclusive but lists a few of the examples to be found in the Worcester Public Library (W), the County Record Office (R), and Birmingham Reference Library (B).

1788	WM. TUNNICLIFFE, *Survey of the County of Worcester*, 1788 (W)
1788	J. GRUNDY, *The Worcestershire Directory* (W:B);
1790, '92, '94	*The Worcester Royal Directory* (W:R:B);
1797	*The Worcester Guide & Royal Directory* (B).
1802, '06	R. GREEN, *Brief History of Worcestershire, or Worcestershire Guide Improved, with a Description of Neighbouring Towns* (B).
1820	S. LEWIS, *Worcestershire General & Commercial Guide* (W:B:R).
1823	R. WRIGHTSON, *Triennial Directory of Birmingham, including a List of Manufacturers in the Neighbouring Towns, in Staffordshire, Warwickshire and Worcestershire* (B).
1828-9	J. PIGOT & CO., *National Commercial Directory for Staffordshire, Warwickshire and Worcestershire* (B).
1830	J. PIGOT & CO., *Commercial Directories of Birmingham, Worcester and their Environs* (B).
1835	J. PIGOT & CO., *National Commercial Directory of Worcester* (W:R).
1837	T. STRATFORD, *Guide and Directory to the City and Suburbs of Worcester* (with Map showing the Boundaries of the Electoral Franchises) (W:B:R).
1840	R. HAYWOOD, *Directory of the City and Borough of Worcester, with an Almanac for the Year 1840* (W:R).
1841	J. BENTLEY, *History, Guide and Directory of Worcestershire*, in 7 parts (W:R).
1850	M. BILLINGS, *Directory of the District Around Birmingham* (B).
1850	H.W. LANG, *Companion to Worcester Beacon, a Panoramic Sketch of the County* (R).
1850, '62	I. SLATER, *Royal National & Commercial Directory and Topography of Derbyshire, Worcestershire, etc.* (B).
1854	LASCELLES & CO., *Directory of Worcester and Neighbourhood* (B).
1854	KELLY, *Post Office Directory*, published every 4 years; available from 1854 (B); 1858 (W) and 1884 (R).
1855	M. BILLING, *Directory & Gazeteer of the County of Worcestershire* (W:R).
1860	E. CASSEY & CO., *History, Topography & Directory of Worcestershire* (W:B:R);
1861	*Guide to the City and Cathedral of Worcester, also a Description of Malvern and other places in the Neighbourhood of Worcester* (B).
1869	W. WHITE, *Directory of Birmingham, Wolverhampton, Walsall, Dudley, Wednesbury, etc., and the Principal Villages in the Hardware District* (B).
1869	J. LITTLEBURY, *Directory of the City of Worcester* (R).
1875	J. LITTLEBURY, *Directory & Gazeteer of the County of Worcestershire* (W).
1879	J. LITTLEBURY, *Directory & Gazeteer of Worcester & District* (Parishes and Villages within 12 miles radius of the City) (W:B:R).
1880	J. LITTLEBURY, *Guide to Worcester & Neighbourhood* (B:R).
1882	J. LITTLEBURY, *Directory & Gazeteer of Worcester & District* (W).
1885	BACON, *New County Guide & Map of Worcestershire, from the Ordnance Survey, with Alphabetic Index to the New Census* (B).
1889	R.N. WORTH, *Tourists' Guide to Worcestershire* (B).
1908	J. LITTLEBURY, *Directory of the City of Worcester, and Towns of Malvern, Droitwich and Pershore,*

followed by Parishes within a radius of 10 miles of the City, 1908 (W); 1905-22 (W).

1911	COPE & CO., *Worcestershire Directory* (R).
1915-20	DEIGHTON & CO., *Annual Appendix to the Almanacs and Worcester Trades Directory* (R:W).
1918	*Bromsgrove & District Directory & Almanac, 49th Year, 1918; 76th Year, 1935* (B).
1919, '27	*Pictorial & Descriptive Guide to Worcester and District, with Plans & Maps* (B).
1926	LEICESTER, *Illustrated Family Almanac and Diary for Worcester City* (W).
1922	F. T. S. HOUGHTON, *Worcestershire* ('Little Guides' Series) (B)
1928 '31	AUBREY & CO., *Warwickshire & Worcestershire Directory* (B).
1933, '34	E. F. COPE, *Worcestershire Directory & Buyers' Guide* (W).
1933	E. M. KEARSEY, *the Malverns & District* ('Homelands Handbooks' Series) (B).
1950	O. BURNIE, *Guide to the County of Worcestershire* (B);
1951	*Directory of Rural Craftsmen in Worcestershire* (B);
1955-58	COUNTY PUBLICITY LTD, *Worcestershire Directory* (W:R).
1956	*Kidderminster Rural District Guide* ('Rural England' Series) (B).
1959	DIOCESAN, *Worcester Diocese* (R).
1965	*Company Information for Worcestershire taken from Kompass Directory of Great Britain* (W).

AN ABSTRACT OF ALL OCCUPATIONS CLASSIFIED IN J. BENTLEY'S *HISTORY, GUIDE AND DIRECTORY OF WORCESTERSHIRE*, 1841

The following figures give some idea of the scope and nature of the surveys made by these 19th-century compilers. They can be usefully compared with the similar analysis of occupations found in 17th-century domestic inventories (see pp.173-5). It must, however, be emphasised that neither of these lists is a census of all those employed in all trades in Worcestershire at the time the documents were compiled. The inventories are a random selection, accidentally occurring; the *Directory* gives, at best, a fairly representative sample of the county's trades. Directories can be particularly misleading in that an analysis of their contents will demonstrate with real accuracy only the relative importance attached by the compiler to any particular trades; the more random nature of the list taken from inventories does at least impose a law of averages. Bentley's high percentage of distribution-trades and manufacturers merely demonstrates the fact that this is, after all, a commercial directory. The relatively low position of agriculture is not an exact picture of the proportion of the county thus employed, as the *Directory* is weighted on the industrial side, including the industrial towns of the northern part of the county alongside the villages and market towns of the predominately agricultural south. Though many towns still, in 1841, numbered a large group of farmers amongst the inhabitants, the northern towns have few, if any. Yet, though exaggerated, this reduced proportion of agricultural classes contains an element of truth; the rural village was certainly less completely an agricultural production unit in 1841 than it is today. One gains a definite impression from the directories of the busy and industrial life of the 19th-century village, which contained a far greater variety of occupations, and many more shopkeepers and craftsmen, than the same village today. None of the occupation-totals pretends to number all those who were employed in each trade, but gives only the names of masters and owners. Very few labourers are included, though many small owners are named. Particularly noticeable in this connection is the prevalence in 1841 of the employment of farmers in other trades, so that one finds numerous references to 'farmer and blacksmith', 'farmer and butcher', 'farmer and wheelwright', 'farmer and shoemaker', 'farmer and shopkeeper', and even 'farmer and coaldealer'.

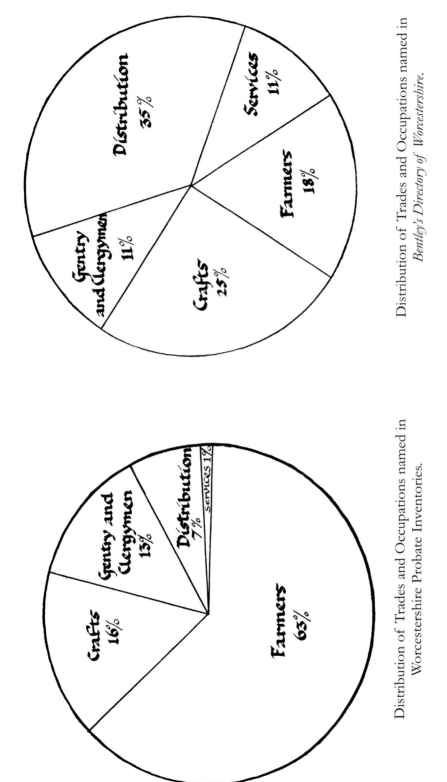

1841

Distribution of Trades and Occupations named in *Bentley's Directory of Worcestershire.*

1650

Distribution of Trades and Occupations named in Worcestershire Probate Inventories.

Fig. 11. Worcestershire Trades and Occupations, 1650 and 1841.

The figures can best be used with a map, to show the distribution of the different occupations and industries in different regions of the county, but they do also reveal other social trends. We note the appearance of many new crafts not mentioned in the 17th century, and the disappearance of some older trades; above all, the figures give a good impression of the tremendous diversity of occupations within a county which was, then as now, partly industrial, partly agricultural. The directories reflect the new importance of the distributor, the carrier, the dealer, and middle-men of all sorts. There is some indication of the increasing specialisation of 19th-century industry, and clear indication of the rise of certain localised manufactures, particularly nail-making, needle-manufacture, carpet-weaving and glass-working; the increase in employment in a more specialised building industry is another of the *Directory*'s more accurate revelations. When counting the trades, several miscellaneous impressions of 19th-century town and village life are strongly felt—the particular importance, for example, of the bootmaker; the fact that few bakers are found outside the towns, and the new importance of the market gardener, greengrocer, milkman and coaldealer.

Comparison with a similar analysis of a 20th-century directory would undoubtedly show a drastic reduction in the number of village shops such as grocers, milliners, shoe-makers, tailors and coaldealers, all remarkably numerous in 1841; the almost complete disappearance of rural crafts and village industries such as wheelwrights, millwrights, coopers, scythesmiths, blacksmiths and carpenters; far less rural 'out-work' for such industries as leatherwork, nail-making and other metal trades. The greatest change statistically would undoubtedly be the immense increase in the numbers of those residents not employed within the village, both of the professional and artisan classes. The proportion of farmers to total population would possibly not have undergone much further change, although farming would now be the occupation of the largest number of those still working within the village; miscellaneous crafts and services, including shopkeepers, within the village would reveal the most drastic diminution. Finally one feels that the comparison would reveal the village of 1961, during the day-time, to be a quieter, emptier place than it was in 1841.

See: G. Hopkins, *A History of Worcestershire based on Bentley's Directory of 1841*, D. Brown & Sons, 1982.

SUMMARY

		Total	Per cent
I. and II.	Gentry, Nobility and Clergy;	1742	11
III.	Farmers and Agricultural Trades	2787	18
IV.	Crafts and Industries:	3959	25
V.	Distribution Trades, Food, Clothing, etc.	5355	35
VI.	Miscellaneous, Services, etc.:	1617	11

The last four classes of occupations can be further analysed as follows:

III. *Farmers and Agricultural Trades. 2787*

Bailiffs, stewards, gamekeepers	8	Market gardeners, nurserymen and	
Cattle dealers, horse dealers, etc.	13	seedsmen	153
Farmers	2412	Millers	144
Hay, straw and corn dealers	57		

IV. *Crafts and Industries. 3959*

Textile Manufacturers:	*304*		
Bombasin Manufacturers	3	Sailcloth makers	4
Cappers	1	Silk mercers	14
Carpet Manufacturers	30	Silk throwsters and ribbon mfrs.	19
Drapers	178	Stocking weavers	10
Dyers	9	Weavers	2
Embroiderers	1	Wool and worsted manufacturers	13
Haircloth Manufacturers	2	Woolstaplers	13
Lace Makers	5		

Ironwork, Metals and Heavy Industries:	*1301*		
Blacksmiths	295	Iron masters	80
Brass founders	5	Machine makers	6
Braziers and tinplate workers	38	Miners	3
Casehardeners	6	Nailers and nailers' ironmongers	626
Chain and trace makers	48	Pump makers	18
Cutlers	6	Scythe makers	9
Engineers	12	Steam engine and boiler mfrs.	8
Firebrick and furnace makers	16	Steel manufacturers	2
Furnace bellows makers	4	Toolmakers	2
Iron bar and hoop makers	13	Vice and anvil makers	29
Iron boat makers	2	Whitesmiths	37
Iron founders	29	Wireworkers	7

Coal Masters:	*45*

Building Trades:	*892*		
Architects	10	Cement and plaster makers	2
Bricklayers, slaters and plasterers	99	Lime burners	4
Brick, slate and tile makers	67	Painters, plumbers and glaziers	153
Builders	105	Stone masons	50
Carpenters and joiners	357	Timber merchants	45

Leather Workers:	*287*		
Curriers	86	Leather stainers	11
Fellmongers	7	Saddlers	66
Glovers	88	Tanners	16
Leather dressers	13		

Miscellaneous Crafts:	*1130*		
Auger makers	2	Cabinet makers and upholsterers	48
Barometer makers	5	Carvers and gilders	8
Basket makers	28	Chair makers	11
Bellhangers	2	Coach builders	19
Blacking makers	1	Comb makers	9
Boat builders	12	Coopers	86
Bone merchants	4	Cork cutters	6
Bonnet-shape makers	1	Distillers	3
Bookbinders	2	Engravers	3
Brushmakers	8	Fender and fire-iron makers	37

Miscellaneous Crafts (cont.)

File cutters	3	Railway contractors	1
Fishing tackle makers	3	Reed makers	2
Gas-fittings mfrs.	1	Rope and sacking mfrs.	29
Glass mfrs.	45	Salt industry	14
Glass stainers	2	Screw tackle mfrs.	2
Glass-house clay merchants	7	Scuttle makers	1
Goldsmiths and silversmiths	9	Sieve makers	3
Gunsmiths	9	Soap makers	3
Harness makers	1	Soda water mfrs.	1
Hook-and-Eyemakers	1	Spade and implement makers	23
Horn powder-flask makers	1	Spectacle makers	1
Horsehair seat makers	1	Spur makers	1
Last makers	2	Stay makers	21
Locksmiths	16	Steelyard makers	1
Malt and coffee mill makers	3	Straw hat makers	126
Mat makers	1	Sword blade and bayonet forgers	4
Mathematical instrument makers	1	Tallow chandlers	29
Millwrights	12	Tobacco-pipe mfrs.	6
Needle and fish-hook makers	138	Trunk makers	3
Organ builders	2	Truss makers	2
Pan makers	5	Umbrella makers	8
Parchment paper makers	8	Watch and clock makers	44
Pill-box mfrs.	1	Wheelwrights	182
Porcelain mfrs.	4	Woodturners	18
Printers	34		

V. Distribution Trades, Clothing, Food, etc. 5355

Bakers and flour dealers	223	Grocers and tea dealers	818
Brewers	7	Haberdashers	53
Booksellers and stationers	45	Hardware dealers	57
Boot and shoe makers	682	Hatters	45
Breeches makers	6	Higglers	2
British wine-makers	2	Hosiers	13
Butchers	345	Hucksters	1
Cheesemongers and Bacon factors	23	Maltsters	254
Chemists and druggists	96	Milliners and dressmakers	305
China, glass and earthenware dealers	50	Patten and clog makers	24
Cider and perry merchants	6	Pork dealers	9
Clothes dealers	34	Tailors	417
Coal merchants	156	Taverns, innkeepers, etc.	1458
Confectioners	40	Tobacconists	6
Eating-house proprietors	17	Toy dealers	9
Fishmongers	16	Tripe dressers	1
Fruiterers and greengrocers	21	Vinegar merchants	4
Furniture brokers	30	Wine and spirit merchants	70
Game dealers	10		

VI. Miscellaneous, Services, etc. 1617

Abbot and Abbess	2	Agents, merchants' and general	39
Accountants	14	Artists and sculptors	16
Actuaries	1	Attorneys, solicitors, barristers	139
Agents for fire insurance, etc.	138	Auctioneers and appraisers	48

Bank managers and secretaries	35	Music dealers	6
Baths and billiard-room keepers	3	Musical composers	1
Boatmen	6	Opticians	1
Bone-setters	1	Pawnbrokers	20
Carriers and haulers	133	Public officials, etc.	
Clerks	10	(including Court Officials, Excise Officers,	
Coach proprietors, livery stable		Governors of Prisons, Asylum Matrons, House	
keepers, etc.	38	of Industry Governors, Tax Collectors, Police,	
Dentists	5	Registrars, Postmasters and Post-mistresses,	
Fossil dealers	2	etc.)	60
Gasworks managers	5	Schoolmasters and mistresses	435
Hairdressers and perfumiers	108	Scourers	1
House agents	6	Stocktakers	1
Huntsmen	2	Surgeons and physicians	136
Ivory turners	1	Taxidermists	2
Labourers	6	Teachers of art, music, languages, etc.	27
Land agents and surveyors	41	Union treasurers	1
Librarians, newsroom proprietors, etc.	49	Veterinary surgeons	11
Lodging-house keepers	43	Waterworks clerks	2
Marine store dealers	2	Wharfingers	19
Midwives	1		

SOME COUNTY PUBLICATIONS

J.E. Norton, *Guide to National and Provincial Directories of England and Wales, excluding London, published before 1856*, Royal Hist. Soc., Guides and Handbooks, no.5, 1984 is an indispensable guide to earlier county directories. For later volumes see a local handlist (as, for example, for Worcestershire, below.)

The following fragmentary county list (*pace* Jane Norton) merely indicates that most Record Offices and libraries can be expected to produce at least one, if not many more, editions of Kelly, Pigot, Robson and Slater to illustrate the 19th-century local history of their county and its towns.

Bedfordshire Pigot & Co., *Royal National and Commercial Directory and Topography of the Counties of Bedford, Cambridge, Essex, Herts. etc.*, London, 1839; G.A. Cooke, *The Modern British Traveller; or Tourist's Pocket Directory*, London, 1802-10: I includes Beds. and Berks.; II Bucks. and Cambridge; III Cheshire, Cornwall, etc.

Berkshire *Robson's Commercial Directory of the Western Counties, including Berkshire*, 1838.

Cheshire Pigot & Co., *A Commercial Directory of Cheshire, 1934* (facsimile edition in paperback), 1982.

Cornwall *Bailey's Western and Midland Directory*, 1783.

Derbyshire Pigot & Co, *A Commercial Directory of Derbyshire, 1835* (facsimile edition in paperback), Derbyshire County Library, 1976.

Devonshire W. White, *History, Gazetteer and Directory of Devonshire* (reprint of the 1850 edition), David and Charles, 1968.

Dorset *Robson's Commercial Directory of the Western Counties, including Dorset*, 1838.

Essex 'Essex Trade Directories', *Essex Journal*, 25, no.3, Winter 1990.

Gloucestershire *Slater's Royal National and Commercial Directory of Gloucestershire and Wales*, 1858-9; *Pigot's Directory for Gloucestershire, 1822-3* (facsimile), reproduced by Brian Stevens Historic Prints, Monmouth, 1973.

Herefordshire *Kelley's Directory of Herefordshire and Gloucestershire, 1891*, E. Hunt & Co., *Commercial Directory for the Cities of Gloucester, Hereford and Worcester*, 1847; *Pigot & Co. National Commercial Directory, including*

Herefordshire, 1835; *Robson's Commercial Directory of the Western Counties, including Herefordshire*, 1838; *Kelly's Directory of Herefordshire*, 1885; J. and M. West, 'Victorian villages' (evidence from Edward Cassey's *Directory of Herefordshire, 1858*), in *A History of Herefordshire*, Phillimore, 1985.

Lancashire   G. Tupling and S. Horrocks, *Lancashire Directories, 1684-1957*, Manchester Joint Committee on Lancashire Bibliography, 1960.

Leicestershire   *Pigot & Co.'s National Commercial Directory, including Leicestershire*, 1835; J.D. Bennet, 'Richard Weston and the first Leicestershire Directory', *Leicestershire Historian*, 2, 1975.

Lincolnshire   *Pigot & Co.'s National Commercial Directory, including Lincolnshire*, 1835; W. White, *History, Gazetteer and Directory of Lincolnshire* (reprint of the 1856 edition), David and Charles, 1970.

London & Middlesex   R.J. Ensing, *Guides to Local History Sources: no.1, Directories*, Wandsworth Hist. Soc., 1985; C. Wade and M. Holmes (intro.), *The Hampstead and Highgate Directory for 1885-6 by Hutchings & Crossley Ltd.*, London Borough of Camden & Camden Hist. Soc., 1986.

Monmouthshire   *Pigot & Co.'s National Commercial Directory, including Monmouthshire*, 1835; *Robson's Commercial Directory of the Western Counties, including Monmouthshire*, 1838.

Northamptonshire   *Pigot & Co.'s Royal National and Commercial Directory and Topography, including Northamptonshire*, 1841; *Pigot & Co.'s Commercial Directory of Northamptonshire* (facsimile edition in paperback), Northampton Library, 1975.

Nottinghamshire   *Pigot & Co.'s National Commercial Directory, including Nottinghamshire*, 1835.

Oxfordshire   *Kelly's Directory of Oxfordshire*, 1887.

Rutland   *Pigot & Co.'s National Commercial Directory, including Rutland*, 1835.

Shropshire   S. Bagshaw, *History, Gazetteer and Directory of Shropshire*, 1851.

Somersetshire   *Robson's Commercial Directory of the Western Counties, including Somerset*, 1838; *Guides, Directories and Newspapers in the Reference Library*, Bath Municipal Library, 1966.

Staffordshire   I. Slater, *Royal National and Commercial Directory, including Staffordshire*, 1835; W. White, *History, Gazetteer and Directory of Staffordshire and the City of Lichfield*, 1851; *Kelly's Post Office Directory of Staffordshire and Worcestershire*, 1876; N. Emery and D. R. Beard, *Staffordshire Directories; A Union List of Directories for the Geographical County of Staffordshire*, Stoke-on-Trent Libraries, Bibliographical series, no.2, 1966; D.F. and S. Radmore, *A Guide to the Directories of the West Midlands to 1850*, Library Association, 1971.

Warwickshire   W. West, *History, Topography and Directory of Warwickshire*, 1830; Francis White & Co., *History, Gazetteer and Directory of Warwickshire*, 1850; W. Showell, *Directory of Birmingham* (reprint of the first edition), S.R. Publications, 1969; D.F. and S. Radmore, *A Guide to the Directories of the West Midlands to 1850*, Library Association, 1971.

Worcestershire   D.F. and S. Radmore, *A Guide to the Directories of the West Midlands to 1850*, Library Association, 1971; G. Hopkins, *Joseph Bentley's History of Worcestershire, written in 1840 and viewed in recent time*, 1985.

Yorkshire   *Pigot & Co.'s Royal National and Commercial Directory and Topography, including Yorkshire*, 1835; E. Baines, *Baines' Yorkshire, a new printing of the History, Directory and Gazetteer of the County of York*, 1: *West Riding*, 2: *East and North Ridings* (reprint of 1823 edition), David and Charles, 1969; P. Wilde, 'The Use of Business Directories in comparing the industrial structure of towns: an example from the South-west Pennines', *The Local Historian*, 12, 1976.

APPENDIX I

Time Chart

✦

— 400. End of the Roman period.
THE DARK AGES
Period of Anglo-Saxon Invasion and Settlement.

— 500.

Benedictine Monasticism established.
Conversion of the Anglo-Saxons.

— 600.

679. Bosel, first Bishop of Worcester.
679-785. The Kings of Wiccia.

— 700.

Bede's *Ecclesiastical History*.

— 800. Viking Invasions begin.
871-901. Alfred the Great.

— 900.

964. The Wolverley Charter (Plate I).

Danegeld instituted.

— 1000.

1066. The Norman Conquest of England.
Population 1¼m.

1085. The Domesday Survey (Plate II).

— 1100. THE MIDDLE AGES
1096. The First Crusade.
Craft Gilds.

— 1200.

1207. St. Francis of Assisi.
1215. Magna Carta.
Population, England and Wales (?) 2½m.

1280. Lay Subsidy Roll (Plate VI).
1280-1303. Romsley Court Roll (Plate III).
1290. Extent of Chaddesley (Plate VII).

— 1300.

1338. Hundred Years' War.

1349. The Black Death.
1381. The Peasants' Revolt.

— 1400.

1455. Wars of the Roses.
1474. Caxton printing in English.

— 1500.

THE MODERN PERIOD

1511. The Chaddesley Brass (Fig. I).

The Reformation begins.
Dissolution of Monasteries.

1538. Chaddesley Parish Register (Plate XI).
1574-1608. Chaddesley Inventories (Plate XIII).
1577. Saxton's Map of Worcestershire (Plate X).

1588. The Spanish Armada.

— 1600.

1637. Chaddelsey Constable's Presentment (Plate XI).

1642. Stuart Civil War.
Interregnum.
1660. Stuart Restoration.
1662. Hearth Tax Introduced.

1666. Chaddesley Hearth Tax Return (Plate XV)

1692. Land Tax introduced.

1697. Chaddesley Map (Plate IX).

— 1700. Population of England and Wales 5½m.
1715. Jacobite Rebellion.
1738. Wesleyan Religious Revival.
1750. Population of England and Wales 6¼m.
Agrarian and Industrial Revolutions accelerate.

1789. Chaddesley Land Tax Assessment (Fig. 8).
1799. Chaddelsey Enclosure (Plate XVI).

— 1800.

1801. First Census. 9m.
Napoleonic Wars.

1822. Greenwood's Map of Worcestershire (Plate X).
1823. Bromsgrove to Worcester Turnpike (Plate XIX).

1825. Railway development begins.
1832. First Reform Act.
1834. New Poor Law.

1835. Pigot's Commercial Directory (Fig. 10).
1839. Chaddesley Tithe Award (Plate XVIII).

1888. Local Government Acts.
— 1900. 1899-1902. Boer War.
1901. Census. 42m.

Elementary Word Lists

✧

GLOSSARY OF SOME WORDS COMMONLY FOUND IN SAXON CHARTERS AND PLACE-NAMES

Ac, Aec, oak-tree
Aecer, acre, strip
Aerest, firstly
Aern, storehouse
Aesc, ash-tree
Aet, at
Apuldre, apple-tree

Baec, back, ridge
Bece, stream or valley
Be suthan, to the south of
Belimpath, belonging to
Beorg, barrow
Betwyxt, between
Big, by, near
Birice, birch-tree
Blaec, black
Broc, brook
Brom, wild broom
Brycg, bridge
Butan, without
Byrig, burgh, township, camp
Byscop, bishop
Byht, a bend

Caerse baece, Caersa waell, watercress
    bed
Cald, cold
Calwan hyll, bare, bald hill
Cirice, church
Cirice stall, church site
Clif, steep slope
Cnoll, knoll
Col, charcoal
Cot, cottage
Croft, croft
Cron mere, heron pond
Cumb, coombe

Cynig, King

Daell, dell
Dene, dean, valley
Deop, deep
Deor, deer
Dic, dyke, ditch
Dun, hill

Ealden, ancient
Eastrihte, due east, eastward
Ecg, edge, ridge
Efen, level with
Eft, again
Embuten, around
Eorth, ploughland

Feld, open field
Fen, fen
Feower, four
Ford, ford
Fos, Fosse-way
Ful, foul, dirty, muddy
Furh, furrow
Furlang, furlong

Gaerstun, grass croft
Gaet, gate
Gar, gore, triangle of ploughland
Geard, yardland, croft
Gebyreth, belongs
Gemaere, boundaries
Geref, reeve
Graf, grove
Grenan weg, green way, lane

Haece, hatch-gate
Haesel, hazel-tree

Haga, enclosure
Halh, Heal, hollow
Heafod, headland
Heahstraet, high-street, made road
Heanleah, high lea
Heaweg, highway
Heg, hedge
Hegeraew, hedgerow
Hens broc, moorhen's brook
Heopan hyll, hill where wild roses grow
Heort, hart, deer
Herepath, highway
Hida, a hide
Hierde, herdsman
Hit cymth, it comes
Hiwan, monastic community
Hlyp geat, 'leap-gate'; gate in an
    enclosure, which deer can leap
    into, but not out of
Holig, holly-tree
Hor pit, mud pit
Hwaete, wheat
Hwit, white
Hyll, hull, hill
Hymel, hop-plant
Hyrst, copse

Laecc, stream or bog
Leag, lea
Lincumb, coombe of lime-trees
Lind, lime-tree
Lond, land, ploughland
Lusthorn, spindle-tree

Maedwe, meadowland
Maerbroc, boundary-brook
Maerc, balk, border, boundary
Maerdic, boundary-ditch

Maerweg, boundary-road
Medland, meadows
Medweland, meadowland, meads
Mere, pond
Micel, great
Middlewarde, to them iddle of
Mor, swamp
Mylensteall, site of a mill
Mythan, meeting-point

Neothe maest, nethermost, lower
Neothewearde, downward
North wearde, on the north side

Of, from
Ofre, bank, slope
On, to
On east healfe, on the east side
On gerihte, straight on
On twa healfe, on two sides of
Onbutan, around
Ondlang, along
Ongean, against
Oxan ers, ox pasture

Portweg, market street
Preost, priest
Pull, brook, pool
Pyrig, pear-tree

Raew, row, 'thorn raew', a row of
  thorns
Rahheg, roe-deer hedge, leap-gate
Risc, rushes
Rith, stream
Ritling, stream
Rod, path
Rycgweg, ridge-way

Sandun, sandy hill
Sceot to, runs to
scire, boundary, division
Sealt, salt
Sealter ford, salt-carrier's ford
Sealtstraet, saltway
Seath, pit
Secg, sedge
Secgmor, sedgey swamp
Set, dwelling-place
Sic, water course
Sihtran, drainage ditch
Slaed, valley
Sloh, slough
Smeth, smooth
Snaeth, enclosed piece of land
Sol, mud, wallowing-place
Stan, stone
Stan gedelfe, quarry
Stapol, pole
Steap, steep
Stig, uphill path
Stigel, stile
Stobb, tree-stump
Stodfold, horse-fold
Stow, place, market, religious place
Straem, stream
Straet, made road, Roman road
Strod, marsh
Suthewearde, southward
Suthrihte, southward
Swa, so, thus
Swin haga, woodland where swine are
  pastured

Thaer hit aer aras, where it first began;
  starting-point
Thaerto, in addition

Thanon, then
The ligeth of, which runs from
Thicce, thick
Thider, there
This sind, these are
Thonne, then
Thorn, thorn-tree
Thurh ut, right through
Togaedere, together
Treow, tree
Tun, village
Twa, two
Twycena, cross-roads

Uferra, over, upper

Wad, woad
Waed, shallow
Weall, wall
Weg, way, road
Well, spring
Weorth, Wyrth, enclosure
Wer, weir
Westmaest, most westerly
Wic, dairy farm
Wictun, dairy farm
Windofre, windbank
With westan, to the west of
Withig, willow-tree
Withutan, outside
Won, crooked
Wud, wood
Wudulond, woodland
Wylla, stream

Ymbutan, around

GLOSSARY OF WORDS AND PHRASES COMMONLY FOUND IN THE DOMESDAY SURVEYS

Abbas, an abbot.
Acciptris, a hawk.
Acra, an acre.
Ad numerum, money paid 'by tale';
  i.e. counted instead of weighed.
Ad peis, money reckoned by its
  weight.
Ad servicium, by the service of.
Ad victum, for the sustenance of.
(se) Adquietare pro, to be reckoned
  at, assessed at.
Aera, an aerie of hawks
Aestivum, in summer.
Aliquantulum, a small amount.

Alnetum, alder-wood.
Ancilla, a bondwoman, maidservant,
  female serf.
Anglicus, Saxon.
Anguilla, an eel.
Antiquorum temporum, by ancient
  custom.
Apendicius, a hamlet, a berewick.
Apud, at.
Arabilis, arable.
Arare, to plough.
Arpenz, a measure of vineyards.
Aula, a hall or manor-house.
Aurum, gold.

Avenae, oats.

Bedellus, a beadle or bailiff.
Berewica, a hamlet or grange farm.
Bloma ferri, a 'bloom', or measure of
  iron.
Bobus, an ox. (Corrupt nominative)
Bordarius, a bordar, free smallholder.
Bovarius, an ox-master, oxman; there
  were two oxmen to team,
  usually tenants of 5-10 acres.
Boves, oxen.
Boveta, a bovate of land, about ¼ of
  a carucate.

Brasium, malt.

Brevis regis, the king's writ, or order; occasionally 'brevis' refers to a Domesday return made elsewhere.

Burgenses, burgesses.

Burgus, a borough, township.

Burh, a borough, township.

Burus, small peasant class.

Canis, a dog.

Capreolis, a roe-deer.

Caput manerii, the chief manor or capital tenement.

Caruca, a plough or plough-team.

Carucata, a carucate, measure of land, one ploughland.

Castellum, a castle.

Causa, a dispute, case or matter.

Ceapstowe, a market.

Censum, a rent.

Circset, 'church-scot'; the payment of horse-loads of grain from manorial land, to the Church.

Civitas, a city.

Colibertus, small peasant, same as 'burus'.

Comes, an earl.

Comitatus, the county, its assembly, chief representatives or shire-court; the jury for the county.

Condonare, to accept.

Consuetudo, customary dues; a custom.

Consuetudines firma, customary rent.

Corpus justitia, corporal punishment.

Cotmannus, a cottar, or cottager; same as 'cottarius'.

Cottarius, a cottar, one of the many categories of free tenants holding small tenements of land.

Curia, a court.

Custodire, to have custody of.

Custos apium, beekeeper.

Daia, a dairymaid.

De, worth; also to hold 'of', or from, an overlord.

Defensio, an enclosure.

Deprecari, to be obtained.

Deservire, to perform services.

Dimidius, half.

Dominicum, Dominium, demesne; the land of the lord, not let out to tenants.

Dum, while, as long as.

Ecclesia, a church.

Emendare, to pay a fine.

Episcopus, a bishop.

Exercitus, a feudal armed levy of troops.

Expeditio, Norman feudal military service.

Faber, a smith.

Falcare, to mow.

Fera, a wild beast, beast of the chase.

Ferrum, iron.

Feodum, Feudum, a 'fee', or fief; a piece of land, or manors, held by feudal tenure and services.

Figulus, a potter.

Firma, the 'farm', or composition of royal taxes and rights in the county ('firma comitatus'), or borough ('firma burgi'), paid by the earl, sheriff, or private undertaker.

Foresta, the Royal forest.

Forestarius, a forester.

Forestellum, 'foresteal'; attack from ambush; a Crown plea, for the royal court.

Foris, outside; outside the jurisdiction of.

Forisfactura, a forfeit, or penalty.

Forum, a market.

Francegena, French.

Frumentum, wheat.

Furnus, a furnace.

Fyrdwite, Saxon military service.

Gallina, a hen.

Gelda, land-tax; Danegeld.

Geldare, to pay geld or tax.

Geneat, a Saxon class, equivalent to villein.

Gurgis, a weir.

Haya, a hedged enclosure.

Heinfara, 'Hamfara' or 'Hamsoc'; an attack upon a man's house and home; a Crown plea.

Herciare, to harrow.

Hida, a rateable value of land. Sometimes it is possible to equate this unit with an area of approximately 120 acres. In Saxon times the Shire and Hundred had occasionally been divided into units of 5 and 10 hides for purposes of defence and government. Most attempts to equate these divisions too accurately prove misleading; e.g. some historians equate the 'hundred' with 100 hides, and distinguish 'double' and 'treble'

Hundreds of 200 and 300 hides.

Hiemale, in winter.

Homo, the dependent 'man' of an overlord, a vassal.

Hospitatus, inhabited.

Iacet, lies; land 'lies' in a certain place.

Ibi, there.

In capite, 'in chief'; land held directly of the King was held 'in chief', and its tenant was a 'tenant-in-chief'.

In fine, within the bounds of.

Lana, wool.

Landfyrd, Saxon military service.

Latus, wide, broad.

Leuca, Lauga, Lewa or Leuua, a league; usual measure of woodland. Four furlongs in Worcvs; elsewhere often 12 furlongs or 480 perches; 1½ miles.

Lewedes, leagues.

Libera terra, land free from tax, exempt.

Liberi homines, freemen.

Libra, one pound.

Licencia, permission.

Lignum, Lignis, wood, timber, firewood, fuel.

Longus, long.

Manere, to dwell, live.

Manerium, the Domesday manor.

Mansio, a town-house.

Massa, a measure of iron.

Masura, a town-house, burgess tenement.

Medietas, a half.

Mel, honey.

Membrum, a hamlet, berewick.

Mensura, a measure of salt.

Mercatum, a market.

Metere, to reap.

Miles, a knight.

Missa in defenso, enclosed, fenced.

Mitta, a measure (e.g. of salt).

Modo, now (i.e. T.R.W.).

Molendinum, a miller.

Monachus, a monk.

Monasterium, a monastery.

Navis, a ship.

Nemus, a woodland.

Nescire, to be ignorant; not know.

Non multa, not much.

Nox de firma, a night's hospitality.

Nummus, money.

Nuper, recently

Ociosus, idle.
Ora, an ounce.
Ovis, sheep.

Parca, a park.
Pasnagio, pannage, fodder for swine, right to graze swine in woodland.
Pastura, pasture.
Pensatus, weighed.
Pensum, weight; money reckoned *ad pensum* was weighed; money *ad numerum* was counted.
Pertinens, belonging to.
Petra, a stone.
Piscare, to fish.
Piscaria, a fishery, pools.
Placitare, the obligation to pleade or accept the jurisdiction of a court.
Planum, a field.
Plumbus, a lead-pan.
Porcarius, a swineherd.
Porcus, a pig.
Praeter, excepting, besides.
Pratum, meadow.
Prepositus, a reeve.
Presbyter, a priest.
Propter, on account of.
Puteus, Puteia, a brine-pit.

Quarentena, a furlong of woodland; 220 yards long.
Quarta pars, a fourth part, quarter.
Quercus, an oak tree.
Quietus, exempt from geld or service.

Radchenistre, Radmannus, a 'riding-

knight', a class whose obligation was to provide mounted escorts or carrying service.
Recedere, to withdraw from an overlord's jurisdiction.
Reddere, to pay.
Regina, queen.
Respondere, to make a return, be responsible for.
Rustico opere, by peasant labour services.

Saca et soca, the jurisdiction of a court over certain minor offences.
Saisitus, held.
Salina, a salt-pan.
Salinarius, a salt-worker.
Scipfyrd, Saxon naval service.
Scira, the Shire.
Secare, to mow.
Seminare, to sow.
Sepultura, burial fees due to the Church.
Serviens, a serjeant; tenant holding by some special rent or service.
Servus, a slave, serf, chattel; the Saxon 'theow'. This class dies out, merging into the less totally unfree class of villeinage, shortly after the Conquest.
Sextarium, sestier, a measure of salt.
Siligus, rye.
Silva, woodland.
Silva minuta, underwood.
Silva regis, the Royal forest.
Sochemannus, a sokeman, freeman.
Sochus, a plough-share.
Stiches, measures or 'sticks' of eels; 25 eels.
Summa, a horse-load.

Supradicta, above-mentioned.

Tainus, a Saxon thegn.
Tale, money paid 'by tale' is counted out, not weighed out (see *Ad peis* and *pensum*).
Tempore regis Edwardi (T.R.E.), in the reign of King Edward the Confessor (1042-66).
Tempore regis Willelmi (T.R.W.), in the reign of King William I (1066-87).
Tercia pars, a third part.
Terra, land.
Teste comitatu, by the testimony and evidence of the county, shire-moot, or jury.
Theloneus, toll, tax.

Uncia, an ounce.
Utlaghe, an outlaw.
Uxor, a woman or wife.

Vaccarius, a cowherd.
Valet, it is worth (T.R.W.).
Valuit, it was worth (T.R.E.).
Vatio, manner, means of tenure.
Vel, or.
Venatio, hunting.
Vestitus, cultivated.
Vicecomes, Shire-reeve, sheriff.
Villa, the vill, village.
Vinea, a vineyard.
Virgata, a virgate; 30 acres; a villein tenement.
Vix, scarcely.

Waliscus, Welsh; literally, 'alien, foreign'.
Wastus or Wastata, waste, derelict, destroyed.

GLOSSARY OF SOME WORDS COMMONLY USED IN MANORIAL RECORDS

For further assistance with technical terms and contractions, see C.T. Martin, *Record Interpreter*, Phillimore, 1982.

Ad mensam domini, a 'wet-boon', i.e. service for which the day's food and drink is provided by the lord.
Agnus, a lamb.
Alauda, a lark.
Allea, garlic.
Allocare, to rebate, allow.
Allocatio, an allowance.
Alveus, a tub.

Anatus, a duck.
Ancilla, a maidservant.
Anser, a gander.
Aparitor, the summoner to an ecclesiastical court.
Aper, a boar.
Arrura, ploughing-service.
Assartum, clearing made in woods or wasteland.
Auca, a goose.

Auxilium, an aid, tallage or payment by unfree tenants.
Avena, oats.
Aver, Averius, a beast of agriculture or burden.
Averagium, carrying-service.
Averoe, payment to workmen.

Ballivus, a bailiff or official.
Bartona, a grange farm.

Bercarius, shepherd.
Berceria, sheep-fold.
Bedellus, beadle, foreman, reeve, often the summoner to the manorial court.
Bederip, harvest boom-work.
Bladum, corn, corn-field.
Bonna, a heifer.
Boon-work, services additional to week-work; see *Precaria*.
Bos, an ox.
Boscum, woodland.
Bouera, thicket or copse.
Brachiare, to brew.
Braseum, malt.
Brechia, a strip of land.
Brevis, a brief, letter or writ.
Burla, rough cloth.
Busca, brushwood.
Busellus, a bushel.
Butirum, butter.

Calumpnia, a challenge or claim.
Calumpniare, to accuse, challenge, disallow.
Campus, an open field.
Caput terra, a headland or capital tenement.
Carecta, Caractata, a cart or cartload.
Carpentarius, a carpenter.
Carrare, to cart or carry.
Carrucagium, liability to do plough-service.
Carta, a charter, or cpy of a court-roll; this was the 'copy-holder's' proof of tenure.
Caruca, a plough.
Celarius, the cellarer of an Abbey, often the lord's Steward, in change of villein lands and services.
Cena, supper.
Cenapis, mustard.
Cepum, lard or tallow.
Cespes, turf.
Cespitare, to lay turf.
Clavus, a nail.
Cliba, a furnace.
Collectio nucium, service of collecting nuts.
Communia, right of common pasture.
Communics, 'common' suit of court, i.e. duty of attendance whether involved in a case or not.
Commutation, the acceptance by the lord of money in lieu of services.
Compotus, an account.
Computare, to reckon.

Consuetudo, a custom of the manor.
Consuetudinarius, a 'customary' tenant, i.e. a villein.
Conventio, an agreement or contract.
Coreus, a hide.
Corporalis pena, corporal punishment.
Cottsettle, a cottager.
Cum secunda manu, an oath taken by the accused with two backers or compurgators, who swear with him.
Cumin, curry-powder, sometimes paid as rent.
Custos, a bailiff or warden.
Custumarius, a 'customary' tenant, or villein.

Datus est dies, a day appointed for further hearing of a case; adjournment.
Daya, a dairymaid.
Decima, a tithe.
Decimator, a tithe assessor.
Denarius, one penny.
Dies, a day's work or service.
Districio, distraint upon property.
Distringere, to distrain upon an accused's cattle or chattels.
Dominicum, the demesne; the lord's lands whether separate or among the common fields.
Domus, a house.

Elemosina, alms, charity.
Essoniare, to send a recognised excuse for non-attendance at court by a neighbour; not permitted to villeins in some cases.
Excambium, exchange.

Fabae, beans.
Facere defaltam, failure to appear in court, without proper excuse of 'essoin'.
Facere legem, to succeed in pledging one's law, i.e. to prove the truth of a statement by personal oath and pledges.
Falcatio, mowing service.
Falcator, a mower.
Falda, a fold.
Famulus, household worker, demesne labourer.
Farina, flour.
Fena, hay.
Feoditas, fealty; the ceremonial pledging of loyalty and service to a lord.

Finis, a 'fee' rather than a fine, e.g. 'relief' or 'merchet', for permission or licence.
Finis mancupator, pledge found by a villein as distinct from the 'pledges' of a freeman.
Finis pro ingressu, a 'relief' or entry fee to an inheritance.
Firma, rent for a leasehould.
Firnum, manure.
Flagellum, a flail.
Forum, a market.
Frumentum, wheat.
Fundere, to brew.
Furca, a fork.
Furniare, to bake.

Gallina, a hen.
Gallus, a cock.
Garba, a sheaf.

Haia, a hedge.
Herbagium, pasture rights.
Hercia, a harrow.
Heriot, payment of the best beast as death-duty by the family of a tenant, at his death.
Hersura, harrowing-service.
Hundredum, the Hundred, a Saxon division of the shire, or its court.
Hutesium, the hue and cry, organised in emergencies, to give chase to thieves and criminals.

Incrementum, extra grain, a bonus, heaped measure, increase or rent.
Inquisitio, an inquiry or inquest as to the facts of a case.
Iumentum, a mare.
Iurati, the jury or jurors of an inquest.

Lerwite, penalty for fornication, paid by girl, or her parents.
Libra, one pound.
Licencia marliandi terram, permission to marl a field.
Licencia se maritandi, licence to marry, by payment of a 'merchet'.
Licencia tradendi terram, prmission to exchange land.
Lineus, linen.
Loquela, a plea or suit.

(in) manum domini, the return of a piece of land into the lord's

demesne.

Manumission, the freeing of an unfree man by the lord.

Marca, a mark; 13s. 4d.

Merchet, fee for permission to marry for oneself, or for members of a family. One sure sign of a man's villein status.

Messura, harvesting.

Misericordia, amercement; a fine, the most common manorial penalty.

Molendarius, a miller.

Molendinum, a mill.

Multura, fee for grinding corn at the lord's mill.

Nativus, a villein or customary tenant who was also unfree in status as opposed to tenancy.

Obolum, one halfpenny.

Opera, works, services.

Optulit se, an absentee presents himself later and proves his excuses or 'essoin'.

Ordeum, barley.

Oretenus, by word of mouth.

Oves matrices, ewes.

Ovila, a fold.

Ovum, an egg.

Pastura, pasture rights.

Pavo, a peacock.

Pelliparius, a skinner or tanner.

Pellis, a fleece.

Peltis, a hide.

Peperis, Piper, pepper.

Pertica, a perch.

Pisae, peas.

Placiam terrae a piece of land.

Placitum, a plea or case.

Plegius, a pledge or surety, found by a freeman and paid by his neighbours to guarantee his appearance in a later court or to pay his fine (bail). Compare the later 'recognisances' found by Tudor villagers before the Quarter Sessions.

Ponitur in respectu, case adjourned, respite given.

Porcellus, a little pig.

Pratum, meadow, hay-field.

Prebenda, fodder.

Precaria, 'boon-work'; extra services done 'ad preces' in addition to normal week-work, at harvest and haymaking time, at the lord's will.

Prepositus, a reeve or overseer.

Purprestura, an encroachment on to another tenant's land, or an enclosure of the waste.

Quadrans, one farthing.

Quietum clamare, to 'quit-claim' or relinquish.

Quintadecima, a tax or subsidy of one fifteenth of all moveable goods.

Reapgoose, a free meal.

Recognosco, to admit.

Redditus, rent.

Redditus assisae, fixed rent.

Relaxatio, remission of a rent or service.

Relevium, 'relief'; the payment of a fee by an heir, for permission to take over his inherited tenement.

Respectus, respite; case held over.

Sarclare, to hoe.

Scilicet, same as *videlicet, viz.* i.e.

Secta curiae, 'suit of court'; the obligation of a villein to attend his lord's court whenever it was held, of a freeman to attend the two Great Courts each year, or when required in a case. 'Suit' is used to express duty of attendance elsewhere, as, e.g. 'Suit of Mill'.

Seisina, 'Seisin'; the ceremonial acceptance of a tenement, the tenant receiving some symbol, a turf, a rod or earth, and acknowledging its receipt.

Selio, a measure of land; a strip.

Senescallo, Seneschal, the lord's steward or estate-manager.

Sepes, hedges or fences.

Serviens, a bailiff.

Siligo, rye.

Solidus, one shilling.

Stagnum, a pond or pool; mill-pool.

Stipendium, wages.

Stipula, stubble-field after harvest.

Stottus, a horse.

Supervenientes, overseers, reeves, or bailiffs.

Sus, a sow.

Sytheale, drink provided for 'boon-service', if it is a 'wet-boon'. For 'dry-boons' a tenant provided his own food and drink.

Tallia, a tally; notched stick used as a receipt.

Tascha, hired work.

Tassator, a rick-maker.

Terminus, a lease; the date for payment of a rent due.

Transgressio, trespass or offence.

Tritutare, to thresh.

Vacca, a cow.

Vadiare, to pledge or swear.

Vadiare legem, to 'wage one's law' i.e. offer to prove the truth of a statement by oaths.

Vadium, a pledge or surety.

Vanga, a spade.

Vastum domini, the lord's waste or commons.

Ventilare, to thresh.

Vescae, vetches.

Vicecomes, sheriff.

Visum, permission; *per visum*, by authority of.

Visum franci plegii, the 'View of Frankpledge'; the twice-yearly assembly of the tithings, and reports of the tithing-men upon the state of law and order in the vill. The rithing (or ten men) was a Saxon institution, a sub-division of the Hundred, within the Shire. All members of a tithing were answerable for each other's good behaviour, the obligation of mutual responsibility known as 'Frith-borh'. This institution was retained by the Normans and is known as 'Frankpledge'. In medieval times it was a very common franchise to be adjoined to manorial authority, the 'view' being held in, or before, the manor court proper.

Vitulus, a calf.

Warrantizare, a person, having sent an excuse, or 'essoin', comes later and confirms it in person.

Week-work, services attached to a villein tenement, so many days' work per week upon the lord's demesne land, instead of money rent.

Suggestions for Teachers and Local Study Groups

✧

The following tasks were devised, 35 years ago, as tokens of one teacher's enthusiasm and his hopes of bringing village records to life for inexperienced students and children. It is, perhaps, necessary in 1997 to measure how much of that hope can be sustained by simple exercises. Much has changed: film strips listed, even some Museums' illustrations and guides are no longer available; the suggestions themselves may seem out-of-date in a hi-tech society, ranging as they do from simple collections of data to fairly obvious lines of interrogation. They are, nevertheless, offered once more for the consideration of another generation of students, both young and old.

I.   ANGLO-SAXON CHARTERS (see pp.15-31, Plate I)

1. Walk the boundaries of your local Charter, recording surviving landmarks on the O.S. 1:2,5000 and 1:25,000 map sheets.
2. Make your own map of the charter bounds and compare them with the O.S. map's parish boundary.
3. Compile your own modern charter for comparison with the Saxon version, e.g. 'from the garage to the poultry farm; from here, follow the pylons to the railway line; along the line to the Ordnance Depot, etc.'
4. Collect specimens from the ground for a Nature Table of specimens named in the charters and place names; find lime leaves at Lincombe, garlick from Romsley, oak, ash, mallow, hassock grass, reeds, etc. Particularly, check for the survival of badger sets, courses of streams, etc.
5. Make a study of place-name origins in your area, and map the distribution of forest-names, water-names, early and later settlement names, in different colours.
6. Help the children to 'forge' their own charters, defining the bounds of their school. Ornate capitals, a suitable pen, and the use of coloured inks, sealing wax, and paper (yellowed chemically, or by heat), produce very attractive and authentic-looking documents.

II.   DOMESDAY SURVEY (see pp.31-45, Plate II)

1. Place the information given in your village's survey on to a conjectural picture-map.
2. Make a class play about 'The Making of Our Village Domesday'.

3. Make a study of a modern farm, and record your information Domesday-fashion. Compare the Domesday land-use with that of the present day, e.g. amounts of ploughed land, numbers of ploughs in use then and now, the number of mills then and now. Try to locate Domesday mills in relation to the surviving streams.

4. Compile pillar graphs for a collection of villages, to illustrate the classes of population, values, etc.

5. Map the distribution of the different land-owners of manors in a limited area around the school. (*Victoria County History* usually gives such a distribution map, for the whole county, which is too large a unit for children's work, but useful for reference.)

6. Combine the use of Domesday with Anglo-Saxon chronicles and Bayeux Tapestry, for a 'patch' study of Norman England.

III. MANORIAL RECORDS (see pp.48-69, Plates III, IV, V)

1. Make your own selection of the most interesting entries in a local printed manor court roll, compiling a source book, for use with children.

2. Make your own class play of 'The Manor Court', using this source book for local material, referring to 'The Court Baron' for samples of the phraseology of these Courts.

3. For a wealth of colourful medieval manuscript illustration, including the entire Bayeux Tapestry and Luttrell Psalter as well as extracts from several Books of Hours, Mappae Mundi, etc., use the British Library's CD-ROM *Medieval Realms* (1995) evaluated by John West and John Lally, with examples of children's work, in an *Historical Association Young Historian's Report* (1996).

4. Past Times shops in most large towns offer a frequently up-dated catalogue and mailing list (from Witney, Oxford OX8 6BH) of authentic medieval reproductions as calendars, postcards and books. See, for example, *The Medieval Woman*, an illuminated book of 30 picture postcards and *The Medieval Cookbook* by Maggie Black, with 142 pages and 85 illustrations.

5. For scrutiny of any source material, picture or document, a hand-held facsimile is preferable to any form of projection. For carefully selected analytical examples, see *Classroom Gallery* by Linda Burridge and John West (Elm Publications, Seaton House, Kings Ripton, Cambs. PE17 2NJ).

6. Using selected Court Roll entries, make up the story behind the bare extract, in dialogue, or as imaginative 'eye-witness' accounts.

7. Make up charter studies of the mediaeval villagers, drawing from Chaucer's *Prologue* as a pattern.

8. Reconstruct a pictorial map or frieze of your manor, identifying surviving farm and field names. Compare this with the previous conjectural maps made up from information supplied by Saxon charters and Domesday Survey. Make a composite map of these, in three colours.

9. (For more advanced students.) Make a statistical analysis comparing the population and economy of the same manor, from Domesday and the Manorial Records, to demonstrate the growth of the manor. Compile a list of occupations on the manor, for comparison with Domesday and later records, down to the present. Use the information gained about population in connection with geography and geology lessons, to show reasons for changes in settlement patterns over the centuries.

IV. LAY SUBSIDY ROLLS (see pp.69-78, Plate VI)

1. Use these Rolls to supply the authentic 'cast', or *dramatis personae*, for your class play about the medieval manor, particularly when Manorial Records are wanting.
2. Identify the inhabitants with those of the Court Rolls, if you have both documents.
3. Develop a study of the origins of the surnames of your class.
4. Attempt a comparison of the numbers, occupations and names, with the directories of the nineteenth century.
5. Using Chaucer's *Prologue* as a pattern, draw up character studies of the knights, reeves, millers, etc. who appear in the Rolls. Search for the names of those who may appear portrayed in church brasses in the county.

V. INQUISITIONES POST MORTEM AND EXTENTS (see pp.78-91, Plate VII)

1. These documents are too advanced for direct use with children. They should be used only for reference, and for a more advanced village study, for information on genealogy an the tenure of the manor.
2. Only in those cases where an extent of a manor is given (as in the Chaddesley document, Plate V), need the document be transcribed and translated to supplement and extend knowledge not otherwise given in the Court Rolls.
3. (For more advanced students.) Map the tenurial changes in your county during the early middle ages. Compile a list, from the P.R.O. calendars, of all those I.p.m. which include extents.

VI. MONUMENTAL BRASSES (see pp.92-100 and Fig. 1)

1. Take the children on brass-rubbing expeditions. Use coloured waxes, or clean rubbings with petrol, and reverse from negative to positive print. Colour the resulting 'white' rubbing. This latter can also be done very effectively with a good rubbing, by photographing the rubbing, and making a positive print from the negative.
2. Brass rubbings are essential for development studies on the history of costume and armour. Combine their evidence with that of the later domestic Inventories and contemporary portraiture, illuminated MSS., etc. Make a collection of local art gallery portrait reproductions, and mount these alongside comparable brass rubbings of the same period. Use them for reference to identify garments shown.
3. Copy the brasses in embroidery and appliqué work, in colourful, authentic materials.
4. Model the figures in clay, and use them as patterns for lino-cuts.
5. Use brasses as a source for a study of the development of armour. Record copies of the brasses on a black ground, using thin sheet metals, foils or silver paint. Connect this with a study of a local family's heraldry.

VII. LOCAL MAPS (see pp.102-112, Plates IX, X)

1. Maps and map-making of all kinds are essential to the most elementary local study. Make your own maps to record every aspect of your study, and, wherever possible, as suggested previously (e.g. with Saxon charters), use maps to record all information gained from

documents. See your county maps for early examples and attractive interpretations.

2. Develop a study, in geography periods, of 'Maps and Map-Making'.

3. Note all local differences and progress from a series of county maps, from the sixteenth century to the present. As with the illustrations shown (Plate VIII), it is more convenient, when faced with a typical series of county maps of varying sizes and scales, to select a section of each map, for a few miles around the school, and have this same section enlarged to a standard size by the Record Office, or reference library. This standardises the scale, and makes it much easier to see how much detail is given on each map for the same area.

4. (For more advanced students.) Read M.W. Beresford's *The Lost Villages of England*, Lutterworth, 1954. Use these maps, along with earlier records (Domesday, Subsidy Rolls, Poll Tax Returns, etc.), to trace deserted village sites in your own neighbourhood.

VIII.   PARISH RECORDS AND QUARTER SESSIONS PAPERS
(see pp.112-138, Plates XI, XII)

1. Develop dramatic work on 'Life in a Tudor Village', using the Quarter Sessions papers to provide the authentic situations.

2. Compile biographies of individual villagers and their families, combining Sessions papers with Parish Registers, Churchwardens' Accounts, Inventories, brasses and later Manorial Records as sources of information.

3. Make a study of the parish church as a time-line for other studies.

4. (For more advanced students.) Use all these documents to study the incidence of recusancy and non-conformity in your area; also for studies of vagrancy, local government, highways repair and maintenance and enclosures. Supplement the knowledge gained by further reference to the indexes and text of printed State Papers Domestic, Star Chamber Proceedings, etc. (For information about these last named, see 'Record Publications', Sectional List No. 24 of Government Publications, H.M.S.O. 1958, obtainable from the local Stationery Office. The books themselves will be found in the larger reference libraries.)

5. (For more advanced students.) Make a comparative study of extracts taken from mediaeval Court Rolls and from Quarter Sessions records about the same village. Look for the differences in local jurisdiction, responsibility for maintenance of roads, for keeping the peace, and any differences in the punishment of offenders, or care for the welfare of the individual villager.

IX.   DOMESTIC INVENTORIES AND HEARTH TAX (see pp.138-188, Plates XIII-XV)

1. Our study of these documents will be incomplete, especially for children, unless the Inventories are fully illustrated and brought to life by constant reference to the contents of museums. The pictures of furniture, utensils and whole interiors of living rooms, kitchens and bedrooms of past generations, which so many museums now produce, add realism and interest to the documents. The Museum of English Rural Life, Reading, has a fine collection of photographs of farm tools and implements, and copies can be supplied on request. The Curtis Museum, Alton, Hampshire, also has an interesting and well-documented agricultural section, and supplies a guide to the remarkable collection of implements, which is delightfully illustrated. The beautiful enlarged photographs of pieces of sixteenth- and seventeenth-century furniture which are available from the Victoria and Albert Museum are indispensable aids to the study of the furniture listed in the inventories; the Geffrye Museum, London, provides not only

a fine series of postcard illustrations of period interiors, but has also produced several booklets by the Curator, Miss Molly Harrison, which are of immense help to the teacher in arranging and recording museum visits. Some of these are:

M. Harrison, *Learning out of School*, London, 1954.

M. Harrison, *Museum Adventure*, U.L.P., 1950.

Handbook to the Geffrye Museum.

Introducing the Geffrye Museum, and supplements on: 1. Furniture; 2. Smaller Domestic Pieces; 3. Tableware.

My Visit to the Geffrye Museum. A work book, with suggested outline for children's records and illustrations.

Outline Picture Books: 1. Furniture; 2. Costumes; 3. Doors, Windows and Walls.

Other leading Folk Museums, with collections of particular interest, include:

Bradford: Bolling Hall Museum, Bolling Hall Rd, Bradford, 4.

Bristol: Blaise Castle House Folk Museum, Henbury, Bristol.

Cardiff: St Fagan's Welsh Folk Museum, St Fagan's Castle, Cardiff.

Cregneash: Manx Village Folk Museum, Cregneash, I.O.M.

Douglas: The Manx Museum, Douglas, I.O.M.

Cricklade: Cricklade Museum, High St, Cricklade, Wilts.

Durham: Bowes Museum, Barnard Castle, Durham.

Forfar: Angus Folk Museum, Rocosbie.

Gloucester: Gloucester Folk Museum, 99-101 Westgate St, Gloucester.

Halifax: West Yorkshire Folk Museum, Shibden Hall, Halifax.

Great Casterton: Rural Life Museum, Great Casterton Secondary Modern School, Rutland.

Leicester: The Newarke Houses, The Newarke, Leicester.

London: Church Farm Museum, Church End, Hendon, N.W.4.

The Pinto Collection of Wooden Bygones, Oxhey Woods House, Northwood, Middlesex.

Keighley: Keighley Museum, Victoria Park, Keighley, Yorks.

Kingussie: The Highland Folk Museum, Am Fasgadh, Kingussie.

Salford: Salford Art Gallery, Peel Park, Salford.

Scarborough: Scarborough Museum, Vernon Road, Scarborough.

Stroud: Cowle Trust Museum, Landsdown, Stroud.

York: Castle Museum, York.

2. Make a collection of illustrations of furniture and interiors. Try to illustrate every item in a typical inventory.

3. Make your own personal inventories at home, to compare with Tudor homes. Collect modern farm sale catalogues for additional comparisons.

4. Trace a surviving house of which an inventory can be identified, and compare its present state of building and contents with the original.

5. Search for evidence of possession of books, Bibles and musical instruments. Compare this picture of cultural life with that given by Pepys in his Diary, and contrast with that of the modern home.

6. Investigate the physical and economic development of the English farm and cottage from the 16th to the 18th centuries.

7. Trace the nature and distribution of village crafts. (see, for instance, in a Chaddesley Corbett Inventory of a scythesmith's workshop of 1620, the listing of '*The sithes, being one hundred dossen, stiell and stiellings and strings and iron: £85*', W.R.O. Inventory of John Smith, 008.7.1620/152.)

8. Make a dictionary of obsolete and regional words. Trace survivals still in use or remembered locally.

9. Make a further study of the 16th- and 17th-century houses of a village. Using the Inventories which list possessions room by room, learn how to draw up conjectural plans of the houses, shewing typical hall, solar, parlour, and kitchen arrangement. Draw large-scale plans of several typical rooms, and 'furnish' with coloured symbols to indicate the amount of furniture in each room. (Illustrate this study with pictures from the Victoria and Albert Museum, and other museums listed above.) Compare these plans with similar plans of your own rooms at home, using comparable symbols. Compare also with the contents of nineteenth-century dolls' houses. (Admirable illustrations of the latter can be found in the Victoria and Albert Museum's booklet, *Dolls and Doll's Houses*.)

10. Make a list of possessions and furniture in a seventeenth-century house, and those in a modern room. Separate the former into three lists, 'Items found in seventeenth-century houses, but *not* found in a twentieth-century house'; 'Items found in twentieth-century houses, but *not* in the seventeenth-century'; 'Items found in seventeenth-century homes which still appear today'. Illustrate these lists with pictures and photographs.

11. Read M. St Clare Byrne, *The Elizabethan Home* (Methuen, 3rd edn. rev., 1949), for additional intimate details of the everyday life of this period.

X. ENCLOSURE AND TITHE AWARDS: LAND TAX RETURNS
(see pp.191-221, Plates XV-XVIII, and Figs. 7, 8 and 9)

1. Trace the history of the fields and land-use of a modern farm.

2. Find out, on the ground, what has happened to the manor farm-land, the common land, glebe, charity and school endowments.

3. Trace the rate of local building from enclosure, tithe and O.S. maps.

4. Compile comparative land-use maps for the whole parish at different stages from the 18th to the 20th century. Account for the changes in crops and farm-units.

5. Make a collection of local field names, and trace their derivation.

6. In the case of surviving 'strip maps', find surviving evidence, on the 6 in. O.S. maps, and on the ground, of curving field boundaries, 'fossilised' boundaries and 'ridge and furrow'.

7. (For more advanced students.) Show, by graph and distribution maps, the progress of Parliamentary Enclosure in your county, using different colours and symbols for each decade. Compare what is thus shown with the geological map, to find reasons for regional differences. In the case of enclosed waste, or marginal land, see how often the bounds of the last remaining commons coincide exactly with the bounds of a poorer layer soil, and often still reveal a poor state of cultivation.

XI. TURNPIKE MAPS (see pp.221-226, Plate XIX)

1. Use a series of county maps from the sixteenth to the nineteenth century, in order to identify the roads developed by local turnpike trusts. Colour these stretches of road distinctively.

2. From a local map of a section of road maintained by a trust, follow the present course of the road on the ground. Identify all surviving toll-houses. Mark wherever the new road now diverges from the original course.

3. If a stretch of 'disturnpiked' road is being dug by road-menders, learn all you can from them about the archaeology of the previous layers of surfacing.

4. Read, in *Tom Brown's Schooldays, Pickwick Papers*, the writings of Arthur Young, John Wesley, Cobbett, Defoe, etc., of the conditions of coach travel and journeys by horseback, if possible in your own area.
5. Use this study as a starting point for a wider study of 'Transport Through the Ages'.
6. Use Turnpike Records in conjunction with the commercial directories, to gain information about the trade and coaching service in your area. Watch for surviving toll-boards and search for toll-gate tickets.
7. Our studies of any 19th-century village must be extended to include the evidence of households and families revealed by decennial national census returns from 1841 to 1891. These are widely available on microfilm in all reference libraries, Record Offices and local history archives and will be updated to 1901 in four years' time. See *Town Records* (Phillimore, 1983) Chapter Eleven for facsimiles and analysis of census ennumerators street-by-street returns, which can be as easily applied to village studies.

XII. COMMERCIAL DIRECTORIES (see pp.226-267, Fig. 10)

1. Construct a frieze, model, or street plan, to show the village as it was 100 years ago. Use this as a convenient starting point for a longer village history.
2. Make up an imaginary village newspaper or magazine for the year of a given directory.
3. Identify all surviving houses, shops, families and trades.
4. Use the material given for development studies in crafts, shops, transport, communications and social services.
5. Make a study of surnames in a village from the various documents illustrated, from the 13th to the 20th century. (For more advanced students) Use this information to reach certain tentative conclusions about changes and mobility of village population.
6. Follow one village through a series of 18th- to 20th-century directories, investigating: (*a*) growth or decline of population, illustrating this with graphs; (*b*) growth or decline of a given craft during the same period.
7. Find the sites and relics of crafts which are now extinct.
8. Supplement the information gained from the directories with the reminiscences of the older villagers.
9. Make a class-room 'Museum of the Recent Past', with family relics and photographs from home.
10. Use the information given in the directories to trace the distribution and development of schools in part of your county (refer to individual Schools' Log Book for more detailed studies).

General Index

✧

Authors to whom reference is made in the text are included here; others will be found in the various bibliographies and documentary gazetteers. Names in *italics* refer to contemporary or nearly contemporary authors; those whose names are printed in **bold** were once inhabitants of Chaddesley Corbett. Documentary references in **bold** print are the gazetteer entries for each county.

ABBREVIATIONS OF COUNTY NAMES

As in E. Ekwall, *The Concise Oxford Dictionary of English Place-Names*, 1980 (Welsh counties added). As far as possible redundant reorganisations such as Cleveland and Avon have been eradicated.

Bd	Bedfordshire	*Ft*	Flintshire	*Np*	Northamptonshire
Bk	Buckinghamshire	*Gd*	Gwynedd	*Nt*	Nottinghamshire
Br	Breconshire	*Gl*	Gloucestershire	*O*	Oxfordshire
Brk	Berkshire	*Gm*	Glamorgan	*Pb*	Pembrokeshire
Ca	Cambridgeshire	*Gt*	Gwent	*Pw*	Powys
Carm	Carmarthenshire	*Ha*	Hampshire	*Rd*	Radnorshire
Cb	Cumberland	*He*	Herefordshire	*Ru*	Rutland
Cg	Cardiganshire	*Hrt*	Hertfordshire	*Sa*	Shropshire
Ches	Cheshire	*Hu*	Huntingdonshire	*Sf*	Suffolk
Co	Cornwall	*K*	Kent	*So*	Somerset
Cvn	Caernarvonshire	*La*	Lancashire	*Sr*	Surrey
Cw	Clwyd	*Le*	Leicestershire	*St*	Staffordshire
D	Devonshire	*Li*	Lincolnshire	*Sx*	Sussex
Db	Derbyshire	*Mr*	Merionethshire	*W*	Wiltshire
Df	Dyfed	*Mon*	Monmouthshire	*Wa*	Warwickshire
Dn	Denbighshire	*Mont*	Montgomeryshire	*We*	Westmorland
Do	Dorset	*Mx*	Middlesex	*Wo*	Worcestershire
Du	Durham	*Nb*	Northumberland	*Wt*	Wight
Ess	Essex	*Nf*	Norfolk	*Y*	Yorkshire

Index of Places

✧

As far as possible, attributions of villages are to their original, historic counties before abortive local government re-organisations which took place between editions. Avon, Cleveland, Humberside etc. have been eradicated but some earlier amalgamations cannot be avoided; Halesowen for example has over the centuries belonged to three counties, including its recent inclusion in the West Midlands, now a Metropolitan District and no county at all; Greater Manchester and Merseyside are no more meaningful. Normally, we have taken the county of publication, though this of course may change from time to time and in some cases (see pages 122 and 129 and notes) can be actively misleading. To trace a village's most reliable county origin, consult the *Phillimore Atlas and Index of Parish Registers*, which takes a useful base line from pre-1832 sources. Otherwise, refer to the index of an old Atlas, such as *The Readers' Digest Complete Atlas of the British Isles* or Ekwall's *Place Name Dictionary*. Failing all else, verify the manor's earliest county in Domesday Book for each of several contenders.

Descriptive words such as Little, Great, North etc. are placed second in order.